Human Development and Learning

Human

Development

and

Learning

NEW REVISED EDITION

LESTER D. CROW
Brooklyn College

ALICE CROW
Formerly Brooklyn College

ROBERT E. KRIEGER PUBLISHING COMPANY
Huntington, New York
1975

Original edition 1965
Reprint 1975

Printed and Published by
Robert E. Krieger Publishing Co., Inc.
645 New York Avenue
Huntington, New York 11743

© *1965 by Litton Educational Pub., Inc.*
Reprinted by arrangement with
Van Nostrand Reinhold Company

PRINTED IN THE UNITED STATES OF AMERICA.

Library of Congress Cataloging in Publication Data

Crow, Lester Donald, 1897–
  Human development and learning.

  Reprint of the ed. published by American Book Co.,
New York.
  Includes bibliographies.
  1. Learning ability. 2. Human growth. I. Crow,
Alice Von Bauer, 1894– joint author. II. Title.
[LB1051.C74 1975]   370.15'2   74-26685
ISBN 0-88275-252-9

Preface to Revised Edition

Human Development and Learning, Revised Edition, aims to help students in Teachers Colleges and Departments of Education of Liberal Arts Colleges to achieve a constructive understanding of the psychological factors inherent in human growth and development and to gain practical insight into the basic principles of teaching and learning. Human development is traced through childhood and adolescence, and emphasis is placed upon the continuous interaction and interrelationship of the natural growth and maturational processes with the environmental forces and conditions that influence individual patterns of growing up and learning.

Throughout the text, attention is directed toward the educational value of the application of mental-hygiene principles in teacher-learner relationships. Consideration also is given to the important implications of differences in ability to learn, attitude toward learning, and behavior in learning situations as related to the teacher's responsibility to help learners achieve adequate personal and social adjustment.

Human Development and Learning includes a comprehensive treatment of the learning process. The theories and principles of learning are discussed from the viewpoint of their practical application to general and specific learning areas, situations, and conditions.

Attention also is focused upon the value to the teacher and the learner of the utilization of various instruments and techniques of pupil evaluation, and of differing approaches to the reporting of learner progress. The purposes and functions of school-organized guidance services are described briefly but succinctly. Of particular interest to the teacher-to-be are the suggestions concerning ways in which a teacher can develop effective interpersonal relations with his pupils, co-workers, and supervisors.

In brief, the authors have aimed to: (1) present the sequence of child and adolescent development, (2) interpret the psychological factors inherent in child and adolescent behavior, (3) alert the prospective teacher to the importance of understanding the

v

adjustment problems of young people, help him gain insight concerning the nature of learning progress, and aid him to achieve competence in the evaluation of the learning process, and (4) inculcate among teacher-trainees an appreciation of the responsibilities inherent in the role of the teacher. To achieve these purposes, the authors have attempted to organize the various areas of discussion in such a way that the reader may experience integrated learning and understanding.

The questions that appear at the end of each chapter and the list of appropriate films at the end of the book are recommended as useful teaching-learning aids.

The authors wish to express their appreciation to all who have offered valuable suggestions for the improvement of the manuscript. They especially wish to thank the many publishers who have given permission to use material from their publications.

Lester D. Crow
Alice Crow

Table of Contents

Tables

Figures

PART 1

Introduction

1 The Nature and Function of Psychology in Education

That the proper study of mankind is man[1] represents a generally accepted point of view. What constitutes a proper study, however, has undergone many changes and probably will continue to change as research and experimentation provide additional information concerning human nature and human interactions.

Interest in Human Behavior

One of the most significant characteristics of a child, an adolescent, or an adult is his interest in people, including himself and all others who touch his life in any way. The influence of the behavior of one individual upon the thoughts, feelings, and actions of another is tremendous. A person may believe that what he wants most is wealth, prestige, or power, when actually his ambition is based on a desire to achieve greater satisfaction to himself in his relationships with others.

Our interest in human behavior permeates every phase of our day-by-day activities. This interest may vary with age, but it is always present. Throughout our discussion of human growth and development in relation to the learning process, we shall emphasize the human interrelationships that play so important a role in life adjustments.

Age levels and behavior interests. The very young child's "interests" are centered in himself and his growth. Soon he begins to study (in his immature fashion) the behavior of each member of his immediate family. He wants his parents to give attention to his physical needs; he learns how to satisfy his wants. He comes to know how to "handle" his mother and how she "handles" him. Before long, the little boy or girl establishes more or less self-satisfying relations with his peer associates and with older people who constitute his narrow environment.

As the child extends his relations with others to include teachers and schoolmates, his opportunities to study human behavior in-

---

[1] Alexander Pope, *Essay on Man*, Epistle II, Line 1: "Know then thyself, presume not God to scan; the proper study of mankind is man."

3

crease. His earlier questions to his parents concerning the *why* or *how* of observed behavior in the home now become self-asked questions about why the teacher or a classmate acts in certain ways, or why he (the child) is treated as he is. A child's curiosity concerning people's behavior may lead him to make illogical but self-satisfying judgments about human behavior, especially in relation to himself.

Older children display great interest in "people of note." They are avid readers of simple biographies of great people. They also become intrigued by the nature and activities of men and women whom they meet personally or about whom they read. The boy wants to grow up to be just like his father, his favorite teacher, a friendly policeman or fireman, a successful businessman, or a notable person about whom he has read. The girl emulates the behavior of her mother, a beloved teacher, an admired motion-picture or television star, or any wonderful woman about whom she has read.

The authors remember a high-school freshman whose one ambition was to become a "lady diplomat." The girl had met a woman who had gained considerable prominence as a member of one of the American Embassies. The young person was not so much impressed by this woman's reputation as she was by her personality. The girl seemed to believe that the responsible position was a direct result of the woman's behavior pattern, which this thirteen-year-old had studied carefully and was determined to use as a model for herself. "I like the way she. acts," said the girl. "She behaves as though she were no better than we are. That's the way I want to be."

One of an older adolescent's chief interests is the study of the behavior of his or her peers, especially the actions of members of the opposite sex. Both boys and girls are very much concerned about the likes and dislikes, and the behavior toward themselves of those members of the opposite sex in whom, at the moment, they are interested. Adolescents also spend much time and thought in analyzing their own behavior, for the purpose of gaining peer-group approval.

An adolescent's interest in human behavior is displayed in many ways. Some are continuations of earlier manifestations; others are related to adult status. The individual continues to be interested in his own behavior and the behavior toward him of his associates.

Specific areas of interest in human behavior. A person's habitual behavior is the key to the kind and amount of satisfaction he achieves in his experiences with others. His behavior in his home, school, occupational, civic, and social relationships reflects the kind of person he is. We are becoming increasingly concerned about the underlying bases of people's behavior and reactions. Psychologists, psychiatrists, sociologists, physicians, educators, industrialists, labor leaders, and businessmen, as well as the general citizenry, are interested in the reactions of those with whom they are associated directly or indirectly.

The community wants "good" teachers; teachers want to motivate learners to become fine men and women; industrialists are as much concerned with the employees' behavior on the job as they are about work competence; voting citizens hope that the leaders they elect will perform their duties satisfactorily. Scientists want to study human behavior to gain greater understanding of human nature; educators attempt to improve the behavior of children, adolescents, and adults. Three questions now face us: What is human behavior? How can it be studied? In what ways can it be improved?

Attempts to Explain Human Behavior

Many attempts have been made to explain human behavior. These include superstitious beliefs, philosophic interpretations, and scientific study.

Superstitious beliefs. A relatively small number of people still cling to superstitions as a means of explaining human behavior. Among the best known of these are astrology (the control of human destiny by the stars) and numerology (the effect of elaborate number combinations upon human behavior). Some people still have great faith in the power of incantations, thought transference, and spiritualism. Fortune telling through the "reading" of tea leaves, coffee grounds, and playing cards still is being practiced, mainly as a social game, but too often with serious intent.

Also in use are palmistry, phrenology (the relation of head formation to the possession of personal characteristics), and physiognomy (the association of physical characteristics with behavior attributes). The earlier superstitions were based on the assumption that conditions and factors outside the individual were responsible for his fate. Palmistry, phrenology, and physiognomy, on the other hand, are attempts to discover reasons for individual potentialities on the basis of physical characteristics. Although these pseudoscientific techniques have failed to meet successfully any scientific check of their validity, they have served to stimulate study and research in the field of personality evaluation.

Philosophic interpretation of human behavior. It is remarkable that some of the great thinkers of the past came so close to those interpretations of human development which, since their times, have resulted from scientific study. Yet the *why* of human behavior eluded even the greatest of the earlier philosophers because of the lack of scientifically obtained knowledge available during their time.

The scientific approach to the study of human behavior. Scattered beginnings in what can be called the scientific approach to a study of living phenomena eventually resulted in discoveries concerning the functioning of the human organism. With an increased understanding of the growing physical constitution came a study of possible relationships between physical growth and behavior development. The experiments of Gregor Mendel and other biologists represent the beginnings of an understanding of inheritance. Further research has provided a core of knowledge concerning the possible effects of environmental factors and conditions on the growing organism. In spite of certain existing inadequacies of knowledge, there are workable principles of human growth and development that constitute the psychological bases of teaching and learning.

The teacher brings to the teaching-learning situation not only his knowledge of the subject but also his *whole self*—his physical constitution, his emotional status, his attitudes, and his interests. So it is with the learner. He brings into the classroom all the potentialities, attitudes, and interests that individualize him as a learner different from, as well as similar to, all other learners. Hence the men and women who aspire to enter the teaching profession need to gain an adequate understanding of the bases of learner reactions and of the values of integrated learning. It is the purpose of this book to help future teachers gain insight into those scientifically obtained psychological facts and principles which later can be applied in their professional activities.

Psychology and Human Development

As can be inferred from reading the foregoing, psychology as a science was not born full-grown. Indeed, some scholars still doubt that psychology should be classified as a science. It is a fact, however, that psychology consists of facts and principles that have grown out of scientifically conducted study and research. At the same time, it must be admitted that psychology is a very young science; most psychologists recognize the need of and the demand for continued study and experimentation in the field.

Meaning of psychology. The origin of the term *psychology* (from the Greek *psycho*—soul, *ology*—study of) is indicative of its relation to philosophy. Psychology began with the study of the soul and gradually shifted its emphasis to the mind.

Since the ways in which an individual's mind functions can be discovered only through his overt behavior, psychologists came to realize that their first concern should be consideration of the individual's observable acts and his expressed attitudes and interests. By studying the outward manifestations of inner processes, psychologists might determine, to some degree at least, the functionings of the total self, and thereby gain an understanding of the relationships that exist between cause and effect in human interactions.

As a result of the change in emphasis from the intangibles to the tangibles, psychology can be defined briefly as the *study of human behavior and human interrelationships*. The term *behavior*, however, needs to be understood in its broadest connotation, as including not only observable acts but also all of a person's reactions, since these are the resultants of inner motivation or environmental stimulation.

Simple as this definition of psychology may seem, psychological study itself is far from simple. The human organism is extremely complex in its functioning: any interactions that take place between an individual and his environment or between himself and other human beings represent multitudinous experiences, each of which may vary in kind and intensity from every other. Studies show that certain specific situations or conditions tend to give rise to relatively similar reactions. From this basis are developed tentative general principles of human behavior.

It is not enough to recognize the relationships that exist between human reactions and the conditions and situations that excite them. The *why* as well as the *what* is important. Consequently, various schools of thought have arisen among psychologists or groups of psychologists in their attempts to explain human behavior.

Schools of thought in psychology. Whatever progress has been made in the study of human development is associated closely with advances in other fields of study, notably anthropology, philosophy, biology, and sociology. Each of the various schools of thought in the field of psychology reflects, to a greater or lesser degree, the influence of the contributions of one or more other fields of study upon the thinking of the psychologists who developed their particular approach to the explanation of human behavior.

The philosophic approach is exemplified in the work of Wilhelm Wundt and his followers. In this school of psychology, usually referred to as *structuralism* or *introspective psychology*, emphasis was placed upon consciousness (sensations, images, and ideas). An analysis of consciousness through mental investigation was expected to lead to the discovery of the principle of association. Introspection may have value as a means of studying human behavior, but it no longer is accepted as the only or best technique.

The work of Sigmund Freud, which was in the area of *functional psychology*, was influenced by the introspective approach. His interest in the diagnosis and treatment of mental illness led him to believe that the roots of a disturbed state can be found in the "unconscious." Helping a patient to probe his unconscious may bring to light memories of past experiences that, directly or indirectly, are basic to his present disturbed condition.

Another school of psychological thought, *behaviorism*, was developed by John B. Watson early in the twentieth century. Watson, who previously had done considerable work in the field of animal psychology, attempted to resolve the disagreements between the structuralists and the functionalists concerning consciousness by evolving a behavioristic explanation of human behavior. Claiming that introspection as a means of studying behavior was no more valid for human beings than it was for animals, Watson ignored consciousness as such, and asserted that human abilities, attitudes, and interests can be studied only through observation of overt behavior.

Although the various schools of psychological thought differed from one another in their approach to the study of human behavior, each was concerned with specific phases of development. Certain German psychologists, including Wolfgang Kohler, Kurt Lewin, and Kurt Koffka, objected to too great analysis of the specific traits or characteristics possessed by an individual. According to these psychologists, a human being's personality consists of more than the sum total of specific qualities or traits. In his relationships with the objects and persons constituting his environment, the individual responds as a totality of form or configuration, or (in

German terminology) *Gestalt*. Gestalt psychology utilizes the technique of insight in studying human behavior.

The trend in the study of human development is away from accepting any one theory in its entirety. Modern psychologists tend to adapt whatever approaches and techniques seem applicable to their particular areas of investigation.[1] Certain assumptions concerning human behavior and adjustment are accepted as basic to continued study. Briefly stated, these are:

1. Human behavior is motivated by inner wants and urges, as well as being stimulated by external environmental conditions and situations, including human interrelationships.
2. Human behavior is dynamic and functional.
3. An individual's personality functions as an integrated and interacting whole, although essential elements or phases of personality may exert a potent influence upon the total personality pattern.
4. Depending on its purposes or aims, a study of human development may utilize any one or more of the following approaches: observation of overt behavior, introspection, insight.

Areas of psychological study. Psychology is concerned with every phase of human development, behavior, and interrelationship. Hence it would be difficult to gain an adequate understanding of the various areas of life relationships through an intensive study of all of them at the same time. Psychologists therefore have found it desirable to organize their study according to artificially classified areas. Some of these are described briefly in the following paragraph.

General psychology deals with the fundamental principles of human growth and development. As their names imply, *child psychology* and *adolescent psychology* are concerned with an intensive study of individual development and behavior from conception to adulthood. The purposes to be served by intensive study in the following areas, respectively, are implicit in their titles: *physiological psychology, study of individual differences, abnormal psychology, human dynamics, social psychology, educational psychology, applied psychology,* and *clinical psychology.*

It is important to keep in mind the fact that no one area of psychology can be divorced from its interrelationship with every other area of human living. Moreover, the techniques of study must be such as to result in valid and reliable conclusions.

[1] See Chapter 10 for a more detailed discussion of learning theories.

Scientific techniques in psychological study. At this point, we shall do no more than refer briefly to some of the generally utilized techniques of psychological study and evaluation.[1] We already have mentioned observation of overt behavior. To be of value, the observational method must be objective, free from bias or prejudice, and controlled in terms of the purposes to be served by the observation.

Introspection as a technique of study is useful to the extent that through its utilization insight can be gained into an individual's thoughts, feelings, attitudes, and inner motivations, insofar as these are not expressed in overt behavior. For the introspective technique to be valid, the subject of the inquiry must be able to evaluate himself with relative accuracy and must be honest in his reporting.

Rating scales, questionnaires, and check lists have been devised (1) to assist an individual to evaluate his degree of possession of one or more personality traits or qualities, and (2) to provide for raters of the individual being studied an organized list of qualities or traits to guide them in their evaluation of him. Validity of response depends upon the intelligence, objectivity, freedom from bias, and honesty of the respondent.

As a result of increased interest in the total reaction pattern of an individual, certain techniques of study and evaluation, called Projective Techniques, have been developed. By means of the application of these techniques, the subject is expected to project his whole personality into his responses. The purpose is to discover the way in which, and the extent to which, an individual's integrated totality of personality functions.

The experimental techniques utilized for scientific study in other fields have been adapted by psychologists to determine the extent to which one personal quality or an environmental condition or situation may influence behavior. The experimental method has been used successfully by educational psychologists to discover differences and likenesses in the ability to learn among young people. To yield valid and reliable results, all phases of the experiment need to be carefully controlled. Because of the complexities of human nature, adequate control of experimental factors sometimes is difficult to achieve.

Clinical and case history methods are extremely valuable as study techniques but require that those utilizing the techniques be well trained and accurate. If appropriate therapy is to be applied to an emotionally disturbed person, for example, it is imperative

[1] See Chapter 15 for a more detailed discussion of Techniques of Evaluation.

that there be a thorough diagnosis of the difficulty. Pertinent, reliable data must be assembled concerning all phases of the patient's life pattern, and must be interpreted intelligently and objectively. Hence no one, except an expert, should attempt to utilize these techniques.

Human Development and the Educative Process

With the foregoing discussion of the meaning and function of psychology as a background, we now are ready to consider the potentials of human growth and behavior development. These potentials are affected by environmental learning stimuli that can be designated as either *informal* or *formal* agencies of education.

The teacher—past and present. Rightly or wrongly, the teacher of the past often is caricatured as a rigidly postured individual, with a book in one hand and a switch in the other. The function of the "teacher" was considered no more than that of a hearer of "lessons" memorized by unwilling learners and recited fearfully, with one eye on the switch. Such a description of the traditional teacher, of course, is a gross exaggeration of the then accepted teaching functions. It probably is true, however, that in the past the mastery of subject matter and the development of needed skills received major consideration.

As a result of psychological findings, not only have educational goals broadened, but also learner needs are better understood. Consequently, teaching techniques and teacher attitudes are geared toward providing for every individual learner whatever assistance he needs to develop those physical, mental, emotional, and social attributes that can enable him to achieve a constructive, well-adjusted life pattern.

Since the concept of teaching has come to include concern for all phases of learner development, teacher-trainees must gain an adequate understanding of the significance of the growth patterns of individual learners. They also should achieve an intelligent appreciation of the teacher's responsibilities for encouraging desirable development.

Human development and learning. The terms *development* and *learning* often are used either as having the same meaning or as being in no way associated with each other. Neither usage is correct. A child's or adolescent's activities help him gain the power to develop whatever inherent potentialities he possesses. He learns to speak correctly, to manipulate objects in his environment, to solve problems, and to engage in creative activities. Success in learning results partly from the learner's potential ability to profit from instruction and partly from the adequacy of instructional materials and teaching techniques.

A young person's development of skills, knowledge, and attitudes is influenced by all the elements in his environment that affect his behavior at any one stage of his growth. These *incidental learnings* may help or hinder desirable development, however. To bring about favorable conditions for continuous and constant development, learning materials must be selected and organized, and techniques should be geared to the learner's needs and capacities at every stage of his growth and maturation.

Educators no longer construct curricula and train teachers on the basis of a "guess" as to what constitutes an effective educational program. Educational theory and practice are being influenced greatly by the application of the results of scientifically conducted studies of human development and adjustment. Educators now adapt materials and procedures in the light of continued studies dealing with (1) the pattern of individual growth, (2) the influence upon the maturational process of external stimulations, and (3) the relationships that exist between the extent and limits of development.

Function of psychology in education. Psychology, interpreted as a study of human behavior, is exerting a tremendous influence upon education. *Education* can be regarded as a *process*—that is, the continuing experiences that are engaged in by the learner as he develops his innate potentialities. Education as a *product* represents the developed skills, knowledge, and attitudes that result from the learner's participation in learning processes. The educational implications of psychologically evolved principles of growth and development have brought about a close union between psychology and education. Consequently, a significant area of psychological study has to do with learning and the outcomes of learning. This particular area generally is referred to as *educational psychology.*

Broadly defined, educational psychology is the science of psychology concerned with the learning experience of an individual throughout his life. Through study and experimentation, educational psychologists are attempting to obtain more adequate answers to such questions as:

1. To what extent and in what ways is learning helped or hindered by biological inheritance and social heritage?
2. What elements inherent in the teaching-learning situation affect learning?
3. To what extent and in what way does a learner's stage of maturation affect his learning?
4. Of what value to educators is a scientific attitude toward learning progress?
5. What is the relationship between teaching procedures and learning outcomes?
6. What are the most effective techniques for evaluating learning outcomes?
7. What is taking place within the learner while he is "learning"?
8. Do the fundamental causes of good adjustment or of maladjustment lie within an individual or in the stimuli situations to which he is exposed?
9. Are geniuses born or made?
10. Is a young person's developmental pattern affected more by incidental learning or by organized, formal schooling?

These are only a few of the many areas of psychological investigation that challenge psychological research and experimentation in education. As teachers work with their pupils and study learner reactions, they too are challenged by the need to understand better how children learn, and what they, as teachers, can do to facilitate learning.

To Edward L. Thorndike, often referred to as the "Father of Educational Psychology," goes the credit for organizing the content of educational psychology in America. During the past seventy years, other worthy contributions have been made by William James, G. Stanley Hall, Charles Judd, Arthur Jersild, Arthur Gates, William Trow, Lawrence Cole, and their confreres. Commendable progress has been made in arriving at workable concepts, but further study and research toward greater understanding of learning differences probably will challenge educational psychologists for many years to come.

Fundamental concepts. Some educators consider the term *educational psychology* a misnomer for the body of factual material that is concerned with growth and development, and with the attitude toward and the appreciation of teaching-learning relationships. An analysis of teacher-learning relationships should constitute a great part of the preparation for entrance into the teaching profession. Regardless of terminology, the degree of attained success in teaching usually is in direct proportion to the degree of sensitivity possessed by the teacher in his relationships with his pupils and their parents, as well as with his supervisors and colleagues.

There are certain psychological concepts that constitute the background of the educative process and that permeate all phases and areas of organized learning. The teacher in the fifth grade of the elementary school, the teacher of any subject-matter field on the secondary level, and the college instructor—all need to understand and, in an integrated fashion, to apply these principles. Briefly stated, they are:

1. A normal child possesses a physical structure and physiological functions that are basic to growth and development.
2. Actively functioning sense organs and muscles, as these are controlled by the nervous system and are properly stimulated, enable the child to achieve awareness of the world about him.
3. To the extent that the nervous system, the ductless glands, and the muscles function in harmony with one another, the child gradually achieves the power to adjust successfully to the demands of his increasingly complex life pattern.
4. The developing individual thinks, feels, and acts.
5. Certain forms of inner activity are automatic, unless there is interference from the outside. These activities are life sustaining and life preserving.
6. From birth to adulthood, growth or maturation is inherent in life itself.
7. An individual's growth and development do not proceed in isolation, but are helped or hindered by environmental factors.
8. The mental and emotional concomitants of the stages of physical growth are significant aspects of the direction of the maturational process.
9. The normally developing organism is adaptable. Hence it can be conditioned, or prepared to meet changing situations or conditions.
10. To the extent that there is made possible for the child and adolescent an integration of the various phases of his developing personality, he is enabled to achieve desirable self-awareness and constructive adjustment to human interrelationships.

The teacher who understands the needs of developing young persons so can adapt his teaching procedures, techniques, and attitudes that he exercises a potent influence upon them. He can help learners achieve desirable behavior patterns, acquire knowledge about them-selves and the world about them that will serve them constructively. The teacher also can help his pupils develop attitudes of emotional control and of motivating interests that will keep them adjusted satisfactorily in meeting their personal needs and in their associa-tions with their fellows.

As the teacher-trainee reads these fundamental psychological con-cepts and considers his responsibility for the welfare of developing learners, he may be overwhelmed by the magnitude of the task that lies before him. He need not be. If, step by step, the prospective teacher follows the detailed treatment of these concepts and their application to himself as they are presented in the remainder of this book, discussed in class, and observed in action, he will develop un-derstandings and appreciations that will become a part of his very being, almost without awareness of his own development as a per-son and as a teacher.

QUESTIONS AND TOPICS FOR DISCUSSION

1. Justify the theory that psychology is the application of common sense to the problems of human behavior.
2. Formulate a definition of psychology, and of psychology in education.
3. To what extent should psychology in education have its own body of subject matter?
4. From your own experiences as a member of a group, indicate some of the influences that affected your behavior, and the ways in which your behavior might have affected group reactions.
5. Describe a study in learning that you would like to see completed. As you continue the study of this book, look for suggestions that may help you to organize a study of this kind.
6. Describe a learning experiment in which you would like to partici-pate.
7. Which is the most important educational agency in your community? Why?
8. What experiences have you had with superstitions? Have you found any of them to be based on scientific data?
9. Why is adherence to the pseudoscientific techniques of personality evaluation still so widespread in spite of the fact that they are con-sidered to be unscientific?
10. Try this experiment. Have a friend and yourself observe, indepen-dently, the behavior of the same child during a fifteen-minute period. Then, without any discussion, each of you list everything you ob-served the child say or do. Compare your lists.
11. Discuss the importance of evaluation in attempts to gain an under-standing of human development.

12. The teacher is important in the whole development of the child. Explain the importance of the teacher's role.

SELECTED REFERENCES

Anderson, R. C., and Faust, G. W., *Educational Psychology*. Dodd, N.Y., 1973.

Blair, G. M., et al, *Educational Psychology*, 3rd ed. Macmillan, N.Y., 1968.

Bolton, N., *Psychology of Thinking*. Barnes and Noble, N.Y., 1973.

Bourne, L. E., *Psychology of Thinking*. Prentice Hall, Englewood, N.J., 1971.

Crow, A., *Educational Psychology*, rev. ed., Littlefield, Totowa, N.J., 1971.

Crow, L. D., and Crow, A., *Educational Psychology*, new rev. ed. Van Nostrand Reinhold, N.Y., 1965.

CRM Staff, *Educational Psychology: A Contemporary View*. CRM Books, N.Y., 1972.

Eson, M. E., *Psychological Foundations of Education*, 2nd ed. Holt, Rinehart & Winston, N.Y., 1972.

Gibson, J. T., *Educational Psychology*, 2nd ed. Appleton-Century-Crofts, N.Y., 1972.

Hawkins, N. E., *Psychology for Contemporary Education*. Charles Merrill, Columbus, Ohio, 1973.

Johnson, P. E., *Psychology of School Learning*, Wiley, N.Y., 1971.

Kalish, R. E., *Psychology of Human Behavior*, 2nd ed. Brooks-Cole, Belmont, Calif., 1973.

Klausmeier, H. J., and Ripple, R. E., *Learning and Human Abilities*. Harper and Row, N.Y., 1971.

Lesser, G. S., *Psychology in Educational Practice*. Scott Foresman, Chicago, 1971.

Lindgren, H. C., *Educational Psychology in the Classroom*. 4th ed. Wiley, N.Y., 1972.

Loree, M. R., *Psychology of Education*, 2nd ed. Ronald Press, N.Y., 1970.

Mouly, G. J., *Psychology for Effective Teaching*, 3rd ed. Holt, Rinehart & Winston, N.Y., 1973.

Sorenson, H., et al, *Psychology for Living*, 3rd ed. McGraw-Hill, N.Y., 1971.

PART II

Human Development during the First Two Decades

2   The Fundamentals of Human Development

The general pattern of growth and development varies from person to person. Moreover, there are differences in rate and extent of development among the various phases of the personality. Although personality represents an integrated whole, there are differences among the patterns of a child's physical, mental, and emotional development. It is important that parents and school people understand the significance of these developmental differences among and within young people.

At one time, for example, when a child reached the age of six, he was supposed to be ready to enter the first grade of elementary school. Differences in school achievement among learners from then on were attributed to factors such as lack of interest, naughtiness, or laziness. Also, parents were accustomed to start training the child in toilet habits, eating, walking, and talking according to what they considered to be the correct chronological age of the child for such training. Psychologists have discovered, however, that the stage of growth and development rather than the chronological age should be the basis of attempted training in any area of activity.

General Nature of Growth and Development

The child is a dynamic human being. He possesses a unique combination of personality traits and characteristics that grow and develop according to certain fundamental principles which do not necessarily make for uniformity. Early studies in child development emphasized age expectancies. Mass studies were made of the one-year-olds, the two-year-olds, and so on in order to discover what might be expected to be "normal" in the way of physical growth and developing behavior at each level. Although valuable information was obtained from such cross-sectional studies of masses of children, this approach did not offer sufficient understanding of the developmental pattern of the individual child. Hence there has been a definite trend among child psychologists toward the study of individual children from birth onward according to a *longitudinal* approach. A combination of the age-group studies and the study of

19

individual patterns of development affords us an opportunity to gain an understanding of the likenesses and differences in both general and specific patterns of growth and development.

Meaning of growth and development. The terms *growth* and *development* have undergone differences of interpretation. In some instances they have been interpreted loosely as relatively synonymous. Some psychologists limit the application of the term *growth* to structural and physiological changes within the physical constitution of the individual from conception to adulthood. According to these psychologists, the term *development* can be applied more correctly to those innate potentialities of behavior that are sensitive to environmental stimulation. Such a dichotomy in terminology, however, is not borne out by facts.

Although it can be expected that, with increasing age, a child will grow in height and weight and that his body organs will increase in size and in power to function, the direction taken by the growth pattern will be affected by environmental factors that either help or hinder its progress. Also, the newborn child brings with him certain potentials of behavior that can be developed through learning. There are, however, certain hereditary limits beyond which the development cannot proceed. Nor can an individual child react successfully to one or another "learning situation" until he is inherently ready to do so. A child's readiness to learn is dependent upon his level of maturation or the existing degree of co-ordination of relationships within the growing neural system. It probably can be asserted, therefore, that growth and development represent two closely related concepts, each sharing in the process of helping an individual in his progress toward becoming the kind of adult that he eventually will be.

An awareness of the effect of a child's maturational pattern upon his degree of success in his educational experiences, both formal and informal, has begun to exercise a potent effect on educational philosophy and teaching procedures. Intelligent and understanding parents do not force "training" upon the young child until he is ready to benefit from their efforts. School people recognize the fact that not all six-year-olds, for example, have reached a degree of maturation that enables them with equal success to learn to read, to grasp number concepts, or to participate in other learning activities. Consequently, there is a growing trend toward individualizing instruction, insofar as this is possible within the limitations of mass instruction.

The developmental sequence. Various factors affect the direction taken by the developmental pattern. Two important characteristics of growth are: (1) In general, structural growth is from the head downward or in a cephalocaudal direction. (2) Body growth and function begin in the center and proceed to the periphery of the body, or in a proximodistal direction. These two generally accepted principles of growth are evidenced not only by the young child's appearance but also by his behavior. His first responses to stimulation are head movements, followed by his gaining the power to sit up and to move his body. Standing and walking are the last controls to be developed. Also, gross body movements, movement of the hips and shoulders, and large muscle control tend to precede finer movements or muscular controls. Experiments with young children, however, have shown that some very young children have reached a stage of maturation that enables them to pick up small objects with their fingers and to manipulate their toes. Even so, much can be said in favor of the trend in early childhood education of providing the young child with manipulatory materials that will develop control of mass movements, with a gradual change to materials that will help the maturing child achieve finer co-ordinations.

Although there appears to be a sequential pattern of development in the area of motor control, psychologists still find it difficult to trace developmental sequences in the more complex phases of the child's behavioral attributes. For example, what changes take place that make it possible for the infant, who seems to be unable to recognize relationships that exist between him and his environment, eventually to develop into a relatively reasonable and reasoning adult, sensitive to the relationships that exist between himself and his physical and social environment? To some extent at least, an individual's development of understanding depends on the culture in which he is reared as well as on his own maturational progress.

Too much emphasis should not be placed upon individual rates of growth. Children may differ in this respect, but they eventually give evidence of meeting what can be termed acceptable normal standards of development. One young child may display signs of rapid early growth. Parents may expect this rate of growth to continue and, consequently, stimulate the youngster to engage in activities beyond his general maturational level of performance. Another young child may be a slow starter who later will reach or exceed that which is considered to be normal for his developmental status. Hence parents and teachers need to be careful in their interpretation of what is "normal" for an individual child's rate of growth. Also, in evaluating a child's stage of development, anyone concerned with the child's welfare must possess an intelligent understanding of all the factors both within and outside the young person that are responsible for his develcpmental progress.

Lawrence Cole succinctly described what takes place in the developmental process:

> As a dynamic energy-consuming system, the active organism must continually replenish its deficits, eliminate its waste products. . . . Viewed from this angle, an organism may be described as a set of compensating mechanisms so operating as to maintain a steady state against assaults from without and against deficits arising from within. This tendency for an organism to maintain such a steady state is called *homeostasis.* . . .
>
> Organisms become persons as they participate in human society. Without the environment of persons, the child could not even maintain himself at birth. He is equipped with reflexes and is reactive at the start, and the tensions of his homeostatic mechanisms arise promptly and automatically. In contrast to the precise and elaborate reflexes of insects . . . the human infant's responses seem random, diffuse, unpatterned, and his road to equilibrium is longer and more variable. Helpless as he is, his cry may prompt an adult to action; but the skill and continuing concern of the adult are what keep him alive. . . . In coming to terms with the vitally important world of persons, the child acquires a personality. He takes on the common patterns of action and belief, even as he organizes these into a unique life style. . . .
>
> Psychology has to look at the individual both as an organism and as a member of a social group. As an organism he is born with certain structures and capacities. As these structures are thrown into their characteristic patterns of functioning by the impact of the environment, adjustment-problems are forced upon the organism, needs or deficits rise and fall, and homeostatic mechanisms set in motion compensatory strivings which tend—in the main—to restore equilibrium. In this process skills and expectancies, habits of acting and perceiving, are established, fixated, or laid aside. Forced to come to terms with a going social matrix, the dynamic trends in his behavior are the joint product of his own bio-physical nature and of environmental pressures, particularly pressures from the world of persons surrounding him.[1]

[1] Lawrence Cole, *Human Behavior—Psychology as a Bio-Social Science,* World Book Co., Yonkers-on-Hudson, N. Y., 1953, pp. 35, 42, 43. Reprinted by permission.

The Impact of Biological Inheritance

Considered genetically, both heredity and environment play important roles in the life of any individual. There must be a living organism upon which environmental conditions can exercise their influence. Contrariwise, an organism cannot live and grow in a vacuum. Human reproduction is basic to the continuance of the human species. Increased understanding of the significance of inherited potentialities exercises a potent influence upon evolving educational theory and practice.

The beginnings of life. The life of every individual begins in the form of a zygote—a one-celled organism. The zygote, or fertilized ovum, formed from the union of a cell from the mother (ovum) and a cell from the father (sperm), is less than one one-hundreth of an inch in diameter. (See Figure 1.) This tiny speck of living matter contains potentialities of growth and development that result eventually in the production of an individual who, at the same time, is like and different from every other person.

Human nature is so complex that we do not yet have an adequate understanding of all phases of human heredity. We do know, however, that the fertilized human cell contains twenty-three pairs of chromosomes, one of each pair having been contributed by the father and the other by the mother. Each chromosome contains hundreds of tiny particles, arranged in linear form. These *genes* are thought to control hereditary traits. There is evidence that physical characteristics (height and weight tendencies, eye and skin color, body structure, and the like) appear to "run" in families and, therefore, can be traced directly to hereditary bases. Variation in the organization of the genes, however, may result in differences among the physical characteristics of children of the same family.

Characteristics of the newly-formed life probably are rooted in gene potential. These characteristics are related to structural growth and functional adequacy of the developing neural and glandular systems and other body organs. Beyond that, we do not know the extent to which mental and emotional traits or disease are inherited tendencies or the outgrowths of environmental conditioning.

The process of growth. Prenatal growth takes place through the process of cell division and specialization. The period of normal prenatal development (approximately 270 to 280 days) is divided roughly into three periods: (a) the period of the ovum or the *germinal*

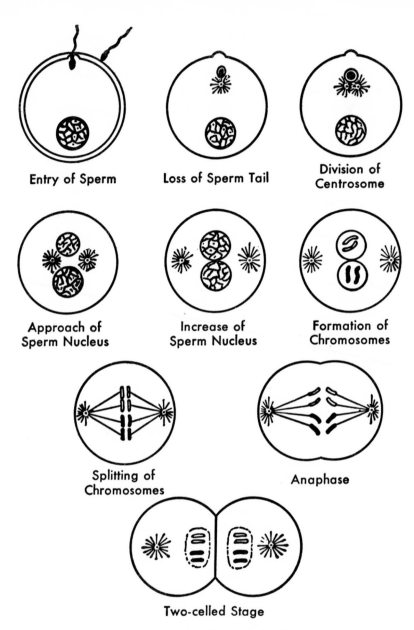

FIGURE 1. The Process of Fertilization

Paternal chromosomes are represented as black; maternal chromosomes as white.

From H. E. Walter, *Genetics*, Macmillan, N. Y., 1938, p. 186. Reprinted by permission.

period, extending from the moment of conception to about the end of the second week; (b) the *embryonic* period, extending to about the end of the second month; and (c) the *fetal* period, extending to birth. Each of these periods appears to serve a particular function. Yet, barring accidents, prenatal development is gradual and continuous.

During the germinal period, the zygote floats freely. It continues to divide and to subdivide at a rapid rate until a cluster of globules containing many cells is formed. Each cell possesses a set of the original genes. Later, two separate clusters of cells are produced— the inner cluster resulting in the formation of the embryo, and the outer cluster becoming the protective and nourishing tissues of the embryo. During the process of cell division, the ovum passes through the Fallopian tube to the uterus and attaches itself to the uterus wall. At the point of implantation is developed the placenta, from which the umbilical cord extends to the ovum and provides nourishment from the blood of the mother for the developing organism.

Many changes occur during the embryonic period. Specific body structures and organs appear. The heart begins to function by the end of the third week. Other organs, such as the liver, become active during the second month. Embryonic development is from the head down and from the trunk outward.

The growth and development that began during the embryonic period continue during the fetal period. The structure of the body is more definite, and certain organs function much in the same way as they do after birth. The heart gives evidence of a rhythmic beat; some body movement, as well as sensory development, is possible; feeble crying may be experienced.

Child psychologists are attaching increasing importance to prenatal growth and development. Various techniques have been devised to study the unborn child's rate and direction of development. Within the circumscribed confines of the prenatal environment, there are various factors of influence that may affect the growth process. Superstitions concerning prenatal "marking" of the child by the mother's behavior have been discarded by most people. There are, however, certain undesirable influences that may affect the organism during the prenatal period. These unfavorable influences, generally referred to as factors of congenital inheritance, include physical difficulties suffered by the mother, such as toxic poisoning, infection, endocrine imbalance, malnutrition, disease, or a severe nervous shock. Birth injuries that may result in some form of abnormality also are experienced, but in a decreasing number of cases.

Functions of biological inheritance, Certain principles of biological inheritance are almost self-evident. As members of the human sp~cies, all individuals have many characteristics in common. Differences among personal traits tend to be quantitative rather than qualitative to the extent that individual patterns of development tend to follow what can be thought of as relatively normal progress. For example, anyone who possesses normal functioning vocal organs can learn to talk. Whether the "silver-voiced" orator is a product of superior biological heredity or of well-guided training is another matter.

Many music lovers still insist that the voice of Caruso has never been equaled. Whence came his unique vocal powers? Psychological study is attempting to find adequate answers to questions such as this. The results of such intensive study can be of inestimable value to parents and teachers in helping young people develop, to an achievable limit, whatever potentialities they may possess. As we gain greater understanding of an individual's inherited potential, we are enabled better to evaluate the potency of environmental influences.

A popular misunderstanding of the functioning of biological inheritance is evidenced by laymen who speak of a child's inheriting a characteristic from his mother or father. Studies in this field have given us the following principle: 50 per cent of a child's characteristics probably are inherited from the mother's line, and the other 50 per cent from the father's. It has been estimated further that one-half of a child's native characteristics are inherited from his parents, one-fourth from his grandparents, one-eighth from his great-grandparents, and the lesser fractions in proportion down the ancestral line. These relationships between inherited traits and family potentials can explain some of the differences (apart from those caused by differing environmental conditions) that are found among siblings.

Determination of the sex of the new organism also is associated with chromosome distribution. It was stated earlier in the chapter that the new life receives twenty-three chromosomes from each parent. The mother contributes twenty-three x chromosomes. If the father contributes the same number of x chromosomes, the child will be a girl. If, however, the father contributes twenty-two x chromosomes and one y chromosome, the child will be a boy. It is the one x

or y chromosome received from the father that is the sex determiner. (See Figure 2.)

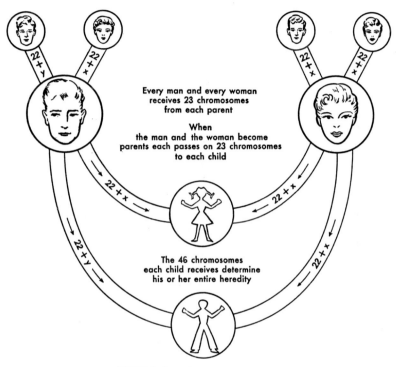

Every man and every woman
receives 23 chromosomes
from each parent

When
the man and the woman become
parents each passes on 23 chromosomes
to each child

The 46 chromosomes
each child receives determine
his or her entire heredity

FIGURE 2. Sex Determination

Furthermore, certain genes give evidence of being stronger than others. The stronger genes are referred to as *dominant* because traits produced by them are more likely to appear in successive generations than are traits produced by the weaker or *recessive* genes. Gregor Mendel, an Austrian Augustinian abbot, in 1866, was the first to propound the theory of dominance and recessiveness of traits, as a result of his experiments in the hybridization of peas.

Environmental and Cultural Influences
upon Human Development

In the foregoing discussion of human growth and development, we attempted to show that an individual is what he is at any stage of his development as a result of the interaction that constantly is taking place between his growing self and the many factors of the environment by which he is stimulated. Biological and psychological studies of the functions of inheritance have provided a workable basis upon which to build comparable studies of the effects of differing environmental conditions and cultural influences upon native traits and maturational sequence. Some of these effects are discussed briefly.

Learning and maturation. An important characteristic of human nature appears to be the inherent ability to respond to stimulation in such ways as to bring about changes in attitudes and overt behavior. This statement implies that every individual from birth on has the power *to learn*—to adapt himself to whatever conditions seem to be of value in his life experiences. This general conclusion does not present the whole story, however. As has been mentioned earlier, what a child learns and how well he learns are dependent upon his existing stage of maturation—his readiness to learn. Moreover, there are wide differences among children, as well as among older persons, in their limits of "learnability." As native constitution differs among individuals, so does the ability to profit from learning stimulation. A more detailed discussion of this point is given in Chapter 3.

A child's relative degree of success in adapting himself to his environment is closely associated with the kind of learning stimulation to which he is exposed and the ways in which he is stimulated. Here again must be taken into consideration the native constitution of the learner and his state of readiness to learn. Before attempting to guide a young person's learning experiences, parents and teachers need to understand the ways in which, and the extent to which, even the children of the same family differ in these respects. Mothers sometimes cause themselves and their children much difficulty because they do not recognize the fact that their children are not all alike.

The attitude of a woman known to the authors illustrates this lack of understanding of child nature. Her first child, a girl, was an extremely alert youngster who responded to learning stimulation so well that she sometimes was expected to react in ways beyond her maturational level. On the whole, she made a good adjustment. As often is the case with the first child, the mother kept a detailed log of the girl's developmental progress, including such matters as the child's first intelligible word, creeping, crawling and walking experiences, toilet training, changes in eating habits, manipulatory progress, and all the other behavior changes that accompany early growth and development. The mother was very proud of her alert daughter.

Then came the second child, a boy. He was a heavier and less active baby than his sister. His developmental process also was much slower than hers. The mother did not keep a written report of his sequences of responses but day by day, almost hour by hour, she compared his behavior reactions with those of his sister when she had been passing through the same stage of development. In every instance, the boy's progress lagged behind his sister's. This disturbed the mother very much. She could not believe that a son of hers could be so "slow." She feared that he was subnormal in intelligence. The fact that he was a healthy boy who ate and slept well only increased her concern about him. Even during the elementary-school years of the two children, this mother continued to compare the boy's behavior at home and his record in his school work with those of his sister at his age.

It was not until they both were in high school, the girl one year ahead of her brother, that the mother discovered that in some areas of study, especially in mathematics, her son was more successful than his supposedly brighter sister. Even then the mother attempted to place the blame of the girl's relative lack of success upon poor teaching, although both young persons had studied with the same teachers. Not until her two children had reached their later teens was the mother finally willing to admit that they were different, and that in many ways, the boy was superior to his sister in learning ability.

Differences in learning ability among the children of the same family become a serious matter if all the children happen to attend the same school and are taught by the same teachers, one after another. It is likely that the first of the siblings to attend the school will achieve a certain reputation for himself as a learner. Nonunderstanding teachers then will expect every other child of that family to perform similarly to the first child. If the first child had demonstrated superior learning ability, he may be held up as a model to the others, some of whom may not be able to achieve so successfully as he did. This is a frustrating experience for a youngster and is likely to inhibit the expressing of whatever other learning abilities he may have, in terms of his maturational status. If the first child were a slow learner, his reputation might result in the teacher's failing to recognize the superior abilities or more rapid maturation of the younger siblings.

The fact that children's maturational patterns do not progress uniformly should be understood by everyone who attempts to guide children's learning experiences. The child whose early maturation is rapid may appear to the teacher of the early school grades to be an extremely bright youngster, and is stimulated accordingly. The child's maturational rate may slow down, however. By the time he reaches the later grades, he may demonstrate no more than average learning ability. Because of his earlier performance, his teachers may expect more from him in the way of learning success than he can achieve. Consequently, his parents and teachers may assign other causes than the real one for his failure to meet their expectations; the child's interest in learning may be inhibited further by their treatment of him. The child who matures slowly at first but who later makes more rapid progress may not receive sufficient learning stimulation in his later childhood years because of non-understanding adults who do not recognize his increased learning readiness.

Environmental influences during early childhood. Many psychologists believe that the first six years of a person's life are the most important. They emphasize the effects of the physical conditions and the cultural pattern of the home on the type of attitudes and the behavior which are being developed in the child. The ways in which the young child's needs and wants are satisfied, the objects in the home by which he is stimulated, the attitudes toward him displayed by his parents and other members of the family, the language spoken in the home, habitual activities of the family, and the relationships that exist among the members of the family and between the family and neighborhood associates and family friends—all these represent some of the factors of influence by which he is surrounded. Gradually, the child learns to react in more or less expected ways to the patterns of behavior that are peculiar to the culture into which he has been born.

During this period, not only is the child being guided by his elders into specific kinds of learning, but also certain habit patterns are being developed without his being aware of them. As the result of a kind of trial-error-trial-success type of response, he learns that some of his behavior responses are approved and others are not. He develops one attitude toward his mother, another toward his father. He soon discovers that he can "get away" with certain forms of activities with one adult and not with another.

For example, a relatively co-operative one-year-old was left in the care of an unmarried uncle while the parents were away for a few hours. When they left, the child was sitting contentedly in his highchair, playing quietly with some toys. As soon as he was alone with his uncle, however, he began to throw his toys on the floor, apparently expecting his uncle to pick them up. As soon as a toy was returned to him, he threw it down again. If the uncle did not return it quickly enough, the child screamed, held his breath, or kicked until the toy was returned. No amount of pleading or scolding made any changes in the child's behavior. By the time the parents returned, both the adult and the baby were in a state of near-exhaustion. At the sight of his mother, the child started to "coo" and to settle back to the manipulation of toys, with no attempts at throwing them.

Unfortunately, we do not know what goes on in the young child's mental processes that causes him to react as he does to environmental stimuli. The best that we can do is to study the child's overt behavior in specific situations and then attempt to discover what factor in the situation is related specifically to the displayed attitude.

By the time the average child enters kindergarten or the first grade, he reflects, in his simple thinking processes, his attitudes toward people and things, and in his accustomed behavior, those environmental influences that either have helped or have hindered desirable personal and social development. At this age, some children exhibit a commendable amount of independence of action, poise, and ease in the presence of adults or their peers, an attitude of co-operation, and a considerable amount of self-control. Other five- or six-year-olds give overt evidence of continued dependence upon their mother or other adult who has cared for their needs, are shy in the presence of strangers, are demanding in their relations with their peers, and appear to have little or no self-control or ability to handle their own affairs. To some extent these differences can be explained in terms of rate of maturation; to an even greater extent they probably are rooted in the kind of home and neighborhood environment in which the children are reared.

Cultural patterns and the developing child. Every child matures in an environment that is peculiar to itself. The effect of all the elements of this environment that gradually stimulate the development of the organism into a social person can be called the individual's *social heritage*. This socializing process sometimes is referred to as *acculturation*.

Several studies have been made of the effects upon the child of the culture in which he is reared. Comparisons between relatively primitive cultures and modern, more sophisticated ones, as these affect child development, have yielded some interesting results. Social anthropologists, sociologists, and psychologists seem to agree that children all over the world are relatively similar in their growth or maturational pattern. The differences that exist in the behavior of children reared in different cultures would seem, then, to be the result of the cultures themselves rather than of the native constitution of the individuals.

In general, competition and aggressiveness among children are cultural outgrowths. Margaret Mead, as a result of her studies of life among primitive people, found, for example, that children in New Guinea were very gentle and noncompetitive, as compared to the children of modern Western cultures. In Samoa, the cultural aim was the development of uniformity of personality rather than the encouragement of many different varieties of personality, as is characteristic of our culture.

In contrast to the Samoan emphasis upon uniformity is the "flattened out" culture that, in the 1930's, was characteristic of the then relatively isolated community of Colvin Hollow, in the Appalachian Mountains, less than one hundred miles from Washington, D. C. This community consisted almost entirely of individually owned and operated farms. Each family was a social unit by itself with little if any community consciousness, or appreciation of what it means to be a citizen of the United States. The children of these families, therefore, developed a pattern of life that was unique to individual family customs and attitudes.

The cultural patterns of some peoples of Europe, Asia, and South America are neither primitive nor modern. Among them, child rearing is in a state of flux. Improved methods of communication and transportation have led to greater intermingling of different peoples, and a breakdown of many of the older cultural traditions. War periods also are responsible for the infiltration into traditional patterns of thought of what might be referred to as modern ideas. Consequently, parental attempts to foster traditional attitudes and modes of behavior come into conflict with youthful struggles to achieve democratic status in the home.

Language patterns still differ, but more peoples are gaining at least a minimum of skill in languages other than their own. In most cultural areas, "modern" dress is taking the place of dress styles peculiar to a particular people. American motion pictures are penetrating far-flung corners of the world; here we enjoy pictures produced outside the country, sometimes presented in a foreign language. Modern toys and games and sports are becoming universal in their appeal. Coca Cola advertisements appear everywhere. These are but a few of the ways in which a modern world culture gradually is supplanting isolated, traditional cultures.

By nature, children all over the world show similar likenesses and differences. It is possible that, as particular cultural beliefs, attitudes, and accustomed behavior disappear, there will be a comparable change in the developmental pattern of all young children. Eventually, we may reach the point where, within limits, all people will share common beliefs, attitudes, and modes of behavior.

QUESTIONS AND TOPICS FOR DISCUSSION

1. What difficulties are encountered by those who attempt to study the prenatal stage of development?
2. Discuss ways in which child development may be affected by congenital influences. Give examples.
3. An average child, seven years of age, is having difficulty with his reading. What are some of the probable causes?
4. What factors affect the rate of increase of mental and physical abilities during childhood?
5. Explain the value in human development of a prolonged period of infancy and childhood.
6. Cite examples of cases in which environmental influences hindered or helped a child's physical growth and development.
7. Discuss the impact of heredity upon human growth and development.
8. What contribution does environment make to human development?
9. Of what value to teachers is an understanding of the relationships that exist between biological inheritance and social heritage?
10. Describe what you would consider to be an optimum environment for a child's physical development; his mental development.
11. Evaluate the statement: Fundamentally, biological inheritance may set the pattern of environmental influences.
12. List some factors or conditions which differentiate primary from secondary sex characteristics.
13. Enumerate adjustment problems experienced by the tall girl in the family or in a group; by the short boy in a family of taller siblings. What can be done to help alleviate tensions that may be experienced by either the girl or the boy?
14. Which, if any, of your customary habits of behaving can you trace to the influence of the culture group in which you live?
15. Show how the child's developmental pattern may become a significant predisposing influence in his life.

SELECTED REFERENCES

Abrahamson, D., *Emotional Care of Your Child*. Trident, N.Y., 1970.

Coleman, J. C., *Psychology and Effective Behavior*. Scott Foresman, Chicago, 1969.

Crow, L. D., and Crow, A., *Child Psychology*. Narnes and Noble, N.Y., 1953.

Crow, L. E., and Graham, T., *Human Development and Adjustment*. Littlefield Totowa, N.J., 1972.

Dichter, E., *Motivating Human Behavior*. McGraw-Hill, N.Y., 1971.

Gordon, I., *Human Development: From Birth through Adolescence*. Harper and Row, N.Y., 1962.

Hurlock, E. B., *Child Growth and Development*, 3rd ed. McGraw-Hill, N.Y., 1968.

Jersild, A. T., *Child Psychology*, 6th ed. Prentice Hall, Englewood Cliffs, N.J., 1968.

Kennedy, W. A., *Child Psychology*. Prentice Hall, Englewood Cliffs, N.J., 1971.

Mussen, P., and Conger, J., *Child Development and Personality*, 2nd ed. Harper and Row, N.Y., 1963.

Robison, H. F., and Schwartz, S. L., *Learning at an Early Age: A Programmed Text for Teachers*. Appleton-Century-Crofts, N.Y., 1972.

Sutton-Smith, B., *Child Psychology*, Appleton-Century-Crofts, N.Y., 1973.

Thorpe, L. P., *Child Psychology and Development*, 3rd ed. Ronald Press, N.Y., 1962.

3   *Physical, Mental, and Emotional Development*

Both biological inheritance and acculturation exert a potent influence upon an individual's integrated personality. Fundamental to a person's adjustment to the world in which he lives and behaves are his physical constitution, his mental abilities, and his emotional status.

Physical Growth and Development

The various phases of an individual's personality pattern do not grow and develop apart from one another. There is a constant interaction among them whereby one area of development is helped or hindered by what is taking place in one or more other areas. At one and the same time, an individual of any age is a physical, mental, and emotional being. His general behavior is affected continuously by the relation that exists among the kinds and degrees of natural growth or maturation that are characteristic of him as his maturational process is affected by environmental factors. To understand the whole child, therefore, one must be aware of these personality interrelations. Consequently, the study of human development should be concerned with a consideration of the general developmental pattern, including the functioning of all the areas.

This concept of the totality of personality represents the authors' point of view. They believe, however, that as the result of many studies in human growth and development, there is available a body of information concerning each of the various areas of development that needs to be known before the interrelationships that exist among them can be appreciated adequately. Hence each of the three areas of development—physical, mental, and emotional—will be considered separately, with whatever crossover of discussion may be needed to indicate pertinent relationships.

Characteristics of physical growth. A study of physical growth and development from conception to adulthood must include two aspects of the physical constitution: anatomical and physiological.

35

Anatomical refers to skeletal growth, including growth of bone structure, changes in height and weight, and body proportions and contours. *Physiological* includes developmental changes in the various systems, such as the nervous, circulatory, respiratory, digestive, muscular, and endocrine gland systems, that in their functioning serve to maintain life. In the total physical constitution can be found the bases of all of a person's thoughts, attitudes, ideals, emotional reactions and activities, as these are molded by the objects, conditions, and individuals that constitute life environments.

In general, physical and physiological growth is continuous and rhythmic. All phases of growth proceed concurrently. The rate and limit of growth vary from person to person and among the different areas of an individual's total of physical constitution. Yet, growth that is relatively normal gives evidence of a pattern of integration at any stage of development. The greatest rate of growth appears to take place during the embryonic and fetal periods, with a slight slowing down toward the end of the prenatal life of the organism.

Although the rate of growth from birth to about four years is slower than it was before the child was born, there is a generally increasing change in anatomical and physiological development, with a slight decline in rate at about the age of ten, followed by an upward spurt during puberty. During adolescence, the rate of growth again is slower but continuous until the early twenties. The trend of growth progress presented in the foregoing represents no more than the general nature of the growth pattern. The many body structures and functions vary in their rate of growth. Each individual differs from others and within himself in the maturation rate of his various physical characteristics.

Nature and nurture. An organism grows in an environment and is helped or hindered by the factors of influence of that environment. Attention needs to be directed, however, to those environmental factors that affect the growth pattern of the living organism. Regardless of the kind or amount of care afforded the young child, physical changes continue to take place. But nurture is needed if the growth is to be healthy.

Deficient social heritage as well as poor biological inheritance may seriously affect a child's adequate growth and development. Improper diet, unsanitary or poorly ventilated living quarters, inadequate sleep, unguided or badly planned play activities, and lack of medical care have a deleterious effect upon natural growth progress. The child's diet is especially significant in its effect upon physical growth. Malnutrition and its concomitants of poor physical health still constitute a social problem. The kind of diet the child receives is more important than the amount of food he eats. Too often, it has been found that children of supposedly intelligent parents of better than average economic status do not eat the proper food conducive to the growth of their bone structure, teeth, muscles, and inner organs.

The development of the endocrine glands, closely related with the young person's pattern of emotional development, is affected also by environmental conditions. Hence the emotional tone of the home environment needs to be such that the child's emotional experiences are nondisturbing.

Structural growth. Much attention has been given by physiological psychology to the study of such phases of structural growth as height and weight, body proportions, and dentition. Detailed discussions of these patterns of growth can be found in any textbook that deals with the physiological bases of human behavior.[1] Hence we present here only a brief summary of the findings of study in this field.

Skeletal changes. The skeletal structure of the fetus and the neonate consists mostly of cartilage. The neonate possesses about 270 bones that are pliable, spongy, small, and loosely connected. There also are soft spots (fontanels) in the skull of the very young child; these usually close before the end of the second year. By the time the child is thirteen or fourteen the number of his bones has increased to 350; they have become ossified or hardened to the extent that calcium phosphate and other minerals have been deposited in the cartilage. As a result of fusion of some of the small bones during the process of ossification, the number of bones is reduced to 206 by the time adulthood is reached. Growth of the bony structure seems to follow a relatively regular course for all human beings, although there may be some slight individual differences, especially insofar as there is a relationship between nutrition and ossification.

Growth in height and weight. Although growth in height and weight is continuous, the rate of growth differs for different life cycles. Growth is more rapid during the early years of children, slows down during the middle years, and then becomes more rapid during the adolescent years. A marked difference in the ratio between growth

[1] Consult Selected References at the end of this chapter.

in height and in weight is important in that it may indicate a health difficulty. Too great a difference between height and weight may cause a child to become embarrassed because of his deviation from a so-called norm of growth, for example.

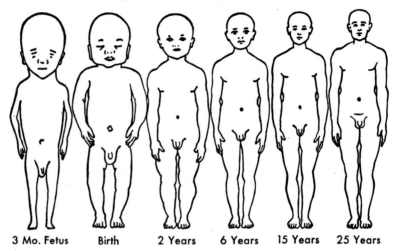

| 3 Mo. Fetus | Birth | 2 Years | 6 Years | 15 Years | 25 Years |

FIGURE 3.   Changes in Body Proportion, Fetus to Maturity

From H. C. Stuart, *Healthy Childhood*, Appleton-Century-Crofts, Inc., N. Y., 1933, p. 55, from drawings by Scammon, Calkins, and Stratz. Reprinted by permission.

At birth, the average boy's length is about 20.5 inches, and the girl's about 20.3 inches. In general, boys maintain a height advantage over girls until about the age of ten, at which time the situation is reversed until the middle teens, when the boys regain height advantage and continue to maintain it.

The same general advantage pattern holds for the weight of boys and girls. The average newborn boy weighs about seven pounds and eight ounces; the newborn girl approximately seven pounds. The boy continues to outweigh the girl until the onset of pubescence, which usually is earlier for the girl. For a time the girl outweighs the boy, but the boy again takes the weight advantage during the early years of adolescence, and continues to maintain it thereafter.

These height and weight figures present no more than possible averages. There are so many deviations from such "norms" that it would be unfair to parents and teachers to lead them to believe that a particular child whose pattern of height and weight growth differs from an accepted form is therefore abnormal. Family tendencies, climatic conditions, and other factors of nature and nurture influence growth sequence and progress.

Body proportions and contours. As has been said earlier, growth is from the head downward. The newborn infant's head is approximately one-fourth of his total body length; that of an adult is about one-tenth. The cephalocaudal pattern of growth applies generally to body growth. The changes that take place in body proportions are illustrated in Figure 3.

Figure 3 shows that body contours also change with increasing physical maturation. Before puberty there is little difference in body contour between boys and girls. Beginning with the early years of adolescence, however, there are significant differences between the sexes. The form of the male is characterized by broad shoulders, narrow hips, and straight leg lines; that of the female by wider hips, curved legs, and relatively narrow shoulders.

Physiological growth and development. There is a close relationship between the maturation of the skeletal structure and of the internal organs. Both develop from birth onward. The rate of growth of each internal organ may vary from that of any or all of the others. The muscular system increases in weight, and in the power to control skeletal movements. From a ratio of about one-fifth of the body weight, the muscles increase in weight to about one-third in adolescence and up to two-fifths at adulthood. In general, males have greater muscular power than females. There are some women, however, who possess as much or more muscular strength than some men, but such cases are exceptional.

Although during the embryonic period there is evidence of frequent but feeble heartbeat, there is no similar evidence that breathing takes place before birth. As postbirth respiration increases, the heart beats more slowly and more strongly than it did during the prenatal stage of growth. The rapid heartbeat of the infant (up to 140 per minute) may decrease to about 62 for men and 63 for women, although a heartbeat of 72 per minute is normal for adults.

At birth, the child possesses his full complement of neurons (nerve cells), and the neural structure is approximately what it will be in later life. The functioning of the nervous system at first is very simple. The sensory, association, and motor neurons gradually strengthen, through maturation and environmental stimulation, so that they serve more or less adequately as the bases of the individual's mental activities throughout his life.

The lymphatic system, active in the elimination of wastes and the destruction of bacteria, increases rapidly for about the first twelve years of life, and then decreases in activity. The genital organs are slow in their growth during early childhood but start to grow rapidly during puberty. The functions of the endocrine or ductless glands constitute one of the most challenging fields of psychological study. Little was known about them before the twentieth century. Although their respective locations in the body, their constitution, and some of their functions now are known, they still offer considerable material for further research. (See Figure 4, Location of the Principal Endocrine Glands.) We also know that they do not follow the same or even a similar sequence of maturation. It would seem, therefore, that they serve specific functions during various stages of physical growth.

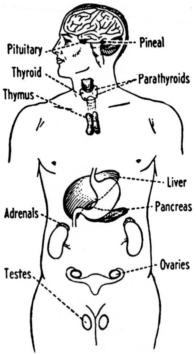

FIGURE 4.   Location of the Principal Endocrine Glands

From J. F. Dashiell, *Fundamentals of General Psychology*, Houghton Mifflin Co., Boston, 1949, p. 295. Reprinted by permission.

The thyroid gland, secreting a hormone (thyroxin) which affects the rate of basal metabolism, apparently serves as a control of development and behavior. Overactivity of the gland, (hyperthyroidism) induces abnormal tensions and extreme physical activity. Generally sluggish behavior can result from underactivity of this gland (hypothyroidism).

The pituitary gland has two lobes. A secretion of one of them (the anterior lobe) seems to regulate skeletal growth. Overfunctioning of this lobe may lead to giantism; underfunctioning is associated with dwarfism. The sex glands or gonads are activated by another hormone of the anterior lobe. Little is known of the functioning of the hormones of the other lobe (posterior lobe), except that one of its functions may be related to the tonus of the smooth-muscle lining of the digestive tract.

The functioning of the adrenal or suprarenal glands is closely related to emotionalized behavior. During a state of anger, for example, an increased amount of adrenin is released into the blood stream, resulting in an increase in blood pressure and greater rapidity of heartbeat. The increase in physical strength that can be characteristic of an angry state results from a combination of these factors and an increased supply of glycogen from the liver.

With the onset of puberty, there begin to be secreted in the testes and ovum the reproductive cells—sperm and ova. The sex glands or gonads also produce hormones that control the development of secondary sex characteristics—breast development and menstruation in girls, and change of voice and growth of beard in boys, as well as changes in facial contours for both sexes and the appearance of hair in the armpits and in the pubic regions.

The pineal glands and the thymus are active during childhood, and seem to have as their function the curbing of sexual maturation during childhood. This theory is borne out by the fact that these two glands disappear or become much less active with the beginning of adolescence.

Health and physical development. Physical growth and development result from a complex pattern of continuous changes that have health implications. The physical constitution can be thought of as a highly organized and delicate mechanism that can be expected to run smoothly and to serve the individual well in all of his life activities if there are no biologically inherited defects and if developmental needs receive proper care.

Adults who are responsible for the health of the growing child need to be alert to any manifestations of developmental difficulties. Hence parents, pediatricians, and teachers should be able to recognize the signs of good health in the young child as these are reflected in his general appearance and behavior. According to Norman

Capon, some of the characteristics of the healthy child that can be observed by the relatively untrained layman are:

1. The mucous membranes (e.g., the lips, and the palpebral conjunctiva of the eyes) are definitely pink in colour.
2. The facial expression is happy, often radiant; smiling is frequent, and the eyes are bright and responsive.
3. The skin is smooth, elastic, and covers a sufficient layer of subcutaneous fat to give the limbs a rounded appearance.
4. The tissue turgor is normal.
5. The muscles are well formed and their tonus is good.
6. The limb muscles are almost straight.
7. The stance is well balanced, erect. and graceful.
8. The spine is straight and the shoulder girdles do not droop.
9. The arches of the feet are well formed.
10. The movements of limbs and body in walking and running are characterized by elasticity, vigour, and poise.[1]

Unfortunately, not all children possess these characteristics of good health. Innate weaknesses and unhealthful environmental conditions may result in early death or in temporary or prolonged periods of illness. It is true that with new drugs and immunization, child mortality has decreased. Fewer fatalities result from pneumonia, and contagious diseases such as whooping cough, diphtheria, measles, and scarlet fever. Pediatricians and health centers try to prevent malnutrition by teaching mothers the principles of healthful child diet.

Other unfavorable conditions are now responsible for death or ill health among children. Too many children are being crippled from birth conditions or from accidents that are caused by the environmental hazards inherent in our present mode of life. Medical science is struggling with the increase among children of such serious health difficulties as heart disease and cancer. Recognition of the early symptoms of either of these dread diseases, followed by proper treatment, may lead to complete or partial recovery. In any case, the mental and emotional strains that result from a nonhealthy physical state may exert an extremely bad influence upon a child's developing personality.

The Development of Mental Abilities

An individual's degree of mental alertness probably influences every phase of his life pattern. From childhood through old age he

[1] Norman B. Capon, "The Assessment of Health in Childhood," *The Archives of Disease in Childhood, British Medical Journal*, London, Vol. 20, 1945, p 54. Reprinted by permission.

constantly is called upon to react to multitudinous elements in his physical environment and to many varied human interrelationships. The more sensitive he is to stimulation and the more able he is to respond adequately to that by which he is stimulated, the more likely he is to achieve success in his daily life activities.

There are available many studies concerning mental growth and the development of what has been termed *intelligence*. Results of these studies have given us some understanding of this phase of human growth and development. Mental processes are so complex, however, that relatively little is known concerning their functional possibilities. In fact, controversies still exist among psychologists concerning cause and effect relationships between demonstrated abilities and factors of influence. Much more extensive and intensive study is needed to achieve some general agreement as to what intelligence really is, how it develops, and why individuals differ in their overt expressions of mental activity.

Mental growth. Mental growth can be defined roughly as the gradual increase in ability to become aware of and to adapt one's self to environmental conditions and, if necessary, to control them. Mentally activated behavior is different from simple reflex responses. The former is consciously controlled toward the achievement of immediate or more remote goals; the latter, such as breathing and eye winking, function automatically as life maintainers and usually do not enter the focus of consciousness unless there is difficulty of functioning.

Mental growth depends upon the growth of the brain and nerves. It follows a pattern of development analogous to that of other phases of human growth and development. The potentialities of mental development lie in the growing physical constitution but require stimulation by the social environment in order for mental ability to be transformed into intelligent behavior.

Mental activity is controlled by the outer layer (*cortex*) of the cerebrum, not by the whole brain. The cortex consists of three layers, the *infragranular* layer, the *granular* layer, and the *supragranular* layer, respectively. The infragranular layer (reaching about 80 per cent of its growth at birth) functions as a controller of the reflexes; the granular layer (reaching 75 per cent of its growth at birth) is connected with the conduction of sense impressions; the supragranular layer (reaching only about 50 per cent of its growth at birth) is most closely related to degree of mental ability. Although the actual number of brain cells is fixed during the prenatal period, the growth continues until maturity. The nerve cells of the supragranular layer, therefore, have much possibility of growth during the maturing years. To the extent that this growth is stimulated, mental development can be expected to progress satisfactorily.

There is evidence that mental growth is continuous, but there is no evidence of any definite stages. Studies indicate, however, that the rate of development varies from age to age. The higher cortical centers, that function very little or not at all at birth, mature rapidly during about the first six months. Although the sensory organs (eyes, ears, nose, mouth, and touch organs) are well developed structurally at birth, their adequate functioning depends upon the maturational process.

A baby's first sensations are simple awarenesses. He then develops the ability to put meaning into his sensations, to associate them and to make simple judgments concerning their relation to one another and to himself. Beginning with sensation, the child's mental abilities can be said to follow a general pattern of development that includes interpreting sensations (*perception*), building upon perceptual material not present to the senses (*imagery*), recalling that which has been experienced (*memory*), and finally, formulating generalizations drawn from experience and dealing with abstractions (*reasoning*).

These various forms of mental activity take place in an integrated and interacting fashion throughout the lifetime of an individual. During the early years, of course, the activities are simple; perceptions may be inaccurate and generalizations illogical. Progress from simple mental activity toward highly complex mental progress constitutes intellectual growth. Overt indications of mental growth follow a pattern that begins with learning word meanings and developing a vocabulary that will make intercommunication possible, and continues with the gaining of factual information and the development of concepts and thought processes. (See Chapter 13.)

Factors that influence mental growth and development. Many studies have had for their purpose an attempt to discover whether mental ability or intelligent behavior is more closely associated with biological inheritance or with social heritage. Hereditarians claim that intelligence is inherited through the ancestral line, and that environmental influences merely help the individual utilize inherent abilities. Proponents of the behaviorist school argue that what the child inherits is of little consequence; eventual intelligent behavior results from the application of environmental influences upon the growing individual. These two emphases still constitute the bases of heated controversy, especially between biologists and sociologists. The generally accepted point of view among psychologists is that both heredity and environment affect mental growth. They are not yet ready to say, however, to what extent. The facts probably are that natural growth and environmentally stimulated development are so closely related that it is almost impossible to isolate either phase for study.

The growth pattern of an individual's mental abilities depends upon the type of brain and nervous system he inherits by way of the genes. Rate of maturation and maturational limits of growth are inherent in the physical constitution, but environmental factors may exercise some effect upon the neural system, even during the prenatal period of life. It probably is correct to say, therefore, that the *limit* of possible mental growth is set by heredity; the *kind* of mental development that takes place within potential limits is dependent upon biological inheritance, congenital influences, and postnatal factors.

A greater or lesser degree of mental alertness seems to run in families. It is difficult to determine, however, to what extent family trends result from inherited potentialities or from the effects of home environment. Studies have been made of identical twins reared apart in different environmental and cultural situations. The results of these studies do not yield any definite conclusions concerning the part played by inheritance and environment in the development of mental abilities, though it would seem that the twin having the more favorable cultural and educational advantages would be likely to earn higher scores on the same intelligence tests administered to both. Studies of foster children reared with the children of the foster parents, when the native capacities of both natural and foster parents were compared with home conditions, have shown that children seem to resemble their natural parents more than their foster parents in the abilities studied.

A child may seem to give behavior evidence of a lower level of mental ability than that which he actually possesses. The reason for this difference may lie in the inadequacy of environmental stimulation or it may be caused by unfavorable conditions such as those enumerated by Grace Archer:

(1) Physical handicaps such as impaired vision, impaired hearing, impaired mechanisms for motor co-ordination, etc., that interfere with academic learning and with success on some scales for measuring intelligence.

(2) Brain injury which occurred at birth or from later accident that interfered with some kinds of intellectual activity but not with others.

(3) Severe early illness that delayed but did not prevent mental development.

(4) Delayed speech that extends far beyond normal limits, but has not prevented development of nonverbal abilities.

(5) Intellectual idiosyncrasies that act as special intellectual disabilities until they are diagnosed and given appropriate treatment, and frequently are confused with general mental deficiency.[1]

Meaning and theories of intelligence. The term *intelligence* is applied to those mental functions that constitute the higher mental processes, such as those utilized in abstract thinking and in complex problem-solving. Intelligence is a concept and hence is difficult to define. It also is a function in that the measure of a person's intelligence seemingly is based on the behavior that results from the degree of successful functioning of the complex combination of the elements of mental capacity. The fact that intelligence is a concept has led to much controversy among psychologists in their attempt to interpret its meaning and to explain differences among individuals in their ability to act intelligently.

Definitions of intelligence during the early 1900's tended to place emphasis upon innate qualities rather than upon the effects of environmental conditions, and upon abstract mental activity. Alfred Binet interpreted intelligence as: "Comprehension, invention, direction, and criticism—intelligence is contained in these four words." [2] An often quoted definition is that of Stern: "Intelligence is a general capacity of an individual consciously to adjust his thinking to new requirements: It is general mental adaptability to new problems and conditions of life." [3] Stern's interpretation of intelligence is based upon the *general* nature of the mental process; it connotes a general mental ability rather than a combination of mental abilities.

Various theories have been propounded concerning the organization of intelligence. Early in the present century, Carl Spearman,

---

[1] Grace Archer, "Some Factors Contributing to Errors in the Diagnosis of Feeble-mindedness," *American Journal of Mental Deficiency*, Vol. 54, 1950, p. 497. Reprinted by permission.

[2] Alfred Binet; quoted in L. M. Terman, *The Measurement of Intelligence*, Houghton Mifflin, Boston, 1916, p. 45.

[3] W. Stern, *Psychological Methods of Testing Intelligence.* Warwick & York, Inc., Baltimore, 1914, p. 3.

an English statistician, formulated the so-termed "two factor" theory of intelligence. Spearman held that in all mental abilities there are two factors—general intelligence or a *g* factor, and specific ability or an *s* factor, the two factors working together as a unit. According to Thorndike, there is no such thing as mental ability *per se;* rather are there "intelligences" that show themselves more or less adequately in behavior as: abstract intelligence, mechanical intelligence, or social intelligence. Hence an individual could be very successful in scholarly pursuits, but mediocre in mechanical activities, and inadequate socially. Any relationship that may exist among these diverse abilities represents overlapping of the functions rather than activity of a general factor. Thorndike's theory would seem to disregard the effect of experience or the influence of environmental conditions upon the expression of mental activity. Other psychologists have attempted to analyze intelligence according to so-called "primary" mental abilities. One of these lists, resulting from intensive investigation by the Thurstones, includes verbal meaning, space thinking, reasoning, quantitative thinking, word fluency, memory, and motor perception.

Results of the various studies in this field indicate that there probably is no one general factor of ability controlling intelligent behavior. Apparently, many complex abilities function in relation to one another. Stoddard interpreted intelligence, in terms of the various theories propounded by psychologists, as "the ability to undertake activities that are characterized by (1) difficulty, (2) complexity, (3) abstractness, (4) economy (speed), (5) adaptiveness to a goal, (6) social value, and (7) the emergence of originals (inventiveness), and to maintain such activities under conditions that demand a concentration of energy and a resistance to emotional forces." [1]

Measurement of intelligence. Degree of intelligence, as such, cannot be evaluated except insofar as mental abilities are expressed in overt behavior. Hence there is a growing trend toward referring to the *intelligent behavior* of an individual rather than to his intelligence. In the final analysis, the most effective way of evaluating an individual's mental abilities is to observe his behavior and the extent to which he achieves success in his many, varied activities. This is a long process, however; it may be necessary to discover,

[1] G. D. Stoddard, "On the Meaning of Intelligence," *Psychological Review,* The American Psychological Association, Vol. 48, 1941, p. 255. Reprinted by permission.

before the individual engages in a particular activity, what his chances of success may be. School people, for example, should obtain some appreciation of a learner's potential learning ability before they stimulate him toward attempted mastery in any area of learning. Consequently, various types of intelligence tests or tests of mental abilities have been devised. These are described in Chapter 15.

Some factors of influence upon intelligence status. In addition to the hereditary, congenital, and environmental factors of influence upon mental development referred to earlier in the chapter, the bases of other possible intellectual differences need to be considered. These include the relationship to intelligence of such factors as sex, racial or national stock, socio-economic status, and home and family environment.

Sex. Traditionally, men were considered to be more intelligent than women. The administration of intelligence tests to large numbers of boys and girls of all ages has shown little difference in the range of scores between the sexes. An item analysis of test performance, however, seems to indicate that boys have a slight advantage over girls in questions that deal with scientific and mathematical concepts, and that girls excel somewhat in materials dealing with the humanities. These differences may result from differing early experiences.

More men than women become eminent. Whether this is the result of greater ability among men or of lack of opportunity for women to achieve recognition for their achievements is a moot question. It probably is true that there are more differences of mental ability within each sex than there are between the sexes. Little difference, if any, seems to be characteristic of boys and girls during the early childhood years. More rapid physical development of the girl during her later childhood and early adolescent years gives her an advantage over the boy. From these age periods onward, any observable differences between the sexes may need to be explained in terms of factors other than innate ability.

Racial, national, and geographical groups. There are many erroneous concepts concerning the intelligence of various groups. Some of these beliefs are based on prejudice. It is difficult to obtain reliable data through the administration of intelligence tests, since materials appropriate to the experiences of one group may be unrelated to the experiential background of another. Hence it is not possible to draw conclusions concerning the intelligence levels of different groups that would indicate greater superiority of one group over the other.

Socio-economic status. An evaluation of socio-economic status usually involves consideration of occupation, reading interests, recreational activities, income, home neighborhood and kind of home, and number and kind of community activities engaged in. There appears to be a definite positive correlation between degree of intelligence and socio-economic status. In general, the children of professional people are mentally superior to children of unskilled laborers. This generalization does not always hold in specific cases, however. Dull children can be found in the homes of the socio-economic superior; some of our most distinguished citizens were born and reared in "poor" home surroundings.

Even if we grant that a relationship does exist between living status and intelligence, we do not know the cause of the difference. Do mental abilities result from biological inheritance or are they concomitants of environmental conditions? The most we can say is that good inherited potential, combined with favorable environmental stimulation, probably will induce superior development; good potential and meager environment, or relatively poor potential and good environment may or may not lead to good development; poor potential and meager environment are likely to result in inadequate development.

Home and school environment. The amount and kind of stimulation that a child receives in the home and in the school exercise a strong influence on his developing personality. Unless a child has been provided with an opportunity to develop one or more phases of his mental potential, he does not know his strengths and weaknesses. Even adults may discover that they possess abilities of which they were unaware. Men and women of sixty years of age or older have earned recognition in fields of endeavor that were very different from their former occupations. For one or another reason, their abilities were challenged and they found, sometimes to their great surprise, that they could produce successfully in the new field.

Analogous situations can be found in the home and the school experiences of the developing young person. Parents who are overprotective in their attitude toward their children deny them the opportunity to learn through doing. Regardless of the advantages that a child may enjoy in his home, he should not be allowed to become "soft" mentally as a result of having his every wish granted and all decisions made for him. Although a parent should not be neglectful of his child's needs, a young person who is expected to do some things for himself has a better chance of developing independence of thinking, planning, and doing *on a mature basis* than does the boy or girl who does not need to engage in such experiences.

Similarly, in the school, the learner should be a doer, not just a recipient of knowledge that, for the most part, represents teacher activity. The child and the adolescent need to be stimulated to want to learn through actual as well as vicarious experiences, each having its proper place. However, whatever is done in the home and in the school to stimulate young people toward maximum mental activity should be based on individual levels of readiness for learning and on the emotional reaction pattern of each learner. In our discussion in Part III of the teaching and learning process, the importance of challenge in learning is discussed at length.

The Development of the Emotions

When we attempt to explain the *why* of human behavior, we are faced with a problem that at times seems to defy solution. Why does a little girl pay no attention to a beautiful new doll and continue to fondle an old rag one that may have lost its eyes and may be coming apart at the seams? Why does a boy resent his mother's emptying his pockets of worthless junk? Why does a usually cheerful and co-operative adolescent suddenly begin to make disparaging remarks to or about the members of his family, his teachers, and his peer associates? Why does a mother constantly "pick on" her child, even though at the same time she cares for the child's every need? Why does a man or a woman who is extremely honest in money matters appropriate for his own use the belongings of others? Why is a person calm and efficient in an emergency but very much disturbed by relatively minor difficulties?

The ready answer to questions like these is "That is the way people are." A more thoughtful response would include recognition of the fact that people are influenced in their behavior by their emotions. The next question would be "What are the emotions, and why and how do they affect human behavior?" Any attempt to provide a satisfactory explanation of the importance of emotions in the life of any individual must include an intensive and extensive study of factors within and outside the person, and the constant interaction that is taking place among these factors. Hence the part played by the emotions in personal and social adjustment cannot be considered in isolation.

In later chapters, we discuss the personal and social development of the child and of the adolescent, and the ways in which teaching and learning proceed. Our present discussion is concerned with some of the bases of emotional behavior, in an attempt to show how emotional development is interwoven with all other phases of developing personality.

Interpretation of emotional states. When a person is experiencing what is generally referred to as an emotional state, both internal and overt behavior changes are taking place. The marked physiological changes, of which the individual himself usually is aware, and the outward manifestations of which can be observed by others, have led to the recognition of an emotion as a *general stirred-up state of the organism.* For a time it was believed that the physiological changes constituted the bases of emotions. Such an explanation of an emotional state does not take into consideration the feelings and experiences of the emotionalized individual. Also, certain physiological changes may be associated with each of various forms of emotionalism.

According to the James-Lange theory of emotions, overt reactions give rise to the emotion. For example, running from an unaccustomed sight results in fear; the more quickly one runs, the more afraid he becomes. Similarly, it can be assumed that fondling a child will lead to a feeling of tenderness toward the child, or that hitting a man will arouse a feeling of anger toward him. Emotion, thus interpreted, would constitute the result of behavior rather than the cause of it. This explanation is not adequate. Although some actors and actresses assert that they live the emotional states that they portray, perhaps the most convincing dramatic performances are given by actors and actresses who present objectively the role that they are playing, without themselves passing through the portrayed emotional experience at that time.

Emotion represents a phase of the total dynamic pattern of human personality. The functioning of an emotion involves physiological changes, overt behavior, and feelings and impulses. Because of the complexity of the interrelations of these aspects of emotion, it is difficult to analyze any emotional state into its component parts. An emotional state varies in intensity and in length of duration. An individual may seem to be giving evidence of one kind of emotional reaction at one moment (either mild or intense) and, at the next moment, shift to another emotional state, sometimes without apparent reason. Why and when does the change take place? Recognizing the elusive nature of the psychological implications of emotion, one needs to be wary in his attempts to formulate a simple and accurate definition. In essence, however, an emotion can be considered to be *an affective experience that is accompanied by generalized inner adjustment and physiological and mental stirred-up states, and that expresses itself in overt behavior.*

An emotional state is closely related to other inherent behavior stimulators. When we say that an individual is stimulated to behave in this or that way, we are implying that an object or group of objects, a person or group of persons, a condition, or a situation activates one or more of the individual's sensory organs; then, through the process of neural association, sensory awareness is translated into one or more forms of behavior. This description of the stimulation of behavior does not take into account the fact that a person may seem to disregard or ignore certain stimulating forces, and to respond to others. A child's, adolescent's, or adult's behavior reactions tend to follow one direction rather than another, mainly because inner impulses or conditions, present at the time of stimulation, motivate or activate him to behave in a particular fashion.

From birth onward, a human being possesses the impulse to achieve desired goals. As we shall show in later chapters, these goals change in form and methods of achieving them in terms of maturation and experience. Throughout life, however, an individual continues to attempt to meet his physical, mental, emotional, and social needs, and to satisfy desires, urges, and interests.[1] Biological and acquired behavior drives are similar to emotions in that they are motivators of behavior. The satisfaction of a drive may have emotional accompaniments. An emotion differs from a drive, however, in that the former constitutes a series of responses to external stimulating situations. The individual is aware of the significance of the emotion-arousing situation which, by its nature, demands a change in inner state and overt behavior from that which is habitual.

"Feeling tones" and emotions. An innate characteristic of human nature appears to be that all of an individual's sensory experiences are accompanied by tendencies to continue or return to them, or to withdraw from or to avoid them. These tendencies are rooted

---

[1] For a detailed description of behavior motivation, see Chapter 6.

in the degree of personal satisfaction or annoyance associated with any specific situation or condition, and are called *feeling tones*. The behavior reactions of a hungry infant are diffused and show little conscious awareness of his reasons for crying, moving his body, and otherwise indicating his need for his bottle. In his immature way he is exhibiting a state of annoyance that, after his hunger is satisfied, changes to one of satisfaction, expressed in relaxed body status, cooing, and gurgling.

As the experiential environment of the young child widens and he becomes increasingly aware of his relationships to it, he *learns* to gain satisfaction from some of his experiences and to be annoyed by others. This process continues through life. What is pleasant or satisfying at one time may annoy or be dissatisfying at another, depending upon the individual's state of responsiveness and existing environmental conditions. Individuals differ from one another in the feeling tones that are attached to similar situations. For example, one person may like eating lettuce, sleeping on a hard mattress, wearing gloves while driving a car, playing bridge, teaching young children, or participating in recreational activities such as swimming or hiking. Another person may find any or all of these activities extremely unpleasant or annoying. Some of the persons who usually gain pleasure from participating in these activities listed in the foregoing sometimes may find them annoying.

There are similarities between feeling tones and the emotions, although they are different in their functioning. An emotion is a conscious reaction to a stimulus situation. We often are not aware of our feeling toward a situation, even though our behavior is affected by it. It is sometimes only as another person calls our attention to the fact that we are reacting in one or another way to a situation or condition that we realize the reason for it. Many of our feeling tones are relatively mild.

We may believe that we are telling the truth when we assert that we have no particular feeling toward an object, a person, or a situation. Yet, the fact is that, without realizing the reason for our choice, we select one object rather than another, give more attention to one person than to another, or tend to relive, in memory, one situation or experience rather than another. Such behavior shows that there is some slight difference, at least, in the feeling tones attached to the object, person, or situation. Teachers often say, for example, that they "like" all of their pupils. Yet, as they recount their classroom experiences, they unconsciously display differences in feeling toward the appearance and behavior of the various members of their classes and their own teaching-learning relationships.

A strong feeling takes on some of the characteristics of an emotion. In fact, emotion is defined loosely by some people as a "strong feeling." We often hear expressions such as, "I feel angry" or "I feel sad." But we also hear people say that they *feel* hungry, sleepy, thirsty, or wide-awake. What these expressions connote is that the happiness, sadness, hunger, sleepiness, etc., represent emotional and physical states that are accompanied by feeling tones of satisfaction or annoyance. The use of the word *feel* is a kind of verbal short cut into which the listener is supposed to put meaning as a result of his own experiences with these states. A feeling is not an emotion, but emotions may have feeling tones that are associated with the individual's reactions in and toward the particular emotional state he is experiencing.

The arousal of emotions. The arousal of an emotion depends on the state of readiness of the individual to be aroused and the kind and strength of the stimulating situation. An individual's maturational level, state of health, degree of mental alertness, extent of fatigue, ideals, ambitions, goals and aspirations, and appreciation of life values are some of the factors that exercise a potent influence on those of his reactions that can be considered emotional. The experiencing of love, affection, tenderness, sympathy, awe, fear, worry, jealousy, anger, rage, or any other form of emotion is possible only when there are present in the environment those factors of influence that have the power to motivate or to stir the particular individual at that specific time.

Many illustrations of this relationship between inner state and outer condition or situation can be found in the everyday life of young people and adults. For example, a boy and a girl play together constantly. They see each other almost daily and enjoy the activities which they share. Of course, they admire each other, but there is no strong attachment between them. Suddenly, during pubescence or early adolescence, one or both of them come to see the other as an attractive young person whose company is sought in preference to that of any other member of the opposite sex. Young love has begun!

Again, a young man may not be particularly interested in small children, but his own child becomes the "apple of his eye." This same young man may be extremely tired when he comes home from work. As a result of his tiredness, he may become very angry with both the child and the mother because the youngster does not want to go to bed, or engages in one or another form of childish behavior which annoys the tired father. One more example is that of the boy who has developed a strong ambition to engage in a particular field of occupational activity. Demonstrated ability to perform may be inferior to that required by the occupation, or there may be no available opportunity for job placement even though he is adequately prepared for it. In either case, the failure to achieve his goal may so discourage the boy that he is afraid to prepare himself for another field, and he comes to regard himself as a failure.

The intensity and duration of an emotional experience are determined largely by the strength and persistency of the stimulating situation and the physical and mental condition of the individual experiencing the emotionalized state. Children's anger, for example, may be intense; but it usually lasts only for a short time, and can be diverted by the removal of the child from the anger-arousing situation. Contrariwise, anger in an older person can persist for long periods of time, even after the original stimulus situation has been removed. Memories of an actual or imagined hurt can give rise to a long-time continuance of the emotion of hostility.

The emotions and other phases of human development. We have referred earlier to the complexities of the human developmental pattern. Development of the emotions is linked with the physical and mental sequences of maturation. The growth and functioning of the nervous system (both central and autonomic) affect the developing emotional pattern. The functioning of the glands (especially the adrenal, thyroid, and pituitary) is basic to the inner changes that take place in the individual when he is emotionally aroused. The great strength that may be displayed by the enraged person is an example of the functioning of the physical system. With increase in mental ability can come greater mental control of the emotions, although a strong emotional state may seem to inhibit an individual's habitually intelligent control of his behavior.

There is closer relation between physical health and emotional status than generally is recognized. The emotions sometimes serve as means of coping with emergency situations. The physiological changes that take place help in meeting the situation, especially one that involves fear or anger. Unless the situation is serious, the emotional state subsides and the physiological emergency reactions return to their normal pattern of functioning. If the individual cannot escape from the situation or does not have a complete understanding of it, these physiological reactions continue.

The individual becomes aware of visceral disturbances that may cause him to believe that he is suffering from a disease. In fact, actual tissue damage may develop. Awareness of symptoms resulting from prolonged psychological reactions as well as actual tissue damage is referred to as *psychosomatic disease*. It often is difficult for the physician to distinguish between actual symptoms of illness or imagined ones, especially if the patient is in a highly disturbed state.

Because of the close relationship that exists between a person's emotional status and his physical constitution, an emotion may affect a person's health. It is a known fact that, although stomach ulcers result from organic dysfunctioning, the origin of the difficulty may be found in extreme emotional stress and strain. If the condition is discovered early enough, removal from the emotion-arousing situation and adherence to a special diet are likely to improve or even to cure the organic difficulty. Moreover, doctors and nurses know the value of helping a patient maintain emotional equilibrium during a period of severe illness. Otherwise, the sick person may become so dependent, or so disturbed over his illness that medication or other forms of treatment may be ineffective as a means of helping the patient regain normal good health.[1]

The emotions and learning. A child's or adolescent's learning progress is affected by many factors that lie both within his inherent nature and in the teaching-learning environment. Since these factors can exert a tremendous influence on the young person's emotional reactions, they have the power to further or hinder satisfactory learning achievement.

As the young child develops physically and mentally, he unconsciously acquires the ability to walk and to talk, and to find a place for himself in the family and among same-age associates. He usually achieves much emotional satisfaction from the growing recognition of his increasing ability to assert himself as an individual among other individuals. At the same time, because he still is too immature to understand his own complex nature and the environmental forces that surround him, he may suffer occasional thwartings and fears. Yet he is responsive to the loving care he receives from his elders. Hence he experiences various emotional states: love, anger, fear and jealousy. To the extent that anger and fear stimuli are minimal, the learning process proceeds smoothly and prepares the child for entrance into his formal schooling.

Most youngsters look forward with much pleasure to going to school. A child who is too dependent on his mother for his satisfactions, however, may find his first school experiences extremely unpleasant. He becomes highly emotional and requires tactful and understanding treatment on the part of his teacher to help him become adjusted to new and more formal learning situations.

As the child progresses through school, his learning achievement constantly is being influenced by his emotional attitudes. He likes or dislikes his teacher. He gets along well with his schoolmates, or he is more or less unpopular with them. If he is successful in his school studies, he probably enjoys school, and is an accepted member of his class group. Unsatisfactory learning achievement may lead to discouragement and dislike of school.

Because of the pubertal changes that are taking place, a young adolescent often finds it difficult to give adequate attention to his school learning responsibilities. He becomes aware of the physical and emotional changes that are taking place within him. He may be eager to learn but the desired learning is associated with his social relationships rather than with school subjects. During the growing-up years incidents and circumstances that to the adult may appear to be relatively unimportant are matters of major emotional importance.

The adolescent is passing through a stage of development that is characterized by a struggle between childhood dependence upon adults and adult independence of action. He is becoming increasingly involved emotionally with peer-group relations. He may be restless; he may find it difficult to concentrate on routine study. His feelings may alternate between high enthusiasm and deep depression. Hence it becomes the responsibility of his teachers to recognize and understand the emotional attributes of the developing adolescent and to motivate him toward the achievement of wholesome emotional outcomes.

QUESTIONS AND TOPICS FOR DISCUSSION

1. Discuss the consistency of growth of intelligence in individual children from birth to twelve years of age. What variables can be found?
2. Describe a school situation in which you observed a child or a group of children experience great emotional excitement. What were the stimuli that aroused the emotional state?
3. In what ways may mental development be affected by the emotions?
4. What are the implications for parents and teachers of the fact that many of our emotions are learned?

5. Describe the developmental stages that usually occur in children's emotions.
6. Mental ability is only one of the factors to be considered in a total evaluation of a person's behavior. What are some of the other factors that should be considered?
7. What can you do to control anger? Fear? Jealousy?
8. Discuss the relationship between emotion-arousing stimuli and overt emotional behavior.
9. Describe the behavior of someone who, you believe, is suffering from a psychosomatic disease. What caused it?

SELECTED REFERENCES

Abrahamson, D., *Emotional Care of Your Child,* Trident, N.Y., 1970.

Cofer, C. N., *Motivation and Emotion.* Scott Foresman, Chicago, 1972.

Crow, A.,* *Educational Psychology,* rev. ed , Littlefield, Totowa, N.J., 1971.

Crow, L. D., and Graham, T., *Human Development and Adjustment.* Littlefield, Totowa, N.J., 1972.

Dichter, E., *Motivating Human Behavior.* McGraw-Hill, N.Y., 1971.

Hurlock, E. B., *Child Growth and Development,* 3rd ed. McGraw-Hill, N.Y., 1968.

Maslow, A. H., *Motivation and Personality,* 2nd ed. Harper and Row, N.Y., 1970.

Stein, P. T., and Rosen, J. J., *Motivation and Emotion,* Macmillan, N.Y. 1974.

4   *Personal and Social Development during Childhood*

Childhood ranges from birth until puberty. The exact number of years included in this period differs with individuals. Except in rare cases, observable pubertal changes may occur as early as the age of ten, or may be delayed until the child reaches fifteen or sixteen. Generally, however, the first twelve years constitute the childhood period of life. A child's patterns of growth, development, and personal and social adjustment during this period strongly influence his later attitudes, interests, emotional reactions, behavior patterns, and interpersonal relations. It is not surprising, therefore, that psychologists, sociologists, and educators emphasize the ways in which the child's inherited potentialities can and should be developed by the provision of those environmental situations that will help him gradually become a healthy, happy, and socially useful person.

The Child's Developing Personality

In an earlier discussion we emphasized the fact that an individual's personality is the total integrating and integrated pattern of all his many characteristics and behavior traits. These function in the continuance of his survival, and influence his relationships with the objects, conditions, people, and situations that constitute his world at any stage of his growth and development. The intrapersonal and the social aspects of personality are stressed in Ruch's definition of personality as "the fundamental organization of the individual which determines the unique nature or individuality of his interactions with himself and with his environment." [1] The kind of personality an individual eventually acquires is rooted in the ways in which he develops physically, mentally, emotionally, and socially during his childhood.

[1] F. L. Ruch, *Psychology and Life,* 4th ed., Scott, Foresman & Co., Chicago, 1953, p. 30.

The growth pattern. Growth in any one aspect of an individual's personality is continuous, though it differs in rate at different stages and does not parallel the growth sequence of other traits. Consequently, it can be said that, at any stage of his total developmental pattern, a child has many "ages," which may vary from one another by as many as two years or more. Some of these differences result from variation in the rate of maturation; others are caused by the kind and amount of environmental stimulation the child has experienced. For example, a child whose chronological age is nine years may have a physiological age of eleven, an anatomical age of twelve, a mental age of nine, a reading age of seven, and an emotional and a social age of eight. Parents and teachers, therefore, are faced with the problem of meeting the developmental needs of each aspect of the child's personality pattern.

The task of the teacher is especially difficult if children are assigned to grade classes on the basis of chronological age. In the same class with the nine-year-old may be another child of the same chronological age whose other "ages" are: physiological, nine; anatomical, eight; mental, thirteen; reading, twelve; emotional, eleven; and social, eight. Each child in a single class may represent differing combinations of maturational ages. In an ideal teaching-learning situation, both learning tasks and techniques of learning motivation would be suited to the differing learning potentials, not only among the members of the class but also for each learner.

Parents encounter similar difficulties. Siblings differ from one another in rate of growth, although such differences usually are less than those between children of different families. As mentioned earlier, parents, in comparing the behavior of their children, often are distressed by the fact that one or more of their children do not seem to meet the developmental standards set by the others. Mothers tend also to compare the developmental progress of their children with that of the children of their friends and neighbors. These mothers either may become unduly proud of a child who seems to progress more rapidly than other children, or may attempt to force the development of a child who seems to be growing and developing at a slower rate than others. Regardless of the child's rate of growth, from birth on he experiences certain needs that must be satisfied if he is to develop satisfactorily within the limits of his potential.

Children's needs. No matter what his age, everyone has needs, urges, or drives that must be satisfied if he is to maintain at least normal adjustment. Some psychologists attempt to differentiate among these three behavior compulsions. Needs are more or less static conditions of the organism. Drives and urges, as motivators of action, differ only to the extent that a drive can be regarded as an impelling force that leads to action, while the urge is more nearly related to the feeling that arouses that drive to action. These differences are slight, however, and relatively unimportant.[1] The recognition of and the provision for the fulfillment of a person's needs should be a shared responsibility of the individual himself and of those who, especially during his developing years, are responsible for his welfare.

Human needs can be arranged in group categories. The following list shows such a grouping—a rearrangement and modification of responses to a questionnaire based upon a selection of needs.

TABLE 1. The Basic Human Needs[2]

A. *Bodily needs*
  1. Need to go on living
  2. Need to avoid danger
  3. Need to relax
  4. Need to recover when ill or injured
  5. Need to overcome handicaps

B. *Personal needs*
  6. Need to grow
  7. Need to be normal
  8. Need to have and keep possessions
  9. Need to overcome difficulties
  10. Need to be loved
  11. Need to feel secure
  12. Need to escape blame
  13. Need to express oneself
  14. Need to seek thrills and excitement
  15. Need to seek some form of sexual expression
  16. Need for independence

C. *Social needs*
  17. Need to have friends
  18. Need to be popular
  19. Need to be a leader
  20. Need to follow a leader
  21. Need to control others
  22. Need to protect others
  23. Need to imitate others
  24. Need to have prestige
  25. Need to seek praise
  26. Need to resist coercion
  27. Need to oppose others

D. *Intellectual needs*
  28. Need to think
  29. Need to acquire facts
  30. Need to think out explanations
  31. Need to relate and interpret facts
  32. Need to organize
  33. Need to work toward a goal
  34. Need to believe in something outside oneself

[1] For a more detailed discussion of drives and urges, see Chapter 6.
[2] L. Cole, *Psychology of Adolescence*, 4th ed., Rinehart & Co., New York, 1954, p. 112. Reprinted by permission.

Since these needs include the wants, desires, urges, and drives of an individual throughout his life span, they are stated in relatively general terms. The fulfillment of many needs begins in childhood. Havighurst prepared a series of what he termed "developmental tasks" which the child needs to learn in order to meet adequately the demands and expectations of his social environment. Havighurst's series of "tasks" of infancy, early childhood, and middle childhood are:

Infancy and Early Childhood

1. Learning to walk
2. Learning to take solid foods
3. Learning to talk
4. Learning to control the elimination of body wastes
5. Learning sex differences and sexual modesty
6. Achieving physiological stability
7. Forming simple concepts of social and physical reality
8. Learning to relate oneself emotionally to parents, siblings, and other people
9. Learning to distinguish right and wrong and developing a conscience.

Middle Childhood

1. Learning physical skills necessary for ordinary games
2. Building wholesome attitudes toward oneself as a growing organism
3. Learning to get along with age-mates
4. Learning an appropriate masculine or feminine social role
5. Developing fundamental skills in reading, writing, and calculating
6. Developing concepts necessary for everyday living
7. Developing conscience, morality, and a scale of values
8. Achieving personal independence
9. Developing attitudes toward social groups and institutions.[1]

These developmental tasks, of course, are not learned in sequential order—that is, the young child does not first complete his learning activities in walking, and then start to learn to take solid foods. Rather, the learnings overlap. Some begin earlier than others; successful learning in one task may aid in the development of another; progress in one may be more rapid than in another. All the learnings

[1] Adapted from R. J. Havighurst, *Human Development and Education*, Longmans, Green & Co., New York, 1953, pp. 9–17, 28–41. Reprinted by permission.

depend on the individual rate and kind of maturation taking place and the efficacy of the learning stimulations provided by the environment. The extent and kind of learning that take place in any of these areas of development during the childhood years will affect later behavior; continued change in or modification of resulting behavior may be expected to occur throughout the entire life span of an individual.

Since the present discussion is concerned primarily with the development of those personality traits that are related especially to a child's increasing ability to meet the demands of his social environment, we shall consider only briefly those phases of development that deal with physical survival. The greater part of the discussion will be devoted to those aspects of the child's personality pattern that have to do with his growing awareness of himself and of other people, his emotional reactions to the world about him, the development of his habitual attitudes, and the changes that take place from infancy through childhood in his relationships with other children and adults.

The Development of Life-Sustaining Activities

If the newborn infant is to become eventually a healthy, actively functioning person, his growing body needs proper care, and he must be helped to develop good physical controls.

Areas of early development. As anatomical structure and physiological functions mature, the child must learn to relate his physical self to the world about him under his own "steam." Physical growth must be accompanied by communication with others through speaking and writing, adequate learnings in the areas of locomotor activities, the caring for body needs, and the control of other forms of manipulatory behavior.

The neonate is helpless as a self-maintaining and self-protecting organism. All of his physical needs are being met. Gradually, he learns to participate, voluntarily and with increasing skill, in such activities as eating, eliminating, creeping, crawling, walking, and running. His first vocalizations, such as ma-ma and da-da (often misunderstood by fond parents as signs of the child's recognition of themselves as his mother and father) gradually take on the form of intelligible words, phrases, and sentences.

Developing patterns of activities. With progressive maturation, muscular activity advances from control of the gross muscles to finer muscle movements. Power to handle objects gradually improves. If a baby is bottle fed, at first the mother must hold the bottle and direct it to the infant's mouth. Later, he may place one of his hands on the bottle; then, he may attempt to grasp it with both hands and even try to place the nipple of the bottle into his mouth. As the growth pattern continues, the child's ability to hold the bottle and to manipulate it also improves.

Recently, a neighbor's son and daughter-in-law flew from Cleveland to New York with their two children, a boy of two years and a ten-month-old girl, to visit the husband's family. They arrived about ten o'clock at night. Soon after their arrival, the young couple brought the boy into our home to say "Hello." The child was very sleepy, but was carrying his sister's bottle (for security, as his mother laughingly said). Being a friendly youngster, the boy proceeded to toddle around the room on a tour of investigation. He closed a door and investigated the door chimes on the wall behind the door, still grasping the bottle in one hand. He was invited to crawl into a large easy chair but spurned the offer. Instead, he proceeded to climb into a higher-seat wing chair. His first efforts were awkward, but he finally seated himself and laughed with satisfaction at his achievement. He pulled himself down from the chair. He then repeated climbing into it several times, each time with greater ease and fewer waste movements, and consequent greater satisfaction to himself. Throughout the series of activities, he held onto the bottle, keeping it in a perpendicular position.

This two-year-old youngster's control of his body and body parts and his degree of alertness, as compared with the fact that his sister had slept during the trip after she had been fed and still was sleeping peacefully while he was learning a new task, illustrate the rapid physical growth and development that take place during the early years of a child's life. The boy's friendliness and ease in the presence of strangers indicated that his parents were doing a good job of helping him develop good interpersonal relationships.

The Development of Language Skill

In general, a child's degree of success in learning to communicate with other people in his environment follows a pattern of development that is similar to progress in the other aspects of his development and is interrelated with them. The infant gives expression to his simple wants through crying and gross body movements. Satisfaction is indicated by way of smiles, coos, and body relaxation. As the baby becomes more sensitive to objects in his environment, he attempts to grasp or to point to something he "wants"; he may push away or turn from things he does not want.

Pattern of language development. Some psychologists believe that vocalization and verbal expression have their beginnings in the explosive sounds, such as cooing, that occur during the first three months of life. These seem to be unlearned, resulting from chance movements of the vocal organs. Usually, between the ages of three to eight months, the baby engages in making more definite sounds, called *babbling*. Gradually these sounds become increasingly meaningful. The child achieves an understanding of simple expressions used by adults in connection with their attempts to meet his needs and to regulate his conduct. He starts to imitate some adult-used words, such as "No," or "Bye-bye."

Many studies have been made of young children's developing speech patterns. Children whose mental growth pattern is normal pass, with relative rapidity, through the developmental stages of language use from babbling, to monologue (talking more or less intelligibly to themselves of their toys), to the naming stage, then to simple question-asking (why, where, when), on to sentence forming, and then to written language, and drawing. Through training and experiences, language patterns are formed that may continue to be modified in terms of individual intercommunicational needs. It is estimated that by the time an average child is six, his speaking vocabulary consists of approximately 2,560 words.

Significant factors of language development. Children use language to obtain the fulfillment of their wants, to give and to receive information, and to express their feelings about all kinds of things and situations. Moreover, just as they delight in having stories read to them, they like to tell stories, the fanciful nature of which is evidence of the child's developing powers of imagination. Although the young child thinks about things and engages in simple reasoning processes, he cannot always explain what he thinks. Even the older child finds it difficult to put the results of his constructive thinking and reasoning into adequate language form. In fact, many adults have similar difficulty.

Young children differ from one another in the time at which they begin to speak, the rate at which they progress in language development, and the adequacy of their language patterns. Various factors are responsible for these differences. Defects in the nervous system or in the vocal apparatus may account for the relatively few cases of seemingly almost complete inability to learn to speak or to speak intelligibly. The age at which a mentally retarded child starts to speak is later than that for the normal child, and his rate of speech progress is slower. Usually, a child with superior mental ability reflects this in his early start, his rapid increase of progress, and his generally superior control of this medium of intercommunication. Not all bright children, however, follow this pattern of language development.

Perhaps one of the most important influences upon a child's learning to talk is the kind and amount of stimulation to which he is exposed during his developing years. Children are great imitators. A child who is reared in a home in which good speech is habitual tends to pattern his pronunciations and enunciations upon the models provided him. His immature vocal apparatus or sensory acuity, however, may prevent his repeating exactly what he hears.

For example, a bright little girl found it difficult to pronounce the word *preserves*. To her it was "dederbs." Patient repetition of the correct pronunciation of the word by the mother and continued serious efforts by the child to hear the word and then say it correctly were needed before she finally was able to pronounce it correctly. This was one of those peculiar kinks in association between stimulus and response that was not characteristic of this child's general speech pattern, since she was an early and fluent talker.

Another example is that of a little boy, also a quick learner, who had difficulty with the term *sweet potatoes,* which he pronounced "weet tatoes." When his attention was called to this incorrect pronunciation, and the words were pronounced for him slowly, carefully, and correctly, he replied in consternation, "But that's what I said—'weet tatoes!'" Occasional blocks similar to these may occur even in the speech patterns of well-trained adults; especially in times of emotional stress, their vocal apparatus and their mental associations sometimes seem to function inadequately. Among normal adults, this condition usually is temporary.

Some young children are late in beginning to talk because they experience no need to do so; their needs are cared for adequately. In some homes, the elders themselves talk so much that the child has little or no opportunity to direct attention to himself by attempts to join in the talking. The type of speech a child develops is related closely to the kind of speech he hears around him. Slurred enunciation, incorrect pronunciation, and inaccurate grammatical structure practiced by his adult associates are certain to find their way into his language. The following case illustrates the influence of environmental factors.

The authors are acquainted with a mature and extremely successful businessman who left school when he was about fifteen and worked at various jobs where he associated with people who made many grammatical errors. Although the speech patterns of his immediate family were adequate, the mode of speech of his co-workers became part of his speech pattern. Now that he associates with men and women whose speech patterns reflect a more cultural background, he recognizes his speech deficiencies and is attempting to correct them. Since his earlier speech habits are so deep-seated, he is finding it difficult to make the desired changes. It is interesting to note that, for the most part, his writing is better than his speech.

Another bad speech practice is the use of "baby talk" when addressing young children. Some adults seem to believe that this artificial form of speech is better understood by young children than is correct speech. Unfortunately, if the practice is continued too long or engaged in continuously, the children respond in kind, especially if adults admire the responses as "cute." Later, adolescents may be embarrassed by their continuing habit of expressing themselves in "baby talk."

Stuttering among children is very common, especially among bright youngsters who are interested in many things and are moved to talk rapidly about them. As they attempt to describe what they have seen or heard or to recount their experiences, their thoughts run ahead of their "tongues," or of their still inadequate skill in expression. They hesitate in their speaking, which usually is at a fast pace, because they are uncertain about which forms of words are correct. With experience and with the reduced tempo in talking that usually accompanies developmental progress, the young person gradually outgrows his tendency to stutter unless adults, by foolishly continuing to call attention to the defect, make him unduly conscious of his difficulty, and so arouse emotional reactions to it.

The Development of Thinking and Reasoning

Whether very young children engage in the kind of mental activity that is termed *thinking* is a moot question. The child is born with a nervous system that, if it has experienced normal growth during the prenatal period, is ready to function. Nevertheless, most of a neonate's early responses are more or less reflex in nature.

The development of thinking. With the gradual maturation of the sensory mechanisms, the young child begins to associate his various sensations, with resulting perceptions, or meaningful sensations. At first, the baby's percepts are simple and often incorrect or inadequate. Repeated experience with the limited environment of his home helps him gain more adequate and satisfying recognitions of the relationships that may exist among these environmental stimuli.

There is disagreement among psychologists concerning the amount or kind of mental manipulation of perceptual materials that takes place during the very early years of the growing child. There is evidence that, before he can talk, the child seems to express in his actions the results of what resembles conceptual thinking in the older person. He responds to one person differently than he does to another. He appears to recognize and to respond to things in the home with which he has daily experience. Some children learn early that, by refraining from the kind of behavior for which they have been punished, they can avoid being chastised for misdeeds.

By the time he is six months old, the child displays some awareness of himself and appears to be able to recognize some of his body parts. He gradually develops a more or less adequate understanding of space relationships. These begin by the baby's reaching his arms above his head and saying "up," or by squirming off an adult's lap as he iterates, "down," or "baby down." Orientation in time is difficult, even after the child has begun his school life. As his language patterns develop, the young child gives evidence through his questioning and story telling that he is developing concepts and that he is relating these concepts to one another through mental association, or thinking.

The development of reasoning. Whatever reasoning the child attempts is limited by his experiences. Even the young child gives some slight evidence of understanding the relationship that exists between cause and effect. He seems to be able to vary his behavior in accordance with expected adult reactions. Because of his meager experiences, the direction that his reasoning takes is very different from that of the adult. Often, to the bewilderment or distress of the child, his reasoning is judged by adults according to their own standards.

Differences between child and adult reasoning may be the basis of much friction, even between adolescents and their parents. Frequently the adolescent's difficulty is that he has developed ideas of right and wrong behavior that differ widely from those the parents evolved as a result of their years of experience. The child, however, may want to do what he believes his mother wants him to do.

For example, a mother took her four-year-old child just outside the home and, pointing to the other side of the street, admonished him not to cross the street unless an older person were with him. Thereafter, he was careful to stay on his side of the street. The mother was satisfied that he had understood her admonition and would be obedient. Imagine her amazement and chagrin when a neighbor told her that the child had been seen crossing a busy high-way at the end of the street, with no one there to escort him. When the boy was asked by his mother how he could be so naughty, he answered, "I wasn't naughty. You told me not to cross here at the house. You didn't say anything about the corner." The child was sincere in his explanation and was much hurt because his mother thought he had disobeyed her.

The number of similar examples of differences between adult and child reasoning is legion. Unless parents and teachers are certain that a child understands adult patterns of reasoning, they must take care lest they arouse emotional tensions in the child by accusing him wrongly of doing things he should not have done or of leaving things undone.

Important factors of learning to think. A child's conceptual thinking, reasoning, and problem-solving, like his language development (to which mental development is closely related), have as their bases the general pattern of his physical maturation and the kind and amount of his experience. Families of high socio-economic status usually can provide for their children a wealth of experiences that lie beyond the reach of the underprivileged. Parental differences in objectivity and accuracy of judgment and reasoning also exert a powerful influence upon the direction taken by and the relative success of a child's mental activities.

The parent who answers his child's questions concerning the reasons for one or another condition or situation with a casual, "Oh, I don't know—just because," is encouraging lazy mental habits in his child. The parent may be busy or wearied by his child's barrage of questions, but it takes only a few minutes to think of a simple answer which will be satisfying for the moment, at least. A parent who consciously tries to satisfy his child's curiosity through short but accurate answers not only is helping the youngster to carry on desirable mental activity, but also is developing in the child an attitude of faith in and admiration for his parent's store of knowledge.

This situation holds for teachers as well as for parents. Teachers should not discourage children from asking questions that they fear may upset the class routines, which some teachers hold so dear. The average and bright (and sometimes the slower) elementary-school child is so intrigued by his enlarging world that he wants to know all about it—the what, the why, and the how.

An especially bright and thoughtful child may ask a question the answer to which the teacher may not know at the moment. The teacher should admit his ignorance frankly. He should follow this by telling the child where he can obtain the information and/or look it up himself and later discuss the matter with the pupil, or with the entire class, if that is appropriate. The teacher can use this procedure occasionally without losing the respect of the children. In fact, they may like him the better for it, since it shows that he too can forget. The teacher who aspires to be a leader of children, however, cannot make a general practice of admitting ignorance concerning matters not directly related to the content of class study, or of brushing children's questions aside. The pupils soon will come to consider him ineffective as a teacher and, perhaps, lose interest in learning what he attempts to teach them.

Teachers as well as parents sometimes are amazed by the maturity of judgment and reasoning displayed by children. An example of such unusual ability recently came to the attention of the authors. An objective test in mathematics, in the process of standardization, was administered to a fifth-grade class. Some of the questions were on the upper-grade levels. Since the class consisted in great part of bright children, many of the more difficult questions were answered correctly.

After the test was administered, one of the boys criticized a question which read, "If the total depreciation of an automobile originally costing $3,000 is $2,000 over a period of four years, the yearly depreciation expressed in per cent is: (a) 6%, (b) 12½%, (c) 16⅔%, (d) 33⅓%." The boy's comment was: "Of course, the answer you want is c, but that's not really right. Everybody knows an automobile depreciates in value more the first year than it does later. You'd have to figure out the actual rate of depreciation, year by year."

In the same situation, a ten-year-old girl objected to a question which dealt with the amount of money a child would save in sixteen weeks, if he saved twenty-five cents per week. She said, "In the test, the right answer is four dollars, but that isn't correct. You might begin by saving twenty-five cents a week, but you wouldn't keep on doing it. I know, because I've tried. I make up my mind to save so much every week. It does not last for more than a week or two. Then I always find something to spend the money for." [1]

The Child and His Emotions

The effect upon a growing child of his emotional reactions is a significant influence upon his developing personality. Every phase of an individual's developmental and experiential pattern is affected by the interrelationships that exist among all the phases of his maturing self. Of no phase is this interrelationship more apparent than it is of the emotions. They permeate all life activities, either advancing or retarding personal and social adjustment. Consequently, emotional concomitants of the various phases of development should be considered directly in connection with them. As we have discussed various areas of the child's personal development to this point, we have made occasional references to the part played by the emotions. Now we shall reverse the approach, stressing emotional reactions as they relate to other phases of personal development.

The developmental pattern of children's emotions. Throughout life, everyone experiences four fundamental personality needs. He needs *status*—he wants others of any age to give him recognition and attention. He needs *security*—he wants his life experiences to be relatively stable, both in interpersonal relationships and in provision for life-sustaining requirements. He needs *affection*—he wants to be loved by someone who understands him and who is willing to share with him his joys and his sorrows. Finally, he needs *independence*—as soon as he has gained awareness of himself as a person, he begins to want to make his own choices and decisions and to be responsible for his own conduct. These needs are closely related to the developing child's emotional reactions. The specific form that any one of these needs may take and the methods employed to fulfill it vary with age and experience. At any age, however, these needs affect behavior. Since their functioning is described in some detail in Chapter 6, we shall limit our discussion of them at this point to the emotional resultants of their fulfillment or denial.

[1] For a detailed discussion of thinking and problem-solving, see Chapter 13.

Beginnings of emotional reactions. The infant gives little or no indication of the kinds of emotional behavior exhibited by the older child, adolescent, or adult. Although some nurses claim that there is evidence of temperamental difference even among the newborn, the most we can conclude, as a result of many observations, is that the very young child may exhibit a general emotional tone. Some babies are described as generally happy and contented; others appear to be "cross" and given to much crying and whimpering. These behavior expressions may be explained as reflex in nature, being stimulated by the general condition of the child at birth.

An older person is able to recognize his emotional state through introspection. He may describe himself as "mad enough to chew nails," "scared to death," "madly in love," "blind with rage," "eaten up with envy." Whether these and similar expressions are true indices of the intensity of the speaker's experienced emotion, they do indicate that he is aware of his disturbed state. We have no evidence of an infant's ability to engage in introspection. Hence our only means of judging his inner states is through our observation of his behavior.

The emotional experiences of the infant present a diffused pattern of responses which appear to fall into two categories: a general feeling of well-being, and a general feeling of discomfort. When the child is healthy, clean, well-fed, and safe in his mother's arms or in his crib, he seems to be satisfied with his state of being. He coos and smiles, his body is relaxed, and his behavior is outgoing. If he is hungry, thirsty, or wet, finds himself in strange surroundings, or is left alone for a long time, he expresses his discomfort through loud crying or continuous whimpering, gross movements of his body, and withdrawing behavior. The general emotional tone of the infant depends in large part on the kind and amount of physical care and parental love and attention he receives.

The development of specific patterns of emotional behavior. Before a child can experience an emotional reaction, he must develop the ability to recognize a stimulus as emotion-arousing and must gain some understanding of his own behavior and the behavior of those about him.

Although the child at birth may give evidence of the arousal of all-over excitement, observable signs of differentiated emotional reactions do not begin to exhibit themselves before the age of three months. It may be possible to distinguish differences between anger and fear responses in the baby only by the time he has reached the age of six months. From then on, changes in emotional expression continue progressively through the childhood years. Further, the development of emotional behavior is closely associated with rate of growth and experience with emotion-arousing stimuli-situations. The changes in emotional behavior from birth to two years are shown in Figure 5.

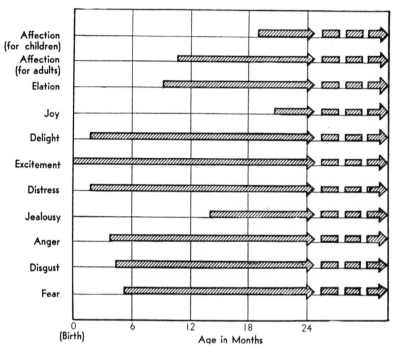

FIGURE 5. Changes in Emotional Behavior from Birth to Two Years

Adapted from data in "Emotional Development in Early Years," by Katharine M. B. Bridges, *Child Development,* March 1932, p. 340.

At first, a child's emotional state is expressed through gross body movements. When he is angry, he lashes out at everything around him; he may kick and scream; he may throw his toys, a cup or other convenient object small enough for him to grasp; or he may attempt to hit anything or any person near him. A fear-arousing stimulus causes him to hide behind his mother's skirts, or run away from the fear-producing object or situation; he may cry or scream, but the crying is different from that of anger. When he is happy, he may jump up and down, clap his hands, and squeal with delight. As the child matures, he is likely to exhibit better controlled expressions of his emotional state. Through experience he has learned that adults do not approve of "wild" demonstrations of emotions. He also gains the ability to recognize the person or object that is the cause of his emotional state, and directs his display of emotional behavior in that direction.

Since children are great imitators, they soon learn to pattern their emotional responses after those exhibited by other members of their family and by close associates. More than that, children learn to respond to situations which, they observe, arouse emotional behavior in persons in their immediate environment. A young child is particularly sensitive to the behavior of his parents and is greatly influenced both by their reactions toward him and toward other members of the family and by the amount and kind of emotional behavior they exhibit in his presence.

The pattern of a child's emotions differs from that of an adult. Although the child probably gives expression to emotional states that are similar to those of an adult, there are age differences between what may arouse an emotional state and how the emotion is expressed. Because of his relatively meager experiences, the child may react emotionally to circumstances or situations that the older person takes in his stride. Contrariwise, an adult may react violently to a potentially dangerous situation which has no effect upon the young person. A child usually responds actively and immediately to that which at the moment is an emotion-arousing situation, but by the introduction of another stimulus he can be distracted easily from it, with a consequent change in emotional behavior. An adult, however, may be able to control his behavior, even when he is inwardly disturbed.

This difference between the child and the adult can be illustrated by the behavior of the two-year-old referred to earlier and that of his grandmother, whom he and his parents were visiting. The authors heard the child (in the garden with his grandmother) crying bitterly. He had not wanted to leave his parents, who were in the house. He flung a toy aside and was in process of dumping clothespins from their container and throwing them in all directions. One of the authors went to the window and tried to attract his attention by calling "Hi" to him. He stopped his angry behavior to locate the sound. When the adult directed his attention to the window, he turned in that direction, sat down on the grass, and looked up at the window, still clutching some of the clothespins which he waved at the neighbor as he kept repeating "Hi." In response to adult suggestion, he began to pick up the clothespins and to replace them in the basket. As he continued to laugh and to talk to the adults, he proudly displayed the progress he was making in retrieving the pins.

The grandmother also was aroused emotionally by a whole situation involving the presence of two youngsters in her usually quiet and immaculate home, irregular eating times, and the indecision of the child's parents concerning their plans for the day, but she gave no evidence of her emotional state as she chatted gaily with the neighbor. Nevertheless, she probably continued to be "stirred up" during the visit. Moreover, she may have decided that future visits of the family to her home would be few and widely spaced, at least until the children were older and more tractable.

We have been emphasizing the fact that the characteristics of children's emotions differ from those of adults. Children also differ from one another in their emotional reactions. What may be an emotion-arousing situation for one child may not affect another. The form of behavior displayed also may range among children from little or no outward manifestations of inner disturbance to extremes of overt behavior demonstrations of an emotional state. A child's degree of maturation and his daily experience in his home and neighborhood may cause his emotional response to differ from those of other children. The fact that a child does not express an emotional state actively should not be interpreted to mean that he is not experiencing it; great overt display of emotion does not necessarily mean that the child is experiencing a strong emotional state. Parents and teachers sometimes make the mistake of believing that the quiet child always is the happy, contented, unemotional child, and that the boy or girl who appears constantly to be indulging in emotional behavior is badly disturbed or unstable. One must be sure to understand the bases of the exhibited behavior before drawing conclusions.

Two cases can be cited by way of illustration. Delores, a junior high-school pupil, was a uniformly cheerful, co-operative, and apparently happy girl. She was well liked by her teachers and her peer groups, and was considered one of the best-adjusted young people in the school. It was not until her counselor asked about her senior high-school and college plans that the girl's inner emotional state was discovered. Her mother was ill, her father had lost his job and could not seem to get another, and there were several younger children in the home. The family was living on the little she earned from after-school jobs (about which the school people knew nothing) and the help of kind neighbors. Her father was too proud to go on relief or even to collect unemployment insurance.

Delores had taken over the responsibility of caring for the home and the children. She was worried about the family's future and her own inadequacy as a mother-substitute. Her only goal was to leave school as soon as she legally could. Asked why she had not explained the home conditions to her counselor earlier, she reflected her father's stubborn pride in her answer that this was her problem and that she did not have a right to bother other people about it. Once her reserves were broken she gave vent to her emotions, remarking later that sharing her trouble with an understanding adult had given her great relief.

It is to the credit of the school that the counselors immediately started to work on the girl's problem. A job was found for the father, the mother received the hospital care she needed, and provision was made for the younger children so that Delores might continue her education. As a result, the girl's tensions were reduced and she became the happy, unworried child that for so long she had pretended to be.

A different situation is that of Harold. From babyhood to about the age of seven, he was a quiet but unusually contented child. He had responded to the loving care of his mother by developing into a healthy, alert, and happy child. During his early years he had few playmates, but he managed to amuse himself in constructive activities. He was always pleasant and unafraid in his relations with adults and other children. Because he was small for his age, he did not participate in some of the rougher forms of play in which larger boys of his age engaged. His father provided well for the family needs; but since his work demanded that he spend long hours daily and sometimes weeks away from the home, he left the rearing of Harold (whom he loved very much) to his wife, a calm, contented woman whose chief ambition was to make the home comfortable and pleasant for her husband and son.

Life went along peacefully until one day the father returned from his work earlier than usual to find his seven-year-old son standing in front of the house, apparently unperturbed by the fact that two other boys had taken possession of his tricycle and other toys and were making fun of him for letting them do so. The father angrily demanded that the boys return his son's possessions. Later, when Harold was asked by his father why he had submitted so easily to the other boys' using his playthings, he replied that it did not bother him—that they often did this and he had fun watching them play. The father suddenly decided that the boy, under his mother's influence, was developing into, what he termed, a "sissy."

Since the man was an aggressive person, he wanted his son to give evidence of similar characteristics and took it upon himself to develop them in the boy. He proceeded, by his own behavior toward the boy and by setting up anger-arousing situations, to try to force the child to give overt expression to supposedly angry inner states. Harold admired his father very much and so did his best to meet his wishes. In school he began to assume the role of a bully, demanding his rights and using what little physical power he had to fight for them. At home he started to defy his mother's wishes, but he, usually ended his tantrum behavior by regretting the fact that he had hurt his mother's feelings or had bewildered her by his changed behavior toward her. The father was delighted by the boy's behavior, asserting that he was starting to develop manly traits.

Harold's overtly aggressive behavior actually was not a true expression of his inner emotional state. As he grew older, his behavior in his father's presence was very different from what it was when he was freed from the man's influence. His teachers were puzzled by the fact that sometimes his conduct was unbearable and at other times, extremely co-operative. The reason for this variation in attitude was not understood by the school people until, in a conference with his mother, the father's ambitions for his son were explained by the wife, who was not in agreement with her husband's point of view. Finally, as a result of his own superior intelligence and the counseling he received from his mother and teachers, the boy recognized the fact that in attempting to please his father he was engaging in behavior which was not a true index of his own emotional nature. Consequently, he developed a behavior pattern that combined needed assertiveness and desirable submission in his relationships with his associates.

The boy's success in his learning activities and his general popularity finally reconciled the father to the fact that his son was a fine lad, even though he was "his mother's son." If Harold's innate nature had been different from what it was and if his early submissive behavior had been the result only of his mother's indulging his every wish, the father's influence might have led to the development in the boy of a very different pattern of emotions.

Characteristic emotions of children. Most children run the gamut of emotions—tenderness, fear, anger, jealousy, nervous tension, and so on. A child's emotional reactions are affected by his personal attributes and his social experiences. At the same time, his emotions influence the development of other phases of his personality and the kind of adjustment he makes to environmental conditions and other people.

The child's outgoing tender emotions are first experienced in his family relationships, though he often may be angered temporarily by behavior exhibited toward himself by one or another member of the family. He may resent restrictions of his freedom; he may be "afraid" of the consequences of his childish misdeeds; he may be jealous of the attention given by one or both of his parents to another sibling, especially a new baby in the home. Fears and resentments experienced in the home usually do not last long, although at the time of their occurrence they may seem to the child to be very severe and important. Overt behavior may give evidence of a strongly disturbed inner state. Some forms of emotionalized behavior are: inordinately shy behavior; refusal to accept the suggestions of others in regard to behavior (negativism); violent temper tantrums, and outward manifestations of inner tensions—refusal to eat, difficulties of elimination of body wastes (often resulting in enuresis, or bed wetting), disturbed sleep or unwillingness to go to sleep, nail biting, handling the genitals, and nervous tics.

Guarding against a serious development of any of these unwholesome emotional reactions in a particular child is the concern of both parents and teachers. The cause or causes should be discovered as early and as accurately as possible, and appropriate remedial techniques should be applied intelligently. Adult behavior must be such that it does not stimulate in the child those emotional states that result from a felt lack of security, affection, achievement, or desired independence. This does not imply that a child should be a completely free agent as he attempts to fulfill his personal and social wants and urges. He needs adult help and, when necessary, adult control of his immature behavior.[1] Perhaps more than anything else, he needs to be stimulated by the behavior of adults who themselves have achieved commendable control of their emotions. Adult temper tantrums almost certainly stimulate tantrum behavior in the child.

It is likely that children do not inherit their fears. The first responses of the neonate that may resemble later fear reactions are the clutching and crying that accompany an apparent lack of body support. Some early fears have their roots in deviations from customary conditions. A child becomes accustomed to the shape, form, and color of the objects in his room as he observes or handles them during the daytime. If he wakes up suddenly during the night, these objects may appear strange. The reactions that accompany this experience may start the development of a strong emotional state that

[1] See Chapter 8 for a detailed discussion of behavior problems and the development of self-discipline.

is referred to as "fear of the dark." Many children rarely, if ever, experience this fear. Other fears, such as fear of thunder, snakes, dogs or other animals, or other possible danger to one's self are the result only of adult example.

Much more could be said here concerning the causes and expression of the characteristic emotions of children. Since the child's emotional life is so closely tied to his social development, we shall discuss his emotions later when we consider his progressing social experiences. Here we shall discuss briefly the importance to an individual of the development of interests and attitudes as these are related to his emotional and social experiences.

The Meaning and Functions of Interests and Attitudes

The terms *interest* and *attitude* often are used to express an individual's pattern of reactions toward himself, his physical environment, his associates, and the situation in which he finds himself. For the most part, interests and attitudes develop as a result of experiences begun in early childhood. Interests and attitudes are personal; they are influenced by the behavior of others and by existing conditions or situations.

Meaning and development of interest. An interest is a motivating force that impels an individual toward participation in one activity rather than another. An interest that motivates achievement in a particular situation may lead to favorable attitudes toward the elements in the situation. Failure in attempts to achieve the goal in which one is interested at the moment may lead to the development of biases or prejudices against the people or things believed responsible for the lack of success. For example, children and adolescents react favorably or unfavorably toward a teacher according to the degree of successful learning.

An individual usually is aware of his interests. They are aroused early in life and are affected by the individual's physical condition, his mental and emotional status, and the social environment in which he has been reared. Individual interests change with experience, not ordinarily becoming stable until after adolescence.

As soon as a child gains some awareness of himself as a person, the development of interest as a motivator of behavior begins. At first, the youngster's interest is centered in himself. Progressive interest in his body and body parts parallels his development of self-awareness. His interests gradually come to include not only himself but also his possessions, as his early intelligible talking patterns indicate. He constantly refers to *baby's* cup, *my* doll, *my* ball, or *my* any other object with which he has experience. The young child is not *selfish;* he appears rather to be *self-centered* during this period of struggle for self-realization.

Gradually the child's interests develop to include his play and play toys, the activities of his parents and other members of his family, and of his play associates. Later, his teacher and his school activities are included. Meanwhile, he is learning to become interested in what other people think of him and what he can do to earn approval from adults and from his peers.

The beginning of interest in appearance and dress varies with the sex of the child and his stimulating experiences. Girls usually become dress conscious earlier than boys, presumably because of a mother's interest in "dressing up" her little girl. A three-and-a-half-year-old came prancing up to her uncle to show off the pretty new dress she was wearing. No sophisticated teen-age girl could display more expert self-preening and attention-getting devices than did this youngster as she danced around her uncle and pointed out all the attractive features of her dress, including her matching socks and hair ribbons.

Increase in maturity and experience is accompanied by a broadening of the child's interests. He becomes intrigued by the activities of great men, past and present. He wants to learn all he can about faraway places. He may develop a great interest in collecting all kinds of objects, experimenting with all kinds of things, and constructing attractive or useful objects.

Most children are interested in having pets, although they differ in their willingness to care for them. At present, many boys of elementary-school age are very much interested in airplanes. They collect pictures of them and make airplane models. These are only a few of the many interests that are characteristic of developing children. In general, however, most childhood interests are short-lived. An interest typically is intense for a short time, only to give way to another equally intense but also temporary interest.

Meaning and development of attitudes. Every human experience is accompanied by affective qualities known as *feeling tones.* Feeling tones are present in all sensations as pleasantness or unpleasantness, satisfaction or annoyance. These experience qualities, which are individual and personal, relate to and affect the way a person thinks or behaves in any situation. Feeling tones are among the components that form the basis of an individual's attitudes. A person is known to be kind or unkind; friendly or unfriendly; tolerant or intolerant. Joy and sorrow are emotional patterns that result from numerous experiences in stimulus situations. An individual's thoughts, interests, and behavior are influenced by his attitudes.

Attitudes act as dynamic forces in human behavior. They give it direction and influence the mental-set of the individual in any situation. Attitudes are not necessarily constant. They vary with the intensity of the individual's interest and with the persons or situations involved. Children are great imitators of attitudes. They learn many of their attitudes indirectly from their parents, teachers, and peer associates. This is the basis for the development of attitudes of which they often are unaware.

When a young child pats a dog, and says "Good doggie, nice doggie," or when he slaps at his mother saying, "Bad mommie" because his mother has denied him something he wants, he is giving expression to an attitude that may be temporary or may have more or less lasting effects upon him. Usually a child's attitudes are fluid; they vary with the experiences that arouse them.

Certain experiences of the child are repeated many times and are accompanied each time by the same or similar attitudes on his part. As a result of these experiences, an habitual attitude is developed that is likely to carry over to adolescent or adult situations or conditions possessing some of the elements of the individual's childhood experiences. In other words, some lifelong attitudes toward people and things have their roots in conditionings that take place early in life.

For example, one child may have been encouraged to stand when older women enter the room, to give his seat in a streetcar or bus to an older person, to refrain from breaking in on the conversation of his elders, to share his toys with other children, to help with the household chores, and to engage in other similar activities. If he receives satisfying approval for doing these things, he is likely to develop an attitude of courtesy and helpfulness that will become an habitual part of his behavior. Another child, however, who is allowed to do as he pleases and who has not been encouraged to consider the welfare of others, is thereby conditioned to develop self-centered attitudes which he may find difficult to change when he is an adult.

Children, as well as adults, may not be fully aware of their attitudes as expressed in behavior until or unless they have their attention called to them. Attitude conditioning usually comes about gradually. Parents, teachers, and other adults may attempt con-

sciously to guide a child's attitude pattern. Yet attitudes thus incul-
cated may not be so effective as those developed unconsciously by
the child as he lives with, observes, and reflects the attitude patterns
of his parents, teachers, and peer associates.

The child of a father or mother who is an ardent Democrat or
Republican is likely to assert proudly that he is a Democrat or a
Republican, without really knowing, of course, what he is talking
about. Many of our prejudices and biases are developed in this way.
In most cultures, customs and attitudes are handed down from generation to generation without question as to the value of the custom
or the validity of the attitude.

The Child as a Social Human Being

The direction taken by a child's physical, mental, and emotional
development is so inextricably interwoven with all the influencing
elements of the social environment in which he is reared that it is
impossible to consider his social development in isolation from the
other phases of his growth and development. This fact may seem
obvious, but at the cost of seeming to repeat over and over again
this principle of the developmental process, we wish to emphasize
the fact that a child can no more escape having his personality
molded by the personal behavior and attitudes of the various persons by whom he is surrounded during his childhood years than he
can escape life itself and the potentialities he inherits from his fore-
bears.

The socializing process. Most infants have achieved some simple
awareness of others by the time they reach their third month. Their
reactions to those around them at this early age depend upon the
extent to which they are played with and talked to. Their first reactions are general, in that infants respond with bodily movements
and unintelligible vocalizations to anyone who comes within their
focus of vision and who reacts to them. They soon come to differentiate among those persons who are most concerned with the fulfillment of their wants. An infant seems to be able to distinguish between his mother and his father, giving special attention to his
mother by smiling at her as he focuses his eyes upon her.

The very young child appears to gain some awareness of others
before he achieves awareness of himself as an entity in his total
small environment. By the time a child is a year old, he will have
developed certain simple patterns of social interaction within his

limited world. He becomes increasingly sensitive to and controlled by social usage and the rules that govern social conduct. He develops an appreciation of the rights of others and his own responsibilities as a member of society. The development of these areas of social consciousness in a child involves a series of learning tasks that can be mastered successfully only with the help of parents, teachers, and other adults who are responsible, directly or indirectly, for the child's development.

Social maturity is achieved only when and if the individual has attained the power to recognize the full import of social behavior. Too many persons end their life span without having reached a complete and socially desirable realization of the proper limitations of their rights in relation to the rights of others or the kind and extent of their personal responsibility for the welfare of others. The accounts that appear daily in the newspapers and over the air attest to the prevalence of asocial behavior. Especially are thoughtful persons concerned about the destructive attitudes displayed by many of our young people.

Many studies have been made to discover the underlying causes of child and adolescent delinquency. It has been found that conditions prevalent in the physical environment in which a child is reared are important factors in social development. More significant is the degree of social adjustment of those individuals by whose attitudes and behavior the child constantly is motivated in his daily struggles to achieve self-realization in his associations with his fellows. Hence all adults who in any way are responsible for the development of a child's social consciousness must give evidence of having achieved social maturity. Fortunately, the socialization of the child is a gradually developing pattern, although there are adults who expect the eight-year-old, for example, to possess a mature understanding of social regulations and to behave in accordance with adult standards. In his home, school, and neighborhood relations and through his play and work activities, a child can be guided, step by step, to develop those attitudes and interests and to engage in those activities that will help him become a constructive and accepted member of society. The kind and extent of guidance he should receive at any stage of his development, of course, should be based on his degree of maturation, his mental status, and his emotional nature.

Developmental progress. During the first year of life, the child is beginning to find himself as an individual among other individuals.

Although he still is primarily concerned with himself and the satisfaction of his physical wants, he is developing interest in and a
relatively satisfactory pattern of responses to other people. Parents
should play with the child but should avoid focusing too much attention upon him and his "cute" behavior. Even at this tender age he
can begin to gain an appreciation of his relative position in the home
and to learn that his parents and their associates have interests in
and participate in activities that, for longer or shorter periods of
time, do and should exclude him and his interests. The acquisition
of this understanding early in life can be of inestimable value to
the child in his later life outside the home. There are limits to the
amount of attention that one person is willing to accord another,
no matter how close the bond between them.

The youngster who has been made to believe that he is the center
of home life and activities is likely to have a sad awakening when
he discovers that he does not hold the same position in his gradually
enlarging world. This may constitute an adjustment difficulty of
an "only child" whose parents lack the wisdom to modify their great
devotion to him. We are not implying here that a young child should
be excluded completely from parental interests and activities and
treated only as a growing organism whose needs constitute no more
than the satisfaction of his physical requirements. The "rejected"
child, whose conception and birth were not desired by the parents,
may react to parental neglect by developing self-minimizing attitudes
that cause him to be shy and unduly retiring in his relations with
others. He may lack self-confidence in meeting the demands of
social situations.

The child's various attitudes and activities that have social impact
upon the progress of developing personality, as we noted earlier,
gradually serve as stimuli-situations to motivate his maturing behavior. Among these social-impact activities and attitudes are
laughter, play, friendship, and group contacts.

Laughter. The more or less reflex smiles of the infant gradually
come to have meaning. By the age of two years, laughter, as a form
of social behavior, has become an easily excited mode of behavior.
Earlier, the child was likely to laugh more when he was alone. Now
he begins to laugh in the presence of other children, and is stimulated to laughter by simple games, pictures, and cartoons that are
within the limits of his appreciation.

Laughter-arousing stimuli show some degree of refinement as the
child increases in age and experience. Yet the ten-or-eleven-year-old
will respond with gales of laughter to situations or incidents which,

to the adult, are not in the least amusing. Little girls tend to engage constantly in "silly giggling" as they exchange whispered secrets.

Play. Children's play activities give evidence of their increasing social consciousness. During the first months of life, whatever the infant does in the form of "play" he does alone. He fingers various parts of his body, shakes his rattle, and may make feeble efforts to push or to throw a ball or any other object within reach. Later, he and another baby of his age may play in the same room but evince no interest in each other.

An awareness of another child as a possible playmate does not show itself until about the middle of the second year. At that age, moreover, the child's interest appears to be mainly that of wresting from another child the toy with which the other is playing. This may result in a tug of war between the two. Such behavior is indicative of the fact that a youngster's concept of *I* as opposed to *you* is strong at this stage of maturation. The urge to possess is a sign of his growing awareness of himself as a person.

The two-year-old may offer an object which he is holding to another person, especially a liked adult, but he immediately proceeds to retrieve it and, perhaps, hold it close to his body. This can take on the aspect of a game to the child as he repeatedly offers and takes back the object, often laughing while he does so. Three-year-olds of both sexes start to show the beginnings of social play. Instead of grabbing the other child's toy, the child now is impelled to offer the other child his toys or other belongings—sometimes almost to force them on him. He may seem to be very generous, but he still tends to take the toys belonging to others and to demand that his own be returned to him when he wants them. Play as a co-operative rather than a parallel activity is not practiced to any extent until the fourth year or later. The child's progressive play experiences are related not only to his rate of maturation but also to the amount and kind of adult encouragement he receives.

Nursery-school experiences can be of great value in helping the child shift from his earlier self-and-other-person attitudes. Some parents believe that a child does not need to attend a nursery school if he has brothers and sisters not too far removed from him in age, or if he experiences many opportunities for free play with children of the same age in the immediate neighborhood. It is true that the presence of other children helps a child gain some appreciation of the rightness or wrongness of his attitudes toward himself and his possessions in relation to similar attitudes displayed by other children with whom he shares play activities.

The planned play experiences provided for the child in the nursery school, in addition to affording much opportunity for the development of individual initiative, help him achieve expression in overt behavior of gradually forming attitudes of co-operation. Moreover, such experiences help to strengthen his self-esteem and to increase his understanding and respect for other nursery-school children. The daily program of activities in a nursery school not only includes many and varied play opportunities, but also provides for continued habit training or retraining that is associated with eating, sleeping, toilet regimens, manipulating outer garments, and caring for communal possessions.

The fact that these habits are being learned not in isolation but in the company of the child's peers helps to advance the child's social consciousness. Mothers are brought into the nursery-school situation. They observe their children's behavior with other children, and they have conferences with the teacher. In these ways a mother gains greater insight into the degree of social adjustment which her child is achieving and the adjustment needs which she should strive to meet during this very important period of her child's social development.

During his elementary-school years, a child's play activities become better organized. Boys and girls of elementary-school age tend to carry on their play activities with other members of the same sex. Boys' play interests include participation in strenuous games that are modifications of the sports engaged in by adolescents and young adults—basketball, baseball, football, wrestling, running, climbing, and other outdoor activities. They engage also in quiet games that can be played around the table with selected pals. It is not uncommon for boys in their later elementary-school years to become quite proficient in checkers, and the authors know several eleven-year-olds who play a passable game of bridge!

Girls are expected to be more interested in forms of play, such as "playing house," that are related to home activities. Modern little girls, however, are indulging more and more in those forms of play that at one time were supposed to be limited to boys. It is not unusual to see boys and girls playing ball together, or participating in other out-of-doors play activities, as well as in quiet home games.

One of the favorite pastimes of elementary-school boys is teasing or tormenting younger or older sisters or girl schoolmates. Sometimes members of either sex will tease others of the same sex. Teasing activity seems to be inherent in the child's development of social consciousness, functioning as a means of learning how other young people will react to annoying situations. It also helps the teaser discover his own power to influence others.

The teasing tendency manifests itself during adolescence and early adulthood in the many seemingly foolish activity-requirements for initiation into high-school and college fraternities. At any age level, teasing is an acceptable socializing medium unless it is malicious in its intent, takes the form of tormenting, or results in physical hurt or emotional shock.

Children's friendships. As early as the fourth year, strong friendships may develop between two children. These attachments usually are temporary. Some friendships may continue for a long time if the two children are close neighbors and attend the same elementary school or religious institution. One of the children usually is more or less dominant and the other submissive, and they may reverse roles under certain circumstances. The friends may be of the same sex or of opposite sexes. Through their friendship they gain a feeling of security that may serve as a potent stimulator of social consciousness. The "twosome" relationship may interfere, however, with social progress. It is desirable that the parents or the nursery-school teacher tactfully attempt to bring other children into the situation.

The friendships of elementary-school-age children are formed on very much the same bases as adult friendships, although age or growth status is much more important with children than it is with adults. A child's friends usually are chosen from among children of the same sex who live near his home, who are in the same school and grade as he, and who give evidence of similar intelligence status, degree of sociability, and kind and amount of experience. Boys seem to be more casual in their selection of friends than are girls, and are not so intense in their friendship relations. Yet boys' friendships seem to be more enduring than those of girls. Perhaps girls are too demanding in their relationships with their friends.

Quarrels are common among friends of either sex. Boys tend to "have it out" with the other fellow and then forget the incident with little damage to the friendship, or they break off the friendship completely. Girls' quarrels or "disagreements" seem to be less aggressive in form, but they may be just as intense. Sometimes the misunderstanding continues in the form of bickering and recrimination, with an emotional concomitant of jealousy or a strong feeling of personal hurt.

Since girls and boys are coming to engage more and more in similar play activities with members of the opposite sex, changing attitudes in friendship relations can be observed. There are many girls who behave toward their friends in much the same manner as do boys. Among the members of both sexes, friendships begun during childhood continue for many years. In some cases, they last a lifetime. Many young people whose friendship results from shared religious experiences find that they are held together by this common bond, in spite of geographic distance or differences in vocational or social status.

Group activity and leadership. Nursery-school and kindergarten children are limited in their capacity to engage in large-group activities. Hence the play group usually consists of a few children who are drawn together by their interest in a particular play activity. These small groups represent only a temporary formation for the carrying-on of a play project. They are dissolved as soon as the members lose interest in the project.

The attempted intrusion of another child into the group while the project is in operation usually is resented by the group members; the intruder may be ejected forcibly from the situation. Later, this same child may be invited by some of the members of the former group to participate with them in another play activity. At this age, denial of participation in group activity does not mean rejection of the child. The denial apparently is related to an existing, though short-lived, recognition of the group as an entity.

As children grow older, group formation for play or other forms of activity becomes relatively more fixed. This is caused in part by the fact that the children's interest span is becoming longer. Toward the end of the elementary-school years, school and neighborhood groups become increasingly more stable.

The groups formed during later childhood usually are organized on a one-sex basis, and often include elaborate organizational and admission rituals. The members are drawn together by a common interest, which they try to develop and to fulfill through group activities. So concerned may the members of the group become about appropriate rules and regulations to govern the behavior of group members that the original purpose for forming the group may be forgotten or disregarded. Girls are more likely than boys to place undue emphasis upon the organizational pattern of group formation. It is not unusual for girls enthusiastically to form themselves into a special-purpose group and then to disagree among themselves so strongly and vehemently about organizational matters that the group is dissolved before there has been any opportunity for it to serve the purpose for which it had been planned.

No matter how long an organized or partially organized group exists, among its most important aspects are these: the selection of a name (one that may have secret significance), the obtaining and wearing of identifying insignia, and the consideration and use of a secret code. The interest of older elementary-school children in ritualism is characteristic of a stage in the development of their imaginative and creative abilities.

Childhood interest in fairy tales, the telling of "tall stories" or "white" lies, playing with imaginary playmates, and similar more or less self-centered imaginative activities gradually take on a more social character. At first, children exchange imaginative stories about themselves, their families, and their possessions. Later, they share in constructively creative activities. Toward the end of this developmental stage, they are beginning to tie their creative abilities to one or another more realistic project. Imagination runs rampant, however, even as, unconsciously, they are attempting to control it.

Group formation and activity may constitute an excellent means of promoting the socializing process. Immature young people can be so stimulated by reports of adult gang activities, unrealistic stories of adventure, and other socially undesirable activities, however, that their own group formations may take on some of the characteristics of adolescent or adult gang behavior. Unless young people can be guided indirectly by parents, school people, and community leaders to organize their groups for socially worthwhile projects, little can be done to stop the continued participation of older children and adolescents in acts of vandalism, stealing, and sex offenses, about which at present we are so concerned.

Left to themselves, children generally are democratic in their selection of other young people with whom they form their groups. It is only as they become the victims of adult prejudices or biases that they grow conscious of such matters as social and economic status, race, nationality, or religious affiliation. A child is not a "born" snob. To the extent that he selects his peer associates on any other basis than similar interests or intellectual level and emotional attraction, adults are responsible.

The success of children's group activities is closely related to the kind of leadership the group is experiencing. Adult leadership must be constructive but indirect. Peer leadership depends upon the general constitution of group membership and the purpose of the group. Children usually select as their group leader a member who possesses the qualities that will be effective in the realization of their purpose.

An aggressive child may attempt to force the group to accept him as a leader. In fact, an overaggressive child who is not accepted by his peer associates may try to gather together a group of more submissive children and constitute himself their leader. Thus he gives expression to his leadership urge. Groups of this kind usually dissolve quickly unless the children gain materially from cont·nued membership—that is, candy or other "goodies" given them by the leader or, in undesirable "gang" situations, the sharing of the loot which they have stolen under the direction of their leader.

Active and worthwhile groups in the school choose as their leader a child who has given evidence of initiative, intelligent comprehension of the purpose of the group's projects, and ability to help plan and carry out these projects. What is most important, they may want a leader who possesses self-confidence, defers to the wishes of the members of the group, and establishes stable emotional attitudes toward himself and among the members.

General comment. We have attempted to give the reader some insight into the developmental changes that take place in the young person as he progresses through childhood to adolescence. In all areas of development, the child may seem to take one step backward for every two or three steps forward. Parents and teachers sometimes feel helpless in the face of all the problems they encounter as they live with the growing child and try to understand the causes of some of his unpredictable behavior. The child himself does not know the "why" of the changes that are taking place within him and in his relationships with other children and adults. In retrospect, however, childhood is probably the most exciting and rewarding period of an individual's life, from the viewpoint both of the child and of his parents and teachers. Herbert Hoover wrote:

> The older I grow, the more I appreciate children. Now, as I near my eightieth birthday, I salute them again. Children are the most wholesome part of the race, the sweetest, for they are freshest from the hand of God. Whimsical, ingenious, mischievous, they fill the world with joy and good humor. We adults live a life of apprehension as to what they will think of us; a life of defense against their terrifying energy; a life of hard work to live up to their great expectations. We put them to bed with a sense of relief—and greet them in the morning with delight and anticipation. We envy them the freshness of adventure and the discovery of life. In all these ways, children add to the wonder of being alive. In all these ways, they help to keep us young.[1]

[1] Herbert Hoover, "How To Stay Young," *This Week Magazine*, August 8, 1954, p. 2, copyright 1954 by the United Newspapers Magazine Corporation. Reprinted by permission of the author, *This Week*, and *Reader's Digest*.

To the parent or teacher who is struggling with childish idiosyncrasies, former President Hoover's description of childhood may appear to be slightly sentimental. If a teacher is to achieve satisfaction and joy in his work with children, however, he needs to exemplify in his attitude toward his pupils much of what is contained in Hoover's words.

QUESTIONS AND TOPICS FOR DISCUSSION

1. Indicate the kinds of behavior we may expect from children of one, two, six, ten, and twelve years of age.
2. What relationships are there between socio-economic status and personality development?
3. Discuss the relationship between social development and character development.
4. In what way is the dynamic nature of child behavior associated with social development?
5. Trace the growth of social consciousness from birth to the age of six.
6. Why is it so important to understand the needs of children?
7. What is the relationship between social development and language development?
8. What are some of the important factors that stimulate children as they learn to think?
9. What is the relationship between social consciousness and the attitude of unselfishness? Illustrate your answer by examples from early childhood years.
10. What may have been the childhood history of an adolescent gangster?
11. Observe several individuals carefully. Try to discover what to them are emotion-arousing stimuli. What seems to be the effect of the same stimulation on the emotional behavior of other persons?
12. Name several ways in which a child may be motivated to control his anger.
13. Evaluate the significance of the emotions in human affairs.
14. Under what circumstances may a child develop fear of dogs? Of the dark? Of people? Of failure?
15. What is the cause of temper tantrums? Indicate ways of coping with temper tantrums at different ages.
16. Give examples of the effect of each of the following upon personality development during childhood: home, school, travel, having many friends.
17. Discuss the role of play in the social development of children.
18. What are the chief criteria upon which children between the ages of ten and twelve years base their friendships?
19. What is the value of insignia to children in the upper grades of the elementary school?

SELECTED REFERENCES

Bales, A. F., *Personality and Interpersonal Behavior.*, 3rd ed. Holt, Rinehart & Winston, N.Y., 1970.

Berkowitz, L., *Social Psychology.* Scott Foresman, Chicago, 1972.

Crow, L. D., *Psychology of Adjustment,* Knopf, N.Y., 1967.

Crow, L. D., *Introduction to Education,* 3rd ed. Christopher, North Quincy, Mass., 1974.

Crow, L. D. and Graham, T., *Human Development and Adjustment.* Littlefield, Totowa, N.J., 1973.

Evans, R. I. and Rozelle, R. M., *Social Psychology in Life,* 2nd ed. Allyn and Bacon, Boston, 1973.

Gordon, J. E., *Personality and Behavior.* Macmillan, N.Y., 1962.

Isaacs S., *Social Development in Young Children.* Schocken Books, N.Y., 1972.

Johnson, D. W., *Social Psychology of Education.* Holt, Rinehart & Winston, N.Y., 1970.

Kalish, R. A., *Psychology of Human Behavior,* 2nd ed. Brooks-Cole, Belmont, Calif., 1973.

Lindsay, C., *School and Community.* Pergamon, Elmsford, N.Y., 1970.

Love, H. D., *Educating Children in a Changing Society.* C. Thomas, Springfield, Ill., 1973.

Margollo, J. and Lloyd, J., *Learning through Play.* Harper and Row, N.Y., 1972.

McLaughlin, B., *Learning and Social Behavior.* Free Press, Riverside, N.J., 1971.

Ottaway, A. K., *Learning through Group Experience.* Fernhill, N.Y., 1966.

Roff, M. et al, *Social Development and Personality Development in Children.* University of Minnesota Press, Minneapolis, 1972.

Thompson, G. G., et al, (ed) *Social Development and Personality.* Wiley, N.Y., 1971.

Wechsler, H. et al, *Social Psychology and Mental Health.* Holt, Rinehart & Winston, N.Y., 1970.

5   *Personal and Social Development during Adolescence*

Personal and social development is an interesting field of study, whether the emphasis is on childhood, adolescent, or adult behavior. This chapter concerns the continued emotional and social experiences of the adolescent. Emotional development and social adjustment are significant personality molders during these active and full years. Almost every aspect of an adolescent's social life is conditioned by his emotional reactions. There are definite reasons for the belief of some adults that adolescent behavior reflects inner stresses and strains, growing pains, teen-age worries, and unreasonable attitudes.

Personal Needs of Adolescents

Like their younger brothers and sisters, adolescents need status, security, affection, and independence. They possess strong interests and urges, many of which have a sexual as well as a social aspect. The adolescent seeks an appropriate social role for himself and strives to experience satisfying relationships with peer and adult associates. Adolescence may be a flowering and a fulfillment, or a series of frustrating experiences.

Basically, the adolescent is the same person he was as a child, but he is confronted now with new physical urges, new patterns of physical growth, new interests and values, and new concepts of life and of self. He becomes increasingly sensitive to his needs, which may be: to gain friends, to be popular, to be a leader, to protect himself or others, to imitate others, to be praised, to be liked by others (especially members of the opposite sex), to resist coercion, to be independent, and to have prestige. An adolescent's experiences in learning to adjust his interests and desires to those of his peer groups are not always satisfying to himself. His participation in social activities during these years results in his emerging as an adult with attitudes and standards that reflect his adolescent experiences.

It was explained earlier that an emotion is the stirred-up state of an organism, the response of an entire human being to a stimulus situation, or an overt manifestation of integrated inner reactions. Sometimes an adolescent's emotions are expressed so vehemently that they arouse strong emotional responses in others. Emotional experiences usually have social overtones. The attitudes associated with these experiences change with the individuals concerned. If, for example, the adolescent wishes to make a good impression on another person, he is more than willing to try to please that person. At the same time, if he becomes antagonistic to the authority of his parents, his behavior toward them may be extremely aggressive.

Change of role during development. The adolescent finds that discarding childhood behavior patterns, as he meets the demands for behavior appropriate to his years, may cause him considerable concern. He faces not only the problem of changing his behavior, but also problems resulting from the reaction of others toward him and his behavior patterns. Group participation and the assumption of new roles require continually new adjustments as he attempts to increase his social skills and to widen his social contacts.

During childhood his peer groupings were, in many ways, relatively informal. He usually was automatically a member of his school or neighborhood groups, so that the matter of acceptance was not important. Now, as an adolescent, he must earn his social spurs before he can wear them. If he wishes to be included in a group, he must have something to offer or be willing to do something to help him become acceptable. Adolescents are often hypercritical of, snobbish with, and cruel to peers whom they find unacceptable.

The adolescent learns, therefore, to be concerned about peer attitudes. In order to be accepted, he may have to prove himself by meeting the requirements of other young people, sometimes in ways alien to his beliefs, attitudes, or inclinations. He believes that he must "cover up" his real self in order to achieve the degree of acceptance he desires. Hence there result the extra hours in bathing and in combing or arranging the hair, the concern with the creases in the suit, the attention to correct speech, and similar newly acquired behavior patterns. These characterize the new role of the adolescent who is attempting to gain or regain status with his peers.

Conduct relating to others is now important, and new codes of behavior must be learned. Moreover, as the adolescent continues toward adult status, he must begin to assume the role of the adult, with a still different code of behavior. As he approaches adulthood, he often is placed in situations in which he is expected to behave as an adult, even though he does not yet know specifically what is expected of him. An adolescent may reach full adult physical stature without having had those experiences needed to develop the social qualities characteristic of adult behavior. Since parents often exaggerate the importance of an adolescent's acting like an adult, it is not easy for the adolescent to be himself at all times.

Desire for peer approval. Fundamentally, an adolescent needs and wants adult approval, but peer acceptance seems much more important. Conformity to the opinions of one's peers is carefully observed, but acceptance of adult points of view may be more difficult. Although a young person may resent adult notions of what his standards of conduct and behavior, dress, or other accepted values should be, he is relatively conservative so far as his own group is concerned.

If the girls of a particular group begin to wear blue jeans, slacks, or other bizarre apparel, those members of the group who at first are not interested or who are denied the privilege by parents face embarrassing situations against which they struggle in one way or another. The fact that "others are doing it" is sufficient reason for teen-agers to have interest in something. Boys also want to imitate the mannerisms of their peers. Because they want to belong, they make an effort to satisfy group demands. Parents who refuse to approve participation in reasonably acceptable activities run the risk of antagonizing their sons or daughters.

Although an adolescent wants to be different, his basic behavior remains within the requirements of his peer group. His attitude might be likened to that of a mature woman regarding clothes. She wants to be in style, yet she dislikes finding herself in the company of another woman wearing the same cut and make of dress, no matter how expensive it may be.

Adolescent-adult interrelationships. Adults who wish to maintain a constructive influence over adolescent behavior must be sensitive to teen-age group opinions and methods of doing things. The adolescent rebels against authority. Hence those persons who represent authority run the danger, merely because they do represent authority, of alienating the good will of adolescents and making them non-co-operative. It is for this reason that indirect suggestion usually is more effective in securing the adolescent's help and co-operation. There is danger in judging adolescent behavior by adult standards. An adult usually is pleased when an adolescent, even momentarily, behaves according to adult standards.

Older men sometimes try to win the friendship of adolescent boys by joining in youthful sports, forgetting that young people have considerable more energy than adults. Hence attempts of an adult to compete with an adolescent are neither understood nor appreciated. Moreover, no matter how hard he tries, the adult cannot quite become a bosom pal of the teen-ager. There is a gap in understanding and interests, since each tends to interpret situations in the light of his own experiences. Nevertheless, the adult must try to place himself in the adolescent's position in order to try to understand his problems. This is difficult for any adult, and almost impossible for most. Adolescents usually believe that their peers understand them better than their parents do. What may seem silly to parents may appear to the adolescent to make perfectly good sense.

Adolescents are sensitive to the behavior of their parents and express to others their opinions concerning them:

> My parents seem to reject me. They act as if I had interfered with their life.
>
> My mother's very kind, but she's a bit old-fashioned at times. What can I do about it?
>
> I don't get along with my father. He seldom believes what I say, and insists I'm a bad example for the younger children. He never says "Hello" or "Good-bye" to me. He says I'm spoiled. I know I'm not perfect, and I'm not asking for pity, but I don't believe I'm as bad as he thinks.
>
> Almost every time I say something, my father passes some sarcastic remark. I'm now afraid to open my mouth.
>
> My older sister has a way of interfering with my social life by putting ideas into my mother's head. Although I never go any place without mother's permission, when I return my sister informs me that I'm never to go there again. If I ask for a reason, she tells me not to answer back. Sometimes I think she's jealous of me.

These examples show some of the problems the teen-ager has as he tries to live in his home environment and still keep up with his peers. In each instance, he fears consequences on the part of the older persons and a struggle for status with other adolescents. The only way in which the teen-ager can learn social skills is to participate in social situations with others, under supervision which, while effective, does not curtail the activities of the group.

Social Development of the Adolescent

The adolescent's social sensitivity and attitudes do not involve the development of a completely new and different behavior pattern. The adolescent's increasing awareness of himself as a potential adult acts merely to modify those social habits which he brings with him from childhood. Consequently, he may seem to adapt himself quickly, if not always successfully, to his new social status.

Characteristics of adolescent social growth. The adolescent becomes acutely aware of social pressures as he associates with his peers, whether in or out of school. He observes what others do and becomes active as an imitator. A study by the Progressive Education Association of the development from preadolescence through adolescence to adulthood shows some of the characteristics of social growth.

SOCIAL GROWTH

Growth from	*Toward*
1. Variety and instability of interests.	1. Fewer and deeper interests.
2. Talkative, noisy, daring with a great amount of any kind of activity.	2. More dignified controlled masculine and feminine adult behavior.
3. Seeking peer status with a high respect for peer standards.	3. The reflecting of adult cultural patterns.
4. A desire for identification with the herd, the crowd of boys and girls.	4. Identification with small select group.
5. Family status a relatively unimportant factor in influencing relations among peers.	5. Family socio-economic status an increasingly important factor in affecting with whom boys or girls associate.
6. Informal social activities such as parties.	6. Social activities becoming more formal, such as dances.
7. Dating rare.	7. Dates and "steadies" the usual thing.
8. Emphasis on building relations with boys and girls.	8. Increasing concern with preparation for own family life.
9. Friendships more temporary.	9. Friendships more lasting.

Growth from	Toward
10. Many friends.	10. Fewer and deeper friendships.
11. Willingness to accept activities providing opportunities for social relations.	11. Individual satisfying activities in line with talent development, proposed vocation, academic interest, or hobby.
12. Little insight into own behavior or behavior of others.	12. Increasing insight into human · relations.
13. The provision of reasonable rules important and stabilizing.	13. Growing independence from adult and dependence on self for decisions and behavior.
14. Ambivalence in accepting adult authority.	14. Seeking relation with adults on equality basis.[1]

As the adolescent mingles with his age-mates and participates in their group activities, his feeling of belonging increases, until it becomes more important than anything else. It may become so important that family ties are neglected as he starts to conform with peer demands and to identify himself with adult behavior. One of the greatest social needs of the adolescent is to be accepted and approved by his peers. If a particular kind of hat is to be worn, its usage is correct for adolescents on any and all occasions; if a hat is taboo, it must not be seen at any time.

Adults often wonder to what extent the characteristics and behavior of peer groups have any real value for the members of the group. Peer-group membership gives the adolescent: (1) a feeling of security, (2) experiences in developing a sense of belonging, and (3) opportunities for achieving individual status. He learns to give and take; he begins to understand something about the rights of others, since each member of the group is bent upon the promotion of his own self-interest. If a problem concerning individual rights arises in the home, however, it is not easy for one adolescent sibling to give in to the other. Each fights for status in a more active way than if strangers were involved. For example, note the troubles of two sisters, ages fourteen and sixteen. As one of them said: "My father definitely takes my sister's side, no matter how wrong she is. This annoys me to such an extent that I fall into fits of silence and

[1] L. H. Meek, *The Personal-Social Development of Boys and Girls*, Committee on Workshops, Progressive Education Association, 1938, p. 121. Reprinted by permission.

resentment. It seems impossible for my father to recognize the fact that my sister is sometimes wrong. My mother is very fair to both of us."

Adolescents constantly are being pulled in several different directions at the same time. Their values are in the formative stage and are subject to change. Hence their behavior is not easy to predict in group situations when they are faced by multiple stimuli. It is unfortunate if the influence of peer groups is such that it weans an adolescent from his parents at too early an age, or if tensions are set up between parents and children because of undesirable out-of-home influences. Teen-agers who defy their parents and eventually run away from home may be responding to undesirable influences outside the home. Difference of opinion between adults and adolescents concerning "rightness" even in small matters may confuse a young person. For example, Mary reports, "When I left my house last Saturday night, I told my mother I would be home about eleven, as she had requested. When I told my friend who was having the gathering that I had to leave, she made some funny remarks because I wanted to obey my mother. I left and she told my girl friends I was very rude and unappreciative. I wish I knew the right thing to do." In such a situation, parents need not only to know what, abstractly, is "best" for the adolescent but also to be aware of the pressures exerted by their child's peers.

Social groupings. The groups formed during late childhood usually are dissolved by young adolescents. Adolescents lose interest in the activities that had occupied them a few years earlier. They pass through a short period of withdrawing from accustomed social groups in attempts to create a social life which they believe will meet their needs and interests. With physical, physiological, emotional, and intellectual changes come changes in attitudes toward friends and associates. Adolescents now seek friends who will give them security in affection.

The selection of friends is not a cold, calculating process, yet the results seem to come out that way. To the adolescent girl, a best friend is an important person. Boys may be content to move in groups of three or more, but a girl tends to want a best friend, even if she quarrels with her occasionally. The diaries of "Mary Y" and "Anne X" furnished Runner the data for determining *social distance* in adolescent friendships. The data from the diaries, covering a two-weeks' period, were used to discover the frequency of contacts of each girl with other people. This and the amount of emotional

warmth shown were the criteria for determining the degree of inti-
macy. Seven zones of increasing social distances are shown in Figures 6 and 7. A close study of the diagrams will help in understanding the effect of Mary's and Anne's social distance upon other
people.

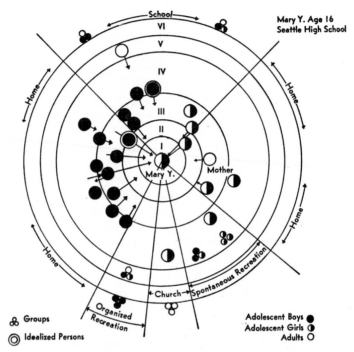

FIGURE 6.   Sociogram for "Mary"

From J. R. Runner, "Social Distance in Adolescent Relationships," *American
Journal of Sociology,* Vol. 43, 1947, p. 435, published by the University of
Chicago Press, copyright 1947 by the University of Chicago. Reprinted by per-
mission.

Runner formulated seven classifications of adolescent friendships:

1. *The Confidante*—an almost inseparable friend in whom the
   individual confides his hopes, fears, successes, and failures.
   Physical contacts of a caressing type and the privilege of
   talking about one's self are rights of the relationship.
2. *The Intimate*—a close friend. Conscious selection is not as
   important as frequency of contact. The conversations are
   about trivialities rather than personal problems.
3. *The Familiar*—a friend who is seen often but for whom one
   feels little emotional warmth.

4. *The Acquaintance*—a person barely known.
5. *The Active Group-Acquaintance*—a person with whom one works in a group but does not know otherwise.
6. *The Passive Group-Acquaintance*—a person who attends the same group meetings but takes no part.
7. *The Spectator*—a person known by name, with whom one has never spoken.[1]

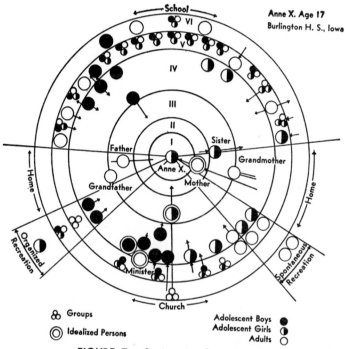

FIGURE 7. Sociogram for "Anne"

From J. R. Runner, "Social Distance in Adolescent Relationships," *American Journal of Sociology,* Vol. 43, 1947, p. 435, published by the University of Chicago Press, copyright 1947 by the University of Chicago. Reprinted by permission.

As a rule, adolescents are keenly aware of social distance, even if they have never heard of or used the term. They know they have close friends with whom they are much more intimate than they are with others. The groups they form usually are small and quite exclusive. Group members are chosen more because of what they, as individuals, have to offer than for financial standing, social back-

[1] J. R. Runner, "Social Distance in Adolescent Relationships," *American Journal of Sociology,* Vol. 43, 1947, p. 435, published by the University of Chicago Press, copyright 1947 by the University of Chicago. Reprinted by permission.

ground, or family approval. Individuals who possess personality traits considered undesirable are excluded from the group.

Group cohesiveness, together with many of the forces that play upon adolescents as they function in their social relationships in a local neighborhood, is revealed through Figure 8, which indicates some of the operative forces and interrelationships. Regular members of the group are indicated by double circles or squares; the single circles and single squares refer to those adolescents who were excluded from the crowd for one reason or another. The ages of the adolescents are from sixteen to nineteen.

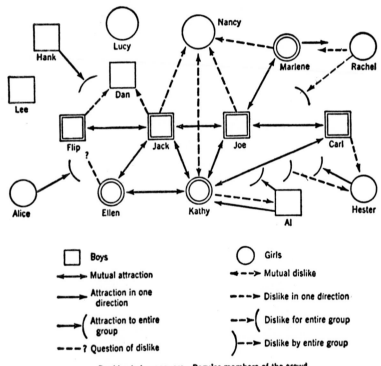

FIGURE 8. Analysis of a Crowd

From L. Cole, *Psychology of Adolescence*, 3rd ed., Rinehart & Co., 1948, p. 216. Reprinted by permission.

Social adaptability in a class. Increased emphasis has been given to those major objectives in education which concern the emotional and social adjustment of the child. Willingness to work with peers who hold differing opinions creates a climate in which skill in human relations grows. Nurturing and maintaining desirable attitudes include concern for the welfare of others, skill in social relations, accepting others as they are, and working to develop group consciousness. These attitudes help promote a classroom climate conducive to happier and more efficient learning.

Teachers have believed that adolescents from the same socioeconomic level tend to form their own groups that sometimes become so exclusive as to disrupt the social life of the school. A study in a small Midwestern community of all the sixteen-year-olds revealed the social behavior and attitudes of teen-agers.[1] The investigators first surveyed all families that had sixteen-year-old children and grouped them into five socio-economic classes. They administered tests, interviewed the adolescents, and studied their social habits. The data as condensed by Cole (Figure 9) are not conclusive, yet they indicate how social stratification operates to throw hurdles in the way of some adolescents who are striving for status.

Adolescent Interests and Attitudes

For the most part, adolescent interests and attitudes grow out of experiences that begin in early childhood. Because of their changing personal and social status, teen-agers become sensitive to stimuli situations that they formerly disregarded. Like children, adolescents are great imitators of observed attitudes. They learn many of their attitudes indirectly from their elders, but they are particularly sensitive to the attitudes of other adolescents. Hence many adolescent attitudes are acquired unconsciously, while others represent conscious efforts to "think" like the peer group.

The development of adolescent interests. Adolescents continue many of the interests developed during childhood but express these interests differently. They play different games, or function under different rules; they watch different television programs and for different reasons; the books they read and the motion pictures they attend are more nearly on the adult level; they plan social gatherings in which they have a vote on the members to be invited. The last fact makes them realize that they must become selective in their friendships since they often cannot invite all the friends they have. As one adolescent girl said, "I have many friends. Some I've had for a long time, and some I've just acquired. When planning a party, must I invite all my friends? If not, how can I face those I don't invite?" As this girl succeeds in meeting this problem, which is very important to her, she gains training for later adult responsibilities.

[1] A. B. Hollingshead, *Elmtown's Youth.* John Wiley & Sons, Inc., New York, 1949.

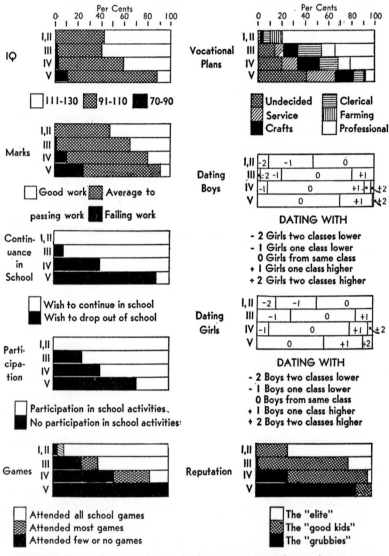

FIGURE 9. Influence of Social Class upon Attitudes and Activities

From L. Cole, *Psychology of Adolescence*, 4th ed., Rinehart & Co., N. Y., 1948, p. 200. Reprinted by permission. Based on figures in A. B. Hollingshead, *Elmtown's Youth*, John Wiley & Sons, Inc., 1949, pp. 172-216.

The interests of adolescents generally are wholesome and constructive. If adolescent interests are thwarted too completely or too frequently, problems of maladjustment may result. It usually is only the emotionally insecure adolescent who develops conflicts as a result of the stresses and strains that may be caused by failures to attain desired goals.

As mentioned earlier, the normal adolescent is interested in his grooming and dress, his voice and conversational ability, his study and independent research, his social and recreational activities, his reading, and his vocational pursuits. To the extent that he gains satisfaction in some or most of these, he will make both inner and overt adjustments that will serve him well in his emotional, intellectual, and social development. Moreover, it is fortunate that during the adolescent period the individual's interests widen to include not only his own welfare and that of his family but also the welfare and activities of other persons and groups.

Attitudes as directive forces in adolescent behavior. Adolescents often behave without being aware of the forces prompting their behavior. Much of adolescent inner conflict is attributable to unconscious attitudes. Hence adolescents may be censured for behavior which they actually believe to be acceptable. They are unaware of the fact that their motives are not understood by others or that others sometimes evaluate their behavior in the light of adult rather than teen-age standards. Consequently, displayed attitudes of selfishness or insincerity can be observed better by others than by the adolescent himself.

Much of an adolescent's behavior is affected by the dynamic nature of sensory and perceptual experiences. At one moment, one idea is in focus, and at the next, another idea or thought process is dominant. An adolescent's attitudes or feeling tones at the moment are the motivating forces that tend to give one idea dominance over another. An adolescent, even more than a child, is mentally set to talk about a particular person or topic of special interest to himself. Hence, unconsciously, he may interpret what is said by another person according to his own interests. For example, a man who was reading a newspaper made the following comment: "The President certainly understands what is needed." His college-freshman son, who is a great admirer of the president of his college, exclaimed, "I didn't know you liked President _____ as much as I do!" Explanations were then in order to clear the issue.

Attitude problems of adolescents. Adolescents have the problem of asserting their independence without hurting others and without themselves being hurt. They want to be independent and yet they want the guiding hand of parents and teachers if it is offered at the time and in the way desired. The teen-ager may seem to flaunt adult authority or refuse to co-operate with his associates in spite of, or perhaps because of, a realization of his insecurity.

This "rebellion" may take many forms. A boy or girl may become unduly aggressive and assume the attitude that the chief function of his parents is to serve him and his wants. He may exhibit a superior attitude toward younger children; or he may attempt to impress his peer groups. Insecurity in relations with the opposite sex may result in behavior as reported by one girl, "I'm fickle. I have an occasional crush for a week or, at the most, three months. This causes me great difficulty because the fellows and girls of my group say, 'She loves to break hearts.' This may be caused by my fondness for my brothers, who are good looking and men's men, the type I would like to have."

The struggles of an adolescent toward self-realization may be intensified by the fact that fundamentally he is an idealist. Through school study, reading newspapers, and listening to news reports on radio and television, he learns about world conditions and becomes deeply concerned over apparent injustices. Hence, in his daydreams, he pictures himself as a reformer. He wants to improve conditions for old men and women, children, and the underprivileged, in general. At the same time, feelings of insecurity in his relationships with his family and with neighborhood groups may cause him to be critical of his grandparents, to be impatient with younger brothers or sisters, and to assume a superior attitude toward schoolmates whose parents are in a lower social and economic class than his.

The adolescent usually is unaware of the contradiction between his idealistic beliefs and his actual behavior. If he does recognize it, he may try to excuse his un-co-operative attitudes toward his close associates as a result of their lack of appreciation of himself and of his high ideals. Yet, fearing that he may be responsible for their inability to understand him, he attempts to impress them through overaggressive behavior, originating in his feelings of insecurity.

Attitudes of parents toward adolescents. An adolescent boy or girl can cause parents great concern. The boy's interest in school sports may be so great that he wants to participate in all or most of them: football, baseball, basketball, and track, to the detriment of his academic achievement. If he is a good athlete, he becomes the school hero, the girls vying with one another for his attention. The personable high-school boy has no dating problems except those that stem from parental disapproval of his excessive demands to use the family car and his late hour of return from social gatherings or dates. The girl is likely to exhibit rebellion that may be centered in the home. For example, she may want to change home customs and conditions because she is ashamed to bring her friends into a home in which the mannerisms, speech patterns, and dress of her parents differ from those which prevail in the homes of her friends.

Regardless of the permissiveness or the rigidity of parental attitudes, many adolescents feel that they have problems in their relations with the family. They often talk freely to other adults about their home difficulties. A few of the many home-rooted teen-age problems reported to the authors are:

My parents are much older than I am and tend to coddle me.

I have a step-father who hates me to the point of perpetual malice. I don't know what to do about it.

If my mother approves of my doing something, my father is sure to disapprove.

My brother, although he's younger than the rest of us, is always loved and cherished more than anyone else by my parents.

My mother constantly tells me, "I'll be glad when you get a home of your own. If you don't like the way I run mine, get out." There's no place else to go, and maybe she doesn't mean it, but it hurts to have her say it.

My brother is sixteen, and at one time he associated with a bad group of boys. The family made him change his friends and now he goes around with a nice group of boys, but they like girls. My father disapproves of his even speaking with girls; and, as these are of another religion, there is constant quarreling in the house. I've taken sides with my brother and, although my friendship with my father was of the best, he and I are now quarreling.

I feel that my brother and I aren't as friendly and chummy as we were when we were younger. Could you please tell me how I could regain this friendship? When we have an argument, who should be the first to apologize? Mother says the younger should be the first. Is she correct?

What can I do with a brother who sometimes is so lovable and amusing that it's a pleasure to have him around until he suddenly gets a domineering fit. Then he begins to discuss my future as a working girl, how much I would contribute to the house, which boys to invite to the house, what time to come home, and the like. He's only three years my senior.

What should you do with a high-strung, nervous sister who's making life miserable for you? She picks on me and finds fault with everything I do or say. My mother and father say I should tolerate her because she's just an unfortunate person. I try to ignore the remarks she makes, but it gets to such a state that I wish I'd never been born.

My sister, who is now twenty, is becoming most disagreeable and very obstinate at home, but on the outside is very agreeable and friendly. My mother traces the cause to too much freedom during her high-school days. She has become very careless about her clothes and keeping her appointments. She takes her troubles out on the family at home. Is there any way that we, the family, might make her correct these bad habits that are known to her family and some friends?

Many more examples can be cited of the problems faced by adolescents in the home. Much also could be said by parents about their problems as they try to understand their teen-age children and thereby reduce or avoid family conflicts. No simple formula can be established to guide parents in dealing with adolescent behavior. One principle is important, however: adolescents must not be given the idea that their wants always should be satisfied in accordance with their wishes regardless of others' interests or welfare.

It is no secret that parental views concerning the kinds of activity to be denied them and the behavior controls to be exercised have a tremendous impact upon the thinking of adolescents. The authors, with the assistance of teachers in the junior and senior high schools of New York City, obtained from about 4,000 teen-agers reports of areas of conflict between themselves and their parents. Some of the items were listed by many adolescents, indicating that what might seem to one adolescent and his parents a problem peculiar to that family situation is common to many parent-adolescent relationships.

The items listed most often by both boys and girls are:

1. To have brothers and sisters held up as models.
2. To eat disliked food.
3. To take younger brothers and sisters with them on trips.
4. To be scolded for low school marks.
5. To account exactly for money spent.
6. To receive inadequate or irregular allowances.
7. To be forbidden to discuss sex matters with other boys and girls.
8. To have to be careful about appearance, manners, and speech.
9. To be denied the use of the family automobile.

Boys objected especially to their parents':

1. Teasing them about their girl friends.
2. Criticizing rowdy behavior.
3. Participating in childish pranks.
4. Deciding what their vocation should be.
5. Controlling the money earned by them in part-time jobs.
6. Talking about them to family friends.

Girls reported that their parents objected to their:

1. Going to parties or dances without a chaperon.
2. Riding in automobiles with boys.
3. Going out with older men.
4. Accepting expensive gifts from boys or men.
5. Selecting friends of either sex without parental approval.
6. Selecting their own clothes and wearing them when or how they wished.
7. Using cosmetics.
8. Having freedom of subject selection at school.
9. "Throwing a party" for boys and girls in the home.
10. Working part-time in local stores.
11. Having as much freedom as is granted to the boys.

One can conclude from reading these reports that many adolescents are too immature to recognize the practical aspects of their parents' attitudes toward teen-age behavior. Young people often are so eager to satisfy their interests and desires that they do not consider the possible harmful consequences of some of their activities. The fact that some of the boys and girls reported no items of conflict between themselves and their parents indicate good relationships in the home.

Boy-Girl Relationships during Adolescence

Adolescents are interested not only in themselves but also in their peers of either sex. They not only seek close friends of their own sex, but also experience an increasing urge to be attractive to and to associate with the opposite sex. Each is concerned with doing for himself what may be necessary to become more attractive to other teen-agers. Young people may be able to change some traits by careful attention to them. Those characteristics that are associated with habits, dress, attitudes toward others, emotional responses, punctuality, respect for authority, and responsiveness to the wishes of others can be improved. Those traits that are associated with intelligence, physical structure, and the like are less likely to be affected by attempts to alter them.

Adolescent attitudes toward members of the opposite sex. The authors recently completed a study among 2,440 girls and 2,360 boys of the

*TABLE 2.   Personality Traits Admired by Members of the Opposite Sex

(Listed in order of frequency of response)

Traits Admired by Boys	Traits Admired by Girls
Good personality	Good personality
Good looking—beautiful face, dress, and figure	Good looking—not necessarily handsome
Looks nice in a bathing suit	Good character
Neatness and cleanliness	Neatness
Helpful to others	Clean and appropriate dress
Consideration for others	Intelligence
Appropriate dress	Good conversationalist
Dependable	Consideration for a girl's wishes
Good talker	Respect for girls—not fresh
Good listener	Willingness to take a girl on dates
Good manners	Boy to be older than girl
Friendliness	Good manners
Ability to dance	Good natured
Acts her age	Smart in school
Courtesy	Clean shaven and hair cut
Politeness	Clean-minded
No show-off	Kind, generous, tall
Interest in hobbies of boys	Acts his age
Modest, but not shy	Has a sense of humor
Acts grown-up, not like a baby	Not too shy
Clean-minded	Honest and fair
Able to take a joke	Respect for rights of girl
	Punctuality
	Not to try to be a big shot
	Able to get along with others
	Has self-control
	The way he kisses
	Good listener

* Tables 2, 3, and 4 are copyrighted by Lester D. Crow.

TABLE 3. Personality Traits Disliked by Members of the Opposite Sex

Traits Disliked by Boys	*Traits Disliked by Girls*
Sloppiness of appearance	Sloppiness of appearance
Overweight or underweight	Boastfulness
Tendency to flirt or "two-time"	Acts like big shots
Talks too much	Display poor manners
Extremes of dress	Stinginess
Little regard for money	Being conceited
Too much interest in self	Poorly groomed
Lack of punctuality	Laziness
Snobbishness	Foolish behavior at parties
Flirting	Exhibits fresh behavior
Talks about other dates	Shyness
Too much make-up	Smoking excessively
Sulking and pouting	Use of bad language
Being conceited	Discourtesy to elders
Bites nails	Talks too much
Smokes and drinks	Wants to be the center of attention
Giggling or talebearer	Moodiness
Inability to dance	Sponging off other boys
Immature behavior	Asks for date at last minute
Mingling with a fast crowd	

TABLE 4. Attempts Made by Boys and Girls to Increase Their Popularity with Members of the Opposite Sex

Attempts Made by Boys	*Attempts Made by Girls*
Develop good taste in dress	Become careful about appearance
Participate in school activities	Try to be friendly
Avoid annoying habits in school events	Develop sincerity
Be considerate of the other person	Be popular with girls also
Develop similar interests	Try not to be catty
Become lively	Try not to go to expensive places on a date
Be as friendly as possible	Be a good conversationalist
Eliminate all annoying habits	Go in for school activities
Always be dependable	Avoid ridicule of others
Be polite to everyone	Have respect for elders

personality traits admired and disliked in members of the opposite sex. Three of the questions asked were: (1) What are the personality characteristics you admire in girls (boys)? (2) What traits do you dislike in girls (boys)? (3) What do you do to increase your popularity with girls (boys) you know?

The results were organized into two groups according to the age of the respondents: the twelve-to-fourteen-year-olds, and the sixteen-to-eighteen-year-olds. Most of the younger group emphasized physical characteristics and overt behavior. The more mature teen-agers stressed attitudes and behavior associated with inner motivations and character traits. There were certain qualities, however, that were considered desirable by all teen-agers. See Tables 2, 3, and 4.

The younger girls dislike boys who want to kiss and paw them, and admire boys who are older than they. They want "boy friends" who are willing to meet their parents, who are interested in sports, and who are willing to work hard. They dislike hot-tempered boys, and rude boys who take a girl to a party and then pay no attention to her. Younger boys admire girls with good figures and girls who are fun to be with. They dislike girls who are fresh and try to act older than they are.

Boys in their later teens seem to admire girls who are even-tempered, lively, less intelligent than they are but not stupid, good listeners, modest, and sincere. Some of the older boys object to a girl's using excessive make-up and wearing slacks or sweaters that exaggerate her figure. The boys want the girls to be a little shorter than they and not fat. Many of the older adolescents stressed good character, consideration for older people, mature behavior, self-respect, and ambition as traits most desired. These qualities outranked having money available for a date. Some girls said they did not want a boy to spend money on them unless he actually had earned the money himself.

These data seem to indicate that sound thinking, high ideals, and wholesome attitudes are characteristic of many of our teen-agers. Since the participants in the study represented a wide range of socio-economic backgrounds in a metropolitan district, differences in points of view and in modes of expression were to be expected. Although some of the responses may not reflect real attitudes but rather imagined responses, there is reason to believe that the responses were not given lightly. As samples of the statements made by several of these teen-agers, we present the following excerpts from their responses as reported in another article by one of the authors:

Traits or qualities admired in boys by fourteen-year-old girls:

(1) To be quite frank, the first thing I look for is looks. Then I make sure he isn't a lemon. I like a boy who can protect me. I also like a boy who is possessive. The boy should be mature and well-mannered. I hate cry babies. I like boys who know when to kid around and when to be serious. I like a boy who does not whistle at another girl when I'm around. I like a boy to be well groomed.

(2) I like a boy who has good manners and isn't a show-off; a boy who acts his age and not like a baby; a boy who knows how to get along with people; a boy who wouldn't leave me flat when he sees another girl; a boy who isn't a sloppy dresser, eater, etc.

(3) Before I like a boy, I look for many things. Above all, he must have a pleasing personality. That is, he should be clean and neat, courteous, kind, and considerate. He should show respect for me and he should be truthful. He should be a nice dresser. I don't actually care if he's good looking or not, but of course it helps, and he shouldn't be too forward. He should be sensible and not silly.

(4) The kind of boy I admire is a boy who is clean, neat, and respected. I would like the boy to be a little taller than I am and a little smarter. The boy must also have a good sense of humor and must stick up for me. He should have good manners, not be too shy, and have a good disposition. I also admire a boy who can tell the truth, is not dull, and knows how to dance.

Traits or qualities admired in girls by fourteen-year-old boys:

(1) I like a girl who acts like a girl and not like a tomboy. A girl who is pretty and talks nice, and a girl who doesn't hang around with a bunch of boys or tough girls.

(2) I admire a girl's appearance, whether she is neat or whether she is untidy. I would like her to be of average intelligence. I don't like girls that put on too much make-up or who giggle or pass notes around the classroom. I wouldn't like her to look like something from a nightmare.

Traits admired in boys by seventeen-year-old girls:

(1) I like a boy with intelligence, someone who knows how to talk about other things than movies and baseball, etc. I also like good looks, even though they're only skin deep. The reason I like them is that first impressions are very important and you notice a person's looks before anything else. I like a boy who's thoughtful and considerate.

(2) At present I like all the traits my boy friend has: He's considerate, polite, ambitious, intelligent, punctual, kind,

thoughtful, complimentary, just affectionate enough, and has a wonderful personality which allows him to mix with all groups of any ages. To top it off, he's dark and handsome.

(3) First, he must be kind and considerate of me. When I go out with a boy, I want him to keep up his end of the conversation. He doesn't have to take me to a big night club to show me a good time. We can have a good time at the movies if he's a pleasant fellow. He should be easy to get along with and be willing to earn the money he spends on a girl. He must be good looking, be a good dancer, well bred, smarter than myself, have a sense of humor, and be able to take teasing.

(4) The boy of my dreams must have a good personality, be lots of fun to be with, but not loud or embarrassing in any way. Most boys feel that being loud and having a good personality are synonymous. They are wrong, since people are most usually attracted to someone who is quiet and a good listener. I like a boy who is firm and stands up for what he thinks is right. I like a boy who can easily mingle with any crowd, young or old, without feeling frustrated. Most of all I like a boy who is considerate of his date and the people he is with. I must look up to the boy I like. Therefore, he must have a sense of responsibility and be able to fulfill his obligations.

Traits admired in girls by seventeen-year-old boys:

(1) I like a friendly smile. I like a good dresser at the right time. I like a girl with plenty of common sense at parties and dates. I like a girl to be a good dancer, a lot of fun, and to have a good sense of humor at the right time. I like a girl who does not stand on ceremony and can make the most of everything. I like a girl to have a nice form.

(2) I like girls to be neat, on time for appointments, to have a man's mechanical mind, to be able to "rough it," to be free and easy, to be able to carry on an intelligent conversation, to be adaptable to all social positions into which we may go, to be musically inclined, and to be a good dancer.

Traits disliked in boys by seventeen-year-old girls:

I hate a boy who is a flirt and makes passes at other girls when out on a date. I dislike insincerity. Even though I'm not punctual, I dislike a boy who is late for a date. I dislike a boy who uses a line to his advantage, who likes to impress you with money, who reads only comics and is proud of the fact, who is cheap, who loves to be pampered, who forgets that you are around but makes it quite obvious that he wants attention. I dislike a boy who is a poor dancer, who constantly brags, who will take you out and then forget that he is with you, who will flirt with every girl he sees while with you. I dislike a boy who does not shave or who is a flashy dresser or who is conceited. I dislike a boy who is cheap, quiet, moody, sensitive, unreliable, dishonest, or who lies, drinks excessively, or uses profane language.

Traits disliked in girls by seventeen-year-old boys:

I dislike a girl who talks too much, who dresses sloppy, who thinks she is cute and isn't. I dislike a girl who gossips. I hate a girl who thinks she's "it." I hate loudmouths. I hate smokers. I hate girls who are always going to sleep. I dislike girls who talk about their last date when they are out with you. I dislike girls who like nothing but dancing, or girls who do not dance, and girls who forget that they're your date.[1]

Adolescent popularity. If the adolescent has had a great deal of experience in meeting people during childhood, he may find it easier to develop traits considered necessary for him to be liked by his peers or to become popular. Reasons for popularity include poise, dignity, social ease, and a genuine consideration for others, rather than loud talking, aggressive behavior, and lavish spending.

Popularity stems from a willingness to do for others or to share with others. Members of a group appreciate and admire the individual who has some leadership qualities and who indicates by his behavior that he is interested in them and is willing to do what he can for the good of the group. If he demonstrates through his actions that he is interested in the others only so long as he can further his personal aims, they soon lose patience with him. The co-operative person is welcomed by all members of a group. He is as much interested in the successful achievement of the other members as in his own. He accepts his responsibilities cheerfully and does his best to carry out whatever is expected of him.

Social status and popularity are fundamental to the personal happiness of the adolescent. Try as they may, many adolescents are unable to achieve the popularity they desire. Some have few friends and have difficulty in making friends. The effect of being "social isolates" may be far reaching. These individuals may decide that social activities are useless, and turn to daydreaming or to an excessive use of imagination for personal satisfaction.

The traits that are characteristic of the popular adolescent are those that are included in the list of personality characteristics admired by adolescents generally. These traits, however, may exist

[1] L. D. Crow, "Personality Traits Admired by Adolescents," *The Clearing House,* Vol. 29, No. 1, September, 1954, pp. 25–26. Reprinted by permission.

in many different forms or patterns. Some popular individuals are aggressive, and others are rather submissive. Some are enthusiastic, talkative, energetic, and daring; others display friendly, sympathetic, and good-natured attitudes.

Leadership and followership. Every group has its leader. Leadership qualities vary according to the needs and requirements of the group. A strong, purposeful leader can exert a tremendous influence upon the activities and attitudes of his followers. An incompetent leader may be the cause of group dissension or even dissolution. The character and purposes of the group may be conditioned or even determined by the kind of leadership given.

An individual *rises* to a position of leadership, rather than *assumes* the role. Before he can exert leadership, he must have the respect and admiration of those about him. His prestige may be built or destroyed by what he does, says, or writes.

Leaders in school usually are found to be superior to their fellow students in physical, mental, and social traits. Since they probably are the more intelligent, they make better marks; they come from homes located in better socio-economic areas, and they tend to be physically attractive. Superior ability and status represent the potentials for leadership. Many adolescents who possess these qualities never aspire to or attain a position of leadership either in school or elsewhere.

Leadership is usually persistent. Many follow-up studies have been made to learn what happens to able high-school graduates. In 1953, Ray G. Wood completed a study, covering a twenty-year period, to discover what became of Ohio's superior high-school graduates. He concluded from the results of a questionnaire that those students who ranked high in the various tests in the Ohio testing program lived up to expectations. Successful school students became well-adjusted and successful citizens with exceptional leadership qualities.

To become a good follower requires social qualities. People who prefer to follow rather than to lead support the individuals who aspire to positions of leadership if the latter display acceptable attitudes. The success of autocratic governments is based in part upon the willingness of the people to follow an accepted leader, regardless of the method of selection. Leadership that results from the democratic approach helps many aspire to positions of leadership. Nevertheless, each potential or actual leader needs also to become a good follower in areas of activity other than that in which he is a leader. For example, if an expert engineer were seriously ill, he would need the services of a good physician.

Followers differ in their reasons for doing so. A *routine* follower is one who lacks initiative but is willing and able to follow the lead of others. A *constructive* follower is an individual who has potential leadership but is afraid of responsibility, and thus becomes the leader's right-hand support. The *impulsive* follower supports a particular leader not because of any interest in what the latter is doing but rather because he likes him or believes that the support will be advantageous to himself.

Vocational Problems of Adolescents

By the time the individual reaches his adolescent years, his aspirations are beginning to take form. Some persons decide upon their life work before they enter high school, but most adolescents do not select a vocation until they are in high school. Some college students still are undecided when they are graduated. Many people change their vocational choice many times until 'they reach their final decision. In any case, choosing a career, getting adequate preparation for entrance into a vocational activity, obtaining a job, and finally adjusting to the job are problems that are solved by some adolescents only with considerable difficulty and emotional strain.

Choosing a career. The choice of a career is not easy for the adolescent. He wants complete freedom of choice; yet he seeks the advice of elders, including his parents and teachers. The fact that his understanding of the requirements of occupational activities is limited does not deter him from protesting against or ignoring suggestions made by his parents and school counselors. Many teen-age boys and girls achieve some understanding of occupational conditions and requirements through part-time employment while they continue their studies in high school and college. More than 50 per cent of high-school youth are doing part-time work as they prepare themselves for later professional and business activities.

Every parent hopes that his child will find a life work that will pay more, be less tiring, and offer greater prestige than his own. No parent, however, should attempt to influence his child unduly to select a vocation solely according to parental interests and ambitions. That the wishes of the parents are troublesome to adolescents in vocational selection is borne out by the questions young people ask and the problems by which they seem to be confronted.

For example, one boy has these questions: "If a parent wishes to set a boy up in business, but the boy wants to go to college, what should he do? Would it be advisable to try to operate the business during the day and go to college at night?" Here is an obvious attempt on the part of the boy to effect a compromise between his and his parent's interests. Another adolescent asks, "Should parents interfere with a girl's choice of a career by telling her that they had plans for her in another field?" Or "Should a parent have the right to prevent a child from specializing in a field in which he is best suited?" One girl is especially concerned with her mother's attitude toward her interest in social work: "I'm interested in social work. I believe unwed mothers and delinquent children have a right to be given a chance through right teaching and proper environment. This has brought about a lot of argument at home. My mother says my ideas are mostly wrong. Do you agree with her?"

Elias asked 5,500 high-school seniors whether they considered their parents' occupation to be ideal, very satisfactory, fairly satisfactory, rather unsatisfactory, or very unsatisfactory. He found that about 57 per cent of the boys rated the parent's occupation "fairly satisfactory" or higher; 42 per cent indicated some degree of unsatisfactoriness. The girls' ratings were about 56 and 42 per cent, respectively.

TABLE 5.   Responses of 5,500 High-School Seniors Who Checked the Statement: "As a Life Occupation for Me, I Consider My Parents' Occupation to Be ————" [1]

	BOYS	GIRLS
RESPONSE	Per Cent	Per Cent
An ideal occupation	8.9	6.4
Very satisfactory	15.9	18.5
Fairly satisfactory	31.9	30.3
Rather unsatisfactory	25.1	20.4
Very unsatisfactory	16.1	21.2

Parental interest in the vocational choices of their children is not harmful if the parents let the final choice be made by the young person. Studies concerning the occupational fields which are entered by young people reveal that children are more than twice as likely

[1] L. J. Elias, *High-School Youth Look at Their Problems,* The College Bookstore, State College of Washington, Pullman, Washington, January, 1949. Reprinted by permission.

to enter the occupational area of their parent as to select one outside that area. This indicates the strength of parental influence upon adolescent vocational choice. There are good reasons for such choices, if the vocation fits the needs, interests, and ambitions of the young person, and if the decision is the child's, not the parent's.

Vocational adjustment. The earlier a final vocational choice is made, especially if the selection is in one of the professions, the more satisfactory it is likely to be. School planning is simplified. Unfortunately, few adolescents are able to make a final vocational choice during the first year in high school. Some adolescents may have occupational interests and aspirations precluded by personality or other limitations. For example, if a boy is unable to meet scholastic requirements or if he lacks financial means to prepare to become a physician, no matter how strong his interest, he should be advised to enter another related activity in which he will have a reasonable chance for success because of lower requirements.

Job placement often causes problems. A young person may be conscious of his personality limitations. For example, one girl believes that her short height and youthful appearance will interfere with her ability to secure the kind of job she wants. She says, "I'm eighteen years old, but look younger. Even though I dress to look older, I'm always taken for a fifteen- or sixteen-year-old. How can I get a position and gain respect under these conditions?" Another student asks, "If you're young when looking for a job but look older than you are, is there any harm in giving a false age?" Another is concerned about how he can overcome feelings of inferiority in applying for a job. He asks, "How can you overcome a feeling of inferiority when being interviewed for a job? How can you present your qualifications without understating or overstating them?"

Age seems to be a serious problem for many adolescents when they want to become gainfully employed. Often there is a strong temptation to advance in age in order to be in a better competing position with other candidates. One boy comments, "When I go out to look for a position, I'll most likely have to state my age. Do you think that my being younger than the average graduate will be a drawback in getting a position? Do you think any employer or personnel manager will check if I say I'm a year older?"

The attitude of the worker on the job is important both to himself and to his employer. The employee should bring to his job thorough preparation to perform his work efficiently. He should manifest personal interest in his work and the organization in which he is an employee. He should manifest respect for his supervisors and co-workers and consistently do an honest day's work. The personal relations between worker and employer should be characterized by friendly respect. An employee should neither seek nor accept favors for himself that are not granted to other workers. It should not become necessary to raise questions such as, "Some of the fellows in my shop are constantly criticizing our foreman when he's not around, but tell him to his face what a good fellow he is. This makes me sore and sometimes I feel like telling the foreman. Would that be right?"

Adolescents start work with full intentions of doing a good job. They are bound to be awkward at first, but if given a chance to prove themselves, they usually become co-operative and efficient workers. If a young person has been prepared by parents and advisers concerning proper attitudes and conduct on the job, he will experience little difficulty. Each young job-seeker should be alerted to the value of dress and grooming, promptness and punctuality, trustworthiness, and care in following directions in work assignment. If the employee enters upon his work with an attitude of co-operation, there should be no need to fear an employer. The young worker should accept praise for work well done, as well as reproof for poor workmanship.

Perhaps one of the most pressing problems, whether employment is part time or full time, is that faced by the adolescent girl. Girl employees need to be especially careful in their attitude toward men employers and supervisors. If they are wise, they will avoid the development of social relationships. The intelligent girl will attempt to keep employer-employee relations objective and businesslike at all times.

QUESTIONS AND TOPICS FOR DISCUSSION

1. What are the problems faced by adolescents in your home or in a family known to you?
2. Write an anecdotal report of an adolescent boy or girl of your acquaintance who seems to be experiencing difficulties in home life.
3. Write an anecdotal report of an adolescent of from thirteen to fifteen who seems to be experiencing difficulties in social life. Of an older adolescent. What can be done to improve the situations?
4. Prepare two lists: (1) adolescent rights in the home, (2) adolescent responsibilities in the home.
5. Prepare two lists: (1) adolescent rights in social situations, (2) adolescent responsibilities in social situations. Compare the two. Ask young adolescents to do the same.

6. Suggest desirable ways of assisting adolescents to gain independence.

7. Name five issues that might arise between an adolescent boy and his parents. Between an adolescent girl and her parents. Evaluate the issues in the light of the parents' interests. The adolescent's interests.

8. Record as many of your interests and attitudes as an adolescent as you can recall.

9. What kind of punitive measures, if any, should be used with non-conforming adolescents?

10. "A dominated adolescent usually is a futile and indecisive adult." Discuss the implications of this statement.

11. What were the chief characteristics of your close friends during your early adolescent years? During your later adolescent years?

12. State briefly your attitude toward three of your close relatives (excluding parents) (a) as a child, (b) as a young adolescent, (c) at present. What differences do you discover? Explain them if you can.

13. Recall a fellow high-school pupil who seemed to have trouble making friends. What was your attitude toward him at that time?

14. Recall the close friends you had during your high-school years. With how many of them do you still associate? What has caused this association to continue?

15. What type of emotional disturbances did you experience during adolescence? How do you explain them?

16. Suggest a good program of social activities for an adolescent boy or girl to follow.

17. To what extent do you agree with the likes and dislikes of traits enumerated on pages 113 to 115?

18. Give the pros and cons of coeducation.

19. How important to adolescents are the opinions of adults? Of other adolescents? Give examples.

20. What values can accrue to adolescents from participating in school-planned social activities?

21. What are the considerations that should enter the selection of a career?

22. If you are preparing to enter a particular occupation, what vocational decisions did you make before you finally decided to enter the occupation of your choice?

23. What are the values that may result from part-time work by adolescents while in school? Evaluate the merits of co-operative high schools.

24. What are some of the important adjustments that adolescents must make on the job?

25. Give examples to illustrate that "The social values of any group influence the behavior of the members of the group."

26. Recall some of your social worries during your adolescence. List three that seemed to be most important to you.

27. In what ways do neighborhood conditions affect group activities of adolescents? Give examples.

SELECTED REFERENCES

Bales, A. F., *Personality and Interpersonal Behavior*, 3rd ed. Holt, Rinehart & Winston, N.Y., 1970.

Crow, L. D., and Crow, A., *Adolescent Development and Adjustment*, 2nd ed. McGraw-Hill, N.Y., 1965.

Crow, L. D. and Graham, T., *Human Development and Adjustment*. Littlefield, Totowa, N.J., 1973.

Evans, R. I. and Rozelle, R. M., *Social Psychology in Life*, 2nd ed. Holt, Rinehart & Winston, N.Y., 1973.

Gammage, P., *Teacher and Pupil: Some Sociological Aspects*. Routledge & Kegan, N.Y., 1972.

Gilbert, G. M., *Personality Dynamics: A Biosocial Approach*. Harper and Row, N.Y., 1970.

Hepner, H. W., *Psychology Applied to Life and Work*, 5th ed. Prentice Hall, Englewood Cliffs, N.J., 1973.

Jersild, A. T., and Alpern, G. D., *Psychology of Adolescence*, 3rd ed. Macmillan, N.Y., 1974.

Johnson, D. W., *Social Psychology of Education*. Holt, Rinehart & Winston, N.Y., 1970.

Kagan, J., *Personality Development*, Harcourt Brace, N.Y., 1971.

Landis, J. T., and Landis, M., *Personal Adjustment, Marriage and Family Living*. 5th ed. Prentice Hall, Englewood Cliffs, N.J., 1970.

Lindsay, C., *School and Community*. Pergamon, Elmsford, N.Y., 1970.

McCandless, B. R., *Children and Adolescents: Behavior and Development*. Holt, Rinehart & Winston, N.Y., 1961.

Rogers, D., *Psychology of Adolescence*, 2nd ed. Appleton-Century-Crofts, N.Y., 1972.

Thompson, G. G., et al, (ed) *Social Development and Personality*. Wiley, N.Y., 1971.

Wechsler, H., et al, *Social Psychology and Mental Health*. Holt, Rinehart & Winston, N.Y., 1970.

PART III

Adjustment in Teaching and Learning

6   The Dynamics of Human Behavior and Learning

The key to constructive guidance of human behavior is an understanding of the forces and influences that energize and direct human beings. The teacher who understands the importance of motivation in learning and who applies his knowledge to problems of teaching is likely to have a fair degree of success in the classroom. Time and energy expended by the teacher to relate school work to pupil needs or to diagnose youthful interests and motives are well repaid by an increase in learner achievement. Pupils can be inspired to acquire knowledge, skills, attitudes, and ideals that will enable them to become effective students or citizens.

The Why of Human Behavior

Since to motivate is to activate, anything that activates is a motive. In current psychological usage, *motivation* pertains to inner control of overt behavior. The motivations with which we are concerned refer to behavior controls that have their roots in a learner's changing physiological status and in his previous experiences.

Arousal of motives. Although an individual's motives often are inferred or deduced from his observable behavior, they have their bases in his urges or drives. An urge or compulsion may be expressed as an aim, a drive, a wish, a desire, a purpose, a craving, a goal, an incentive, an attitude, a choice, or an interest. Each suggests inner regulation of overt behavior. These terms do not necessarily explain why an individual does what he does; they do point to the fact that an individual's behavior is based upon a choice, a purpose, or a desire.

An individual's response to a specific activity-arousing stimulus is dependent upon the strength of his inner state. For example, an ardent golfer is invited to participate in a golf tournament. Ordi-

125

narily he would accept, but he is involved in an important business deal. Hence he declines.

Influence of motives. Man constantly is trying to explain his own behavior or the behavior of others. Why do some people return to work when they could continue a vacation? Do men play baseball because they wish to go through life engaging in play? Do individuals spend long hours at arduous work merely to occupy their time? Are there reasons other than economic and environmental for some people to live in houses, others in huts, still others in apartments? Why do some people enjoy watching a baseball or football game, while others prefer a concert or a play?

Human behavior is conditioned by individual urges and desires, as these are modified by experience. Human beings do countless things as a result of complex and little-understood motives. They are impelled variously to swim rivers, climb mountains, build houses, play canasta, fight wars, compete in various sports, or participate in civic projects. At times, human motives are expressed in daring and heroic feats. The aerialist who performs without a net, a man who risks his life to save someone from drowning, a soldier who faces danger to help a buddy or who endures torture to protect his country's secrets—all illustrate the dynamic nature of human motives on a level that is dramatic and emotion-arousing.

Motives are especially important in the classroom. Before a teacher attempts to guide his pupils, he should know their characteristic drives and urges. He then can utilize this understanding in devising techniques likely to arouse pupil interest in applying themselves to mastering learning materials and situations.

Importance of Human Drives and Urges

Needs, drives, or urges are the roots of those inner dynamic potentialities that motivate human behavior. These urges are satisfied by the child or young person as he lives and develops in his home, school, and community. The extent to which and the ways in which they can be satisfied are conditioned by environmental influences.

Nature of inner drives. Everyone is born with potential dynamic impulses which serve as motivating forces throughout life; his thoughts, attitudes, emotions, and overt behavior are influenced by them. As has been said earlier, some of these drives grow out of physical, life-sustaining needs; others are acquired through experience. Social recognition plays an important role in the direction taken by overt behavior that is stimulated by inner urges. Whether the behavior is motivated through inner drives or by social forces, there is always an impulse toward action. Overt behavior usually reflects the total of influences that affect the individual at one time.

In general, individuals are motivated (1) to satisfy organic needs, (2) to achieve a constructive purpose or goal, or (3) to gain social prestige. In spite of intensive study in this area of human development, however, there still is no general agreement among psychologists as to the exact nature of human urges, how they are stimulated, or what their relative importance is in human behavior. Indeed, writing as late as 1950, Cattell was impelled to call his list of drives only a "preliminary list."

PRELIMINARY LIST OF DRIVES

I. Organic needs:

To seek air; to avoid physical pain, heat, cold; to seek water; to urinate and defecate.

II. Propensities which are organic, viscerogenic, appetitive:

1. (a) To seek stimulation, exercise, activity when well rested.

(b) To play.

2. To avoid stimulation, lie down, sleep, and rest when tired.

3. To seek food. This may be functionally connected with storing food, with restless wandering (as in the herbivorous animals), or with hunting readiness (as in carnivorous).

4. To court and mate (sex drive).

5. To feed, protect, and shelter the young.

6. To reject and avoid noxious substances.

III. Propensities showing no clear organic rhythm, nonappetitive:

7. To escape from violent impressions by (a) flight, (b) "freezing" to the spot.

8. To defer, obey, abase oneself in the presence of superiority and dominance behavior in others.

9. To appeal, cry aloud, and seek help when utterly baffled.

10. To acquire, collect, possess, and defend whatever is found useful or attractive.

11. To explore strange places and things or manipulate and pull to pieces strange objects.

12. To remain in or seek the company of one's fellows. . . .

13. To assert oneself, achieve, domineer, lead, display one-self.
14. To resent resistance to the expression of any propensity; to attack and destroy such resistance.
15. To laugh and destroy tension in certain tension-provoking situations.
16. (Questionable.) To construct shelter and implements.[1]

Importance of stimuli in the arousal of urges. Directly or indirectly, environmental stimuli tend to activate inner urges. The individual then responds according to the degree of readiness engendered by a particular urge at the time. Strong interests, high aspirations, or frustrations impinge upon the individual, thereby arousing behavior that may be highly satisfying or extremely annoying. A person who has not reached the level desired or expected by himself, by someone in authority, or by someone whose opinion he values, may be driven to attempt tasks beyond his endurance, with a resulting break in health. A man may be able to take care of his family comfortably as a truck driver, but his family may demand luxuries which he cannot provide. As a result, he may be driven into behavior that is antisocial, such as hi-jacking.

Is a young man or woman stimulated to enter the teaching profession, in spite of relatively low salary status, by long vacations, security in the job, or a strong desire to teach? Why is a motion-picture or television star willing to submit to rigid training? Is it to boast that he has participated in a certain number of performances, plays before large audiences, earns a fabulous salary, enjoys prestige? Is the willingness to work hard motivated by sincere interest in and love for the profession? Regardless of the field of activity, some type of anticipation is valuable to the individual who is willing to sacrifice immediate satisfactions for possible long-range benefits.

Urges Associated with Biological Needs

Biological drives are the results of organic conditions in which there is aroused behavior based upon change in equilibrium. *Inner* imbalance of an organism arouses activity which attempts to restore *homeostasis.* Thus, a need for food leads to the hunger drive, although the hunger drive does not necessarily become stronger as the intensity of the need increases. Hunger pangs come and go in

---

[1] By permission from *Personality*, by R. B. Cattell. Copyright, 1950. McGraw-Hill Book Company, Inc.

persons who refrain from eating for long periods of time; yet their food need persists.

Need for food and drink. The origin of hunger is not fully understood. Hunger pangs result from the contraction of stomach muscles, but experimental evidence seems to indicate that the hunger drive is present in the absence of stomach contractions. Consequently, the origin of hunger may be chemical in nature, and the stomach contractions may be by-products of other basic conditions in the hungry individual. The balloon technique has been used to study the relationship between the hunger drive and general body activity. It has been discovered that there is a close relationship between the rhythmic occurrence of hunger and the rhythmic occurrence of striated muscle activity.

Hunger sensations usually are more pronounced under conditions of semistarvation than of total fasting. The satisfaction of hunger and the eating of tasty food differ in that considerable conditioning is required to develop eating habits and food tastes. For example, the frequency and the precise hour of eating are matters of custom or habit. The preparation of food, its color, or its seasoning may contribute to the liking or disliking of that food, regardless of its nutritional value.

There are certain food allergies, the cause of which is unknown, that sometimes result from a developed attitude toward the food. The attitude may be caused by the extent to which the eating of the food causes stomach distress. Likewise, the environment in which it is eaten may cause the food to disagree with the eater. Good steak taken from the loin of a prize steer may be refused by the boy who raised the animal. Individual conditioning is important in food values. Yet, if the hunger pangs are strong enough, the individual easily surmounts these psychological hazards to satisfy his hunger.

The effects upon a child's behavior of the hunger drive and the food habits peculiar to his home have important classroom implications. It is annoying to have pupils eating candy or cookies in class, but teachers should realize that growing bodies need plenty of food. The adult's "three meals a day" do not satisfy the child's food wants. Hence he is motivated to have "snacks" to satisfy his hunger. In an increasing number of schools, children can buy milk at cost and buy or bring cookies for a mid-morning recess period. Many schools also provide well-balanced lunches for their pupils, at little or no cost.

Teachers are beginning to alert themselves to the customary diets of their pupils. School people are attempting to educate parents, either directly, or indirectly through the children, toward a better understanding of children's food needs and of healthful diets. One of the authors remembers her experiences with a fifth-grade student of average intelligence. During morning sessions, the girl was alert and co-operative. When she returned from lunch, however, she was phlegmatic and noninterested, and sometimes fell asleep. Investigation disclosed that the girl's lunch usually consisted of wine and rich cake! According to the mother, the child liked them and they were easy to serve.

Water as well as food is needed for human endurance and survival. The need for water arises earlier than does that for food. If the body is deprived of water for a substantial length of time, it starts to make certain adaptations aimed at the correction of the imbalance. Excessive loss of water damages body tissue more quickly than does loss of food. Therefore, some believe that, among the biological drives, thirst is second in strength only to the maternal urge.

Need for oxygen. Need for oxygen is seldom experienced under normal circumstances, but, under certain conditions, air hunger can become an intense drive. Persons in a high altitude, where oxygen content is reduced considerably from that to which they are accustomed, may suffer from acute oxygen deficiency without being aware of it. They may experience dizziness or confused feeling; they may shout, burst into tears, or even fight.

Not so extreme as the effects of lack of oxygen are those upon the teacher and the pupils of an insufficiently ventilated classroom. Very few schools have air conditioning systems. Hence, in most classrooms, ventilation is achieved by way of open windows. During the winter, children who sit near the windows complain rightly about the cold air that blows in on them. In order to relieve this situation, the teacher may close the classroom windows. Temporary comfort results, but before long the air in the room is likely to lack sufficient oxygen to meet the needs of the group, thereby producing lethargy and restlessness. Unfortunately, those in the room become accustomed to the bad air until someone (often a supervisor) comes into the room from the outside and calls the teacher's attention to its condition. Even though the pupils may object to cold air, it is the teacher's responsibility to "freshen" air from time to time and to maintain sufficient oxygen content.

The sex urge. A physiological drive which may or may not be rooted in homeostasis is the sex urge. This drive is a potent factor of social living. Associated with this drive are the maternal urge and the urge to experience sensory pleasure. The physical manifestations of the sex drive concern us at this point; the intellectual, emotional, and social manifestations were considered earlier.

Although sexual satisfaction contributes to physical and mental health, sexual activity is not essential to the life of an individual. It is essential to the survival of mankind, however. The androgens and hormones secreted in the pituitary gland affect the sexual development of the male. If the androgen supply is not affected by operation or disease, sexual appetite in the male remains fairly stable.

The principal sex hormones of the human female are the estrogen and progesterone secreted by the ovaries. The sexual appetite is controlled by the estrogen; progesterone is important in pregnancy. Each is involved in the human female's sexual cycle but is active at different times.

The sex urge is one of the most important influences in the psychic life of an individual, often dominating his entire being. Hence conflicts arise between expression of this urge and the restrictions and inhibitions of social conventions and moral codes. When it is properly controlled, the sex drive can be of great service to mankind. The persistency of the sex urge, however, makes necessary a psychological development of the person for the good of himself and of society.

Psychosexual urges include the thoughts, feelings, and emotion that accompany the maturation of the sex organs. Individual atti tudes are influenced greatly by the inner nature of the individua as he is conditioned by his environment. Each individual condition his sex drive by the thinking and feeling he develops toward se and toward others. Parents and teachers should have an understanc ing of the sexual development and behavior of the adolescent.

> The sex drive begins to function early in life. His early experience in the home and family develop in the child the basic patterns of sex and love life that will be guiding influences in his later life. If strong and wholesome attitudes are to be developed by the child, he will need all the constructive help that he can receive from his parents, relatives, playmates, and teachers. The nursing experience may become, through pattern fixations, the basis of later sex conflicts. These sensory stimuli that are experienced at regular intervals during the

first year of an individual's life are his first erogenous satisfactions.

Because to adolescents the meaning of sex is still vague and sometimes faulty, they tend to expand upon their supposed sex escapades. The subject of necking and petting is very popular. Boys try to gain prestige through tall stories of their conquest of girls, the use of vulgar language, or a display of unusual knowledge about sex matters.

Girls boast, either truthfully or untruthfully, about their dates and their popularity with the opposite sex. Environmental restrictions and insufficient or improper training cause sex conflicts to arise partly because of societal denials and partly because of the belief of adolescents that they should experiment in order to demonstrate their adulthood.

Sex conflicts during adulthood arise from numerous causes. The aging individual or the alcoholic who recognizes growing impotency may accuse his wife of being unfaithful. The alcoholic satisfies through excessive drinking his desire to prove his potency, and the older man may cohabit with a younger woman in order to demonstrate his virility. A young woman, as a result of too rigid training during her girlhood, may be overmodest or frigid in her sex relations. As she approaches the menopause, conflict may arise between her recognition of her changed sexual life and her sex interests or if she is still unmarried between her desire to experience sex activity and the knowledge that she is probably no longer sexually attractive.[1]

Social Drives and Urges

Individuals are social beings. In their relations with others, they are impelled to behave, through the strength of their inner urges, in different manners. The resulting behavior may be pleasing or annoying to others. Most of our motives are social in origin (whether or not they are grounded in physiological needs) and are conditioned by the behavior of others. Socially conditioned motives are present in all human beings. Some of these motives, as for example, the competitive drive, are widespread in one culture but are not found in another. Although these motives are so strong that they seem to be inborn, they probably are learned through close and long association with others. Among the inner urges that have social significance are those concerned with success and mastery, recognition and approval, superiority, sympathy, security, and adventure.

[1] By permission from *Mental Hygiene*, by L. D. Crow, and Alice Crow, pp. 49–50. Copyright, 1951, 2nd ed., by McGraw-Hill Book Co., Inc.

Urge for successful achievement. To be successful is a personal experience. It is the kind of experience an individual likes to share with another as a fact of personal accomplishment. Success that is earned only partly through one's own efforts is not completely satisfying. An individual experiences satisfaction from a realization that he has completed successfully a specific task, assignment, or request. This satisfied state strengthens the body tonus for further activity, and also gives him a psychic lift. It motivates him toward further accomplishment in the area. The individual who makes headway toward a goal in which he is interested has a feeling of accomplishment, which is important in the development of ego-awareness.

The feeling of accomplishment is especially important in the classroom. Every learner needs to experience success in what he considers worthwhile activities. The slow learner needs to achieve successfully in his daily activities just as much as does the bright learner. The modern school is attempting so to gear its curriculum offerings to individual capacity as to permit successful achievement for each child, according to his ability to learn. This procedure enables each child to "find himself"; to be freed from those conflicts which, in the past, restricted the learning activity of many children. Participation in an experience wherein the child achieves what he sets out to achieve is most satisfying.

That individual learners differ from one another in their interests, goals, and capacity to learn is recognized by most teachers. School people are organizing their curricula in the light of the ability, the interests, and the experiential background of the learner, thereby encouraging him toward further and better achievement. If each pupil is given work within his mental and physical capacities, he will be more likely to achieve a feeling of satisfaction as he strives, often for long periods of time, toward completing tasks he has been encouraged to believe he can master. The actual pleasure derived from planning an action, perfecting a skill, or solving a problem may become the motivating force that will stimulate similar attempts at later times.

Urge for mastery or superiority. Each individual gets satisfaction from excelling in at least one form of activity. Human happiness is believed to rest heavily upon the urge to perform well. Observe the face of any child—bright or dull—when he believes he has done something well. Success not only radiates from his face but also seems to come from every part of him. Although satisfaction is gained from doing something well, the greatest satisfaction results when an individual knows that he has done something better than others can do it.

Harm as well as good may result from an attempt to satisfy an intense urge for mastery. Many cases of lying, cheating, and stealing can be traced to an unwise use of the drive. Such behavior may occur if a person faces unequal competition, or if his level of aspiration is much lower than that set for him by others, such as parents or teachers. In every instance, the individual must be helped to crawl before he can be expected to be able to run. An individual who is motivated toward the achievement of goals by the utilization of any one or more antisocial methods needs help badly. Usually, careful guidance, rather than punishment, is the best method to help him raise himself to a level of achievement in which he can earn success without socially disapproved acts. He should be given numerous opportunities to earn self-respect and the good opinion of his peers and elders. Too often, a single misdeed results in permanent stigma.

Urge for recognition and approval. Success becomes most satisfying when others are aware of it and applaud it. Everyone needs and seeks the approval of others. The child displays early that behavior which earns approval from parents or any other individual who provides for his needs. He learns which behavior is approved and which is not. He conforms to the standards set by his mother. Her touch, her smile, her words (even though the meaning of the words may not be understood) are important to him and are the conditioners of behavior that make him co-operative.

The child possesses a strong drive toward ego-fulfillment. Hence a conflict situation may be established. He may learn that, for his own good, he cannot be granted all his wishes or desires. In a child's refusal to accept denial of his wishes are found the roots of the negativistic attitude that often is associated with early childhood.

Because his ego must be satisfied, the child craves attention. He soon develops numerous ways to gain the attention of those on whom he depends for his survival. The child actually works at securing social approval. The successful completion of any activity that commands the attention of elders assures him a degree of approval. Positive drives toward desirable achievement are stimulated through the efforts of others to give attention to his interests and plans. The feeling of satisfaction is intensified when his achievement receives group approval and recognition.

The practice of gaining approval at home is carried over into the school. If the child has received approval at home, he may attempt to gain similar recognition and approval in school from either his teachers or his peers. All will go well for him if he gains it; if he fails, he may try to attract attention by antisocial techniques that may bring him unexpected and undesirable results. Use of a water pistol or peashooter may satisfy an immediate craving for attention or approval, but such behavior earns only temporary admiration from his classmates and disapproval or punishment from his teacher.

Teachers can make wise use of praise in their daily evaluation of class work and of co-operative child behavior. Good work warrants the recognition and approval of the teacher. Behavior that is satisfactory also is worthy of an occasional word of praise. It is true that co-operative behavior should be habitual among children, but good interpersonal relations are encouraged by the teacher who gives approval to individual good behavior.

The fact that children and adolescents go to great lengths to satisfy the expectations of their peer group has excellent socializing values. It is normal to want to be approved by others. School groups, sororities, and fraternities know the pressure they can put on individuals who have a strong desire to enter a popular club or organization. Sometimes the drive is so strong that the individuals perform antisocial acts, or engage in activities that border on rowdyism, if called upon to do so by the members of the group they desire to enter. They want to meet the test of acceptance. During a time like this, adult supervision may be needed to ensure harmless activities on the part of adolescents.

The striving for success—social, political, or business—is based upon the fact that at any one time of life an individual's level of aspiration usually is higher than his actual status. He therefore wishes to please those he considers his superiors. Even among people to whom success seems to come easily, efforts are made continuously to please someone. For example, at the height of his success, Babe Ruth never had to wait for approval. When he began to be less successful on the diamond, he still yearned for the approval which he did not receive. The stories of many leaders-- in sports, in politics, or in education follow this pattern. When the individual is at his peak, he gets approval in abundance; when he loses his touch, he also loses the responsiveness of his erstwhile admirers which he continues to desire.

In the classroom there are children who receive approval because they are successful in their studies. The children who should be the teacher's concern are those who seldom win an honor or rarely complete their work sufficiently well to merit a favorable response. At the same time, they may be eager for the kind of recognition that others receive with little effort. Careful observation of the less successful learners is necessary in order to provide learning projects for them in which they can succeed sufficiently to receive praise from the adult and from their peers.

What may be sufficient praise for one person may not be adequate for another. Approval must be suited to the individual and the situation. Sometimes children compete for approval of parents or of teachers; sometimes there is a conflict between children and parents, or between children and teachers concerning the giving and receiving of coveted approval. Behavior problems arise as a result of the child's attitude toward desired approval that is denied, or approval that is distributed inequitably.

The teacher should give approval only when it is earned. Favoritism by a teacher soon becomes apparent to the pupils. Normally, children avoid disapproval and seek approval. Praise based upon careful evaluation of achievement and behavior is a strong factor in the development of desirable attitudes that serve the growing child in all his social relationships.

The urge for security. A feeling of security leads to good adjustment; a feeling of insecurity leads to maladjustment. Individuals have strong drives "to belong." Behavior is conditioned by an urge to be secure in the good opinion of another. If the other is one in whom a person is especially interested, he will change, sometimes even radically, to make himself acceptable to the other person. All efforts at co-operation with others earn for the individual their respect and admiration. Conformity to social mores is based in part upon the urge for security. Loyalties of members of social groups and political parties emanate partly from the fact that each wishes to be secure in the respect of the other members of the group.

In addition to wanting emotional security, the individual needs economic security. Problems associated with financial security haunt most individuals throughout life. Children need to be inducted gradually into an understanding of the responsibility that goes with financial security. Some parents discuss family finances with their children as soon as the latter are old enough to understand the value of money. School banks are organized to help young people to save money and then to spend it wisely. Care must be taken by school people, however, that they do not urge children so strongly to put money into the school bank that young people are impelled to obtain this money dishonestly.

Men and women struggle long hours to avoid insecurity. Because many older people, unassisted, cannot provide for their old age, social security was voted by the American people to serve them during the period of declining years and diminishing income. At times, the urge for some form of security is the prime motive for marriage.

The urge for adventure. The human being exhibits curiosity as a normal activity, since each individual has a strong urge to experience the new and different. The classroom teacher has learned that an idea introduced with a new approach has greater interest for the learner. Thus, within limits, novelty can serve as a learning motivator.

Individuals may spend as much time, money, and energy to satisfy this urge as they do for the satisfaction of any other urge. The problem becomes more difficult as the individual grows older and accumulates a wealth of experience. Nevertheless, there is always something that is different and new, even for the most talented and the most experienced. Children make opportunities to satisfy this drive. In school, the teacher has abundant opportunities to aid children in satisfying their curiosity about people and things. Today, through the use of audio and visual aids there are almost unlimited possibilities of opening new vistas to the learner.

Fortunately, the young child's spirit of adventure is satisfied easily. Diversified material becomes important to the teacher who deals with pupils of this age level. The child is not restless; he is active. His curiosity should be challenged as much as possible; he should be given opportunities to explore many phenomena at first hand. Then, when the child becomes an adult, he is ready to satisfy his spirit of adventure through traveling, watching television or motion-picture programs, attending plays, joining one of the armed services, getting married and having a family, engaging in community or church activities, or planning and participating in elaborate social activities.

The Motivating Process

We are concerned especially with the motivating process related to the teaching-learning situation. Of necessity, motivation includes the arousal of interest; yet, the mere arousal of interest is not, in and of itself, good motivation for best learning. Each learning situation is unique and can be helped or hindered by the motivation used. Consequently, motivation is one of the most vital devices for stimulating learning.

Function of motivation. The purpose of motivation is to bridge the gap between the learner's background experiences and new learning material. All learners come to class with some experience background. It is difficult, however, for some students to draw upon that experience. Through proper motivation, the skillful teacher can help them apply experience that may have a bearing on the question at issue. This means that what is done to arouse interest must have a functional relationship to the problem under consideration. Thus learners become interested in solving the problem and, at the same time, are helped to bring into the discussion what they may know relative to it.

For example, a unit of study deals with heart action. The pupils, in pairs, measure each other's pulse rate, and the identified results are recorded on the blackboard. They then run up and down a short flight of stairs outside the classroom, three times. When they return, they again measure the pulse rates and record them. The demonstrated fact that their hearts beat more quickly after exercise motivates them to want to discover the reason. Interest in studying heart action has been aroused.

No more time should be spent on the motivating introduction of a lesson than is needed to effect an adequate transition from the known to the unknown. Motivating illustrations, questions, or experiments should be stimulating enough to arouse interest, but they should not be stressed unduly lest their effect may be negative rather than positive. For example, a class is reading Scott's *Ivanhoe*. To arouse interest in and an understanding of jousts, the teacher begins the lesson by asking the pupils to give the needed skills, "plays," and rules of some present-day sports such as baseball, basketball, polo, and tennis. The purpose is to encourage the pupils to discover likenesses and differences between modern competitive sports and a former popular skill game. However, the sports enthusiasts may become so interested in discussing their favorite games and players that the teacher has difficulty in shifting their attention to jousts.

Teacher imagination is needed to guide the learners, indirectly and smoothly, toward willingness to attend to the new study material. If children and adolescents are motivated to believe a subject fitted to their learning capacity is interesting and worthwhile, they usually can master it. There are other learning requirements, but interest-arousing motivation is a potent factor of learning success. Even mathematics, which is considered by some young people to be an extremely difficult subject, can be mastered by a learner of average intelligence if interest in it is aroused.

Much can be learned about the power of motivation and then applied to classroom situations through observation of the behavior of young people engaged in out-of-class projects selected according to personal interests. For example, Bob, who is a good athlete, may devote most of his free time to practice and never be late or miss a practice session. Jane, editor of the school newspaper, expends much energy and spends many hours after the school day in preparing copy for the weekly issue.

Successful participation in interesting activity satisfies ego status by affording approval from schoolmates. Similarly, through the utilization of appropriate, small-group projects which permit reasonable freedom of activity, a teacher can motivate his pupils to achieve results that not only help them master learning material but also satisfy their self-bolstering needs.

What an individual wants to do is rooted in his basic need to satisfy his developing potentials—the intellectual, emotional, physical, social, economic, and spiritual. The power to be motivated toward activity lies within the individual; the teacher directs learner attention to a wise choice of problems and questions, and makes adequate evaluation of responses.

Incentives and motivation. An incentive is any force or stimulus that impels an individual to do something which otherwise he may be uninterested in doing. The incentive for a tired child to want a ride is a carriage near him. If he previously has enjoyed the experience of riding in it and an adult is now available to afford him a repetition of this experience, the presence of the carriage becomes an even stronger incentive for him. A stimulus serves as an incentive if there is an achievable goal within the reach of the individual in time, space, and comprehension.

The motivating power of incentives varies with individuals. Incentives do not become potent action arousers unless, or until, either adequate maturation or a sufficient degree of developed skill has been achieved. Maturational readiness for walking, talking, or reading, for example, must have been reached if stimuli are to serve as incentives for their activity. Otherwise, the child is not likely to be motivated toward walking, talking, or reading, regardless of the strength of the incentive.

A learner needs an incentive to motivate him toward successful achievement. Incentives may be *extrinsic* (lying outside the learning situation, such as a "star," a medal, or a money award) or *intrinsic* (lying within the learning situation, such as developed pride in achievement, power gained to engage in related activities, or strengthening of self-confidence). Intrinsic incentives usually produce the best results as motivators of successful learning. The learner, however, needs to recognize the value to himself of being motivated by an intrinsic incentive.

During the child's early learning experiences, it may be necessary to stimulate his interest in achievement with extrinsic rewards to bolster his ego. Care must be taken by the parent or teacher that these are incidental to the learning goal, and that there is not aroused a spirit of extreme competition in relation to others. Rather there should be an attitude of competition with one's own record of performance. Commendation for successful performance and constructive criticism of inadequate achievement in terms of the learner's ability are incentives that usually motivate learners, of any competitive level, toward improved performance. If no attention is given by the teacher, the learner is likely to lose interest or to become discouraged.

A principle of the mental hygiene approach to teaching and learning is applied when competition is transferred from that of competition between learners to that of a learner's competing with his own records. There often is an unfortunate psychological impact on learners who are expected to measure up to the achievement of their brighter classmates. If competition can be kept on an equitable basis of ability and experience, it may serve as an incentive to further progress. Competition can be an achievement-motivating incentive for young persons who generally are successful learners. Therefore, in competitive efforts, one individual should be so well matched in ability with his colearners that he cannot be at the top at all times, but rather, can be beaten occasionally.

The harmful effects of competition are experienced by those unfortunate young people who have been placed into unequal competition with others who always are the winners. The emotional impact of a situation of this kind can be so great that even the bright who succeed most of the time become emotionally disturbed if others win part of the time. The grouping of learners on a heterogeneous basis may have as one of its weaknesses the inequality of competition. Of course the theory is that each learner is to compete with his own record, but the facts are that humans are always more stimulating than any record, even if it is the individual's own.

Children who are left to their own devices have ways of equating for competitive purposes. The boys on the baseball field draw up teams that are sufficiently well matched for a good ball game. Teachers too can utilize many devices or can plan situations in which competition can be so equalized as to stimulate an interest in the work and in successful results.

Incentive through co-operation. Competition and co-operation are not complete opposites. At least there need not be an antithesis between them. It is possible to engage in competitive activity through the utilization of some of the qualities of co-operation. In fact, the best kind of competition makes use of the spirit of co-operation. Those who guide individuals in their attainment of best achievement can help learners strike a balance between co-operation and good competition. Children should be provided with incentives to enable them to cultivate the ability to work co-operatively with their classmates. On the other hand, best results are achieved by some who in one situation or another need to be stimulated by an appropriate incentive toward competitive activity.

If too much emphasis is placed upon competition at the expense of co-operation, however, undesirable behavior habits may result. Unequal competition may stimulate behavior that is undesirable for an individual as he attempts to avoid failure. Unwittingly, the teacher may encourage him to try to win by cheating, copying, or having others prepare his study assignments. Personal integrity should be stressed at all times, even though it may mean defeat. It must be borne in mind that in any contest there must be both a winner and a loser.

Goals and Human Behavior

The establishment of specific and relatively permanent goals varies with individuals and their early experiences. Some parents and teachers, for example, seem to expect a child of elementary-school age to decide upon his adult vocational goals. Vocational decisions may be made during the junior or senior high-school years;

some young men and women do not select their life work until they are in college or later. A relatively few individuals, unable to make any final choice, drift from one job to another. There are numerous reasons for a young person's vocational goal to center in profes-sional work, business, skilled labor, or creative production.

Importance of goals. The roots for differences in goal-setting spread in many directions and in most cases are almost impossible to dis-cover. One individual may be motivated toward a vocational ac-tivity as a result of experiences he had during early childhood. An-other's interest may have been aroused during later developmental experiences. In both instances, there may have been a common motivating factor. At one time the motive may be a desire for recognition; at another time the desire is to become economically independent. A study of personal histories reveals that, in many instances, predominating motives are established in childhood as the individual was influenced by his social environment. Later, there may be a deviation from this dominant motive, yet there usu-ally can be found some likeness to it even though the activity of childish interest may vary widely from the final occupation.

Levels of aspiration. The life goals selected or the extent to which everyday activities are undertaken differ widely among individuals. The demands made upon one's self and the expectation of accom-plishment vary among individuals in groups or within families. One child may aspire to become a fireman, another an explorer, and still another an electrician. One individual will be satisfied to make just enough money to feed and to clothe himself and his family; another will aspire to accumulate wealth beyond his own personal needs and requirements. Likewise, in the amount of work that may be turned out, one individual will set for himself a high level of ac-complishment; another will be content to produce a minimum.

Success or failure in the attainment of goals tends to influence levels of aspiration. Some persons whose goals are indefinite obtain a college degree and then enter a nonacademic occupation. Others are influenced during their college experiences to a different level of aspiration and set new goals for themselves.

In the final analysis, a person's goal depends on his inner motives and the degree to which he perceives the goal as contributing to his maintenance or prestige. Both individual goals and the demands of others influence the decisions that are made and the levels of aspiration that are attained. An individual gains or loses self-esteem as he succeeds or fails to reach his goals. His level of aspiration is influenced by his attitudes toward himself and by his estimate of his status in a group. An individual experiences a drive to reach a second goal after he has successfully achieved the first. This was illustrated by an experiment in which 151 students related incidents which affected their goals.

One incident involved frustration which prevented the individual from reaching his goal, one involved goal attainment after frustration, and another, simple goal attainment without too much, if any, frustration. Following this, the students were invited to tell the effect of the incident on their level of aspiration. The results are summarized in Table 6.

TABLE 6.   Summary of Frequency of Reported Shifts in Level of Aspiration Produced by Each of Three Types of Incidents[1]

TYPE OF INCIDENT	FREQUENCY OF EACH SHIFT IN LEVEL OF ASPIRATION		
	Lowering	None	Rise
Complete frustration	66	36	33
Frustration followed by goal attainment	15	15	95
Simple goal attainment	3	17	121

Individuals learn from experience the level of aspiration they reasonably may expect to attain in any given task. Many frustrating experiences are avoided by lowering the level of aspiration. If the level of aspiration is high, a young man may complete college and professional school in spite of the fact that he may have to work his way through. If the goal is simply to attain a college degree, the student may select the easy courses that will enable him to secure the degree.

Some individuals prefer to occupy a routine position which makes few demands upon their energy or talent. Others prefer to keep their goals to themselves, thus avoiding the necessity of declaring publicly what goals they have set. In the latter case, they avoid admitting to others any defeat or frustration. Still others work for many years in their attempt to reach the goals that to them repre-

[1] From I. L. Child, and J. W. M. Whiting, "Determinants of Level of Aspiration: Evidence from Everyday Life," *Journal of Abnormal and Social Psychology*, Vol. 44, 1949, p. 308, published by the American Psychological Association, Washington, D. C. Reprinted by permission.

sent a high level of aspiration. To attain these long-range goals requires considerable faith in one's ability to persist in the long struggle for something that is remote in time and often unrewarding
when it is attained.

Fortunately, the level of aspiration for ambitious individuals continues beyond the level of achievement. Men and women who
achieve greatness strive constantly to reach higher levels of achievement, usually to the last years of their lives. Less ambitious or less
talented persons usually are motivated to function successfully in
their particular field of activity but are not stirred to reach higher
levels. The experiences of two women who started their teaching
careers at the same time illustrate differences in aspiration levels.
One woman started on the elementary-school level but subsequently
taught on the junior and senior high-school levels and in college;
then she became a school administrator, and ended her teaching
career as chairman of a college graduate curriculum. The other
woman, after a few years in an elementary school, became a junior
high-school teacher and remained in that position until her retirement. Both were able teachers; one was motivated by higher levels
of aspiration, the other was satisfied to continue to do a good job
on the same level.

Occasionally an individual holds a concept of himself that is
considered lower than the evaluation placed upon him by others.
This is probably characteristic of a person with very strong interests.
His associates react toward him according to what they have come
to expect in terms of his ability. He is likely to be satisfied with the
results of his behavior because of the social approval received. An
individual interested in developing a motor skill may be uncertain
about his chances to become a skilled performer. A person learning to skate, for example, at first is satisfied to master the rudiments:
leg and foot movements and body balance. He then wants to skate
as well as others in his group. The successful beginner, encouraged
by the approval of his group, is motivated to continue practice until, as he perfects his skill, he surpasses others in competition.

QUESTIONS AND TOPICS FOR DISCUSSION

1. List your motives for attending college, studying this subject, training for your particular profession or vocation.
2. Indicate ways in which your levels of aspiration have changed during
   the past two years; ways in which they have held more or less constant.
3. What are the motivations of young people toward acceptable group
   or individual behavior?

4. What motivated you toward the selection of your career?
5. What motivates individuals to run for political office?
6. Discuss the importance of understanding the motives of friends, candidates for office, or fellow workers.
7. To what extent are motion-picture or television stars motivated toward the entertainment of people? Toward their own self-satisfaction?
8. Give examples of thwarting of motives and indicate how adjustments can be made in each instance.
9. How do the motives of people of one country compare with the motives of the people of other countries?
10. Discuss the effect on achievement of giving praise or reproof to a learner.
11. Compare the strength of socially-derived motives with the strength of basic drives.
12. Evaluate the importance of the goal in motivation.
13. To what extent and in what ways is the level of aspiration an individual matter?
14. Discuss the extent to which individuals are motivated by symbolic rewards.
15. Discuss the importance of stimuli to the motivation of behavior.
16. Explain the meaning of homeostasis.
17. Indicate how motivation can be achieved through competition, cooperation, punishment, praise, or reward.
18. What is meant by motivation of learning?
19. Explain differences in motivating forces at different age levels.
20. Explain motivating factors that operate in gang life.
21. To what extent have you been frustrated by failure? In what ways has failure stimulated you to greater accomplishment?

SELECTED REFERENCES

Arkoff, A., *Adjustment and Mental Health.* McGraw-Hill, N.Y., 1968.

Burton, W. H., *The Guidance of Learning Activities,* 3rd ed. Appleton-Century-Crofts, N.Y., 1962.

Cofer, C. N., *Motivation and Emotion.* Scott Foresman, Chicago, 1972.

Coleman, J. D., *Psychology for Effective Behavior.* Scott Foresman, Chicago, 1969.

Crow, L. D., *Psychology of Adjustment.* Knopf, N.Y., 1967.

Crow, L. D., and Crow, A., *Psychology,* rev. ed., Littlefield, Totowa, N.J., 1972.

Dichter, E., *Motivating Human Behavior.* McGraw-Hill, N.Y., 1971.

Donelson, E., *Personality: A Scientific Approach.* Appleton-Century-Crofts, N.Y., 1973.

Gilbert, G. M., *Personality Dynamics: A Biosocial Approach.* Harper and Row, N.Y., 1970.

Kalish, R. A., *Psychology of Human Behavior*, 2nd ed. Brooks-Cole, Belmont, Calif., 1973.

Kagan, J., *Personality Development*, Harcourt, Brace, N.Y., 1971.

Kaplan, L. (ed), *Education and Mental Health*, rev. ed. Harper and Row, N.Y., 1971.

Keezer, W. S., *Mental Health and Human Behavior*, 3rd ed. William C. Brown, Dubuque, Iowa, 1971.

Klausmeier, H. J., and Ripple, R. E., *Learning and Human Abilities*. Harper and Row, N.Y., 1971.

Love, H. D., *Educating Children in a Changing Society*. C. C. Thomas, Springfield, Ill. 1973.

Lyon, H. C., *Learning to Feel: Feeling to Learn*. Charles Merrill, Columbus, Ohio, 1971.

Maslow, A. H., *Motivation and Personality*, 2nd ed. Harper and Row, N.Y., 1970.

Murphy, G., *Freeing Intelligence through Teaching*. Harper and Row, N.Y., 1961.

Rogers, C., *On Being a Person*. Houghton Mifflin, Boston, 1961.

Russell, I. L., and Bentley, J. C., *Motivation*, rev. ed. W. C. Brown, Dubuque, Iowa, 1971.

Strongman, K. T., *Psychology of Emotion*. Wiley, N.Y., 1973.

Vernon, W. M., *Motivating Children: Behavioral Modifications in the Classroom*. Holt, Rinehart & Winston, N.Y., 1972.

7   *Personal and Social Bases of Adjustment*

One of the primary purposes of education is to aid individuals to adjust to personal, social, and economic problems. To the layman, to adjust means to make sufficient change to bring about success and contentment in any activity. To the psychologist, sociologist, or educator, to adjust includes both inner and overt changes that are made by individuals as they grow and develop.

Impact of Needs on Individual Adjustment

Adjustive behavior may or may not be conducive to personal or social welfare. An individual is faced with the problem of so ordering his attitudes and behavior that he achieves maximum satisfaction in his home life, his school, his social activities, and his work, without limiting or interfering with the satisfactions that are the rights of others. Adjustment to people and to environment begins in infancy and continues gradually throughout life.

Fundamental human needs. In earlier chapters we referred to the basic needs which the human being constantly is activated to satisfy.[1] The child is especially active and seems always to want something. He eats, sleeps, drinks, rests, strives for social approval, seeks affection, and struggles for independence. Hence he may continue to engage in behavior that is considered aggressive, impudent, non-co-operative, or delinquent, as he attempts to adjust to life. Whether these adjustments satisfy his elders may not concern him enough to deter him from unacceptable behavior. His chief purpose is to satisfy one or another organic or social need.

When a need exists and is not satisfied, the individual becomes restless, tense, and motivated toward action. He sets out to do something about the inner state of affairs in order to alleviate inner tensions. If a person is hungry, he seeks food; if thirsty, liquids; if tired, rest; if warm, coolness; if unloved, affection; and if restricted by others, independence. Contrariwise, food has no interest to a person who has just eaten, and water is not desired by an individual who

[1] See page 61.

has had his thirst quenched. Similarly, other wants that have been satisfied cease to be drives to action. As needs are satisfied, an individual can continue for a certain length of time before his needs again arise and must be satisfied. Viscerogenic needs (including air, water, food, sex, lactation, urination, defecation, etc.) can be satisfied completely for a short period of time, but seldom does an individual achieve completely his psychogenic needs (recognition, status, approval, security, affection, or success).

Areas of life adjustment. Life consists of many experiences that, from time to time, need to be interrelated or integrated. The majority of persons, at one time or another, are motivated by the desire to marry, rear children, experience a happy home life, and earn success in a chosen vocation. In addition, the average person wants to enjoy the companionship of friends and associates of his choice and to spend his leisure time in what he considers worthwhile and interesting activities. From birth on, each of us constantly struggles toward the attainment of self-expression, self-realization, security, or adventure.

Inner desires, wants, and ambitions are expressed through overt behavior. Both our inner compulsion toward expression and our overt behavior are influenced by environmental factors. If the individual sets for himself ego-satisfying rather than socio-satisfying goals, he may be confronted with conflict in his struggles for individual adjustment. This conflict is likely to create unhappiness, discontent, resentment, or maladjustment.

An individual constantly is stimulated by animate and inanimate factors in his environment. We are interested especially in the relationships that exist between overt behavior and the total personality pattern of the reacting individual. Human behavior is a dynamic interaction between the individual and his environment. It is a continuous process involving various phases of an individual's "self," and affected by inner drives and external factors.

Conditions That Create Frustration

Whenever an individual meets a more or less insurmountable obstacle in the satisfaction of a vital need, he is frustrated. Frustration can occur only if the individual is aware of the barrier or obstacle and understands that it serves as a stress force. A feeble-minded person, for example, is not frustrated at his ineligibility to enter college. He knows little about college, has no interest in attending, and has no insight into his condition. Another person may have the requirements to enter college but is faced with family problems that require his working to maintain the home. Consequently, he may experience considerable frustration because he is denied the opportunity to attend college. Hence a condition in which extreme tension is experienced can be thought of as a frustration.

Stresses and strains in frustration. A frustration results when a strong emotional tension arises from the blocking of drives. Many minor obstacles cause annoyances or stresses that are not actual frustrations. The individual stubs his toe; breaks his glasses; misses his train; or misplaces a letter. Each of these tends to provoke stresses that may produce frustrations, but most persons usually take them in stride and adjust quickly to such temporary emotional stresses and strains.

There are, however, many thwarting situations and conditions which present problems that are difficult to solve. Sometimes environmental conditions or events act as obstacles to the fulfillment of strong interests or desires. A sudden fire, the contraction of a contagious disease, the death of a relative, prolonged drought in a farm area, or other serious happenings may become a basis of frustration. Or the source of the frustration may be "social" in nature. The individual may be charged with guilt in an automobile accident, or he is caught in a traffic violation. Perhaps he has broken traffic regulations so often without being caught that he is stunned when he is called to account for a violation.

Moral, ethical, and legal codes are evolved to regulate behavior for the good of the general citizenry. At one or another time, regulations will interfere with an individual's immediate interests or desires. A "No Parking" sign provides a space for a car. May this space be used by one individual and not by another? Why should any person be privileged to make use of it? If an individual decides to park his car in this restricted zone, does he have a right to protest if he receives a police summons for this violation? The degree of his frustration in this situation may depend upon the extent of inconvenience the "ticket" causes him.

Many individuals want to keep up with the living standards of their neighbors. There is nothing wrong with this ambition if it is possible.to achieve this desire without financial strain. This attitude tends to bring families into neighborhoods inhabited by other householders who are similar in their ability to provide home comforts for their families. Occasionally, there is a husband or wife who suffers strong feelings of frustration because of inability to match the possessions or neighborhood status of others. Some individuals cannot hear about or see a neighbor's new washer, ironer, stove, automobile, or other luxury without wanting the same or a better article. These persons are frustrated, but are not always aware of the extent of their frustration.

An individual can be thwarted in the attainment of a strong ambition. It is desirable to keep aspirations on a high level, yet the individual must be prepared to make adjustments downward if he meets conditions with which he is unable to cope. He should learn that he may experience thwarting, but not necessarily frustration, by his failure to fulfill an ambition because of unforeseen circumstances, over which he may have no control. If one goal eludes an individual, he can direct his efforts toward the achievement of one of numerous other equally worthwhile goals, success in the attainment of which may prove to be more rewarding to him.

For example, a young man started out in life to become a salesman. After having gone through two depressions, he decided to engage in farming at a time when most farmers were finding it difficult to eke out a living. Yet, his persistence, the growing demand for hybrid seed corn, and his interest in scientific farming resulted in his finding that, within several years, his beginning activities in this area had mushroomed into one of the largest hybrid seed corn businesses in the world.

It is easy to become frustrated. The seeds of frustration are imbedded in one's everyday experiences. Yet, the individual who learns how to adapt himself to varying situations and who is flexible in goal selection may avoid deep frustrations. If normal individuals are denied participation in activities common to others like themselves, or if they are not given adequate recognition for their accomplishments, there may be sown the seeds of discontent, resentment, and frustration. Unfair competition also is a potent arouser of frustration. To the individual who is interested in the attainment of goals aspired to by his peers, but who does not realize that his capabilities are inadequate, may come a sudden feeling of frustration that he blames on forces outside himself. Self-realization in an achievable area of activity is significant as a tension releaser to this frustrated individual.

The intellectually gifted individual experiences problems of frustration that are peculiar to his superior mental status. He is more alert to problem situations than are his less able peers. His interests and desires are more numerous, and he is more aware of his potentialities. It may be difficult for him to try to explain something in simple language to less able associates in terms that they can understand. If his analysis of the situation is not understood by the others, he throws up his hands at their stupidity and exclaims, "What's the use? No one understands what I am saying, anyway." To him this is a frustrating situation.

The bright child faces the fact that he understands much of what is happening around him, but is not mature enough to comprehend fully the significance of many of these happenings. For example, a twelve-year-old may be bright enough to participate in an academic discussion on the level of the college freshman, but he has difficulty in appreciating the full impact of human relations on the level of the nineteen-year-old. Consequently, he is frustrated in that area of understanding.

Responses to frustrations. Frustration has both immediate and long-range consequences. When an individual believes he is being blocked in his goal-seeking, his immediate response may be the display of restlessness, tension, or even rage; his long-range reaction may become one of indifference to, or of patient waiting for, eventual outcomes.

During a state of frustration, children are likely to indulge in some form of destructive activity. In a frustrating situation, they usually show rage, becoming extremely active as they direct aggressive behavior toward persons or things. If the source of the frustration is vague and intangible, there may be expressions of diffused aggression. When a direct attack upon the known source of the frustration does not seem advisable, the young person (sometimes the adult) commits an aggressive act against an innocent person, or an object. For example, a child who has had an argument with his playmates may come home and hit his mother, break a dish deliberately, or slap his cat or dog. A teacher who is annoyed at a new departmental ruling may snap at his students or give an unusually long assignment.

Four important factors are operative in determining an individual's response to a frustrating situation. The first is *age*. Infants respond to restraint of muscular activity by aggressive behavior— crying, kicking, or holding the breath. The young child tends to express his anger immediately in the form of a temper tantrum. The child, and sometimes the adolescent, may respond through body and vocal activity to the frustration of a desired goal. The more sophisticated adolescent or adult has developed sufficient control of his overt responses to enable him to utilize more subtle ways of overcoming obstacles.

The second factor is *health status.* Illness predisposes the person toward lack of control. If an individual has not had sufficient sleep, has suffered prolonged digestive difficulties, is susceptible to severe colds, or is an excessive smoker, he usually is more easily upset than if he is physically healthy, and temperate in his habits.

A third factor is *past experience.* For example, the first tantrum may be the natural response of the infant or young person to a feeling of frustration. If he learns, however, that through its use he can attain his desired but denied goals, he becomes predisposed to make use of the tantrum procedure again. Unwittingly, overindulgent parents often encourage their children to perfect the tantrum technique in meeting frustrating situations.

A fourth factor is the *nature of the motive that was thwarted.* Some individual desires are fleeting and of minor importance. To such interests or desires, the individual adjusts quickly. Other desires may be so strong and may be considered by the individual to be so important to him that they must be satisfied at any cost. The person who believes that special titles are important will do all he can to become a member of an organization which uses them. It is possible to provide substitute gratifications for many frustrated desires by reading books, daydreaming, attending movies and plays, or watching television. If a strong desire can be satisfied directly through proper application of energy and talent, however, the thing to do is to carry it through. Direct meeting of a situation that may contain elements of frustration is better than attempting to compensate for a possible frustration.

Frustration tolerance. Frustration tolerance refers to the extent to which an individual can endure frustrations without undue overt emotional expression. Life is full of frustrating situations and disappointments. There is a wide range in the degree and extent to which people experience frustrating situations. There are also significant differences in the ways in which individuals behave in the presence of obstacles. The level of aspiration is important as a determiner of the nature and extent of the frustration. A situation that would constitute a bitter disappointment for one person may not in any way become an emotion stimulator for another. Also, some persons are more easily aroused than others by disturbing factors in situations, whereas some people are able to accept frustrations without great alarm or disorganization. Everyone meets failure at one time or another. Sometimes, failure aids an individual to rally his strength and overcome the factors and forces that caused the failure. He is said to have high frustration tolerance. When failure so discourages an individual that he is unable to muster his energy and talent to try again, he gives evidence of low frustration tolerance.

The following examples illustrate high and low frustration tolerance. A middle-aged teacher who had qualified for the profession when the requirements were low found herself facing a frustrating situation when the law was changed to require a college degree of all teachers. The new ruling caused a strong state of frustration among some of the older teachers, and many resigned. This teacher, however, persisted in her efforts to meet the qualifications. She not only took advantage of the summer sessions, but also continued her training during the school year, at night, and on Saturdays. She did not consider herself too old to learn or too frustrated to do what was expected from her. She was not the kind of person easily to be defeated by this or perhaps any other frustrating situation. Those teachers who resigned probably had low frustration tolerance.

Another example concerns a young woman who had achieved only moderate success in the classroom during her student-teaching. She later failed an examination to qualify for a license. Since she was discouraged by the experiences, she did not retake the test. Later, when she needed a job, she regretted her decision. Again, a high-school pupil was interested in dramatics, but because she was not selected to fill a role in a particular play, she never again attempted to participate in the school dramatics program. In both these examples the frustration tolerance was low.

Conditions That Create Conflicts

Conflicts arise out of failure to adjust rather than out of satisfactory adjustment. When an individual's desires are blocked and he is unable to shift to other interests, there is established an inner disturbance that affects his mental and emotional life. Inner conflicts may have their roots in the thwarting of a personal satisfaction or in the denial of a social ambition.

Factors in arousal of conflicts. The affective side of man's nature results from his inner urges, his interests, his desires, his training, and the milieu in which he lives and grows. The emotions that represent generalized inner experiences change constantly with changing environmental stimuli and serve as motivators of individual behavior. As an individual experiences anger, fear, affection, or any other emotional state, he may stimulate other persons near him toward similar experiences. Emotional experiences are contagious, and spread easily throughout a group.

The experiencing of stress, strain, and frustration is closely associated with the arousal of conflicts within the individual. *A conflict may be considered to be an inner state, attitude, or behavior pattern that results from mutually exclusive or opposing tendencies, impulses, or desires.* Unresolved conflict may be the cause of maladjustment. Conflict arises when habitually motivating stimuli are opposed by another set of stimuli that ordinarily may or may not motivate a person. The specific urge experienced by the individual at the moment may increase the power of the stimuli-situation, and bring about the conflict.

Conflict situations. In a discussion on the characteristics of conflicts, Symonds suggested the following:

> Maslow sees four types of conflict. Type one is sheer choice, as when one has to choose between flavors of ice cream or whether to wear blue or green. Type two involves the choice between two paths to some one vital goal. Type three involves a choice between two important goals. Type four is a pure threat in which the person is so hemmed in and bound down that there is no possibility of choice.
>
> Conflict implies that these opposing forces are of approximately the same strength and importance to an individual. If one action system is stronger either because it serves a more basic purpose, or points to a more direct and easy way of achieving a desired end, or because learning has been more adequate, this behavior will have the preference and the conflict will not be so acute.
>
> In general, the stronger the cravings or the stronger the avoidance tendencies, the more intense the conflict. One does not feel a very strong conflict about things for which he cares very little. Conflicts over minor wants are not likely to be very intense. If there are signs of intense conflict over apparently trivial decisions, one may feel assured that the desires involved go deeper than they appear to on the surface and probably unconsciously are connected with broad and underlying trends in the personality. For instance, one may apparently have great difficulty in selecting some simple gift and the conflict seemingly causes great mental distress. One does

not know, however, to what extent the difficulty in selecting the gift is related to conflict of friendly and hostile attitudes toward the person for whom the gift is meant.[1]

Many examples of conflict can be cited. A conflict is experienced by a motel attendant who finds a watch. Should he keep the watch, or should he turn it over to the manager of the motel? Perhaps he resolves his conflict by not reporting it and then by denying he had seen it in the cabin. Once he has made the decision to retain the watch, he is faced with the problem of justifying his behavior by finding self-satisfying reasons for his dishonesty.

A coat is left in another motel by an overnight guest; the manager forwards the coat to its owner. The owner then is faced with a conflict concerning a reward. Should he send an appropriate sum of money to the manager to be turned over to the attendant for his honesty, or should he merely write an expression of appreciation? These examples are typical of relatively simple conflicts that do not lead to maladjustment, but they do illustrate the factors involved in conflict.

A conflict may arise between two forms of motivation, each of which in itself represents desirable behavior. A student-teacher, for example, is motivated to follow the procedures of the co-operating teacher in whose classroom he is working. He also is supervised in his teaching by a college supervisor. The teacher and the supervisor are not in agreement as to what the best procedure is in certain situations. Each has presented his point of view to the student teacher. The latter is torn between these conflicting forces. How should he resolve his conflict? If the difference is great enough, he usually lives with his conflict until the student-teaching assignment is completed.

Some degree of personal conflict is inevitable. Our drives are so strong and our interests are so different from one another that conflicts are almost certain to arise in the lives of some individuals, in their day-by-day activities. Problems of adjustment are rooted deeply in all areas of group living; frustrations and conflicts are certain to arise. Antagonism arises between one set of values or standards and another. Many conflict-arousing situations, for example, are faced by people who marry and attempt to work out a satisfactory marital adjustment.

[1] Percival M. Symonds, *The Dynamics of Human Adjustment*, Appleton-Century-Crofts, Inc., N. Y., 1946, p. 338. Reprinted by permission.

Adjusting to Frustration and Conflict

A situation may occur in which a person's outgoing motivated behavior or organized plan of action is temporarily or permanently prevented from reaching consummation by delay, thwarting, or conflict. The individual experiences frustrations that require action in order to be resolved. The young child can see and hear what he cannot reach or have. Obstacles seem to the small child to be large, but he continues to be outgoing in his patterns of expression. As social patterns (including talking, reading, and thinking) develop, the child's horizons of wants expand still further. At each stage of his development, his wants exceed his capacity of fulfillment. Consequent thwartings may be immediate and direct, or they may be derived and symbolic.

Aggressive behavior and frustration. Aggressive impulses inevitably are aroused by thwarting situations and are set in motion by frustration. The young child may give overt expression to his feelings. As he becomes sensitive to the responses of others, he may suppress and restrain these expressions of feelings. Adjustments are rapid for the child. They are increasingly more complex, however, as he meets new situations. For social reasons, the individual is expected to repress his aggressive responses and emotions; yet, for good mental hygiene, it may be bad for him to repress all hostile and aggressive inner feelings. "To blow off steam" occasionally is good for the individual, and sometimes for others in his presence because emotional tensions are thereby released.

The teacher is faced with meeting these tensions and with the responsibility of helping the pupils live with others. Each child may desire the same thing as the other. Fights among children are common. It is more important to settle the strife quickly than to give prolonged attention to the fact that the individuals had a fight. Suggestions for handling aggressive behavior in the classroom and the question of punishment were considered by Hilgard and Russell:

> The first [situation is that in which] punishment is appropriately combined with reward. Punishment may occasionally be used to redirect behavior so that the desired behavior can occur and be rewarded. Even though the effect of punishment is temporarily disturbing, it may under some circumstances permit the more permanent effect of reward to become operative. For example, a shock through mishandling an electrical appliance in science may be effective if supplemented by help in correcting the hazardous condition.

The second situation in which punishment is appropriate is that recognized clinically as one in which the need for punishment is great. A child sometimes tests the authoritative adult by provocative behavior to see how far he can go. If not punished (in order that the limits may be defined for him), his anxiety mounts as he does things which seem beyond the law.[1]

Introjection. An individual unconsciously acquires ideas, emotional attitudes, and ideals from people in his environment. As the child lives with his parents, brothers, sisters, and others, he absorbs those emotional attitudes and ideals exhibited by his associates. His feeling tones are personal; they contribute to the ideals and standards he gradually develops. The impact of all the forces and influences about an individual results from a process known as *introjection*.

The beliefs and ideals of parents, brothers and sisters, and others in the child's early environment become the beliefs of the child. Thus moral and social values are acquired. The interaction between home experiences and later educational experiences helps the child develop values of his own. He thereby becomes less dependent upon the forces that stimulate him. Yet, the environment of the home is the important influence that affects the child as he develops his political and social beliefs, as well as his attitudes toward others. His prejudices are born in this milieu. If attitudes develop that differ from those of parents, feelings of resentment toward parents or even defiance of parental authority may result.

Since the process of introjection is automatic, parents and teachers are expected to be models of behavior. However, in the acquiring of these unconscious ideals, the child's own developing attitudes help him to accept the ideas of someone he likes, but deter him from agreeing with someone he dislikes.

Compensation. In an individual's attempts at adjustment, he does not use one method to the exclusion of others. Compensation is an excellent example of adjustment that operates in one way or another when an individual changes his behavior to adapt in his human relationships. Added effort that may be utilized by an individual to alleviate the tensions caused by a real or imagined defect or shortcoming illustrates the process of compensation. Short men who be-

[1] E. R. Hilgard, and D. H. Russell, "Motivation in School Learning," in Part I, the *49th Yearbook of the National Society for the Study of Education, Learning, and Instruction,* University of Chicago Press, Chicago, 1950, p 50. Reprinted by permission.

come assertive and aggressive, tall girls who further accentuate their height, the cripple who attempts to participate in activities too strenuous for him, the unpopular student who buries himself in his books—all are indulging in one or another form of compensating behavior.

Compensation may take the form of developing to a greater proficiency one's strong points, of covering up or minimizing a weakness, of boasting, of assuming an attitude of superiority, or of attempting to be overhumorous. The most common and perhaps the simplest form of compensation is illustrated by the individual who tends to overact in the same general function. For example, a short man becomes overtalkative. There are compensations, however, in which the overactivity is of a function other than the deficiency.

A parent who has not satisfied his vocational wish may attempt to persuade his child to take an interest in it. A child who cannot meet with success in his classroom may be able to perform physical feats that give him personal satisfaction and approval from others. A gifted child may substitute academic superiority for his lack of success in physical activities which might cause him to develop attitudes of inferiority. A child who is successful in social situations but below average in scholastic achievement may become a "wise-cracker" to compensate for his learning deficiencies.

Identification. An individual may gain personal satisfaction from imitating the behavior of another person. For example, he may want to be like an admired successful person, or he may wish to be like an undesirable person, such as a criminal, a delinquent, or a notorious celebrity. Identification may function in such a way that personal tension is reduced through respect for the achievements of others in whom the individual is keenly interested. In any group there are those who carry the ball, or achieve success. Others in the group get a lift from the fact that they are members of that group, and personally assume some of the credit for the achievement.

Strong loyalties are built through the functioning of this technique. The child in the home stands by his parents, the child in school is likely to be loyal to his particular school, the member of the gang fights for his buddies. Examples are numerous. When these influences are wholesome, they are most effective as ingredients of character formation. When they are antisocial, they are just as effective, but the tendency is toward delinquent behavior.

If in the home a girl identifies herself with her mother and a boy with his father, the young person experiences a feeling of security. At the same time, a child should be helped to develop strong personal traits rather than to bask in the glory of the achievements of others. Children are constantly identifying themselves with teachers, class heroes, motion-picture stars, supermen, and other heroes who strongly appeal to them at any one time. Social groups and other organizations are formed and held together partly because individuals want to be identified with a particular club, fraternity, religious or political organization. This is wholesome because it gives the individual something for which to live and fight.

Identification also can be most undesirable. If, through identification, a person loses his own individuality in the personality of his hero to the extent that he considers himself to be that person, and believes himself capable of the latter's achievements, he is faced with a serious maladjustment. For example, a boy interested in a Western yarn, may become so much a victim of identification that he actually injures others. A person who announces and believes he is Churchill, Eisenhower, or even God is the victim of identification to the point of mental disorder.

Projection. This kind of adjustment mechanism has two major components: (1) the inability to accept blame for errors made, and (2) the inability to admit personal shortcomings. In the first, the individual places the blame for his undesirable behavior on another; in the second, he calls attention to the shortcomings of others in order to divert attention from his own undesirable behavior or motives.

The driver blames an accident on the other driver; the pupil traces his lack of success to the teacher; the housewife's failure with a cake is due to the grocer's having sent her stale baking powder. All such attempts to shift to others the responsibility for personal failure, rather than to accept one's share of blame, are examples of projection.

Another form of projection is excusing one's acts by stating that, "The other fellow is just as bad," or "If I don't do it, someone else will." The boy caught in the act is not so bad as the one who did not get caught. The motorist arrested for speeding was not driving so fast as the other fellow who was not caught. Most persons apprehended in asocial behavior believe that the behavior of others is much more asocial. The swearing, cheating, stealing, and lying of associates are more serious than the acts of those who are reprimanded. These comparisons may be imaginary as well as real, but

the fact remains that any attempt to temper unsatisfactory consequences of one's own bad behavior is an experience in undesirable
projection.

Rationalization. Making excuses or reasons for behavior that one
knows is undesirable or foolish is known as rationalization. It includes those thinking processes by which the individual deceives
himself by concealing the real reason for his act. With seeming
honesty, he gives specious explanations rather than truthful reasons for his behavior. In this way he attempts to save face and to
maintain his self-esteem.

Rationalizing experiences are daily occurrences. It is not always
easy for an individual to admit to himself or to others the actual
reasons for his behavior. Rationalization is a form of self-deception
whereby the individual believes that through this means he can
make it easier for him to live with himself. One's level of aspiration and the expectations of others have much to do with the extent
to which an individual is likely to make use of rationalization. Attempts at self-deception may increase as the standards of conduct
or ideals of living become higher, especially if the means of attaining them are inadequate.

Some of the generalizations in our language patterns are expressions of rationalizations that are used without much thought. Some
common self-deceiving expressions are: lucky at cards, unlucky in
love; people with ability are not expected to be able to spell; good
thinkers are poor penmen; details are for the less able; he who can,
does, he who can't, teaches; the grapes were sour anyway, and the
like. In these examples can be discerned attempts to explain behavior in terms of a desire to build up self-esteem and prestige,
and to belittle other people.

An individual may be aware of much that is inconsistent in his
behavior, but there may still be an aversion to resolve mental conflicts by putting one's thinking in order. On occasions, rationalization
may seem to be the easiest and best way out. If the rationalization
is accompanied by a determination to improve behavior, these self-
bolstering devices may serve the individual's best interests. If
rationalization is indulged in consistently as a means of self-justifica-
tion for undesirable conduct, others soon learn to resent the implied
dishonesty, and unfriendly attitudes arise.

Daydreaming. Imagination serves a useful purpose in solving problems that defy solution in reality. Through daydreaming, an in-

dividual can attain many imaginary satisfactions. If he is confronted with a seemingly unsolvable problem, he can find refuge in his daydreams. This tendency to gain success in imaginary achievement when success in real situations eludes one is a much-used form of attaining self-satisfaction.

Daydreaming is a mental function that need not be harmful to the healthy child, adolescent, or adult. An individual is in a constant state of awareness during his waking hours. Because of the many associations of ideas, it is impossible to attend completely to one thought for any length of time. Consequently, differing ideas and images seek attention. This is wholesome, and sometimes provides the ideas through mental association that are essential to the solution of problems. It is dangerous, however, if the individual indulges in these mental wanderings to the extent that he is unable to bring his mind back to the problem to be solved. It is only when normal and necessary activities are interfered with that daydreaming may become harmful.

The fairies, goblins, brave princes, and beautiful princesses that people the world of fancy constitute the real world to the young child. They are as real as the people and objects about him. Children should not be permitted to live too long in a world of fantasy and imagination, however. They gradually should be inducted into the real world of people, objects, and experiences, so that they develop a realistic understanding of human relations. Children's literature might well provide many experiences of actual life. Imagination is more rewarding if it is stimulated by an understanding of some of the basic facts in a situation.

Long before they are old enough to participate in adult activities, children are stimulated by success stories of adults. It is not uncommon to find an adolescent deep in daydreams of things he aspires to do. These dreams of conquest may inspire him sufficiently so that he will embark on efforts toward the achievement of high ideals and noble purposes. On the other hand, he may be engrossed merely in what he expects to do during the week end just ahead. Dreams of future achievement, if they have a basis in reality, may serve as incentives toward self-improvement and self-realization. If the daydreams are not related to real situations or are used as a device for wish fulfillment, however, they may lead to dangerous consequences.

Idealization. For personal satisfaction, an individual may place far greater value on something than its real worth. In doing this, he uses the technique of idealization. He can idealize either himself or others. The person or object idealized becomes the most beautiful in the world. The emotions take over and help the individual discover traits that others cannot see or experience. Exaggerated expressions concerning the beauty, for example, of one's fiancée are frequent.

Within desirable limits, idealization is wholesome. A person must have faith in his own ability to succeed. Poise and perspective result from a proper balance in idealization. Yet, if an individual idealizes himself, or other persons or things too much, he may become conceited or arrogant. Inability to see one's faults or unwillingness to admit mistakes are evidence of a wrong use of idealization that may lead to serious emotional disturbance.

Sublimation. If a child's conduct has met with interference, it may be possible to lessen the disturbance by guiding him into a substitute activity. The meaning of sublimation sometimes is limited to the redirecting of the sex urge away from immediate expression and toward higher, more socially acceptable forms of behavior. The purpose is to up-step an individual's expression of his urges and drives from lower to higher forms of behavior. Thus, primitive emotional reactions are directed toward socially approved goals.

Socialization of individuals requires that children learn to control their strong drives toward love and hate and to give them expression through behavior that is in accordance with our laws, customs, and moral codes. Selfish interests must be replaced by those of the societal group. Undesirable attitudes and behavior thus can be avoided.

Sublimation can be the basis of much creative work. The sublimated outpourings of emotional energy sometimes find expression in art, music, and literature. Childless men and women may become active in providing for the health, safety, and welfare of all children, or engage in social welfare work. Sublimation is a tension-reducing device that operates for the benefit of the individual and the group.

Egocentrism. Constant attention and praise given to children sometimes result in egocentrism. Young children need praise and all the help they can get to give them a feeling of security. They become accustomed to receiving attention to their demands. As they grow older, they may use many devices to continue to receive attention and help. They have been the center of attraction and may wish to hold that position. Temper tantrums are types of behavior exhibited during an attention-getting experience. The child is and should be egocentric. Yet, the time comes when he has need for interest in others, what they are doing, and in what they are interested. If egocentric traits are highly developed in the child, he later may experience frustration when he finds that other children are unwilling to give him the consideration he craves.

Withdrawal. When an individual finds himself in an unsatisfactory situation or in one to which he cannot adjust, he has an urge to retreat from it, and usually does. This method of adjustment shows itself whether the individual withdraws from situations completely or partially, for long periods of time or temporarily, as a result of vocational failures, to avoid meeting people, or to evade responsibility. This withdrawal may be so strong that the individual retreats from any normal associations with others.

There are at least four types of withdrawing behavior: (1) shyness, (2) negativism, (3) regression, and (4) daydreaming. Daydreaming, although it possesses some of the characteristics of withdrawal, has other characteristics which were discussed previously.

Shyness. Shyness is a characteristic of most individuals in certain situations. The courageous fighter may be the shy person in a social situation; the confident driver, the shy pedestrian; the daring football player, the shy student in class. But if an individual is shy in every situation in which he finds himself, he has personality difficulties that need strengthening.

If a child has been overprotected, has experienced a childhood without companions of his own age, or has been disciplined too severely by his parents, he may develop an attitude of retreat from many life situations. The timid, withdrawing child may be the joy of the teacher in the classroom because he creates no disturbance. The shy child, however, is likely to be hindered in his social development by lack of activity. He experiences great fear, but hesitates to share his difficulties with anyone. Usually, beneath his quiet external behavior are emotional tensions and frustrations that are caused by a strong desire to participate in the activities of others. He is afraid to do so. As the child gets older, this conflict is likely to get worse unless the teacher and the parents grapple with the problem and help the child participate in group activities.

The following example illustrates the need of the shy child for adult understanding and co-operation.

Jane, a first term student in high school, was the daughter of a relatively ignorant and apathetic mother and of a father who had died, when Jane was a baby, in a sanitarium for the mentally ill. Jane's mother remarried a poor but sincere man who treated his stepdaughter with kindness, but gave her little attention. The girl received her elementary-school training in a parochial school, where she was a good and obedient child. However, in high school, she found it difficult to adjust to the freedom of behavior that was exhibited by other students. She developed a mild case of acne, which resulted in her refusing to attend school because she thought all the girls were looking at her. She was persuaded to return to school, and her program was adjusted to meet her interests and needs. She still found it difficult to mingle with large groups, and developed the habit of disappearing from her classrooms. For a semester her teachers escorted her personally from one recitation room to another. Since she was a bright girl, her good marks helped her overcome her aversion to school. Each term, however, she needed to become adjusted to new teachers and to new student groups, with the help of her teachers and guidance counselor.

Negativism. To give a negative response is characteristic behavior of a young child. A negativistic child deliberately refuses to recognize a real situation, pleasant or unpleasant, and is rebellious against authority or suggestion. The child passes through the stage of saying "No" to any request even though, while saying "No," he may begin to carry out the request. Before he enters school, however, he should have advanced beyond this stage. If his negativism persists and is accompanied by temper tantrums, there may be danger of the development of behavior maladjustment.

Negativism, expressed vocally or by gesture, is not deep-seated and does not persist in a child unless parents and teachers overtax his physical strength or mental ability. If tasks and assignments are kept within the child's ability to understand and to perform, he is likely to move away from the negative attitude rather easily and quickly. Of a more serious nature and more difficult to correct are the contradictory attitudes and overt rebellion against authority by the adolescent or adult, whose negative reactions have had their beginnings in lack of behavior control during childhood.

Regression. Using behavior patterns that brought satisfaction during an earlier developmental period is known as regression. Great satisfaction may be derived from shifting any responsibility for decision-making. The importance of training in decision-making, no matter how simple the decisions may be, at each stage of development is evidenced when we discover individuals who attempt to fall back on their earlier levels of response in order to avoid the necessity of making decisions. An individual who is unable to meet the demands of his environment may revert in his behavior to an earlier stage in his development in which problems were solved for him.

This form of behavior is not restricted to children, but may show itself at any time during life. A four-year-old who believes his baby brother is receiving too much attention may insist upon being helped in eating, dressing, and getting his toys. However, before the arrival of his brother, he was able to perform most of these activities unaided.

Habit patterns that were useful on earlier levels are resorted to only when an individual faces a difficult situation in which he may experience frustration, real or imagined. Any person who has been coddled and protected at home faces a challenge in marriage. It is no surprise to find that, shortly after marriage, a girl wants to retreat to the protection of her home. College students and others away from home for the first time often find the desire to return to the place of their comfort and protection so strong that they are impelled to do so, even if it means giving up something they thought they wanted.

Pleasant memories are more lasting than unpleasant ones. Hence the urge to revert to earlier experiences for the comfort and satisfaction seemingly lacking in the present is a strong one. However, memories of childhood pleasures are less likely to cause an individual to retreat or regress to childhood behavior patterns if he is provided with well-planned activities in which he participates with others. A full day of interesting activity so will occupy the time and the mind of the individual that he will have no desire to return to an earlier stage of development. Training in the acceptance of responsibility will avoid the danger of the development of regressive behavior.

Neurotic behavior. Physical illness, fear or anxiety, if experienced over a long period of time, may cause neurotic behavior. If the individual is confronted with issues he considers important, and if solutions are not forthcoming, mental conflicts may arise. Thus patterns of behavior may become fixed and result in neurotic behavior. Neurotic symptoms are not fixed at first, but as the malady continues, neurotic behavior patterns are not easily changed. Neurotic behavior is characterized by *phobias, obsessions*. and *compulsions*.

Phobias. A phobia is an unusual fear of something for which there is no sound reason to fear. A person who has developed a phobia often is unable to explain its cause or to give a clear description of his feelings during the emotional experience. For example, a child who fears crowds may not be fully aware of the exact experience or experiences that cause it. A person whose phobia makes it difficult for him to stay in a closed room probably has suffered an unpleasant experience in a room or other inclosure that did not permit an easy escape. Phobias or strong irrational fears, as abnormal fear of the dark, high places, dirt, closed rooms, insects, or possible illness, may be attached to generally harmless situations.

Obsessions. Unreasonable ideas that tend to persist or recur are called obsessions. In spite of the fact that they are recognized as illogical or unreasonable, they persist and interfere with clear thinking. Obsessions may relate to the attitude of others toward an individual, or to an individual's own attitudes toward himself or that which may affect him. For example, an obsession might take the form of a fixed belief that certain foods are poisonous, or that something terrible is going to happen.

Compulsions. Behavior continued because the person has a strong desire to engage in it without good reason is called a compulsion. The urge to participate is so strong that emotional tension is relieved only after the act has been performed. The neurotic person often exhibits pronounced reactions if he is denied the privilege of satisfying the urge to complete the compulsion. For example, a sixteen-year-old boy who had set many fires reported during an interview that he had difficulty sitting in school until the end of the school day because he wanted to get out to set another fire.

Some compulsions represent normal adjustive behavior; others are definite maladjustments. Among some of the common compulsions of children are: touching or counting objects, stepping over cracks on the sidewalk, throwing a stone at a target, and imitating elders. An abnormal compulsion would be an urge to take property belonging to another, regardless of its value (kleptomania), or the compelling desire to start fires (pyromania).

Impact of a Handicap on Learning

The physically handicapped child faces special adjustment problems in his behavior and learning. For our purpose, this group includes those children who, because of some defects or deficiencies in their physical make-up, are unable to participate in a normal manner in all phases of the school's program. Physically handicapped children may vary from those who are seriously crippled to those who are extremely sensitive because of a skin disfigurement; the number in the latter group is large. The physically handicapped are classified according to the following types: (1) the delicate individual; (2) the cripple; (3) the child with defective vision; (4) the child with hearing defects; (5) the child with defective speech.

The delicate individual. Since the delicate child usually is coddled from the early years of life, he stands a good chance of becoming "spoiled." He has many experiences in gaining the attention of his elders for the satisfaction of his needs. If it is at all possible, care should be exercised in the home to avoid pampering the delicate child. Before he is old enough to attend school, his parents should attempt to orient him to the fact that he may need special attention, but that other children also deserve consideration of their wants, desires, and problems. Too often, disharmony results in a home in which there is a delicate child. Other children cannot understand what to them seems like parental favoritism.

The school problems of the delicate child may be more acute than those for children with other more noticeable handicaps. If delicate children are forced, because of illness, to miss stimulating school experiences, they may not have the strength to make up the work, and they fall behind the others. Parents and teachers should be informed concerning the common ailments or diseases of children so that these children may become adjusted to their condition as they associate with their more healthy schoolmates. Here is a situation in which co-operation between the teacher and the parents is most important.

The cripple. Like the delicate individual, the child who has been crippled from birth receives special care at home and learns early to lean upon others for the satisfaction of his needs. During his developing years he must be helped to acquire a proper attitude toward his infirmity. A well-planned program on the part of parents can give sufficient help to the physically handicapped child so that he develops a wholesome attitude toward his handicap, toward himself, and toward others about him.

Parents and teachers must keep in mind that the crippled child has hopes and ambitions similar to those of other children. The cripple often has a drive to do more things at home and at school than he safely can undertake. He develops a restlessness that increases as he reaches adolescence. At this time his schooling is often terminated. During recent years, however, considerable attention has been given to the training of handicapped adults.

The prevailing point of view among many educators is that handicapped individuals should be educated in classes with normal children. Some cities still have schools and segregated classes that are limited to children with physical handicaps. Others are trying to train them in regular classes with other children, at the same time giving them the special care and attention they need. Advantages are to be found in either practice; a combination of the two might be the solution for individuals with certain types of handicaps. Special schools can provide physical facilities, but they cannot provide the human experiences that come to individuals only as they live and work with others.

The child with defective vision. The infant with defective vision cannot understand his limitations. With increasing maturity there comes an awareness of his limited experiences. He develops a realization of the fact that he has problems that are different from those of others. In his adjustments, he may attempt to retreat into himself unless his parents and teachers concern themselves with him and his special problems. The young child is satisfied with his mother as his companion. Later, he usually is shy, and tends to limit the number of his companions to one or, at the most, two.

He may become impatient at school partly because he believes that he is a nuisance to his peers. During play activities, he often is helpless. He tends to withdraw and to engage in an activity he can perform alone. He needs social experience with the sighted. Hence, although success has been achieved by training the near blind and the blind in special schools, there is a movement on foot to have these children trained together in regular schools and classrooms. Schools for the blind, now found in most states, provide training in personal, educational, and vocational adjustment.

Within certain limits, the blind child is accepted in social situations. Normal social experiences are extremely difficult for the blind, but not so severe for the partially sighted. The blind child may not be so conscious of social disapproval as are children with other kinds of handicaps, such as those of the hard of hearing child. Blind children crave social experiences, but they also build up a defense against the development of friendships. The fact that they do not want to impose on others may tend to inhibit their social drives. They are satisfied if they make and keep one or two close friends.

There is a great range of ability among the blind, especially since the widespread use of the system of raised point writing invented by a French teacher, Louis Braille. Helen Keller, whose hearing as well as her sight was destroyed by illness before she was two years old, is an excellent example of what can be done for a person who is severely handicapped. The encouragement she has extended to other handicapped persons, through her fine attitudes toward life and her achievement in spite of her handicaps, will long be an inspiration to others.

The child with hearing defects. The totally deaf child usually starts his formal school training without the use of language. In this respect his adjustment problems are much more severe than those of the hard of hearing. It is now known that the deaf child can develop language ability if patience is exercised in training him. Miss Keller learned to speak after she was ten years old, primarily through the skill, patience, and encouragement of her teacher, Anne Sullivan.

Since the totally deaf child lacks the ability to imitate the voices of others, he strives to imitate the facial movements of a speaker after studying, through eyes and touch, the movements of his own throat, lips, and tongue in attempted speech. This is a time-consuming activity and one that tries the patience of a teacher.

The problems of the hard of hearing are quite different from those of the completely deaf, but equally important. Many children hesitate to admit that they cannot see or that they cannot hear. They are willing to "cover-up" to the point of failure in school rather than to admit the handicap. These difficulties are discovered, however, through teacher observation and through physical examinations. Present-day hearing aids make it easier to correct hearing difficulties.

In social situations, the deaf often are more irritable than the blind. The former can see that comments have been made, but they are not able to hear them and may imagine they were derogatory.

During the fall of 1954, the Board of Education of New York City inaugurated an experimental program designed to help deaf children by bringing them into contact with children with normal hearing. Under the plan, a third-grade class of deaf children in the school for the deaf is taking part in the classroom work of a third-grade class of children in a near-by school, for a half-day session each day.

The aim is to try to give them ability to use both written and oral language. Deaf children do not provide the best examples for one another to imitate. The teacher of the deaf provides correct speech patterns, but the children tend to imitate the incorrect language pattern of their deaf classmates. It is thought to be better for deaf children to mingle with hearing children, under proper guidance and supervision. A satisfactory time to begin this may be about the third grade, after the deaf have been given some training in lip reading and oral expression.

In this experiment, teaching responsibilities are shared by the teacher of the hearing children for the half-day session in which both the normal and the deaf children are in attendance together. The deaf children are escorted to and from the school for the deaf by their teacher. They return to their school in time for lunch, and their afternoon session consists of special work for the deaf. This experiment will be watched with great interest, for it may set a new approach to the education of this or other types of handicapped children.

The child with defective speech. There are many forms of speech defects. Some children have unattractive speech habits as a result of imitation of inadequate speech: others exhibit various forms of stammering, stuttering, or lisps caused by defective dentation or improper use of the tongue. Some defects are organic, but most of a child's speech defects are functional and can be traced to factors in his early environment. As was said in Chapter 4, speech patterns are formed through the child's imitation of the speech of others. If adults have careless, inaccurate, or sloppy speech habits, the child is likely to learn to speak in the same way.

The "cute" utterances of the child often receive so much adult approval that they are cultivated by the child as desirable speech. Once these patterns are set, the establishment of new and different patterns is not easy. If a child is delayed in talking, parents need not become unduly alarmed. Speech maturation often is delayed. If a child uses odd speech, help rather than ridicule should be given in order that he may not lose his self-confidence as he attempts to correct his difficulties. The parent who talks baby talk, with the idea that the child understands it better, is as mistaken as is the teacher who attempts to have a child learn to write by imitating copy that is on the level of a fourth-grade child. Children can attain certain levels of accomplishment in various activities, but they should have a good model before them at all times.

Speech defects caused by improper use of the tongue, irregular or badly formed teeth, or throat or nose difficulties can be remedied if adequate medical and dental care is provided. Sometimes, however, members of a family are more interested in what the child says than in the way he expresses himself. Outside the home, the child is confronted with the necessity of using speech that expresses his ideas to others. His speech patterns in school, therefore, must be such as to be understood by both his teachers and his associates. Any speech inadequacy includes a fear of social situations. If the speech difficulty is severe, there may be a consequent maladjusting effect upon the personality of the individual concerned.

Some speech difficulties, such as stammering and stuttering, seem to accompany disturbed emotional states. Fear is basic to the problem. If and when this emotional state can be relieved or reduced, the stuttering may disappear. Too much overexcitement or undue stimulation of a young child may result in nervous tension and a consequent speech defect. As a child becomes conscious of a speech defect, he may tend to be overcareful in his speech and thereby intensify the defect.

Speech is the medium of expression in school and social situations. As such, it is one of the most important factors of personality adjustment. Care must be exercised by parents and teachers not to permit a speech defect to undermine a child's confidence to the extent that he develops a tendency to withdraw from the activities of the school or of the group.

The attitudes of others become important to a child who has a speech problem. He needs a psychological lift during these trying experiences. The child who could not say "seven" or "twenty" used various devices to avoid saying those numbers until he was forced by his teacher to include them in his counting. He had substituted "wan-wan" for the seven and "chenty" for twenty. The teacher wisely continued to emphasize the desirability of change, rather than to make light of the defect. With proper help, the child learned to say both numbers correctly.

A child with a speech defect must be motivated to want to correct it. Routine drill is ineffective unless there is awakened in the child a desire to improve his speech difficulty. He needs encouragement so as to bolster his confidence. Insofar as possible, he should attend regular classes. Speech specialists should be available to give special help, but he needs careful guidance that will assist him to correct his difficulty, in order not to emphasize its importance. If inner conflicts arise, his problem is intensified, especially in such defects as stammering and stuttering.

Speech is receiving greater attention in school than ever before. Teacher-training institutions are producing an increasing number of speech specialists who know how to help individuals with speech defects and who understand the adjustment problems involved. Some of these teachers are assigned to special classes in which the children give evidence of one or another type of speech problem; other speech teachers are functioning on a school basis, wherein they give assistance to pupils in the school whenever and wherever it is needed.

QUESTIONS AND PROBLEMS FOR DISCUSSION

1. How may the attitudes of the teacher toward his pupils become a motivating force to the child?
2. What attitude should a parent or a teacher display toward a child who engages in excessive daydreaming?
3. What experiences have you had that may have contributed to self-deception?
4. Discuss the effects of a feeling of inferiority.
5. Observe a small child and try to discover as many attempts at attention-getting as you can. Which, if any, of these are undesirable?
6. Describe a situation in which you were faced with many changes in order to adjust to the requirements of a group.
7. Give examples to illustrate that daydreams may result in creative production.
8. To what extent do you adversely criticize others? To what extent do you speak in praise of others?
9. If you have had experiences recently that threatened your self-respect, indicate how you met them.
10. Describe the behavior of anyone you know who has a tendency toward repression.
11. What have been limiting factors in your experience in overcoming phobias, obsessions, compulsions?
12. How much stick-to-itiveness do you have? In what way is your frustration tolerance affected in your school work; your other activities?
13. Give examples of the four types of conflicts referred to by Maslow. (See page 154.)
14. Suggest some of the important adjustment problems that arise in the teacher-pupil situation. Show how one of them may be resolved.
15. Observe the behavior of any handicapped children you know. How do they differ in their reactions to their respective handicaps? How do you explain observed differences?

SELECTED REFERENCES

Chernow, F., and Chernow, C., *Teaching the Culturally Disadvantaged Child.* Prentice Hall, Englewood, N.J., 1973.

Crow, L. D., et al, *Educating the Culturally Disadvantaged Child.* David McKay, N.Y., 1965.

Crow, L. D., *Psychology of Human Adjustment.* Knopf, N.Y., 1967.

Cruickshank, W. M., *Psychology of Exceptional Children,* 3rd ed. Prentice Hall, Englewood Cliffs, N.J., 1971.

Fass, L. L., *Emotionally Disturbed Child.* C. C. Thomas, Springfield, Illinois, 1970.

Kaplan, L. (ed) *Education and Mental Health,* rev. ed. Harper and Row, N.Y., 1971.

Klausmeier, H. J., and Ripple, R. E., *Learning and Human Abilities,* Harper and Row, N.Y., 1971.

Kolstoe, O. P., *Teaching Educable Mentally Retarded Children.* Holt, Rinehart & Winston, N.Y., 1970.

Lindgren, H. C., *Educational Psychology in the Classroom,* 4th ed. Wiley, N.Y., 1972.

Moustakas, C. E., *Psychotherapy with Children.* Harper and Row, N.Y., 1960.

Pai, Y., *Teaching, Learning and the Mind.* Houghton Mifflin, Boston, 1973.

Sauliner, L., *Personal Growth and Interpersonal Relations.* Prentice Hall, Englewood Cliffs, N.J., 1973.

Shelton, B. O., *Teaching and Guiding the Slow Learner.* Prentice Hall, Englewood Cliffs, N.J., 1971.

Wenar, C., *Personality Development from Infancy to Adulthood.* Holt, Rinehart & Winston, N.Y., 1971.

8   *Adjustment through the Development of Self-Discipline*

"What is happening to our children?" "Why do they do the things they do?" "Modern children have no respect for authority." "When *I* was a child, I was taught to behave." "Parents have no control over their children." "Children are allowed to do as they please in school. That's why they think they own the world."

Questions and statements like these are frequent, especially among the members of the older citizenry. Elementary- and secondary-school people, and college instructors who are preparing young men and women to become teachers, are the targets of constant criticism. It is believed by the critics that teacher-education programs are not preparing future teachers to use proper disciplinary methods in the classroom. Educational psychologists and sociologists are accused of advocating "soft" pedagogy, by which the critics mean that all the emphasis is placed upon the children's need for self-expression, with no regard for the assumption of responsibilities by young people.

Behavior Difficulties of Young People

The attitudes toward child behavior and child-training described in the opening paragraph have been somewhat exaggerated in order to focus our discussion concerning behavior difficulties. There are certain elements of truth in the criticisms presented. The present increase in youthful delinquent acts would seem to indicate that something needs to be done by parents, school people, and community leaders to bring about desirable changes in the attitudes and behavior of at least some young people. Our problem is to discover what that *something that needs to be done* should be, and how we can go about doing it. It is no mere truism to say that behavior at any age is the result of many complex and subtle elements inherent in the stimulus-response pattern of reaction.

Behavior as cause and effect. It is easy to say that the causes of general or specific asocial behavior should be discovered and removed or

174

ameliorated. The causes, however, may defy detection. Some causes are so deep-rooted that it is almost impossible to remove them; we do not always know the best techniques for the possible amelioration of behavior-inducing causes. To improve child and adolescent adjustment to the behavior-motivating stimuli inherent in their own constitution and in environmental components is a difficult task. All the changes that take place within an individual during his progress toward adult maturity affect what he thinks, feels, and does. Hence one needs to understand every phase of the developmental pattern in order to gain insight into the causes of any one form of overt behavior requiring reconditioning.

The authors approach this area of discussion with humility. Parents and teachers constantly seek help from those who are supposed to know about these matters. Both parents and teachers want to know what they can do to motivate young people to channel their immature urges and interests into socially acceptable behavior paths. Unfortunately, there are no quick-acting panaceas that, when they are applied, can be guaranteed to bring immediate results in all or even one case of behavior conditioning. Every child differs from every other child. The form of the undesirable behavior, as well as the fundamental causes of the behavior, differs from individual to individual and sometimes within the individual himself. Hence, as we consider some of the behavior problems common to various age levels and their possible causes, we are attempting to do no more than to guide the reader's thinking toward the possible application of our discussion to the specific behavior difficulties of particular children or adolescents.

Significance of behavior deviations. Socially unacceptable behavior may range in degree of seriousness from harmless pranks or the occasional display of un-co-operative behavior to more or less permanent personal and social maladjustment that shows itself in behavior that may harm the individual who engages in it and/or others who may be the victims of his disturbed behavior. Every teacher probably has had experience with pupils who display some of the less serious forms of asocial behavior. From time to time, many teachers also have had in their classes one or more young people who gave evidence of extremely serious behavior difficulties. The term *behavior problem* probably does not apply to mild behavior deviations, except as the handling of such behavior constitutes a problem for the inexperienced teacher. Behavior that deviates greatly from what is considered to be "normal" for a particular developmental level may take on the nature of a problem situation for those affected in any way by the behavior—the individual himself, parents, teachers, siblings, schoolmates, school and agency counselors, physicians, and religious leaders.

Certain behavior difficulties are recognized more easily than others by the person with relatively less training. Overt aggression or un-co-operative behavior on the part of a member of a group, either grade class in school, or school or neighborhood play group, usually affects group attitude if observable aggressive or un-co-operative acts interfere with group projects. Perhaps more serious behavior difficulties are unnoticed because the accompanying behavior is quiet and does not disturb the activities of the other members of the group.

Some thirty years ago, a study was made of the relative importance of behavior difficulties displayed by children. This study is one of the first in the field. The conclusions that resulted from the study have exercised a tremendous effect upon the point of view of school people concerning the relative importance of various forms of behavior exhibited by children. Wickman, who conducted the study, compared the opinions of 30 mental hygienists and 511 teachers concerning the relative importance of children's behavior problems.[1]

Both groups (teachers and mental hygienists) rated as *serious* certain forms of behavior, such as suggestibility, cruelty and bullying, tattling, temper tantrums, stubbornness, nervousness, selfishness, sullenness, stealing, physical cowardice, and lack of self-confidence. The two groups considered the following characteristics of the growing child to be of relatively little significance at certain stages of development: inquisitiveness, attention-seeking, thoughtlessness, imaginative lying, quarrelsomeness, and enuresis (bed wetting).

There was difference of opinion between the groups concerning some other forms of behavior. The mental hygienists tended to place greater emphasis upon the less overt forms of behavior as the more serious. Teachers indicated by their ratings that they were more concerned about active, overt "misbehavior." These differences of opinion are shown in Table 7 on page 177.

Adult attitudes toward children's behavior. Teachers and teacher-trainees are gaining greater understanding of the significance of

[1] E. K. Wickman, *Children's Behavior and Teachers' Attitudes*, Commonwealth Fund, Division of Publications, New York, 1928, pp. 124–125.

TABLE 7.   Behavior Difficulties Emphasized by
Teachers and Mental Hygienists[1]

Teachers emphasize:	Mental hygienists emphasize:
Masturbation	Shyness
Profanity	Suspiciousness
Smoking	Unsocialness
Heterosexual activity	Sensitiveness
Obscene notes and talk	Fearfulness
Destruction of school property	Unhappiness, depression
Impertinence and defiance	Overcriticalness of others
Disobedience	Resentfulness
Untruthfulness	Dreaminess
Truancy	Domineeringness
Disorderliness in class	
Tardiness	
Interrupting	
Whispering	
Inattention	

child behavior. Through reading, discussion, and leadership experience with children's groups, they become alert to differences
in behavior and the relative significance of these observed differences. Parents also are becoming increasingly aware of the diffi-

TABLE 8.   Behavior Difficulties Related to General Experiences[2]

Refusal to eat	Dawdling
Careless toilet habits	Lying
Bed-wetting	Stealing
Masturbation	Deliberate property damage
Thumb-sucking	Cruelty to animals
Nail-biting	Neglecting home chores
Temper tantrums	Doing things without permis-
Carelessness	sion
Noisiness	Misbehaving in school
Roughness at play	Disinterest in school work
Fights and quarrels	Overinterest in play
Profanity	Impertinence
Obscenity	Stubbornness
	Staying up late

[1] E. K. Wickman, *Children's Behavior and Teachers' Attitudes,* Commonwealth
Fund, Division of Publications, N. Y., 1928, pp. 124–125. Reprinted by permission.

[2] L. D. Crow, and Alice Crow, *Child Psychology,* Barnes and Noble, New York,
1953, p. 173. Reprinted by permission.

culties of adjustment experienced by their children during the developmental years. The authors obtained from parents and teachers a number of reports concerning behavior aberrations believed by these adults to be the most· common forms of difficulties experienced by children and adolescents. The items most frequently mentioned in these reports then were organized in the form of the following lists of children's behavior difficulties that require adult help in their reconditioning.

TABLE 9.   Behavior Difficulties Related to School Experiences[1]

Tardiness	Physical attack
Truancy	Extreme timidity
Restlessness	Vandalism
Whispering in class	Name-calling
Writing notes in class	Cheating
Poor school work	Smoking
Profanity	Drinking
Temper tantrums	Gambling
Defiance of authority	Puppy-love behavior

As one reads these lists, he probably can recall a young person who has been guilty of behavior that falls into one or more categories. Perhaps the reader himself has been the guilty one. No young person is perfect; neither is any adult. The fact that a developing young person occasionally may take a pencil without permission, for example, or whisper in class does not necessarily mean that he is badly adjusted. It may indicate no more than that he does not yet appreciate the importance of directing his behavior in accordance with what adults believe to be best for him. He may believe, rightly, that no harm will come from his actions.

As an illustration of this point, the case may be cited of a woman who is well known for her success as a college teacher. She was a bright child who mastered her school work easily and quickly. She and several of her equally bright pals sat together in the eighth-grade class. During the "lessons," they were accustomed to writing notes to one another. At that age the note exchanging usually consisted of that favorite pastime of preadolescent girls who are becoming conscious of boy-girl relations but who have not experienced the desired thrills of "dating." Each girl would write on a piece of paper her own name and that of a boy who was the current object of childish adoration. Then she proceeded to cross out the common letters in both names in order to discover whether

[1] *Ibid.*

the relationship between them was one of "hate, love, or friendship.".

Much pleasure was derived by the youngsters from comparing results. They had sufficient control over their behavior, however, not to lose awareness of what was going on in the classroom; they always were ready to take their proper share in class discussions. They derived a twofold satisfaction from their activities: giving expression to their budding interest in the other sex, and "getting away with" supposedly disapproved classroom behavior. The teacher did not seem aware of their extraclass activity, but rather expressed great approval of their learning success. Perhaps the teacher was more alert to their behavior than her attitude showed and did nothing about it because she understood preadolescent interests and urges.

As a high-school student, this woman was so deeply interested in her studies that she had no time for "such nonsense." This attitude was carried over to her college undergraduate days. She was experiencing a satisfying social life outside the school; time spent in the classroom was devoted to the serious business of studying. During her graduate study, however, she returned to her childhood habits. When class discussions seemed nonstimulating she was accustomed to engage with her seatmate in private, written intercommunication, usually having to do with their respective philosophies of life. Now, as a college teacher, she constantly is alert to any activity, unrelated to the regular class discussion, that may start in her classes. Indirectly, she brings the "offenders" into line by challenging their thinking on the topic of class discussion. Perhaps her own earlier experiences with, to her, insufficiently motivated learning situations bear some relation to the fact that she is considered by her students to be an unusually stimulating and thought-provoking instructor.

The experiences of this woman can be compared by the reader to instances of his own youthful misdemeanors or the seemingly undesirable conduct of other young people. At the time of their occurrence, such acts may have caused nonunderstanding adults, even intelligent parents and teachers, to become unduly concerned about the future adjustment of these young people to adult acceptance of responsibility for their behavior. The important considerations in dealing with the behavior difficulties of young people, therefore, are to recognize the consistency of the display of such behavior, the seriousness of its social implications, and the deeprootedness of its causes.

The child or adolescent who, day after day, in the various areas of his associations with other people, gives evidence of uncontrolled behavior or of emotional upsets needs the kind of adult help that results from: (1) a mature understanding of the bases of his lack of behavior control, and/or his emotionally disturbed state, and (2) the knowledge of and skill in applying those therapeutic measures that can assist him to discover what is wrong and guide him toward achieving a more wholesome outlook on life, with consequent improvement in his overt behavior and his emotional reactions. Parents and teachers should learn to recognize the symptoms of severe emotional disturbances or of definite mental illness so that provision can be made for immediate treatment by a psychiatrist or for admission to a hospital for the mentally ill. One of the difficulties of handling cases of this kind is that too many parents and teachers are not prepared to recognize the first symptoms of mental and emotional breakdown. Therefore, they may consider the behavior aberrations of the child to be no more than forms of childish nonconformity to adult standards of proper attitudes and behavior.

Causes of Behavior Difficulties

The basic causes of the arousal and, perhaps, habituation of socially nonacceptable attitudes, emotional tensions, and nonconforming behavior usually are associated with physiological, personal or social status or conditions, or with elements of the situation in which the behavior difficulty is evidenced. The subtle interaction among the elements of physiological, personal, social, and situational causes of behavior is so great and so consistent that rarely, if ever, can one of these factors be considered to be the sole cause of maladjusted behavior. The influence of any one of them upon the developing individual may become so potent a behavior drive that the other areas of influence may be affected adversely by it.

For example, during a young person's pubertal stage of growth, glandular disturbances may be so great that he becomes either extremely nervous or very phlegmatic; his behavior is characterized by irritability or sluggishness; his emotional reactions to his elders and among his peers reflect his inward state. He may develop patterns of un-co-operative attitudes that give some evidence of becoming habitual for him even after the original physiological difficulty has been overcome. He may experience emotional unrest when he transfers from the relatively sheltered environment of the elementary school to a strange and more rigidly organized junior or senior high school that places greater responsibility upon him for his learning activities. This may present adjustment difficulties which he is unable to meet. He thereby becomes increasingly un-co-operative and nonconforming. He may attempt to escape from the realities of the situation into a dream world in which he achieves the fulfillment of those drives and urges that are denied him in his actual school experiences. Keeping in mind the interactions that constantly are taking place among the various phases of the life pattern, we shall consider briefly each of the basic causes.

Physiological status. Structural and organic deviations sometimes give rise to what commonly is referred to as "undisciplined" be-havior. The child or even older person who is short for his age may experience the need to compensate for his stature by engaging in attention-getting activities that may disrupt group activities. Con-trariwise, a boy who has matured physiologically far beyond the average for his age may be stimulated to become a bully in his relations with his less mature associates, especially if other factors of development have aroused the drive to achieve leadership in this way.

A young preson who has matured sexually more rapidly than other children in the group may be mentally retarded as compared with the others. Consequently, he may attempt to gain status among his classmates by discussing matters pertaining to sex. Usually he gives them much misinformation, thereby inducing shock or fear of sex among the more "innocent" and sensitive children. Hence an important parental responsibility in child-rearing is to acquaint the child gradually with correct factual material concerning life proc-esses, in terms of the child's ability to comprehend. In addition, parents should encourage the child to develop wholesome attitudes of respect for his own body and body functions, and of sexual con-trol in his relationships with members of both sexes.

Temporary or more prolonged ill health, and physical defects, such as poor eyesight, partial deafness, and delicate or crippled condition, may adversely affect a child's behavior. Denial of par-ticipation in activities common to the normal child may cause the young person to become embittered, resentful, and self-pitying. Unless he has been encouraged to engage in and gain satisfaction from the kinds of activities that are appropriate to his physical con-dition, he is likely to withdraw from social situations or to achieve the fulfillment of his normal urges in nonsocial behavior. His ac-tions may be characterized by malicious teasing and tormenting, temper tantrums, and excessive demands upon others (often his sisters and brothers) for special attention or the giving up of their wants and interests, or of their possessions, to meet his whims or fancies.

In fairness to parental attitudes, it must be noted that there are many homes in which the presence of a physically-handicapped child has brought about a commendable family unity. There is a willingness on the part of all the members of the family to care for those needs of the child which he himself cannot meet. The child, in turn, displays a wholesome attitude toward the family and toward the defect, and a spirit of independence, insofar as this is possible.

Personal interests and attitudes. We must keep in mind the fact that a child's overt actions are motivated by the relative strength of various inherent urges and drives. Behavior patterns that are associated with the fulfillment of drives result from physical and social environmental influences to which the child is exposed during his developing years. We know also that the child's progressing interests are not inborn, but develop through learning. Since the growing young person has not yet succeeded in achieving supposedly adult control of the expression of inner drives, he may engage in behavior that is immature and harmful to himself and to society. He manifests, in his attitudes and overt activities, his degree of possession of personal qualities, such as overawareness of self, self-interest, unawareness of consequences, and imitation of undesirable behavior. Expressions of these interests and traits may interfere with classroom procedures and standards; hence they constitute some of the most serious problems faced by teachers.

Overawareness of self. Some children and a great many adolescents suffer from an overawareness of their personal appearance, degree of successful achievement in learning, social acceptance, and emotional reactions. The elementary-school girl who usually hides her hands behind her back because they seem to her to be so "big and ugly"; the adolescent boy whose voice squeaks; the girl whose mother's ideas about children's clothes seem to the child to differ from the ideas of other mothers (a kind of little Lord Fauntleroy attitude); the child or adolescent who refrains from taking part in class discussion because other members of the class "can say things much better than I can"; the boy or girl who is shy and retiring in social situations because he cannot recognize in himself any of the fine qualities he admires in other young people of the group; the boy, and especially the girl, whose feelings are hurt easily, who applies any generally expressed criticisms as directed at himself, who is inclined to experience strong feelings of personal guilt if things seem to go wrong in a situation of which he is a member—all of these young people display attitudes that give evidence of undue awareness of the self as an individual in the group.

Too great or too long-continued manifestations of self-consciousness may have serious effects upon the individual's ability to adjust satisfactorily to present and future life situations and relationships. The parent or the teacher who notices that a child is unduly self-conscious in his behavior needs to do something about it at once. The child's attitude may be a manifestation of the presence of unfavorable personality difficulties or situational conditions. It may be that expert help is needed for the solution of the problem.

Self-interest. Another personal quality that may be a strong motivator of child or adolescent behavior is an undue concern with and about the self. Self-interest, as opposed to self-consciousness, motivates the individual to "get what he wants when he wants it," without regard to the effect upon his associates. Self-interest and self-concern are normal characteristics of the very young child, whose one purpose in life (interpreted from the adult point of view) is to *grow*. During his early stages of social development, even socially stimulated behavior is directed toward the self. As development continues to maturity and through the adult years of life, all but a very few individuals are motivated in their behavior by their personal needs, desires, and interests. Yet they learn, more or less effectively, to modify their self-seeking and self-aggrandizing interests and conduct in accordance with the interests of others and the approval they want to receive from others.

The extremely self-centered young person may use any means available to satisfy his selfish interests. This characteristic appears to become more evident in the behavior of the adolescent than it is in a child's behavior. There are children in the elementary schools, however, who pout and sulk if the teacher denies unreasonable requests, if other children seem to be more successful in the completion of a project than they are, or if others seem to gain greater approval from the teacher. Individualistic young people tend to defy the authority of parents and teachers. They rebel against rather than seek the approval of their peers. On occasions, however, if it suits their purposes, they can be very agreeable.

Although a child gains much personal satisfaction from giving a favorite teacher little gifts, such as flowers from his garden, or cookies or other goodies that his mother has made, his reason for doing this grows out of his admiration for the teacher. He behaves in much the same way as a nursery school, kindergarten, or lower elementary-school child does when he throws his arms around the teacher and tells her how much he loves her.

The self-centered adolescent, on the other hand, will "apple-polish" the teacher so that (as is believed) he will be given better marks or win a coveted privilege. An adolescent girl of this type may go to great extremes to "catch" the school hero. She may have no interest in him as a person but may want the prestige that comes of having him escort her to social functions. Some self-centered boys and young men achieve much personal satisfaction from "stealing another fellow's best girl." Behavior of this kind is likely to set up strong resentments among other young people that eventually result in the young person's not being accepted by the group, to his great chagrin. He may bolster his ego by convincing himself that the group is not worthy of his attention. He shifts to another group, where he may make a good first impression but again arouses resentments, leading to nonacceptance. Each such experience may do no more than strengthen his self-interest, unless someone helps him overcome or modify his attitude.

Unawareness of consequences. Every mother knows that when a baby starts to toddle around, nothing in the home is safe, especially any object that is movable or small enough to be pushed or grasped by the child. He may chortle with joy as he picks up a piece of bric-a-brac, throws it on the floor, and then hears the sound of its breaking. During the baby's creeping and crawling days, anything on the floor that is small enough to go into his mouth, goes there.

One baby must learn the hard way that he must watch his step and his hand as his mother continues to admonish him, "No, no," "No touch," or "Don't touch," perhaps accompanied by a shake of the head and a slapping of the baby's hand. Another baby begins his early exploratory process in a room or a playpen in which there are no breakable objects and in which there is nothing harmful to him, even though he does try to eat whatever he touches. No matter what the mother's approach may be as she attempts to control her baby's urge to find out about the new and the different, she realizes that the baby does not understand the consequences of his behavior.

Adults sometimes fail to recognize the fact that the child's appreciation of values does not parallel his growth status, unless he is helped by patient and understanding elders to learn to discriminate between behavior that is right and proper and acts that may harm him and others. No matter how well the child has been trained, however, he sometimes finds himself in a situation which is different from those for which he has developed habitual behavior patterns of right doing. In a situation of this kind, he may be too immature to apply the simple principles of right and wrong that are attached to accustomed situations, and his reactions may have more or less harmful consequences.

A little boy has a pet cat who permits him to hold her, carry her around, or play with her. When he attempts to make her pretty by tying a ribbon on her tail, in much the same way that his sister decorates her doll, the situation changes; a scratched little boy runs to his mother for comfort, and expresses bewilderment caused by the fact that his kitty did not want to be made pretty.

Immature recognition of values associated with behavior is exhibited by elementary-school children, as well as by little tots. As a child continues to give expression to his urges to seek attention and to explore the new and the different, he may engage in many so-called mischievous acts that may try the patience even of an understanding teacher. He sticks his foot into the classroom aisle as a classmate is passing, partly to tease the other child and partly to discover what the other's reaction may be. He puts some mucilage on the hair of the girl who sits in front of him, not because he does not like the girl but because he wants to find out whether the mucilage will stick to hair as it does to paper.

Many acts are committed by young people that may be considered by parents and teachers to give evidence of malicious intent, but that in reality are well-meaning attempts at exploration, engaged in by energy-filled, curious, but immature individuals. In the high-school chemistry laboratory, even a co-operative student may be tempted to experiment with chemical elements, if he can get the chance to do so. That there are relatively few serious accidents in high-school "labs" is a result of the watchful care exercised by teachers, in addition to the fact that by the time adolescents elect chemistry, they have reached a more mature appreciation of values. Moreover, chemistry usually attracts the more intelligent students, who have achieved some control over their impulsive behavior.

Mentally slow children are likely to engage in behavior that will get them into trouble. They observe that brighter children "try their wings" in areas of novel experiences, without any harm to themselves or others. The bright youngsters seem, to the less able children, to "get away" with undesirable exploratory behavior which, when imitated by the slow child, earns for him either parent or teacher disapproval, or both. Intelligence differences are closely associated with the suffering of consequences for antisocial acts, even on the adult level. It sometimes is said that there are more criminals and delinquents walking around the streets than are found in jails and reform schools. One explanation given for this statement is that the mentally dull are more easily caught than are the bright.

Imitation of others. We already have made reference to the child's desire to imitate behavior exhibited by his associates. We have referred also to the fact that much of a child's developing behavior and many of his attitudes result from conscious or unconscious imitation of the behavior or attitudes of adults and peer associates. The personal and social desirability of the imitated behavior depends upon the kind of model imitated. The child may shock his teacher and classmates by expressing dissatisfaction with a classroom situation in a string of profane words that he unconcernedly rattles off. He is not the one who should have his mouth washed out or should receive a more psychologically desirable punishment. His adult model is the one who deserves the mouth washing!

There are many and varied ways in which a child can become the innocent victim of undesirable, harm-inducing models. Patterns of behavior in the home become *his* patterns of behavior. As a result of undesirable home attitudes and behavior, he may learn to be dishonest, to cheat, to use vulgar language, to be careless in his dress and general appearance, or to reflect in his conduct or attitudes an undesirable pattern of home life. This is an extreme portrayal of unhealthful home conditions. Most modern parents attempt to inculcate desirable child behavior patterns, both by precept and by example. See Chapter 19 for discussion of desirable traits and characteristics of teachers.

There are instances, however, of parents who forget that a child cannot always distinguish between those forms of behavior that may be permissible for an adult but wrong for him. His father smokes, but if the child attempts to imitate him the youngster is told in no uncertain tone of voice to "wait till you're old enough." A mother impresses upon her child that he always should tell the truth; the child then hears her refuse an invitation to a social event, saying that she has another engagement. When the child asks the mother where she is going, the mother may answer, unmindful of the effect upon the child, "I'm not going anywhere, but I don't intend to be bored at one of her stuffy parties!" When is a lie a lie and when isn't it? Examples like these could be continued *ad in-finitum*.

The developing child is bound to be stimulated to action within his limited sphere of operation by the stories that he hears or reads that deal with all kinds of ways of "beating the game." It seems almost impossible for parents to protect their children from the influence of radio and television programs, motion pictures, some comic books, and newspaper accounts of asocial activities, in which wrongdoing fails to receive immediate punishment or reconditioning. It is the parents' responsibility, therefore, to attempt to help the child appreciate the eventual consequences suffered by persons who do not respect the rights of others. However, it is easier *to say* that this should be done than it is *to do* it.

The physical and social environment. A growing child must develop, through experience, the ability to become aware of all the elements that constitute his broadening environment, and to recognize their relation to himself as well as his relation to them. In terms of his home environment and the care that he is expected to exercise in dealing with it, his attitude toward the classroom and learning materials will be either to take pride in an attractive school building or classroom, or to be unconcerned about such acts as defacing the walls, throwing papers on the floor, and/or more serious acts of vandalism.

The child's or adolescent's overt reactions to environmental conditions do not always reflect home influence. Emotional states may be induced by his degree of relative success or failure to achieve desired goals or to meet others' expectations for him. This may cause him to attach an affective attitude to the environmental situation in which he has achieved either satisfaction or annoyance in the activities in which he has engaged. For example, teachers usually find that the successful learners exercise more care in handling school materials than do those who fail to attain learning goals. Another factor related to lack of success is the child's directing of his energy. The unsuccessful learner, bored by learning activities, may be driven by his need for activity to do those things that will give him immediate satisfaction, even though his behavior receives teacher or class disapproval. In fact, it may be more satisfying to be disapproved of than to be ignored. The tearing up of paper, the throwing of a blackboard eraser against the wall, the carving of his initials on the desk, or any other form of destructive behavior may earn for him the attention he craves.

An individual's reactions to his physical environment cannot be divorced from his social interactions. In his home, school, and neighborhood environments, the child is motivated in his behavior by his intense desire to find a place for himself in his group. We already have devoted considerable attention to the functioning of this strong drive as the child gradually passes through the progressive stages of his social development. In this discussion, therefore, emphasis is placed upon a child's possible modes of expressing this attention-seeking drive as he attempts to adjust himself and his behavior to what is expected of him by his teachers and his peer groups during his school experiences.

In his struggle for school status, the child usually is motivated by (1) the desire to belong—to be an accepted member of the group, (2) the desire to receive attention, often by means of spectacular bits of behavior, and (3) the desire to conform to classroom routines and learning demands, insofar as the conformity does not interfere with his desire for freedom of activity.

Desire to belong. The reader probably can apply here much of what already has appeared in this book concerning the need of a child to feel secure in the affection and approval of others. Especially does the child seek to earn the esteem of those adults or peer associates whose good opinion of himself means much to him. Hence most school children are eager to do what an admired teacher requests; they may refrain from the kind of behavior that would lower them in the estimation of class members or schoolmates whom they admire.

Freshman and sophomore high-school boys and girls, for example, sometimes seem willing to become the slaves of the school athletic hero or the leader of the important school activities. These younger adolescents imitate the dress and manners of their hero and are ready to fight with anyone who dares to say anything disparaging of him. It is partly for this reason that teacher advisers attempt indirectly to guide pupils' selection of their student group leaders. The child or adolescent who patterns his behavior upon that of an admired peer leader often finds that thereby he has acquired qualities that later may earn for himself a position of school leadership.

Desire to be spectacular. The motivating desire that causes a young person to engage in spectacular behavior is rooted, of course, in his strong drive to gain attention from his associates. As we said earlier, the child is not intentionally cruel or malicious, or consciously disobedient when he performs pranks or in other ways appears to be showing off.

A high-school boy known to the authors was an extremely bright and successful student. His superior performance in the classroom came to be taken for granted by his teachers and classmates. If a particularly difficult problem were to be solved, the students were accustomed to say, "Oh, let Gerald do it. He can do anything." This continued approving attitude no longer satisfied his desire for attention. Consequently, one day when asked to present the results of some research he had done, he gave his report in words that, except when he had to do otherwise, were extremely technical and at least four or more syllables in length. He startled both his teacher and his classmates, who challenged him to explain the technical terms. He did a good job with most of them. When the teacher had to explain the meaning of a few of them and point out that he had used them inappropriately, he joined the class in their good-natured laughter at his expense. But he had accomplished his aim—the class accorded him a new kind of attention. They would greet him with, "Hi Gerald, got any big words for us today?" or, "Here comes the walking encyclopedia!" His "stunt" was written up in the school newspaper. Finally, he could not take the "gaff" any longer; he told them to "dry up" and to stop picking on him. This led to a different form of attention-getting. Throughout all of this experience, however, there were no hard feelings. He still was the class leader in study matters, as well as in social activities.

Desire for freedom of activity. Many children seem to be able to strike a nice balance between their desire to conform to established patterns of behavior and their extremely strong urge to experience freedom of activity. Their attitude toward adult authority in relation to the strength of their felt need to become independent arbiters of their fate grows out of the kind and amount of faith they have developed in the soundness, consistency, and humaneness of adult expression of authority in relation to the fulfillment of their needs, urges, and interests. For example, a child or an adolescent believes that his parents, teachers, or any other adults who are in the position of authority in regard to himself are fair and intelligent in their judgments concerning the amount of independence of action or decision-making a young person rightfully should experience. Consequently, the young person is willing to be guided in his behavior by the decisions of his elders. Willingness to conform also is affected by the extent to which the developing person is given opportunities to share with the adult in the making of decisions concerning what should be done, and to help in the planning of how it should be carried out.

Unfortunately, some children have not learned how to adjust their desire for freedom of activity to the restrictions upon their freedom by rules and regulations devised by adults to guard the safety and welfare of the members of a group. A child observes an adult break a regulation that supposedly is aimed at the achievement of general welfare, and which the child is expected to obey. The effect of an incident of this kind is likely to be loss of respect for both the regulation and the adult who forces the child's acceptance of it.

For example, a teacher in charge of a high-school study room admonishes the pupils to refrain from talking, lest they interfere with the studying of surrounding pupils. Then the teacher proceeds to carry on an animated conversation, in a loud voice, with another teacher. The pupils in that room are justified in wondering why a teacher's talking should interfere less with studying than the talking of a pupil. Although the teacher or parent should not engage in an activity which he claims will interfere with general welfare, even adolescents may not be mature enough to understand that one person's talking may not be too annoying in this situation, but that the cumulative effect of general conversation among the students would interfere greatly with concentrated study on the part of even a few pupils.

We have made no reference so far to the teacher's relation to behavior control in matters dealing with classroom routines and learning activities. One of the most serious problems of teachers, especially those who lack the self-confidence that is born of experience, is that of dealing with young people who seem to possess little or no respect for the authority of the teacher and who are determined to exercise what they consider to be their right of doing as they please. The attitudes toward authority and personal freedom that children bring with them to their school experiences usually reflect the amount and kind of training they received in the home during their preschool years.

Long before he enters school, the child's attitude toward authority has been formed by that which he has known in his own home. The properly disciplined child thinks of the adults he has known as wise, kind, and supporting; accordingly, this is the attitude he will have toward teachers. If discipline represents to him arbitrary, interfering, unfair, punishing parents, he will expect the same treatment from teachers, and his reaction will be that of self-protection through escape or rebellion, attitudes that may continue into adult life. Persons with these points of view have difficulty in keeping jobs, because they regard their superiors as unfair.

As soldiers, they will be AWOL, when leave might be had for the asking.

These undisciplined, emotionally immature adults hate all authority; they are always *against,* but seldom *for* anything. Throughout life they live apart from the herd. They may be successful in certain ways, and frequently they are financially prosperous, but they remain unhappy, lonely individualists who find it difficult to get along with others. If they marry, their homes are seldom stable, and they pass on to their children their unfortunate emotional attitudes and patterns of life, and thus the cycle is repeated.[1]

Problems Associated with the Development of Self-Control

Some parents still regard the school's chief function to be that of "making Johnny behave." Too many mothers of young children are heard to remark, "I can't wait until he (she) is old enough to go to school. I can't do anything with that child." Often, after a speech similar to this, the mother will turn to the child, who may be in the midst of a parent-induced tantrum, and shaking her finger at him will say, "Just wait till you go to school. The teachers won't stand for anything like this. They'll take it out of you!" It is small wonder that children who are prepared in this way for entrance into school begin their school life afraid of "teacher" but ready to fight it out with her as they have done with their mothers. With increasing emphasis upon parent education, situations such as these are decreasing in number, although there still are too many parents who tend to shift their responsibilities for the development of the child's behavior control to school people. They then complain bitterly if Johnny or Mary does not discard immediately all the bad habits that had developed under parental tutelage during the preschool years.

Discipline as related to self-discipline. One of the greatest concerns of teacher-trainees and beginning teachers is associated with the fear that they will not be successful in maintaining "good discipline" in their classes. This attitude is displayed even by the graduates of our modern colleges and teacher-training institutions who have gained academic understanding of the principles of child development and have had some experience in working with young people. They are perturbed over the difficulties that may arise when they attempt to

---

[1] F. S. DuBois, "The Security of Discipline," *Mental Hygiene,* Vol. 36: No. 5, July, 1952, p. 367. Reprinted by permission.

help a young person overcome undesirable attitudes or bad behavior.

Discipline, as control, always has been recognized as an element of human living and of human behavior. The connotation of the words, *discipline* and *control*, differs with the point of view from which the meaning of these terms is approached. Who is to do the disciplining? Who is responsible for the control? Until recently, schoolmasters regarded discipline as referring to those measures utilized by them to force learners to order their conduct according to rigid rules and regulations set down by the schoolmaster or teacher, and enforced by devious methods, including the application of a switch. Control of behavior, therefore, was thought of as the power of the teacher to gain overt obedience to his commands. Silence in the classroom was imperative, except for the voice of the teacher or of the child as he recited his "lesson." Rigidity of position, and prompt response to the teacher's orders were supposed to characterize a class that was well disciplined.

Harm of negative approach. It is possible for a teacher *to control* the overt behavior of a class by means of threats of punishment which are carried out. Constant emphasis upon rules and regulations can cause pupils to look upon the classroom as the place where the main function of the teacher is to teach them to be "good"; any other phase of learning is secondary or incidental. This attitude is displayed by the child when he says to another child who is engaging in one or another form of misbehavior, "Look out! Teacher is watching."

A class controlled in this way is likely to be an orderly group. Anyone who passes the door of such a classroom may be impressed by the apparent calmness and the attentive attitude of the students, unless he happens to arrive when the teacher is shouting at the group for a misdemeanor of one of its members; is preaching to them concerning their obligation to obey rules and regulations set down by him; is informing them about their parents' failure to teach them good manners, or is reminding them of all their past and present transgressions, and of their stupidity, laziness, or unwillingness to learn. This description of a teacher who attempts to control his class through fear of consequences is not a figment of the authors' imagination. Too many such disciplinary situations still are extant, although their number is decreasing. The function of the teacher—to *guide* learners' activities, rather than to keep order in the classroom—is coming to be better understood by teachers.

The orderly child or the behavior-inhibited adolescent in the classroom is not necessarily a well-disciplined young person. When he is removed from the eagle eye of the demanding teacher, he is more than likely to feel impelled to give expression to the energies that have been pent up within him during the school day. He runs; he shouts; in a streetcar or other public conveyance, he pushes older people aside in order to get to an available seat. When he is seated, he broadcasts his opinion of his teachers, his school subjects, or of the school in general. He may tease his peer companions. He and his companions may tussle, without regard for the feet or the feelings of other passengers. If an adult in the car disapproves such behavior, the young person probably will taunt the adult for being an old "fuss box," or disregard him completely. This description of the uncontrolled young person may fit the behavior of boys, but girls also give evidence of similar behavior, sometimes in a more modified form.

The laissez-faire approach. These are the possible disastrous effects upon the general attitudes of young people of a teacher's emphasis upon rigid control of classroom conduct. We have referred to a parent's or a teacher's need to understand a child's or adolescent's drive to express his inner wants and urges. Early in this century, psychologists attempted to advise parents how to rear their children, and teachers how to teach them so as to meet the child's growth and developmental needs. It was pointed out that a child should be given an opportunity to learn through self-expression. At first, psychologists' suggestions were misinterpreted and misused by parents and school people, alike.

For a child to be allowed to "express himself" and to "learn through doing" were understood by enthusiastic followers of these psychological principles to mean that a young person should grow and develop "naturally," without any adult control or inhibition of his inner drives to action. Hence parents interpreted child-rearing to mean that they should not thwart their child's wishes or disapprove self-centered behavior, lest he suffer feelings of frustration and consequent emotional disturbance. Teachers were expected to remove themselves from the front to the rear of the classroom, and to encourage the pupils to follow their own learning interests. A child was to be permitted to follow his own desires. If he did not experience an urge to learn, it was considered good pedagogy to allow him to engage in whatever activity his immediate interest prompted him to do.

The reader can imagine, or may know, what might be and what

were the results of such parent and teacher procedures. There was little or no attempt to regulate the developing child's behavior. Child behavior was as uncontrolled by inner motivations as it had been under rigid teacher disciplining. There were fundamental differences, however, in the effect upon the child of these two diametrically opposed attitudes toward child adjustment. Rigidly exercised control of a child's overt behavior often gave rise to bitter feelings of resentment toward the imposed control. In the presence of the teacher, he attempted to fit his behavior into the pattern demanded of him. He might display complete, or almost complete, lack of behavior control when he was on his own. He believed that then he need not fear punishment for his undisciplined behavior.

The newer concept of child-rearing, that resulted in removal of externally applied controls of behavior, tended to result in the child's having no fear of unpleasant consequences, in the form of punishment by adults, for conduct that was undesirable in terms of adult standards. He was expected to learn control through the effects upon him of the "natural" consequences he might suffer as a result of his acts. It cannot be denied that "the burned child fears the fire," but the doctrine of "natural punishment," carried to extremes, might not stop at burning the child—it might kill him! Moreover, *freedom* in activity very easily can become *license* in activity. The young person not only may come to develop, through no fault of his own, an attitude of defiance of all authority, but also fail to acquire a clear or definite understanding of what constitutes personally or socially wholesome behavior.

Some parents and teachers still practice a kind *of laissez-faire* mode of child-rearing and teaching. They refrain from curbing a child's inner drives to action. Most modern parents, however, are striking a happy balance between rigidly controlled and completely uncontrolled child behavior. Difficulties arise when children who are reared differently attempt to play or work together. The results of differences in behavior control are illustrated in the following account of child and adult reactions to discipline.

This story concerns two brothers, each of whom is married. One brother and his wife have two children, five and three years, respectively. The mother believes that children's behavior should not be inhibited by adult control. Hence these youngsters are undisciplined. In the words of another member of the family, they are un-co-operative "brats."

The other brother and his wife have one three-year-old child who is expected to control his behavior in terms of simple but socially acceptable attitudes that he has been helped by his parents to develop. When the three children meet, the better controlled child is inclined to refrain from participation in the unrestrained activities of his cousins. He appears to be bewildered by their behavior. Who knows what the effect upon him might be if he were frequently in their company! This is not likely to happen, however, since cordial relations between the two families are strained because of differences in parental philosophies concerning child-rearing. This story does not represent an isolated instance. In neighborhoods where differently trained children are accustomed to play together, parents who desire to inculcate ideals of socially desirable behavior in their children struggle constantly to overcome the effects of companionship with uncontrolled youngsters.

Value of a well-balanced approach. A child's conduct may reflect the utilization of too rigid or too lax control of overt behavior. As adults, we know, to some extent at least, that we cannot always do what we want to do, or in the way we would like to do it. Much of our behavior is controlled in terms of accepted cultural standards. The well-disciplined adult considers that other persons as well as himself may be affected by his behavior patterns. He has some appreciation of the extent to which his personal desire must be modified to meet group standards. This indicates that, somewhere and somehow during the course of his development, he has been helped to achieve an understanding of personal responsibility for social welfare.

A young person needs to learn why he should control the satisfaction of some of his wants, and how he can develop such control. The very young child can respond to simple cause-and-effect relationships. Hence the parent and the nursery-school teacher may need to employ a relatively direct and specific disciplinary approach, whereby the child is guided to appreciate the fact that if he does this, a specific consequence will follow. Even during these early years, it is possible to give him some understanding of the *why* of the relationship between "naughty" conduct and parent or teacher disapproval.

As the maturing child becomes increasingly active in his participation in home, neighborhood, and early school situations, he can begin to form certain conceptual generalizations concerning the degree of rightness or wrongness of his behavior drives. This developing consciousness of behavior standards in relation to himself and his attitudes can be achieved by the child only (1) if he learns that these standards should control his behavior in all the situations of which he is a part, either temporarily or for a longer time, and (2) if adults are consistent in their appraisal of and treatment of his childish misdeeds.

The parent or teacher who evaluates a young person's actions on the basis of adult physical or emotional condition is likely, at one time, to punish a child severely for a specific form of misconduct that, at another time, he either overlooks or condones. As a result, the child may respond to the mood of the adult as the restraining factor of undesirable behavior, rather than to his own recognition of it as the wrong thing for him to do in any situation or under any conditions.

To the extent that a young person is encouraged by parents and teachers to "think through" his reasons for his behaving in one way rather than in another, and is helped to achieve inner satisfaction from engaging in socially acceptable behavior, he gradually develops the power to control his actions in accordance with personally established and habituated ideals and standards. His behavior is coming to be motivated by inner controls rather than by forces outside himself. His behavior now reflects *self-control* or *self-discipline*.

The Teacher and the Development of Self-Discipline

The average child or adolescent usually spends no more than six hours per day for fewer than 190 days of the year in the classroom. Yet, the successive teachers of the young person are expected, through their guidance of his learning activities, to increase his knowledge of the world about him, to improve the skills needed by him, to help him adapt himself to this world and the world to himself, and to develop attitudes and interests that are centered in the welfare of his world rather than to remain ego-centered. As a result of his school training, a mature adult is supposed to have achieved and to maintain the status of a constructive, well-adjusted member of his ever-enlarging world.

Teacher personality and pupil behavior. A teacher's attitudes and the kind of behavior he displays in and outside the classroom exert a powerful influence upon teacher-learner relationships and on pupil progress in every area of learning. So important is the personality pattern of the teacher that the personal qualities of men and women who aspire to enter the teaching profession are evaluated by their instructors, both before entrance into the teacher-education program and during their period of training. Through this procedure, those who give definite indications of being unsuited in personality for entrance into the profession can be guided out of it and into other occupational fields in which personal qualities are not so clearly related to success. Those who give evidence of potential fitness for teaching are helped to bring about any personal improvement that may seem to be needed.

We are concerned here with the mental hygiene approach to the development of self-control or self-discipline among young people. Hence we emphasize the teacher's expressed attitudes toward and ways of dealing with pupils' behavior, as he attempts to prevent the arousal of unsocial behavior, to preserve desirable behavior, and to help in the reconditioning of behavior that gives definite evidence of deviation from socially acceptable standards. It might seem needless to emphasize the fact that a teacher should be sincere, honest, and conscientious; should like and understand young people; should know the subject matter he is expected to teach, and should be skilled in techniques of learner motivation. Yet, there are some teachers whose personality shortcomings induce uncontrolled behavior among the members of a class.

The teacher and his behavior in class situations exert a most powerful influence upon each member of the class. A discussion of class discipline should include consideration of the attitudes of the teacher and the techniques employed by him: to prevent the arousal of possible behavior and attitude difficulties among those pupils who are predisposed toward their arousal, to preserve those desirable behavior patterns already developed, and to treat intelligently those pupils who tend to display habitual nonconforming behavior.

Prevention of behavior difficulties in the classroom. The characteristic behavior of the teacher in the classroom has a potent influence upon class behavior. The teacher's personal qualities, his understanding of the capabilities and attitudes of his pupils, his own mastery of the subject matter he attempts to teach, and his management of classroom routines set the pace for class progress.

Personal qualities. Children are keen observers and usually are outspoken critics of teacher behavior. They tend either consciously or unconsciously to reflect in their behavior the attitudes and behavior displayed by teachers. Pupils resent to be told by the teacher to be honest, for example, and then to hear the teacher give a supervisor what they recognize to be a false reason for failure to submit a report by its due date. They are sensitive to lack of sincerity in a teacher.

A member of the class tells his teacher something in confidence, after being assured by the teacher that the matter will go no further. Unfortunately, there are teachers who cannot refrain from gossiping with their confreres about their pupils. Hence this young person's confidence may become the subject of teacher lunch-table conversation. When or if the pupil concerned hears, by way of the grapevine, that the teacher was insincere when he made the promise not to disclose information that was given in confidence, the young person is likely to have no further faith in the teacher. In addition, the pupil may suffer feelings of resentment, embarrassment, or even emotional upset, if the matter represents a serious experience.

The teacher who is conscientious about the fulfillment of his own responsibilities has the right to expect his pupils to follow his example. However, a teacher may meet the class without having prepared himself properly for the day's work; be careless about home study assignments, and fail to check pupils' completion of them; neglect to return test papers and written work; and forget to discuss with the class those learning errors that require attention. Such teacher behavior soon results in lack of pupil interest in, and effort to engage in, diligent study.

The few examples cited are sufficient to impress upon the reader the fact that the characteristics displayed by the teacher in the classroom are the prime motivators of the kind of attitudes and behavior that become typical of the members of the class. Young people of all ages react to their teachers. In terms of observed teacher qualities, they may attempt to imitate him or to develop attitudes of contempt, resentment, or defiance of his authority. What the teacher *does* speaks much more loudly than what he *says*. Appearance and appropriateness of dress and grooming; mannerisms; voice quality and diction, and clearness of speech; temperament and degree of emotional maturity, and degree of adaptability —these and other personal characteristics are factors of influence upon pupil behavior in the classroom, and upon pupil memories of their teachers that may last a long time.

For example, one of the authors still has a vivid memory picture of a teacher who seemed always to wear a purple skirt and a yellow blouse, who never got up from her seat at the front of the room, and who constantly "treated" the less able members of the class to expressions of biting sarcasm. The author's reaction, as a pupil, to this woman was an attitude of contempt, and the reading of novels during class periods. The contempt was intensified by the fact that the teacher appeared to be unaware of her pupil's behavior and gave her an "A" at the end of the term. A combination of yellow and purple still has an unpleasant effect upon this former student.

Teacher-trainees usually are very much concerned about becoming thoroughly prepared in the areas of subject matter mastery and teaching skill development. These are important, of course. Their greatest concern probably should be to develop the. kind of personal characteristics that will win friends for them among their pupils and, by their influence, to prevent the arousal of disapproving, un-co-operative, and resentful behavior.

Understanding individual pupils. Little need be said here concerning the value of teacher understanding of children. Much of the discussion in this book deals with the acquisition of this understanding. The teacher's task is to apply what he has learned about young people in his relationships with the members of his particular classes. A teacher should avail himself of all the accumulated information that can be obtained from the school guidance records. Furthermore, he must be alert, at all times, to the displayed behavior of individual pupils, and should interpret what he observes in terms of his understanding of young people's nature.

A teacher's success in gaining an adequate appreciation of each child's or adolescent's potentialities and habituated behavior patterns and needs depends to a great extent upon the availability of official records, size of class, and his own ingenuity in setting up situations that will help him to gain the desired understanding. A few simple suggestions concerning techniques that can be started on the first day of a school term include: early identification of each pupil by name and seat; constant alertness to what is going on in the classroom; awareness of differences among pupils in their ability and willingness to participate in class discussion; recognition of posture and other physical characteristics; appreciation of existing relations among the various members of the class, in addition to other more subtle factors that attract the teacher's attention early in his acquaintance with the group. Why are some children identified and at least partially understood very soon, and others hardly understood by the end of the term?

Knowledge of subject matter. Most elementary-school children regard their teachers as fountains of wisdom that constantly can be expected to gush forth with new and intriguing knowledge. Adolescents may not have such great faith in their teacher's extensive and intensive mastery of all fields of knowledge, but they do expect these adults to know thoroughly their own teaching material. Most teachers are able to meet expectations in this respect. They do not always give evidence of the ability to get across to their pupils their possessed knowledge in a form that can be understood by their learners. The authors can recall a noted psychologist who was an impossible instructor in beginning psychology. His students did not know what he was talking about, since his terminology as well as his attempted explanations went beyond their ability to comprehend. At the same time, he was a brilliant and challenging instructor of graduate psychology majors.

It is not unusual for high-school and college teachers to overrate their students' background of understanding. They do not realize that young people cannot skip some of the intermediary steps of thinking that have become part of their own thinking pattern. A college teacher of statistics was an unusually able statistician, but he kept many of the members of his college classes bewildered and confused as he attempted to explain to them some of the more simple statistical concepts. A high-school boy was heard to remark about one of his instructors: "He sure knows his subject, but he can't teach it to us. He leaves us up in the air."

In teaching-learning situations such as these, the more able and interested learners are likely to "dig out" the learning on their own, or seek the help of other adults who are acquainted with the subject. The less able probably will give up in despair, decide that the subject is too hard for them, spend class time in participation with others of their kind in classroom pranks, or resort to daydreaming. Sometimes, the more aware the teacher becomes of his own ineffectiveness, the greater will be his annoyance and his consequent emotional reactions to class-disturbing activities of supposedly unco-operative and lazy pupils.

The opposite of such teacher handling of learning material is that of the man or woman who tends to talk down to his pupils. His expressed attitude seems to be that no one in the class has the "brains" to understand what he is talking about. This attitude may be accompanied by a general attitude of superiority toward the class. Any mistake in oral discussion or written work by even a few of his pupils stimulates him to expound upon their dullness, stupidity, or inattention, since they cannot understand even one-syllable words. There are teachers, however, who oversimplify their teaching because of a sincere belief that they cannot leave anything to learner imagination. This characteristic is displayed especially by elementary-school teachers of the early grades who, for one or another reason, are teaching on the secondary or college level.

The effect upon young people of this teaching approach differs with the individual. Bright learners become bored; they usually are at least one step beyond teacher explanation. Whether they then indulge in antisocial behavior depends upon their habitual patterns of behavior control. Poorly motivated class-learning situations sometimes afford able young people excellent opportunities for the preparation of homework or study for their more challenging classes.

A teacher may know his subject matter well and be able to stimulate the interest and learning efforts of his pupils when all of his pupils possess relatively similar ability to profit from instruction. If the class is composed of young people who vary widely in mental ability, readiness to learn, or learning background, the task of motivating differing learning potentials constitutes a problem that is difficult for any teacher to meet. The many and varied behavior problems that can arise in this class are not primarily the fault of the teacher or of the pupils, but are rooted in the teaching-learning situation.

Management of class routines. Most young people are helped to experience an attitude of emotional security if their daily activities follow a well-planned, but not too rigidly enforced schedule. The generally satisfying adaptation of the baby to established routines finds its counterpart in the reactions of elementary-school children and adolescents to organized routines that are characteristic of good class management. Young people like to feel that the school day or the recitation period can be expected to proceed according to a pattern that was established early in the term. They know what they have to do and the way in which it should be done. They usually are willing or eager to carry out the regular class schedule with dispatch and acceptable performance.

There are several principles that underlie the setting up of good class routines. These should be understood and applied by a teacher on any school level. Routines should not be practiced so rigidly that they become boring to the pupils or interfere with their achieving habits of adaptability. An occasional change in routine usually is welcomed, unless the change is too different from accustomed routines. If possible, it is good psychology for the teacher to give the members of the class the right to share in setting up the plan of general class procedures. Young people (like adults) tend to take pride in activities which they have helped organize.

An excellent co-operation inducer is to find jobs for all the members of the group. On the elementary-school level this is relatively easy to do. Committees can be appointed or elected to be responsible for various class duties: distribution of writing or drawing materials, care of the blackboards and bulletin boards, care and distribution of learning aids and library books, as well as responsibility for the various other phases of good classroom management that make the classroom a pleasant place in which to be. The time schedule for learning activities and other phases of classroom living also should follow a relatively regular plan except for interesting and worthwhile deviations from it.

The assumption of responsibilities in terms of ability to perform them keeps young people out of mischief and encourages the development of good behavior control. The teacher who himself is disorganized in his thinking and supposedly habitual modes of behavior is almost certain to act on impulse in the management of class routines. His pupils may not know what will happen next, but will be expected to perform adequately. They may become restless. Since they have no personal responsibilities for class management, they must find something to do to keep them busy. So they get into mischief, develop habits of inattention and, in their behavior reactions, reflect the disorganized attitudes of the teacher. The potential trouble makers find many ways to interfere with or to influence the behavior of their less aggressive classmates. It takes skill and patience, however, for a teacher to bring every member of the class into the group situation in a constructive way.

Preservation of good behavior control. Many of the presented suggestions dealt with teacher techniques, aimed at preventing the arousal of uncontrolled behavior. They apply also to ways in which a teacher can help generally well-adjusted learners to maintain their habitual good attitudes and behavior patterns and, with increasing physiological maturation, strengthen them. If pupils possess good learning and personality potential, and their learning activities are guided by a well-adjusted adult who is a good teacher as well as a good manager of class affairs, they enjoy their learning activities and can be expected to make commendable progress.

Mentally slow as well as bright children, whose earlier experiences in the home and in the school encouraged the development of acceptable behavior patterns, can gain much from their school experiences if they continue to experience favorable motivation of their activities. The classroom teacher is responsible for helping well-adjusted young people to develop even greater awareness of themselves as persons and as members of their various groups. Each of them needs many opportunities to participate in worthwhile learning activities. Teacher emphasis should be placed upon a satisfying recognition of acceptable performance. Needed criticism of failure to achieve or of inadequate production usually is more effective when it is constructive. Even co-operative young people resent having their work or their behavior pulled to shreds, with no credit for whatever effort was made by them to complete the project in which they failed to meet required standards. They may not have understood directions, or they may not have been ready for that particular form of activity.

Even the most well-adjusted individual may have his "off moments." Other interests or temporary emotional strains, resulting from circumstances that are removed from the present situation, may impel a person, young or old, to engage in behavior that is not appropriate. When a situation of this kind arises in the classroom, the teacher's understanding of the young person is an aid in handling the unaccustomed behavior. The teacher does not say, in the presence of the class, "What has come over you today? I have never seen you act like this before." An attitude of this kind displayed by the teacher can lead only to the intensifying of the child's emotional strain. The ignoring of the incident, or a sympathetic attempt to discover privately the cause of the difficulty is appreciated and serves as a means of improving the situation. Through this experience, the young person may gain greater awareness of himself and increased social consciousness.

Treatment of behavior difficulties. The causes of personally harmful and socially unacceptable behavior lie in all the factors of influence to which we refer repeatedly in this book. Because they are related to school situations, these causes are summarized here briefly as:

(1) Inherited potential in: physical constitution, mental ability, emotional status, strength of inner drives.
(2) Kinds of life experiences in: the home, the school, the neighborhood, or the community.

In some school communities, there seem to be clustered biological and cultural influences that militate against a child's probability of developing personally and socially desirable attitudes and overt behavior patterns. In general, however, most teachers will admit that developing young people respond satisfactorily to learning motivation within achievable limits. At the same time, in the majority of classrooms, there can be found at least a few young people who do not fit into the general behavior pattern of the class. These nonconforming or non-co-operative members of the class often give the teacher much concern. In attempting to help the recalcitrant pupil improve his behavior, the teacher has several purposes in mind. He utilizes whatever may seem to be the most effective procedure to (1) help the individual himself gain better control of his behavior, (2) prevent the spread of uncontrolled behavior to other better-adjusted pupils, and (3) keep teaching-learning activities running smoothly.

The what, when, and how of remedial techniques to be employed in behavior reconditioning vary with the offender's total personality pattern and the nature of his offense. Reconditioning of behavior, then, must be specific in terms of specific individuals and circumstances.

Teacher attitudes toward behavior difficulties. The form of treatment employed may need to vary. Regardless of what a teacher does in a particular situation, however, his attitude toward the offense and the offender should reflect a high degree of emotional control and of intelligent understanding of what he hopes to accomplish. A teacher who meets temper tantrum with temper tantrum, who gives evidence of lack of self-confidence in the situation, or who flounders in his attempts to help the young person will be ineffectual in his treatment of the offender and the offense.

Disciplinary action undertaken by a teacher or by any other school official should be accompanied by the display of certain desirable attitude characteristics. Whatever treatment is utilized, it should be:

1. Definite and understood by the offender.
2. Objective and impersonal.
3. Directed at the offense—not at the offender.
4. Administered privately, if possible, although in case of minor infractions of class regulations, both individual and class morale are aided by immediate action.
5. Related to the offense.
6. Devoid of anger. A "cooling off" period usually helps both the teacher and the offender gain a better perspective.
7. Adjusted to the offense and the offender. Offenses differ in their degree of seriousness; offenders differ in their ability and willingness to respond to treatment.
8. Applied to the guilty person, not to the entire group.
9. Administered in such way and at such time that there will be little if any interruption of teaching-learning activities.

10. Effective in that the offender is motivated to try to exercise greater control of his behavior.

These suggestions are general, but they may serve as a check list whereby the teacher can examine his own attitudes in specific situations involving one or another form of behavior difficulty. However, if the offense is extremely serious and reflects definite behavior maladjustment, the teacher should not hesitate to seek help in its treatment. Too often, young teachers, especially, struggle with a behavior problem because they fear that if they report it to an administrator or counselor they will be considered "poor disciplinarians."

Suggestions for correcting misbehavior. Since everyone desires approval, emphasis should be placed upon the inner satisfactions that can be attained from success-achieving behavior. This induces a pleasurable appreciation of the fact that one is earning a commendable reputation among his associates. There are times, however, when a young person experiences satisfaction from the display of un-co-operative behavior that must be corrected by disapproval, rather than approval.

Attitudes of school people are changing toward the forms of punishment that should be utilized to help a young person "mend his ways." Punishment inflicted mainly as a warning to the offender and others of the consequences of misbehavior is not sufficient. We want the child or adolescent to become conscious of the fact that he has acted in an undesirable way, to be sorry that he has transgressed, and to grow in power of inner control.

To demand that an offender apologize to the teacher and/or the class for his offense may have little value. Unless the individual is unusually stubborn, it is easy for him to say glibly, "I'm sorry." There may be no inner contrition. It is only to the extent that an apology is *meant* when it is given overt expression, that it is a means of reconditioning behavior.

The giving of demerits falls into the same category as the awarding of stars. A demerit may serve as a temporary deterrent of anti-social behavior. If demerits are distributed too generously among the members of the class, the result may be that they lose their significance as penalties. Children may compete among themselves to receive the largest number of "bad marks." There is little, if anything, constructive in this technique.

Threats that are not carried out soon become a source of increased misbehavior. The young person learns early that some adults "take out" their emotional feelings in dire but idle threats of future penalties. Objective and unemotionally given warnings usually are heeded, however, especially if disregard of the warning is followed by an appropriate penalty.

Enforced penalties, such as standing in the corner of the room, writing, "I am sorry" one hundred times, or being detained after school hours, are following the "dunce cap" as discarded methods of punishment. Teachers are becoming interested primarily in bringing about changes *within the offender.* Corporal punishment is not permitted in most school communities, although some parents and school people recognize its value, if it is administered infrequently, judiciously, and without causing physical harm.

An offender must be made to suffer for his offense. We do not advocate the continuance of some of the "soft pedagogy" that still is being practiced. A young person should learn that he must obey just and reasonable authority, and consider the rights and property of other people. To be deprived temporarily of a much desired privilege that is related to his offense can be understood by the child and can help him develop greater self-control. To "lose face" in a group or with an admired teacher constitutes a severe penalty for most young people. Finally, one of the most effective ways of helping an average young person improve his attitudes and behavior probably is to let him "talk out" his difficulties and the reasons for his behavior. The teacher or counselor with whom he talks should be sympathetic but not sentimental, and must refrain from preaching. Rather should the teacher try to motivate him toward greater self-disciplining of his antisocial attitudes and behavior. Such changes in youthful behavior can be achieved only through adult patience and perseverance.

QUESTIONS AND TOPICS FOR DISCUSSION

1. Why is the development of self-discipline so important to the individual?
2. Show the value of self-discipline to a democratic way of life.
3. Discuss the influence on child behavior of the home, the school, and the class.
4. What are some of the causes of behavior difficulties of children?
5. To what extent should teachers be alert to the behavior of each child in class?
6. Study the lists of differences in emphasis concerning undesirable child behavior between teachers and mental hygienists; report on the probable bases of those differences.
7. By using examples, report on physiological status as a cause for behavior disturbance.

8. Outline an attitude-development program that can exert a positive influence upon the displayed attitudes of all the pupils in a school.
9. How does self-centeredness affect the behavior of a child? What can parents or teachers do to broaden the interests of the child and help him develop interest in others?
10. Why are children often unaware of the consequences of their acts?
11. To what extent do the mores of the group affect child behavior?
12. Discuss the relationship between inner urges and self-discipline.
13. What is the role of the teacher in the development of self-discipline?
14. Cite examples of disciplinary problems in which the teacher-pupil conference or interview relationship should have been used.
15. Discuss the importance of teacher personality in the development of good class discipline.
16. What are the dangers of too much teacher domination or of too much class freedom in relation to the development of self-discipline?
17. Enumerate five typical classroom behavior problems and analyze the factors that may be operative toward their arousal.
18. Prepare a statement which you believe constitutes a good code of behavior for children in the elementary school; in the junior high school. What differences, if any, should there be in these codes?
19. Discuss the correction of misbehavior through the use of demerits or of other forms of punishment.

SELECTED REFERENCES

Bernard, H. W., *Child Development and Learning*. Allyn and Bacon, Boston, 1973.

Coleman, J. C., *Psychology and Effective Behavior*. Scott Foresman, Chicago, 1969.

Crow, L. D., *Introduction to Education*, 3rd ed. Christopher, North Quincy, Mass., 1974.

Crow, L. D., and Crow, A., *Student Teaching in the Elementary School*. David McKay, N.Y., 1965.

Dreikurs, R., and Cassel, P., *Discipline without Tears*. Howthorne, N.Y., 1973.

Gammage, P., *Teacher and Pupil: Some Sociological Aspects*. Routledge & Kegan, N.Y., 1972.

Gnagey, W. J., *Psychology of Discipline in the Classroom*. Macmillan, N.Y., 1968.

Jessup, M. H., and Kiley, M., *Discipline: Positive Attitudes for Learning*. Prentice Hall, Englewood Cliffs, N.J., 1971.

Kujoth, J. S., *Teacher and School Discipline*. Scarecrow, Los Angeles, Calif. 1971.

LaGrand, L., *Discipline in the Secondary School*. Prentice Hall, Englewood Cliffs, N.J., 1969.

Miller, D. R., and Swanson, G. E., *Inner Conflict and Defense*. Holt, Rinehart & Winston, N.Y., 1960.

Ottaway, A. K., *Learning through Group Experience.* Fernhill, N.Y., 1966.

Rivlin, H. N., *Teaching Adolescents in Secondary Schools*, 2nd ed. Appleton-Century-Crofts, N.Y., 1961.

Rosenshine, B., *Teaching Behaviors and Student Achievement.* Fernhill, N.Y., 1971.

Sayre, J. M., *Teaching Moral Values through Behavior Modification.* Interstate, Danville, Ill., 1972.

Shaw, M., *Psychology of Small Group Behavior.* McGraw-Hill, N.Y., 1971.

Weiner, I. B., *Psychological Disturbances in Adolescence.* Wiley, N.Y., 1970.

PART IV

The Educative Process

9   *Learning: Principles, Theories, and Transfer Values*

By definition, the terms *development* and *adjustment* imply that learning is taking place. When we traced the developmental progress of the individual from conception to adulthood, and emphasized the significant bases of adjustment to various areas of life experiences, we were in effect discussing *learning*. The word *learn* is a commonly used term. The child *learns* his lessons; the adult refers to the fact that he *learns* about this or that person, condition, or situation through his observation, reading, or conversation with others.

People use the word *learn* loosely, to mean that they have discovered something new about someone or something, or have acquired a new point of view. They seldom stop to consider *why* they learn, *what* they learn, or *how* the learning occurs. Since it is the teacher's responsibility to guide the learning of his pupils, he needs to have a clear understanding of what learning is, why we should learn, and how learning takes place, both among different learners and in various areas of human development. Hence in this chapter we discuss principles and theories of learning; in later chapters we consider the application of learning principles to specific areas and phases of learning.

Essential Characteristics of the Learning Process

The kind and amount of learning achieved by any one learner in any area of learning are affected by many factors. Some of these are inherent in the learner himself; others are rooted in the conditions under which and the situations in which the learning takes place.

Learning—general and specific. Learning connotes change. Throughout his life an individual acquires new patterns of inner motivations or attitudes, and of overt behavior. These result from the changes taking place within himself. At the same time, he may be strengthening attitude and behavior patterns that are in the process of forma-

211

tion, or weakening old patterns that already have been established.

Learning takes place whenever an individual finds himself in a situation to which he cannot adjust through the utilization of customary modes of response, or whenever he must overcome obstacles that interfere with desired activities. The process of adjusting to or of overcoming obstacles may take place more or less unconsciously; without thinking much about what he is doing, the learner tries out one or another already formed habit of behavior until he hits upon a satisfactory response. Much of what is generally called "school learning," however, is engaged in with more or less awareness of the reason for the learning, what is being learned, and how the learning is taking place.

Learning is complex. At one and the same time, an individual is (1) learning new skills or improving those that already are operating, (2) building a store of information or knowledge, and (3) developing interests, attitudes, and ways of thinking. All of these areas of learning are interrelated; to varying degrees, as phases of the general educative process, they are dependent upon one another. The learner does not engage in one kind of learning to the exclusion of the others; he is helped or hindered in one area of learning by the kind and amount of learning that has been achieved or that is taking place in other areas.

For example, a woman attempts to bake an angel-food cake. She needs certain skills; she must be able to measure the ingredients exactly, combine them correctly, and beat them lightly. Required knowledges include the kinds and amounts of ingredients needed, the order of their combining, the kind of baking pan to be used, and the oven temperature and length of baking time. The reason for her to attempt the project may be her family's fondness for the cake. Her attitude toward this baking not only is motivated by her desire to please her family, but also reflects the extent of her experience in this form of activity and the degree of success achieved in former attempts.

Much of our learning consists of the formation of habit patterns as we are stimulated by conditions that surround us to imitate the behavior of others or to try out various forms of response. Learning satisfaction probably is greatest when we consciously attempt to make changes in our behavior that will bring about more successful ways of dealing with people and things. When school people began to emphasize self-motivation in learning, many children complained that they were tired of doing as they pleased; they wanted to know what they should do and what they were expected to learn. In their participation with other children in nondirected activities, these children probably were acquiring certain desirable habits and knowledge. Since they could not envision expected outcomes, however, and were unable to evaluate their degree of progress, they often became bored by their apparently useless activities. Some of these children acquired habit patterns that were neither personally satisfying nor socially constructive.

Enforced learning can have equally undesirable effects upon young people. The supposed learner may have little or no understanding of the reasons for his engaging in the learning; he may not recognize any need for it; he may give an outward semblance of "learning," but no fundamental changes are taking place within him. Here learner criticism is pointed toward the uselessness to him of the whole learning situation, since he cannot or will not accept its challenge. He becomes bored and turns to personally interesting activities. From participation in such activities, he may learn something that is far removed from what the teacher expects or hopes that he will learn.

Learning is engaged in consciously or unconsciously; it may be informal in that it represents learning as an aspect of an individual's daily situational experiences, or formal to the extent that the learning situation is organized according to definite objectives, planned procedures, and expected outcomes. The direction of the learning can be vertical and/or horizontal. *Vertical learning* applies to the addition of knowledge to that which already is possessed in a particular area of knowledge, the improvement of a skill in which some dexterity has been achieved, or the strengthening of developing attitudes and modes of thinking. *Horizontal learning* means that the learner is widening his learning horizons by attaining mastery of different kinds of knowledge, achieving competence in new forms of skill, gaining new interests, discovering new approaches to problem-solving, and developing different attitudes toward newly experienced situations and conditions. As learning proceeds both vertically and horizontally, that which is learned is integrated and organized as functioning units of expanding experiences.

Changes in learning progress. Viewed broadly, learning outcomes can be evaluated best in terms of their effects upon the kind of behavior displayed in every situation in which the individual is afforded an opportunity to give evidence of successful development and adjustment, as these are related to his learning. Ideally, learning would be based upon the premise that once learning activity is started, the learning will proceed on an even keel until complete mastery is achieved. For example, in the development of any skill, it might be assumed that the infant begins with no learned ability; learning would start and continue, step by step, until skill perfection is attained. This means that if learning begins at birth and continues regularly until complete mastery is reached, learning is cumulative, with no breaks, until a 100 per cent mastery has been achieved.

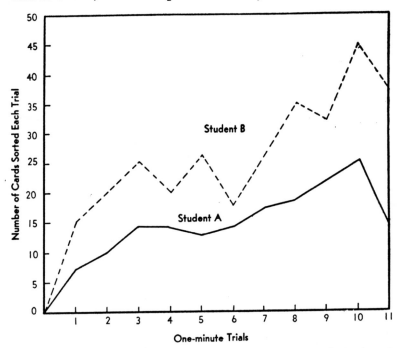

FIGURE 10. Number of Cards Sorted by Student A and Student B during Ten Consecutive, One-Minute Trials, and After a Lapse of Two Weeks of No Practice

In no area of learning does progress proceed in regular sequential order. Implicit in the interpretation of learning as change, however, is the fact that gradually the learner changes, during a learning activity in which he participates, from what he was when he started. His position on a learning curve at the end of a particular unit of learning will be different from what it was at the beginning. Certain factors that are inherent in the learning project, in the learner, and in the teacher's techniques may cause individual learning curves to show irregular but upward trends, the rate and limit of achievement varying from one learner to another. Figure 10 illustrates the relative performance, during the first ten trials, of two psychology students in a manual card-sorting experiment. Each trial consisted of one minute of practice in sorting numbered cards. Speed and accuracy of sorting were emphasized. The eleventh trial represents the amount of loss of skill after a two-week interval during which there was no practice.

The two students displayed differing ability to achieve success in this learning situation. Although the slower learner, A, achieved less, his learning progress was more consistent than that of the faster learner, B. Student A was a relaxed, conscientious student of average ability; B was an extremely bright student who wanted to excel. He became emotionally upset if his achievement did not parallel his ambitions. He was able to "pull himself together," however, and eventually achieve his goal. Trials four and six represent periods of frustration that served as self-motivators toward his achievement of the greatest number of cards sorted by the class. In the delayed-response trial, he also showed least "forgetting." Student A worked quietly and calmly and seemed to be satisfied to show some improvement in the project; B, on the other hand, was very much excited during the experiment. Throughout the ten trials, he commented upon the difficulties he was experiencing, and changed his position from standing to sitting.

A teacher should understand differences in rates and limits of learning, and relative speed of forgetting after practice or learning has ceased. Specific causes of success or failure in learning are discussed at length in subsequent chapters.

Factors that influence learning progress. Learning is self-initiated. A learning situation is set up, and a teacher attempts to guide the learning. Whatever change takes place within the supposed learner, however, depends upon *what he does to bring about the change.* This interpretation of learning is well stated in the following definition.

> Learning is a modification of behavior accompanying growth processes that are brought about through adjustment to tensions initiated through sensory stimulation. This definition brings out the important fact that all learning situations place the learner under stress, i.e., the need for doing something about the situation or the necessity of resolving motive forces. It further implies that the learner's habits or possibilities for action are inadequate to relieve these tensions except through adaptation or modification of behavior.[1]

[1] H. H. Remmers, E. R. Ryden, and C. L. Morgan, *Introduction to Educational Psychology*, Harper & Bros., New York, 1954, p. 252. Reprinted by permission.

The *stress* or *tension* referred to in this definition can initiate learning only insofar as the individual is aware of the need to do something about the situation. If this recognition is not present, there is no stress or tension. For example, an adult might agree that the more he knows and the more things he can do, the better able he might be to meet novel situations in which he is unprepared to participate at the time. An accomplished linguist once was heard to say that an individual who speaks many languages fluently has many personalities. Languages other than their own are studied in foreign schools. In America, students usually exhibit little more than an academic interest in the study of a foreign language. There is no recognition, here, of a felt need.

The lack of drive among Americans to achieve fluency in a language other than English probably can be explained by the fact that we have learned through experience that there are few places in the world in which a visiting American cannot find someone who has acquired sufficient command of English to meet the English-speaking visitors' needs. Since American tourist trade is welcomed by other countries, the people of these countries experience English-learning stresses. The import of differences of interest in learning a language holds for many other learning areas.

Adult attitudes toward learning. By the time an individual has reached adult status and has developed a relatively satisfactory adjustment to his accustomed life pattern, he not only forgets much that he had learned in school, but also his attitudes change toward some of his former school subjects. He generally is satisfied with what his "schooling" did for him in the way of preparation for adult responsibility. At the same time, if he discovers that he needs more education in order to meet a newly aroused need, he is likely to be motivated by the sensory stimulations from the conditions that aroused the need, or the situations in which his need was aroused.

Adult attitudes toward their learning experiences tend to influence them in their attitudes toward what the growing child should learn. Probably every parent wants his children to be better educated than he is, or at least as well educated. Parents often make the mistake of believing that their children are different from themselves. For example, during his developing years, a parent may have had no interest in continuing his education beyond the age required by law. Yet he expects his child to be able and willing to respond to every learning situation with success-achieving attitudes toward learning. As an adult he has come to recognize what the value to him would be now if he had continued his education, as his own parents probably had wanted him to do. Hence he expects the child to learn from his experiences.

To those of us who have studied about, worked with, and observed many such children participating in learning situations, such parental attitudes may appear to be unreasonable. Unconsciously, teachers may display similar attitudes. They expect all adolescents to be equally interested in and able to master high-school studies. That young people differ in their ability to learn and in their interest in certain learning areas is a fact that we, as teachers, must accept.

Learner attitudes. Learners differ greatly in their mental capacity to engage in the more difficult phases of learning and their readiness to start learning at a particular chronological age. Other factors also affect their degree of learning achievement. Some of these factors function so subtly that a teacher of a large class may have difficulty in discovering their presence or the strength of their influence upon a particular learner.

A person's background of learning, his interests, his social sensitivities, as well as his physical health and emotional condition, also exercise a potent effect upon his degree of learnability. The child who enters high school with a reading grade of five is not able to gain much thought from the pages of textbooks that have been written for children with a reading grade of nine or higher. A high-school student who starts the second year of a foreign language in a new high school after supposedly completing the first year's work in another school finds that he has completed the equivalent of only a half-year's work in his present school. Consequently, he is not likely to succeed in the second year's work.

During his early school years, the average child is so curious about his expanding world that he usually is interested in whatever he is stimulated to learn. He is relatively unself-conscious, and he participates cheerfully and sometimes eagerly in all learning activities. Learning situations become more complex and challenging, however. His degree of success, in competition with his classmates, becomes less satisfying. A consequent loss of interest may accompany his relative lack of success in a particular area of learning. Moreover, as he embarks upon secondary-school learning, changing interests and ambitions may cause the young person to be stimulated by his new desires and urges to respond to the challenge of learning in some areas, and to be completely uninterested in others.

The efficacy of the motives and incentives by which the learner is stimulated to learn differs with age, degree of readiness, interest, and sensitivity to elements in his social milieu. Nursery school, kindergarten, and elementary-school children thrill to the praise that they receive from their parents and teachers for their learning progress. The young child will repeat often a little verse or ditty which he learned at school. He proudly displays to anyone who will look at them his drawings and other craftwork. He informs his family concerning all the bits of information he has learned at school. He delights to share in adult conversation. He wants to learn. Unless other factors of influence interfere with his learning activities, he is motivated easily, and responds quickly to appropriate learning incentives. For most children, going to school becomes a major life activity. Adolescents, however, usually view their school learning activities as only one part of their entire experience pattern. To the extent that other interests and activities seem to make demands upon their time and energy, they may need to be strongly motivated toward a recognition of the value to them of achieving success in school learning.

Interest in learning can be stimulated best among adolescents through the utilization of incentives that are related to the fulfillment of their other adolescent interests and activities. At the same time, teen-agers may begin an interest in learning for its own sake. Thirst for knowledge itself, rather than interest in the practical application of knowledge, may stimulate an adolescent to study assiduously in one or another academic field.

Both children and adolescents respond to those elements in their social relationships that act as spurs to learning. In more restrained and less obvious ways, an adolescent may attempt, as does the child, to earn parental pride in his learning success, to win the approval of his teachers, and to gain prestige among his schoolmates. Learning that goes along with relative smoothness, and in which the learner is interested, usually is accompanied by a mild, pleasurable, emotional state. The satisfying pleasure that is derived from participation in the learning serves as a stimulator of continued learning activity.

If learning appears to be difficult or if the degree of desired success is not achieved, the learner of any age may experience strong emotional states of discouragement and/or anger. During a thwarted or frustrated state, learning is inhibited. The more discouraged or angered the individual becomes, the less able he is to improve in his learning. If the condition continues long enough, the young adolescent especially is moved to give up, and directs his energies into what appear to him to be more satisfying kinds of activity. Many high-school boys and girls who terminate their formal education as soon as the law allows them to leave school illustrate the effect of discouragement upon learning.

External factors. A young person's emotional refusal to continue learning activities may be caused by the fact that he is attempting to engage in learning activities that are too difficult for him. Curricular adjustment to learner needs, therefore, is a significant factor of influence upon learning success. Equally important are the teaching-learning conditions and the attitudes and methods of the teacher. A classroom situated on the first floor of a school building, with windows facing a noisy street, for example, makes learning difficult, as teacher and pupils must shout at one another to be heard above the din of passing automobiles and the loud talking of passers-by.

The methods used by the teacher to present learning materials, the techniques employed to stimulate learning interest, and the kind of results expected are closely related to the success-realization that the learners achieve. For example, at one time, the children of every grade were expected to achieve writing that was an exact imitation of a perfect model. It was not until Thorndike, as a result of his study of children's handwriting, constructed a handwriting scale, that grade standards in penmanship were developed.

Although the mental processes involved in learning are relatively the same for most learners, it does not follow that all techniques utilized to stimulate learners and learning activities will serve all learners effectively at each maturational stage of development. In other words, proved teaching techniques that are effective in the kindergarten, and in the first, second, third, and fourth grades may not be adequate either for the teachers of more mature learners or for the learners themselves.

Sensory and Perceptual Aspects of Learning

We have referred to the fact that learning is initiated through sensory stimulation. Learning cannot take place adequately unless the learner has sensory awareness of objects, people, or conditions, and is able to interpret the sensation correctly, or to *perceive* it.

Sensation and learning. In order that sensory stimulation initiate learning, the sense organs must function in such a way that the learner actually is stimulated. Defects in any sense organ may interfere with proper recognition of the elements of a learning situation. Especially is this true for sight and hearing. Inability to see well or to hear distinctly places a learner at a distinct disadvantage in the classroom. A child who cannot see the blackboard clearly from his seat must use so much energy in trying to decipher the writing on it that he is slow in attending to the content of the writing. As a result he may lag behind the others in responding to the task assigned.

Fortunately, most school people are aware of the effect of visual defects. The sight of each child is checked periodically, and recommendations for the wearing of glasses are made when necessary. Recommendation is not enough, however. Some parents foolishly refuse to obtain glasses for their children; others cannot afford them. Much teacher persuasion is needed, sometimes, to convince unwilling parents to meet the child's need.

There are cases in which eyesight is so poor that even the wearing of glasses does not help the wearer to decipher what is written on the blackboard. In such instances, the teachers should allow the pupil to sit in one of the front seats, and to change his seat to read what may be written on a blackboard or a chart in another part of the room. For the good of all learners, regardless of how adequate their sight may be, teachers should take great care that whatever appears on a blackboard is written clearly and in large enough letters or figures so that everyone in the room can read the writing easily. One common fault of teachers is to erase inadequately what had been written on the blackboard and then try to write over the former material. This is particularly bad if colored chalks are used. In some schools, *green* rather than *black* boards, and dustless chalk are used effectively to achieve greater readability.

Defective hearing is much more difficult to deal with than de fective sight. The teacher can become aware of the fact that a child "squints." There is no such obvious overt sign of a child's poor hearing. Young people are extremely sensitive to their suffering from a hearing defect. Many children try to disguise the fact that they are more or less hard of hearing; some children are not aware of the fact that their hearing is less acute than that of their classmates. Too often a teacher may accuse a learner of inattention, daydreaming, or lack of interest and effort, if the young person does not respond quickly to a question or directive or asks that it be repeated, or if he appears not to have heard what another pupil said during a class-discussion period.

Before a teacher decides that a learner is uninterested or "stupid," he should make sure that there is no hearing difficulty. Moreover, as we have said earlier, the teacher needs to speak clearly and distinctly at all times, but should refrain from shouting or loud talking. Similarly, as children participate in class discussions, their speech, too, should be clear and distinct, and what they say should be addressed to the class—not remain a secret between the teacher and the pupil. Mumbling and indistinct speech are especially characteristic of some students who sit in the front seats of a classroom in which the teacher is accustomed to sit or stand at his desk rather than to move around among the pupils.

Regardless of the adequacy of the sense organs of individual learners, it has been found that the combining of various sensory stimulations aids learning. For exámple, to see, to hear, and to touch provide greater opportunity to obtain correct sensory impressions of learning materials than is possible if only one sense organ is stimulated. The recognition of this learning principle has led to an increasing trend toward the utilization of many learning aids. In most modern classrooms there can be seen a great variety of specimens of one kind or another about which the learners read or talk, and examine by taking them in their hands and getting the "feel" of them. If an obtainable object merely is read about, children who have had no previous experience with that object may get queer notions of what it is like. Field trips are excellent learning aids to acquaint learners with objects, situations, or conditions that cannot be studied at first hand in the classroom.

It cannot be emphasized too strongly that success-achieving learning involves learner activity that includes reading and talking about, and *personally experiencing* the learning materials, insofar as the last kind of learning experience is possible. Personal experience does not constitute the whole of learning activity, however. Complete understanding involves correct perception as stimulated by touching or working with materials, and discovering *through appropriate reading* and *discussion* what are the inherent qualities, areas of usefulness, and relationships to others of its kind of any material of learning.

Perhaps we can illustrate our point of view in this respect by reference to preparation for teaching. Occasionally, a school administrator says to a beginning teacher, "Now you can forget all that you were taught about teaching. I'll make a good teacher of you as you work in your classroom with your pupils and learn through experience what you should do." It is interesting to note that the principal who makes a fine speech about learning through experience usually does all he can to procure an outstanding teacher-trainee from the point of view of what he terms "academic learning."

We admit that the reading of the material in a book, without some experience in dealing with young people, might afford insufficient sensory stimulation for accurate perception of children in action. Hence teacher-trainees are stimulated toward a better understanding of the young people whom they expect to teach and of the teacher's part in the teaching-learning situation: by *reading about* and *discussing these matters;* by *observing* the techniques and attitudes of their own instructors, as well as of teachers in the lower schools, and by *participating* in teaching-learning situations under guidance. The orientation programs for beginning teachers described in Chapter 18 gives evidence that *learning about* school ideals and procedures and teacher activities is desirable before one attempts to participate in the actual experience of teaching.

Gaining correct percepts. We have shown in the foregoing that adequate perception or the association of correct percepts with that which is sensed is dependent upon the ability to sense accurately. Inadequate sensation results in faulty perception. Not all errors of perception are the resultants of sensory defects, however. For an individual of any age to gain a complete and accurate percept of whatever stimulates him by way of the senses requires that he be exposed to all the facets of that which is sensed, and that his degree of mental alertness and interest and his background of experience enable him to recognize the relationships that exist among the various elements sensed.

"Pure" sensation probably is experienced only at birth. Perception begins when the baby's taste buds are stimulated by the milk that he receives; his body senses the action of being picked up or laid down; his skin sense organs respond to warmth or cold; he "hears" loud noises; he is hungry or thirsty. At first these perceptions are very simple and often inaccurate. Adults do not always realize that meager experiences during this early period of life (at any age, in fact) results in incomplete and faulty perception.

For example, a baby who customarily is served his orange juice in a particular glass or mug, drinks it with gusto. He has gained a perceptual pattern of the juice in that particular receptacle. His sensations and learned perception of the entire situation are satisfying because he likes the taste of the juice. Unwittingly, one morning, the mother serves him the juice in another cup or glass that is very different from the one that means good orange juice to him.

He refuses the juice and may even try to push the cup away from him. Although the adult takes a sip of the juice and engages in all the other eating and drinking stimulations that are common among mothers, she neglects to do the one thing that is needed to help the child drink his juice—put it into his regular cup. Instead, both the child and the mother may go into a tantrum, or the latter may call the doctor in haste because she believes the child to be ill. The belief that the baby is sick is strengthened by the fact that the child's emotional state may be accompanied by a fever condition. In this situation, both the child's and the mother's behavior is activated by false perception.

The achievement of accurate perception usually parallels experience with many different sensory stimulations, maturing mental abilities, and changing interests and ambitions. To the child, a watch is a bright and glittering plaything; to the wearer, the watch is a timepiece which may or may not keep accurate time; to the watchmaker, it is a delicate mechanism consisting of many tiny parts that must bear certain relationships to one another if the wearer is to perceive it as an accurate timepiece.

Shifts in perception. During his waking hours an individual is perceiving one thing or another, unless he is absorbed in thought. The experienced teacher has learned to shift his attention so quickly and so efficiently that apparently he perceives, at the same time, what each child is doing, the room temperature, weather conditions outside, the time of the day, his lesson plan and learning materials, sounds outside the classroom, persons that pass his open door, condition of the classroom floor, and his own fatigue, thirst, or hunger. He so has trained himself. that, although he perceives all of the sense-stimulating factors and conditions of the situation, he keeps many of them on the fringe of attention and focuses his attentive perception on pupil activity and his own reactions in the teaching-learning situation.

In the same classroom situation, the pupils differ in what they are able and willing to perceive. Their attention may wander from their learning activities, if they perceive that it is snowing, that a pencil needs sharpening, that their leg muscles pain because they have been in one position too long, or that their arm and finger muscles are tired from writing. An adolescent boy or girl may be so much interested in a classmate of the opposite sex that little if anything else in the classroom is observed except the object of budding "puppy love." Every movement of the other is perceived, especially glances thrown in the direction of the adorer. As he observes the object of adolescent adoration, he may be getting false percepts concerning the one observed. Because of his emotional state, he does not perceive the other's true characteristics but idealizes them in terms of what he wants to perceive. This statement is corroborated by the comments made by adults when, in retrospect, they review their adolescent "love affairs." Invariably they are likely to say, concerning one or more of the young people who during high-school days seemed to be paragons of attractiveness, "I can't understand what I saw in her (him). Why, she (he) actually was ugly and stupid."

Value of correct percepts. Correct percepts are basic to learning. The inner emotional state, interest, or attitude at the time of the sensory stimulation has a potent effect upon the way the stimulus is perceived. We all know about usually normal perceivers who make occasional errors, such as perceiving the ringing of the doorbell to be that of the telephone; erroneously recognizing a stranger as an acquaintance because of similarity of voice, dress, or some other characteristic; in the dark, mistaking a gravestone for a ghost; evaluating length or size of objects to be smaller or larger than they are; reading what is not written, or hearing things differently from the way they are said. You can recall many similar examples of false perception that have been experienced either by yourself or by your associates. These illusions are not serious, unless they are experienced continually and are accompanied by emotional upsets; they then can be symptoms of emotional disturbance or mental illness.

Many adults show evidence of inadequate or incorrect knowledge or understanding of things about them or of past events (especially historical), or display relatively immature attitudes. In most instances, these errors can be traced to earlier inadequate formation of percepts. Parents and teachers are responsible for the development of a young person's perceptual understanding. Sometimes, adults seem to believe that the child, unaided, will come to perceive and to identify objects, and to understand situations in an adult fashion. Learning cannot proceed without the experiencing of sensation and perception. Perception must be accurate and suited to comprehension level. Progressively accurate and complete perception of sensed material is achieved through learning. A few simple reminders concerning the learning of adequate percepts may be helpful to teachers.

1. The infant focuses on movement, thereby gaining perceptual understanding of space relationships and object identity.
2. Usually, first percepts include general outlines; details are filled in later.
3. The child does not perceive all the details in his environment.
4. Mental set and interest influence what is perceived.
5. The child should not be expected to respond to a variety of sensory stimuli simultaneously with accurate perception of all of them.
6. As the child or adolescent is stimulated toward learning in any area, he should begin by achieving simple, *correct* percepts upon which can be built gradually increasing perceptual understanding.
7. The process of broadening and intensifying the meaning of any one percept may be a lifetime job. New facets constantly are discovered by an individual because his interests and needs initiate the experiencing of new sensory stimulations, and he attempts to gain a usable understanding of them.
8. Concepts are built upon percepts. All of an individual's mental activities are influenced by the correctness and adequacy of the percepts that he has been helped to form.

Various Explanations of the Learning Process

Too many young people fail to achieve success in advanced areas of learning because their earlier learned percepts were so badly formed that they lack the background of understanding needed for continued study. Various psychologists have attempted to explain the ways in which sensory awareness is transformed gradually into perceptual and consequent conceptual understanding and problem-solving.

Some experimental studies in animal learning. In the early days of experimentation, the subjects were rats, dogs, and other animals. Rats were stimulated under controlled conditions to learn to find their way through a maze, for example, in order to reach food that had been placed at the exits of the mazes. Experiments in animal learning were popular because fully controlled learning conditions could be set up for animals more easily than for human beings.

Experimental studies of animal learning dealt mainly with the development of simple skills. The fact that the maturation period for animals is much shorter than that of human beings gave experimenters an opportunity to study the developmental cycle much more quickly than would be possible in the case of a child. It was assumed that a child's early learning parallels the behavior of the lower forms of living organisms.

It could not be discovered to what extent, if any, animals can reason on the human level. Hence experimentation in animal learning has been limited to observable behavioral changes that seem to take place in terms of appropriate motivating stimuli, including the extent to which and the rate at which animals tend to "forget" or to lose competence in the form of behavior that is experimentally conditioned. Several principles of learning were propounded as a result of such experimentation, especially from those experiments conducted by Thorndike and his associates, and by John B. Watson. The most significant of these principles probably are: (1) behavior of an animal can be conditioned if he is stimulated to engage in the activity as a means of fulfilling a felt need, such as obtaining desired food which he sees or smells when he is hungry; (2) the number of times that the learning activity is practiced, first as goal-seeking, later in the form of a habit, affects the length of time that the particular form of activity will remain a part of the learner's general behavior pattern.

The behavior of a rat, for example, in his first attempt to find his way through a maze in search of the cheese at its exit is characterized by many wrong turns before he eventually reaches his goal. A second trial, motivated in the same way, gives evidence of fewer waste movements and a consequent reduction in time of performance. Each succeeding trial, even when the food is removed, shows that learning habits are being formed. The rat goes quickly and directly from entrance to exit of the maze. The more he practices the activity, the more expert he becomes in performance. One practice session results in his barely learning what he should do. As his behavior pattern becomes fixed with practice, it can be said that he has *overlearned* the activity. The greater his extent of overlearning, the greater will be his ability to engage successfully in the activity even after a period of no practice. If the stimulating reward of food is removed too early in the total learning experience, the habit may not be fixed firmly enough for him to continue in a nonrewarding situation; he may refuse to continue the practice. His refusal will be more definite if he is punished in some fashion when he reaches the exit of the maze.

Evolving theories of learning. Human learning resembles that of animals. Young people respond to the earning of a reward as the goal to be achieved through learning practice. As has been said earlier, for the young child the reward usually needs to be extrinsic and immediately obtained; with increasing maturity and continued building of self-realizing attitudes, the desired reward becomes intrinsic and further removed in time from the learning practice. Moreover, with human beings, as with animals, permanency of learning and delay of forgetting bear a positive relationship to the amount of overlearning that has taken place.

As a result of much experimentation in animal-learning and greater emphasis upon setting up laboratory experiments involving the learning of young people, valuable knowledge has been gained concerning the influence upon the degree of learning success of such factors as: physical and mental maturation, readiness, emotional reactions, interests and attitudes, and motivation. We talk and write glibly about stimulation of learning behavior changes and general and specific educational objectives and outcomes. Yet, if we are honest, we must admit that our understanding of *what actually is taking place within the learner,* as he changes in knowledge mastery, skill competence, or attitude expression, is incomplete, vague, and still in the realm of theory. According to studies, the inner reactions that accompany the functioning of what generally are referred to as the "higher mental processes" appear to be especially elusive. The most significant of the theories that have been propounded as explanations of the way in which human beings learn are reviewed here briefly.[1]

Connectionism in Learning

From the days of Aristotle, it has been recognized that, as an individual learns, relationships of one kind or another are present. Psychologists, biologists, and other students of human nature and behavior development have attempted to discover what the associations in mental life are, and how they function. Some of the hypotheses concerning mental associations, that had been presented by earlier writers, were organized in applicable form by Edward L. Thorndike. During the early part of this century, he propounded the *bond hypothesis,* based upon the physiological aspects of stimulus and response patterns, as representing synaptic connections between neurons.

According to Thorndike, learning consists of the relaying of impulses that start when elements of the external world stimulate

[1] For a more detailed and intensive treatment of these theories, consult L. P. Thorpe and A. M. Schmuller, *Contemporary Theories of Learning,* The Ronald Press Co., New York, 1954.

the sensitive neurons of an appropriate sense organ. By way of these *afferent* neurons, the impulse travels to the brain or spinal cord and then is transmitted through the *efferent* neurons to the appropriate muscles and glands. Thus, an intricate pattern of neural impulses, which may be electro-chemical in nature, is set up in the form of stimulus-response reactions.

Thorndike described his neural bond theory of learning briefly in the following words:

> The essence of my account of the physiological mechanism of learning may be stated as follows, independently of any hypothesis about the power of the ends of a neurone to move. The connections formed between situation and response are represented by connections between neurones and neurones whereby the disturbance, or neural current, arising in the former is conducted to the latter across their synapses. The strength or weakness of the connection means the greater or less likelihood that the same current will be conducted from the former to the latter rather than to some other place. The strength or weakness of the connection is a condition of the synapse.[1]

Thorndike's "Laws of Learning." Thorndike's concept of the synapse as the axone-dendrite connection of the nerve impulse led him to the formulation of his well-known laws of learning: the Law of Effect, the Law of Exercise, and the Law of Readiness. Basic to these laws is the interpretation of learning as a series of connections between a possible external stimulus, (S) and an inner expected response, (R).

The Law of Effect means that, when an organism is stimulated and a reaction follows, the connection is strengthened, provided that a feeling of satisfaction accompanies the stamping-in process. The connection, however, may be weakened and eventually discontinued if the reaction is dissatisfying or annoying to the organism. The effect of feeling-tone upon learning leads to the continuance of practice in learning. Hence the implications of the Law of Exercise are that a neural connection between a stimulating force and the organism is strengthened through satisfying repetition of the response (Law of Use); contrariwise, an unsatisfying or annoying S-R connection that is not used for a length of time results in the weakening of the connection (Law of Disuse). Readiness to

---

[1] E. L. Thorndike, *Educational Psychology:* Vol. I, *The Original Nature of Man,* Teachers College, Columbia University, New York, 1913–1914, p. 227. Reprinted by permission.

react strengthens the neural connection or the S-R bond. The functioning of these laws was illustrated earlier in the behavior of a rat in a maze.

Thorndike formulated other corollary or secondary laws that affect learning. These can be described in essence as follows: (1) if a person at first cannot find the correct response to a novel situation, he will proceed to attempt various responses until a satisfying response is discovered by a kind of trial-error-trial-success learning (Law of Multiple Response); (2) an individual's response to a situation depends upon his inner condition, and his attitude toward or interest in the stimulating situation (Law of Attitude, Disposition, or Set); (3) an individual has the ability to select from among the elements of a situation the one or more which are best suited to his present needs (Law of Partial Activity); (4) an individual's response to a novel situation is influenced by the extent to which there are elements in this situation that are like those with which the individual has had previous experience, or are *identical elements* (Law of Assimilation or Analogy); (5) as the result of sufficient practice in responding to a specific situation, a response becomes habitual in situations that are like it, even though the original stimulating situation is absent (Law of Associative Shifting).

By 1929, Thorndike had modified his original laws of learning. He discovered that practice may yield successful learning results only when it is satisfying practice. Satisfaction from participation in a learning activity strengthens the S-R connection, but annoyance or punishment does not necessarily weaken the connection.

Critical comment. That learning brings about observable changes in behavior and that the processes by which these changes are effected seem to follow Thorndike's principles to a greater or lesser extent cannot be denied. His bond hypothesis, based upon the interaction of the million of neurons composing the nervous system, may be doubtful; the theory of brain connections as propounded by Thorndike is not substantiated by research concerning the structure of the brain. We know that the changes in behavior that take place during learning are associated with inner changes that operate according to certain regulating principles. Whether Thorndike's bond hypothesis is correct still needs to be verified through continued research.

Some psychologists accept the practical implications of S-R connections as propounded by Thorndike. They are not certain, however, that his explanation of learning in terms of synaptic connections gives the answer to the way in which inner changes occur during learning, although this hypothesis probably is as logical as any theory that, to the present, has been presented. Thorndike did imply that we probably cannot view learning only as a series of mechanical S-R connections.

We know that the degree of success gained by a learner in any learning situation is closely related to his *inner states* at the time of the learning. Consequently, we need to know something about the inner states of the organism and their effects upon the kind of response made to the stimulating situation. If we include the general state of the organism at the time of learning stimulation, learning then can be described as S-O-R connections; the O represents all those inner states or conditions that affect the extent to which a stimulus situation is able to arouse and to continue to satisfy exercise of the connections. These inner states or conditions include: physical and mental status; felt needs, urges, and drives to action, and personal attitudes, interests, and ambitions.

Learning as Conditioning

The explanation of learning as conditioning also is based upon the functioning of the nervous system. Conditioning follows a pattern similar to Thorndike's theory of learning as S-R connections. Behavioristic systems, however, tend to emphasize reflex patterns that involve the functioning of nerve fibers.[1] In learning viewed as conditioning, the stimulus situation, such as a list of numbers to be added or a bit of verse to be memorized, is presented to the learner. The correctness of his addition or the degree of his retention of the memorized material then is measured. Guthrie's explanation of what takes place during conditioning follows:

> . . . it is our desire to apply the principle to material that can be observed and material with which the principle can be verified. Our position is that what is associated is a stimulus and a response. It would perhaps be more exact to say that what is associated is some stimulation of sense organs and a corresponding muscular contraction or glandular secretion. By calling them associated, we mean that the stimulation has become the occasion for the response because of a past association of the two. Both stimulus and response are observable.

[1] For a more detailed discussion of the structure and functions of the nervous system, consult C. T. Morgan, and E. Stellar, *Physiological Psychology*, 2nd ed., McGraw-Hill, New York, 1950. Also, J. F. Fulton, *Physiology of the Nervous System*, 3rd ed., Oxford University Press, New York, 1949.

Only by using observable and nameable items in our theory can we hope to illustrate it, apply it, or to verify it.[1]

Pavlov's experiments. Pavlov's experimentation with the conditioning of the responses of dogs is well known. The classical example is that in which Pavlov attempted to induce a dog's flow of saliva by ringing a bell. A tube was attached to the salivary glands of the dog through an incision in the cheek. Each time that food was given the dog through automatic devices (the observer was hidden from the dog's view), a bell was rung. This combination of presenting food and ringing a bell was repeated until the production of salivary secretions, that, before the experiment had been associated with the presentation of food only, now was stimulated by the ringing of the bell without the food. The response (salivary flow) had become associated with a new stimulus (ringing of a bell). The dog had been conditioned to respond to a new stimulus with an habitual response.

As a result of his experimentation, Pavlov discovered that desired conditioning was achieved more quickly under rigidly controlled laboratory conditions; that the new response to a stimulus tends to be less strong than it was to the "old" stimulus, and that the mental set of the subject of an experiment is an important factor in degree of conditioning achieved.[2] It generally is impossible to conduct experiments in children's learning in rigidly controlled learning situations. Moreover, human learning must take into account many extraneous factors which are not found in a simple stimulus-response situation, as exemplified by Pavlov's experiment. Hence simple conditioning of human behavior can be found only in specific learning situations such as associating an English word with its French counterpart until an habitual relationship is established as "Yes = Oui." Achieving comprehension and skilled use of a foreign language represents a much more complex learning situation, however.

Behaviorism. Experimentation aimed at conditioning children is associated with the name of John B. Watson, whose theory of learning

[1] E. R. Guthrie, "Conditioning: A Theory of Learning in Terms of Stimulus, Response and Association," in the *Psychology of Learning*, 41st Yearbook, The National Society for the Study of Education, 1942, Pt. II, University of Chicago Press, Chicago, 1943, p. 23. Reprinted by permission.
[2] See I. P. Pavlov, *Conditioned Reflexes*, Oxford University Press, London, 1927.

usually is termed _behaviorism_. Behavior itself, not consciousness, is the fundamental factor in learning. According to Watson, it would be possible to make whatever changes one wished in the behavior of an individual if one were able to take the child at birth and continue to expose him to carefully selected and controlled learning situations.

In one of his well-known experiments, Watson conditioned an eleven-months-old child to fear a white rat (with which the child had been friendly) by making a loud noise behind the child's back as the latter was patting the rat. By repetition of this situation, Watson succeeded in bringing about extreme fear responses on the part of the child at the sight of the rat alone. He also reconditioned, or unconditioned, a child's attitude of fear of a white rabbit to that of friendliness toward the animal.

Like those of Pavlov, Watson's experiments were conducted under rigidly controlled conditions. However, he presented suggestions for the early conditioning of young children that emphasized caring for the physical growth needs of the child and of disregarding his emotional needs. For a time, Watson's theory of baby-rearing was practiced enthusiastically by some parents.[1]

A modern exponent of behaviorism is Edwin R. Guthrie, who emphasizes the _principle of contiguity_ in learning. According to Guthrie, "A combination of stimuli which has accompanied a movement will on its recurrence tend to be followed by that movement." [2] Basing his theory upon the S-R hypothesis, Guthrie regarded the response as consisting of two types: _movement_ and _act_. The former concerns glandular and motor functioning; the latter represents the form of behavior (act) that results from stimulated movements.

Learning takes place when associations are made among S-R units through contiguity in time and space. Acts of behavior are set in motion by "drives" initiated by the many S-R associations that are made. To Guthrie, learning is action. Since there can be associative inhibition as well as associative drive, he believes that "effective practice is conducted in the general situation in which we desire the future performance to be given." [3] Habit formation, forgetting, and

[1] See J. B. Watson, _Psychology from the Standpoint of a Behaviorist_, J. B. Lippincott Co., Philadelphia, 1919; also, J. B. Watson, _Physiological Care of Infant and Child_, W. W. Norton & Co., New York, 1928.
[2] E. R. Guthrie, _The Psychology of Learning_, Harper & Bros., New York, 1952, p. 23.
[3] _Ibid._, p. 32.

motivation are explained in terms of stimuli and response association.

Application of conditioning. A habit is formed by one association replacing or supplanting another when or if a continuous, disturbing stimulus produces activity by which is set up a series of associations and movement sequences. Forgetting consists of associative inhibition. The elimination of undesirable acts or responses is best achieved by the substitution for them of opposite desirable responses, or *reconditioning*. In this way, the former responses are inhibited or forgotten. To prevent the "forgetting" of desirable responses or acts, continued stimulus-response associations must be practiced in the form of associative conditioning. Motivation is regarded by Guthrie as the initiation by appropriate stimuli of activity directed at the achieving of a goal that has been attained previously by such activity. Goal-directed activity represents effectively stimulated bodily movements.

Hence school learning consists of the bringing about of sequences of movements through associations with appropriate stimuli that will lead to desired behavior changes. Learning then is explained by behaviorists as a continuing exchange of stimulus-response patterns rather than as rooted in association of ideas. The forming of ideas (ideation) implies movement. Learning as conditioning is dependent upon change of stimulation, not upon mental processes as such. Emphasis is placed upon the associations of stimulus situations with behavior responses, the elements of which can be measured objectively.

Learning as Gestalt Organization

In opposition to other explanations of learning that emphasize the strengthening of specific responses which are initiated by appropriate stimulus-situations, learning such as gaining *insight* is based upon the assumption that there exists in each natural phenomenon an essential unity which represents more than the sum of its parts. This whole is the *Gestalt* or configuration. One perceives not a single part or figure of a whole or ground. According to Koffka: "The figure depends for its characteristics upon the ground on which it appears. The ground serves as a *framework* in which the figure is suspended and thereby determines the figure . . . we can demonstrate the framework character of the ground by its influence on the shape of the figure." [1]

[1] From *Principles of Gestalt Psychology* by Kurt Koffka, copyright 1935, by Harcourt, Brace & Co., Inc., New York, p. 184. Reprinted by permission.

Functioning of insight. According to the Gestaltists, the universe is patterned. It can be assumed that there is some similarity between the objective, stimulating structure and the structure of the perceptual pattern. The concept of "form" is applied also to experience. The perception of a form, configuration or Gestalt does not result from an analysis or breaking down of its parts. For the Gestaltist, recognition of the significance or meaning of the configuration is through a kind of cortical or neural organization that can be called power or insight. For example, the solution of a creative problem comes to you suddenly, after days of struggling with it. Again, appreciation of an artistic production is not dependent upon the elements that compose it. The total form or configuration impresses you favorably or unfavorably. The gaining of insight depends upon the degree of maturity and background of experience. However, once insight into a situation or experience has been achieved, the insight will help the understanding of similar situations.

Application to learning. The implications of the Gestalt theory can be found in our current attitudes toward learners and learning. Concerning personality development, Thorpe and Schmuller wrote:

> In the process of protecting integration, with which the school is concerned, there should be continual care regarding the child's personality problems, his intellectual growth, and his psychological needs. Since Gestalt theory is conceived of as movement of an individual in a field, such situations should be presented as will serve as stimuli suitable for motivating pupil learning to its fullest extent. The teacher in the classroom will play no small part in this process. Upon him will depend many of the judgments which must be made from time to time in the maintenance of integrated pupil personalities. In both elementary and secondary schools, the individual instructor will need to assume the role, not only of mentor, but of counselor and confidante as well.[1]

Piecemeal and unrelated learning is giving way to attempted integration of a young person's learning experiences with the total pattern of his life experiences, past, present, and future. We are stressing the need of every child to be a part of the class group. The teacher no longer is considered to be outside the learning situation, directing learning activities and measuring results. In a modern classroom one is likely to find everyone in the room, including

---

[1] Louis P. Thorpe, and Allen M. Schmuller, *Contemporary Theories of Learning,* copyright 1954, The Ronald Press, New York, p. 251. Reprinted by permission.

the teacher, sharing co-operatively in all those many activities that constitute a teaching-learning situation. Viewed thus, the classroom itself, its equipment, and all those who meet in it would constitute, ideally, a program of learning based upon the Gestalt theory.

Functionalism

The functional approach in education has grown out of the acceptance of the concept of individual adaptation to environment. The child needs to learn to adjust to the requirements of his life experiences. Functionalism, basically, is not a theory; it is an outgrowth of many physiological and psychological concepts. Robert Woodworth, one of the outstanding proponents of the dynamic, functional approach in learning, was accustomed, in talking with his confreres, laughingly to label himself as a "middle-of-the-roader." His associates still are applying to educational philosophy and practice whatever of each current theory of learning seems appropriate.

In the functional approach to learning, the developing of ideas and other mental activities are necessary components of the learning process. Emphasis is placed, however, upon the direct and immediate overt activity of the learner. The learner, through his own activity, can be expected to make whatever changes in his thinking seem needed to reach his goal-directed activity. This point is discussed further in Chapter 12.

Perhaps the operational point of view, interpreted to refer to the changes in performance that result from learning practice, may seem to emphasize observable, measurable performances to the extent that the more subjective and abstract phases of learning may be underplayed. This is not necessarily true. The dynamic approach to learning, influenced by the philosophy of Dewey and his associates, is concerned with observable activity, but takes into consideration also the mental concomitants of observable and measurable behavior.

Dewey's contribution. John Dewey viewed learning as problem-solving. Regardless of the way in which changes in observable behavior are linked with inner changes, Dewey claimed that life constitutes a series of problems, all of which are more or less serious. These problems need to be solved by the individual if he is to survive. Hence learning should revolve around problems that are suited to the maturation level and experience background of the learner. The child learns through *thinking* and *doing*. In Chapter 12, we consider the learner as a problem-solver. At this point, we are interested only in the relationship that exists between Dewey's contribution and functionalism. Dewey was a functionalist to the extent that he believed in the dynamic approach to learning. He viewed the child as the center of learning. He was concerned with the overt behavior of the learner. At the same time, he emphasized, without explaining inner structural and functional bases, the importance of *reasoning* as the means whereby an individual achieves social competence.

The eclectic point of view. There probably are few if any educators who, in their procedures and practices, conform completely to any single theory of learning. Thorndike's laws of learning, conditioning, and the gaining of insights function in learning situations. There is much to commend the functional or dynamic approach to learning. Learning implies activity. Hence functionalism has exercised considerable influence upon modern education. Objections to its emphasis upon *overt activity* as the basis of learning certainly need be considered. Yet, many practical followers of the functional point of view are achieving an effective balance between subjective and mechanical explanations of learning.

The reader probably will discover for himself, as he reads about, discusses, and observes or participates in teaching-learning situations, that the utilization of the eclectic approach to learning principles attempts to apply whatever is desirable in the various theories to the task of guiding the learning of young people toward the achievement of constructive educational outcomes.[1]

Integrating Learning through Transfer

Transfer of training is a popular term among educators. The idea inherent in the phrase is not new. For many years, school people have recognized the value to an individual of his ability to apply what he learns in school situations to life experiences. Hence psychologists have made many attempts to explain how transfer takes place. Educators have been and still are concerned with the problems of selecting curriculum materials and of devising teaching techniques that will enable the learner to carry over what he learns in one situation to other learning situations or to out-of-school activities.

Meaning and importance of transfer. Transfer of learning or transfer of training can be defined broadly as the carry-over of knowledge,

[1] For an interesting treatment of the eclectic point of view in learning, see L. P. Thorpe, and A. M. Schmuller, *op. cit.*, chap. 13.

skill, thinking, or attitude habits from one learning situation to another. This concept of transfer includes the extent to which and the ways in which skills, knowledges, attitudes, or thinking patterns that are acquired through learning, either formal or informal, become a part of an individual's total behavior pattern and function in his life relationships. Transfer, thus interpreted, permeates every area of life activities. It exerts a powerful influence over the degree of success which an individual attains in solving problems of adjustment to, and in, all the many experiences that constitute his daily reactions to people, things, and situations.

We constantly apply to any one situation those recognitions, attitudes, and modes of behavior that functioned successfully in another situation. The other depended, in turn, upon how we reacted in a situation previous to *it*. For the average adult, and probably also for the developing child, there are few if any *new* situations. Rather are there *novel* situations, in that they bear some likeness to those which have been experienced previously. The novel situation introduces one or more differences that, as they form the whole, require responses that give evidence of recognition of the presence of that which is different. The problem then is to discover ways in which the likenesses and the differences can be combined so that the situation is met successfully. If there is no ready pattern for meeting the differences that have been recognized, additional learning may be needed before the entire situation is understood. Situations like these occur often in the life of an average individual.

The school's responsibility. In all learning situations, the time factor is extremely important. One of the common "gripes" of teachers is that curricula are so full that everything cannot be covered. Their problem then becomes one of selecting, from all the material included in the syllabus, those learning areas that to them seem to be most significant from the point of view of usefulness to the learner. What are the areas of general competence in which an individual should be proficient to participate constructively in the world of affairs? What knowledge, skills, and attitudes should result from his formal school experiences that will fit him to meet out-of-school activities? In what ways and how can his learnings in various school areas become so interrelated that they function in an integrated fashion when he needs them? These are questions that must be considered carefully by curriculum constructors, college instructors of methods classes, school administrators, and teachers in the classroom.

Many subtle factors influence the extent to which transfer of learning constitutes a carry-over from one field of learning to another. The more intelligent a learner is, the more likely he is to grasp relationships. Learner interest also is important. If a young person experiences a strong drive to master certain learning materials because of their value to him, he tends to view his learning personally. He constantly applies mentally, if not actually, what he is learning to the ways in which it can be used. He notes relationships that may exist between one area of learning and other areas that can be associated with his practical interests and activities.

Curriculum-makers who are concerned with learning materials in various areas no longer limit the expenditure of all of their efforts in decision-making concerning the content to be mastered in their own particular field. Specific-field experts are getting together to discover to what extent educational objectives, general and specific, and common grounds of learning are related to their particular field of curriculum building, so that the learner's concepts can be enlarged in terms of transfer among various areas of learning.

Bases of transfer. There is no doubt among educators concerning the value of producing constructive and desirable changes in a learner's behavior that will function in various situations. There is considerable uncertainty, however, concerning the ways in which transfer takes place. Before the twentieth century, the accepted basis for the functioning of transfer in learning was rooted in faculty psychology. It was assumed that exercise of the mind, or mental discipline, would prepare the learner to meet all practical situations. He would become so well trained in general approaches to problem-solving that all he needed to do would be to apply these general mental disciplines to specific situations.

Hence subjects such as mathematics, Latin, and logic were taught as mind discipliners, regardless of their practical application to life activities except as a particular learner might become a "teacher" of the subject. With the death of faculty psychology, the disciplinary aspect of learning lost favor, although some teachers of abstract subject matter areas still defend these areas in terms of disciplinary values.

Thorndike, as could be expected, believed that transfer from one area of learning to another took place only to the extent to which there was identity between the elements of the transferred learning. These identical elements may be in the form of content, method, aim, or attitude. Any elementary fact of experience that is repeated to the point of completeness in various situations will be transferred to all situations in which it is a factor. For example, the color *red* first might be associated by the child with his *red* ball. As he enlarges his experiences with the color red (red dress, red pencil, red flower), he learns to identify this color in any situation it is found.

Different shades of red may cause difficulties. In the beginning, anything is red that is the shade of his red ball. It is only as he experiences many shades of the color and hears all of them called *red* that he attaches redness to shades of red. The specific descriptive terms that are appropriate to various shades of red may not serve as identifiers of similarity, even to the adult. Recently, a man referred to a brick-red object as a "funny shade of yellow."

Thorndike modified his original concept of "identical element" to refer not entirely to identity in the object or situation but rather to the mental processes which have the "same cell action in the brain as their physical correlate." [1]

Woodworth and other psychologists later modified Thorndike's concept of identical *elements* to that of identical *components* or constituents. There may be great complexity of a functional or partly functional component that may be present in two situations, giving them identity or likeness.

Charles Judd [2] introduced the concept of transfer as synonymous with *generalization*. Transfer in behavior takes place when the individual comes to recognize the general meaning or implication of various specific situations. A child learns to be punctual in his arrival at school in the morning. It is only as he experiences the need of being punctual or prompt in the fulfillment of other responsibilities and activities that he achieves a general idea of punctuality that carries over into all situations in which punctuality or promptness is involved. These may include promptness in submitting written reports or assignments, punctuality in returning home from a date, and punctuality in arriving at a friend's home or at a place of entertainment. In terms of Judd's theory, many American adults have not yet gained a full understanding of the meaning of punctuality nor of the ability to apply this generalized term to many phases of their *own* behavior. The perennial lateness of Mr., Mrs., and Miss

---

[1] From E. L. Thorndike, *Educational Psychology, Briefer Course,* Bureau of Publications, Teachers College, Columbia University, New York, 1916, p 269.

[2] C. H. Judd, *Educational Psychology,* Houghton Mifflin Co., Boston, 1939, chapter 27.

America illustrates this point. Lack of punctuality, however, may be the result of the transfer of other learned generalizations that to an individual may seem to be more important than punctuality.

The Gestaltists modify the theory of generalization as an explanation of transfer in learning. To them the learning of a meaningful configuration or Gestalt represents a kind of organization that, with continued learning, modifies the organism. A learner acquires an integrated system of responses as he participates in a learning situation. This is repeated as a whole in other situations in which it is applicable. If the learned configuration or Gestalt is not appropriate to a specific situation, the individual seeks further modifications of his behavior until a satisfying configuration is achieved. This then remains habitual, until or unless further modification and changed Gestalts seem desirable. The successive gaining and utilization of insight, of course, will affect the degree to which an individual adapts himself to changing situations, each of which constitutes an integrated whole.

Areas of transfer. Transfer effects may be positive or negative. If the same response is appropriate to two stimuli, there is positive transfer; if one stimulus requires two responses, the transfer can be said to be negative. Negative or detrimental transfer can be illustrated in the spelling of the word *receive*, for example. Having learned to spell words such as believe, relieve, or retrieve correctly, a child tends to spell receive as *recieve*. Another example is that of a person whose accustomed language is German. He may experience considerable difficulty in mastering correct forms of English expressions. To the foreigner the English language appears to be made up of exceptions. For example, according to their spelling, the pronunciation of the words *though, through, tough, bough,* and *cough* could be expected to be similar.

The method of approach in learning and teaching techniques constitutes a factor of the extent to which transfer of learning can be encouraged. At the beginning of a school year, a teacher receives pupils who had been taught by different teachers during the preceding year. Habits developed in the previous class may have a positive or a negative effect upon a learner's adjustment to his present teaching-learning experience. A pupil whose former teacher used teaching approaches and methods very similar to those of the present teacher will find that there is considerable positive transfer for him from the old to the new learning situation. The positive areas include: accustomed study and work habits, the display of teacher-expected attitudes, and favorable responses to general classroom management. Contrariwise, the child, whose former teacher's procedures were very different from those of his present teacher, may come to believe that everything he does is wrong.

The situation may be even more serious if, in a teacher's class, some of the pupils had been taught by him during the previous year. They know what to expect; they are accustomed to his method of questioning; habituated patterns of behavior now serve them well. Difficulty of adjustment by the "new" pupils is intensified if the teacher, inadvertently, gives expression to the differences between the two groups, with emphasis upon the superiority of his former pupils.

A learner's mental set and his attitude toward a learning situation or subject area also affect the extent of achieved transfer. In the foregoing illustration, the former pupils of the teacher perceived the new school year's work in terms of a background understanding of what their teacher would do and expect them to do. They were *mentally set* to continue to respond in their accustomed ways. The others, perhaps, were mentally set to continue as they had been behaving. When they discovered that things were different in this class, their accustomed mental set failed to function. Successful learning thereby could be inhibited temporarily, at least. Attitudes that have developed in one learning experience may function favorably or unfavorably in any other learning situation. It has been found that the way in which testing directions are given, home assignments made, or questions asked by the teacher affects the attitudes of learners, either positively or negatively, toward all tests, home assignments, or teacher-questioning situations.

A high-school student may refuse to elect a particular subject, or fail to achieve success in it because other students have warned him concerning the difficulty of the subject or the ineffectiveness of the teacher. The student may have the ability to succeed, but, unless his attitude toward the situation changes, he may be unable or unwilling to apply his background of learning experience toward mastery in this subject.

Transfer of learning does not just happen. Learners must be alerted to the extent to which and the ways in which behavior in one situation carries over to another. For example, a high-school student writes well in his English classes and gains commendation for his achievement. In another subject area, social studies for example, his penmanship is sloppy and illegible, his spelling is incorrect, and his sentence structure is poor. Unless he is stimulated to carry writing habits learned in his English class into other writing situations, he honestly may believe that adequate writing is not needed in other classes where the emphasis is on knowledge and not on the way in which it is expressed.

Transfer in learning becomes more worthwhile when learners know what is expected of them and are provided with material which helps them discover relationships among learning materials. It is helpful when they realize that their learning can be furthered through the utilization of the problem-solving approach and are given numerous opportunities in which to participate in situations that permit transfer. They should be encouraged to give attention to the process of learning as well as to be concerned with the material learned.

Learning can be integrated through correlated, fused, core, and experience curricula. What is taught in school can be learned in such a way that achieved knowledges, skills, and attitudes can be applied toward the solving of school and other life problems of adjustment. We know that transfer takes place; we do not yet know exactly what happens within the learner that makes transfer possible.

Programed instruction. Programed instruction represents an application of learning theory and involves curriculum content and learning practice. The learning material is referred to as *the program* or *programed learning material* and is presented to the student in the form of questions or statements by way of a teaching machine or a programed text.

The programing system can take one of two forms: *linear* or *intrinsic*. The *linear* method is a step-by-step process of learner responses. Correct answers to each step are available and enable the learner to progress through the program by correcting any incorrect responses. The *intrinsic* or branching method involves the presentation of multiple-choice items which are checked for correctness by means of the responses resulting from this branching.

Proponents of programed instruction claim that through its utilization self-instruction is made possible. They hold that it has various advantages. The teacher is freed from performing some of the less creative teaching functions. Each learner can progress at his own rate. As the student is presented with a series of related learning materials, he responds to each item and then checks his answer with the correct response which is immediately available to him. Student interest is aroused and maintained as understanding is gained through the immediate feedback and reinforcement.

Programed instruction still is in the developmental stage. There is difference of opinion among educators concerning its value. It is generally conceded that machines can be useful in assisting learners to master factual materials that require more or less rote memorization. There is grave doubt, however, concerning the possibility of a machine's supplanting the master teacher who guides his students in achieving deep perceptions, gaining correct insights, analyzing problem data and making wise decisions. The teaching-learning process involves the synthesizing of relevant materials. This requires the functioning of an imaginative teacher who is well grounded in subject matter. Programed instruction, textbooks, and audio-visual aids can be used by the teacher as instruments to further the learning process; they cannot be expected to replace the human interaction that is essential to learning progress.

QUESTIONS AND TOPICS FOR DISCUSSION

1. Define learning in your own words.
2. In what ways does vertical learning differ from horizontal learning?
3. Discuss the importance of awareness of learning progress.
4. To what extent do the emotions aid or hinder learning?
5. Report all the perceptions that come to you as you sit where you are.
6. By the use of specific examples show the value of a learner's receiving correct sensations.
7. Look at a picture for one minute. Report immediately everything that you saw in it. How accurate was your perception of it?
8. Discuss the relationship between correct perception and effective learning.
9. Explain the value of using visual and auditory aids in the classroom.
10. Evaluate the utilization of each of the following in education: radio, television, sound films, film strips, slides.
11. In what ways may illusions interfere with learning?
12. Explain what is meant by overlearning. What value does overlearning have for the learner?
13. Explain how gaining insight assists learning.
14. What is the value of selecting certain implications from each or all of the theories of learning in an attempt to explain how learning takes place?
15. After studying the underlying ideas of the respective theories of learning, with which do you agree? What combinations among the theories would you make to explain learning?

16. How is learning through insight associated with the concept of whole learning? See Chapter 14.
17. To what extent does all learning partake of transfer?
18. Even though a subject-matter area seems to have little to offer in the way of transfer, should teachers concern themselves with teaching for transfer? Defend your conclusion.
19. What does attitude or method or procedure have to do with the amount and kind of transfer that takes place?

SELECTED REFERENCES

Bourne, L. E., *Psychology of Thinking*. Prentice Hall, Englewood Cliffs, N.J., 1971.

Crow, A., *Educational Psychology*, rev. ed. Littlefield, Totowa, N.J., 1971.

Deterline, W. A., *An Introduction to Programmed Instruction*. Prentice Hall, Englewood Cliffs, N.J., 1962.

Green, E. J., *The Learning Process and Programmed Instruction*. Holt, Rinehart & Winston, N.Y., 1962.

Haber, R. N., *Psychology of Visual Perception*. Holt, Rinehart & Winston, N.Y., 1973.

Hilgard, E. R., and Marquis, D. G., *Conditioning and Learning*. Appleton-Century-Crofts, N.Y., 1961.

Kay, H., et al, *Teaching Machines*. Penguin, N.Y., 1968.

Keller, F. S., *Learning: Reinforcement Theory*, 2nd ed. Random House, N.Y., 1969.

Klausmaier, H. J., and Ripple, R. E., *Learning and Human Abilities*. Harper and Row, N.Y., 1971.

Medwick, S. A., *Learning*, 2nd ed. Prentice Hall, Englewood Cliffs, N.J., 1973.

Peterson, L., *Learning*. Scott Foresman, Chicago, 1974.

Robison, H. F., and Schwartz, S. L., *Learning at an Early Age: A Programmed Text for Teachers*. Appleton-Century-Crofts, N.Y., 1972.

Travers, J. F., *Learning: Analysis and Application*. David McKay, N.Y., 1972.

Underwood, B. J., and Schulz, R. W., *Meaningfulness and Verbal Learning*. Lippincott, Philadelphia, 1962.

10   *Retention and Effective Study in Learning*

Unless learning has occurred, there is no opportunity for either remembering or forgetting to function. The child must give evidence through his behavior that he can utilize past experience. The changes that are produced through experience of one kind or another are retained. Thus learning and retention are essential to remembering. Any loss of the effects of learning is referred to as *forgetting*.

Retention in Learning

Since all learning implies retaining, it also includes remembering. To remember is to deal with past experience, to be able to recall or to recollect the circumstances surrounding an event, an idea, or a fact. It does not follow, however, that if one has learned he also can remember all that he has learned. Recall depends upon many factors including the emotions. For example, although you know the names of your close friends, it is possible to be in such an emotional state that, at any one moment, a mental block interferes with recall. Likewise, a mental set may so involve one's entire thinking at the moment that nothing outside the existing association focus can be recalled.

Importance of retention. To experience a clear mental image at the time of sense stimulation is basic to the development of correct perceptions. Yet, it is equally important that, if the individual so desires, he will be able to recall clearly what he has learned. Learning can be demonstrated only through the ability to bring to the level of conscious recall what has been experienced. If a formula, fact, or point of view can be repeated, there is evidence that it has been learned. An individual's ability to make progressive achievement depends upon his power of memory.

Recall functions more effectively when the material has been understood and completely learned. It is not correct to think that learn-

245

ing has taken place unless or until that which is presented verbally or in written form is understood by the learner. The type of material learned usually has an effect upon an individual's degree of success in retaining it. For example, meaningful materials usually are retained more easily than meaningless material; likewise, materials which are associated with pleasantness are retained more easily than are those associated with unpleasantness, dissatisfaction, or annoyance. Associating ideas with other ideas that have been thoroughly learned also is an effective aid to memory. Perceptual and integrated learning functions through this process.

Overlearning and retention. Facts that are to be used in further learning need to be learned beyond the point of simple recall. They need to be *overlearned* so that they may be used easily and quickly by the individual in his thinking and problem-solving. Many of our habits are overlearned through their constant use from early childhood onward. Among the early established habits are walking, handedness, throwing, and language usage. One reason for correct language usage by adults in the hearing of the growing child is to insure the child's formation of good speech habits. It is less important for him to know why he is speaking correctly than it is for him to imitate correct patterns during his early years.

There are many facts and principles that are used constantly in the daily life of individuals. When many of these responses become automatic, energy can be directed toward productive thinking. For example, the addition and multiplication combinations and the spelling of words are so necessary to an individual that he should have mastered them to the point of immediate recall when they are needed. Fortunately, we are discovering improved ways for the learning of these combinations and the spelling of words. No longer are drill exercises staged as drill exercises only; rather are the combinations learned in activity situations in which there is some degree of usefulness.

The good student discovers the value of rethinking the various topics in his lesson. He knows that recall is easier when ideas have been repeated or rethought. Many students attempt to rely upon one reading of an assignment to fix the ideas firmly in mind. They believe recall will follow if they understand what they read. What they do not always realize is that it is one thing to understand and to retain, but another to recall. A little overlearning is good insurance for effective recall.

Much information or learning is retained, but cannot be recalled.

Names, places, dates, or ideas that have been learned can be recognized to have been a part of our former experience even though they may not be recalled, without assistance, at the time they are needed. One difference between the short-form examination and the typical essay type is that, in the former, fewer recall demands are placed upon the responder than there are when he writes complete answers to essay questions. The true-false or the multiple-choice type of question places the data required for thinking before the responder. This lessens his need to search his memory for the once-learned facts that have a bearing on the question.

Individuals differ greatly in the extent to which or the ways in which they remember exactly what they have learned or experienced. This fact can be illustrated by the two widely differing stories of an accident reported by two witnesses. Each observer may have perceived different aspects of the situation. One may remember certain details; the other may remember the thing that impressed him most. What a person remembers in any situation is influenced by his personal needs at the moment, his emotional state or mood, his interest in the situations, the kinds of material he has learned, and the extent of his overlearning. For example, in the case of an automobile accident, a physician would be able to give an accurate report concerning the physical condition of the occupants of the cars. The damage to the cars could be reported more adequately by an automobile mechanic than by the physician.

Numerous experiments have been conducted that deal with ability to recall learned material. One study made by Lawshe and Dawson concerned the recall responses made by six hundred students as they listened to the reading of a list of words. The entire list of words was read once; during the reading, the eighth word was pronounced much more loudly than the others; the twelfth word was repeated five times. The students then were asked to write the words which they recalled. A study of the results, presented in Table 10, shows that the first, eighth, twelfth, and last words were recalled most frequently by the students. This illustrates that recall is aided by the application of the principles of primacy, intensity, frequency, and recency in learning situations.

Forgetting as a Factor in Learning

The act of remembering implies forgetting. If we cannot recall or remember a name, an object, a person, or an event, it is because we have forgotten it. Hence forgetting concerns itself with the loss of or the lack of retention of experiences, ideas, or skills. It is affected

TABLE 10. Per Cent of Students Recalling Each of Twenty Words After One Reading[1]

WORDS	PER CENT	WORDS	PER CENT
1. jewel	97	11. river	39
2. color	88	12. house	98
3. field	90	13. value	33
4. charm	49	14. watch	48
5. world	45	15. study	61
6. lover	72	16. cheat	58
7. water	74	17. paper	60
8. enemy	97	18. think	78
9. great	22	19. queen	54
10. spoon	25	20. clear	90

by every factor that determines the rate, efficiency, or extent of learning. Numerous experiments have been performed to determine the rate and extent of forgetting. One of the most extensive projects of this type of research was conducted by Ebbinghaus. He discovered that an individual who has learned nonsense syllables retains only about 59 per cent of what he has learned after a period of twenty minutes; 44 per cent after one hour; 34 per cent after one day, and slightly over 20 per cent after thirty days. The curve of retention for nonsense syllables is given in Figure 11.

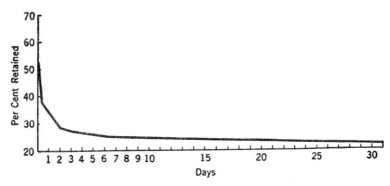

FIGURE 11. A Typical Curve of Forgetting

The curve takes this shape when material to be mastered verbatim is learned to the point of a single correct reproduction.

[1] See C. H. Lawshe, Jr., and R. I. Dawson, "A Procedure for Demonstrating the Secondary Laws of Association," *Journal of Educational Psychology*, Vol. 37, 1947, p. 249. Reprinted by permission.

In the experiment concerning the value of home study reported by the authors on pages 260–261 of this chapter, the extent of retention of material learned between the date of the final examination and twenty-eight days later, when the delayed recall test was given, varied with the groups, from a low of 86 per cent for one group during Experiment II to a high of 91 per cent for another group, with an average retention for all groups of 88 per cent. In other words, within one month the students had forgotten about 12 per cent of what they had learned, even though this was regular subject-matter material, instead of nonsense syllables.

In a study of retention of college classes in zoology, psychology, and chemistry, Greene discovered that, four months after the final examination, the percentage of retention was 42, 42, and 48 respectively. These percentage figures compare with the class averages on the final examination of 76, 70, and 80 respectively. After twenty months of no learning, they fell to 32 and 24 per cent for zoology and psychology; no figures were available for chemistry.[1]

It is now known that meaningful material usually is retained longer than is meaningless. Even so, since forgetting sets in as soon as learning ceases, material that is memorized requires much overlearning for retention over a long period of time.

TABLE 11. The Per Cent Retained for Nonsense Syllables and Poetry[2]
(From Ebbinghaus and Radosavljevich)

PERIOD AFTER LEARNING	EBBINGHAUS Nonsense Syllables	RADOSAVLJEVICH Nonsense Syllables	RADOSAVLJEVICH Poetry
5 minutes	. .	98	100
20 minutes	59	89	96
1 hour	44	71	78
8 hours	36	47	58
24 hours	34	68	79
2 days	28	61	67
6 days	25	49	42
14 days	. .	41	30
21 days	. .	37	48
30 days	21	20	24

[1] E. B. Greene, "The Retention of Information Learned in College Courses," *Journal of Educational Research*, Vol. 24, 1931, pp. 262–273.

[2] F. C. Dockery, and G. G. Lane, *Psychology*, 2nd ed., Prentice-Hall, Inc., New York, 1950, p. 182. Reprinted by permission.

Learning experiments conducted by Ebbinghaus and by Rado-salvjevich deal with comparisons in forgetting between nonsense syllables and poetry. In these experiments, learning had progressed to one correct repetition (Ebbinghaus), and to two (Radosavlje-vich). The data are presented in Table 11.

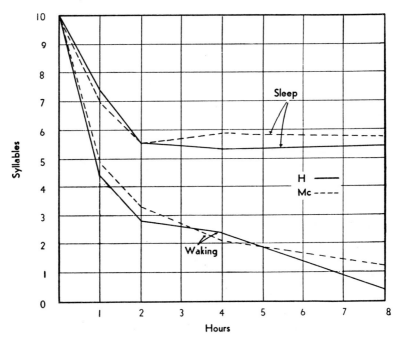

FIGURE 12.   Forgetting as a Function of Retroactive Inhibition

Two subjects learned ten nonsense syllables. The graphs show for each subject the number of syllables recalled after one, two, four, and eight hours when the subjects remained awake, and when they went to sleep. Forgetting is less during sleep and almost nonexistent when sleep has become sound two hours after learning.

From J. G. Jenkins, and K. M. Dallenbach, "Forgetting as a Function of Retro-active Inhibition," *American Journal of Psychology,* Vol. 35, 1924, p. 610. Reprinted by permission.

From the results of these and other studies, it can be observed that forgetting starts as soon as learning has been achieved. It also is evident that the rate of forgetting is great at first. After the first few days, factors other than time operate to determine the extent of reten-tion. There is some experimental evidence to the effect that retention during active waking hours is poorer than retention during sleep. That is, when we awake Monday morning we recall better what we did before we went to bed Sunday night than we recall what we did Monday morning by the time we retire Monday night. This is illustrated in Figure 12.

The fact that material having meaning for the learner is likely to be retained longer than meaningless material has teaching implications. Also, if the learner has a personal interest in the material or if there is a special purpose for the learning, the impact of these factors may be so great that the material is retained on the level of recall for a long time.

Developing Habits of Effective Study

Learning competence cannot be achieved without the application of energy to learning material or situations. Study is essential to learning, and fundamental to school life. Acquiring knowledge, perfecting skills, and developing attitudes constitute the main purposes of learning. The term *study* usually is associated with reading and reference work which will be helpful in interpreting ideas, making judgments, and creating new ideas. Sometimes, the study of a situation requires more than merely reading about it. For example, to locate the difficulty in a television set that has stopped functioning may require the direct research of the mechanic who must check every part of the machine to discover the cause of the breakdown. In this discussion, "study" is limited mainly to reading and reference work.

Factors of effective study. At one or another time in his life every child, adolescent, and adult has recognized his need for improved study habits. So much energy may be required for effective study that, for many learners, studying becomes distasteful. Although habits can be developed that will serve the individual well during his study sessions, other habits also can be formed that will interfere greatly with success-achieving, protracted study. It is the function of parents and teachers to help learners find ways in which their study may become as pleasant and as successful as possible. Many learners are able, unaided, to develop good study procedures; others need careful and continued guidance.

The physical conditions under which an individual attempts to study are important factors of the degree of successful studying. Poor lighting, bad ventilation, extremes in temperature, or excessive dryness of the air may interfere with learning efficiency. When the physical conditions are ideal, the learner has little excuse for not getting started in his study without wasting a great deal of time. A favorable mental set or attitude toward study is likely to accompany good physical conditions. If there are few distracting influences, the learner should be better able to attend to the task at hand.

The teacher can influence the attitude of the learner toward the mastery of a subject. If a learner dislikes a particular subject, the teacher should try so to motivate the learning of it that the student will develop a change in attitude toward it. If the displayed attitude of a bright learner toward a subject is that it is difficult, the fault may lie with the teacher rather than in the subject. If the learner's study experience is pleasant, he is impelled toward continuing it; if it is unpleasant, he tends to avoid studying. Attitudes that cause a learner to believe he can do a school or home assignment will send him into it with enthusiasm.

It is relatively easy for a learner to plan a program of study when he understands the study assignment, when he recognizes the fact that the assignment is not to be completed merely to satisfy a teacher, and when he believes that the material is worth learning. The learner should know not only the purpose of the assignment but also in what way the studying will contribute to his subsequent learning requirements. The learner experiences a greater drive toward study if he is aware of the goals toward which he is striving.

The ability to concentrate on what one is doing for a period of time that is long enough to complete it successfully is a great asset in the preparation of home-study assignments. A learner may possess a wealth of experience, but he needs to be able to recall it as an aid in his present study situation. During a period of concentration, he can bring to the focus of attention those background facts and experiences that may be essential to the solution of a problem. His correct analysis of an assigned problem will depend upon his capacity to bring into clear focus those knowledges that have a bearing upon the situation before him. To do this requires ability to give exclusive attention to the task at hand. It may be more satisfying, however, to shift attention to another activity, if thereby one can achieve an immediate, recognized goal.

Sometimes, there are present in the study situation certain conditions that produce feelings of fatigue. In spite of the fact that a great amount of energy is required, the *mental* activity involved in study seldom causes fatigue. A condition of boredom rather than of actual fatigue may result if a pupil engages in study activity against his will. An enthusiastic attitude toward what one does, an interest in subject matter mastery, and a desire to achieve success contribute to effective study outcomes. Even so, a learner needs an occasional change of activity if he wishes to avoid physical fatigue.

Studying printed material. Much learning that takes place originates from the printed page. If ideas are to be gained from printed material, the reader not only must be able to read the words, but also must be able to read with understanding and a purpose. Knowledge of the meaning of each word in a sentence is important to the reader's gaining an understanding of what he is reading. He brings to any reading attempt his experience up to that time. When he reads, he is seeing his experiences reflected in the words of the writer.

He often interprets what an author has said in terms of his own experience pattern. This may be very different from the knowledge and experience pattern of the person who wrote the passage or of another person who reads the same selection. Hence the same combination of words may be given different meanings by different persons, including the writer as well as the readers. A few suggestions for improving skill in studying printed material are presented. A teacher can help learners improve their study habits by encouraging them to incorporate these suggestions in their study procedures.

Using the dictionary. The dictionary is a useful book for discovering the exact meanings of words. Since some words have a variety of meanings, however, the context of the sentence may be necessary to get the precise connotation of a word used by an author. The meaning of words must be understood before a learner can interpret any passage correctly. Consequently, if the dictionary habit can be developed at an early age, the individual later will be saved time, energy, and perhaps embarrassment.

Improving rate and comprehension. It now is well known that poor reading habits often are basic causes of study and learning difficulties. Usually, best study results are achieved by the quick, careful reader. Rapid readers are more likely to get correct ideas from the printed page than are slow readers. A slow reader attends too much to each word or to separate phrases, thereby decreasing his ability to carry the thought in mind, as his reading progresses. If he is not rushed, a slow careful reader can gain mastery of ideas, however. There are wide differences among individuals in reading rate and comprehension. The reading rate of either the rapid reader or the slow reader is greater if the individual is reading for a definite purpose.

The results of a remedial reading program for college students at Northwestern University, reported by Witty and others, revealed that the remedial work led to an appreciable gain not only in rate of reading but also in comprehension.

The results of the reading-improvement program show conclusively that great gains in reading skill can be made by college students if they follow a systematic program. Since the program described in this paper was in operation for a single term only, the largest gains were made in such skills as rate of reading and simple comprehension rather than in broader abilities such as critical reading or discrimination in the selection of reading materials. Greater gains would undoubtedly result from longer periods of sustained effort. However, the gains made are extremely important and are individually serviceable. To be able to read at 474 words instead of 272 words a minute constitutes an important acquisition for any student. This gain is particularly valuable when one recognizes that scores on tests of comprehension as well as reading speed showed considerable improvement. Then, too, improvement in other reading skills such as in the vocabulary of the subject fields represents a great asset for the college student.

The fact that some reading skills most needed by college students are acquired slowly indicates the need for developmental reading programs in the college as well as the high school. As long as reading instruction is terminated in the upper grades of the elementary school and reading instruction is infrequently given in the high school, there exists a great need for corrective or remedial programs in college. The limitations of such programs are clearly evident and are the best argument for giving continuous attention to reading skills throughout the educative process. However, the gains that can be made in a short period devoted to remedial work certainly justify this effort.[1]

The status of the two groups at the beginning and at the end of the study are presented in Table 12.

Outlining and notetaking. The student who makes a practice of outlining his study material learns to look for the main points and to organize them in his thinking for use when they are needed. Difficult facts are remembered more easily if they are associated with the main ideas in the study material. Teachers can give aid in techniques of good outlining procedure by stimulating the learners to organize carefully the important points in the lesson. Either the teacher or one of the members of the class can write these points on the blackboard while they are being organized or shortly thereafter.

[1] P. Witty, et al., "Some Results of a Remedial Reading Program for College Students" School and Society, Vol. 76, December 1952, pp. 379–380. Reprinted by permission of the authors and of School and Society.

It is possible to make mental outlines or mental notes of the difficult or important points in an assignment, but it is more fruitful to summarize these ideas immediately in written form so that they can be reviewed for better learning before the next meeting of the class. Any notes taken by the reader as he works on his assignment are more useful if they are arranged in an organized form. Notes taken in haphazard fashion, or notes that are poorly written, often are not worth the time required for their writing.

Students differ in the kind of outline they find most useful. Each one must discover a form that is usable, and then modify it for his own use. The taking of good notes, as the teacher is developing a topic or as a speaker discusses an issue, comes only through practice. Usually, the learner will find it helpful to rewrite, as soon as he can, the notes taken during a learning session. At the second writing he should fill in details that lack of time prevented his including in his first writing. If the writing of outlines or the taking of notes are well done, these learning activities become excellent educational experiences. They help in the development of greater understanding of study material, and they aid remembering.

TABLE 12.   Gains Made on the Iowa Test[1]

	AVERAGE STANDARD SCORE		GRADE PERCENTILE OF AVERAGE SCORE (13TH–GRADE NORMS)	
	Initial	Terminal	Initial	Terminal
Freshmen	171	182	28	52
Upperclass students	180	191	48	76
Total (all students)	176	187	39	64

Outlines that are made or notes that are taken during a first reading of an assignment can be supplemented at the next reading. As the reader concentrates on study material, the ideas become fixed and he develops a mental readiness for recall through the practice of associating one idea with another. Good notes in outline form also are most helpful during review. Note-taking and outlining, however, cannot be substituted for intelligent recognition and understanding of the relationships that are inherent in the thinking and expression of a teacher or of a textbook author. The following

[1] *Ibid.*, p. 379. Reprinted by permission.

account of the different approaches to subject-matter study of two teacher-trainees illustrates this fact.

A young woman who was preparing herself to become a teacher was meticulous in her preparation of learning assignments. During class periods she took copious notes which later she transcribed carefully, adding details the inclusion of which was impossible during the class discussion. She also outlined, in minute detail, the content of assigned home reading. Unfortunately, she spent so much time and effort in her preparation of outlines and reading notes that she failed to understand their proper relationships. One reason for this, of course, was the fact that she was a slow thinker who could not grasp quickly those relationships in learning material that would enable her to select from among them the significant elements. When she was expected to contribute to class discussions, she was able to reproduce almost exactly what she had "studied," but failed miserably if she were asked a "thought" question which required the selection of appropriate concepts and a reorganization of them in terms of the posed question. As a teacher, this woman has earned an enviable reputation as a conscientious, industrious member of her school faculty. Her pupils learn subject matter, but their approach to problem-solving reflects her lack of ability to stimulate independent thinking.

Another teacher-trainee was a less industrious student. She took few class notes, but these included pertinent points. She did not rewrite her notes, and she put into outline form only what to her were the significant topics of a reading assignment. In class, she might not have been so accurate as the other in reproducing details, but she was extremely successful in thinking through problem questions. Moreover, she earned excellent grades in examinations, especially in short-answer questions that were based upon textbook and reference reading.

After this student had finished her training, she admitted to her former instructors that her preparation for a short-form quiz on reading material consisted of going through the material in terms of what she thought the instructor would include in the test. She not only had learned to emphasize significant points of study material, but also had achieved an understanding of the customary thought processes of her instructors.

Alertness is important, but so is interest in the mastery of thought-provoking situations and the kind of learning that takes place in the acquisition of knowledge. For example, a college student was an English major. His great interest in the field of literature motivated him to read widely and intensively. Both on the high-school and the college level, he also had taken a considerable number of required and elective courses in mathematics and science. His performance in these courses was satisfactory, but his achievement in the study of literature was outstanding. He himself believed that his interests and abilities lay in the field of the humanities rather than in the sciences.

Some twenty years after he had completed his formal education, he chanced to see a graduate-record examination. He decided to administer it to himself in order to discover how much he had forgotten of what he had studied in college. To his amazement, his performance on the part of the examination that dealt with literary knowledge was not nearly so successful as were his responses to questions that were based upon the application of scientific principles.

The man answered correctly questions in every area that represented problem situations, but he found some questions concerning literature to be extremely difficult. The difficult questions included the identifying of people, incidents, or plots associated with various literary masterpieces. At one time, these would have been "on the tip of his tongue." He decided that he had not been so good a student of literature as he had thought.

The fault, in this instance, did not lie so much in the mental ability of the man as it did in the way in which he had learned. Mathematics and science had challenged his power of problem-solving. In his study of literature much of his attention was devoted to the acquisition of memory images. With the passage of time and the shifting of interest from the study of literature to other fields of endeavor, he had forgotten many of the ideas associated with his former study. His memory did not function in the recall examination situation; there had been too long a lapse of time between memorization and recall. The exercise of his thinking processes in relation to the solving of problems in his study of the sciences, combined with the problem-solving techniques he continued to use in his adult activities, however, was a causative factor of his success in solving the thought questions of the examination.

Importance of raising questions. The main purpose that is served by reading is to get ideas from the printed page. Anything that can be done, therefore, to help the learner receive correct ideas, or to understand the material better will be of service to him. The reader is helped if he knows what to look for as he reads. The teacher or other person who previously has read the material can help the learner gain the ideas in written material by raising a question to which the answer can be found in the passage. Well-phrased questions motivate the reader to become mentally set to search for the particular idea in the selection that relates to the question.

Thought processes are started by problems. Questions are stimulators of mental activity if they are within the experience range of the individual. Questions that usually appear at the end of chapters in textbooks are placed there for the purpose of stimulating thinking in class discussion on topics related to chapter content. Some of the questions may encourage learners toward original investigation. Questions posed by the teacher when he makes an assignment are aimed at directing the thinking of the learner as he prepares himself to participate in discussion of the material of study. Both reading and lesson preparation can become more success-stimulating if adequate questions are raised to help pinpoint the meaning.

During the first reading of a selection, a student can develop the practice of formulating his own questions. Learners who study in groups find this an excellent practice. Each one can try to find the answers to the questions that have been raised. This procedure serves the added purpose of integrating the learning. The pertinent ideas, rather than petty details, then can be remembered longer.

A few general questions may not be sufficient to bring out all of the ideas that should be learned. The type of question to be raised will vary with the subject, however. For example, in the social sciences, questions dealing with detail should be used to supplement key questions, thus helping the learner get the complete picture. This procedure is good for any learner, but it is especially helpful for slow learners. It enables them to follow the sequence of ideas, and thus gain an understanding of what is being read or being presented orally.

Importance of whole and part methods of study. "Whole learning" means that the entire unit to be mastered is considered together, without giving special attention to or practice of any part of the material. For example, an entire poem is read repeatedly in order to learn it as a whole, rather than to memorize one line or one stanza at a time until every line or every stanza of the poem is memorized. Students should read an assignment in its entirety rather than dwell on any one part for special study.

Many experiments have been conducted to determine the relative value of the *whole* versus the *part* method as a procedure of effective study and learning. The results indicate that, unless the material is unusually long, it is better to learn by the whole method than to break the material into fragments. The size of the unit of material to be mastered determines largely whether there should be whole or part learning. Daily assignments are based upon that premise. During the term or the year, material in the entire textbook is to be learned; yet, no teacher assigns the reading of the entire textbook at the beginning of the term. Although an attempt to master the contents of an entire book by the whole method may seem to be an impossible task, the study of one unit of the book may be within the reach of most learners. Likewise, a poem that is relatively short should be learned by reading it through time after time.

The whole method is becoming effective in the learning of a foreign language, shorthand, typewriting, and in other learning areas where it can be applied. Intensive study will need to be given to difficult parts or to parts that seem to be difficult for any one learner. Unless learners recognize the value of the whole method of learning, they may become discouraged by their apparent failure to learn. During the initial periods of practice, little progress can be observed. This has a negative effect upon the learner. Yet, it has been found that if the learner has stick-to-itiveness, functional learning through the whole method will be most rewarding.

For best results, both methods probably are needed. However, whether the learner utilizes the whole method, the part method, or a combination in his attempts to master learning material, he should be encouraged by his classroom teacher to make use of the study procedures that serve him best. Successful learning achievement depends upon those study habits that have been formed by the learner.

Whole learning leads to better understanding through integration. The Gestalt concept is utilized through the whole process. This method avoids the piecemeal approach in which overlearning of some parts takes place at the expense of the learning of all the parts. For example, a reason for our remembering the first and not the second stanza of "America" is that the first has been sung again and again, while the second is sung infrequently.

Value of reviewing. The importance of overlearning already has been stressed. Reviewing is simply a continuation of learning beyond the first recall. Much of what is learned may be forgotten. Hence additional learning is necessary beyond the point of immediate recall in order to insure satisfactory recall at a later time. The student should review, either mentally or by reference to class notes or printed material, whatever is taken up in class on one day before he begins the preparation of his next assignment in that area. These are known as preparatory reviews, since they aid the student to understand the next topic to be discussed. The primary and perhaps only reason for teachers to announce that a quiz or an examination is to be given is his desire to stimulate the learners to review the material for better understanding and better retention. The main purpose for giving unannounced quizzes is to make certain that each pupil prepares his assignments daily. Adequately assigned home-study tasks have learning value.

A study was conducted by the authors to compare possible differences in retention of study materials that might result from (1) home study in addition to recitation class experiences, and (2) recitation class experience without additional home study. The participants in the study consisted of 155 college students who were enrolled in classes in Educational Psychology. Included in the study were two classes of college freshmen (61 students) in Virginia and three classes (94 students) of second-semester students of a college in New York City.

The students participated in a twelve-week experiment. During six weeks, their study included both classroom experiences and home study; the other six weeks were devoted to classroom experiences with *no home preparation.*

Before each part of the experiment was started, a pre-test was administered to all students to discover what they already knew in the field of educational psychology. At the end of each six-week period, an equated final examination was administered. Four weeks later, a delayed-recall examination was given to discover the extent to which the students had forgotten what they had learned.

In all classes, the students showed in their final examination that they had learned more when they studied outside the classroom than they did when they limited their study to classroom experience only. Moreover, as evidenced by the results of the delayed-recall tests, *less* forgetting had taken place, at the end of the four-weeks' period of nonlearning, for the six-weeks' session during which the students had studied at home as well as during class periods. Table 13 presents the results of the three examinations. Each six-weeks' session of the total experiment was termed Experiment I or Experiment II. The extraclass study groups are indicated as follows: Experiment I, 1A', 1A, and 1C', Experiment II, 2B', and 2B.

TABLE 13. Mean Scores Made in Preliminary, Final, and Delayed
Recall Examinations (Perfect score for each, 300)

	VIRGINIA		NEW YORK CITY		
Experiment I	1A'	1B'	1A	1B	1C
Preliminary	42	43.5	98.9	95.2	87
Final examination	193.4	157.5	222.3	189.1	200.6
Delayed recall	142.6	122.3	215.3	188.5	182.5
Experiment II	2A'	2B'	2A	2B	2C
Preliminary	52.3	48.2	114.4	99.8	106.2
Final examination	149.7	166.0	201.8	247.1	184.3
Delayed recall	136.4	146.5	181.7	213.3	157.4

An interesting result was the fact that the students who participated in the experiment appeared to have greater self-confidence
when they were permitted to study outside class. Restriction to class
study tended to arouse an attitude of insecurity concerning mastery
of learning materials.

The mastery of some facts requires the use of drill. We are not
using the term *review* as a synonym for drill. Through review,
summarizations can be made that contribute to an integration of
ideas. Although memorized facts have value for the learner, it is
through the integration of learning experience that learning is made
functional. That is, during review of material, an individual's concepts are expanded as he reflects on and evaluates the ideas associated with the learning material.

Importance of a study program. It is easy to procrastinate in the
preparation of home assignments that appear to be difficult or that
may seem to interfere with more interesting activities. The people
who perform the important work in the world are those who work
according to a schedule. The child who learns early to plan his
study program and to follow it has started to develop habits that
will assist him throughout his school years—in fact, throughout
life. It is difficult for children or young people to realize that those
who succeed in life tend to organize and to follow a well-planned
schedule of activities.

The home-study requirements of children are being reduced. There are arguments on both sides of this issue. For the pupils in the elementary- and junior high-schools, home-study requirements probably can be kept to a minimum. However, this is said with the understanding that effective supervised study will continue in the classrooms of our schools. All children need to learn how to study; this is accomplished through practice under guidance. The high-school and the college student should be expected to complete a definite program of home study.

As part of his orientation to high school, the learner can be helped to construct a workable study program. The student must learn to plan a time schedule that will make intelligent use of all the hours of the day. Some time should be allowed for recreation and leisure-time activities. It is surprising what can be accomplished in study if a carefully constructed time schedule is followed consistently. Some provision can be made for flexibility, but the changes in the schedule should be kept to a minimum. It is best to draw up a tentative schedule and then to make needed changes in it. Once a good schedule is constructed, it should be adhered to.

A significant reason for the large number of failures among college freshmen is that they do not know how to budget their study time, or they do not follow a study schedule after they prepare it. The extent of lack of self-discipline in this area is reflected in the low marks made by some college freshmen. Many of these students were among the top 10 per cent in their high-school classes. Greater enjoyment and greater efficiency are the inevitable outcomes of following a study schedule. Worry about finding time for study is reduced thereby to a minimum or is eliminated.

The primary purpose for this discussion concerning the development of good study habits is to alert the beginning teacher to ways in which he can help his pupils improve their study procedure. In addition, the reader, himself, may discover inadequacies in his own study habits which can be remedied. Hence the following practical suggestions may have value for him as a teacher or as a student.

1. Study with a definite purpose in mind.
2. Evaluate immediate and remote goals.
3. Provide a definite place for study.
4. Seek physical conditions that are conducive to study.
5. Plan and follow a definite time schedule.
6. Look for the main ideas of reading material.
7. Cultivate the habit of reading rapidly and carefully.
8. Outline the study material.
9. Take brief, well-organized notes.

10. Evaluate the difficulty of the material.
11. Raise significant questions on the material to be learned; then answer them.
12. Study with intent to recall.
13. Give careful attention to all illustrative material.
14. Complete all study assignments.
15. Intersperse active study with rest periods.
16. Employ the "whole" method of learning whenever possible.
17. Concentrate on what you are studying at the time.
18. Shut out emotional distractions.
19. Overlearn sufficiently for delayed recall.
20. Learn to review and to summarize.
21. Be alert to ideas emphasized by the teacher.
22. Reflect on and challenge questionable statements made by authors.
23. Investigate points of view of several authorities.
24. Apply subject matter learned in as many practical situations as possible.
25. Make intelligent use of the dictionary.[1]

QUESTIONS AND TOPICS FOR DISCUSSION

1. Jot down the names of as many objects as you can remember that are in your sitting room at home. Do the same for the sitting room in the home of a friend you have visited recently. Check the correctness of your lists.

2. What special aids do you use to assist you to remember facts or ideas?

3. The following is a good test in memory that can be made a learning exercise. Read each series of digits to one of your friends to discover how many numbers he can repeat after one hearing. Next, try each series backwards. Then, read the numbers of the last series and have your friend repeat them until he can write the numbers exactly as given. Note the number of trials taken.

```
4  8  2  7
2  6  8  9  5
7  3  8  5  4  8
6  9  3  5  2  7  4
8  3  5  6  2  4  1  7
4  2  8  1  5  3  6  9  7
3  8  7  4  6  8  1  4  2  5
```

4. What are the effects of a summer vacation on the retention of school-learned material?

5. What values may result from neat and orderly note-taking?

[1] L. D. Crow, and A. Crow, *Understanding Interrelations in Nursing*, Macmillan, New York, 1961, pp. 71–72. Reprinted by permission.

6. Discuss the relationship between ability to concentrate and effectiveness of study.
7. Write a six-paragraph summary of this chapter without rereading the chapter. Then reread the chapter and try again.
8. Learn the numbers and words in the following lists by reading each list from top to bottom—(the whole method). Note the number of trials required to be able to reproduce each list exactly as it is given.

53	Does	Table	AZR
64	Among	Paper	PLX
81	Through	Ceiling	TMU
72	Allow	Apple	EMT
65	Deal	Music	AUY
48	Correct	Light	ZHM
26	Present	Hammer	ARI
34	Focus	Face	NGR
89	Written	Kite	UTP
17	Utilize	Nail	DYJ

9. What suggestions can you offer for the improvement of retention?
10. What values can come from attending to the points of emphasis given by the teacher?
11. What can you do to improve your study effectiveness?
12. Name five factors of effective study, and discuss the impact of two of them on your present study effectiveness.
13. Secure an Advanced Battery Test for the Ninth Grade and determine, through taking this test, how well you remember material learned in high school or earlier. The results may be surprising, especially if you allow yourself only two-thirds of the time allotted for ninth-grade pupils.
14. Discuss the value of frequent reviews; of tests covering material studied.
15. Construct a study schedule. After changing it to meet your immediate needs, follow it for at least two months.
16. Among the various learning aids used by your instructor, which do you find most valuable? Indicate why you believe this to be so.
17. Make a list of the influences or factors that interfere with your study effectiveness. State in writing what you can do to eliminate them.
18. To what extent do you tend to study with others? Indicate circumstances in which group study may be an excellent supplement to individual study.
19. Enumerate some difficulties you experience when applying the "whole" method of learning. To what extent do you attempt to use the "whole" method in your study of printed material?

SELECTED REFERENCES

Carter, L. J., and Cheers, A. L., *Teaching-Learning Process.* Exposition Press, Jericho, N.Y., 1973.

Cole, L., *Students' Guide to Effective Study*, 4th ed. Holt, Rinehart & Winston, N.Y., 1960.

Crow, L. D. and Crow, A., *How to Study.* Collier Books, N.Y., 1963.

Ehrlich, E. H., *How to Study Better and Get Higher Marks.* Crowell, N.Y., 1961.

Farquhar, W. W., et al, *Learning to Study.* Ronald Press, N.Y., 1960.

Kintsch, W., *Learning, Memory and Conceptual Procedure.* Wiley, N.Y., 1970.

Robinson, F. P., *Effective Study*, rev. ed. Harper and Row, N.Y., 1961.

Robinson, F. P., *Effective Reading.* Harper and Row, N.Y., 1962.

II   The Acquiring of Skill Competence

As a self-initiated, teacher-guided process, learning involves the acquiring of improved ways of doing things. To satisfy his learning interests, the individual must apply his energies toward goals. Included among the areas in which satisfying achievement is sought are: memorization of factual material, development of conceptual understanding and problem-solving, acquisition of skill competence, and attitude development. This chapter deals with habits that are formed in the acquisition of skill competencies.

The Acquisition of Motor Control

To meet life demands, an individual's acquiring of adequate motor skill is as important as is his mastery of abstract ideas. There are few situations in which both are not needed. Those bodily movements that result from the co-ordinated functioning of nerves and muscles usually are referred to as motor activities. These activities involve the movements of gross muscles and the muscular co-ordinations of the fine muscles. Gross movements appear in such activities as walking, running, jumping, skating, swimming, dancing, and bicycling. The smaller muscle co-ordinations are especially active in grasping, writing, drawing, painting, sewing, typing, and the use of tools of various types. Most motor skills involve both gross and finer movements.

Bases of motor control. The development of competence in a motor skill depends upon an individual's sensory acuity and perceptual power, as well as upon the adequacy of his muscular co-ordination. External or internal stimuli are needed to motivate muscular activity of any kind. Consequently, accurate perception of sensory stimuli is necessary for the perfecting of motor skills. Foremost among the early motor skills that are developed is the ability to hold a bottle for getting food. Walking is another motor skill that, after maturation has taken place, becomes habituated through many trials. The body balance that is achieved is a result of much activity, both successful and unsuccessful. This motor skill becomes so much a part of an individual that he often can be identified by his walk.

Handedness also results, in part, from the early development of motor habits. What causes a child to give preference to one hand over another as he holds a spoon with which to eat, a ball to throw, or a toy to manipulate is not certain. Yet, as he exercises one hand more than the other, he develops a degree of skill that causes him to become either right-handed or left-handed, from practice. The various motor skills needed for survival are developed day by day as the individual spends much time in planned or unplanned practice toward their perfection. The skills needed for social competence are developed similarly. Although many early motor habits are acquired without any formal training, there is an increasing need for the development of certain motor skills through organized learning situations.

Value of skill development. Motor skills are more important to growing youth than we sometimes permit ourselves to believe. The hero of the football field gains his social prestige because of his skill at running, tackling, or passing. The popular dancing partner is the one who has developed skill in many dance steps. The admired cheer leader is the one who has developed skill in vocalization and body movement. In other words, there is great social value in the attainment of highly developed motor skills. No adolescent wants to be called "butterfingers" if he drops things easily, or a "lummox" if he accidentally upsets something in the room. Some children whose general intelligence is lower than that of others in the group but whose aptitudes in mechanical areas are high have a chance to gain desired attention through their motor superiority.

Early Motor Development

Motor growth does not take place at random, but improves in an orderly sequence. Movements begin during the prenatal stage and are basic to the later development of posture, locomotion, and prehension. Many mass activities continue during the neonatal period and into early infancy. Later, motor abilities develop from these relatively random expressions of motor activities. The fact that maturation or inner growth determines the rate and pattern of early motor response, rather than training and experience, is borne out by numerous experiments made by Gesell,[1] McGraw,[2]

[1] A. Gesell, *et al.*, *The First Five Years of Life*, Harper & Bros., New York, 1940.
[2] M. B. McGraw, *The Neuromuscular Maturation of the Human Infant*, Columbia University Press, New York, 1943.

and others. In general, children follow similar patterns of motor growth.

Muscular growth of the neonate. The neonate has little control of his head muscles at birth, and requires much care in handling. His head will wobble if he is picked up carelessly. His head and neck muscles are so weak that he needs support for the back and the head for the first three months. At the end of the first month, however, when the infant is lying prone (on the stomach), he is able to hold his head up for a few seconds. Motor control begins in the head region of the infant, and continues posteriorly. He first learns to hold his head erect and to fixate his eyes. His eyes begin early to follow a moving object. His attention is gained as easily through a controlled moving object as through the use of the voice. Next he reaches for and, if they are within his reach, grasps objects that he can hold and that interest him.

Locomotor development. Posture begins posteriorly and develops until the child can sit erect, crawl, stand, and eventually walk. It is difficult for the infant to change from a prone to a sitting position or from a sitting position to a prone position. These motor responses may be mastered by about the tenth or eleventh month. A child who is placed on the floor may be stimulated to *crawl* in order to reach a nearby object in which he is interested. After he learns to crawl, he may try to "go it on all fours." Plenty of space needs to be provided for these activities. Individual differences show themselves in the methods of locomotion used by children. Some children crawl on all fours, others hitch or scoot. In Figure 13 are illustrated the transitional stages from crawling to creeping.

A child may develop so great a proficiency in a particular method of crawling that he prefers it to attempting to walk, even after he has learned to take steps. To be able to walk, a child first must be able to pull himself up to a standing position. These attempts usually occur, during the time he is creeping, when he is near an object that is stable enough so that he can hold on to it. A child is fascinated by the experience of standing; he wants to repeat it again and again. With a little encouragement, the child gradually shifts from crawling and creeping to walking. The child who creeps at an early age usually is likely to learn to walk at an early age. The postural sequence from a prone position through the various developmental stages to walking alone is illustrated in Figure 14.

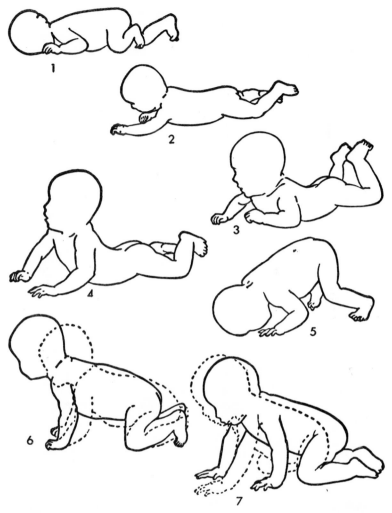

FIGURE 13.   Postural Phases in Development of Crawling and Creeping

1. Newborn crawling movement. 2. Less activity in lower extremities; begins to hold head up. 3. Increases control over movements of head and shoulder girdle. 4. Marked development in upper part of body; pelvis rests on the surface. 5. Conflict in action of pelvic and shoulder regions; when pelvis is raised, head and shoulders are lowered. 6. Rocking movements; maintains abdomen above surface. 7. Associated creeping movements.

From M. B. McGraw, *Growth: A Study of Johnny and Jimmy*, Appleton-Century-Crofts, Inc., N. Y., 1935, p. 70. Reprinted by permission of the publisher and the author.

269

Table 14 is a summarization of a study, over a two-year period, of the developmental sequence of the sitting up and walking of twenty-five babies.

0 MONTH
Fetal Posture

1 MONTH
Chin Up

2 MONTHS
Chest Up

3 MONTHS
Reach and Miss

4 MONTHS
Sit with Support

5 MONTHS
Sit on Lap Grasp Object

6 MONTHS
Sit on High Chair Grasp Dangling Object

7 MONTHS
Sit Alone

8 MONTHS
Stand with Help

9 MONTHS
Stand Holding Furniture

10 MONTHS
Creep

11 MONTHS
Walk when Led

12 MONTHS
Pull to Stand by Furniture

13 MONTHS
Climb Stair Steps

14 MONTHS
Stand Alone

15 MONTHS
Walk Alone

FIGURE 14.   The Motor Sequence

Adapted from *The First Two Years, Vol. II,* frontispiece, by Mary M. Shirley. Copyright 1933 by the University of Minnesota Press, Minneapolis, Minn. Reprinted by permission.

TABLE 14. Sequence for Walking[1]

I. *First order skills:* Passive postural control

Activity	Median Age (weeks)
On stomach, chin up	3
On stomach, chest up	9
Held under arms in erect position, makes stepping movements	13
On back, tenses or stiffens spine for lifting	15
Held erect, keeps knees straight	15
Sits on lap (support at lower ribs and complete head control)	18.5

(This marks the end of the first third of the walking sequence.)

II. *Second order skills:* Postural control of entire trunk and undirected activity

Sits alone momentarily	25
Makes knee push or swimming movements when placed on stomach	25
On back, rolling	29
Held erect, stands firmly with help	29.5
Sits alone one minute	31

(This marks the completion of one-half of the walking sequence.)

III. *Third order skills:* Active efforts at locomotion

Makes some progress on stomach by crawling (i.e., drags or pushes abdomen along on the floor by his arms)	37
Scoots backwards on stomach	39.5

IV. *Fourth order skills:* Locomotion by creeping

Stands, holding to furniture	42
Creeps (abdomen lifted off floor; goes on all fours) (By this stage the child has accomplished two-thirds of the walking sequence.)	44.5
Walks when led	45
Pulls to standing position by holding on to furniture	47

V. *Fifth order skills:* Postural control and coordination for walking

Stands alone	62
Walks alone	64

[1] Adapted from *The First Two Years*, Vol. I, Table III, p. 99, and chap. 6, by Mary M. Shirley, copyright 1933 by the University of Minnesota Press, Minneapolis, Minn. Reprinted by permission.

One of Gesell's intensive studies of child growth dealt with the series of developmental stages in a child's learning to walk. Other studies in the field of early child growth and development also include the tracing of the maturational stages in a child's learning to walk. The results of these studies are similar to those shown in Table 14. We must remember, however, that these patterns of development in walking are normative. A mother should not expect her baby's locomotor growth to follow exactly the sequences as they are outlined here. Some babies seem to skip one of the stages by gaining an early control of motor co-ordination. Other youngsters are retarded in their power of locomotion. Excessive weight, ill health, or physical defects may slow down what would seem to be normal development. The significant point to be made here is that adults should not try to hasten individual maturational motor processes. The child should be allowed to develop his motor co-ordinations at his own rate. At the same time, his development should be watched carefully by a pediatrician so that remediable difficulties are not allowed to persist.

Development of prehension. The reflex grasping movements of the neonate represent the beginnings of the fine muscular co-ordinations that later become skilled manual activities. Muscular maturation accompanied by increase in tactual, visual, and kinesthetic sensitivity makes it possible for a developing individual to achieve commendable manual skill to the extent that muscular and sensory development is guided toward facility and accuracy of performance.

At first, the infant's grasping reflex is digital. By the time the baby is a year old, however, the palmar grasp, or grasping with the thumb and the forefinger, is developed and is continued through adulthood.

A child's early manipulatory movements are awkward and fumbling. A relatively consistent pattern in the development of arm and hand movements can be observed as one studies a child's progressing facility through the first six years of his life in manipulating blocks, drinking equipment, playthings, and other objects in the home. With the child's entrance into formal schooling begins his acquiring specific skills that will continue to help him gain control of objects in his physical environment.

Learning and Skill Competence

The value to the individual of motor learning lies in the degree of proficiency he can develop in his finer muscular responses. His skill will depend upon the correct motor responses' becoming automatic. The effectiveness of these voluntary movements depends upon the extent to which the individual develops *speed, precision* or *accuracy, steadiness* or *control,* and *strength* in them. Although these abilities are relatively independent of one another, long periods of practice are required for skill development. During the practice periods, errors are eliminated from the habits that are being established. Not only is practice required, but the practicing also should be accompanied by a desire to succeed and confidence that successful performance can be attained.

Finer motor development. Motor learning is receiving an increasing amount of time and attention in both elementary and secondary schools. The child is being given many opportunities to develop motor co-ordination of various kinds through planned school activities, such as penmanship, drawing, typewriting, laboratory experimentation, shopwork, cooking, and sewing. In addition, learning in the more academic subjects is accompanied by participation in motor activity as "projects" are planned and constructed.

Present educational emphasis upon intramural sports and games attempts to satisfy the need of every child to develop some proficiency in the motor skills involved in such activities. Success cannot be attained in the use of gymnasium equipment unless and until the individual has had considerable experience working with it. A person can be a skilled performer in any form of sport only after he has had extensive training and experience in controlling his muscular system and dealing with needed equipment. Overlearning is a *must* in the development of motor skills.

The aim of motor learning that involves movement of the fine muscles is to develop skill in the activity. The importance of forming correct habits at all times is recognized by the individual who has an urge to improve his degree of skill. Such motor co-ordinations as those required in learning to drive an automobile, to ride a bicycle, or to play a musical instrument are conditioned in part by the habit patterns possessed by the individual at the time he starts his specialized learning.

After the learner has gained some control of the muscular co-ordinations that are basic to the learning of a particular skill, the goal toward which he strives is the development of good form, or method of performing. An acceptable form for a particular motor performance is one patterned after that of successful men and women in the specific activity. There are general aspects of good form. In the final analysis, however, good form in an activity is based upon the learner's innate ability and his previous experiences. For example, the stance taken by the successful baseball player at the homeplate illustrates good batting form; the body co-ordination and the swing of the racquet by a tennis champion illustrate good form in tennis.

A learner must realize that his earlier habit patterns may help or hinder his progress in the development of any particular skill. He should be concerned with discovering the finer muscle co-ordinations that are made by the skilled technician, and should do his best to imitate the model. He needs to realize that he must make adaptations that are suitable to his individual traits, limitations, and capacities. Hence, in the development of a skill, the learner should be permitted freedom to achieve competence in terms of his own potential patterns of development.

Suggestions for the development of motor skills. In order to avoid too much loss of time in the mastery of skill in any one of various areas of motor learning, the understanding and application of certain underlying principles of motor learning may be helpful both to the teacher and the learner. Activity on the part of the learner is important in all learning, but the immediate value of activity seems to show itself clearly in motor learning. If the individual does not practice, he cannot expect to gain skill in performance. Tennis cannot be learned merely by observing the game, nor can an individual become a good dancer merely by watching others on the dance floor. Skill habits become a part of a person only as he himself participates in the activity. Emphasis upon the need for practice does not imply, however, that knowledge concerning what to do is not valuable and cannot be gained, in part, on the sidelines.

Perception of goal or objective. It is important that in mastering a skill the learner know what is expected of him and something about how it is to be done. Refinement of responses accompanies increased perception of the exact goal to be achieved. An awareness of the component aspects of a total situation helps an individual to orient his thinking and attitude toward his specific activities in the achievement of that particular goal. For example, the absence of a bat in the hands of a baseball player at the home plate is easily perceived by an observer. It is more difficult, however, to discover that the batter may not be holding his bat correctly or that the bat is too light for him. The performer who is able to perceive small differences in ways to improve his skill is in a position to make additional progress. The child who has motor speech difficulties is able to correct his speech patterns after he becomes aware not only of the fact that his speech is unsatisfactory but also of his specific speech faults.

In the learning of a skill, the perceiving of a good model helps the learner to appreciate the goal toward which he is striving. He must realize that he cannot achieve perfection at one "fell swoop." It is known, for example, that a child in the third grade cannot duplicate the form and style of a model of perfect penmanship. Yet, for best learning results, he needs to have the model before him, but he also should know what the teacher considers to be adequate imitation of the model for this particular age and grade level. Handwriting scales have been developed; yet no teacher would think of teaching children in the fourth grade to write by utilizing the fourth-grade level of the penmanship scale as the model for them to imitate. An understanding of the goal is important, as well as are the suggestions that teachers may be able to give to enable the learners to reach desired goals.

A skilled person may not know all the underlying reasons for his high degree of skill. It may be difficult for him to attempt to tell another person exactly what he does, or the manner in which he does it, as he gives skilled performance. There also are times when words are inadequate to describe some of the aspects of skill, even if the individual knows the reasons for his success. The artist knows in general what he does when he paints a beautiful picture; rarely can he convey this information to another person through the use of words. At the same time, he is able to evaluate critically the attempts of a beginner in the field. He helps the learner through suggestions.

Value of knowing what to do. If the individual knows what to do as he participates in activities, his confidence thereby is bolstered. Children and young people have an enormous amount of energy and seek ways to release it. The young girl who decides to bake a pie may not achieve perfect results the first time she tries, but she is willing to undertake this new adventure because she has a recipe to follow. She therefore believes that she knows what to do. She has confidence in her own ability to follow the directions explicitly. Sometimes a young person must learn through humiliating failure that he does not know and cannot do as much as he thinks.

The teacher often can be of assistance in pointing out what to do and in suggesting ways of proceeding. Anything that will alert the learner to a desire to want to master a skill constitutes half the battle. Teachers who have had much experience with skill-development procedures inspire confidence in the learners through the utilization of the correct approach. Also, if teacher suggestions are given at the psychological time, many errors can be avoided or perhaps eliminated, and adequate progress achieved. A teacher-motivated attitude of "I think I can" is likely to be most fruitful in motor learning and skill development.

The early stages in the learning of any skill are filled with much fumbling and many false movements. Therefore, correct speech patterns should be developed early, social dancing experienced before the end of high-school years, typewriting practiced as it is to be used later, and driver training received during the teen years so that there will be fewer interfering habits or emotional blocks. In the same way, any skills that are to be developed in the gymnasium or on the athletic field should have their beginnings during childhood so that later the performer will experience less fear of ridicule from his peers if or when he fails to perform successfully.

Importance of practice in motor learning. Once the learner understands the preliminary techniques to be used, there is only one way by which he can achieve perfection in any motor skill—that is by practice or drill. It is important, however, that the learner practice correct movements; otherwise, he is likely to form habits that will inhibit adequate performance. Success does not always greet the initial attempts of the learner. If the learner is mentally set to improve in the skill, his practice periods will be satisfying to him; even though he does not make speedy progress, he is stimulated to keep at it.

The importance of the kind and amount of practice needed in the development of a skill can be illustrated by the experiences of a boy who possesses considerable musical ability. Because of his interest, at the age of six, in drumming on the piano keys and picking out little melodies by ear, his parents arranged for him to take piano lessons from a teacher who was so amazed by his musical ability that she permitted him to play difficult musical selections. His rendition of these compositions was remarkable for his age, but lacked accuracy of performance. His teacher failed to give attention to good techniques of playing. By the time he became a pupil of a well-known school of music, he went through a difficult period of relearning. He was required to practice finger exercises. Playing became annoying drudgery rather than self-expression through music. Eventually, his poor techniques were reconditioned, and he now is achieving considerable success in the interpretation of musical themes that are performed with excellent technique.

The effectiveness of practice includes more than mere repetition. The outcomes of motor learning depend in part upon (1) the nature of the skill to be learned, (2) the age and special interest of the learner, (3) the conditions under which the practice is conducted, (4) the amount of time available for practice, (5) the spacing of the practice periods, and (6) the degree of proficiency desired.

Learning effectiveness is furthered through the practice of the skill in the way in which it is to be used later. There also should be developed the power to adapt the skill to meet modifications that may be required in certain situations. One learns what he practices; it is also important that he practice what he should learn. The learner, therefore, should have a clear idea of what he is attempting and should continue his practice accordingly.

It is the function of the teacher to help the learner focus on the degree of efficiency that can be attained. The level of achievable proficiency differs among individual learners as well as does the time required to achieve a desired goal. The rate of the learning and the degree of skill to be attained should reflect the abilities and interests of the learner.

Drill is effective when it is well motivated and properly spaced. Practice as mere repetition may create unfavorable attitudes toward the task and thereby defeat its own purpose. The length of practice periods and their spacing depend upon the age and ability of the learner and the type of skill to be mastered. Practice periods of young children should be shorter than those of older children, adolescents, or adults. Relatively short practice periods once or twice a day are likely to be more productive of learning achievement than long protracted, less frequent periods of practice. It should be noted, however, that practice periods should not be so short that little is accomplished during them; they should not be so long that fatigue or boredom enters the situation.

The learning curve resulting from practice of most motor skills shows a rapid initial spurt, with a leveling off after the first stage of achievement. After a time, a plateau may develop. During the "plateau" period, there is little or no rise in the learning curve, in spite of continued practice. No gain is evident. Learning is taking place, however; the plateau usually is followed by a spurt of improved performance.

The curve of learning in typewriting illustrates what happens during a long period of practice. The curves indicate initial rapid progress which becomes more gradual until there is no further upward movement. Plateaus can be seen at numerous places on the curve in Figure 15.

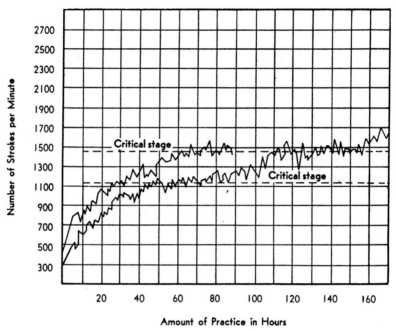

FIGURE 15.   Improvement in Typewriting

By permission from *Improvement in Typewriting,* by W. F. Book. Copyright 1925. McGraw-Hill Book Co., Inc.

There is a wide variation among individuals in the matter of practice. Some persons are more consistent than others in their practicing, in their attending to what they are doing, and in their goal of achievement. The progress of any one individual is likely to be irregular from day to day, however. Fluctuations are caused by such chance factors as variations in the individual's physical condition or in his motivation. Each learner also has his own individual limit. It is true that the four-minute mile has been broken, yet there is a point beyond which no human being can reduce the time required to run a mile.

Significance of speed and accuracy. The problem of emphasizing speed at the expense of accuracy confronts men and women who give instruction in certain motor skills. The problem seems to be one of interest in learning experiences such as eye-movements in reading, handwriting, learning to type, learning to play a musical instrument, or mastering similar motor activities. For example, in training individuals to become rapid typists, consideration is given simultaneously to both speed and accuracy. It is certain that a trained worker does more work with less effort than does the untrained worker. The champion skater seldom loses his balance, the bicyclist seldom falls, and the tightrope walker usually gets across the rope. As a result of his consistently successful achievement, the trained person possesses the necessary confidence to perform on any occasion.

Speed and accuracy can go together. In the development of a high degree of proficiency, speed and accuracy should be joint goals toward which to strive. Accuracy should not be sacrificed for speed, however. Beginners should try to complete the motor pattern, regardless of the errors that may be made. Complete patterns should be practiced as a continuity, eliminating minor errors, until definite progress is shown. After initial progress has been achieved, any weakness in the performance can be singled out for improvement through concentrated practice.

Value of effective guidance. One of the considerations in the teaching of motor skills is to get the learners to relax. The beginner usually is tense. Anything that can be done to reduce the tensions already present in a learner will be beneficial. This is especially true in the learning of handwriting, golf, or swimming, as well as in participation in a ball game or in playing a musical instrument. The skilled person can relax because he has confidence in his ability to perform; the untrained person has a desire to perform without mistakes but emotional tensions usually prevent him from doing as well as he otherwise might do.

A child cannot run until he has learned to walk; neither should the adolescent or adult expect to exhibit fineness of response during early stages of motor learning. In the beginning stages of the development of any skill, the movements of the learner are likely to be hesitant and awkward. As practice proceeds, errors are reduced; useless and clumsy movements are eliminated. Praise directed toward correct responses will build confidence in the learner and inspire him toward further practice and consequent improved skill. During the beginning stages of practice, gross errors only should be corrected; later, attention can be directed toward the improvement of finer responses. Instruction helps to avoid gross errors in the integrative period; expert guidance is needed to perfect the skill in the precision stage.

Parents and teachers should encourage freedom of movement. They should praise achievement to the degree of the learner's need of encouragement and to the extent of progress made. Those responsible for the guiding of motor co-ordination should help the learner give attention to the skill to be achieved, not to the movements involved. The total learning situation must be considered. Insofar as it is possible, all phases of performance should be approached simultaneously, rather than giving attention to each phase separately.

The "whole method" is important in the learning of a skill. The child attempts to ride a bicycle as a whole, rather than to attend to balance alone; he pedals, steers, and sees where he is going. In studying shorthand, the learner no longer is expected to learn various separate skills and then combine them into a total pattern of efficiency. Newer methods place the emphasis upon fitting all of these separate skills together. Dictation is given to beginners from the outset as if they were trained stenographers, except that care is exercised to choose material that is relatively simple at first; the material is increased in difficulty only after there has been some progress in the motor skill. Rate also is slow at first; but it too can be increased with improvement in the skill.

Once a skill has been perfected to the point of adequate or superior proficiency, the degree to which the habitual behavior remains fixed and efficient depends upon the extent to which the individual continues to use the skill in his daily living. A long period of disuse results in loss of efficiency. An earlier level of efficiency can be attained, however, by a relatively short period of relearning. A motor skill is kinesthetic; it is never completely lost. For example, if you have learned to ride a bicycle, it is likely that you will be able to ride it even after a long period of disuse.

Motor co-ordinations are transformed into skilled performance through drill and the integration of inner needs. Teaching techniques must be adapted in terms of these differences among learners. These include the amount of previous experience and practice in the skill, general physical condition, interest, general intelligence, special talent, and behavior habits that may have been utilized earlier.

The teacher is responsible for providing stimuli, as they are needed, for the correction of responses. These stimuli must be recognized by the learner and incorporated into his reacting mechanism so as to serve him as methods of procedure. The importance of effective instruction is evidenced by the improvement that is made through the employment of coaches for special skill functions in ball playing: a special coach for baseball pitchers, a special coach for infielders, or a special line coach in football, and the like. After an individual has mastered the fundamentals of a sport or of another skill, he is ready to master the fine points. He can profit from help given by a specialist.

Films are very effective aids in the teaching of a skill. A film that shows the various activities included in a game or in any other form of sport, for example, çan be slowed down so that the player can see for himself what his activities should be during a play in baseball, football, golf, swimming, or other sport. The grosser bodily movements can be improved through the viewing of well-selected films. If teamwork is filmed, it is possible, during the showing, to direct special attention to any one man on the team or to several men. Films have found their way into the teaching materials of good athletic coaches. They are helpful also for the teaching and learning of other skills.

Acquiring Skill in Expression

In addition to developing meaning and understanding in the area of human relationships there is need to develop some degree of competence in written expression, reading, spelling, and handwriting. A few of the psychological factors involved in the development of skill in these areas are presented in this section.

Developing skill in reading. During the past sixty years, the question of improvement in skill in reading has commanded the attention of educators and psychologists, to the extent that thousands of studies dealing with the various phases of reading skill have been published. Foremost among psychologists who are interested in the development of reading skill can be included such men as Gates, Witty, and Betts.

The term *reading* includes both *oral* and *silent* reading. Oral reading is not so effective as is silent reading for the gaining of ideas. It has been found that when the emphasis is placed upon oral reading the reading rate is reduced considerably, approximately one-third. Nevertheless, oral reading should not be neglected during the early stages of learning to read. Although there is kinesthetic and visual action during silent reading, oral reading brings into play a synthesis of visual, auditory, and kinesthetic sensations. Reading readiness also is important in the development of skill in reading, whether silent or oral.

For greatest improvement in reading skill to be achieved, reading material should be graded according to the maturity status and interests of the learner. Skill in the mechanics of reading should be developed early in the child's schooling through the use of material within his level of maturation and experience comprehension. Skill in reading, therefore, is dependent in part upon the material selected. As a result of the administration of reading comprehension tests, we now know that understanding of what is read cannot be

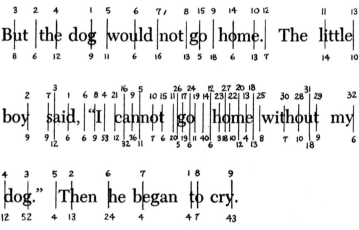

FIGURE 16.   Record of Silent Reading by a Pupil in Grade 1A

From G. T. Buswell, *Fundamental Reading Habits: A Study of Their Development*, Supplementary Educational Monographs, No. 21, published by the University of Chicago Press, p. 79, copyright 1922 by the University of Chicago. Reprinted by permission.

assumed, whether a learner is studying in the fifth grade, in the first year of high school, or even in the first year of college. Hence, in competitive school situations, the poor reader is at a distinct disadvantage.

Eye movements in reading. Eye movements are important indicators of reading competence. Experimental work on eye movements has helped increase the speed of reading. If you check the movements of your eyes as you read a line on a page, you will become aware of the fact that your eyes do not sweep across the page in a single movement. They move along jerkily, stopping for a moment at various points in their progress. These movements can be observed more easily if you watch the eyes of another person as he reads. Experimental evidence reveals that successive fixations do not move regularly along the print but tend to cut back (regress) to words already passed. In Figure 16 are illustrated the eye movement record of a pupil in Grade 1A when the child was reading silently. The fixations of a high-school sophomore are shown in Figure 17. At the upper end of the lines are numbers which indicate the number of the fixations; at the bottom of each line is a number which shows the duration of the fixation in twenty-fifths of a second. It seems clear that a fluent reader fixates phrases rather than words or letters. It can be seen by reference to Figure 16 that

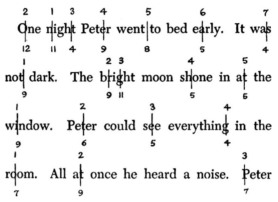

FIGURE 17.   Record of Silent Reading by a High-School Sophomore

From G. T. Buswell, *Fundamental Reading Habits: A Study of Their Development,* Supplementary Educational Monographs, No. 21, published by the University of Chicago Press, p. 132, copyright 1922 by the University of Chicago. Reprinted by permission.

fixations made by the Grade 1A pupil were long and irregular; those made by the high-school sophomore were short and fairly regular in duration (Figure 17).

Other studies have shown that:

It is evident that a speed fixation of from 5 to 6 twenty-fifths of a second satisfies the demands of maturity in reading. It is also evident that it is entirely possible to reach this level by the end of the fourth grade. Rate of recognition, therefore, is one element of reading which can be carried to the level of maturity very early in the school period.[1]

[1] From G. T. Buswell, *Fundamental Reading Habits: A Study of Their Development,* Supplementary Educational Monographs. No. 21, Copyright 1922 by The University of Chicago, University of Chicago Press, p. 33. Reprinted by permission.

The amount of time devoted to eye-movement averages from 6 to 8 per cent of the reading time for usual reading material, the maximum time being about 10 per cent; if difficult material is involved, the eye-movement time may decrease to 2.8 per cent of the reading time. In general, the more skilled the reader, the fewer will be the fixations of the eyes, the shorter the duration of the fixations, and the greater the conformity to a definite reading rhythm.

Value of remedial teaching. When weaknesses of one kind or another show themselves in the development of reading skill, individual instruction is needed. There are numerous reading hazards that interfere with progress. One of these (verbalism) may not be recognized by either the teacher or the learner. The child may read the word correctly without grasping the thought or ideas involved. The 100 per cent promotion plan increases the need for giving remedial reading instruction to retarded readers. Successful learning cannot continue unless and until reading difficulties are corrected or alleviated.

Important headway has been made in remedial reading through the work of people such as Betts, Fernald, and Witty. Yet, there is still much to be done to discover the best techniques to be used in the development of reading skill. Specially trained teachers are needed to develop in the child those attitudes that will impel him to improve his reading skill by gaining some of the mechanics of reading necessary to increase the power of comprehension.

Developing skill in spelling. The ability to spell varies among individuals. Ability to spell is not, in and of itself, an index of brightness or of dullness. An individual's spelling competence accompanies his writing requirements. It is helpful to him that, when he wishes to use a word in written expression, he also is able to spell it. Learning to spell is an individual matter and the teaching of spelling should be aimed at a pupil's mastering those words that he will use in his daily life. It is not always a wise practice to advise a pupil to substitute a word that he knows how to spell for another word that he wishes to use in composition. It is better for the teacher to use the situation to motivate the pupil to discover the correct spelling of the desired word.

Learning to spell includes the perception of the sound and the written form of the word, the interassociation of its parts, and its meaning. Since some words are not spelled as they are pronounced, visual rather than auditory imagery is preferable for learning to write a word correctly. As an individual writes a word, he is engaging in a kinesthetic experience which may be of assistance to him in spelling the word at another writing.

Practice in learning to spell a word should not be required of those pupils who already know how to spell it. The words that a pupil spells correctly can be discovered quickly by the teacher's giving of pre-tests. Spelling rules probably are less significant in the development of skill in spelling than the actual learning of the letter association of each word. Another helpful suggestion is to have pupils keep individual word books in which are listed those words (spelled correctly) which they have failed to spell correctly. Drill in these correct spellings will eventuate in spelling mastery. Yet, a recent list of words that are misspelled by college students included such apparently simple words as *exist, existence, extent, occasion.* Words that they frequently misuse are: *their, there, to, too, two.*

Developing skill in written expression. The young child gains a great deal of pleasure from scribbling with a soft pencil or a crayon. He will cover a sheet of paper with many kinds of forms which to him represent this or that common object in his environment. The adult may not be able to recognize the resemblance, yet the child can describe it vividly. When the child begins to express his ideas in written form, however, he encounters many difficulties.

At first, the child is confronted with the necessity of developing a vocabulary for expression, of acquiring the facility to form the characters needed in writing, and of expressing his thoughts in acceptable patterns of grammatical usage and sentence structure. Intelligent guidance during his early attempts in written composition helps him avoid later difficulties.

Even though the mechanics of writing are important, free expression should not be inhibited by overemphasis upon mechanical form and structure. Most individuals improve their ability to express themselves in writing as they increase in age and maturity. The skill achieved by the child in correct oral expression is likely to help him improve his written expression. Eventually, a learner may be expected to develop a characteristic style of composition.

Developing skill in handwriting. Just as inner maturation is required for walking, reading, or talking, so is muscle readiness needed for handwriting. It is believed that a child has reached a stage of readiness for instruction in penmanship when the control of his finer muscles is sufficient for him to manipulate objects such as chalk, a crayon, or a pencil. When the child in the nursery school is given crayons and large sheets of paper, he may mark the paper or scribble on it, but he is not ready to engage in the co-ordinated muscular movements that are essential for writing legibly.

The average five-year-old is ready to adapt his developing muscular control to skill training. By this time he has gained manipulatory control and can associate visual and kinesthetic sensations. He needs freedom of motion; hence his handwriting is large. Later, he can be expected to acquire greater control over his finer muscles. Consequently, he refines his handwriting. Penmanship is a complex sensori-motor-skill that is developed gradually as the child matures. In order to improve in penmanship the child must acquire dexterity in hand, wrist, finger, and arm movement. He also should possess good perception and memory for details.

There are wide differences in the handwriting proficiency among children of any age. Hence penmanship scales have been prepared to guide teachers in evaluating the handwriting achievement that can be expected from learners on each grade level. Two such scales are the Ayres Handwriting Scale and the Thorndike Handwriting Scale.

Certain techniques help the child develop skill in penmanship. Six suggestions given by Trow are worthy of attention.

1. Motivation. Children will want to write if there is need for it, beginning with simple directions and labels. They will want to improve if they can scale their own handwriting and chart their progress.

2. Fatigue. Much time spent in practice is harmful, especially small writing for small children. Until they are ready for the fine, eye-hand co-ordinations, large writing is better.

3. Exercise. Practice there must be, but intervals are important, norms of speed and quality should be known by the teacher, and the same standard should be demanded of a pupil in all written work.

4. Interval. Short, spaced practice periods are better than long.

5. Maturation. Readiness is determined by the ability and desire of the pupil. Manuscript writing is more easily learned first, because it is more like print, and because the separate letters form simpler perceptual patterns and shorter performance units than when imbedded in the whole word as in cursive writing.

6. Individuation. The forming of letters is affected by the position of the body, which need be no more awkward for left- than for right-handed pupils, and by the total arm and

wrist as well as the finger movements. Illegibilities can be corrected by attending to part movements.[1]

The development of legible handwriting includes instruction in body position, hand movement, rhythm and position. Studies have shown that correct position, and desirable movement and rhythm are fundamental components. Each of these must become so automatic, however, that the trained penman need not give conscious attention to any one of them as he engages in the writing process. Once this muscular co-ordination has been achieved, it is likely to remain a functioning skill.

QUESTIONS AND TOPICS FOR DISCUSSION

1. Trace motor development from infancy through childhood and adolescence, showing changes that may be expected in walking; in language usage.
2. What motor skill have you developed to a high degree of perfection? Report what you have done to attain this proficiency.
3. Evaluate the importance of knowledge of the goal in skill development.
4. In what way may knowledge of progress assist an individual to develop motor skills?
5. Specifically, what help can a teacher give to a child who wishes to learn to ride a bicycle? To swim? To drive an automobile?
6. Discuss the relationship of the development of motor skills to maturation.
7. What purpose may a good model serve in the teaching of penmanship?
8. Discuss the effect of spaced practice periods upon the learning of a skill.
9. What use can be made of "whole" learning and "part" learning in the development of skills?
10. What pitfalls should a person avoid who attempts to teach motor co-ordination to another?
11. Discuss the factors that cause children to retreat from practicing the piano? Why do most boys enjoy practicing basketball?
12. Using the same passage of a newspaper, ask each member of the class to cross out all the e's that he can in a minute. Count the number of letters crossed out by each member of the class. What was the median number of letters crossed out?
13. Discuss the extent to which learning transfers from one skill to another.
14. In what way do emotional responses affect the development of motor skills?

[1] W. C. Trow, *Educational Psychology*, Houghton Mifflin Co., Boston, 1950, pp. 618–619. Reprinted by permission.

15. Name some techniques that can be utilized to help learners develop good reading habits; good spelling habits; good handwriting habits; good habits of written expression.
16. Discuss any difficulties in the learning of penmanship that you have experienced.
17. Discuss the disadvantages of a teacher's placing emphasis upon formal grammar in the writing of a composition.
18. How effective are your own reading habits? To what extent do you believe that your reading rate can be increased?
19. What outcomes can result from the teaching of English with emphasis upon usage rather than upon grammar?

SELECTED REFERENCES

Biehler, R. F., *Psychology Applied to Teaching*, 2nd ed. Houghton Mifflin, Boston, 1974.

Crow, L. D., and Crow, A., *Educational Psychology*, New Rev. ed. Van Nostrand Reinhold, N.Y., 1964.

Crow, L. D., and Crow, A., *Psychology*, rev. ed. Littlefield, Totowa, N.J., 1972.

Dawson, M. A., and Bamman, H. A., *Fundamentals of Basic Reading Instruction*. David McKay, N.Y., 1963.

Gowan, J. C., *Guidance of Exceptional Children*, 2nd ed. David McKay, N.Y., 1972.

Hurlock, E. B., *Child Growth and Development*, 3rd ed. McGraw-Hill, N.Y., 1968.

Jersild, A. T., *Child Psychology*, 6th ed. Prentice Hall, Englewood Cliffs, N.J., 1968.

Kirk, S. A., *Educating Exceptional Children*, 2nd ed. Houghton Mifflin, Boston, 1972.

Mainord, J. C., and Love, H. D., *Teaching Educable Mentally Retarded Children*, C. C. Thomas, Springfield, Ill., 1973.

Trow, W., *Psychology in Teaching and Learning*. Houghton Mifflin, Boston, 1960.

Wright, B. A., *Physical Disability—A Psychological Approach*. Harper and Row, N.Y., 1960.

12   *Thinking and Problem-Solving*

We have stressed the fact that learning is evidenced by changes in behavior. We have implied that these behavioral changes refer not only to the observable actions of the learner but also to something that is happening within the learner himself. His sensory mechanism is stimulated by factors and forces that gradually bring about both the outer and the inner changes that constitute the learning process. Regardless of what explanations we accept concerning the ways in which inner changes take place, we know from our own experiences that overt behavior, barring reflex activity, is an expression of inner motivation. Motivation does not represent a blind groping for a response; it is the result of a systematic organization of inner reactions that enables an individual to achieve appropriate relationships between his inner and outer worlds.

As we mature and develop, sensation stimulates the forming of percepts; percepts change to concepts; concepts become the tools of thinking; thinking promotes understanding; conceptual understanding and thinking form the bases for problem-solving; the solving of problems is fundamental to effective learning and living. The significance in learning of the various phases of "mental manipulation" or ideation comprises the content of discussion in this chapter. To think is to initiate action; *how* we think is reflected in *what* we do. The primary responsibility of a teacher is to help his pupils learn to utilize their thinking powers in such ways that learning outcomes represent organized systems of constructive and wholesome inner and overt activity.

Conceptual Learning

Perceptual learning is basic to the development of understanding. If learning stopped with the forming of percepts from sensed material, life would consist of nothing more than a continued recognition of the meaning of that which is present to the senses. Mental activity can progress profitably only as adequate percepts become a part of our mental framework, so that thinking can proceed in the absence of sensed and perceived material.

Remembered images. Imagery is closely related to the functioning of memory. One perceives an object. Later, when the object is not present to the senses, an *image* of that object can be recalled. The extent to which the mental "picture" is an exact representation of the imaged object depends upon the complexity of the object, the degree of attention that was given to details, and the attitude of the observer toward the object when it was perceived.

For example, a small boy was telling the authors about his red ball. The child seemed to think that the adults did not know what a red ball looks like, so he tried to draw a picture of the ball on a piece of paper. Although he selected a red crayon for his drawing, he was not able to reproduce the roundness of the ball and seemed unable to decide upon its size. When he was asked how big the ball was, he said it was a little ball, but at the same time he spread his hands far apart. After the boy had gone to bed, the authors noticed a small red ball lying on a bookcase and asked the mother of the child whether that was John's red ball. It was. The interest aroused by the child's attempt to describe it caused them to look at the ball carefully and to pick it up. The simplicity of the object, the carefulness with which it was examined, and the attitude of the observers toward it resulted in the formation of what seemed to be a clear and vivid image of it.

Although the authors saw the ball a year previous to this writing, they still can describe it better than the child did. As a result of their greater mental maturity and wider experiential background, they are able to express in words that the ball is bright red, made of rubber, and about three inches in diameter. The fact that the exact diameter of the ball cannot be given reflects the describers' faulty evaluation of precise size. If exact size had seemed important, rather than relative largeness or smallness, a caliper could have been procured to measure the ball's diameter. The image itself would have remained the same; the description of the object would have been more accurate. The important consideration at this point is not the description of the image, but the image itself. Was the child's inability to give the adults a correct idea of it caused by the fact that his own image was inadequate or that he lacked adult-developed tools of expression?

Even young children have the ability to remember what they have experienced. It is difficult for an adult to discover the adequacy or correctness of a child's imagery, however. Incorrect perceptions, especially those that fall into the category of illusions, may result from inadequate or careless observation; they also may be based upon expectation or mind-set to observe what one wants to observe. Hence the image is distorted in terms of what the observer unconsciously puts into it.

Most adults have seen an American flag suspended from the windows of a building. A friend of the authors, whom the latter were visiting on a national holiday, hung his flag flat against the house. Then there was started a discussion as to whether the flag was hung correctly. There was no question concerning the straightness of hanging. The question was: Should the blue square containing the stars be at the left or right as viewed from the street? Although all agreed about the correctness of having the blue background at the top, everyone attempted to recall his image of a flag displayed on a building. As there was no agreement of opinion, a research problem was initiated that resulted in the reversal of the flag's position. Has the reader's perception of a displayed flag been so adequate that he has a correct image of it? Should the blue background be on the left or on the right of an observer facing a flag hung flat against a building?

When one's remembered image of a perceived person or object is far removed from actuality, the error is not merely a matter of inattention to details. Expectation or mind-set causes the observer to disregard that which he supposedly is sensing, except as he is stimulated by the presence of an element of his environment which is perceived and imaged to be what he *wants* it to be. A person who is disturbed by the absence of a close relative hears footsteps which in no way resemble those of the absent person. Later, he insists that the other person has returned but has not come into the room. The latter knows that the other is in the house because *he still can hear in his mind the sound of the familiar footsteps.*

Children tend to live in two worlds—the world of fantasy and the world of reality. As a result, they may confuse memory images of things that they perceive around them with the products of their vivid imagination. The teacher is well aware of this childish tendency. A child's descriptions of objects in his home may differ greatly from what they really are. The youngster is not deliberately lying. He shifts so easily from the real to the fanciful that he believes that he is describing honestly the images that he has built up through supposed perception of objects in the home. A child describes his toys or tells about the other fine things he has seen. He may become very much disturbed if his teacher seems to doubt the truthfulness of the descriptions; to him the things he imagines are as real as those with which he has had actual experience. One of the responsibilities of parents and teachers is to stimulate in the child an appreciation of the real as being as attractive and as satisfying to him as are the things and people that inhabit his imaginary world. Hence conceptual learning requires that the child's remembered images, the bases of *ideation,* grow out of accurate perceptions of realistically sensed materials.

The development of concepts. A concept is more than a memory image. The child builds many percepts of the elements of his surroundings, and these are transformed into more or less adequate images. Percepts and images are not formed in isolation; the percept and also the remembered image are related to other percepts and images, and to the background of experience in which they are formed. A continual mental process of organization and reorganization of relationships among percepts and images gradually leads to the achievement of meaningful associations or *concepts.* These concepts can be applied in the building of more complex perceptions and more accurate interpretations of symbols that are used to signify or describe percepts or images.

Concepts can be defined as generalized meanings, expressed in understandable symbols, that represent relationships in experience. A concept is abstract; it is built upon many experiences or situations in which are present the elements that constitute the concept. The young child's concepts are simple and associated with relationships that exist in his immediate environment. The concepts of *moreness* and *lessness, tallness* and *shortness, bigness* and *littleness,* and *goodness* and *badness* grow out of his home experiences with words, gestures, and other forms of behavior. Parents stimulate the child to perceive the relationship of these meanings in differing situations. The big ball, the smaller orange, and the little marble are round; they are not all the same size. The big bear, the middle-sized bear, and the little bear are bears; they all differ in size.

In a similar way, the child learns that a cup is a cup because you can pour something into it which you then drink. At first, a cup is *his* cup; it next becomes the cup on the table from which his mother or father drinks; later, a cup is that from which one can drink, regardless of its size or where it is standing. The child's learning of concepts that have realistic and correct meaning is hindered, however, by his relatively meager background of experience and his limited vocabulary. He may have a concept of two objects and of their relationship to one another in situations that have been experienced by him, but he is unable to combine his concepts in such a way that he will achieve a new concept that represents a different meaning.

For example, a child reared in the country probably knows what a goose is; he also has learned that his neck is what his head rests upon, or that his neck is between his head and the rest of his body. Then, one day, the child watches his father trying to repair the plumbing in the home and hears the adult say that he must go out to get a new "gooseneck." The father is astounded by the fact that the child begins to cry and to protest vehemently that "bad daddy" must not take the neck of the child's pet goose. The country child also may be bewildered by having an adult refer to him as a "little goose."

A city child also forms false concepts that are based upon lack of experience. Returning to our example of the young child's developing concept of a cup, we can appreciate what happens when he hears the two words *cup* and *butter* (the meanings of both of which he understands in his limited way) put together by the adult in form of *buttercup*. To him that combination can mean only one thing—a cup into which one puts butter. Since he has had no experience with the flower, he cannot understand the meaning of the new word or recognize its derivation.

Many similar examples of children's incorrect concepts could be cited. A child's expression of an incorrect concept may seem very amusing to adults. At the same time, in their dealings with even older children and adolescents, parents and teachers can never assume that young peoples' concepts of objects, persons, or situations are those of the mature and experienced adult. Even on the college level, an instructor may assume a conceptual understanding on the part of students of background material that does not exist. Learning based upon learner misconceptions does no more than increase the amount of misunderstanding, and decrease the extent to which clear and accurate thinking can take place.

A teacher may err in his presentation of learning materials by expecting children to become acquainted with so many new concepts that they become confused. It might be better procedure for the teacher to reduce the number of new concepts, while he helps the learners gain enriched understanding of those concepts which they currently are learning.

Basic factors of concept building. No matter how intensive and extensive his educational experiences may have been, nor how expert he is in one field of knowledge or skill, there is no adult who possesses complete conceptual understanding of all phenomena. There are certain concepts, however, that are basic to the development of successful and satisfying life patterns of behavior. We often hear one person say of another that the latter possesses "half-baked" ideas. This expression can be interpreted to mean that the individual referred to had accumulated, during his school days or later, a large number of inadequate concepts. These resulted from meager experience and/or lack of training in the forming of correct percepts and/or in the organizing of accurate concepts.

The implications of the foregoing discussion is important to teachers. Concepts are built out of experience. Hence learning should be the experiencing of enriched percepts that are acquired through learner participation in many forms of activity; through appropriate reading and viewing of visual learning aids (film strips, motion pictures, and television programs), and through classroom discussions which will help the learner build concepts both vertically (enriching the meaning) and horizontally (increasing the number).

The atmosphere of the classroom and the relationship between the teacher and the learners should be such that learners are encouraged to admit their lack of background understanding of learning content, and are motivated to recognize any existing misconceptions and to recondition them, without embarrassment to themselves. Too often a learner is loath to have his teacher and his classmates discover that he does not understand the meaning of the terms or statements that are used. Rather than admit his ignorance, he is willing to be considered inattentive or unwilling to learn.

Not only are differing experiences needed in the building of concepts, but the order in which these experiences are graded also is important. A young child cannot comprehend the concept of *morality* or *ethical values*, for example. He soon learns, however, what constitutes *goodness* and *badness* of behavior, in terms of the standards of behavior that are set up by his parents.

The child is *good* when he eats or drinks what is given to him. He is naughty or *bad* when he refuses to eat his food, pushes it away from him, or throws it on the floor. Likenesses among what he does that is good or among his bad or naughty acts, respectively, are accompanied by a limited understanding of differences between good and bad behavior. Yet, he is bewildered sometimes by the fact that he has done something that he "thought" was good but was treated by his mother as though he had been bad. Gradually, good and bad come to be recognized as *right* and *wrong*, and more realistic concepts concerning adult standards of rightness and wrongness are achieved.

Conceptualization on lower-level relationships among many particular experiences is needed by the immature child before he is able to achieve the power to deal with increasingly complex relationships on higher levels. The recognition of concepts as abstract generalizations that can be applied in all appropriate totals of inner and overt behavior (the configuration of the Gestaltists) is a long process of intensive and extensive experience. When can an adult be said to have achieved a completely adequate concept of moral or ethical behavior? What are the standards by which society or his particular cultural group evaluates behavior that has been motivated by his concept of morality or ethical conduct? To what extent does the concept itself reflect his experiences among the members of his group and their effect upon the direction of concept-building in this area? To what extent, and why, do different peoples differ in their concept of *honesty, industry, loyalty, universe, world-mindedness, beauty, usefulness, life on Mars,* or any other form of abstraction? Is truth absolute or relative?

We purposely have posed questions which have not yet been answered to everyone's satisfaction, although they are terms that can be found in the vocabulary of most adults. We cannot give concepts to learners. Each learner must develop his own concepts; we can provide for him, however, the kinds of experiences that help him evolve concepts that will be of value to him as behavior motivators in the society of which he is a member. Parents and teachers should be the key persons to guide his learning. Their responsibilities include concern with the development not only of ideas but also of symbols—usually words or phrases—through which concepts are expressed.

Language and Conceptual Learning

It is almost a truism to say that learning depends upon the power to communicate ideas. Robinson Crusoe managed to survive on a deserted island by adapting himself to the island and it to him, through a trial-error-trial-success kind of learning. His adaptations, however, were made possible by the fact that before he was shipwrecked on the island, he had achieved many conceptual patterns of relationships that he was able to apply in this unaccustomed situation. Moreover, his mastery of the obstacles that confronted him was helped greatly by the presence of his man, Friday, and the method of communication that gradually was developed between them.

Since primitive times, human beings have been able to "think," but the thoughts of one individual cannot be perceived directly by another. Hence one or another vehicle of expression must be found. The gestures, grunts, and symbolic marks and crude forms of writing that were characteristic of early primitive peoples have become refined through the ages to those forms of communication that now are represented by a complex hierarchy of oral and written symbols. Yet, primitive forms of communication find their way into modern culture, because we employ facial grimaces, and hand and body movements to assist us in expressing our thoughts. As a person attempts to explain the meaning of the word *spiral*, for example, he needs to exercise considerable self-control not to move his hand or arm in a spiral movement. These are mannerisms, however, that can be overcome to the extent to which an individual finds a satisfying word description of that which he is attempting to define or explain, or is willing to take sufficient time to communicate his ideas adequately in verbal language.

Words and phrases as symbols of concepts. We have referred to the fact that one of children's difficulties in conceptual learning is their inability to express their concepts or ideas in adequate language. By definition, a *concept is a generalization expressed in a symbol that usually is a word or phrase.* As new concepts appear, word symbols are attached to them. By common consent, a word symbol can be changed if a more meaningful term is available.

For example, in the early days of power-driven vehicles, the term "horseless carriages" was applied to them. The concept expressed by the term was not the same for all people, however. To some it denoted a marvelous step in mechanical progress; to others it was an invention of the devil that was aimed at killing off the people; to still others, those who could afford to own one, it represented wealth and daring. Relatively soon, however, the word *automobile* came into use. It was a more appropriate word symbol of the concept of that which is self-movable (from the Greek *auto*, self, and the Latin, *mobile*, moving).

A study of semantics, a relatively new method of discriminating more accurately among words as tools of thinking, alerts one to the differences of meaning that are attached by different individuals to the same words. These differences result from differences in experience; hence it can be understood readily that the concepts which are connoted by the terms also differ. For example, to some people, the word freedom means to do as one wishes within a framework of social acceptability of one's actions; to others freedom is a symbol that connotes uninhibited and self-satisfying behavior. The second concept of freedom is more nearly associated by the first group with the term *license*. Yet the word license has various connotations. According to dictionary definition, *license* can mean: (1) *Authority or liberty granted to do or omit an act;* (2) *A written or printed certificate of a legal permit;* (3) *Unrestrained liberty of action, abuse of privilege, disregard of property;* (4) *Allowable deviation from established rule, variation from a standard for a purpose.*

A young person simultaneously (1) is attempting to combine his experiences in such way that there will emerge for him certain generalized meanings or concepts, and (2) is groping for correct words or terms in which to express his evolved concepts. This is a difficult task, especially if adults, more especially parents and teachers, use words carelessly in the presence of a child, or assume that a particular word or phrase represents the same concept to him that it does to them. It is imperative, therefore, that when a teacher consciously introduces a new word into a child's vocabulary, the word is explained simply in terms of the adult's concept of it, lest the child confuse the meaning of the term as used by the adult with a concept that he has associated with the term through previous and different experiences. The learner's mental set toward use of words or phrases to express ideas may be in opposition to the mental set of the teacher. Such differences in attitude and consequent understanding may interfere greatly with the child's ability to build new learnings upon supposedly learned material.

College students, as well as their instructors, constantly are encountering accepted concepts couched in new terminology. Sometimes, the unaccustomed term adds precision of meaning. At other times, it may appear to the person who must add the new term to his vocabulary or substitute it for an already habituated word that the change of terminology represents no more than an attempt on the part of its deviser to gain attention from his confreres by seeming to introduce a "brand new idea" by dressing up an old concept in new clothes. The fields of psychology, sociology, and education include many examples of changes in terminology. Some of these are desirable, to the extent that continued study not only is refining our concepts of personal and social behavior and the learning process, but also is adding precision in the expressing of these growing concepts.

Other new terms puzzle even those who possess relatively clear concepts of what is intended. The word *communication* has been accepted generally as indicating *an exchange of ideas.* With modern advances in the development of mechanical devices for communication purposes, a new term has appeared—*intercommunication system,* which is defined as *a two-way communication system with two-way microphones and loudspeakers at each station for localized use in a ship, airplane, or building.* There is creeping into usage, however, the term *intercommunication* in connection with the leveling of attitudes, customs, and mutual understandings of people who may differ from one another in these respects. To what extent does the term *intercommunication* give greater precision of meaning or difference in concept from the word *communication?* Some of the new forms of terminology for the expressing of known concepts include: for degree of mental deficiency, *mild* for *moron, moderate* for *imbecile,* and *severe* for *idiot; psychosomatic disorders* may become *psychophysiologic disorders.*

Modern language is dynamic. New words constantly are being introduced to express ideas or concepts. At first, some of these terms constitute what is referred to as colloquialisms or "slang" expressions. Later, they find a place for themselves in accepted usage, and become dictionary-defined expressions of concepts. The word *Roger* is used specifically as the response of an airplane pilot to instructions that come to him from the ground or another airplane, and means that the pilot understands the instructions and will follow them. The term now is coming to be used by the general public, with an implication similar to its technical meaning. Hence it may not be too long before it is an accepted dictionary-defined term for common usage.

Adults do not experience difficulty only with adult-coined words. The terms used by children and adolescents often (in colloquial phraseology) "throw them for a loop." Unfortunately, by the time one child-or-adolescent-coined word has come to be attached by the adult to the concept which it seems to express, that term has been outmoded, and another term that carries a generally accepted connotation for an adult may be substituted by young people for the discarded term. The new-style expression is imbued by them with a meaning that again must be "learned" by their older associates. Among the not so old expressions of young people can be included: *groovy, tacky, beaver, cat, chicken, cool, scrambled eggs, snafu, hot rod, and dreamboat.* We shall leave to the reader the task of relating these terms to the particular concepts which they are supposed to express, unless by the time they are read, these terms have given way to new expressions. This general comment should be added, however. If a teacher wishes and expects to achieve satisfying relationships with his elementary- or high-school pupils, or even with his college students, it behooves him to learn *their* language as well at to attempt to refine their conceptual expressions according to *his* word usage.

Learning through communication. We have devoted considerable attention to the usage of words. When words or terms represent the same concepts to teacher and pupils, then teaching and learning are effective. There can be little if any learning unless concepts or ideas are formed and applied to the mastery of whatever area of learning is engaged in. Meager or incomplete concepts are enriched through reading and observing; they also develop vertically through the introduction of new facets by way of classroom discussion, questioning, and answering, and other methods of oral communication. Even as a young person learns by doing, communication of one kind or another is involved.

The appropriateness of the words used by the teacher, the sentence structure in which he presents his ideas, his word or phrase emphasis, and his manner of presentation exercise a potent influence upon his degree of success in communicating his own conceptual understandings to his pupils. A teacher may be accustomed to expressing himself in technical language when he is discussing his subject content with fellow teachers who are well acquainted with the field. He cannot expect learners in the classroom to profit from similar modes of explanations or attempted discussions. One of the outstanding characteristics of a successful teacher is his ability to meet learners on their level of understanding and interest, and gradually to lead them to come as near his level of understanding as it is possible for them.

A former chairman of a high-school English department and instructor of teacher-trainees in the field of methods of high-school English was accustomed to criticize adversely some of the reading materials that then were (and in some schools still are) used in the teaching of English literature. High-school freshmen were expected to gain an understanding of and an appreciation of literary classics that were far removed in time of writing and conceptual background from the experiences of most immature learners. This teacher constantly stressed the importance of starting the teaching of literary appreciation on the level of the learner's interest and ability. This might mean the bringing into the classroom of the reading and discussion of simple stories that deal with known situations and experiences. From that beginning, the high-school learner should be introduced to stories and other reading materials that represent a gradual inclusion of experiences that are more removed in time and space from learner experience, and that are written in more involved literary style. To plan a course in literature to meet the different appreciation levels of a heterogeneously organized class is extremely difficult, however, especially if the members of the class vary widely in reading comprehension.

When reading matter or the content of class discussion goes beyond the experiential or expression level of the learner, his overt expression of ideas may constitute no more than verbalism. He may memorize words, phrases, or sentences and repeat them parrot-fashion without having any understanding of what he is expressing. If a question is worded in such way that a memorized answer is suitable, the teacher may mistake verbalism for an expression of real understanding. A common example of the use of verbalism, resulting from verbatim memorization, is the proving of theorems in geometry. The well-intentioned learner memorizes the steps of proof as these are presented in his textbook, including in his memorization the placing of the figure on the page as well as the identifying letters of each part of the figure. If the teacher allows him, in class, to place the figure on his paper or on the blackboard and use the identifying letters that he has memorized, he may appear to understand the theorem. If the teacher is "mean" enough to change the position on the blackboard of the figure and to use identifying letters different from those in the textbook, the learner is lost. He has no concept of the relationships that are involved in the theorem.

Learning situations in which memorization of learning materials is substituted for understanding of them can be illustrated from performance in almost any area of learning in which correct ideas or concepts are needed to further the learning. The child reports to his mother that he is learning "gosinter" examples. (He is referring to his having been taught that "two goes into eight four times, etc.) During their school life, young people sing "The Star-Spangled Banner" or "America," at least once a week. If a teacher is brave enough to ask upper elementary-school or even high-school students to write the words that they have been singing, he is likely to be shocked by the kind and amount of meaningless jargon they produce. The proverbial examination "boner" is not limited to the lower schools. College students and even candidates for teaching licenses give evidence in written examinations of inaccurate and, sometimes weird, concepts.

Effects of mass communication upon learning. Parents and teachers often are heard to express the wish that they might have the power to control the media of communication to which young people are exposed. If children could be exposed only to what some persons consider to be desirable stimuli-situations, and all others avoided, the adults contend that maturing young people would be more likely to achieve at least relatively accurate and wholesome concepts of life relationships. Fortunately or unfortunately, mass communication is an inherent factor of community life. Neither young people nor adults can escape from it.

Although the point of view expressed in the preceding paragraph is untenable in our present culture and may not even be wise, one cannot help be sympathetic to the attitude of the parents and teachers. Young people, as well as adults, are exposed continually to a tremendous amount of one-way communication in the form of propaganda. The purpose may be directed toward' the achievement of self-perpetuation or aggrandizement on the part of political parties, social or economic groups, advertising agencies, or other local or more general factions that are interested in molding public opinion. These attempts at one-way mass communication operate through many media of influence: radio, television, motion pictures, public lectures, magazines and newspapers, and open discussions.

Children are encouraged by their parents and teachers to enlarge their experiences through many and varied contacts. There probably are few homes, except those in the hinterlands, in which one or more radios cannot be found; television sets are becoming almost equally popular; the reading of a newspaper is a *must* in the lives of most individuals, young as well as old. Magazines of all kinds can be purchased at the corner newsstand. Without enlarging upon available media of propaganda, we wish to emphasize the undesirable effects of inaccurate, prejudiced, or actually dishonest propaganda upon the developing conceptual understanding of the child. As a young person is exposed to intriguingly presented half-truths or deliberate lies, he sometimes finds it almost impossible to evaluate propaganda properly in terms of what he learns in school. "Glittering generalities" and emotional appeals that characterize most propaganda media' are much more exciting to the young person than are the more objective and perhaps less interestingly presented materials of school learning.

There is an excellent approach for parents and teachers to employ, however. If they wish to combat the influence upon children of inaccurate and unwholesome propaganda, they can attempt the utilization of two-way mass communication. Children should not be forbidden to read or to listen to specious arguments; that would be the most successful method to increase their interest in them. Rather should young people be encouraged to become acquainted with the various points of view expressed by opposing propagandists. These points of view then should become the bases of intelligently organized and interesting class or group discussion. This can be supplemented by learners' participation in research that is suited to their level of performance and that will produce factual information in terms of which a discussed bit of propaganda can be evaluated.

An adult often is surprised by the interest and understanding displayed in children's responses to such propaganda-evaluating techniques. A ten-year-old boy remarked one evening that he was glad he had not yet begun to smoke cigarettes because he would not be able to decide just "which brand actually is the best for one's health." He continued to say, "Maybe by the time I grow up, they'll really know which is best and they'll stop all this foolish advertising." A girl of about the same age, who was watching a dentifrice commercial on television, said, "We were talking about tooth paste in school the other day, and some of us checked on what is put into tooth paste to keep the teeth clean. When we found out about it, my teacher said that all tooth pastes that are made by good laboratories will help our teeth, if we clean them at least twice a day. Why do they waste all their money in advertising?" To this her brother answered, "They don't think they're wasting their money. They know others are good, but they want you to buy theirs. That's what advertising is for; but they are not supposed to tell lies about other kinds and they should not say that theirs is the best unless they can prove it. We discussed that in school last week." These children were not verbalizing. Their thinking gave evidence of objective and intelligent evaluation that had been motivated by their teachers.

Thinking in the Learning Process

What we have said to this point has been to prepare the way for a consideration of the importance of constructive thinking as a phase of learning in any area. From time immemorial, people have engaged in thinking. To say, "I think," followed by a presentation of one's thought, is common practice. What we think and the thinking process by which we arrive at our overt expression of mental activity vary from person to person and from one age and experience level to another. In the following consideration of the thinking process, we shall limit most of our discussion to the educational aspects of thinking and the responsibilities of teachers in their guidance of the development of effective thinking.

Purposes of thinking. As we implied earlier, thinking can be regarded as a kind of manipulation of concepts and ideas that bears some likeness to our manipulation of objects. In both forms of manipulation, there is attempted an organization of the material manipulated; the manipulation usually is aimed at the achievement of a goal or purpose that is inherent in the reason for the manipulatory activity. If we already had been achieving the goal through habitual reactions, there would be no need of manipulation. At this point, however, the analogy stops. Mental activity in the form of thinking goes beyond what is required of, or is done in, the manipulation of objects.

Thinking involves the manipulation of symbols that represent images of objects not present to the senses, and complex concepts or ideas. In thinking, these symbols are recognized in their existing relationships, and are manipulated and organized into different or new relationships for the purpose of attaining a desired goal. Participation in an activity for which an individual has developed patterns of behavior that have become habitual requires little or no need to think about the activity. It is entirely or almost automatic. A person walks along an accustomed path or street, for example, without giving thought to which foot he should put forward first. In fact, he may be so engrossed in thinking about something else that he is unaware of his walking; he may walk beyond his destination before he realizes that he has walked too far. If the individual is walking along a new road, however, or on a street that is partially torn-up, he literally must "watch his step." He brings to the focus of his attention whatever he has learned through actual or vicarious experiences about the best way of getting himself from where he is to where he wants to go. If walking on the broken pavement is an entirely or comparatively new experience, he may stumble or fall several times until or unless he can apply appropriate thinking to the solution of the problem.

Essentially, thinking is problem-solving. To the possible solving of the "problem," the individual concerned first applies all of his already formed thinking habits of responding; he then modifies or reorganizes these in terms of whatever is needed in the way of new knowledge or techniques of approach in order to arrive at a satisfying solution.

The thinking process. One might raise the question: "Do we learn to think or do we think to learn?" Viewed differently, we do both. Success-achieving thinking is not inherent in the original constitution of a growing and developing child. Although the newborn infant may possess all the physical potentials that later make it possible for him to engage in thinking, he needs to acquire a continuously changing body of percepts, images, concepts, and conceptual relations that form the basis of whatever he does in the way of thinking at any stage of his development. Hence *we learn to think*. At the same time, learning connotes change that is brought about by the gradual acquiring of refined and enriched percepts, concepts and patterns of relationships within the individual and between him and the external world. Organizing functional mental relationships is, by definition, thinking. Hence *we think to learn*.

An individual's thinking is influenced by the thinking of others. We presented evidence of this fact in our consideration of the effect of mass communication or propaganda. Throughout our discussion of human development, we also have emphasized the potency of the effect upon the developing young person of the thought patterns and attitudes of his adult and peer associates. Some individuals are more suggestible than others. Lack of confidence in one's own ability to "think through" a situation may be the result of meager experience or of low intelligence status. An individual may find it easier and more satisfying to have someone else do his thinking for him.

The mother of an adolescent may complain that her daughter expects her mother to do all the thinking for her. This is not a usual characteristic of teen-agers. The facts in this situation may be that, during childhood, the girl was not permitted to share with her mother in decision-making about the child's activities. Eventually, she learned to depend almost entirely upon her mother's decisions, especially if any attempts at thinking on her own were disapproved or ridiculed by adults. Now, however, the parent has become just as definite in her opinion concerning the fact that with adolescence should come the power to think for one's self, rather than to annoy the adult with adolescent problems.

The teacher's responsibilities. Thinking does not "just happen." One of the responsibilities of teachers is to motivate learners to think clearly and effectively within the limits of their experiences and abilities, rather than to have learners' thinking done for them by the teacher, leaving to the learners merely the responsibility of reproducing "what teacher thinks."

There is danger, however, in a teacher's removing himself completely from a thinking situation in the classroom. In a broad interpretation of the "activity" program, learning to do by doing is interpreted also to mean learning to think by thinking. There can be no disagreement with the underlying philosophy of learning through activity, provided that the theory is understood and applied intelligently. If it could be assumed that, by nature, every individual is a competent thinker, and that all he needs is the provision of thinking "materials," teaching would consist mainly in providing learners with sources from which a learner could select whatever he deemed best suited for his particular needs.

One of a teacher's functions is to provide materials about which the learner can *think,* and with which he can *do.* The teacher has an even more significant function. It is the teacher's responsibility to help learners achieve understandings and appreciations of relationships that they can manipulate and organize toward the developing of competent thinking habits. Hence the teacher needs to be a very definite participator in whatever thinking processes are active among his pupils.

In their struggles to form their own opinions, to achieve increased understanding, and to solve their problems, learners of all ages and levels of maturity need the help of those whom they consider to be more experienced thinkers than themselves. Graduate university study places emphasis upon self-initiated, self-organized, and self-achieved competence in areas of study that involve the "higher mental processes." Hence the instructor of graduate students attempts to keep himself out of the learning situation as much as possible by refraining from imposing upon the learner his opinions, attitudes, and appreciations of the learning unit. Consequently, in graduate classes, discussions usually are student-initiated and student-conducted within a framework of specific learning areas. Students do not always appreciate this democratic approach, however. Comments addressed to the instructor are common: "What do *you* think?" "We're not here to listen to our own futile meanderings." "We want to learn something."

Teachers cannot keep out of thinking or problem-solving situations; neither should teachers dominate the learner's thinking. Every teacher is a propagandist to the extent that it is his job to guide the development of immature thinking processes. For that reason, it is imperative that the thinking of the teacher is clear and definite, based upon rich conceptual understandings, and unbiased. Prejudiced thinking that is displayed by a teacher may be extremely harmful in its effects upon learners' attitudes and opinions. Controversial issues in any area of human relationships should not be avoided. Young people need to have their thinking cleared on many matters, especially on those that involve emotional concomitants. The teacher must take care, however, that he motivates the learners to consider every aspect of a controversial topic, that they are encouraged to assemble as much correct data as possible, and finally, that they develop their own point of view concerning what to them seems to be the best point of view, in terms of the actual facts available.

We subscribe heartily to the psychological principle that a young person's opinions should be his own, in that they have resulted from his own thinking activities. We fear, however, that sometimes children are expected to think through situations that are beyond their maturity level or their experiential background. Their expressed views, or opinions, or attitudes are likely to be verbalistic reproductions of what they read in the newspaper, or what they learn from adults outside the school. A teacher may be amazed at a child's apparently mature expression of attitude or opinion concerning a complex issue; tactful but searching questioning may reveal that the child possesses no real understanding of what he has been talking about.

Kinds of thinking. In its broadest interpretation, all thinking represents one or another form of problem-solving. The kind of problem that requires the functioning of the thinking processes, the goal to be achieved, and the manner in which the problem is approached make it possible to differentiate among kinds of thinking. The kinds of thinking in which an individual may engage during a day, a week, a month or a whole lifetime range from autistic, or self-directed thinking to logical, objective reasoning that is applied in attempted solution of difficult or complex problems.

Thinking may constitute the mental components of the emotional factors that are operative in the appreciation of the arts, or of objects, situations, or peoples' achievements. Studying to acquire knowledge or information requires that one meet the problem of discovering the source of the information, or of selecting that which should be emphasized as having particular significance or usefulness. In each of these kinds of thinking there is present a problem that needs solution. Some problems can be solved with only slight modification of existing organizational thinking patterns, however.

Autistic thinking implies the presence of emotional self-concern that is accompanied by a strong drive to satisfy motives in terms of release of tension. The individual may be experiencing a serious personal problem. Because of his self-involvement, he is unable to attack it realistically. His emotionalized state interferes with an objective, realistic approach to the problem. His reactions in the situation are impulsive; his failure to achieve his goal may result in the cessation of overt activity; he continues mental activity in the form of daydreaming. This may become so intense that eventually he loses partial or complete contact with reality, and may be adjudged mentally ill.

We may be confronted by a situation which is different from those to which we are accustomed. We first try to meet the novel elements of the strange situation with habitual responses. This is referred to by some psychologists as a "reproduction attitude." For example, a woman is asked by a neighbor, who is preparing his dinner in the absence of his wife, how long it should take to cook corn-on-the-cob. The first, automatic response is, "Till it is done." This is a thoughtless answer that is based upon the fact that the woman has had so much experience in the cooking of corn that she knows, without much thinking about it, when the corn is ready. She immediately recognizes the fact that this answer means nothing to the inexperienced man. She then proceeds to think about what she really does, and gives him careful directions. This situation posed a problem to the woman to the extent that she needed to meet the man's problem of cooking the corn. The difficulty lay in differences between them in cooking experience.

Much of the thinking that is associated with everyday activities follows a kind of trial-error-trial-success pattern. We must make decisions concerning the meeting of this or that slightly different situation. A man receives a letter asking him to participate in a forthcoming conference. His first thought, resulting from many experiences of this kind, is to notice the date of the conference and decide whether or not he is free to accept the invitation. He is, so he starts to write an acceptance. By rereading the invitation, he discovers that he is supposed to make certain suggestions concerning other possible speakers and to hold himself in readiness for a preconference meeting with all the participants. This poses a problem. He tears up the letter he has started to write. After some consideration of the problem, he starts another letter in which, he hopes, he has responded satisfactorily to the suggestions included in the invitation.

This man gave some thought to the new situation. If an impulsive or relatively inexperienced thinker recognizes the inadequacy of the "reproduction attitude" of approaching an everyday unfamiliar situation, he may attempt various reorganizations of his ideas. His recognition of the unfamiliar elements of the situation may be vague; he may not have a clear understanding of the facts needed to help him solve this problem-like situation; his response is inadequate, or it may shift aimlessly from one solution to another. Children's thinking processes in meeting the daily requirements of classroom learning too often are disorganized and uncertain. They are based upon vague incomplete ideas. The factors responsible for much of children's inadequate thinking are presented in the following quotation:

> Many of the problems which the child encounters do not have their setting in a definite sequence of thought-steps so that he may solve them in a direct fashion. . . . Facts that should be known before the problem is attacked are not known, or perhaps only vaguely known. The problem becomes a number of problems which then must be dealt with in a piecemeal fashion.
>
> It is conceivable, perhaps . . . that the problems of formal education might be so well "paced" in difficulty and sequence that a child need never have recourse to trial-and-error thinking. This must be very difficult to realize in practice. It does seem, however, that we can take advantage of the suggestion to increase the mental efficiency of the pupil. By encouraging him to adopt a problem attitude and to inhibit reproductive tendencies, his method of attack will be more comprehensive and direct. "Crowding" the child with assignments on which he must get something done, right or wrong, tends to favor partial insights and trial-and-error thinking which is never completed. In order to resist the internal and external pressure calling for "results," the child needs to have a wholesome confidence in his own ability and to set a definite value on the products of his own mental life.[1]

Factors that influence thinking. An individual thinks when he needs to solve a problem of one kind or another. The degree of success with

[1] W. D. Commins, and Barry Fagin, *Principles of Educational Psychology*, 2nd ed., copyright 1954 by The Ronald Press Co., pp. 690–691. Reprinted by permission.

which the problem is solved depends upon various factors that are associated with the readiness of the individual to relate his thinking to the elements of the situations which stimulated him to think.

The conceptual background of the thinker is an important factor of influence upon the direction that is followed in the thought process. The mentally-slow child whose experiences have been meager cannot grasp relationships easily. He does not have a sensory background sufficient to assist him in forming correct percepts that eventually become the memory images and concepts of thinking material. An alert or intelligent person may possess superior ability in organizing and reorganizing concepts or ideas. Yet, his mental manipulation of ideas is conditioned by the kinds of ideas he has developed and the way in which they were learned. The more intelligent person is able to gain insight into a whole situation and the interrelations of its elements that elude the slower learner, no matter how eager the latter may be to profit from instruction.

Some parents are not so much concerned with the subject matter of their child's learning as they are with the development of his power to *think*. These parents are both right and wrong. We do not think about *nothing;* problems that need to be solved grow out of situations or conditions that are external to the solver. In order to *think* about the problem we need a background of information and conceptual understanding that give us something to think about. For example, the question: "What would happen to Jean Valjean today if he committed the offense described by Victor Hugo?" constitutes a problem. The learner who attempts to answer the question must be able to evaluate the offense and decide upon the way it should be treated. To solve the problem, there is needed a background of knowledge and understanding. He must know who Jean Valjean was; identify the offense and its treatment; know how such offenses are treated now; understand present attitudes toward poverty, etc.

The factors that affect the thinking of young people can be summarized to include: conceptual background; degree of intelligence; habitual patterns of thinking; teacher motivation of thinking; fluency of expression; learner appreciation of the worthwhileness of the thinking expected in a particular area of learning; effect of adult-initiated propaganda, and opportunity to engage in independent thinking. Although all thinking (broadly interpreted) is problem-solving, we now consider the mental processes that are involved in attempted resolutions of difficulties that are recognized to be problematic situations.

Problem-Solving

A problem arises when an individual is confronted with a situation in which he must respond, but realizes that his habitual patterns of response are not adequate for satisfactory adjustment to the "problem situation." We have pointed out that many minor problems can be solved more or less satisfactorily by the application of trial-error-trial-success techniques. Much waste of time and effort may be involved in such haphazard approaches to the meeting of problem difficulties, however. Hence, through their learning experiences, children need to develop a more orderly thinking procedure toward the solution of problems that are suited progressively to their maturing and developing stages of thinking ability.

Problem-solving and reasoning. In order for problems to be solved adequately, a person's concepts and memory must reflect correct perceptions of materials with which the problem deals; fruitful relationships then must be achieved through the tracing and retracing of thoughts until a satisfactory solution of the problems is reached. Such mental manipulations are characteristic of reasoning. Hence reasoning can be regarded as a form of thinking that is concerned with the orderly manipulation of memory images and concepts or ideas, until workable relationships are discovered. The science of valid and accurate thinking or reasoning is known as *logic*. According to the nature of the problem one of two approaches can be employed—the *inductive* or the *deductive*.

Inductive approach. Induction is the process of inferring or aiming at the general from observation of the particular. A law of causational connection can be inferred or derived from observing and analyzing some particular instances which appear to the reasoner to have either one or more characteristics in common.

Many scientific laws or principles are inferences based upon many accurate observations of certain phenomena that, upon analysis, give evidence of a common factor that then is assumed to be a general characteristic of the group observed. For example, Thorndike first promulgated the Laws of Exercise and Effect in learning as a result of his maze experiments with hungry rats. Pavlov's explanation of learning as conditioning was based upon his observation and analysis of the carrying over of a habitual response from the stimulation situation that included it to a new stimulus. Through his observation of the behavior of many adolescents, G.

Stanley Hall concluded that adolescence is a period of storm and stress.

The validity of a general conclusion reached by utilization of the inductive approach depends upon the number of instances observed and the actual similarity among them. Lay people and even men and women trained in their field may draw conclusions from too few cases of a large group that then are accepted as generalizations for the entire group. Consequently, young learners are encouraged to draw conclusions from several isolated studies. Teachers should be careful that their pupils do not make "snap judgments" without adequate observation and analysis. Perhaps one of the learning areas in which inductive thinking or reasoning is likely to produce inadequate or partially adequate conclusions is that of the social studies.

Deductive approach. Deduction means reasoning from the general to the particular. If a conclusion or principle is assumed to be valid, the problem becomes one of discovering whether the general principle applies to particular phenomena or instances. This approach to problem-solving is referred to as the logical form of reasoning. Formal logic takes the form of syllogistic reasoning. A syllogism consists of three propositions. The first two are called the premises (accepted facts or generalizations) and the third is the conclusion, in which the common term in the premise disappears, after furnishing the logical connection between the premises.

Problem-solving through logical reasoning implies the evolving of an adequate solution of the problem. Much of our thinking follows the syllogistic pattern, but subtle elements in the premises may not be recognized, thus leading to erroneous conclusions. Insight into the significance of each idea is needed. Unless children are helped to discover the actual implications of a stated idea, thinking and reasoning continue to be fuzzy even on the college level.

Although the syllogistic approach to problem-solving is helpful in that the syllogism deals with relationships in thinking, syllogisms are constructed upon relatively artificial materials. Logic, as it usually is taught, does not necessarily induce the student to apply syllogistic reasoning to his own life situations. Logical reasoning places emphasis upon *techniques* of thinking, rather than upon the *materials* of thinking. The application of syllogistic techniques has value, however, in helping an individual gain insight into thought relationships. A few examples of syllogisms may help to clarify this point.

Major premise—All men are mortal.—(correct general concept)
Minor premise—He is a man.—(correct specific idea)
Conclusion—Therefore, he is mortal.—(correct conclusion)

This syllogism represents accurate reasoning. Let us change the wording of the syllogism:

All mortals are men.—(incorrect generalization)
She is a mortal.—(correct specific idea)
Therefore, she is a man.—(incorrect conclusion)

In the second syllogism, the generalization is factually incorrect; therefore, the conclusion cannot be correct. Here is another syllogism:

Some flowers are red.—(correct partial generalization)
Violets are flowers.—(correct specific idea)
Therefore, all violets are red.—(incorrect conclusion)

The error in this syllogism is caused by the fact that the first premise tells us about the color of *some* flowers, not all. Hence there may be flowers that have other colors. One cannot conclude from the ideas included in the premises that violets are red; they may be any color.

Phases in problem-solving. In Chapter 10, we referred to John Dewey's belief that children learn by thinking their way through problem situations. In his book, *How We Think*, Dewey presented five phases or steps that are involved in the solution of a problem. These can be described as:

1. Awareness and comprehension of the problem. (Realization of the problem.)
2. Localization, evaluation, and organization of information. (Search for clarity.)
3. Discovery of relationships and formulation of hypothesis. (The proposal of hypothesis.)
4. Evaluation of hypothesis. (Rational application.)
5. Application. (Experimental verification.)[1]

In scientific experimentation these five phases usually are clearly indicated. The scientist becomes aware of a problem that requires careful reflective thinking. He then interprets the problem in order to make certain that he understands the implications that are inherent in the problem situation. If he possessed ready-made re-

[1] Adapted from J. Dewey, *How We Think*, D. C. Heath & Co., Boston, 1910, pp. 106–115.

sponses to all of these elements, the situation would be no problem to him. Since the situation involves unrecognized implications, however, he attempts, through research and perhaps experimentation, to gather all of the information for understanding that he believes he needs. He then organizes and reorganizes relationships among all of the concepts until he comes up with what seems to him to be a workable answer or hypothesis, or tentative solution. He mentally checks the hypothesis against the elements of the problem situation. He may modify and remodify his original hypothesis by reflecting upon the extent to which his tentative solution meets the requirements of the problem.

When the reasoner is satisfied with the rational validity of the hypothesis, he attempts to verify his conclusions by applying the hypothesis in the solution of problems that are similar to the one on which he has been working. If the hypothesis "works" in many situations, all of which contain the problematic element or elements, the hypothesis becomes a scientific law or a principle. The law then is applied generally until it fails to solve difficulties that are found to be common to problematic situations in which the principle is supposed to function adequately.

At this point a new problem is posed: What problematic elements are there in these situations that require solution? The five phases of problem-solving then are repeated until a better solution of the difficulty is achieved.

Factors of adequacy in problem solutions. If problem-solving is to result in correct and usable solutions, problem-solvers must possess an adequate background understanding of the elements of the problem. They must be able to discover sources of necessary information and to relate that information to the requirements of the problem until a workable hypothesis emerges, which then is thought through to check its validity. The verifying of the hypothesis through its application in appropriate problem situations may be the responsibility of the original problem-solver or of other persons who are experiencing problems in similar situations.

The verification of an hypothesis is as important as the development of the hypothesis itself. Too often a principle or law is evolved and accepted without sufficient verification through application in many situations. Consequently, the principle, law, or conclusion is found to be inadequate for general application.

We have lived through the establishment of many educational policies and philosophies that appear to function successfully in certain limited educational situations but fail to bring about expected results when they are applied in larger or different learning situations. For example, every educator is vitally interested in the problem of learner stimulation toward successful learner achievement. Consequently, many attempts have been made to solve this problem. Learning situations and learning activities can be controlled somewhat adequately in relatively small school systems. Hence many principles, techniques, and approaches to learning have been evolved and applied in small school communities or in selected schools of a larger community. When these apparently workable solutions to an educational problem have been applied to learning situations that represent mass education, they usually fail to function, or they need to be greatly modified before they are usable. In the field of standardized measurement, the same difficulty may be experienced. A test is devised to measure a certain area of learning. Unless its usability is verified by application to a large cross section of the learning level for which the test has been constructed, its value will remain local rather than general.

Reasoning that is applied to the attempted solution of a problem may be ineffective because the reasoner does not have sufficient power of insight or richness of background experience to recognize the elements of or the extent of the problem. Learners on all levels, from the elementary school through the college graduate level, may find it difficult to comprehend the problems which they are attempting to solve. Children experience this difficulty when they are motivated by their teachers to engage in the solving of problems that are associated with learning content. They might find a way to solve the problem if they understood its meaning and significance.

It is good learning procedure to challenge children with questions or problems that require the establishment of new or different conceptual organizations. The teacher must be certain, however, that a posed problem is suited to the understanding level of the children who are expected to solve it. Especially does the teacher need to be careful concerning the thought problems he assigns for home solution. The learner soon becomes discouraged if he does not understand the statement of a problem. Either he returns to school the next day with uncompleted homework, or, before the school session begins, he attempts to copy the work of another pupil, without any understanding of what he is copying.

Older learners may attempt to solve problems that they themselves propound and that are outgrowths of their desire to further their learning in a particular area of study. Usually, a student-initiated problem tends to include practically all of the subject content and relationships. A few examples of students' too-broad questions are: What is wrong with labor organizations? What are the problems of the producer of hybrid seed corn? How does modern music differ from classical music? What should be done about juvenile delinquency? How are climatic conditions related to health?

To obtain completely accurate answers to these questions would necessitate considerable research. Moreover, most, if not all, of these questions could be separated into specific questions, each of which might require a great deal of information-gathering and reflective thinking to evolve an adequate answer.

Young people tend to think in generalities. They become impatient if they are asked to deal with what to them may seem to be unnecessary details. It would be possible, of course, to reproduce the opinions of experts in any of the fields included in the list of questions presented. These experts, however, arrived at their conclusions through patient and careful consideration of the many subproblems that can be analyzed out of the general, over-all question or problem.

A college student, for example, presented to her English instructor a long and carefully prepared study-report that dealt with a critical evaluation of the literary writers of the nineteenth century. She had spent days of research to discover what literary critics had to say about the literary products of that period. When the instructor returned the document to the student, it contained this comment: "This is an excellent piece of research, but where are *you?*" The student's reply was, "I thought that this was what you wanted. I've read all the writings of the nineteenth century referred to by the critics and I don't agree with everything that they say, but I was afraid that my criticisms would not be valid since I don't have their background of critical evaluation."

An adult's ability to solve problems is dependent upon the self-confidence that he had achieved, during his earlier learning years, through successful attempts to solve problems which became progressively more difficult. Skill in problem-solving is associated with interest in the problem, ability to understand it, and recognition of its practicality. When or if problem-solving situations are graded to a learner's ability and interest, he probably will develop an attitude of willingness to solve his personal problems, and the mental power to reach satisfactory situational adjustments. Emergency problem situations may arise, however, which seem to go beyond his ability to comprehend and/or to meet. In such instances, he should be encouraged to seek the assistance of someone who is more experienced than himself in the solving of emergency problems. Personal problems are discussed in greater detail in Chapter 20.

Problem-solving in everyday life. We referred earlier to the inadequacy of hit-or-miss attempts to resolve problems. The trained thinker tends to attack problematic situations or conditions through the utilization of a relatively orderly process of reflective thinking. He usually is not aware of the fact that, in his reasoning, he is following the five phases of problem-solving. Several or all of the steps may seem to be telescoped, especially if he encounters a problem that requires immediate solution. The following account of an emergency situation illustrates this point.

Because the connecting wires of an automobile cigarette lighter were damaged, the family refrained from using the lighter. Recently, before starting on a trip, the man had his car conditioned, but neglected to have the lighter repaired. When the group was traveling through a sparsely populated area, however, the owner's wife used the lighter. It worked; but when it was returned to its socket, it became jammed and could not be released. Later, a sudden pushing of the lighter into its socket caused a short, which became evident to the occupants of the car as they smelled and saw smoke. The man's first response was to pull out the lighter and, with it, the flaming piece of wire which was attached to the socket. As he blew out the flame, he noticed more flames in the vacant space. His wife ran hastily to a house by the side of the road to obtain water. Instead of waiting for her return, the man picked up handfuls of dirt from the side of the road and threw them onto the burning wires, thereby extinguishing the flames. The man's next move was to use some tape, which he kept in the car, to bind the ends of the exposed wires. He then tested the ignition which appeared to function satisfactorily, and he started to drive on.

The motor continued to operate satisfactorily. Throughout the remainder of the trip, however, all of the driving was done during daylight hours because the driver did not know what might happen if he were to turn on his lights.

In this illustration, all of the phases of problem-solving were covered. The driver of the car became aware of the problem when he smelled and saw the smoke. He comprehended what the problem might be and, as he pulled out the lighter, located it and took immediate action: he procured the dirt, threw it on the flames, and examined the open ends of the wires. He then carried the solution to a conclusion by wrapping the wires. All of this was completed in less than an hour.

As the man drove, he continued to verify his solution of the problem by checking the wires from time to time and reflecting upon whether the car was driving smoothly. One possible problem he could not solve—the effect upon the operation of the car of his battery's losing its charge, as a result of a short in the light circuit. He knew that he did not have and could not get the proper equipment to correct this difficulty until he reached a city. Moreover, he recognized his own lack of expertness in dealing with serious car difficulties.

This man would be described by the man in the street as a "quick thinker." He did give evidence of alertness. His speed of successful action was evidence not only of his intelligence but also of his acquired background of knowledge, and of his trained power to recognize conceptual relationships and to organize them into new patterns of thinking that resulted in effective action. His problem-solving activity did not represent mere reproductive thinking. This was his first experience with an emergency problem of this type. The kind of thinking and action exhibited in this situation was characteristic of this man's attitude and approach to other problematic situations which differed in nature from the one described but in which he responded with equal speed and good judgment.

A poorly trained or emotionally uncontrolled person might have found it difficult to do anything about the described situation. Although he would want to take action, adequate thinking could be inhibited by his slowness to comprehend the situation and his inability to start action. The emotional state brought about by the suddenness of the emergency would hinder his effectiveness in the total situation. Two of the most important outcomes of learning should be the attainment of ability to reason quickly and the power to control the emotions during an emergency problem situation.

We have illustrated the application of reasoning to an emergency problem situation. The average individual meets relatively few such situations in his life. There are many times, however, when training in problem-solving functions in situations that are less exciting but perhaps equally important to the individual involved.

For example, a young woman is requested by a busy friend to

purchase some greeting cards for her, without giving any indication of the number and kinds of cards desired. This shopping assignment poses certain problems: the total number of cards to be bought; the variety of each kind, and the number of each kind; the style of card, and the amount to be paid for each.

The time and place of buying are problems that can be met by the young woman in terms of her daily activity schedule and her previous experiences in the purchase of greeting cards. The number, varieties, proportion of each variety, style, and price must be decided in terms of her understanding of the friend's needs, tastes, and attitude toward the spending of money.

While the purchaser is engaging in the selection of cards, each card examined constitutes an individual problem of judgment concerning its suitability in terms of the criteria to be met. A few of the cards are selected especially for relatives and friends of the woman who had requested the purchase. A final selection is made and the cards are given to the friend for her approval, which they receive. The final verification of success in meeting the problem of shopping for another person will come later. The two women will check the number and kind of each variety of cards that will be used as situations arise that require the sending of cards for special occasions such as: birthdays, weddings, arrival of new babies, wedding anniversaries, illnesses, graduations, and other occasions that are associated with card-sending.

This appears to be a simple problem, yet it necessitates the application of the steps in problem-solving without immediate awareness of their functioning. Conceptual understanding and thinking organization are required. An assignment of this kind could result in inadequate performance and dissatisfaction on the part of both women, if either or both lacked confidence in the young woman's ability to carry out the commission. Learning, as thinking and reasoning, should be aimed toward competence in solving simple problems as well as in dealing with problems of greater significance.

Creative thinking as problem-solving. A young child's first attempt to create is centered in the manipulation of materials that usually are handled in a relatively unthinking manner. The youngster is more interested in the creating than in the product created. He molds clay, scribbles, covers sheets of paper with crayon or paint. He experiments with other media of expression. He soon attempts to identify what he has created, and he tries to create something that he has seen or that has attracted his attention. Sometimes, he wants an adult to interpret for him what he has done.

With maturing motor control, increasing experience, and developing interest in his surroundings, the child consciously begins to create something in one form or another. In school he is encouraged to "express himself" through handicraft activities, writing of stories, dancing, and one or another form of musical activity. He is being motivated to develop whatever creative potentialities he may have.

The more mature individual may be moved to engage in one or another form of creative thinking. Creative thinking involves mental processes that are characteristic of other forms of thinking, i.e., experience, association, and expression. Creative thinking is similar also to other forms of problem-solving in that there is a felt need or problem that motivates mental manipulation and organization of conceptual relationships. The thinking activity is aimed at the realization of a goal to be reached through overt expression of mental activity. Creative thinking differs from the logical reasoning employed in problem-solving, however, in that the stages of creative thinking usually include preparation, a time of incubation, and insight.

The writing of a book, the painting of a picture, the composing of a musical work, the building of a bridge, the making of a dress—in fact, any activity that is creative requires that the creator experience a strong desire to create. The desire is accompanied by emotional and imaginative factors that influence the thinking of the individual. During the preparatory period, the creator may assemble and integrate materials, and investigate various aspects of the problem. Except in rare instances, there then occurs a longer or shorter period of time, during which no conscious thinking is present. Any attempt to hurry the thinking process may interfere with eventual creative production. Associations and vague aspects of creative thinking may take place but, generally, the period of incubation shows little or no effort to produce. In fact, the individual may come to believe that he cannot produce. He seems not to know how to get started. Insight into the situation usually comes suddenly. The individual now is ready to start thinking creatively and to keep going until thinking is transformed into creative expression.

Many students have had an experience of this kind when they wanted to write a story or to engage in any other creative project. They are intensely interested in the project; they make careful preparations for starting it. Then nothing seems to happen. They cannot even find an appropriate beginning. Sometimes, when they are about ready to discard the project, they suddenly get an idea. They have gained needed insight into the problem. How simple it is! Creative thinking is in full swing. The apparent period of incubation was not a time of thinking inactivity. The mental associations that were being made and the relationships that were formed were acting subtly but surely toward the gaining of necessary appreciation of appropriate relationships, or toward functional insight.

QUESTIONS AND TOPICS FOR DISCUSSION

1. What contributions to your present learning activities can be made by your past experiences?
2. Explain how habits of thinking may be acquired.
3. Give examples of trial-error-trial-success learning from your own experiences other than those associated with motor learning.
4. Why does reading a passage aloud in the presence of others sometimes interfere with an understanding of it?
5. Evaluate the importance of reflective thinking to an individual who lives in a democracy.
6. What is the relationship between ability to think effectively and general intelligence?
7. Illustrate the steps in scientific thinking or problem-solving.
8. To what extent is thinking required in the solving of crossword puzzles?
9. What role should be taken by the teacher in helping learners improve their ability to think?
10. By keeping in mind possible transfer values, compare rote learning with logical learning.
11. Discuss the relationship between memory and the development of concepts.
12. Trace the mental stages through which a child probably passes as he develops the concept of conscientiousness.
13. Why can the learning of a language be considered to be conceptual learning?
14. What are the bases of communication between two or more persons?
15. Discuss the effect upon learning of oral and written communication.
16. Differentiate between autistic thinking and daydreaming? To what extent do all persons engage in either or both?
17. Recall an experience that you have had in creative thinking and expression. Explain the mental processes through which you passed until your desire to create was expressed in overt behavior.

SELECTED REFERENCES

Anderson, R. C., and Faust, G. W., *Educational Psychology: The Science of Instruction and Learning.* Dodd, N.Y., 1973.

Bolton, N., *Psychology of Thinking.* Barnes and Noble, N.Y., 1973.

Bourne, L. E., *Psychology of Thinking.* Prentice Hall, Englewood Cliffs, N.J., 1971.

Crow, L. D. and Crow, A., *Educational Psychology,* new rev. ed. Van Nostrand Reinhold, N.Y., 1963.

Getzel, J. W., and Jackson, P. W., *Creativity and Intelligence.* Wiley, N.Y., 1962.

Gibson, J. T., *Educational Psychology,* 2nd ed. Appleton-Century-Crofts, N.Y., 1972.

Hawkins, N. E., *Psychology for Contemporary Education.* Charles Merrill, Columbus, Ohio, 1973.

Johnson, P. E., *Psychology of School Learning.* Wiley, N.Y., 1971.

Lesser, G. S., *Psychology in Educational Practice.* Scott Foresman, Chicago, 1971.

Lindgren, H. C., *Educational Psychology in the Classroom,* 4th ed. Wiley, N.Y., 1972.

Murphy, G., *Freeing Intelligence through Teaching.* Harper and Row, N.Y., 1961.

Peterson, L., *Learning.* Scott Foresman, Chicago, 1974.

Stein, D. G., and Rosen, J. J., *Learning and Memory.* Macmillan, N.Y., 1974.

Stevenson, K. T., *Children's Learning.* Appleton-Century-Crofts, N.Y., 1972.

Wellington, C. B., and Wellington, J., *Teaching for Critical Thinking.* McGraw-Hill, N.Y., 1960.

13   *Individual Differences in Learning*

The fact that learners differ in many respects poses important questions for educators. Since children differ greatly in their abilities, interests, needs, and motives, it is no easy assignment to set up an educational program that will enable mass education to proceed, and yet give special attention to the individual learner. His learning readiness, his intelligence, his aptitudes, and his relative degree of successful achievement become the concern of all who are responsible for stimulating and guiding the learner as he grows and develops.

Ability Differences among Learners

A child enters school at about the age of six and is expected to progress sequentially in his schooling. Formerly, it was assumed erroneously that all children are able to profit similarly from instruction at each age or grade level. Inability on the part of the learner to master minimum essentials or to keep pace with the work of the class was explained in terms of laziness, stubbornness, or indifference to learning. Our failure to take into consideration the fact that learners differ in their ability to perform in various areas of learning, and that there are many factors of influence in child-learning has complicated the problem of child-training.

Psychologists and educational leaders have been grappling with this problem during the past half century. They are discovering some of the facts that no doubt will assist in the solution of the problem of educating all children in mass situations. Research has revealed many of the individual differences with which the teachers have to cope; it has helped to determine the educational objectives and the content and techniques that are needed to improve the adjustment of differing young people to learning situations.

There are literally hundreds of studies that have been made to evaluate individual differences among children, adolescents, and adults. Educators and psychologists have considered both the nature and extent of the differences as well as the factors that cause them. Although it was believed at one time that there are racial and

322

national bases for these differences, study and experimentation have revealed that differences based upon either race or national origin are less important than are differences that exist among the individuals of any one group. The differences between the sexes also are becoming less and less apparent as men and women are given equivalent training, and engage in similar activities.

We are interested in differences in learning ability that may be found among children of the same age, as they progress through successive age levels. We shall present the findings of various studies which clearly show the range of abilities among students in one class. A study of the data will convince the reader of the wide range of problems with which a teacher must deal as he attempts to stimulate learning. The teacher who hopes to motivate the learning of every child in his class is confronted with the need to plan different lessons for each individual and to organize his class into small groups, each of which will represent some similarity in learnability among its members.

Studies showing differences among individuals. Some of these studies have been made by the authors; others are the results of experiments performed by various experts in the field of education. The first study concerns data based upon learners who were tested on a Reading Comprehension Test.

The scores earned by a fourth-grade and a seventh-grade class, respectively, on a reading comprehension test, their intelligence quotients obtained from the administration of the Otis Group Intelligence Scale, and their chronological ages in years and months are presented in Table 15. The pupils, by initial, are arranged in descending order according to the score made on the reading test.

Significant differences are found among the children. The data illustrate that children with high intelligence quotients do not always have superior reading comprehension. It is an interesting fact that the pupils with the highest intelligence quotient in both the fourth grade and the seventh grade did not make the highest score on the reading test; likewise, the pupils with the lowest intelligence quotients did not score the lowest on the test, although these pupils were next to the lowest in both grades.

The same reading comprehension test was administered to classes ranging from the fourth grade through the ninth grade (including the two classes presented in Table 16. The spread of scores made by more than three hundred pupils in *each* grade is shown in the following table.

TABLE 15. Scores Made by the Members of a Fourth-Grade Class and of a Seventh-Grade Class on a Reading Comprehension Test, together with Their Intelligence Quotients and Their Ages (Crow-Kuhlmann-Crow)

	PUPILS IN FOURTH–GRADE CLASS				PUPILS IN SEVENTH–GRADE CLASS				
Pupils' Initials	Score on Reading Test	IQ	Age		Pupils' Initials	Score on Reading Test	IQ	Age	
			Year	Month				Year	Month
N.K.	59	116	8	6	B.R.	86	109	11	11
D.S.	53	127	8	6	M.R.	83	128	12	6
W.F.	49	119	9	0	H.G.	83	123	12	2
R.H.	46	120	8	6	V.S.	83	102	12	2
K.P.	45	125	8	6	H.E.	81	115	12	7
A.Z.	44	116	8	5	S.V.	81	115	12	6
P.S.	44	112	9	0	R.C.	81	114	12	2
R.F.	36	110	8	10	F.C.	79	109	12	2
D.V.	34	104	8	9	D.E.	79	125	11	8
M.D.	32	105	9	4	P.F.	77	106	12	4
E.S.	31	101	8	10	B.P.	76	106	12	6
R.F.	29	112	9	2	F.M.	75	111	12	4
C.A.	29	106	8	5	G.T.	72	111	12	4
S.G.	29	107	8	5	W.B.	70	108	12	5
E.T.	27	107	8	8	M.J.	68	102	12	11
V.C.	27	104	8	10	S.R.	66	106	12	4
G.D.	27	104	9	9	S.L.	64	107	11	8
C.J.	25	106	9	1	S.A.	63	109	11	8
J.A.	25	114	8	5	S.R.	62	102	11	10
S.C.	25	108	8	8	O.E.	62	105	12	7
E.D.	23	102	8	9	M.B.	62	104	11	8
L.L.	23	102	8	5	P.D.	61	102	12	1
J.D.	21	106	8	1	S.M.	61	101	11	9
R.R.	20	103	10	2	D.V.	60	109	12	4
F.H.	20	105	8	5	D.F.	58	101	11	9
H.Z.	20	101	8	7	L.T.	57	109	11	9
M.C.	19	107	8	3	D.C.	57	91	12	3
S.D.	17	101	8	11	P.W.	54	80	13	4
V.P.	15	85	9	7	F.Q.	49	89	12	3
R.S.	11	94	10	0	W.J.	42	84	13	9
					F.R.	39	99	11	10
					C.D.	30	75	11	8
					F.P.	27	80	11	11

TABLE 16.   Spread of Scores Made by Pupils in Each Grade (Grades 4 through 9) on a Reading Comprehension Test

GRADE	LOW SCORE	HIGH SCORE	RANGE OF SCORES	MIDDLE SCORE
4	3	59	56	28
5	10	79	69	40
6	14	89	75	51
7	22	100	78	64
8	31	105	74	70
9	41	110	69	76

The spread of individual differences in any one grade is evidenced by the fact that the *low* for each grade including the ninth (low-41) is lower than the *high* for any grade including the *fourth* (high-59).

The foregoing data and the distribution of scores for each grade shown graphically in Figure 18 indicate that overlapping in ability to read was great on all grade levels from the fourth through the

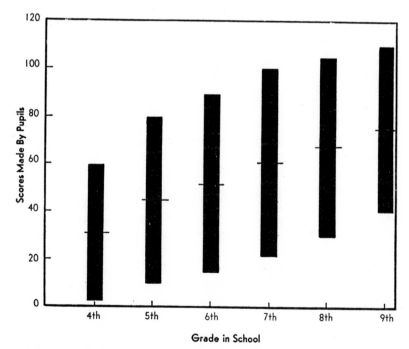

FIGURE 18.   Spread of Scores Made by Pupils in Each Grade; Also the Point on the Scale Below Which and Above Which 50 Per Cent of the Grades Fall

ninth. It can be seen that 50 per cent of the scores made by the pupils in each grade fall as follows: fourth grade, below 28; fifth grade, below 40; sixth grade, below 51; seventh grade, below 64; eighth grade, below 70; and ninth grade, below 76.

These data are based on school grades; for all practical purposes the data apply also to age levels. The schools from which these scores were obtained are organized into classes on an age basis for teaching-learning purposes. Teachers in similar situations, therefore, should be aware of the fact that there probably are vast differences among their pupils in ability to learn. Hence teachers should have available, for their use, data that result from this kind of testing. Objectively-obtained information concerning the reading-comprehension status of each of his pupils is of particular interest to the teacher who is confronted with the task of helping his pupils get information from the printed page.

These data reinforce the need for studying learners in order to know more about them than the fact that they have a high intelligence quotient. Learning achievement seems to be based upon many factors other than ability alone. Sometimes, it is a great challenge to the teacher to discover exactly what will motivate any one learner to further achievement in a particular area of learning. Complete information concerning a pupil may help the teacher gain insight into the problem and may permit emotional or other disturbances to be removed if they interfere with learning progress.

The data obtained from a study reported by Courtis also indicate the extent to which differences are found among children of the same grade. Each of 240 fifth-grade boys and girls was compared to the respective norms of grades 9A and above, through 2A and below, in the following areas: chronological age, height, weight, number of teeth cut, intelligence level, and reading ability. Courtis organized the data in tabular form. (See Table 17.) The number of children in each category in the 5A level is usual for that grade. A close study of Table 17 gives evidence of the wide range of difference among the children in each category. For example, a comparison of these differences in relation to intelligence levels shows that of the 226 children to whom an intelligence test was administered, only 33 met grade standards. The others ranged from a high of Grade 9 and above to Grade 3B, 131 exceeding and 62 falling below 5A norms. The reader may be interested in comparing relative spreads of all the categories. These data reveal how futile it is to put all children into the same mold.

Indicative of the problems confronted by a teacher in the class-

TABLE 17.   The Scores of Approximately 240 Boys and Girls in a Variety of Tests and Measurements (Grade 5A)[1]

GRADE LEVELS	NUMBER OF CHILDREN MAKING EACH GRADE–LEVEL SCORE						
	Chronological Age	Height	Weight	Number Teeth Cut	Intelligence Kuhlmann-Andersen	Reading Stanford Achievement	Reading Thorndike McCall
9 & above	1*	7*	20*		2	8*	5*
8A	2	6	9		0	3	0
8B	0	9	15		0	7	5
7A	5	36	23	18*	7	5	7
7B	6	25	19	25	24	21	10
6A	10	44	29	55	34	22	51
6B	19	18	25	44	64	42	23
5A	34	39	31	42	33	38	31
5B	135	22	23	23	39	43	48
4A	29	19	12	14	17	26	25
4B	7	9	15	7	5	21	17
3A		2	11	9		7*	14*
3B					1		
2A & below		2*	6*				
Total children measured	248	238	238	237	226	243	236

* These scores mark the limits of the available scores or norms for the given test. The scores so marked should be read "or above" or "or below" as the case may be.

room are differences in abilities as illustrated by Smith in an excellent graphic presentation of the range of mental ages within each of five chronological age groups. At a glance, the reader can become aware of the spread of ability as well as recognize the concentration of ability for each age. Smith's graphic presentation and his accompanying comments follow.

Since we know that M.A. is our best indicator of ability to learn, let's examine the mental age distributions that we find among five chronological age groups (four, six, eight, ten, and twelve-year-olds). These are shown in Figure 19.

[1] S. A. Courtis, "The Rate of Growth Makes a Difference," *The Phi Delta Kappan*, Vol. 30, April, 1949, p. 320. Reprinted by permission.

It is easy to understand why the bright and the dull children (the upper and lower ends of the five distributions) grow further apart in mental age as they grow older. At age 6, a child of 125 I.Q. has a mental age of 7½; at age 12, he has a mental age of 15. Thus, at age 6 he was but 1½ years above average in mental age, but at age 12 he is 3 years above average. The child of 70 I.Q., on the other hand, is 1.8 years below average in mental age at age 6, but 3.6 years below average by the time he is 12 years old. As we can see from Figure 19,

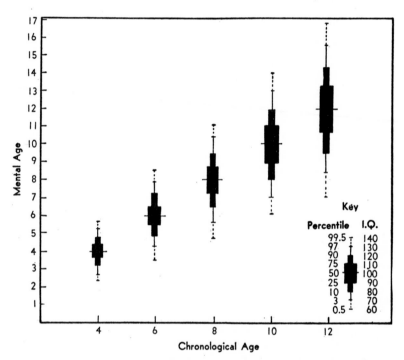

FIGURE 19. The Range of Mental Ages among Each of Five Chronological Age Groups

the mental age between any two 4-year-old children doubles by age 8 and triples by age 12. Although the spread of mental ages within the middle 80 per cent of the group (I.Q. 80 to 120) is only slightly more than 1½ years at age 4, it is 3 years at age 8 and nearly 5 years by age 12. We can see, then, that although many of the children with the lowest I.Q.'s drop out of school after about the eighth grade, the gross differences in mental age are greater in the high school than in the elementary school.[1]

From the results of these studies, it can be concluded that a class on any grade or age level includes learners who differ from one another in mental ability, interest, or readiness to master learning materials supposedly appropriate for their grade or age levels. No matter how carefully learners are assigned to their classes, the range of difference will be wide in one or more areas.

Problems created by spread of mental ability. In terms of their general intelligence, children are classified as feeble-minded, dull or borderline, normal, above average, superior, very superior or near genius. A classification often used is the one based upon data obtained from the administration of the Terman and Merrill revision of the Stanford-Binet Scale.

Classification of Intelligence Quotients

Classification	IQ
Near genius or genius	140 and above
Very superior	130–139
Superior	120–129
Above average	110–119
Normal or average	90–109
Below average	80– 89
Dull or borderline	70– 79
Feeble-minded: moron, imbecile, idiot	49– and below

The children who are in the group having IQ's that fall below 70, and the children whose IQ's are higher than 130 need special consideration in their school learning. Those children who are classified as idiots (IQ below 25), and imbeciles (IQ below 50) usually do not constitute a problem for the regular class teacher. In most school systems, provision is made for these feeble-minded children in special schools or institutions.

This discussion deals with those learners whose intelligence quotients are above fifty, as determined by the Stanford Binet test. Education of children includes much more than helping them gain academic knowledge. If learning were restricted to this area, the job of the teacher would be lightened considerably. Parallel to the gaining of abstract knowledge are emotional and social develop-

[1] H. P. Smith, *Psychology in Teaching*, copyright, 1954, by Prentice-Hall, Inc., New York, pp. 278–280. Reprinted by permission.

ment, improvement of skills, and habituation of behavior that will serve the child in his daily living.

For the intelligence quotient to be below a hundred is neither the fault nor the choice of the child. Boys and girls are born with capacity to learn, but they must be helped to adjust to slow rate and low limit of learning achievement.

It is our duty as educators to organize learning situations for them in which they may experience some degree of satisfaction as they struggle to attain whatever learning outcomes are possible. As learning content becomes increasingly more abstract, dull children experience more and more difficulty in keeping pace with their normally intelligent or bright associates. Each child can master much of the simpler learning material; there is a limit beyond which many of them cannot go. These limits are far from set. Properly motivated slow learners usually can gain sufficient usable knowledge and skill to prevent the arousal of feelings of frustration. In any case, the slow learner will reach his limit of educability sooner than will the normal or superior learner. For example, some high-school subjects cannot be mastered unless the learner has an IQ of 100 or over; acceptable learning progress on the college level is likely to be achieved only if the student has an IQ of 110 or above.

Wide individual differences in learning achievement persist even among those learners whose mental ability is at or near the norm for the group. Special plans must be made to awaken and to continue to motivate the average learner toward adequate achievement. Furthermore, the bright child usually succeeds in school study. Since he is not in a closely competing situation, however, he does not need to work to his full capacity. Hence he may develop lazy habits of thinking. If conditions are favorable, both the slow and the bright can be stimulated to advance as far as their interests and available educational opportunities can take them.

Readiness for Learning

The readiness of the pupils of a class for participation in any area of learning is so variable that a teacher rarely can expect to reach all of them through utilization of the same procedure. It is known that maturation is an individual matter and that one child may be mentally ready for a learning activity long before another child of his same age or school level is. Data now available for educators can help them gain a better understanding of the relationship that exists between learning readiness and learner achievement, as well as help them discover individual readiness in any learning function.

In a survey study of the book-reading levels of children from nursery school to the tenth grade, Olson found the percentage of children in each grade who were ready for each book level. Study of Table 18 reveals that there is much overlapping in readiness to read certain books. For example, 7 per cent of the sixth graders are not ready for books above the second-grade level, yet 7 per cent of the children in the same grade are able to read books that are on the tenth-grade level.

TABLE 18. The Percentage of Children in Each Grade Ready for Each Book Level [1]

GRADE—BOOK LEVEL	AGE	GRADE—ACHIEVEMENT LEVEL					
		I	II	III	IV	V	VI
Nursery school	5	2	2	2			
Kindergarten	6	23	8	5	7		
1	7	50	24	11	9	7	
2	8	23	33	20	10	9	7
3	9	2	24	24	16	10	9
4	10		8	20	17	16	10
5	11		2	11	16	17	16
6	12			5	10	16	17
7	13			2	9	10	16
8	14				7	9	10
9	15					7	9
10	16						7

Factors of readiness. Inherent readiness is determined genetically by growth; attitude readiness is dependent upon the experiences and interests of the learner. At this point we are concerned with maturation which takes place along with growth. There is little that anyone can do either to promote it or to defer it. Numerous experiments have been performed to determine the extent to which such activities as sitting, crawling, walking, and bladder and bowel control are the results mainly of maturation.[2]

[1] W. C. Olson, "Seeking Self-Selection and Pacing in the Use of Books by Children," *The Packet*, Vol. 7, D. C. Heath & Co., Boston, 1952, p. 7. Reprinted by permission.

[2] M. McGraw, "Neural Maturation as Exemplified by the Achievement of Bladder Control," *Journal of Pediatrics*, Vol. 16, 1940, pp. 580–590; W. Dennis, *Readings in Child Psychology*, 2nd ed., Prentice-Hall, Englewood Cliffs, N. J., 1963, pp. 68–71, 86–89.

Maturation is considered an essential prerequisite to learning. Readiness to learn is especially important in reading. One of the aims of education is to prepare the child to put meaning into the printed page. The child should be trained as early as possible to master the tools of reading so that he may be prepared to interpret the ideas of another person when they are presented in written form.

A mental readiness or predisposition toward learning also is based upon a learner's previous experience. Thorndike's principle of readiness in learning was based upon the maturation and experience aspects of readiness:

> (1) that when a conduction unit is ready to conduct, conduction by it is satisfying, nothing being done to alter its action; (2) that for a conduction unit ready to conduct not to conduct is annoying, and provokes whatever responses nature provides in connection with that particular annoying lack; (3) that when a conduction unit unready for conduction is forced to conduct, conduction by it is annoying.[1]

Achievement of success in reading comes with experience in reading. Hence it is inevitable that a child will be a poor reader unless he is encouraged to read material that is fitted to his maturation level. The problem then concerns the best time for him to start his reading experience. The answer, of course, is as soon as he has matured sufficiently for reading. It takes uncommon sense, however, to discover just when he has reached that stage of maturation. Reading readiness tests have been devised but are not yet completely reliable.

If a child is delayed in reading, we know that the cause of the retardation may be his delayed maturation. Although it may be possible to stimulate a child to read before he has reached the state of reading readiness, the gains from that effort are not likely to be great.

The state of reading readiness may appear suddenly, however. For example, a primary-school boy was experiencing considerable difficulty in learning how to read. He dreaded the class's daily reading period. Illness kept him from school for about two weeks. He could not engage in regular play activities. For the lack of something better to do, he started to read the story of Hansel and Gretel

---

[1] From E. L. Thorndike, *Educational Psychology, Briefer Course*, Bureau of Publications, Teachers College, Columbia University, New York, 1914, p. 55. Reprinted by permission.

in the *Book of Knowledge.* To his great surprise and delight he discovered that not only was he able to read, but also he was enjoying it. Consequently, he read everything on his maturity level that he could find. He returned to school, ready to become one of the best readers in the group. Had he suddenly reached maturational readiness for reading? Did he gain sudden insight into the total reading situation?

Experiences gained from the home and the immediate environment are important factors in learning readiness. The attitude of parents and of the children themselves toward school plays an important role in learner readiness. If the school is admired and respected, the displayed approving attitudes of community members toward the school have a positive effect on readiness to learn. If the community seems to believe that the school is attempting to educate children away from interest in and concern about home and community life, the children are likely to reflect this attitude. Learning readiness will be at a minimum.

The interests of children are important factors in readiness. We have discovered that slow readers can be taught to read if the reading material stimulates them to become interested in it. It may seem surprising that the interest factor may be more significant than word difficulty. Words that are within the experience of the child and are understood by him become for him psychologically simple. The size of the word may not be the criterion for determining its difficulty. A word such as *automobile,* although long, may be easy for the young child to recognize.

Appraisal of readiness. As suggested earlier, well-constructed tests can be used to appraise learner readiness. Aptitude tests by their very name and nature are supposed to evaluate an individual's readiness for a particular activity. Testing for reading readiness perhaps is one of the most important areas of aptitude evaluation for two reasons: (1) reading is begun during the early days of development, and (2) much of a young person's learning success depends upon his reading efficiency. Among the items used to measure reading readiness are included simply-drawn pictures of things, people, or situations with which the child is acquainted. The tasks of a test generally are: to identify objects or persons; to recognize likenesses and differences; and to respond to directions. The administrator *tells* the children what to do, and they place marks on the appropriate picture, or on an object in a picture. Some reading readiness tests are given individually (to one child at a time). Others are administered to groups of children. The test of which a few items are illustrated here is a *group* test.

The Binion-Beck Reading Readiness Test for Kindergarten and First Grade[1] includes three major tests, each with seven parts, in the form of pictures in rows. The constructors of the test state the determining factors involved in this reading readiness test to be: "Development in observing likenesses and differences in position, forward or backward, direction and reversals." Three items of the five that appear in Test II, Row 1, are presented in Figure 20.

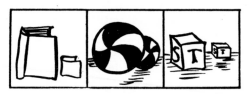

FIGURE 20.   Test II, Row 1

Directions for administering Test II, Row 1: The test administrator says; "Place your markers below the first row. Be sure to make a cross on the one that I tell you in each picture."

The test administrator is instructed to:

              1. Show children a big book and a little book. Hold the little book above the big book.
[Then say:]   "Make a cross mark on the book in the first picture which I am holding up the higher." Repeat directions.

              2. Show children a big ball and a little ball. Hold the big ball above the little ball. "Make a cross mark on the ball in the second picture which I am holding up the higher." Repeat directions.

              3. Show children a big block and a little block. Hold the little block above the big block. "Make a cross mark on the block in the third picture which I am holding up the higher." Repeat directions.

In Test II, Row 5, the determining factor involved is: "To associate picture meaning and objects, to identify pictures of objects, to match object to picture." (See Figures 21a and 21b.)

[1] H. S. Binion, and R. L. Beck, *Binion-Beck Reading Readiness Test for Kindergarten and First Grade,* Courtesy Acorn Publishing Company, Rockville Centre, New York, 1945. Reprinted by permission.

Directions for administering Test II, Row 5: the test administrator holds up this picture and asks the children to:

1. "Draw a straight mark on the picture that is like the one that I am showing you." Hold up the picture of the soldier. (Figure 21b.) Repeat directions.

As a means of prognostication of the probable degree of successful learning that will be achieved in high school by entering fresh-

FIGURE 21a.   Test II, Row 5

men, the authors have constructed a *Test for High-School Entrants*, which in effect, is a learning readiness test, based upon training and experience during the learner's elementary-school years. The test consists of four parts: English; Reading Comprehension; Arithmetic Reasoning and Computation; General Information. A sample question taken from the sub-test in English is:

Find the sentence in which there is a mistake.

    a. They were lying on the grass.
    b. I laid down for a nap.
    c. The shoes have lain in the closet for a long time.
    d. Lay the book down.

As we have said repeatedly for emphasis, maturation is the primary factor which determines when a child begins to learn and how much he learns. In this connection, Courtis wrote, "Individual growth is cyclic in character. The various cycles of growth occur at different times in different individuals. Each child is unique as to times and amounts of growth. Each should be judged in terms of his own natural standards, not in terms of norms derived from mass measurements." [1]

Specific Plans for Meeting Individual Differences

It is the function of the school to provide adequate schooling for every learner no matter how much he deviates from other learners.

[1] Courtis, *op. cit.*, p. 323. Reprinted by permission.

School leaders who are responsible for the education of young people, therefore, (1) must formulate their educational plans with the
knowledge that children should be afforded learning experiences
within the limits of individual ability to achieve; (2) must provide
adequate buildings in and facilities with which to work; (3) must

FIGURE 21b.   Test II, Row 5

provide sufficient and well-trained teachers who regard children as individuals to be taught; (4) must construct curricula that meet the needs and interests of individual learners; (5) must provide adequate teaching and learning materials, including audio-visual aids, for proper stimulation of learning; and (6) must encourage the co-operation of all members of the community toward implementing the individualization of education—teachers, administrators, parents, and others.

The entire guidance program of the school is based upon the premise of serving better every learner in school. The emphases that are to be placed on this aspect of child-training are discussed in Chapter 20. During the past fifty years, school people have been struggling to provide ways to meet the needs of individuals. Numerous plans have been evolved. Some of the earlier attempts are no longer used in the form in which they originated. Others have been discarded. Even if plans formulated earlier have not been continued in their original state, various aspects of those plans have been salvaged and utilized in modified form by school people throughout the country. Several of the well-known plans that are exerting a variety of influence upon present-day procedures are discussed here.

The Dalton Laboratory Plan. The Dalton Plan was instituted for the purpose of meeting the problems of individual differences. It was initiated by Helen Parkhurst and put into operation on the high-school level in the early 1920's. This plan stressed the principles of freedom of expression, individual initiative, and group interaction. Through the operation of this plan the learner is motivated to understand what he is to do as well as to decide which activities within the limits of the learning jobs are to be completed by him within a given period of time.

The learner may choose the job he prefers to attack first. The decision is his to make. According to the Dalton Plan, the school is to be regarded as a "house" in which the learning activities are to be performed. Traditional classrooms become laboratories in which the function of the teacher is that of preserving "an atmosphere of study!" The learner's assignments are arranged in the form of contracts that spread over an entire month. The learner is free to prepare his assignments in his own way, assisted by the teacher who guides him in the budgeting of his time and who, as well as the pupil, keeps "graphs of his daily progress." In this way the learner may proceed at his own rate and according to his own ability to achieve. The teacher also suggests activities, answers questions, and holds conferences with the learners.

A set of mimeographed assignments or guide sheets are furnished each pupil as his job book. A contract is for one day's work. Each pupil plans his day by consulting the bulletin board at the beginning of the day. During the first fifteen minutes, each pupil meets in his "house" with a regular teacher for the purpose of planning his day's work. The pupil then spends the morning working on his chosen jobs, after which he engages in a group conference with teachers who meet assigned classes. The afternoon session usually is devoted to participation in specialty subjects, such as art, music, physical education, and industrial or household arts.

Learners are given opportunities to engage in such group activities as games, athletics, dramatics, and similar programs of social value; they also have discussions of literary, historical, or other topics of interest. All this is to be completed within the framework of the regular school, thus making it easier to be experimented with in many schools. Although the Dalton Plan is not now accepted in its entirety, it influenced the giving of individual attention to the educational needs of each child.

The Winnetka Plan. A technique for individualizing instruction was started in Winnetka, Illinois, by Carlton Washburne in 1919. This plan, which took its name from a town near Chicago, was initiated to meet the needs of children who lived in that select community. Although the plan began in a special situation, it was based upon a sound philosophy of education and became a jumping-off point for the kind of individual education that may be best for learners, no matter what their ability, or where they live.

The educational philosophy underlying this plan is that a learner should be allowed to follow his own rate of learning in each of the subject fields that comprise his full curriculum. In order to implement the plan, it is necessary to discover the individual's stage of learning in each area of learning. The plan is to build upon learner readiness for continued study in the respective areas rather than to have the learner move in lock step fashion with a group of learners who differ from him in stage of learning readiness. It becomes necessary, therefore, to administer examinations of various kinds before a specific learning unit is undertaken.

In order to discover rate of learner progress, a pre-test is administered. For example, a pre-test is used to discover which of the spelling words of the term the child does not know. It then becomes the child's responsibility to master these words before the end of the term. The same technique can be applied to reading and, later, to other subjects, such as language, arithmetic, geography, and history. At its inception, the plan concerned itself with pupils in the elementary school only, since at that time there was no high school in Winnetka.

The Winnetka Plan allows the child to proceed at different rates in different learning areas. This is quite different from the Dalton Plan in which, through a contract, the learners, month by month, were kept on the same achievement level in all subject fields. In the Winnetka Plan, the child may be a year ahead in arithmetic, six months ahead in reading, and at his expected learning level in another subject. Learning units are arranged in the forms of tasks or goals. Progress is checked by the learner himself, by means of self-administered tests. In this way he prepares himself for a teacher test which he must pass with a high score, or re-study the material in preparation for another test.

Achievement is continuous; no child is confronted with failure, in the traditional sense of the word. The learner's achievement is measured against his own achievement rather than in terms of the achievement of other learners. No skipping is planned for the bright learners; they are permitted to complete all the work in less time. Likewise, the slow learner is expected to complete his work, but more time is needed by him to complete it. Variations of this plan have found wide acceptance of application.

The Project Method. Another plan to meet the individual problems of pupils was suggested by Kilpatrick. This plan gives learners a chance to work together in the planning and execution of definite projects. Kilpatrick suggested four types of projects that might be effective for use in a school with learners of various ability levels. The projects are: producer's project, consumer's project, problem project, and drill project. Through these activities, learning can be individualized for each member in terms of his interest and ability. In general, this formal approach has been discarded in favor of other types of activities that emphasize learning through direct experience or doing.

The Activity Program. The activity program appears to be an outgrowth of many attempts to individualize learning. Its name was applied to it during a period of extensive experimentation with it. The plan received much criticism while in an experimental stage.

Although the program as developed on the elementary level had many excellent aspects, parent and teacher disapproval became so great that the name had to be dropped with the hope that some of its good qualities might be salvaged.

In this newer educational approach, children participate in planning their daily activities; they engage in research and expressional activities, and they help plan and engage in field trips. This program, like the others described, permits great flexibility in adaptation to individual differences. Active participation in learning situations rather than passive acceptance of teacher-dominated learning "tasks" constitutes the basic ideal of this program.

According to Wrightstone, "The core of the usual activity program has these central ideas: first, that children should be treated as individuals; second, children's interests and needs should be considered in shaping the curriculum; third, children should learn by actual participation in many activities; fourth, children should practice democracy and should learn to solve the same kind of problems that they will meet after they finish school. Today, in a typical activity school, children treat teachers as friends instead of as masters. In place of fixed desks and seats, are chairs and workbenches. In addition to textbooks, pupils use newspapers, magazines, and reference books, and take excursions or trips. Instead of studying subjects in separate capsules only, as reading, spelling, and arithmetic, they study them combined into projects." [1]

The Experience Curriculum. As the activity program came into disfavor, an effort was made to utilize as many as possible of its values and to continue them under the aegis of the New Education Program, with emphasis upon the experience curriculum. At first, teachers were not trained to follow the procedures in which the experiences of the children were to be used. When experience is understood to mean living through an event involving a "skill, a facility, or functional knowledge gained through personal experience, feeling or action," the underlying educational philosophy seems to be sound. Early in this century, John Dewey helped develop a working concept of experience in relation to the school program. He believed that experience starts with a dynamic interaction between the child and his environment.

[1] J. W. Wrightstone, in *Elementary Educational Psychology*, 2nd ed. (ed. C. E. Skinner), copyright, 1950 by Prentice-Hall, New York, p. 197. Reprinted by permission of the publisher.

The nature of experience can be understood only by noting that it includes an active and a passive element peculiarly combined. On the active hand, experience is *trying*—a meaning which is explicit in the connected term experiment. On the passive, it is *undergoing*. When we experience something we act upon it, we do something with it; then we suffer or undergo the consequences. We do something to the thing and then it does something to us in return; such is the peculiar combination. The connection between these two phases of experience measures the fruitfulness or value of the experience. Mere activity does not constitute experience. It is dispersive, centrifugal, dissipating. Experience as trying involves change, but change is meaningless transition unless it is consciously connected with the return wave of consequences which flow from it. When an activity is continued *into* the undergoing of consequences, when the change made by action is reflected back into a change made in us, the mere flux is loaded with significance. We learn something. It is not experience when a child merely sticks his finger into a flame; it is experience when the movement is connected with the pain which he undergoes in consequence. Henceforth the sticking of the finger into the flame *means* a burn. Being burned is a mere physical change, like the burning of a stick of wood, if it is not perceived as a consequence of some other action.[1]

The experience approach implies integration; yet, the integration that occurs takes place within the learner. Experiences can be provided but their significance to the learner will depend upon the extent to which he is stimulated to make them functional in his thinking and behavior.

The so-called new education program has much of value in it. Authorities who plan according to it must realize that much more material in the form of learning aids is needed for its operation than formerly was the case. The experience procedure provides for children to engage in various activities with some degree of interest, since they are invited to participate in the planning of the work of the day or of a particular unit of activity.

Homogeneous grouping versus heterogeneous grouping. There has been and still is great diversity of opinion concerning what is the best plan of grouping children for learning. One thing is certain: pupils

---

[1] John Dewey, *Democracy and Education*. The Macmillan Co., New York, 1916, pp. 163–164. Reprinted by permission.

must be organized into groups of some kind for teaching-learning purposes. Ability grouping fell into disrepute because groups were organized on the basis of degree of intelligence, without regard for other important learner characteristics. Homogeneous grouping is based on the principle that teaching is more effective with children who are similar in ability to learn, than it is with a heterogeneous group that may have a wide ability range. During the kindergarten and first three grades in school there should be a period of living together and learning to master the fundamentals of learning, including reading. Beginning with the fourth grade, however, after the development of some skill in reading, the children should be given a chance to learn in groups that are of the same age but have achievement ability that is not too divergent.

Groupings by school authorities. Recently, there has been an attempt to organize all the classes in a school on a completely heterogeneous basis, i.e., if there are five fourth-grade classes in a school, any mechanical basis for grouping, such as alphabetic listing, is used to avoid classification according to ability. The purpose of this procedure is to help all learners live together as a social group; to curb possible attitudes of intellectual snobbery among the members of "honor classes," and to prevent children in slow-learner classes from becoming unduly aware of their low-group status. The fundamental question concerning learner groups should be: Does this grouping best meet the needs of the learners, and of the teachers who are assigned to motivate the learning of every learner?

Advocates of heterogeneous grouping claim that present educational philosophy emphasizes the need of every member of a class group to progress in learning in terms of his own ability to achieve, regardless of the learning capacity of any other member of the class. Therefore, a learner of any degree of ability would be better able to make social and personal adjustments if he were permitted to associate with other children of all ability levels. In some school communities, however, class size is large. The amount of time and energy that a teacher can give to any one child is so little that those who need help most are neglected. Moreover, if similar background experiences are fundamental to successful motivation in learning, the teacher is faced with an impossible task. He attempts to reach every learner in a group that represents a wide range of ability and background. The result is likely to be that teachers come to believe that they are not motivating anyone. Consequently, completely heterogeneous grouping is being modified considerably, especially in the large school communities.

If complete homogeneity of grouping is practiced, the mentally retarded are grouped together for learning purposes; the bright are assigned to special classes, such as honors classes. Too great emphasis upon rigid grouping that categorizes young people may have undesirable social implications. Some form of grouping, which takes into account the learning ability of the individual, seems to be sensible. Yet, the school must provide for the intermingling of all children, regardless of ability. Social and emotional development is as important as is mental progress. A child who has any form of handicap, physical or mental, should have provided for him some opportunities during a part of the school day to associate with other children. Grouping in terms of mental status may be needed in learning areas that offer differing kinds of mental challenge. There are many learning situations that can offer relatively similar stimulation to all young people, however. A few of these learning situations are: physical education and hygiene, music and art, some cocurricular activities, assembly programs, arts and crafts, and other special offerings that can be found in one or another school.

It is important that the more able children learn to live with those who are not able to compete with them mentally. Slower learners need to meet and become acquainted with their brighter schoolmates. Society is composed of individuals of differing mental abilities and aptitudes. Yet, these people must learn to adjust to one another. It therefore is the responsibility of the school to plan for some daily activities in which all learners can share experiences together.

Pupil participation in planning. If the learner is helped to understand the purpose of an activity, he is motivated toward more enthusiastic participation in it than otherwise might be the case. Especially does the principle of learning by doing become a reality when pupils share in the planning of the activity. Even though help that can be given by pupils in the planning of the day's work is limited, the motivation value is great. In the lower grades, teacher-pupil planning may be limited to topics to be considered and the order in which the work of the day is to be scheduled.

The teacher who chooses to make use of pupil-shared planning in his classroom must have confidence in the ability of his pupils to co-operate in this process. The extent of responsibility that can be assumed by pupils depends upon such factors as their background of experience, mental and physical maturity, individual interests, and willingness to participate. If a good social climate is achieved, the pupils can be encouraged to share responsibility with the teacher. To those children who have not had previous experience in this kind of co-operative project, should be given only that responsibility which they can assume successfully.

Pupil participation in planning learning situations in the upper grades or in high school might include the evaluation of a general unit of study to discover important ideas related to the unit. For example, a junior high-school class may be launching a project that requires committee work. The pupils and teacher may spend a class period or longer in raising questions to be considered by the committees to help them carry on the research that is needed to gain a better understanding of the projects. The entire class might engage in a consideration of a particular topic such as "Silk." The interests of the members of the class can be aroused and discovered by asking what they would like to know about silk. These questions could be placed on the blackboard. The pupils are likely to raise such questions as: Where does silk come from? How is it made? How does it grow? What do the silkworms feed on? Why does it not grow in large quantities in the United States? Why is it used less today than formerly? Where are the factories for silk processing located? How is it gathered?

A long list of questions can be written on the blackboard to guide the learners in their search for information concerning silk. Before the "unit" is completed, the class will have touched on most of the important activities such as: agriculture, finance, transportation, manufacturing, distribution, and consumption. Most of all, the pupils will have participated in this activity with interest and understanding because they had raised questions to which they themselves want the answers. Teachers know that significant questions are those that stem from the curiosity of the learners. They respond to these questions because the teaching-learning situation thereby comes to life.

Meeting the Problems of the Mentally Retarded

No parent likes to believe that his child is mentally retarded; relatively few teachers desire to have the mentally retarded learners in their regular classes. This discussion is concerned with the learning and adjustment problems that are faced by those children whose Intelligence Quotients fall between fifty and seventy as determined by the administration of an individual intelligence test. Since the mentally retarded child has not enjoyed the kinds of school experiences that lead to successful learning achievement, he is in danger of becoming emotionally maladjusted. In the past, the school program was geared to the level of the average pupil or his more able brother. In a school situation of that kind, the retarded child had too many experiences of failure and frequently developed feelings of frustration.

Characteristics of the mentally retarded. A descriptive listing of the characteristics of mentally retarded children at different ages has been so well summarized by Ingram that we present her findings for ages eight, nine, and ten.

General Description of Certain Physical, Social, and Mental Traits of the Mentally Retarded at Different Age Levels (8, 9, and 10 Years)[1]

Physical Traits

Height and weight for the majority approximate normal standards for their respective ages—50 inches, 58 pounds, for the eight-year-old; 52 inches, 64 pounds, for the nine-year-old; 54 inches, 70 pounds, for the ten-year-old.

Muscular control of limbs is well developed. Walking, skipping, running, and jumping are done with ease, except in occasional cases of especially inferior coordination. Muscular control of hands tested in baseball throw and catch at distance, bean-bag toss for accuracy, and standing broad jump are slightly inferior to the norm for children of average ability.

Muscular control of fine muscles of hands and arms is fairly well developed. Chalk, pencil, crayon, and brush are used with neatness and considerable precision. Paper cutting, hammering, and sawing are carried on, but construction in woodwork is likely to be crude.

Senses are well developed. Variation from the normal results from a lessened capacity for discriminating and interpreting sensations. Failure to carry out directions is due to lack of comprehension rather than to lack of auditory acuity.

Speech defects such as stammering, lisping, and infantile speech are found in about 15 to 18 per cent of the children[2] as compared with 5 or 6 per cent of regular grade groups.

Social Traits

Period of individualization is past and transition to social group has been made to the extent that the child has more or

[1] Christine P. Ingram, *Education of the Slow-Learning Child*, 2nd ed. Copyright 1953 by The Ronald Press Co., New York, pp. 20–21. Reprinted by permission.

[2] Based on average per cents found in Rochester special classes over a period of two years. Includes incapable children placed for observation.

less learned to expect certain reactions from persons and things around him, and realizes that certain things are in turn expected of him. Cooperation in personal cleanliness, the use of expressions of courtesy, and the exercise of some self-control in satisfying wants are developed. Attempts to win approval of adults and satisfaction of desires dominate conduct.

The majority want to have a place in the family group and enjoy sharing in the housework and the care of younger children. They are likely to be quarrelsome with siblings of comparable ages.

Suggestion and imitation dominate in conduct and play. Running games with "choice" element such as tag; singing games like "The Farmer in the Dell," "The Mulberry Bush"; seasonal games like marbles, jackstones, and spinning tops; and ball playing, are enjoyed. The ego is too dominant to allow for being a "good sport" in play. Make-believe play must involve elements that have become very familiar through actual experience or pictures, such as playing school, house, policeman, aviator, Indian, and the like.

Stories to be successfully dramatized must be familiar. Satisfaction is obtained from much repetition of stories, plays, and games. Rhythm, music, folk dances, and mimetics set to music are enjoyed, as well as picture books, fairy stories, animal stories, and descriptions of child life. The distinction between true and imaginative stories is appreciated. Independence of appreciation of humorous situations is generally lacking; an explanation is necessary even for the "funnies."

Play interests of group of twelve ten-year-olds in order of preference were tag games, hide-and-seek, ball games, playing catch, checkers, lotto, playing house, playing school, playing with dolls, playing with pet kitten, picture puzzles, jumping rope, spinning tops, flying kites, marbles, and table games such as spinning for turn and matching cards.

Mental Traits

Mental development approximates that of average children five to seven years of age. Situations such as playing games, making toys, and listening to stories are of interest to the more retarded. Gradually, from the mental age of six years on, activities like reading and writing, calling for periods of voluntary attention, will be undertaken. Rote memory is good at all three age levels, but memory of images and logical memory are poor. Concepts of time are weak. The names of the days of the week and the date can be named because they are read daily. The idea of months is very vague. Hours on the clock are associated with daily routine by a majority of nine- and ten-year-olds—"9 o'clock, school begins," "12 o'clock, lunch time," etc.

At eight years weakness of power of association, fundamental to language development, is noticeable. Differences and similarities between two common objects, like a baseball and an orange or an airplane and a kite, are not readily noted. The power to call up ideational representation of objects may be weak or there may be an inability to recognize any associations between the two. At ten years more ability to associate is evident, but development continues to be consistently slow.

Mere activity and manipulation may continue to satisfy at these ages, but there is greater stimulation to think and to talk about pursuits. Expression in play or conversation is less than that of the average child. Estimated vocabulary is 25 to 35 per cent below the eight-year-old standard. Objects are generally defined in terms of use, as "a stove is to cook with," "a ball is to play with." Little description or classification of objects is in evidence. There is a lack of awareness of qualities and characteristics that are of interest to average eight-year-olds.

Picture description is largely a naming of objects or of action. Spontaneous drawings show few relationships and a lack of detail.

Little ability for self-criticism is evident at eight years. Any response tends to satisfy until some basis for and help in judging effort are provided.

New things in the environment are more readily observed without direction.

Lack of adaptation in a new situation seems due to failure to recognize similarities and to make associations.

The Pollocks, who have devoted twenty years to the education of retarded children, have discovered the potentials of these young people and have formulated the following evaluations of the status, problems, and capabilities of the retarded.

1. Mentally retarded children are born to parents of all social and economic classes.
2. The mentally retarded child is not an unfavorable reflection on his parents.
3. Normal children who play with mentally retarded children do not become "dull" from associating with them.
4. The mentally retarded child is not a dangerous child.
5. The mentally retarded child is neither overly affectionate nor unaffectionate.
6. It is not difficult to satisfy the mentally retarded child.

7. The mentally retarded child can enjoy life as much as can the normal child.
8. Teaching mentally retarded children is not more difficult than teaching those of normal intelligence, but the problems involved are different.
9. The mentally retarded child is not lazy.
10. The mentally retarded child should be taught the tool subjects before he is introduced to the social studies.
11. The mentally retarded are capable of religious devotion.
12. The mentally retarded child can "amount to something." [1]

Importance of understanding the problems. All children should be educated together during the first two or three years of their schooling. Education should be continuous for the mentally retarded, and promotions should be made on an age basis. This principle should be maintained into the high school. It is important that these children associate with other children of their age. Hence provision should be made for them to live together with other children during recreational periods, at least. The slow learner should be one of a group, whether he is in the regular class or in a special class. Emphasis should be focused on the growth and development of the whole child for each year he is in attendance at school. A carefully planned program that enables the slow learner to move from one experience to another must be made available to him. He should be given a chance to experience successful achievement even though the standard of achievement for him is not so high as that reached by his more able associates.

The mentally retarded child is receiving special attention from many sources. Educational leaders are providing special classes and specially trained teachers to work with them in groups that are small enough to allow each child to receive individual attention. Many mentally retarded children are able to achieve commendable success in learning activities that are suited to their limited abilities. The learning must revolve about the respective interests of the children; simple vocabulary and reading material must be used, and the pace of attempted achievement must be slowed down. If attention is given to these considerations, most of these learners, within their mental limitations, can profit from learning experiences.

The mentally retarded child has a short attention span and has limited ability to concentrate. In the classroom, he has a great need for individual attention and instruction. He needs many concrete experiences, since he is unable to work successfully with abstrac-

[1] Adapted from Morris P. and Miriam Pollock, *New Hope for the Retarded,* Porter Sargent, Publisher, Boston, 1953, pp. 3–13. Reprinted by permission.

tions. He requires praise and commendation to keep him interested in learning activities, no matter how simple they may be.

The value of having specially trained teachers work with mentally retarded children is that such teachers understand the problems of these children and know how to discover their interests as well as to provide learning material that will be within their ability to comprehend and master. These children need special help which requires both time and energy to provide. Not only are these children misfits in a regular class, members of which are able to succeed in most of their learning activities, but they resent the attempts of teachers to force them to master something in which they are not interested, and in which they are not mentally equipped to perform successfully.

Parents and the mentally retarded. The parents of retarded children need to adjust to the realization that the child's ability is such that learning is difficult for him. The recently organized association of parents of mentally retarded children has done much to help parents who have children with these handicaps. They learn how to adjust to their child's mental status. When parents meet the problem realistically, the school and the parents can work together toward better adjustment of all concerned.

In the home, the mentally retarded child can be trained to do many things that he likes to do and can do effectively. The mother can help him develop a belief that what he is doing is of great value to her, and that he is doing something worthwhile when he empties the wastepaper basket, dusts the lower rungs of chairs, hangs up his pajamas, and takes his clean clothes from the bureau drawer. There are innumerable opportunities for him to help in the kitchen, the living room, or other parts of the home. If the parents encourage him to think that he is a wanted and useful member of the family, he thereby experiences emotional satisfaction. It is especially valuable for the parents and teachers to learn to work closely together in order to give the child the kind of individual help that is best for him. Co-operative efforts of various kinds can alert the child to the fact that others are interested in him. Such adult attitudes bolster his feeling of security. Parents alone cannot achieve this; neither can teachers succeed in this task without parental co-operation.

Meeting the Problems of the Gifted

The gifted child also experiences problems. Fortunately for him, they are of a different kind. They are no less significant than those faced by the mentally retarded. The parents who discover that their child has ability far beyond that of other children of his age often publicize this fact, to the detriment of the child. At an early age, the gifted child is called upon to exhibit, in the presence of family, relatives, and friends, his outstanding abilities. Parental behavior of this kind affects his attitude toward his parents and other supposedly admiring adults. He may resent his parents' attempts to "show off" his wonderful accomplishments. As a result, he either becomes stubborn and refuses to perform, or attempts to withdraw from the situation.

Characteristics of the gifted. The possession of a high level of general intelligence, as measured by the administration of standardized intelligence tests, or the possession of special aptitudes that may not be associated with high general intelligence, such as those in art, music, or science, is characteristic of the gifted individual.

Gifted children, in general, give evidence of superiority in character, personality traits, emotional stability, and school adjustment. They tend to display their superior abilities at an early age. They show early signs of leadership but seem to be overaggressive in their attitude toward less able children in the playing of some games, especially when they attempt to formulate new rules for the game. In the Stanford study of the gifted, it was found that the gifted children are characterized as follows:

> First of all, the average member of our group is a slightly better physical specimen than the average child of the generality; the evidence obtained from the medical examinations, the health histories, and the anthropometric measurements is unanimous and conclusive on this point.
>
> Educationally, the average gifted child is accelerated in grade placement about 14 per cent of his age, but a three-hour achievement test of subjects in grades 2 to 8 showed that in mastery of the school curriculum he is accelerated about 44 per cent of his age. The net result is that the average gifted child is held back two or three full grades below the level which he has already attained in school subjects.
>
> The achievement quotients of the gifted were not equally high in all school subjects. For the fields of subject matter covered in our tests, the superiority of gifted over unselected children was greatest in reading, language usage, arithmetical reasoning, and in science, literature, and the arts. In arithmetical computation, spelling, and factual information about history and civics, the superiority of the gifted was somewhat less marked. However, in no school subject was the average

achievement quotient of the group below 130, and no quotient
in any subject for a single child was as low as 100.[1]

Acceleration. The gifted child is sometimes permitted to advance
rapidly from grade to grade. The moving of a child from one level
of instruction to another without leaving any learning gaps in the
material to be mastered is referred to as *acceleration*. Acceleration
must not be confused with skipping. By skipping is meant that a
child is promoted from one grade to the second higher grade. He
thereby may miss many valuable experiences, or information that
should have been learned. Acceleration implies full coverage of
the material of all grades, but at a more rapid pace than is possible
for the less bright.

Controversy continues relative to the advantages and disadvantages of acceleration. The arguments revolve mostly around
the potential social and emotional adjustment problems that may
be created if, or when, young people complete their school learning
at so young an age that they are socially and emotionally too immature to participate in adult activities. One major problem is the
extent of the risk if the child is promoted solely on his ability to
achieve. Practical school leaders have decided the question in favor
of a limited amount of acceleration. There is some evidence, however, that experimentation is under way to meet the educational and
adjustment problems of the bright. Colleges are co-operating in an
attempt to discover how well the gifted young person can adjust
to the total life of the campus.

Enrichment. In an attempt to meet the academic needs of the gifted,
there has been developed an interest in the concept of giving them
more to learn at any one grade level than is expected of average
learners. This procedure is called *curricular enrichment*. For those
pupils whose inquiring minds find the usual educational offerings
to be too meager to satisfy their curiosity and lively interest in
learning, the enrichment concept was suggested and applied in
varying forms. Unfortunately, in some learning situations, enrichment became *more* of the *same*. Those learners, however, who have
readiness to learn at a more rapid pace and at a higher level need
the kind of stimulation that comes from *new material* and *thought-
provoking situations*.

The task of meeting the requirements of enrichment is over-

[1] Paul Witty (ed.) *The Gifted Child*, D. C. Heath & Co., Boston 1951, p.
23. Reprinted by permission.

whelming to a teacher who has children in his class showing a range in ability from a low IQ of 85 to one or more of above 130. The time and energy required by a teacher to meet the needs of each child in this spread of ability class are greater than most human beings can muster. If the entire class group consists of gifted individuals, however, it is relatively simple for the teacher to meet the enrichment needs of the learners. The very able learner clamors for the privilege of doing extra "research."

Concerning the importance of enrichment in the education of the gifted, Witty suggested:

> Enrichment, too, is indispensable in the education of the gifted. Yet in three decades surprisingly few enrichment programs have been developed in our schools. At the present time there is a renewed interest in the formation of special classes and schools in which enrichment of experience is planned for gifted pupils. . . .
>
> The manner of providing enrichment of education for gifted children will perhaps become a local responsibility in every school system. In large cities, it may be feasible and desirable to group the gifted for instruction; in smaller communities the gifted child may be given an enriched program in regular classrooms supplemented by individual instruction and guidance.[1]

Importance of understanding the gifted. In a democratic society the boys and girls who are able to advance at a faster rate and to a greater achievement level than is characteristic of the majority of learners should be stimulated toward maximum development. Many gifted children have not been adequately challenged to develop their superior abilities. Special classes are being provided in many schools to assist these children to work up to their maximum capacity. However, Townsend Harris High School, affiliated with City College in New York City, was established for the purpose of meeting the educational needs of bright boys but was closed as an economy measure. At this writing, there is agitation to have it open its doors again. The Hunter College Elementary School and High School, in New York City, are providing excellent learning experiences for those learners who are fortunate enough to gain admission. A recent study of the work of the elementary school was made and reported by Hildreth and her associates.[2] A reading

---

[1] Witty, *op. cit.*, p. 273. Reprinted by permission.
[2] G. Hildreth, *et al.*, *Educating Gifted Children at Hunter College Elementary School*, Harper & Bros., New York, 1952.

of this report convinces us of the values that can accrue to bright learners who are fortunate enough to have this kind of school experiences included in their enriched program.

There is value in identifying the gifted child at an early age in order that a long-term program of education may be planned. This program should include careful and continuous counseling in order that the gifted pupil may become a well-adjusted individual throughout all of his developing years and into adulthood. This is especially important since it is estimated that one out of twenty gifted individuals may develop serious maladjustments; one out of five may suffer minor personality difficulties.

In Hildreth's study it was suggested that:

> The picture of the gifted child as a warped, one-sided individual appears to be due to unwise training at home or limited goals of a narrow school program; perhaps a combination of the two. If gifted children become eccentric misfits, it is because of injudicious handling in their background. . . .
>
> The gifted tend to become unnecessarily one-sided in early childhood when their surroundings overstress bookishness. Feelings of inadequacy and inferiority due to lack of prowess in sports in comparison with others of their age may develop. Lack of friends and other indications of inadequacy in social adjustments may result from age-grade displacement at school. It is unfortunate to see a young gifted child concentrating on intellectual achievement as compensation for inferiority feelings due to social ostracism.[1]

The importance of giving the bright pupils an opportunity to gain more from their school experiences is becoming clearer daily. It is through their creative efforts and genius that life is made more pleasant and endurable for other people who do not have the inventive ability to discover special drugs, or invent mechanical aids and other energy and time-saving devices. It is a good investment for a state or a local community to provide better teachers and teaching-learning conditions for the especially gifted. Humanitarian rewards are important both to the gifted themselves and to others.

In a recent study covering 735 high schools (371 junior, 110 senior high schools, and 254 regular high schools), the United States Office of Education discovered the instructional provisions and procedures that are being used to meet the needs of rapid and of slow learners in English, social studies, mathematics, science,

[1] G. Hildreth, et al., *Educating Gifted Children at Hunter College Elementary School*, Harper & Bros., New York, 1952, p. 192. Reprinted by permission.

TABLE 19. Instructional Provisions and Procedures in Social Studies for Rapid Learners and for Slow Learners, Arranged in Rank Order, for 735 High Schools[1]

	INSTRUCTIONAL PROVISIONS AND PROCEDURES	RANK ORDER OF ITEM	
		Rapid Learners	Slow Learners
1	Use current events as an important part of class work..................................	1	1
2	Teach pupils to use the layman's reference books: the dictionary, encyclopedia, World Almanac..	2	4
3	Teach pupils how to register and vote; give experiences in studying party platforms and personal views of candidates....................	3	2
4	Encourage pupils to engage in conversation in school and at home on current events, politics, government, and news of school and neighborhood.....................................	4	3
5	Encourage pupils to use references in a large library......................................	5	11
6	Use critical thinking when the class is seeking a solution for a social problem.................	6	13.5
7	Teach pupils how to read a newspaper. (Learning to distinguish between fact and opinion, recognizing the use of propaganda devices, etc.)....	7	7.5
8	Use the socialized recitation to develop major ideas......................................	8	7.5
9	Assign individual research projects on selected topics....................................	9	21
10	Encourage pupils to select and plan to see and listen to radio, television programs, and movies of social significance........................	10	6
11	Teach basic skills in reading and writing (including mapreading) to build social-studies vocabulary and concepts.........................	11	5
12	Encourage and advise pupils to organize and operate student governments and manage extra-class activities.............................	12	16
13	Plan learning experiences in large units.........	13	13.5
14	Encourage pupils to set up personal goals and to engage in self-evaluation to see progress.......	14	9
15	Evaluate the work of the class in terms of changes in behavior toward better citizenship.........	15	10
16	Assign biographies of recognized literary merit of men and women who have made important contributions to civilization.................	16.5	21
17	Utilize resources of the local community for study.	16.5	12

[1] *Teaching Rapid and Slow Learners in High Schools,* U. S. Department of Health, Education, and Welfare, Washington, D. C., 1954, pp. 34–37.

	INSTRUCTIONAL PROVISIONS AND PROCEDURES	RANK ORDER OF ITEM	
		Rapid Learners	Slow Learners
18	Encourage pupils to read classics of historical significance.............................	18	28
19	Use group process in which all pupils use information to find solutions for social problems....	19	19
20	Give pupils practice in reading all parts of news magazines. (Include medicine, music and art, science, as well as national and international news).................................	20	23
21	Provide experiences for pupils to examine prejudices and attitudes that are provincial........	21.5	17.5
22	Lead the class in an evaluation of how well a job carried out by the whole class has been done and how group work can be improved........	21.5	15
23	Encourage pupils to make individual studies of the history of areas in which they have special interests—art, music, medicine, etc..........	23.5	24
24	Use pupil-teacher planning in studying social problems.................................	23.5	25
25	Use several textbooks for pupils of different ability rather than a single textbook...............	25	17.5
26	Supervise the planning of culminating activities by class to organize major ideas of a unit......	26	26
27	Have pupils make charts and graphs based on statistics.................................	27	27
28	Encourage participation in local adult movements	28	29
29	Provide experiences to help pupils learn how to find and apply for jobs....................	29	21
30	Arrange for preparation and presentation of radio and television programs...................	30	30

home economics, and industrial arts. In Table 19 are presented the thirty instructional provisions and procedures that are utilized in social studies. These have been ranked in the order of their greatest frequency of use among the reporting schools.

These findings clearly indicate that, throughout this country, a great deal of thought has been given to planning for bright and slow learners. Each of the suggestions in the list can be expanded considerably to meet the educational needs of these deviate learners. The value of the suggestions emerges as the specific applications are made in child development. They all have merit for inclusion in a program in which the chief concern of the educator is to guide the individual learner.

The teacher of the gifted. It is both an opportunity and a responsibility to be permitted to guide the learning of gifted students. To be successful in the role of leadership for the able student, the teacher must possess those personal qualities which will be admired and respected by his charges. The extent to which an individual needs to be gifted himself to become an effective teacher of academically able students is not clear. It is believed, however, that in order to stimulate them to greater achievement, the teacher must not only be intelligent and emotionally stable but also adaptable and resourceful. His drive and enthusiasm for learning will stimulate the gifted toward the attainment of reachable goals. Evidence of solid scholarship and creative ability will earn the confidence of gifted learners.

The successful teacher of gifted learners directs his energy in such a way as to motivate them to optimum learning achievement. The fact that an individual is gifted does not insure his attainment of desirable learning goals. He needs supervision of both his behavior and his learning activities. He learns good social behavior as he lives with his peers under the supervision of good adult leadership; he learns in the academic world as he is adequately stimulated by teachers and others who know how to motivate gifted individuals.

Gifted students need many opportunities to explore on their own. They tend to question what they read or hear. This questioning attitude can be directed toward constructive conclusions. The skillful teacher helps them gain intellectual discipline in their pursuit of learning. In brief, the effective teacher of gifted learners has (1) a willingness to adapt his teaching to the needs of his learners, (2) an understanding of the teacher-learner relationships, (3) a knowledge of his learners' potentialities, (4) a rich background in the material he is teaching, (5) leadership ability in personal and social development, and (6) a willingness to utilize scientific procedures in the teaching-learning situation.

QUESTIONS AND TOPICS FOR DISCUSSION

1. List persons whom you have met during your school years who seemed to show marked differences in their ability to learn. What was your attitude toward them at the time? How has it since changed?
2. Explain with examples what is meant by learning readiness. Reading readiness.
3. What are the frustrating effects of failure to achieve in an area in which the learner has ability deficiencies?

4. As a teacher, what kind of grouping would you prefer for the class to which you are assigned to teach?

5. What are the fundamental differences between the Dalton Plan and the Winnetka Plan? What are the advantages of each in learner achievement?

6. Study a group of ten children of any one age to discover how they differ. Record the differences.

7. Discuss the value of organizing special classes for mentally retarded learners.

8. What are the advantages and disadvantages of groupings based upon the results of a reading comprehension test?

9. Describe the behavior and interest of children who are up to their level in accomplishment but who are physically and socially immature.

10. What advantages may the mentally retarded derive from high-school attendance?

11. If home conditions of the mentally retarded group tend to hinder their educational advancement, suggest ways in which the school may alleviate the situation.

12. What are the important reasons for a thorough and careful study of pupils placed in special classes for the mentally retarded?

13. How is a general view of expected attainment helpful to the mentally retarded child?

14. If children are promoted on an age basis, it is possible that they are more homogeneous socially than the typical heterogeneous group. Discuss.

15. Evaluate these procedures: (1) enrichment of curriculum; (2) acceleration of pupils to the level of their ability to achieve.

16. Suggest a usable plan for the meeting of individual differences.

17. Discuss the extent to which bright pupils are neglected in their education.

18. What help can be given to bright children whose school performance is very poor?

19. Interpret the story that can be found in Figure 10 on page 214.

20. Study the behavior, interests, and mental development of a gifted individual and report your findings.

21. Compare the difficulties of mentally retarded learners with those of gifted learners. Report differences.

SELECTED REFERENCES

Chernow, F., and Chernow, C., *Teaching the Culturally Disadvantaged Child.* Prentice Hall, Englewood Cliffs, N.J., 1973.

Cruicschank, W. M., *Psychology of Exceptional Children and Youth,* 3rd ed. Prentice Hall, Englewood Cliffs, N.J., 1971.

French, J. L., *Educating the Gifted. Readings.* Holt, Rinehart & Winston, N.Y., 1964.

Hunt, J., *Intelligence and Experience.* Ronald Press, N.Y., 1961.

Jenkins, G., *Helping Children Reach Their Potential.* Scott Foresman, Chicago, 1961.

Jensen, A. R., *Educability and Group Differences.* Harper and Row, N.Y., 1973.

Kirk, S. A., *Educating Exceptional Children,* 2nd ed. Houghton Mifflin, Boston, 1972.

Kolstoe, O. P., *Teaching Educable Mentally Retarded Children.* Holt, Rinehart and Winston, N.Y., 1970.

Mainord, J. C. and Love, H. D., *Teaching Educable Mentally Retarded Children.* C. C. Thomas, Springfield, Ill., 1973.

Miller, H. L., *Education of the Disadvantaged.* Macmillan, N.Y., 1967.

Rothstein, J. H., *Mental Retardation,* 2nd ed. Harper and Row, N.Y., 1971.

Sanderlin, L., *Teaching Gifted Children.* A. S. Barnes, N.Y., 1973.

Wallace, C., and Kaufman, J., *Teaching Children with Learning Problems.* Charles Merrill, Columbus, Ohio, 1973.

PART V

Evaluating and Reporting

14   *The Study of the Learner in the Classroom*

Increasing attention is being given by educators to the specific learning needs of individual learners. Educational goals are being expanded to include for every learner whatever plans, procedures, and material he may need to help him develop, within the limits of his capacity for achievement, toward adult status in all areas of life. This chapter is concerned with some of the ways in which the teacher can discover the readiness of each learner to benefit from instruction that is aimed at the mastery of knowledge and skills and the improvement of attitudes, emotional control, and social adaptability.

Importance of Studying Pupil Characteristics

To be effective in their stimulation of learners toward wholesome mental, emotional, and social development, teachers must possess a thorough understanding of the psychological factors involved in child development and child training. Through their study of psychology, teachers have learned that the developmental pattern of one child differs from that of another. A practical application of this knowledge would be the teacher's attempts to discover the needs, capacities, interests, and habit patterns of each learner, in order that the co-operative process of teaching and learning may be adapted to individual needs, interests, and potentialities.

Teacher's awareness of the problem. Every classroom teacher recognizes overt behavior differences among learners. The teacher on any school level needs suggestions that will enable him to deal intelligently with young people who, at the same time, are alike and different in their ways of responding to classroom routines. The teacher knows that the child's personality does not consist of a single functioning entity but is composed of a complex of many traits or characteristics that are more or less integrated to serve his existing needs. Unfortunately, these personality components do not always parallel one another in their rate and extent of development, either between individuals or within the individual himself.

Experimentation is under way concerning phases of the developmental pattern that should constitute the basis of classification for training purposes. Some educators prefer grouping learners on a mental ability basis; others prefer a chronological age basis. Regardless of which form of grouping is used, the teacher is likely to have a range of abilities of one kind or another in his class. If the classification is based upon chronological age, the teacher soon discovers that he has a decidedly heterogeneous group. Some individuals are stout; others are thin; some are short; others are tall. Some are bright; others are dull. Some seem to be happy; others may be moody and sad.

Distribution of individual differences. Any measurable trait of human beings gives evidence of differences among individuals. For example, to discover the distribution of differences in any one meas-

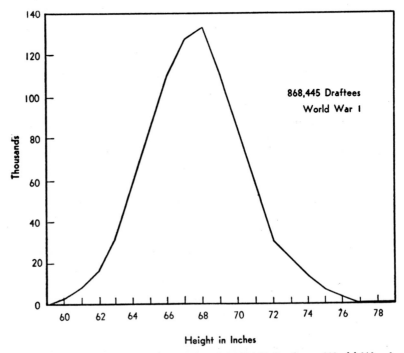

FIGURE 22.   Distribution of Height of 868,445 Draftees, World War I

From *Introduction to Psychology*, by Ernest R. Hilgard, copyright 1953 by Harcourt, Brace & Co. Reprinted by permission.

urable characteristic of fourth graders, we can select all the fourth graders in a particular school or city school system, measure individual possession of the characteristic, and arrange the obtained scores on a scale so that we may see how many fall at each point. If we want to discover the height of all the fourth graders in a city with a population of ten thousand, each child is measured and his height is placed on the chart. It is likely that a wide variation will be found in the range of height among these fourth-grade pupils. It also is probable that at least half of them will tend to cluster around the national norm for fourth-grade children. (See Figure 22 for adults.)

Likewise, if mental ability status is measured, there will be found a wide range from those with very low ability to those with exceptionally high ability, the majority clustering near the middle.

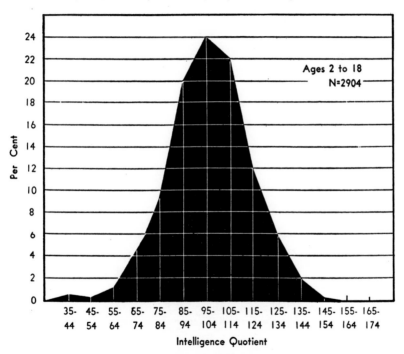

FIGURE 23.   Distribution of IQ's for 2,904 Children and Youths, Ages Two to Eighteen

This is the group upon which the Revised Stanford-Binet was standardized.

From L. M. Terman, and M. Merrill, *Measuring Intelligence*, Houghton Mifflin Co., Boston, 1937, p. 37. Reprinted by permission.

Individual differences in any characteristic are so varied that, if the sampling is large enough, the results tend to arrange themselves according to the data shown in Figure 23.

If a reading comprehension test is administered to an average seventh-grade class, subsequent arrangement of the scores will be such that they indicate the reading ability of the members of the group to range from that of a pupil with third-grade reading ability to one who has twelfth-grade reading ability. Difference in reading ability is shown in Figure 24, indicating the distribution of scores obtained from the administration of a reading comprehension test to seventh-grade pupils.

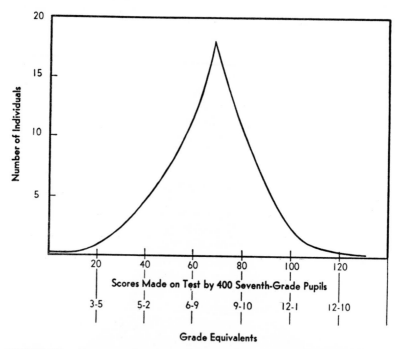

FIGURE 24.   Range in Reading Ability of Four Hundred Seventh-Grade Pupils as Determined by the Crow-Kuhlmann-Crow Reading Comprehension Test

Problems faced by teachers. To become effective as a teacher, a person needs broad and specialized training. His interest in teaching and his fine personality can carry him a long way toward successful teaching achievement. To these must be added knowledge of the nature of the child, knowledge of subject matter, and skill in the utilization of techniques for learner stimulation. Since beginning teachers usually lack experience in dealing with children, they need to become acquainted with them in one situation or another as they develop the know-how of working with children.

Among the kinds of experiences with which the teacher-trainee can gain some personal acquaintance are those that:

1. Provide conditions that make learning situations effective.
2. Guide the learning process toward the attainment of worthwhile goals.
3. Include learning situations that emphasize child activity rather than teacher activity.
4. Furnish data helpful to the gaining of an understanding of individual differences.
5. Stimulate leadership that will motivate the child toward continued learning.
6. Provide opportunities for the young learner to solve problems within the limits of his interests and capacities.
7. Direct functional learning and review opportunities for the child.
8. Create learning situations that will enable the young learner to draw heavily upon his past experience.
9. Create learning situations that have some relationship to the child's life.
10. Provide opportunities for the extremes in ability—the dull and the bright.

Problems of children. Each child is unique. He presents a variety of problems to himself and to others. Two children may appear to parallel each other in chronological age and rate of physical, mental, and emotional development, yet the problems each faces as he goes through school may differ greatly. One has musical talent; another has good memory. One is a good reader; another is a poor reader, or a nonreader. These likenesses and differences are better understood if identical twins are studied. They may and generally do have different personalities. They may develop differences in temperament and personality even if they are reared together; they usually do develop differences in these areas if they are reared apart. Fraternal twins may differ in sex and may display extremes of differences in physical, mental, and emotional development.

Most problems of children are fleeting. Yet, almost all children tend to have problems. It probably is more accurate to say that children have problems rather than that a young person is a "problem child." A child who is experiencing a problem behaves as he does only because his problem has not been solved; perhaps he has received no help in its solution. Individual behavior should be studied by the teacher in the classroom for two reasons: to help the "difficult" child make better adjustment and to avoid the spread of his influence to other members of the group.

Teacher Responsibility for Studying Learners

It is becoming increasingly evident that the teacher needs to learn as much as he can concerning each member of his group. If the principle of teaching the *child through subject matter* rather than the *subject matter to the child* is adhered to, a complete profile must be available concerning every pupil in the class. The person who is responsible for gathering the data concerning the child must utilize appropriate techniques for securing pertinent information. The following discussion is concerned with the effectiveness of studying children in classroom situations.

Purpose of individual study. Teachers constantly are confronted with the problem of estimating the results of learning and degree of behavior adjustment. They are concerned with evaluating the knowledge acquired, the skills perfected, and the attitudes developed. The results of the evaluation then should be interpreted in terms of the educational goals which the teachers are expected to reach.

In order that he may give individual attention more effectively to each learner in terms of the latter's learning capacity and interests, the teacher should be acquainted with the child's background, his inherent ability, his interests, his health status, his aspirations, his degree of sociability, his emotional reactions in various situations, and similar aspects of his personality. Some of these data can be made available for the teacher by an efficient school guidance staff, but there are many data that he must be trained to secure for himself.

The teacher probably has been trained to evaluate learning achievement; he also needs to be trained in effective ways to study child behavior, to discover for himself why children behave as they do and what can be done to guide their behavior into more suitable channels. Above all, the teacher must know for what he is searching, regardless of whether he is evaluating general learner progress through the administration of classroom tests or whether he is evaluating the ability of the learner to succeed in a particular area of learning activity. In short, the teacher attempts to understand his pupils so that he is more effective in assisting each learner to achieve the greatest possible success.

Special classroom procedures. With the change in emphasis from the mastery of learning content to the development of the physical, intellectual, emotional, and social aspects of a learner's personality, has come a need to expand appropriate approaches to evaluation. Experimentation already has produced some useful procedures that are helpful to the teacher as he attempts to meet his broadened responsibilities for learner development. Some of the *informal ways* of studying learners are: (1) teacher observation of learner behavior, (2) anecdotal records or reports prepared by the teacher, (3) autobiographical sketches, (4) sociograms, (5) oral recitations and short quizzes, (6) individual or group projects, (7) learner's notebooks, reports, and themes, (8) creative expression of learners, and (9) teacher-pupil interviews.

Teacher Observation of Learner Behavior

Careful observation is basic to pupil study and is associated with most of the other techniques used. Although teachers have many opportunities to observe their pupils, it is surprising what they miss unless they are trained to look for certain behavior and personality traits. Insight into the causes of behavior displayed by a child or an adolescent is increased as the teacher carefully studies accumulated data about the young person. Teachers need to develop not only the attitude of observing carefully the behavior of all learners but also the habit of recording the data thus obtained at the time it is observed or shortly thereafter. Accuracy is possible only if the record is made within the span of memory of the facts observed.

Classroom opportunities. The alert teacher is aware of much that is taking place in his class. He may observe that during a class activity a particular pupil is engaging in a bit of unusual behavior; he may overhear an interesting and perhaps startling remark; he may notice a peculiar expression on the face of a pupil. At the time of their occurrence, the teacher may be so concerned about the activity of the class that he forgets what he has observed or recalls it only after the school day is over and he is recounting the day's doings to the members of his family or to friends. Unusual behavior, remarks, or facial expressions may have no more than momentary significance; they may be symptomatic of a situation that needs rectifying, however. It might seem to be asking a great deal of a busy teacher to make note of the many things that happen in the classroom. Yet, an apparently unimportant bit of behavior may be a significant element of the personality status of a child.

The teacher is interested in all the patterns of behavior that are exhibited by the members of his class. Since it is impossible for him to evaluate all of them at the same time, he must be selective. He may give close attention to several behavior traits at one time and organize his findings in the form of a report which he presents to the class. A correct report on the punctuality, neatness, accuracy, and responsiveness of the members of the class may stimulate pupils to improve their behavior in these areas.

Either one of two different approaches can be utilized in the study of behavior: (1) The teacher can select a long list of possible traits, and check the behavior of each of the children in relation to all of them, or (2) He can attempt to record the behavior of each of the learners while they are busily working on a project. Efficiency experts constantly are studying the behavior of individuals as the latter attempt to carry out assignments.

The teacher often is a less critical observer in his classroom than a visitor may be. The stranger may observe behavior to which the teacher is so accustomed that he overlooks it. Hence observations must be made with a definite purpose in mind. It perhaps is impossible for a teacher-observer to perceive everything that transpires in a classroom situation at any one time. He therefore learns to observe for one purpose at one time and for another purpose at another time. For example, at one time the teacher may wish to discover what he can do concerning the general sequence of activities of one or more children; at another time he may wish to study the behavior of certain individuals in definite stimuli-situations. In either instance he attends to definite items and records his findings.

The teacher must learn to be accurate and objective in his recordings, avoiding the intrusion of his own personal biases or prejudices. He records everything that is observed; he does not list only those data that interest him at the moment. There are vast differences among teachers as observers of children. Some are careful, reliable, and accurate; others tend to be subjective and careless. Proficiency in observation increases as the teacher gains experience in the utilization of it, however. We repeat for emphasis that valid results in observation demand that the teacher be able to rise above personal bias of judgment and be accurate in recording. He also should be mindful of the fact that his interpretation of child behavior may not always be completely adequate.

Training in observation. As the shift was made from emphasis upon subject matter in the teaching-learning situation to attention to the child, it became necessary that teachers be trained well in the study of children. Consequently, the teacher-training institutions began to give attention to ways in which teachers-in-training might be assisted in the utilization of observation during their student-teaching experiences. Too often, these students were uncertain about what to observe. As a means of giving teacher-trainees *purpose* in observation, a plan was devised to encourage student-teachers to become aware of pupils as individuals, as well as to become acquainted with the activities of the class as a whole and the methods of the teachers. These student-teachers observed the characteristic behavior of each pupil; they prepared and kept daily records. At the end of the term, they reported their observation of class activities, teaching procedures, and identifying information relative to each of the members of the observed class.

Student-teachers become better observers of pupil behavior if and when they are furnished with specific items to observe. Numerous lists have been devised for this purpose. These items may be specific or they may be given in the form of generalizations. If the student is given functional areas to evaluate concerning learners, he might be expected to:

1. Observe the behavior of individuals as they strive to gain attention and approval from teachers or associates.
2. Observe the tendency of the individuals toward mastery or submission.
3. Observe the extent to which each pupil attempts to participate in class discussion.
4. Observe the habits of study of each member of the class.
5. Observe the proficiency with which each prepares the assignment.
6. Observe the reading ability of each member of the class.
7. Observe the types of responses to questions.
8. Observe the extent of interest in the work.
9. Observe the extent of self-discipline demonstrated by each member of the class.
10. Observe the social climate in the classroom.
11. Observe the kind and number of questions asked by the pupils.
12. Observe the speech or language difficulties.
13. Observe the nature and extent of physical handicaps.
14. Observe the nature and extent of cheating.
15. Observe the willingness to begin the work of the day.
16. Observe the extent of attention given to the lesson.
17. Observe the individual responsiveness to punishment.

18. Observe the behavior of individuals who may be classified as "teacher's pet."
19. Observe the behavior of the members of the class toward you as the observer.
20. Evaluate your attitude toward the members of the class during your period as an observer.

The time and attention of the student-teacher should not be given exclusively to pupil reaction. He also should give attention to what is being done by the teacher. In fact, he should attempt to discover what the teacher does to better his understanding of the children in his class. In this, the student-teacher is helped by knowing some of the things for which to look or to which to direct his attention as he observes. Among these are:

1. Evidences concerning the usefulness of anecdotal records.
2. Motivation value of visual aids, such as blackboards, charts, slides, motion pictures.
3. Extent to which pupils are motivated to learn.
4. Motivation toward creating learning readiness.
5. Extent to which learners are given a chance to participate.
6. Extent to which the interests of the learners are taken into consideration.
7. Extent to which learning is motivated through fear.
8. Extent to which, and means by which, self-discipline is developed.
9. Extent to which time is used effectively by the teacher.
10. Extent to which learners are acquiring good habits of work.
11. Kind and nature of techniques of problem-solving that are utilized.
12. Leadership given to develop desirable personality traits among the learners.
13. Importance of personality of the teacher in child development.
14. Possession by the teacher of personality traits that may interfere with teacher success.
15. Pupil reaction to the teacher.

The reader may be interested to read two reports prepared by student-teachers who participated in this kind of experience during their student-teaching work. Each student was instructed to write a report about the class, giving the high lights of the term's work as related to: (1) the general reaction of the class to the teacher and teaching, and (2) a detailed report on each learner who was observed. Excerpts from two of these reports follow.

Student-teacher A. During my observation of classroom activities as a student-teacher, I have seen many phases of the learning process in operation. I have seen the importance of teaching at the learning and experience levels of the learners. As a specific example of this, I refer to the physics honor class which I observed. This class is supposed to be a homogeneous grouping of all the best science and mathematics students in the school. In reality, however, there were at least three students in the class who did not belong there. As a result of this, the course was conducted on a level which was a good deal higher than the learning level of these three students. This is one of the main dangers of improper planning for homogeneous grouping. Speaking for homogeneous grouping, the teacher, who is also chairman of the department, said that such grouping enables the good students to get more work done and to discuss among themselves topics which would not come up in an ordinary class.

In a science class, such as physics, experiments and demonstrations are integral parts of the daily lessons. I was surprised to learn that films were not at all used in this class. I have seen some very interesting science films, and when I spoke to the teacher about this, he said that there are films for the second-term physics classes, and then added something about budget restrictions. . . .

I have always conferred with the teacher before he allowed me to take over a class. It was during these discussions that he stressed the importance of stimulating class interest when introducing a new lesson or a new topic. Whenever I had difficulty in finding a method of gaining and maintaining class interest, he would come up with a wealth of wonderful suggestions. These suggestions would be in the form of statements, questions, demonstrations, or experiments, and they helped to make my teaching more enjoyable. He was always ready to help me by drawing from his years of teaching experience.

It seems to me that at times he was more concerned with teacher-activity than with pupil-activity. For example: When he sets up and operates a class experiment, he seems to be enthralled by it and forgets momentarily that the demonstration is for the benefit of the class. This results in a loss of class attention which, in turn, detracts from the value of the lesson. He was doing this when he taught me in high school and he is still doing it. Despite this unchanging pedagogical fault, he is a dynamic department head.

He is continually striving for certain courses which would help many of the students. At present he is trying to inaugurate a course called "Applied Physics." This course would be similar in form to the "Applied Chemistry" course which has been instituted in many high schools. He is always well informed concerning the latest scientific developments. He maintains a science library, which is always open to the students. He was instrumental in forming science help classes and special help classes for those students who intend to take science award examinations. I was fortunate, one day, to hear him confer with a member of his department for the purpose of passing judgment on the latter's pedagogical methods. He did this in such a genial manner that it did not seem as though a department head was criticizing a member of his department, but it appeared as though two good friends were conversing about the value of a variety of pedagogical methods.

As a result of his years of teaching experience, he is able to anticipate the reactions of the class during any particular lesson. In fact, he once gave me a list of five questions which he said would be asked by pupils during a specific lesson. During the lesson, four of the questions were asked. This is knowledge which can be gained only through experience.

As far as discipline is concerned, he and I differ as to the value of the following disciplinary method. He will not hesitate to reprimand a student in front of the whole class, whereas I would try to avoid this as much as possible. I have never seen him punish the class when an individual was responsible for the disorder. I have seen him stare at an offender for about ten seconds in order to bring him back to order. This proved to be very effective. Every student seems to know just what is expected of him with regard to behavior controls. I was not present at the first few meetings of the class, so I do not know what methods he used to bring about this desirable result. He must be well acquainted with disciplinary problems, because, as head of the department, many teachers come to him for advice before embarking on any drastic disciplinary measures.

I have seen him use praise to bring about many desirable results. For example: one student had no intention of completing a special project. With a few well-chosen words of praise about the incompleted portion of the project, the teacher provided enough motivation for the student so that the project was soon completed.

As soon as the bell rings, work begins. One student takes the attendance, another clears the boards, and still another arranges materials. This and other means of delegating authority to the students seem to make them feel that they have some part in each day's work. The teacher is prepared to stimulate thinking immediately, and there is no wasted time before the day's work is begun. At times, when there is a delay caused by the misbehavior of a student, the teacher makes it a point of showing disapproval of the behavior, and not of the student. He does not merely tell the student that the behavior is wrong, but he tells him why it is wrong.

When I sat in on the class for the first time, the teacher introduced me to the students. He mentioned that I was a student teacher from ———— College and asked them to have the same respect for me that they had for him. Not a single student spoke to me until the teacher told them that I would be glad to help them with their term projects. After I had answered their questions concerning the projects, the questions were extended to cover homework assignments, topics which were not clearly understood, and certain phases of laboratory work. Before the period began, and after it had ended, I would have a group of students gathered around me with a barrage of questions. I didn't mind this and neither did the teacher, so these short question and answer periods have continued throughout the term.

My first reaction to the class was that most of the students were very much interested in the course and that they possessed a great desire to learn. This reaction was justified by their attention in class, their response to questions, their ability to ask meaningful questions, and their ease in handling themselves in the laboratory. I was not at all surprised to learn that this class was a physics honor class and was composed of some of the best science and mathematics students in the school. The teacher referred to the teaching of this class as an example of the ideal teaching situation. He would cover the required work for the day in less than the allotted time and spend the remaining time discussing advanced topics of science which would never have been mentioned in the regular physics class. He believes that this is one of the greatest advantages of homogeneous grouping, such as an honor class.

Student-teacher B. Art appreciation 23AA was, according to all standards, a unique class. To me, of course, it seemed individual because it represented my first contact with a group of people as a teacher. Even to an experienced teacher, 23AA would have seemed unusual. The class was small. It had fewer than thirty students, most of whom were seniors. The fact that about three-fourths of the class were girls and that almost all the students were following a commercial program presented a problem in curriculum.

Since the class was relatively homogeneous according to grade level and curriculum, it was easy to plan a special program of work. I was delighted to be assigned to this class. Here was a chance to design a program to fit their specific and immediate needs, and to watch their growth and progress. I knew that this course would be the only art or design instruction for almost all of them.

During my first week of observation, I watched the opening procedure carefully. The relations between teacher and class, and within the student body itself also interested me. Since I sat in the rear of the room, little or no attention was paid me and so, unnoticed, I could observe and take notes on all that went on.

Usually, the class began work immediately. At first there were some whispering, gossiping, and giggling, but within ten minutes, there were complete order and attention to work. I had no way of knowing at this point what the assignment had been or how it had been presented; therefore all I could do was to acquaint myself with the class and their general work habits.

Watching students at work and the teacher criticizing their work without leaving his desk disturbed me a little and reminded me of my own days in this same school. No matter what we as students did, decisions were made and instructions to go ahead were given from the front of the room. Before one did anything, it had to be checked and approved lest it turn out to be different from the ideal that the teacher had set.

I discovered later that this procedure was used only while classes were being equalized and clerical changes made. I still feel that even this period of adjustment can be used to establish good working relations in the class. As soon as the class started the regular work of the term, however, the situation improved greatly.

The teacher in charge, Mr. M., showed interest in stimulating the class as individuals on their own levels. In presenting new work, he utilized visual demonstrations and discussions to stimulate student participation. Although at times his methods seemed inconsistent (sometimes he allowed them to work freely and at other times he insisted on supervising every move they made), his attitude gradually became more relaxed and friendly.

Mr. M. had a pleasant, subtle way of handling discipline problems, and he showed that he knew his students well. When one of the truants of the class would return after prolonged and inexcusable absence, he would tactfully inquire about the present state of the student's health and would smile sympathetically as he listened to a tale of woe. He then would quietly suggest methods of making up the work missed. Never did he display anger or annoyance; he often tried to help the truant by inviting him to his office for a friendly "Dutch uncle" talk. The class respected and admired his attitude and accepted him as a friend.

Once, when the class did not co-operate in cleaning up after a problem in cut paper construction, he handled the situation by appealing to their sense of responsibility. In spite of the fact that we gave the class a five-minute warning period to pick up paper scraps and clean up, we found ourselves performing the janitorial task after they had left. Very quietly the next day, as they were about to leave, he mentioned the fact that on the day before he had had to use his lunch period to clean up after them. In a body, they put their books aside and started to straighten up the room, and we never again had trouble with that problem.

During the early part of the term, I wondered if he were being a little too easy with the students. Yet, because he never was authoritarian, he earned their respect. He always treated them as individuals and adults and delegated responsibilities to them. For the most part, only a hint was needed for them to meet forgotten responsibilities. Some students, of course, thought he was just an easy guy who let them get away with murder. For the majority of the students, however, his system provided opportunities for social and intellectual growth.

On Friday, October 15, Mr. M. asked me to prepare an informal lecture with demonstration material for a problem in mobiles. During the term, the class had been working in three-dimensional form and color, and most of the constructions had been in cut paper which had to be mounted or glued down. The subject and the material to be prepared gave me no trouble, but I wondered whether the students would accept me in the teacher role. Seated at the back of the room, I had been unnoticed; some students even thought I was a member of the class. I wondered how Mr. M. would introduce me to the class, or whether he would at all. He was able to control the class, but I worried about what I would do if they became bored or disinterested and started teen-age pranks. I decided that I would have to do more than prepare a lesson to teach. I would have to prepare a thoroughly interesting and mystifying demonstration that would surprise them.

Monday morning, after doing research on the concept of motion in time and space and Einstein's Theory of Relativity, I sat patiently awaiting my introduction to the class. I had several bits of equipment to set up. The demonstration, keyed to adolescent interest and knowledge, was clear in my mind. I wasn't even nervous, but Mr. M. apparently had forgotten it was the day for my lesson and carried on till the bell rang. My reaction was more one of frustration than relief. The following day I taught the lesson and it went very well.

Within a week the class was turned over to me because Mr. M. felt that I was ready. I received a copy of the Art Appreciation, Term 2 curriculum, and was told to select, organize, and create a program for the class. In choosing work topics for my students, I eliminated stuffy, overacademic topics, and chose those having a definite, practical, and creative appeal. The average maturity of my students convinced me that they would appreciate realistic work with practical applicational value. My job, therefore, was to introduce the qualities of good taste and design and to stimulate creative efforts along these lines.

Of all my student-teaching experiences, those of most importance in 23AA revolved directly around the students. Most important in a class are the personality qualities of the students. Whether the teacher is experimenting to arouse interest, guiding them in their work, evaluating their abilities, or watching their social and creative development, adolescent students are always the stars of the show.

I will never forget my experiences as a student-teacher, both the good and the bad. The mistakes that I made were the best guides to improvement and understanding of my pupils, myself, and the situation. I learned more from the students than anyone could have forewarned me about. Even if I never teach, I feel that I am a better person because of the characteristics I developed and strengthened as a student-teacher.

Some Commonly-Used Study Approaches

The teacher has within his classroom situation all that is necessary to evaluate learners in their day-by-day activities. Information concerning behavior and achievement can be obtained from anecdotal records, autobiographical statements, oral and written quizzes, class projects, reports and themes, and individual conferences.

Anecdotal records. A systematic recording of data concerning an individual often is called an anecdotal record of that individual. If behavior relative to an individual is recorded systematically and the records are kept in cumulative form, the total story during a term or a year becomes significant as representing a profile of the individual. There is nothing unique about anecdotal records. The teacher who assiduously keeps daily or weekly records of significant sayings or happenings in the classroom is the teacher who gradually gets to know his children in different and more complete ways than do those teachers who believe that they can rely upon remembering all the significant happenings that occur. At the time of their happening, some events are so vivid that the observer believes he never will forget them; yet in one short week some of the important details may be forgotten.

If a teacher inaugurates a plan whereby he uses cards or sheets of paper to record incidents that occur in the classroom, eventually he will have accumulated considerable data that will be of service to him as he counsels and works with his learners. The record may contain notes on behavior that is satisfactory as well as that which gives evidence of poor adjustment on the part of the learner. Teachers who attempt to write anecdotal reports need to be encouraged to observe behavior carefully and to make accurate recordings of observations. Above all, they should evaluate the behavior in light of the background of each individual concerned.

The teacher who follows the practice of preparing and keeping written reports of observations discovers that they (1) promote balanced judgments, (2) save him time and the time of school counselors, (3) reveal developmental patterns of behavior, and (4) can be summarized on permanent records for use by counselors and other teachers who may wish to discover how teachers react toward a particular child.

A written record may be most helpful as a teacher confers with the supervisor, the principal, or a parent regarding the learning problems of a child. The recency of a boy's failure to prepare his lessons, the extent to which he correctly completes his work, or the level of his achievement can become matters of record which, when needed, can be referred to by the teacher, with assurance that he is not merely guessing at the facts. When some of the important findings about the learning habits and behavior characteristics of learners are recorded, teachers have the facts at hand and are not confronted with loss of memory or with uncertainty as to the possible application of the data to the wrong child. The record remembers for them.

In summarizing some of the limitations of anecdotes, Traxler made the following recommendations concerning their preparation and use.

1. It is apparent, of course, that an anecdotal record can be valuable only if the original observation is accurate and correctly recorded; otherwise, it may be worse than useless. . . .
2. Many persons find it extremely difficult to write with complete objectivity, but practice will do a great deal to over-

come the tendency to intersperse the report of behavior with statements of opinion. . . .

3. A pernicious but fortunately rare use of anecdotal records is their employment for the defense of the person making the report. The central purpose of every anecdotal record is to help the entire school staff to obtain better understanding of a given student. . . .

4. It is evident that there is danger in lifting a behavior incident out of the social setting in which it occurred and in reporting it in isolation. . . .

5. At best, only a small proportion of the total number of significant behavior incidents for any pupil will find its way into anecdotal records. . . .

6. Some persons fear that anecdotes, through preserving a record of unfortunate behavior incidents on the part of certain pupils, may prejudice their success long afterward, when the behavior is no longer typical of them. There is ground for this fear if the school carelessly allows the anecdotes to fall into the hands of irresponsible persons. . . .

7. It cannot be emphasized too strongly that the adoption of a system of anecdotal records is no small commitment and that it will add inevitably to the load of the entire school, particularly the counselors and the clerical staff. . . .

8. It is obvious that the indications in the anecdotal records should be studied and an attempt made to improve the adjustment of the pupils when the anecdotes show that better adjustment is needed. . . .

9. Undesirable behavior, because of its nuisance aspect, is likely to make a stronger impression on teachers than desirable behavior. There is some danger, therefore, that the total effect of anecdotal records will be negative rather than positive. . . .

10. Occasionally teachers will observe incidents that are not at all typical of the behavior of the pupil concerned.[1]

In studying his pupils, the teacher may find it helpful to record such information as: projects completed; test scores made on various types of tests, e.g., achievement, personal and social adjustment, or scales showing attitudes and interests; library books taken out by pupils; field trips made; and extraclass activities.[2]

[1] A. E. Traxler, *Techniques of Guidance*, Harper & Bros., New York, 1945, pp. 141–142. Reprinted by permission.
[2] Standardized tests, case studies, and other forms of evaluation are discussed in Chapter 15.

As a part of student-teacher observation of classroom activities, each student teacher should make an individual study of every pupil in his class. Sample reports follow.

Joe. Joe is the most likable boy in the class and it is indeed an effort not to show favoritism. (It is not shown.) He is always alert, interested, and participating. He, more than any of his classmates, has the ability of making the subject meaningful for him. He extracts important ideas and characteristics and applies them to everyday life, particularly in terms of his own experience. He sees a value in school and learning, and for him the value lies in the learning's practicality and whether or not it is applicable to and useful in day-to-day living. Furthermore, it increases in value if it aids him in finding and maintaining a good position. He feels that progress cannot be assured without education, but that it must be meaningful and practical. He is very direct in stating his beliefs, and hardly a day passes without some participation on his part. He is very well liked by all the boys in the class as well as the teacher. His work is good. He had some difficulty in another class during the semester which necessitated his being out of class for most of the group activity. When he attended class, during the time the difficulty was being straightened out, he was in a depressed state and did not participate at all. His appearance was also altered as a result of his difficulty. When matters were once more back to normal, his recuperative powers were amazing. He regained his usual liveliness and interest. He appreciates and responds to constructive criticism, as well as to praise. A very important motivating factor in his performance is his desire for a high mark and, perhaps, exemption from the final. He is not different from the other boys in this respect in that it is the ultimate goal of all. Marks do not, however, account for his attitudes and behavior since they seem to be totally natural to him. He may very well be a leader, though I believe that he would much rather follow, or be a part of the group. I think it is because he would rather not accept full responsibility. His IQ is 127, and he is enrolled in the College Preparatory Course, although he may not attend college, and he may change his major in the spring term.

Arline. Arline is fifteen years of age, has an IQ of 128, and is a member of the "Leaders Club." The girl is of medium height with a boyish figure. Her hair is cut short, and she is very sloppy about her appearance. She likes to act and dress like a boy. She is very awkward in her movements and is generally unsure of herself.

Arline is a very good athlete. A few weeks ago she participated in a P.A.L. basketball tournament in Madison Square Garden. Her team won the tournament and Arline received a beautiful gold wrist watch as an award. She is a member of the school band and plays the drums. She is enthusiastic about everything she participates in. Her speech is very poor and her vocabulary even worse. She uses a great deal of slang and seems proud of it. Arline told me that she would love to go to ———— College when she is graduated from high school but is afraid that her grades will prevent her from doing so. She asked me if I knew anyone that could give her the answers to the entrance examination. When I told her that I had never heard of anyone getting the answers to the test in advance, she informed me that I just didn't know the right people.

This adolescent seemed to admire me a great deal. She would follow me wherever I went. I asked my supervisor what to do about her when she would run up in back of me, put her hands over my eyes and ask me to guess who it was. She is very pessimistic and has no confidence in her mental ability.

Autobiographical sketches. Some teachers are successful in working with children who can express themselves in writing by having them prepare comprehensive autobiographical sketches. The individual is given an opportunity thereby to give expression to his interests, attitudes, and ideals. Because of their fear to give honest expression to their inner feelings, and because some individuals are not skilled in telling about their hopes, aspirations, and true feelings, these sketches may be meager and often worthless. In the upper grades and in the junior and senior high school, however, much can be learned concerning the personality and the personal problems of individuals by way of biographical sketches.

Each individual who writes an autobiographical sketch possesses a wealth of experience, but he may have difficulty in selecting that which he believes to be pertinent to his story. His inhibitions may not permit him to write freely and fully concerning his experiences. He may be tempted to write what he believes the teacher wants or what he wants the teacher to know about him. He may have difficulty in distinguishing fact from fancy.

One value of an attempt to write an autobiography is that it gives the learner an opportunity to evaluate himself in a more objective fashion than he otherwise might do. These sketches also can be handled on a cumulative basis. Each week, the pupils might be invited to write their most interesting experiences for that period; they might be encouraged to prepare detailed diaries that cover a stated period of time. These might engender a great deal of interest among the learners and become helpful to those who guide them.

An interesting factual account of his work experiences was reported by Frank who always had been interested in the value of money. As soon as he was able to do so, he began to work after school and during summers at jobs suitable to his age. In connection with a high-school assignment, he gave the following autobiographical account of his work experiences.

During my seventeen years of existence, my working experiences have been many and varied.

Shortly after our family moved from a small town to a city (I was in the third grade at the time), I started selling magazines. Each night, rain or shine, snow or otherwise, I would go from door to door selling magazines. I can never remember making much money, but from the small amount I did earn, I learned the value of money. Even yet, when I spend money, I think of how many houses I would have to go to sell magazines enough for the prescribed amount of money. My next job along this line was a paper route. My first route was an afternoon edition, but when I became twelve years old I got a morning route. Getting up at five in the morning required going to bed early; a job that requires regular living is worth much more than its pecuniary returns.

My grandparents live in a small town, where they operate a general store, a feed mill, and a coal business. They also buy large quantities of maple sirup. My first selling experience, that is in a store, was in my grandparents' general store selling groceries, hardware, and clothing. Also at their place of business I learned to operate a feed mill, to run grinders and mixers. Here I learned, by contrast, the value of a white-collar job. I also learned something about the process of making maple sirup, a product which I have been retailing in this city from door to door for the past year.

Other relatives operate farms, and I have had the opportunity of working on their farms. Learning many of the activities of a farmer has been quite interesting and healthful.

I have spent many days caddying, and working in a parking lot. These contacts with people have proved invaluable. During Christmas vacations I have worked in a post office, helping to deliver mail. An experience such as this is interesting at first but after a few weeks becomes dull and boring.

My next job was helping a milkman deliver milk. The milkman has a rather hard job, with long hours starting at three in the morning. However, through this contact I learned the workings of a modern dairy.

I've been working this summer while attending summer school. I first got a job in an ice-cream bar, selling cones, sodas, and sundaes. It did not pay very well, so I got a position as a salesman in a Western Auto Store. This is rather interesting because we sell ten thousand different items.

The day summer school is over and until my college term starts, I expect to get a job as a coal passer on a ship on the Great Lakes.

All the different types of work in which I have been engaged have been of great importance in helping me to determine my future lifework.[1]

Sociograms. The sociogram is used to give a structural picture of a child as a member of a group. The purpose of the sociogram is to discover those children who may need help in peer relationships, and to discover those who may need assistance in the development of social living in the classroom. Such expression of interests as the classmate with whom a child would like to sit, walk with on an excursion to the park, or work with on a report are suitable considerations for a sociometric study. It is possible to arouse sensitive children to be alarmed concerning the teacher's motive for asking the question, however.

Sociograms are easily constructed. The accompanying sociogram, Figure 25, resulted from the question asked of a group of fifth-grade children, "Who are your three best friends in this room?" The girls are represented by the circles and the boys by the squares. Those members of the class who were chosen most frequently are nearest the center of the sociogram. Mutual choices are shown by double arrows. It is easy to discover from this sociogram that P.T. is the most popular girl of the class and that S.D. is the most popular boy, since each was chosen by the largest number of other children. Also, the one who was not chosen as a "good friend" by any child is easily detected. Any good teacher is likely to be aware of these facts without the need of this device. Unless it is wisely used, this technique may lead to maladjustment as well as to good adjustment among the children.

Oral recitation and quizzes. Many factors influence a learner's attitude toward reciting in class. Unless the teacher distributes his questions equitably, there usually are a few pupils who want to answer all of them whether or not they have given thoughtful con-

[1] By permission from *Our Teen-Age Boys and Girls*, by L. D. Crow, and A. Crow, copyright 1945, McGraw-Hill Book Company, New York, pp. 170–171.

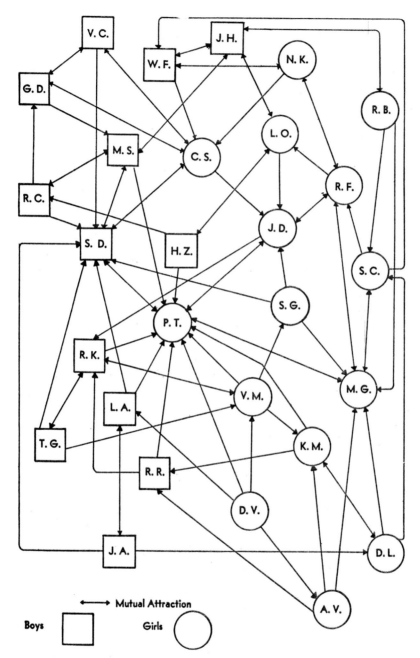

FIGURE 25. Sociogram Showing Best Friends (Three Choices) in a Fifth-Grade Class

sideration to the question or topic to be discussed. Less aggressive young people are likely to be afraid to enter into competition with the others; they assume an attitude of letting the others take over. A learner may not hear or understand the question, may not be prepared to answer it, or may lack sufficient self-confidence to participate in class discussion. It is the teacher's responsibility not only to discover the underlying reasons for differences among learners in oral recitations, but also to do something definite about what he has discovered.

Periodic short quizzes serve as excellent motivators of serious and consistent learner application to his studies. Some teachers have found the utilization of the following technique to be satisfactory: at the beginning of the recitation period there is administered a five-minute quiz based upon a significant phase of the topic to be discussed. Sometimes the papers are exchanged among the pupils and the answers evaluated or used as the starting point of the day's discussion. The class activity then is not so much a matter of recitation as it is a meeting of minds. The teacher and the members of the class participate in an informal, relaxed discussion that, through teacher guidance, is prevented from going too far afield.

Some young people who are unaccustomed to this type of class procedure may give the impression of being unable or unwilling to take their rightful share in the discussion. Here again the teacher, recognizing the reason for the behavior, can use appropriate techniques for changing the situation. A study of this pupil's performance on the short preparatory quiz helps the teacher discover the reason for the nonparticipation in the discussion.

The utilization of pre-tests as a means of discovering gaps in learner background is coming into wide use. Another value of administering a pre-test is to enable the teacher to discover what the learners *already know* in this area of study. If the group is relatively homogeneous, much learner boredom and the development of laziness in studying can be avoided by the teacher who picks up from what the learners already know rather than start from the beginning of the teaching unit.

For example, in some schools and school systems, a course in *General Science* is a freshman requirement. The students then may continue the study of biology, chemistry, or physics. Unless the teacher knows what was included in the first survey course, he may assume little learner knowledge in the field and start with beginning principles and facts. This is "old stuff" to the learners. Hence they lose interest or find that they do not need to study. As a result, many of these young people are not able to recognize new material when it is introduced, and they continue to maintain their first-of-the-term's attitude toward the subject.

Individual and group projects. Research or construction projects in which learners engage either alone or with other classmates afford an observant teacher excellent opportunities to study personal qualities that are displayed by a learner. The teacher can discover a great deal about a learner as he observes the ease or difficulty with which the learner approaches the project, his degree of interest in it, his ability to plan and to execute whatever needs to be done, his degree of persistence, the amount of assistance he requests, the successful completion of the project, and his pride in accomplishment.

If the project is a group activity, the teacher also can evaluate the kind and extent of co-operation exhibited by each member of the group, differences in the display of leadership qualities, malingering on the job, and special aptitudes or abilities. To be worthwhile as a means of developing desirable personal and social attitudes, however, the project must be suited to the capabilities and interests of the learners; it must possess realistic and practical significance.

Learners' notebooks, reports, and themes. The authors do not favor the keeping by learners of elaborate, detailed, meticulously written, and copiously illustrated notebooks. The teacher's time and attention should be given to the resultants of learning as these are displayed by the learner's exhibited increase in knowledge or skill and improvement of attitude, instead of "marking" notebooks.

There may be learning situations, however, in which a notebook can become the receptacle of materials that are of value to the learner after he has completed a particular course, and that may not be available to him in printed form. Such materials might include: special food recipes in home economics; research material in science or social studies that is garnered from many original sources and that has practical significance; special teaching approaches that have resulted from personal experience and class discussion in methods courses of teacher education.

Whether the written work of learners is in the form of a notebook, a theme, or a report, a teacher can use it as a means of evaluating: a young person's habits of neatness and care; attention to significant material to be included, and extent to which individual differences show themselves in such phases of performance as mode of thinking, creative expression, and persistence of effort in responding to challenge.

The out-of-class preparation of themes, reports, and notebooks may motivate a young person to engage in forms of activity that are detrimental to the development of good character. We shall illustrate this point by citing a few common examples taken from specific school situations.

The pupils of a school discover that a certain teacher places considerable emphasis upon the inclusion of illustrative material in the

FIGURE 26a.   Drawings of a House Made by Two Children in the Same Kindergarten Class

notebooks prepared by the pupils and submitted to the teacher for his evaluation. Too great interest in competition and in the receiving of high marks may motivate a young person to include in his notebook as many illustrations as he can obtain honestly or otherwise. Hence books and magazines found in the home, as well as those taken from the school or public library, are mutilated because of the student's strong urge to excel. He does not appreciate the enormity of his crime until or unless the teacher, who was the cause of his committing it, discovers what he has done and uses drastic measures to correct the practice. One boy who was "caught" in this kind of offense (his first major antisocial act) expressed his feelings about the situation in these words: "I tried to please the teacher and look what happened! Did she think I could pull those pictures out of the air?"

The utilization of the same theme or report in different classes is another form of deception that is practiced frequently. Still another undesirable form of behavior may be displayed by the young person who is required to describe, in the form of a class theme, his out-of-chool activities, or his attitudes toward matters that have significant emotional meaning in his life. A teacher cannot be certain that he is receiving completely truthful accounts of situations, con-

FIGURE 26b.   Drawings of a House Made by Two Children in the Same First-Grade Class

ditions, or personal attitudes. To the extent of his understanding of the learner's life pattern, however, he can learn much about the child or adolescent through what he says in a theme of this kind. Teachers are becoming increasingly sensitive to learner's reactions.

Creative expression of learners. Young children often reveal many of their inner needs and cravings through what they draw and the way in which they draw it. In the kindergarten and in the lower grades of the elementary school, the children engage in finger painting, water coloring, drawing with crayons, and craft activities. Each of these activities serves its particular function in helping the child develop his imaginative and emotional interests and possibilities.

A wide variation of expression is given by different children as they manipulate the mud in finger painting. The teacher may suggest and encourage, but the resulting pattern should be that of the child. In this freedom of movement we observe a form of play in which the child is given an opportunity to express himself without too much concern for his clothes or the material employed. Insight can be gained into the child's emotional state by an experienced teacher as he watches the child at work with these finger painting materials.

MARY J.   CARL

FIGURE 27a.   Drawings of a Man Made by Two Kindergarten Children in the Same Class

This type of activity also is believed to have therapeutic value for some types of maladjustment.

Easel painting, to which children usually are introduced later, is a stimulating experience. After they get experience with prepared paints, they are permitted to mix one color with another to get the hues in which they may be interested. By the time children reach the sixth grade, they should have attained some facility with paints and brushes. One technique for studying changes in children's interests and progressing abilities in this area is to keep cumulative samples of their work from the nursery-school days through elementary school.

Parents, and teachers of the early grades know that the young child gains a great deal of satisfaction from drawing or scribbling with a soft pencil or crayon. He will cover many sheets of paper with various forms which are not recognized by adults as having meaning but which, to the child, represent objects or persons in his environment of current interest to him. The creative ability of children is expressed in the drawings of a house and a man, Figures 26 and 27. Each pair exemplifies poor and good drawings.

Children also enjoy working with materials such as clay, blocks, yarn, wood, cloth, and puppets. They have a strong urge to manipu-

ELLEN

DOROTHY

FIGURE 27b.   Drawings of a Man Made by Two First-Grade Children in the Same Class

late, and to construct, or to take apart. The child is happy as he molds a lump of clay into many shapes. He also is fascinated as he cuts, tears, folds, and decorates paper with which he has had a chance to play. By means of any of these media, he engages in activities that provide a wide range of expression of creative abilities and interests.

Children differ greatly in their handling of these media. Some show initiative and originality in their ideas and their ways of producing that which they want to produce. Other children appear much more conventional in their approach. Others ask the teacher what they should make. These differences are significant.

Similarly, after children have mastered the mechanics of writing and have developed a workable writing vocabulary, much can be learned by teachers from children's writing interests and their modes of expressing themselves. Some children seem to be full of ideas but find it difficult to express these ideas intelligibly. Other children appear to be interested in correct form of written expression but have meager content. One cannot fail to be impressed by differences among children if he compares even the short compositions of thirty fifth-grade pupils, for example. If the members of a class, representing a relatively homogeneous group, on any school level above the third grade through high school, are motivated to write a story about a topic of their individual choice, the range of interests, emphasis, kind and amount of content, degree of correctness of structure, spelling, and legibility of handwriting is surprisingly great. Yet, these young people supposedly have experienced similar learnings. What causes the difference? Attempts to gain insight into the background of creative performance through the medium of creative writing offer a fascinating challenge to interested teachers.

Young people's responses to rhythm in instrumental or vocal music, or the dance also serve as indicators of the great differences that exist among them. The authors know a high-school music teacher who asserts that the most interesting phase of her teaching is her students' reactions to their learning experiences in this field: their differing abilities to carry a tune; their musical tastes; their power to interpret musical themes—in fact all of their reactions to musical stimulation. This woman claims that after she has gained some understanding of the reasons for observed differences, she achieves relatively satisfying success in stimulating them to greater musical appreciation, some of them even to creditable performance. This teacher's attitude is characteristic of many teachers in the various fields of creative expression who have a keen interest, not only in their area of study but also in pupil reactions in it.

Pupil-teacher interviews. The term *interview* probably is used incorrectly to describe the face-to-face talks that take place between a teacher and a pupil, either before or after the regular school day, during the lunch period, or at any other time. These talks usually grow out of an immediate interest, a need for information or personal help that is experienced by the pupil. These talks rarely are planned, seldom require teacher preparation, and may or may not require a follow-up meeting. "Interviews" that are used by the teacher as scolding or preachment sessions have doubtful value. Other informal, relatively short teacher-pupil talks may be extremely valuable both to the young person and to the teacher. For the student, they serve as builders of self-confidence and as satisfiers of the urge "to belong"; for the teacher, they represent mediums through which he can gain insights that have evaluating significance.

If a teacher talks privately with a pupil who has been extremely un-co-operative instead of scolding the pupil publicly, he is likely to earn the confidence of the other learners in his class. Not all teachers avail themselves of the opportunity, however. There are some teachers to whom children will tell everything they know, and there are other teachers to whom children tell as little as possible. In these face-to-face talks, the teacher can discover the specific difficulties of learners in learning areas as well as any deep-seated behavior problem.

The teacher should avoid a tendency to talk too much. He should learn to listen, since he can learn so much by becoming a good listener. A willingness to listen may be rewarding in that thereby is created a warm, permissive, and informal atmosphere that can be expected to facilitate a flow of confidential information. The teacher refrains from asking a question that might instill fear or appear to take the form of a threat. These talks can provide much data concerning a child; they also help the child to gain security and self-confidence.

As we have indicated, a pupil-teacher interview may serve one of several purposes: (1) the teacher may give the pupil certain information needed by the latter, (2) the teacher may receive desired information from the pupil, or (3) the pupil may consult the teacher about a problem which is bothering him. The first two types of interviews usually can be handled easily by the teacher. Of course, he should be careful about giving correct information to the pupil who is seeking it, and should refrain from asking the pupil questions about himself that might be embarrassing or regarded by him as prying into personal matters.

The teacher who attempts to help a pupil solve a personal problem needs to be extremely tactful and have confidence in his ability to guide the pupil's thinking along constructive lines. Unless the problem is a simple one, such as the choice of one of two dresses to be worn at a party, the teacher probably would do well to recommend to the pupil that he or she talk the matter over with a guidance counselor. There are several reasons for this advice. The counselor usually has training beyond that of the teacher in the conduct of interviewing. He has more time available than most teachers for helping the pupil analyze his problem and work out his own solution. Of course, the individual himself must solve his own problems. All that a wise teacher or counselor can do in one or more interviews is guide the thinking of the young person.

QUESTIONS AND TOPICS FOR DISCUSSION

1. Ask five to ten eight-year-olds to draw pictures for you. Then ask each child what his picture tells and record the description on the back. What have you learned about the children from these pictures and these descriptions?
2. Follow the same procedure with a group of twelve-year-olds. Compare the results.
3. Note the play interests of a group of ten-year-old girls. Compare them with the play interest of a group of twelve-year-old girls.
4. From your own experience give several instances in which meeting the child's present need prepared him for a future need.
5. Evaluate the responsibility of the teacher to develop an understanding of the potentials of the learners in his class.
6. To what extent do you make use of observation in the evaluation of your pupils? In the evaluation of your associates?
7. Discuss the limitations of observation as a technique to secure information.
8. Visit a class on the level for which you are preparing to teach and make use of the suggestions given to student-teachers as you observe. Report your experiences.
9. Write an autobiographical sketch. Indicate how this procedure may be useful in studying an individual's behavior.
10. What are the problems faced by the teacher of a class in which the reading grades range from that of a pupil who has a reading grade of third grade to that of a pupil who has a reading grade of twelfth grade?
11. Differentiate between the types of problems of the teacher that are likely to be created by dull learners and extremely bright learners.
12. Practice the taking of anecdotal records in one of your college classes. What can you learn about individuals through this technique? What are its limitations?
13. Play the role of an interviewer and present what might be a good opening for an interview with an eighth-grader who is coming to you for vocational advice.

14. Plan to observe the behavior of a child at play for one hour or more. Report all that you observed.
15. What use can be made of the sociogram by an elementary-school teacher?

SELECTED REFERENCES

Anastasi, A., *Psychological Testing*, rev. ed. Macmillan, N.Y., 1961.

Aiken, L. R., *Psychological and Educational Testing.* Allyn and Bacon, Boston, 1971.

Chase, C. L., *Measurement for Educational Evaluation.* Addison-Wesley, Boston, 1974.

Crow, L. D., and Crow, A., *Student Teaching in the Elementary School.* David McKay, N.Y., 1965.

Durost, W. N., and Prescott, G. A., *Essentials of Measurement for Teacher.* Harcourt Brace, N.Y., 1962.

Gronlund, N. E., *Measurement and Evaluation in Teaching,* 2nd ed. Macmillan, N.Y., 1971.

Karmel, L. J., *Measurement and Evaluation in the Secondary School.* Macmillan, N.Y., 1972.

Lien, A. J., *Measurement and Evaluation in Learning,* 2nd ed. William C. Brown, Dubuque, Iowa, 1971.

Nelson, C. H., *Measurement and Evaluation in the Classroom.* Macmillian, N.Y., 1970.

Nunally, T. C., *Educational Measurement and Evaluation.* McGraw-Hill, N.Y., 1972.

Smith, F. W., and Adams, S., *Educational Measurement for the Classroom Teacher.* Harper and Row, N.Y., 1972.

Thorndike, R. M., *Educational Measurement,* 2nd ed. Appleton-Century-Crofts, N.Y., 1970.

15   Functions and Techniques of Evaluation

Among the common terms included in the vocabulary of psychologists and educators are: *stages* of development, *degree* of adjustment, *outcomes* of education, *realization* of educational goals, skill *competence, extent* of knowledge, *maturity* of attitude, and *progress* in learning. Other terms could be added to this list, but these are sufficient to indicate that when terms such as these are employed, there is implicit in their connotation a recognition of the existence of accepted *standards* of development and learning, in terms of which individual status or performance can be judged. We constantly are judging or measuring something. The psychologist's or educator's judgment usually is based upon the results obtained through the utilization of evaluation procedures that may vary in kind and in adequacy.

In the preceding chapter we considered some of the relatively informal ways in which the classroom teacher can discover learner potentiality and evaluate learner progress. We now shall discuss the various types of more formal evaluating procedures, including a brief description of and the purpose to be served by each type.

Basic Principles of Evaluation

Opinions have varied concerning the practical usefulness of some or all types of formal evaluating procedures. There still is no general agreement among school people concerning the extent to and the ways in which any one or another particular technique of measurement or evaluation should be utilized. That measurement of some kind is needed cannot be disputed, however. For example, a study of child development requires the establishment of more or less accurate "growth norms," in accordance with which any child's growth progress can be compared.

Beginnings of educational evaluation. Traditionally, progress in learning consists mainly in the child's advancement in knowledge and skill competence. In the past, learning progress was checked by the teacher's giving weekly or term "tests," which often consisted of no

394

more than the verbatim reproduction of memorized material. Skill competence was judged in terms of comparison with what were considered to be "perfect" models. The more subtle areas of learning were disregarded. A recognition of the significance of evaluation in education is of relatively recent origin; for the most part it was born of necessity.

We shall not discuss the historical background of the present utilization of evaluating techniques. Several early developments in the field warrant attention, however. Psychological testing began during the last quarter of the nineteenth century when Wilhelm Wundt set up his laboratory in Leipzig to analyze consciousness into its elements. His experiments necessitated that he measure reaction time in sensory responses. Galton employed quantitative measurement in his study of free association and initiated the application of statistical methods to the interpretation of data. It was not until Alfred Binet, a French psychologist, constructed a scale of test situations and standardized it in terms of predetermined criteria that "measurement" came into its own. Binet's first scale of intelligence was published in 1905. This date marks the beginning of an interest in testing that, to the present, has resulted in the construction of thousands of measuring instruments which are designed to test practically every phase of personality.

Binet's first scale and its modifications and adaptations are intended for administration to one individual. In order to differentiate among the relative intelligence levels of servicemen during World War I, it was found necessary to devise a test that could be administered to a group rather than to one person. Hence, as a time-saving measure, the Army Alpha was constructed and became the model upon which were based many of the group intelligence tests that later were devised for use in the schools.

For a period of time, enthusiasm was high in respect to the testing movement. Tests continued to be constructed and to be administered, often with little or no application of test results. The earlier, conventional forms of tests gradually have been giving way to newer and different kinds of measuring instruments. Psychologists and school people are not discarding standardized tests but are becoming more discriminating in the use of them. Moreover, other methods of studying personality characteristics are being devised to evaluate individual development and adjustment.

In the past, much of what can be termed educational theory was of the "armchair" variety. The application of scientifically derived methods to discover learning needs of young people and learning outcomes has exercised a potent effect upon educational philosophy, curriculum construction, and teaching approaches and techniques. Continued research is needed to settle the still unsolved problems associated with learning and learning outcomes, however.

The evaluation of learning outcomes must represent a functional approach. The results of the various techniques that are utilized have significance only when they are interpreted in relation to other factors that influence development and adjustment. For example, the fact that an individual rates high on an intelligence test does not mean necessarily that he is certain to be an outstanding learner or that his attitudes will be desirable. Characteristics other than intelligence alone need to be measured as accurately as possible. The extent to which and the ways in which all of the traits or qualities are interrelated also must be considered. It is the purpose of evaluation to discover, through the administration of appropriate evaluating techniques, what the learner brings to any learning situation in the way of physical health status, mental ability, emotional tendencies, interests, attitudes, and ambitions. Then, as learning progresses, one can measure the degree of success that is attained in terms of the individual's learning potentialities and the adequacy of learning materials and methods.

Meaning and purpose of evaluation. The terms *measurement* and *evaluation* often are used interchangeably. Such usage of the terms is incorrect, however. To measure is to compare with a fixed standard, or to estimate in comparison with something else; to evaluate is to fix the value of, or to estimate the force of. Evaluation has a broader connotation than the term measurement. The utilization of any measuring instrument can be regarded as *one* of the techniques employed to evaluate status or extent of progress. Hence any device that is utilized with an individual or a group of individuals to gain added insights concerning personal characteristics can be called a *tool of evaluation.* Parents, psychologists, and educators are concerned with the continuous evaluation of a young person's progress toward the achievement of desirable life goals. To aid them in the process of evaluation, school people and psychologists utilize many and varied testing techniques and other devices.

Errors in evaluation are possible. It is difficult to evaluate the subtle personality factors that influence overt behavior. An adequate evaluation of learning progress must include all phases of the learner's complex total of abilities, attitudes, and overt behavior patterns. Evaluating techniques are being evolved that, it is hoped, eventually may result in a greater understanding of all the factors of personality that operate in making a child or an adolescent the kind of person that he is, at any one stage of his development. Perhaps we are beginning to scratch the surface. Yet, much more research is needed before we achieve a satisfactory degree of competence to measure personal characteristics and to evaluate their significance in relationship to the external situations and conditions to which a young person is exposed.

Tools of Evaluation

Interest in personal characteristics probably is as old as the human race. In Chapter 1, reference was made to some of the pseudopsychological techniques of personality evaluation that represent man's attempts to study man. During the twentieth century, however, there have been constructed many and different techniques that are designed to measure objectively the various phases of an individual's total, integrated personality.

Function of measurement. Measuring instruments and other tools of evaluation should function only as a *means to an end*. Whatever is discovered through the administration of a standardized or teacher-made test, or is a result of information obtained from observation of performance or face-to-face contacts, should constitute a background body of knowledge concerning the individual. Upon this basis of understanding can be built the teaching and counseling procedures that may be of most benefit to the young person whose characteristics are evaluated. The mental hygiene approach in education, vocational and personal guidance, and character development necessitate the application of as many appropriate evaluating techniques as are available for use by those who are responsible for young people's progress in any area of learning.

If administrators and teachers hope to motivate worthy and effective educational growth, they need to know as much as they can discover about what a young person brings to his new school experiences. From that point onward, what he does with what he has is conditioned by (1) his own capacity and willingness to benefit from guidance and instruction, (2) the educational objectives which the school is attempting to achieve, (3) the curricular offerings and the organization and techniques of instruction that are utilized, and (4) the validity and reliability of the evaluating media that are employed. By means of these evaluating techniques the young person and his teachers determine the extent to which he is benefiting from his school experiences, the possible reasons for apparent failure or mediocre performance, and the means that can or should not be used to motivate learning.[1]

Formal evaluating techniques. Evaluating techniques may be administered by the classroom teacher or the teacher counselor under the direction of trained counselors, by the counselors themselves, or by the specialist in a particular area of evaluation. Some of these tools need not be utilized with all individuals. Limitations in personnel, time and budget in a school or school system probably would preclude a general application of all the techniques. Since these evaluating techniques are administered at specific times, for specific purposes, and by trained administrators, they usually are referred to as formal evaluating techniques. They include: (1) Standardized tests, scales and inventories, such as (a) Intelligence tests (general classification tests), (b) Differential aptitude batteries, (c) Tests of special aptitudes, (d) Scholastic achievement tests—comprehensive, subject areas, (e) Personality tests and scales, and interest inventories, (2) Projective techniques, (3) Situational tests, (4) Observational evaluation, (5) The interview, and (6) The case history.

The remainder of this chapter is devoted to brief descriptions of the various kinds of tools of evaluation and the purposes to be served by them. Of necessity, the discussion of tests and other media of evaluation is limited here to the general, salient aspects of their purpose and use. More detailed descriptions of these measuring instruments can be found in books listed in the *Selected References* at the end of the chapter.

Standardized Tests, Scales, and Inventories

The thousands of standardized measuring instruments that now are available for administration vary greatly in their degree of usefulness. Some of the earlier tests and scales have become well standardized through much usage, but test items are so well known that their present value is doubtful. Those measuring instruments that have been constructed recently may not yet be completely standardized; hence their norms may be only tentative.

Familiarity, on the part of the taker of a test, with its content material militates against the value of the test as a measuring instrument. The general public is interested in these instruments. Parents may attempt to procure copies of tests that they expect will be ad-

[1] See L. D. Crow, H. E. Ritchie, and A. Crow, *Education in the Secondary School,* American Book Company, New York, 1961, p. 368.

ministered to their child so that they can "coach" him. Too frequently, items from a good measuring instrument are presented in popular magazines for the edification of readers. It is possible for an individual to become "test wise." It has been found that performance on a second form of a test, after the first form has been taken, tends to yield higher scores than were earned on the first form. Psychologists, school people, or other individuals whose function it is to administer testing materials should exercise extreme care that standardized testing material is not distributed indiscriminately. For example, the Psychological Corporation distributes their tests only to authorized users of these materials.

Classification of standardized tests and scales. Classified according to their form, standardized tests fall into two categories, (1) rate or speed tests, and (2) quality or power tests. Technically, a *test* consists of a number of items of uniform quality and difficulty to which responses are made in a specified time. A *scale* represents a series of projects or objective samples of different quality or difficulty. The items usually are arranged in an ascending order of merit or difficulty in order to discover the extent of the quality or power of the testee or subject to respond correctly in terms of the increasing difficulty of the items. Most tests are *scaled tests* in that they are confined to one area of material arranged in ascending order of difficulty. The scaling allows for the first items to be simple enough so that all the testees can respond correctly, and the last items to be so difficult that few if any of them can be completed correctly in the given time. Most standardized tests have a time limit for response.

Standardized tests also are classified as *individual* or *group*. An individual test is administered to only one person at a time; a group test can be given to as many persons as the need of administration or available space dictates. Standardized tests also are classified according to the function they are supposed to serve. *Survey* tests usually are achievement tests that measure the total performance of a learner in a field of knowledge, or that compare a group against another group or against itself. Relative extent of achievement in specified learning areas can be discovered by the administration of a survey test to different classes, schools, or school systems.

The administration of a *diagnostic* test in a given unit or area of learning is useful to a teacher as a means to discover or diagnose specific learning difficulties of pupils. The utilization of diagnostic tests is extremely valuable in that it yields data concerning specific learning inadequacies that may need remedial treatment before continued study in the particular area is begun. It prevents the accumulation of error upon error. The function of a *prognostic* test is to yield a measure of prediction concerning a learner's expected success in a field in which he has participated very slightly, or not at all. Prognostic tests serve some of the functions of subject pretests. Differential and special aptitude tests fall into this category, as do tests of learning readiness.

Standardized tests as objective measuring instruments. Most standardized testing materials are concerned with recognition and recall; some deal with the discovery of relationships in the form of analogies, identifications, or rearrangement of item material. The items of a test to which the subject is expected to respond may be presented in the form of printed material (paper-and-pencil test); the test may consist of materials that are to be manipulated in one or another fashion (performance test).

Some paper-and-pencil tests for use with young children and illiterates consist mainly of pictures, mazes, and similar materials which require little, if any, reading. Responses are marked in one or another way according to the directions that are given orally by the test administrator. These tests are called *nonverbal* paper-and-pencil tests. The items of *verbal* paper-and-pencil tests usually are presented as short-form questions or statements. The responses selected by the subject as correct may be indicated in any one of several ways; underlining, circling, inserting a word, letter, or number in an appropriate space, checking, crossing out, etc.

The form of a verbal test usually consists of one or more of the following types of short-form items: true-false, multiple choice, completion, or matching. The construction of an objective or short-form type of test requires that the constructor so phrase the individual items that his intended meaning is clear, that the item contains realistic material, and that there is only *one* best response.

Tests of intelligence. The primary purpose of an intelligence test is to determine an individual's learning capacity. Supposedly, an intelligence test is based upon material with which the subject has had no formal learning experience. The content of intelligence tests usually includes items that deal with vocabulary, memory of form, numbers, number series, sentences to be interpreted, the following of directions, drawing, completion, analogies, space perception, abstract ideas, reasoning, or similar material. Differences in out-of-school background experience, as well as in degree of mental alertness, may affect the test performance of respective individuals.

Intelligence tests are graded in difficulty from tests designed for preschool children through those for use on the adult level. By this we mean that certain tests (usually nonverbal paper-and-pencil and performance tests) are constructed for utilization only with young children; others are suitable for elementary-school-age children; still others are on the secondary-school age level; difficult tests, involving the functioning of the higher mental processes, are designed for college students and mature adults. The Stanford revision of the Binet Scales is an individual test. It is administered when there is needed an index of mental status that will be more accurate than the results obtained from a group test. This test consists of a series of tasks for each age level from the age of three years to that of the superior adult. Most intelligence tests, however, are intended for use on specific age or grade levels. Another point that is worthy of attention is the fact that intelligence tests for the middle years of development are better measures of mental ability than are tests designed for either children or adults.

Scales to measure general intelligence that are popular with clinicians are the *Wechsler-Bellevue Intelligence Scale,* the *Wechsler Intelligence Scale for Children,* and the *Wechsler Adult Intelligence Scale.* These are similar to the Stanford-Binet scales in that they are administered individually and serve somewhat the same purposes. The Wechsler scales, however, include an equal number of verbal and performance subtests. Hence both a verbal and a performance IQ can be computed.

The Wechsler-Bellevue Intelligence Scale provides a scale that is suitable for use with adults. It avoids the inclusion of content that, for the most part, deals with school experiences. The contents of the verbal scale, arranged in subtest form include: general information, general comprehension, arithmetical reasoning, digits forward and backward, similarities, and vocabulary. The subtests of the performance scale include: picture completion, picture arrangement, object assembly, block design, and digit symbols. The order in which the subtests of the whole scale are administered is not important; subtests may be interspersed in terms of interest or the gaining of rapport.

The Wechsler Intelligence Scale for Children is a modified form of the Wechsler-Bellevue and is intended for use with children. The general organization of the WISC is similar to the other; both verbal and performance subtests are included, but the content material is much simpler. Although the Wechsler-Bellevue supposedly can be administered to individuals from ages ten to sixty years, the WISC has proved itself to be much more valid than the other for use with children. The WAIS (1955) is a carefully standardized revision of Form I of the WBIS. It is intended for use with individuals ranging in age from sixteen to seventy-five.

Degree of successful performance on an intelligence test, usually expressed in the form of the IQ, represents *general* status only. It does not indicate the degree of strength or weakness in each of the particular mental functions that are being tested. For example, the same intelligence test is administered, at the same time, to a group of children. Each of two individuals earns an IQ of ninety-eight. The performance of the two is not identical, however. One may have answered correctly all the items that dealt with mathematical concepts and analogies but failed to respond correctly to the items that had to do with vocabulary, directions, etc.; the performance of the other subject may have been reversed, in that the least success was achieved in items dealing with mathematical concepts. Hence performance in *each type of item* needs to be considered.

Differential aptitude batteries. Factor-analysis, based upon the multiple factor theory of trait relationship, has resulted in the construction of intelligence tests that are based upon what have been termed by Thurstone the *primary mental abilities*. These abilities include: verbal comprehension, word fluency, number, space, associative memory, perceptual speed, and reasoning. A differential aptitude battery comprises a group of tests, each of which would be designed to measure ability in one of the various phases of mental ability.

The Thurstone Test of Primary Mental Abilities was designed for administration on the high school and college levels. Similar batteries of tests have been constructed for utilization with younger children and for adults. Appropriate differential aptitude batteries also are designed for special testing programs as, for example, those used by the United States Employment Service and the Army. Experience with these batteries seems to indicate that they have greater value than have general intelligence tests as techniques to discover and utilize available human abilities.

Special aptitude tests. An aptitude can be regarded as a quality or ability that all individuals possess to some degree. A *special apti-*

tude refers to superior ability to respond to learning in a limited area of performance. The aptitude is one aspect of an individual's whole personality. Intelligence comprises a number of "special aptitudes" or, as Thurstone termed them, "primary mental abilities." There may be other specific aptitudes, however.

Attempts have been made to construct measuring instruments to determine the degree to which an individual may possess potentiality of successful achievement in a specific field of learning. Some special aptitude testing is designed to discover superior possession of a quality, such as sensory capacity (vision, hearing) and motor dexterity. Such special aptitudes are "general" in nature to the extent that various occupations require superior ability in these areas. Tests are available to determine special aptitude for training toward participation in a vocation, such as mechanical and clerical work, law, medicine, teaching, or other areas of occupational work. Success in any of these vocational fields however, is dependent upon a complex of abilities. Hence it is difficult to isolate those factors that pre-eminently represent special aptitude for success-achievement in any one of these fields.

Whether superior performance in music, the graphic arts or design, mathematics, or literature is the resultant of a superior innate aptitude for it is a matter of controversy. It is the belief of some biologists and psychologists that no amount of training can produce a *virtuoso;* others contend that superior performance in these areas can be achieved when or if training begins early and is geared to the development of superior achievement. It probably is true that aptitude in any one of these areas represents a complexity of abilities. In order to achieve superlative mastery, all of these special potentialities need to be relatively higher than those of the average individual.

There may be prognostic value in a test that is designed to measure degree of possession of a specific aptitude. Yet, the results of the test need to be interpreted and applied with caution. An individual may seem to exhibit a quality or a complex of qualities that gives indication of future superiority of achievement in the particular skill or ability involved. We must keep in mind, however, that *present* display of special potential does not guarantee *future* realization of that potential capacity or tendency. It is probably a fact that "genius consists of 1 per cent of inspiration and 99 per cent of perspiration." The individual who apparently possesses the aptitude must be willing to engage intensively in appropriate learning experiences.

Achievement tests. An achievement test is designed to measure the extent to which a learner is profiting from instruction in a given area of learning. Achievement tests are available in nearly every school subject or field of study.[1] Table 20 presents a list of the kinds and number of achievement tests now available. Each year sees others added to this list.

TABLE 20.   Achievement Tests Listed in the Fourth Mental Measurements Yearbook[2]

26 Achievement Batteries	50 Reading Tests including
30 English Tests	Seven Reading Readiness
2 Composition Tests	Tests
18 Literature Tests	11 Study Skills Tests
15 Spelling Tests	7 Science Tests
16 Vocabulary Tests	11 Biology Tests
5 Art Tests	16 Chemistry Tests
6 Music Tests	7 General Science Tests
34 Foreign Language Tests	1 Geology Test
15 General Mathematics Tests	2 Miscellaneous Science
18 Algebra Tests	Tests
24 Arithmetic Tests	11 Physics Tests
17 Geometry Tests	8 Social Studies Tests
3 Trigonometry Tests	4 Economics Tests
2 Agriculture Tests	5 Geography Tests
21 Business Education Tests	19 History Tests
4 Etiquette Tests	10 Political Science Tests
13 Health Tests	2 Sociology Tests
12 Home Economic Tests	16 Education Tests
2 Industrial Arts Tests	6 Engineering Tests
2 Philosophy Tests	2 Law Tests
3 Psychology Tests	1 Medicine Test
3 Religious Education Tests	6 Nursing Tests
5 Safety Education Tests	

The purpose of some achievement tests is to measure learning achievement either in one area of learning or in several areas: arithmetic, vocabulary, social studies, reading comprehension, and the like. Since standards or norms may differ from test to test, it is difficult to compare the relative status of performance in different learning areas. For this reason, school people are becoming in-

[1] Consult: O. K. Buros, editor, *The Fourth Mental Measurements Yearbook,* The Gryphon Press, Highland Park, N. J., 1953.
[2] G. M. Blair, R. S. Jones, and R. H. Simpson, *Educational Psychology,* The Macmillan Co., 1954, p. 432. Reprinted by permission.

creasingly interested in administering batteries of tests. Performance in each test of a battery can be equated in such a way that relativity of performance can be evaluated. Achievement tests, as was mentioned earlier, can serve as survey, diagnostic, or prognostic (learning readiness) instruments of measurement.

Achievement tests are used extensively on the elementary-school level; their utilization on the secondary-school level is limited. One reason for this is that elementary-school learning materials deal with fundamental skills and knowledges that are relatively the same for all schools and school systems. Hence statistically obtained norms of performance can be applied as achievable standards to be attained in any particular school community. On the higher-school levels, however, instructional emphases vary, in terms of selectivity of learning materials that is based upon teacher and learner interests. A standardized achievement test on the higher levels, therefore, can do no more than include essential learning minimums. Even here there may be differences of opinion concerning what constitutes *essential* learning. Certain supposedly fundamental knowledges, skills, and appreciations of relationships comprise the content of various batteries of tests for use at strategic points in progress on these levels, e.g., College Entrance Examinations and Graduate Record Examinations.

Techniques of Personality Evaluation

"Personality" testing is a misnomer. The use of this designation for measuring certain personal traits, qualities, or characteristics could lead one to assume that intelligence, aptitude, and achievement tests measure conditions or qualities that lie outside an individual's total personality pattern. We know this is not true. The justification for this apparent dichotomy is the fact that the measurements we discussed earlier are commonly used by school people. The measuring instruments to be discussed here attempt to evaluate what probably can be regarded as the more subtle elements of personality.

Techniques of personality evaluation involve one of two concepts of personality. The test constructor may place emphasis upon the amount of possession of, and kind of functioning of, one or another *individual phase* of the total personality; or he may attempt to construct an instrument of evaluation that will help in the gaining of insights concerning the functioning of the *integrated total* of an individual's personality pattern. *Trait* analysis is related to the Thorndikian theory of identical elements; attempted evaluation of the functioning of the *whole pattern* of integrated traits, qualities, or characteristics reflects the Gestaltist theory of configuration or form.

The measuring of personality traits takes the form of (1) inventories or questionnaires to which the individual himself responds, or (2) rating scales, through the utilization of which another individual evaluates the specific attitudes or forms of behavior that customarily are displayed by the subject of the rating. The evaluation of the interfunctioning of the subject's total of qualities or traits is attempted usually through the utilization of *projective techniques, situational tests,* and interviews.

Self-evaluating questionnaires. These measuring devices are of the paper-and-pencil variety. The traditional type of questionnaire is exemplified in Woodworth's Personal Data Sheet, which was devised originally to be administered to servicemen during World War I. Later, a modified form of this questionnaire was constructed for use with children.

Woodworth's Personal Data Sheet became the model for the many measuring instruments that have been designed for self-appraisal. At first, questions were asked to which an absolute affirmative or negative response was to be given. For example, Are you afraid of the dark? Yes. No. It was recognized that some questions cannot be answered in terms of *all* or *none.* Hence, to encourage more accurate self-appraisal, changes were made in the form of the answer. In most tests therefore, the response is given in one of the following forms:

Yes		?		No
Always		Sometimes		Never
Always	Often	Usually	Frequently	Rarely

In some instances, explanatory terms are used as dividing points on a line; the responder can check himself on the line at the phrase which he considers describes himself best in relation to the item. For example,

How well do you control your temper?

Rarely become angry·	Seldom get annoyed	Usually control my temper	Frequently become annoyed	Easily angered

In some personality tests, various situations are described and the subject is asked which of the listed attitudes or overt acts would most accurately fit his habitual behavior. For example:

You are engrossed in a piece of work which you wish to complete. The telephone rings. What would you be most likely to do?

a. Ignore the ringing of the telephone.

b. Answer it, but report immediately to the person at the other end of the line that you are too busy to talk to him.

c. Answer the telephone, say that you are busy, and arrange for another time for him to telephone you.

d. Talk to the person who telephoned, but, without telling him that you are busy, show by the abruptness of your responses that you are not interested in talking to him.

e. Answer the telephone and, disregarding your work, carry on a lengthy conversation.

Self-applying questionnaires and inventories have been constructed to assist an individual to evaluate various phases of his attitudes or behavior, i.e., degree of introversion or extroversion, social dominance or submission, emotional security, social maturity, sociability, self-sufficiency, and similar qualities or traits. By the inclusion of a long list of questions to which different keys are applied, some questionnaires attempt to evaluate various personality states. An example of this kind of measuring instrument is the Bernreuter Inventory which attempts to measure, by way of 125 questions, six different aspects of personality, including: neurotic tendency, self-sufficiency, introversion-extroversion, dominance-submission, confidence in one's self, and sociability.

The Minnesota Multiphase Personality Inventory is considered by some psychologists to be one of the best measuring instruments in the field. It has been devised for use with older adolescents and adults. The 550 questions included in the questionnaire are designed to discover the degree to which the subject evaluates himself as deviating from supposedly normal persons in many areas, including health; social, civic, and religious attitudes; family, educational, and occupational relations; and the pressure of abnormal drives, phobias, and other neurotic or psychotic manifestations.

Interest and attitude inventories. Interest and attitude inventories are similar to self-administering questionnaires in that they are presented in relatively the same form. The personality test tends to place greater emphasis upon behavior habits, whereas interest and attitude inventories, as their designation implies, are more nearly associated with the way in which a person "feels about people, objects, conditions, and situations." Some interest inventories have vocational implications in that, like Strong's Vocational Interest Blank and the Kuder Preference Record, they are aimed at discovering the extent to which an individual's interests are related to interests of successful workers in respective occupations (Strong VIB) or his relative interest in broad occupational areas (Kuder Preference Record).

Other interest and attitude inventories and scales include many areas, such as (1) opinions concerning political, social, religious, or economic issues, and (2) attitudes toward conditions or personal relationships in the home, or the school, or toward parents, teachers, supervisors, co-workers, or other associates.

Rating scales. Rating scales differ from self-applied questionnaires in purpose. Through the utilization of the rating scale, a person who knows the subject evaluates the latter according to the former's appraisal of significant attitudes and behavior as these are compared with the attitudes and behavior of other persons with whom the rater has had comparable experiences.

Value of personality tests and inventories. Personality tests and inventories have value as measuring instruments to the extent that the self-evaluator or the rater of another's personality is aware of the presence of specific attitudes and behavior patterns. The results of the administration of one of these instruments cannot be taken too seriously, however. A self-rater may respond to the items as he thinks he is expected to do. What he *says* that he does or thinks may be different from what he *actually* does or thinks. Unless the instrument is so constructed that the items check one another, the most that can be said about many of a subject's supposedly desirable responses is that they indicate his awareness of what is "right," regardless of his own behavior.

Similarly, a rater of another person may fail to be completely honest in his responses. Personal prejudices or biases, either conscious or unconscious, are likely to influence the extent of objectivity with which he can evaluate the other person. Furthermore, the rater may not be sufficiently acquainted with the subject to make a completely accurate evaluation of some traits, yet hesitates to refrain from rating them. Rating of an adolescent, for example, by only one person rarely yields an adequate or even correct judgment. Hence an individual's personal qualities should be rated by two or more persons. A group of raters, each rating the subject separately, may display general agreement in their evaluation of certain qualities. To the extent of such agreement it can be assumed that the subject of the rating gives overt behavior evidence of the trait or quality.

Another weakness of attempted trait evaluation is the fact that qualities, traits, or conditions do not function in isolation. When one studies the results obtained from the utilization of one of these measuring instruments, he must ask himself whether he can be certain that other personality aspects have not entered into the picture. The recognition of these weaknesses in attempts to measure isolated traits or trait groups has been responsible, in part at least, for the development and utilization of other evaluating techniques, such as projective techniques, situational settings, and interviewing.

Projective Techniques

The personality tests and inventories that were discussed in the preceding pages can be regarded as containing "structured" material. The subject or the rater responds to definite items according to an assigned pattern of responses from which he has to select the one that seems best to meet his reactions to the task. His responses are limited thereby to the *what* and the *how* of the stimuli-situations that comprise the test. The techniques here described do not place these restrictions upon the responder. For the most part, these techniques are individually administered. A projective technique presents a supposedly *"unstructured"* situation or task to which the subject responds freely. The administrator offers only brief general suggestions or directions and/or asks relatively vague questions. The situation is informal; the subject is permitted to give free rein to his imagination. Instead of being restricted in his responses, he is encouraged to *project*, through his responses, his characteristic opinions, aggressions, hopes and aspirations, fears and worries, likes and dislikes, and other expressive attitudes. However, the subject will co-operate with the clinician only to the extent that the atmosphere is informal and relaxed.

Because of the relative vagueness and ambiguity of the stimuli and the "looseness" of the entire evaluating experience, interpretation of responses is difficult. Explanatory manuals that accompany the materials suggest possible interpretations of various combinations of responses. A projective technique should not be administered by anyone except a clinician who has received intensive training in its administration and interpretation.

Many projective techniques have been devised, and more are in the process of construction. This new approach to personality analysis still is in an exploratory stage and needs much study and application before valid conclusions can be reached concerning its value. There are several of these techniques that have gained ᶜome attention among psychologists and are used in clinical testing situations.

The Rorschach technique. Probably the most widely known and most generally discussed projective technique is the Rorschach Inkblot Technique. The material consists of ten cards, each of which has printed on it an ink blot or an apparently meaningless, bilaterally symmetrical figure or form. On five of the blots, the shades are gray and black; two of them contain touches of bright red, and the other three have assorted colors.

The subject is given the following instructions:

> You will be given a series of ten cards, one by one. The cards have on them designs made up out of ink blots. Look at each card, and tell the examiner what you see on each card, or anything that might be represented there. Look at each card as long as you like; only be sure to tell the examiner everything that you see on the cards as you look at them. When you have finished with a card, give it to the examiner as a sign that you are through with it.[1]

The person who is being tested then is given the first card and encouraged to describe everything that he sees on the card. He may turn the card to any position. On a blank prepared for this purpose, the clinician notes down everything that the subject says. After the ten cards have been examined and described, the subject goes through them again, pointing to the areas of the respective ink blots that represented to him what he had described. Meanwhile, on a duplicate set of ink blots, the examiner marks the areas indicated by the subject.

The interpretation of the responses includes: location (area) determinants, color, shading, forms, "movement," contents (kind of figures: human, scenery, food, etc.), and popularity (frequency of response among different subjects). Differences can be found among scoring systems, especially for content. As yet, there are no definitive norms. Hence the clinician needs to interpret data carefully. He must give special attention to behavior and attitude

---

[1] S. J. Beck, *Rorschach's Test*, Grune and Stratton, New York, 1944, p. 2. Reprinted by permission.

tendencies that show themselves with relative consistency in reactions to all the inkblots. Although this technique is concerned primarily with emotional reactions, degree of mental alertness and educational background are reflected in the kind of responses given.

Pictorial techniques. There are various techniques that utilize pictures as the materials of evaluation. The pictures may seem to be a little more structured than are ink blots, but pictured material varies in degree of situational ambiguity and figure portrayal.

The Thematic Apperception Test (TAT). This test is relatively unstructured. It consists of nineteen cards, each of which presents vague pictorial material in black and white, and one blank card. The subject is asked to tell a story about each of the nineteen pictures, including: what probably has happened, what is happening now, what is going to happen, and how the depicted characters feel about the whole "situation." While the subject looks at the one blank card, he is supposed to imagine a picture on it and tell a story about it.

There is no general agreement regarding a scoring system. As the clinician listens to the subject talk, observes his behavior, and takes notes, he usually finds a relatively consistent pattern of emotional reaction running like a thread throughout the stories. For example, one adolescent boy to whom the TAT was administered was consistent in his interpretations of the fact that someone had been murdered, would be murdered, or was doing something for which he deserved to be killed. This boy was known to resent his parents and teachers, and was suffering from deep-seated feelings of frustration. Another subject interpreted every picture as a "happy" picture. Several of her stories were accounts of young lovers who had been separated but were together again. This adolescent girl was irresponsible, extremely romantic, and given to much daydreaming.

Children's Apperception Test (CAT). Other pictorial techniques have been devised for specific age ranges. The TAT can be given to children as young as seven, but better results are obtained with older children, adolescents, and adults. The Children's Apperception Test (CAT) substitutes animals for humans, but the animals are portrayed in human situations. Stories about these pictures may reveal a child's emotional reactions to parent-child and parent-parent relationships, sibling rivalry, and other problem situations that arise in the child's home or neighborhood environment.

Situational Tests

The purpose of a situational test is to observe the subject's behavior in a situation that has been set up to resemble what might be an everyday situational experience.

The Character Education Inquiry. One of the earliest of these testing approaches includes the situations set up by Hartshorne and May when they were conducting the Character Education Inquiry. As part of their study of children's behavior in relation to character development, they established situations in which children's behavior was observed, without the subject's being aware of it. Many of these situations dealt with dishonesty in the form of cheating: accepting more change than was coming to them when they purchased something in a store, changing answers as they marked their own test papers (duplicates of which had been made), using materials to help them during the taking of a test and similar situations.[1]

As a result of their findings, Hartshorne and May concluded that extent of cheating is determined by the ease or difficulty of cheating, and that probably no one is completely honest. To this conclusion were added other conclusions based upon situations that involved the degree of displayed generous behavior or of other forms of behavior that are associated with ethical and social values. Much protest was elicited from parents and from educational and religious leaders as a result of the published findings of Hartshorne and May. The Inquiry has continued to be a subject of controversy.

Value of the situational technique. The situational technique employed in the Inquiry has been applied to situational stress tests, such as those that were employed during World War II to discover reactions of men under stress. This technique was one of the "screening" devices by which men were evaluated for assignment to strategic and perhaps dangerous forms of service.

Tests that involve participation in disguised or partially disguised "lifelike" situations are difficult and costly to set up. Moreover, they may not give complete or adequate insight into "habitual" behavior as such, unless the individual can be exposed to many such structured situations. The Committee on Human Development of the University of Chicago organized and conducted a study of

[1] These situational tests are described in H. Hartshorne and M. May, *Studies in Deceit*, Macmillan, New York, 1928.

youth development in "Prairie City." Although the committee utilized, in modified form, some of the techniques employed by Hartshorne and May, they did have modifications regarding the use of invented test situations.

> Good as the tests might be, and the Character Inquiry Tests were good, observation of behavior in test situations must always be a doubtful substitute for observation of everyday behavior. The great variety of everyday situations cannot be duplicated in a small number of tests, and there is always the question whether the test situation is lifelike enough to motivate the subject to behave as he would in real life.[1]

The fundamental idea is sound, however. The best test of personal behavior is controlled observation of behavior itself.

Observational Evaluation

Direct observation of behavior in normal settings yields data that are likely to represent much more accurate samples of the observed person's accustomed modes of activity than can be obtained by means of the artificial settings utilized in the situational technique. As was suggested in Chapter 14, teachers can learn a great deal concerning their pupils by observing the latters' behavior reactions. Unless direct observation is carefully controlled, however, resulting data may reflect the personal prejudices of the observer or his failure to note significant details.

Control of observation. In order to reduce to a minimum the inadequacies of general parent or teacher observation of children and young people, observation is becoming more systematized, and the recording of observation is gaining in objectivity. For example, samplings of a child's behavior under different conditions are observed and recorded periodically, or the child is observed carefully in a situation of which the conditions have been set up to encourage a specific type of behavior. In these forms of controlled observation, the adequacy of the resulting data depends, of course, upon the ability of the observer to perceive accurately and to record exactly.

The trained clinician who observes the behavior of a client in a laboratory setting probably is in a position to control all phases of the evaluation. Hence his obtained data will be correct and free from the effects of personal prejudice or preconceived expectation concerning client behavior during the experiment. The clinic

[1] R. J. Havighurst, and H. Taba. *Adolescent Character and Personality.* John Wiley & Sons, Inc., New York, 1949, p. 9. Reprinted by permission.

atmosphere may inhibit naturalness of response on the part of the client. Moreover, some kinds of behavior cannot be studied adequately in a clinic situation. To obtain an understanding of a child's general emotional pattern and of his accustomed reactions in social situations, he must be observed as he is reacting freely and naturally, without consciousness that his behavior is being observed for the purpose of evaluation.

The utilization of special devices. Outstanding examples of the utilization of special devices for observational study are the Yale University child development studies that were planned and directed by Arnold Gesell. The subjects of study were placed in a dome-shaped compartment, the walls of which consisted of one-way-vision screens. The child, unaware of the fact that he was being observed, responded naturally to various stimuli situations to which he was exposed. In addition to the one-way-vision screen through which the child's behavior could be observed, an exact record of his reactions was obtained by means of motion-picture cameras placed at concealed, strategic points in the domed compartment. In this way, motion pictures of the child's behavior were secured from different angles.

Observation by means of the one-way-vision screen is coming to be accepted as an excellent device for studying the behavior of children and adolescents. It is especially useful for the evaluation of behavior that deviates from what is considered to be normal. Play therapy, as a technique to help young children give expression to their resentments, inhibitions, or other pent-up emotional states, often is conducted in a room that has a one-way-vision screen through which qualified observers can watch the child's reactions to toys and other play equipment. Concealed microphones enable the observers to hear as well as to see the child in action.

These special observational devices are utilized in an increasing number of institutions for teacher education. At Brooklyn College, for example, students who are preparing to become teachers are provided excellent opportunities for using these study aids. A nursery school attached to the college is equipped with these observational devices. Class-size groups of students thus are enabled to enrich their study of child development by actual experience with young children who represent a cross section of the kinds of children with whom they later will be working.

The Education Clinic of Brooklyn College has a dual function.

It serves children of the community who are experiencing problems of adjustment and also provides opportunities for the college students to become acquainted with the behavior symptoms of various forms of maladjustment. As an aid for this kind of study, the facilities include two rooms that are equipped with one-way-vision screens and microphones: the play therapy room, and the conference room in which tests are administered by members of the clinic staff for observation by groups of students. In addition, another similarly equipped room is available for the use of students who are majoring in speech therapy.

Important factors of reference. Much valuable information concerning human development and adjustment can be and has been obtained through the utilization of various techniques of observational study and evaluation. A trained and experienced professional, business, or industrial leader constantly is employing observation as a means of evaluating the behavior of persons who work with or for him. Some supervisors and administrators have greater confidence in their judgments based upon their personal observation than they have in the results of standardized tests and other formal techniques of evaluation. To secure, through observation, a complete understanding of all phases of an individual's personality pattern may be a difficult and time-consuming process, however. Moreover, even a carefully conducted observation is subject to error of interpretation that needs to be checked by the utilization of other evaluating techniques.

The age of the observed is an important factor of the validity of data obtained through observation. The younger child usually is not sensitive to the possibility that his behavior is being observed in any except a casual fashion, unless he is urged by his elders to "show off" for an admiring audience. Rarely is the behavior of a young child inhibited by a recognition of the fact that he is being observed through a one-way-vision screen. Older children and adolescents often become self-conscious under observational conditions.

At Brooklyn College, for example, older observees sometimes are suspicious of the mirrorlike walls in the conference room where they are taken for testing and interview purposes. They want to know what is behind the mirrors, even though the observers are completely hidden from view. Moreover, adolescents, especially, read and hear about these observational devices. Hence they are quick to recognize anything that is "peculiar" about a room in which they are interviewed. One thirteen-year-old boy who was being interviewed in the conference room pointed to a small gadget on the wall and asked "What is that—a mike?" He was correct in his assumption and evidently did not believe the interviewer's casually given explanation of it as a part of the electrical equipment. Consequently, in his interview responses, the boy proceeded to "put on an act" that was not representative of his natural behavior.

A fundamental principle of observation is to evaluate the display of interrelated and comprehensive behavior, rather than to analyze specific segments of the total personality pattern. In this Gestalt approach are rooted both the study advantages and difficulties of utilizing this evaluating technique. Patterns of development and adjustment are not formed in isolation. Throughout the book we have stressed the effects upon the maturing individual of the constant interaction that is taking place among the various phases of his total personality. Overt behavior in any situation or at any stage of development, therefore, represents the observable outcomes of these inner reactions and interactions as they are stimulated by inner or outer factors or influence. Hence, as one observes and evaluates behavior, his recordings, interpretations, and judgments are based upon observed comprehensive behavior, situational motivation, and background history.

The Interview

The interview as an instrument of evaluation and therapy may serve one of various purposes:

(1) Giving information, (2) Obtaining information, (3) "Screening" for educational or occupational purposes, and (4) Helping in the solution of an adjustment problem.

Regardless of the purpose to be served by the interview, much can be learned in this face-to-face situation by the trained and experienced interviewer concerning the interviewee. As in the utilization of a projective technique, the interviewing situation should be informal and relaxed. Unless the purpose of the interview is to give definite information to the interviewee, the counselor or interviewer remains in the background to as great extent as possible. By the interviewer's few and tactfully worded questions or comments, the interviewee or client is encouraged to talk about himself, his interests, his emotional reactions, and his ambitions. The nondirective or little-directed approach is especially desirable if a young person is seeking the help of a counselor in the meeting of a difficult situation or in the solving of a personal problem.

As the interviewer listens and occasionally comments upon what is said, he has an excellent opportunity to study the reactions, expressed attitudes, and modes of thinking of the client. Interviewing, employed as a tool of evaluation, differs from a teacher's talking with his pupils. The interview is planned for the achieving of a definite purpose. The conduct of the evaluating interview, therefore, can be regarded as a structured situation. From the point of approach, however, the interview is unstructured, informal, and inducive of self-expression on the part of a relaxed subject. The latter, unwittingly, may provide the interviewer with much information concerning personal qualities and characteristics.

The Case History

We said earlier that measurement of any kind is a tool of evaluation. We cannot reach an adequate evaluation of an individual, his behavior, or his problems through the utilization of *one or even a few* tools. A teacher may want to achieve an understanding of one phase of an apparently normal individual's personality or to acquire knowledge concerning one life area. Such understanding or knowledge probably can be gained by the teacher or counselor through the utilization of a few media of evaluation.

If a problem is associated with an individual's personal characteristics or his overt behavior, we need to accumulate as much correct information concerning him as is possible. This information then is arranged in an orderly form so that a reasonably adequate evaluation of all the factors of influence can be achieved. The study of accumulated data enables us to gain insights that will guide us in helping him. All of the accumulated information takes the form of a *Case History*.

The case history technique is utilized by child guidance clinics, hospitals for the mentally ill, or any other organization or institution that is concerned with the application of therapeutic techniques to an emotionally or mentally disturbed patient or a person who deviates seriously from what is considered to be normal behavior. The various kinds of information that are included in a case history should be accumulated and arranged by a trained person, preferably a psychiatric social worker. It is imperative that all items of information are accurate; otherwise, evaluation will not constitute an adequate and functional basis for appropriate treatment.

A complete case history includes the following general areas of information and evaluation: (1) Identifying data, (2) Information concerning home and neighborhood conditions, etc., (3) Symptoms of the problem, condition, or situation, (4) Examinations, (5) Physical and Health, (6) Psychophysical, (7) Psychological, (8) Educational, (9) Health and physical history, (10) Family history, (11) School history, (12) Occupational history (of an adult), and (13) Social history and contacts.

In terms of insights gained through the information obtained from the case history, diagnosis of the difficulties is made, recommendations for treatment evolved, and therapy applied. Then, when or if the client responds to the therapy, a follow-up program is planned and carried on until the client gives evidence of good adjustment.

QUESTIONS AND TOPICS FOR DISCUSSION

1. List the values as you see them of the short-form type test.
2. Present values that you have experienced from the participation in programs of evaluation.
3. What relationship do you believe should exist between educational objectives and the content of examinations?
4. Discuss the difficulties inherent in the construction of each type of standardized test discussed in the chapter.
5. If possible, get five copies of an intelligence test that has been administered to children. Analyze the items that were correct on each test. Indicate the differences in kinds of performance among these five children.
6. What use can be made of the results of intelligence tests and of aptitude tests?
7. Suggest learning outcomes that do not adapt themselves readily to the paper-and-pencil measurement.
8. In what ways can the use of evaluation affect the curriculum or teaching procedures of a particular school or class?
9. Why, in a true-false test, is the number of items important?
10. What are the differences between a differential aptitude test and a special aptitude test? Illustrate.
11. Analyze the qualities needed for success in clerical work. Discuss the possibility of a person's having an aptitude for clerical work.
12. As a class project, construct objective-type tests for the material in any two chapters of this book. Compare the tests for definiteness of items.
13. List the values of projective techniques in personality evaluation.
14. How does the Rorschach technique differ from the Thematic Apperception Test?
15. Compare the projective techniques with other standardized techniques as instruments of evaluation.

16. Plan a situational test that you would like to apply. How would you go about it? What trait or quality would you be interested in studying? Discuss some of the difficulties.
17. Recount an interview with a teacher or a prospective employer. Evaluate the behavior of the interviewer in light of the procedures discussed in the chapter.
18. What are among the difficulties encountered by a social worker in attempts to obtain a complete and accurate case history of a learner who needs special help?
19. What is the value of the case study technique in pupil evaluation?
20. Explain why personality is so difficult to evaluate.

SELECTED REFERENCES

Aiken, L. R., *Psychological and Educational Testing.* Allyn and Bacon, Boston, 1971.

Anastasi, A., *Psychological Testing,* rev. ed. Macmillan, N.Y., 1961.

Buros, O. K., *Mental Measurement Yearbook,* 7th ed. Gryphon Press, Highland Park, N.J., 1972.

Chronbach, L. J., *Essentials of Psychological Testing,* 2nd ed. Harper and Row, N.Y., 1960.

Crow, L. D., and Crow, A., *Student Teaching in the Secondary School,* David McKay, N.Y., 1964.

Durost, W. N., and Prescott, G. A., *Essentials of Measurement for Teachers.* Harcourt Brace, N.Y., 1962.

Gottman, J. W., *Evaluation in Education: A Practitioner's Guide.* Peacock Pub., N.Y., 1972.

Gronlund, N. E., *Measurement and Evaluation in Teaching,* 2nd ed. Macmillan, N.Y., 1972.

Karmel, L. J., *Measurement and Evaluation in the Secondary School.* Macmillan, N.Y., 1972.

Lien, A. J., *Measurement and Evaluation in Learning,* 2nd ed. William C. Brown, Dubuque, Iowa, 1971.

Lindvall, C. M., *Testing and Education: An Introduction.* Harcourt Brace, N.Y., 1961.

Nunally, T. C., *Educational Measurement and Evaluation.* McGraw-Hill, N.Y., 1972.

Smith, F. W., and Adams, S., *Educational Measurement for the Classroom.* Harper and Row, N.Y., 1972.

Thorndike, R. M., and Hagen, E., *Measurement and Evaluation in Psychology and Education,* 2nd ed. Wiley, N.Y., 1961.

16   *Interpretation of Learner Progress*

The implications of data that result from the administration of tests should be understood by (1) the pupils, (2) the teachers, (3) the principal, and (4) the parents. Test results have functional value only when they are utilized to improve learning conditions and situations.

Using Standardized Achievement Tests

Among the most useful evaluating instruments in education are the various kinds of standardized tests. Evaluation becomes more meaningful in a testing situation when and if comparisons can be made with the results that are obtained by testing other pupils with the same or equivalent tests. In the evaluation of functions such as attitudes or personality characteristics, measurement still is relatively inadequate because of the nature of the traits measured and our inability to interpret results objectively. Tests that have been devised for the measurement of achievement, however, can be utilized by a teacher as one aspect of evaluation of learner progress and teaching success.

Selection of standardized tests. The need for careful selection becomes greater as more standardized tests are developed. This is especially true of achievement tests. Teachers probably use achievement tests as much as or more than they use any other type of standardized test. Important, therefore, are criteria to help a teacher evaluate these tests before he recommends their use. When a specific test is ordered, the publisher includes with the copies of the test the directions for administering and scoring it, as well as a statement of its reliability and validity, and the standardized norms of expected performance.

Interest in reliability. All test constructors are careful to make certain that, if administrative conditions are similar, the results obtained through the utilization of a test will be the same (consistent) each time it is administered. When a test yields consistent results upon successive administrations, it is considered to be

421

reliable. The degree of a test's reliability depends upon the degree of consistency in its results. For example, a reading comprehension test is administered to three hundred fourth-grade pupils. The range of scores falls between thirty and sixty, with the mid-score at forty. If this same reading-comprehension test is administered to another group of three hundred fourth-grade children and the range of scores is between twenty-eight and fifty-nine, with the mid-score at forty, there is evidence that the test has good reliability. A more accurate index of reliability can be determined through statistical treatment of the two sets of results.

One of the methods employed to discover test consistency (reliability) is to administer a test to no fewer than three hundred pupils in any grade. Then, after a lapse of time, the same test is administered to the same pupils to discover what differences, if any, appear between the scores made by each individual in each administration of the tests. The test-retest method is acceptable to discover reliability; but another method—the split-half method—is used more widely. In the split-half method, the pupils take only one test. The test constructor then compares, statistically, the scores made on the first half of the test with the scores made on the last half of the test, or the scores made on the odd-numbered items with the scores on the even-numbered items.

The teacher is less concerned with the methods of computing reliability than he is with the fact that the reliability of the test is adequate. Except for a few achievement areas, the reliability of achievement tests should exceed .90, provided that the test is administered properly. A teacher probably can use a test with confidence if its reliability exceeds .90. (See page 441.)

Interest in validity. The test user is not only interested in consistency of test results, but also is concerned with the extent to which test items cover adequately the curricular area included in the test. The stated objectives of the test become important considerations in test validity. A reliable test in arithmetic achievement would not be a *valid test* to discover the achievement of an individual in algebra. In other words, *test validity means that a test measures what it purports to measure.* For a test to be valid, therefore, it must include an adequate sampling of items that cover all phases of the subject area to be measured.

Interest in norms. The practical value of a standardized test lies in the norms that are established through the administration of a test to a relatively large group of individuals of the same grade or age level. The scores are recorded and analyzed. As these scores are analyzed, the average of performance becomes the norm for the group. For example, as the result of the administration of a Reading Comprehension Test (Grades 4 to 9), the average performance or norms for the respective grades were as follows:

TABLE 21.   Grade Norms for 2,200 Children in Metropolitan New York and the Midwest on Crow-Kuhlmann-Crow Reading Comprehension Test, Grades 4 through 9

GRADE LEVEL		TEST GIVEN AT THE END OF	GRADE NORMS
Grade	Month		
4	2	October	28
4	7	March	31
5	2	October	40
5	7	March	45
6	2	October	51
6	7	March	57
7	2	October	64
7	7	March	67
8	2	October	70
8	7	March	73
9	2	October	76
9	7	March	79

No geographic differences were found among the scores. In fact, after an analysis of the first three hundred scores, the norms were practically set. As the scores of class after class were added, only small changes were evident, even in the decile ratings (cumulative ratings by intervals of ten). This would seem to mean that the norms of the test are reliable and can be applied to the results that are obtained from the administration of a test in similar school systems.

Other factors of interest in test selection. The teacher or principal who selects a test also needs to know the cost of the test; whether there are several forms of the same test; whether the test can be used for diagnostic purposes; if it can be given in the time available; if it covers the mental functions desired; if it consumes much or little time to score, or if it can be machine scored. The last-named factor may seem to be incidental to the selection of tests; yet, if the utilizer of the test is responsible for scoring, it becomes very important that tests be selected that are as easy to score as is possible. Moreover, there is little value in ordering forms for machine scoring unless machines are available. Scoring service may be provided by publishers who furnish forms for machine scoring. However, since machine scoring may be delayed, a school that needs to know test results immediately can hand-score tests, even though the test are devised for machine scoring.

The administration of standardized tests. The directions for administering a test should be stated clearly and simply. A teacher who has minimum training and experience with test administration should be able to administer any standardized achievement test. All questions that might be asked by the pupils taking.the test are included in the manual of directions to avoid individual interpretation of directions by the teacher who administers the test. Uniformity of directions must be maintained by the test administrator if the test results are to be compared with established norms. A test administrator should not deviate from the specific directions that are given in the test manual.

The time factor in the administration of timed tests is extremely important. Great care must be exercised that the pupils will be given the exact number of minutes allotted for performance in the test. Any departure from the techniques of administration that have been established by the standardizing group reduces the validity of the comparison of pupil results with standardized norms.

The scoring of standardized tests. Directions for scoring the test usually are stated simply and clearly in the manual of directions. The reliability of test results is based partly upon the objectivity of the scoring. Tests that require teacher interpretation of answers may reduce the value of the norms. Considerable experience and training are essential to evaluate the results of tests in which the expected answers are not completely objective. Since correct interpretation is difficult for some personality tests and for a few intelligence tests, instructions for scoring and interpretation should be followed exactly.

Use and Misuse of Evaluation Techniques

Standardized tests are excellent for discovering something about learners in comparison with other learners in similar school communities. For example, it usually is desirable to become alerted to a child's level in reading comprehension and his ability in arithmetic computation. Carefully selected and properly administered tests can provide objective data that help the teacher to understand learners better and to improve teacher-learner relationships.

Use of test results. As we mentioned earlier, test results can be used to classify pupils for the attainment of stimulating teaching-learning conditions. We know that there are values in learner classification according to measures other than those obtained from intelligence tests. Many tests can be used to obtain a good estimate of a child's ability in various learning areas, such as reading and arithmetic. Upon a child's entrance into high school, a good test to aid in pupil classification for effective learning is one in an area other than intelligence. The authors have devised a Test for High School Entrants that has been used widely for guidance purposes. The results of this test not only give evidence of the readiness of a pupil to do work on the high-school level but also enable freshmen counselors to organize classes in terms of readiness for high-school study. Although there is a high correlation between results obtained from the administration of this test and levels of intelligence as obtained through the Henmon-Nelson Intelligence Test, the test for high school entrants is not an intelligence test.

Standardized tests should be used to measure learner progress, but they should not be used to evaluate teacher success or failure. Many factors enter into the evaluation of learning progress in any class. Teachers have feared the administration of standardized tests because, in far too many instances, the test results are utilized by the principal or other school supervisor to evaluate teacher effectiveness. Perhaps the teacher, himself, may believe that his success is based upon these test results. Before too great value can be attached to test scores, a great deal more must be known about the learners and their ability to master particular subject matter. A teacher who has a class of gifted pupils may not experience pride in the test results of the pupils that merely reach the standardized norm; a teacher who has a class of dull learners rightfully can gain much satisfaction from the test results of his pupils who exceed the standardized norm.

The goals set by these tests, however, should never become the purposes of education, nor should results secured from the administration of standardized achievement tests be the sole basis of a term's mark. For many years in New York State, a uniform examination has been given to students in various subjects. It is called a Regents' Examination because it is supervised by the Board of Regents in New York State. This examination is not a standardized test. It is never administered twice in the same form; hence no norms are established for it. There are, however, standard questions that are used frequently in one or another form. A teacher usually wants to stimulate learner achievement far beyond the mere passing of a Regents' examination. When emphasis is placed upon the passing of this examination as the goal of learning, other educational values are likely to be lost.

One of the difficulties of teaching has been the use of objective marking criteria. Marks indicative of pupil progress must be prepared for parent scrutiny. It is a misuse of the results of standardized tests to have them serve as an "easy way out" for the teacher when he assigns the final mark for the school term or year. It is equally bad for the teacher to issue marks on the basis of personal impressions. Measures other than scores obtained from the administration of standardized achievement tests and a teacher's personal impressions should be utilized as the bases of marks.

Cautions in interpreting test results. Interpretation of test scores can be undertaken effectively only after the evaluator has gained some information relative to the factors that influence test performance. It is difficult to evaluate, on a verbal intelligence test, the intelligence of a child who has little or no reading ability; likewise, it is impossible to measure the achievement of individuals for comparative purposes on an improperly administered test. If the test conditions are changed in any way, the results cannot be compared to standard norms.

The success of the teacher cannot be measured in terms of this type of test. It would be unfair to hold teachers rigidly responsible to meet minimum standards on these tests in order for them to obtain salary increments, for example. To do so might invite an unprofessional approach to testing, on the part of teachers. It is difficult to deter some teachers from reviewing specific items on a test before the test is administered to members of their classes. This is not only unprofessional, but also is harmful to the child.

If the same test has been used in the school for a number of years, it is possible for some pupils to obtain copies of it and to study it. Moreover, whenever standardized tests are to be used, some teachers who are directly concerned with the results become interested in discovering the test questions or items. If the learners are stimulated to master the subject-matter area on which the test is based, they will give a good account of themselves on the test. If, through drill, they are stimulated toward learning the answers to test questions, they may master specific bits of information at the expense of other more important learning outcomes.

Understanding of Simple Statistics

Measurement and evaluation become more meaningful as the reader develops an understanding of statistical procedures. It is coming to be recognized that it is essential for a teacher to understand simple statistical interpretation of data in order that he can understand better the individual child with whom he is associated in the teaching-learning situation. The likelihood that a classroom teacher will use statistics as a tool of research is remote. Nevertheless, he can become a more effective teacher if he understands some of the terminology and procedures essential to study and research in his profession.

Throughout this book, reference has been made to terms and to data that require a minimal knowledge of statistics in order to be interpreted and understood. For dealing objectively and intelligently with scores on tests or examinations, methods have been devised to reduce these scores to units of comparison for purposes of interpreting their significance. The teacher, therefore, should know some of the devices that are used from time to time to organize and to treat collected data.

The discussion that follows is devoted to a brief explanation and illustration of some of the techniques that are used commonly in simple educational statistical interpretation. The presentation is as practical and as simple as possible. For those techniques that can be used by teachers, examples of their computation are included. Among the terms that should be understood by teachers are: range, frequency distribution, normal curve of distribution, measures of central tendency (mode, mean, median), spread of scores, and correlation.

Frequency Distribution

For the purpose of illustrating range in scores and frequency distribution, we are including the scores on a survey test of Competence in Social Studies, Health Education, and Science that were made by forty-five pupils in each of three seventh-grade classes. In Table 22 are presented the initials of the pupils in each class, and their accompanying scores. In Table 23 are presented the frequency distribution of the scores (ungrouped data) according to the number of pupils who had the same score. In Table 24 appear the same scores (grouped data) organized in step-intervals of five.

TABLE 22. Scores Made by Pupils in Three Classes, A, B, C, on a Test of Competence in Social Studies, Health Education, and Science (Bristow-Crow-Crow)

CLASS A		CLASS B		CLASS C	
Student's Initials	Scores	Student's Initials	Scores	Student's Initials	Scores
M.A.	81	T.B.	85	G.A.	80
K.A.	72	U.B.	80	S.B.	70
R.A.	76	S.B.	81	Z.B.	59
A.A.	53	H.C.	42	K.B.	70
V.B.	59	R.C.	56	R.C.	46
M.C.	73	S.C.	60	S.C.	41
S.C.	50	J.D.	78	O.C.	64
T.D.	44	N.E.	71	G.D.	71
Y.D.	48	W.F.	69	K.D.	53
G.D.	81	G.G.	54	D.E.	67
B.E.	65	B.H.	46	A.E.	67
M.F.	68	S.H.	49	Y.F.	78
V.G.	77	E.H.	70	R.G.	46
R.H.	50	R.J.	52	N.H.	70
P.H.	47	B.K.	77	S.H.	68
B.J.	63	M.K.	86	L.I.	54
F.J.	70	B.K.	66	C.J.	80
J.K.	78	R.L.	52	S.K.	69
R.K.	51	W.L.	48	B.L.	57
A.L.	63	B.L.	66	S.L.	46
G.M.	45	S.M.	68	B.M.	53
S.M.	62	R.M.	71	R.M.	78
S.N.	80	M.M.	41	B.N.	64
C.N.	77	S.N.	68	A.N.	58
W.O.	51	A.N.	55	G.O.	48
C.P.	45	B.O.	44	B.O.	55
F.P.	72	K.O.	55	R.O.	70
K.P.	48	J.P.	70	M.P.	58
J.P.	74	F.P.	80	K.P.	56
R.S.	50	G.P.	57	A.P.	46
R.S.	47	M.P.	73	P.P.	45
M.S.	52	W.R.	86	E.R.	76
D.S.	71	W.R.	70	Z.R.	62
J.S.	72	B.R.	83	B.R.	59
E.S.	49	G.R.	85	K.S.	72
S.T.	67	F.R.	67	G.S.	54
M.T.	58	R.S.	49	P.S.	54

CLASS A		CLASS B		CLASS C	
Student's Initials	Scores	Student's Initials	Scores	Student's Initials	Scores
S.T.	54	S.S.	55	C.T.	60
T.V.	77	G.S.	49	A.T.	37
G.V.	45	K.T.	44	P.V.	59
M.V.	43	O.T.	82	L.V.	57
L.W.	42	G.W.	59	T.W.	70
E.Y.	52	K.W.	72	V.W.	74
R.Y.	70	R.W.	77	B.W.	68
B.Y.	77	L.W.	70	J.W.	53

Analysis of data. The same data appear in each of the three tables but are organized for different purposes. In Table 23 the *range* (the distance or the spread of scores between the lowest and the highest score) can be obtained easily through inspection. In Class A, the range is between the scores of 42 and 81, or 39 points; in Class B, it is between the scores of 41 and 86, or 45 points; in Class C, it is between 41 and 80, or 39 points. It can be seen that the range varies slightly among these classes. Although the range of the scores for each of these three classes is approximately the same, the scores distribute themselves in different patterns.

The scores earned by each individual are arranged (Table 23) according to the number of individuals earning each score on the test [a frequency distribution, (f)]. A frequency distribution is arranged on the basis of the number of individuals making the same scores. In order to facilitate the treatment of data, individual scores can be grouped according to a selected group interval, i.e., step-intervals of 2, 3, 5, 10, etc.; in Table 24 these scores have been arranged in step-intervals of 5.

The distribution of scores can be illustrated pictorially by using a *bar graph*, Figure 28, or a *frequency polygon*, Figure 29. These forms of visual material are useful for presenting data, for better understanding of data, and for making comparisons among groups of data. When the data are recorded on a bar graph (sometimes called a *histogram*), the number of students making any particular score is indicated on the graph by the length of the bar (Figure 28). When the data are recorded as a profile (usually called a *frequency polygon*), the line is drawn through the points that represent the number of pupils who make the respective scores (Figure 29).

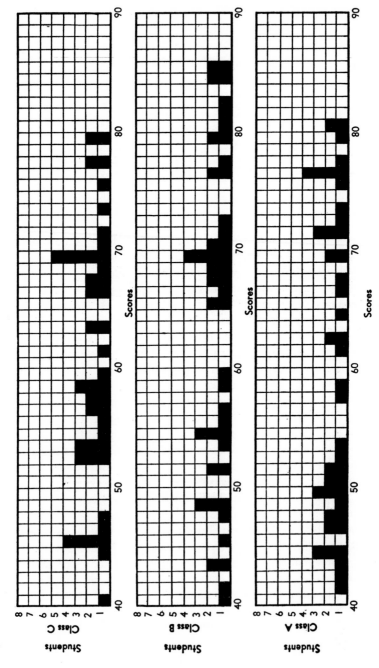

FIGURE 28. Histogram Based on Individual Scores

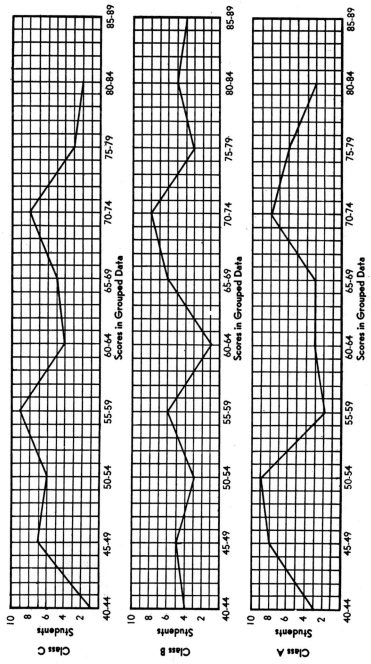

FIGURE 29. Frequency Polygon Based on Grouped Data

431

TABLE 23. Frequency Distribution of Scores Made by Three Classes, A, B, C, on a Survey Test of Competence in Social Studies, Health Education, and Science

CLASS A			CLASS B			CLASS C		
Score	Tally	Fre-quency	Score	Tally	Fre-quency	Score	Tally	Fre-quency
86			86	//	2	86		
85			85	//	2	85		
84			84			84		
83			83	/	1	83		
82			82	/	1	82		
81	//	2	81	/	1	81		
80	/	1	80	//	2	80	//	2
79			79			79		
78	/	1	78	/	1	78	//	2
77	////	4	77	//	2	77		
76	/	1	76			76	/	1
75			75			75		
74	/	1	74			74	/	1
73	/	1	73	/	1	73		
72	///	3	72	/	1	72	/	1
71	/	1	71	//	2	71	/	1
70	//	2	70	////	4	70	ﬅﬀ	5
69			69	/	1	69	/	1
68	/	1	68	//	2	68	//	2
67	/	1	67	/	1	67	//	2
66			66	//	2	66		
65	/	1	65			65		
64			64			64	//	2
63	//	2	63			63		
62	/	1	62			62	/	1
61			61			61		
60			60	/	1	60	/	1
59	/	1	59	/	1	59	///	3
58	/	1	58			58	//	2
57			57	/	1	57	//	2
56			56	/	1	56	/	1
55			55	///	3	55	/	1
54	/	1	54	/	1	54	///	3
53	/	1	53			53	///	3
52	//	2	52	//	2	52		
51	//	2	51			51		
50	///	3	50			50		
49	/	1	49	///	3	49		
48	//	2	48	/	1	48	/	1
47	//	2	47			47	/	1
46			46	/	1	46	////	4
45	///	3	45			45	/	1
44	/	1	44	//	2	44		
43	/	1	43			43		
42	/	1	42	/	1	42		
41			41	/	1	41	/	1

**TABLE 24.   Frequency Distribution of Scores of Data in Table 23
(Grouped Data)**

CLASS A			CLASS B			CLASS C		
Step Interval	Tally	Fre-quency	Step Interval	Tally	Fre-quency	Step Interval	Tally	Fre-quency
85–89			85–89	////	4	85–89		
80–84	///	3	80–84	ЖΗ	5	80–84	//	2
75–79	ЖΗ /	6	75–79	///	3	75–79	///	3
70–74	ЖΗ ///	8	70–74	ЖΗ ///	8	70–74	ЖΗ ///	8
65–69	///	3	65–69	ЖΗ /	6	65–69	ЖΗ	5
60–64	///	3	60–64	/	1	60–64	////	4
55–59	//	2	55–59	ЖΗ /	6	55–59	ЖΗ ////	9
50–54	ЖΗ ////	9	50–54	///	3	50–54	ЖΗ /	6
45–49	ЖΗ ///	8	45–49	ЖΗ	5	45–49	ЖΗ //	7
40–44	///	3	40–44	////	4	40–44	/	1

The normal curve of distribution. At this point, we shall explain briefly
what is meant by a "normal curve." A large and unselected group
of phenomena or data tends to be distributed according to a definite
pattern. For example, if a large cross section of the population is
measured for degree of possession of any trait or characteristic, it
can be discovered that relatively few persons possess the characteristic to a much greater or lesser degree, respectively, than do the
majority of the individuals who have been measured. These represent the extremes of distribution. The greatest number of cases,
however, will cluster around a point that is midway between the
extremes. For example, out of a thousand men selected at random,
there will be very few tall men and about an equal number of very
short men. The largest number of the group will be about average
in height and will fall midway between these two extremes. If the
deviations from the center point follow a regular pattern in either
direction, the distribution of the measures can be presented in the
form of a curve that is bell-shaped. This curve is called a *normal
curve of distribution.*

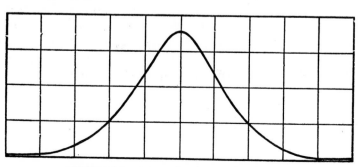

FIGURE 30.   Normal Curve of Distribution

If the group is small and represents any kind of selectivity, the frequency polygon is unlikely to take on the form of a normal curve. Reference to Figure 29 shows the irregularity of distribution of the scores presented in Table 22. Each of the three classes was small; each represented selectivity in that it was a seventh-grade class. Hence the scores spread themselves from 40 to 85 with no mid-point clustering.

Measures of Central Tendency

The three units of measure that commonly are used to express the degree of concentration of scores in any set of data are *mode, arithmetic mean,* and *median.*

The mode. The largest number of pupils who earned the same score on the survey test for each class is the *mode* of the class for that test. For example, in the ungrouped data, for Class A in Table 23, four pupils earned the score of 77; in Class B, four pupils earned a score of 70; in Class C, five pupils earned a score of 70. The score representing the highest frequency among the pupils in each class is the *mode* for that class.

In *grouped* data the mode is obtained differently. (See Table 24.) Here the mode falls in the step-interval in which the largest number of pupils have scored. For Class A, the step-interval is 50–54; with nine pupils having scores within this range. The mode then is considered to lie at the mid-point of this step-interval, i.e., 52.5. In Class B, the mode is in the 70–74 step-interval, or 72.5; in Class C, the mode is in the 50–54 step-interval, or 52.5. In other words, in group data the mode is the mid-point of the step-interval in which the largest number of scores fall.

The mean. The arithmetic mean (usually referred to as the *mean*) is a commonly used measure of central tendency. It represents the average score of the group. The mean can be obtained by adding all the scores made by the pupils who took the test (Table 22) and dividing the sum by the number of pupils. In class A, the total of all the scores is 2,750. Since there were 45 pupils in Class A, 2,750 is divided by 45. The result is 61.1; the average, the arithmetic mean, or the mean score of Class A. The mean can be computed in the same way for Class B, and Class C.

The formula for computing the mean in ungrouped data is:

$$\text{Mean} = \frac{\text{Total of all scores}}{\text{Number of pupils}} \text{ or } M = \frac{\Sigma X}{N}$$

TABLE 25. Computation of the Mean from Frequency Distribution.

TEST SCORES OF PUPILS IN CLASS A

Score	Number of Students	Score Times Frequency	Computation
82		0	
81	2	162	
80	1	81	
79		0	
78	1	78	
77	4	,308	Number of pupils = 45
76	1	76	
75		0	
74	1	74	
73	1	73	61.1
72	3	216	45)2750
71	1	71	270
70	2	140	50
69		0	45
68	1	68	50
67	1	67	45
66		0	5
65	1	65	
64		0	
63	2	126	Mean 61.1
62	1	62	
61		0	
60		0	
59	1	59	
58	1	58	
57		0	
56		0	
55		0	
54	1	54	
53	1	53	
52	2	104	
51	2	102	
50	3	150	
49	1	49	
48	2	96	
47	2	94	
46		0	
45	3	135	
44	1	44	
43	1	43	
42	1	42	
41	0	0	
		Total 2,750	

The symbol Σ represents *the sum of*, the X represents the scores made by the pupils, and the N represents the total number of scores.

The mean also can be computed from tables of frequency of scores. For example, if we wish to use the scores in Table 25 for the purpose of finding the average score or the mean, we must consider the number of pupils earning any one score. In Class A, two pupils made the score of 81, hence 81 is multiplied by 2. Four pupils made the score of 77, hence the 77 is multiplied by 4, and so on. We shall illustrate how this is done. In Table 25 is found the frequency distribution of the scores made by members of Class A (See Table 22) together with the total of each score multiplied by the number of pupils making that score. The results are shown in Table 25. The mean is 61.1. The mean of Classes B and C can be computed in the same way and the means for the three classes compared. By the computation of the mean, the teacher can discover differences in average achievement among the classes.

The mean also can be computed from grouped data. In grouped data, the mid-point of the step-interval is used as representative of all the scores of each interval. The method with grouped data is illustrated for Class A in Table 26. Note the slight difference of the mean score when using grouped data as compared with the true mean obtained from the use of actual scores.

TABLE 26. Computation of the Mean from Grouped Data, Class A

STEP-INTERVAL (5)	X	F	FX	COMPUTATION
80–84.99	82.5	3	247.5	N = 45
75–79.99	77.5	6	465.0	FX = 2,777.5
70–74.99	72.5	8	580.0	Substituting in the formula:
65–69.99	67.5	3	202.5	
60–64.99	62.5	3	187.5	$M = \dfrac{\Sigma FX}{N}$
55–59.99	57.5	2	115.0	
50–54.99	52.5	9	472.5	
45–49.99	47.5	8	380.0	$M = \dfrac{2,777.5}{45} = 61.7$
40–44.99	42.5	3	127.5	
				The *Mean* based upon
		45	2,777.5	grouped data is 61.7

The formula to be used to compute the mean for grouped data is:

$$\text{Mean} = \frac{\text{The sum of the scores multiplied by the frequency}}{\text{Number of pupils}}$$

$$M = \frac{\Sigma FX}{N}$$

The *F* represents the number of pupils making each score, the *X* represents the mid-point in each step-interval, and the *N* represents the total number of scores.

Since the scores represent continuous rather than discrete series, a score of 80, for example, extends from 80.0 to 80.99+. Hence the step-interval of 80.0–84.99 includes all the values from 80.0 through 84.99+ or five steps.

The median (Mdn.). A measure of central tendency that is more easily computed than the mean is the *median*. For this reason, it is used by teachers and administrators to discover quickly how one group differs from another, or the relative standing of an individual in a class. This measure represents the mid-point of the range of scores on the test. A "rough" median or middle score can be obtained by using the score of the middle pupil in the total range of scores. For example, in a class of twenty-five pupils, the middle score would be that made by the thirteenth pupil, if the scores are arranged in order from high to low. If there are twenty-four pupils, the middle score would lie between the twelfth and thirteenth score.

It is relatively easy to discover which pupils receive scores that are higher than the middle score if we (1) arrange all the scores in a descending order from high to low, (2) count down to the score made by one-half of the pupils. The score made by this middle pupil is the score that represents the rough median of the group. Statistically, the *median refers to the point on a scale above which and below which 50 per cent of the cases fall.*

By referring to Table 23 we discover by counting down that the middle pupil, the twenty-third on the scale, made a score of 62. As a check, we count the number of pupils falling below his score and find that there are as many below as above. By following this procedure, we learn that the middle score in Class B falls at 68, and in Class C, at 59.

The procedure to find the median with grouped data is more complicated and requires the use of the following formula (Table 27):

$$\text{Median} = \frac{N}{2}$$

When we divide the number of scores by 2, the quotient is 22 1/2. The problem then is to find a point on the scale at which this case falls. By beginning at the lowest score at the bottom of the column in which the number of pupils is listed for each step-interval, and count-

TABLE 27.   Computation of Median (Grouped Data) of Class A

STEP-INTERVAL (5)	NUMBER OF PUPILS	COMPUTATION
80–84.99	3	
75–79.99	6	
70–74.99	8	$\text{Median} = \dfrac{N}{2} = \dfrac{45}{2} = 22\ 1/2$
65–69.99	3	
60–64.99	3	
55–59.99	2	$\text{Median} = 60 + (1/6 \times 5) = 60.83$
50–54.99	9	$\text{Median} = 60.83$
45–49.99	8	
40–44.99	3	
	$N = 45$	

ing up to and including 22 1/2 cases, we discover that the median falls somewhere in the step-interval 60–64.99. There are 22 pupils who have scores up to the 60–64 interval. Therefore, in order to obtain the 22 1/2 point that is needed, we must take 1/2 score of the 3 in step-interval, 60–64.99. Consequently, we take 1/6 of 5 (size of step-interval) and add the result to the 60.0, the beginning of the step-interval. The result is the median, or 60.83. The same procedure can be used to find the median of the scores made by the pupils in Classes B and C.

Spread of Scores

The spread of scores sometimes is measured by means of technical statistical procedures. Chief among these are *range, quartile deviation, standard deviation, and percentiles*. The range was explained earlier. The standard deviation is too technical for this discussion. However, a teacher should understand something about the spread of scores as well as their concentration. This information is especially valuable to school principals and guidance personnel who have to organize classes for instructional purposes.

Quartile deviation. Quartile deviation (Q) refers to *fourths* of the range of scores. Quartile deviation is measured from the median. The median represents 50 per cent of the cases, computed from the lowest case upward or from the highest case downward. The *first* or lower quartile (Q_1) represents the lowest 25 per cent of the scores. These fall below the median. The highest quartile (Q_3) represents 75 per cent of the cases: 25 per cent of these fall above the median.

Half of the cases, therefore, fall between Q_3 and Q_1. Hence half of the distance between Q_3 and Q_1 represents the quartile deviation from the median, or $\dfrac{Q_3 - Q_1}{2}$.

The computation of the quartiles follows that for locating the median, except that we now want to find the fourths, rather than the half. Hence starting at the bottom of the distribution, the formulas for finding the quartiles are:

$$Q_1 = \frac{N}{4} \qquad Q_3 = \frac{3N}{4}$$

To find Q_1 for grouped data, Table 28, we divide 45 by 4, or 11¼. Then counting up 11¼ cases, we find that Q_1 equals ¼ of the interval 50–54. To compute Q_3, we take ¾ of 45 cases, which gives us 33¾ cases. Counting up from the bottom of the distribution, we find that the 33¾ case falls in the interval 70–74.99. We need 5¾ or 5.75 of the 8 cases in that step-interval.

To discover the *quartile deviation* we substitute in the formula as follows:

$$Q = \frac{Q_3 - Q_1}{2}$$

TABLE 28.   Computation of Quartile Deviation (Grouped Data) of Class A

STEP-INTERVAL (5)	NUMBER OF PUPILS	COMPUTATION
80–84.99	3	$Q_3 = \dfrac{3N}{4} = \dfrac{135}{4} = 33.75$
75–79.99	6	
70–74.99	8	
65–69.99	3	$Q_3 = 70 + \dfrac{(5.75 \times 5)}{8}$
60–64.99	3	
55–59.99	2	$= 73.6$
50–54.99	9	Median = 60.83
45–49.99	8	
40–44.99	3	$Q_1 = \dfrac{N}{4} = \dfrac{45}{4} = 11.25$
	N = 45	$Q_1 = 50 + \dfrac{(1 \times 5)}{36} = 50.14$
		$Q_1 = 50.14$
		$Q = \dfrac{Q_3 - Q_1}{2} = \dfrac{73.6 - 50.14}{2} = 11.73$
		$Q = 11.73$

The quartile deviation from the median in either direction is 11.73 and contains 50 per cent of the cases. It can be concluded from these grouped data that within a range of scores on the test from 40 to 84.99, this Class A is heterogeneously grouped in terms of reading comprehension.

Percentile distribution. The measure of dispersion that indicates the distance between percentiles is easy to compute and to understand. Distribution according to percentiles, centiles, or deciles is finding its way into much of present-day professional literature. Teachers will want to become acquainted with percentile distribution so that they may be able to read educational literature with greater understanding as well as be able to utilize it in the construction of pupil marks.

The percentile is used to designate where a pupil ranks in relation to the other members of his class. The median score is the fiftieth percentile. If a pupil makes a median score, it means that half of the pupils in the class have scores that are higher than his, and that the other half have scores that are lower than his. Likewise, if a pupil's score falls at the seventy-fifth percentile (Q_3), it means that 75 per cent of the pupils in the class have scores that are lower than his score.

Percentiles, as measures of relative standing, can be used to compare a learner's achievement with that of the other members of the group. For comparison purposes it is more effective than either the percentage mark or the letter grade. A *percentile* represents one point on a one hundred-point scale. Deciles are decade percentiles that appear at every ten, twenty, thirty, etc., percentile. For example, in Class A, pupil S.M., with a score of 62, is the one nearest the fiftieth percentile. (It will be remembered that the median is 60.83.) This means that S.M. has a score higher than half of all the members of the class. However, J.P., with a score of 74, is at or near the seventy-fifth percentile (Q_3, 73.6). This means that J.P. has a score higher than three-fourths of the class.

Relationships among Data (Correlation)

The classroom teacher may have occasion to determine the relationship among various phases of pupils' personality better to appraise their nature, their learning responses, their reaction to teaching procedures, and their achievement in different areas of learning. In order to apply statistical procedures, it is necessary to have measures of pupils' achievement or traits. Hence the relationships with which we are concerned are those between quantitative variables of individuals.

Coefficient of correlation. Teachers often want to use information concerning the relative standing of the members of a class on two tests. For example, a teacher may be interested in: the relationships that exist between the scores made on a test and the intelligence quotients of the members of the class, or the relationship between the scores made on a reading test and scores made on a survey battery taken by the same pupils. It is possible to treat the data (scores made by learners on any two tests) statistically and discover an index of relationship between them. Further, teachers' interests may lie in the relationship that exists between the scores earned by two classes on the same test, for example, reading comprehension, intelligence, arithmetic, social studies, etc. The index that represents the extent of agreement between the two sets of scores is known as the *coefficient of correlations*. e.g., +.89, or −.47.

The sign (+ or −) of the coefficient of correlation must be considered in an interpretation of the significance of the correlation. Relationships may be either positive or negative. The sign indicates the direction of the relationship. When there is a tendency for two series of scores to vary in the same direction, they show a positive correlation; if a tendency toward inverse relationships is shown, there is a negative correlation. The size of the coefficient index indicates the degree of relationship that exists between the sets of scores. When no sign is placed before the decimal, a positive coefficient is indicated; a coefficient that represents an inverse relationship must be preceded by a minus sign. No correlation between the scores is indicated by .00. Correlations vary from this point and increase in both directions either to 1.00 (perfect positive correlation), or to −1.00 (completely negative correlation).

What constitutes a correlation that indicates a close relationship between data depends upon several factors—the nature and purpose of the tests, and the conditions under which they are administered. For example, the results obtained by the administration of one intelligence test should have a high positive coefficient of correlation with the results obtained from the administration of another, to the same individuals. Again, the scores that are earned on one reading comprehension test should show a close relationship to the scores that result from the administration of another standardized reading comprehension test.

The extent of correlation between two tests in the same area depends upon the suitability of both tests for the subjects of the test. For example, the results of the administration to a fourth-grade class of a fourth-grade reading comprehension test and of another reading comprehension test that is valid for high-school entrants are likely to yield a low coefficient of correlation. Even for two tests that in content would seem to be suited to a group of subjects, the coefficient of correlation might be low if either or both of the tests were statistically unreliable, and/or invalid, measuring instruments.

We shall attempt to explain, through the use of data from Table 15, page 324, what is meant by a coefficient of correlation in an actual situation. For convenience the scores are repeated in Table 29.

TABLE 29. Scores Made by Pupils on a Reading Comprehension Test and Their IQ's

PUPIL'S INITIALS	SCORE ON TEST	IQ	PUPIL'S INITIALS	SCORE ON TEST	IQ
N.K.	59	116	V.C.	27	104
D.S .	53	127	G.D.	27	104
W.F.	49	119	C.J.	25	106
R.H.	46	120	J.A.	25	114
K.P.	45	125	S.C.	25	108
A.Z.	44	116	E.D.	23	102
P.S.	44	112	L.L.	23	102
R.F.	36	110	J.D.	21	106
D.V.	34	104	R.R.	20	103
M.D.	32	105	F.H.	20	105 ·
E.S.	31	101	H.Z.	20	101
R.F.	29	112	M.C.	19	107
C.A.	29	106	S.D.	17	101
S.G.	29	107	V.P.	15	85
E.T.	27	107	R.S.	11	94

The scores on the Reading Comprehension test have been arranged from high to low. The pupil making the highest score is placed at the top; the IQ of each pupil is placed next to the reading score. A perfect positive correlation index of 1.00 would result if: the pupil with the highest score also had the highest IQ; the pupil with second highest score, the second highest IQ; the pupil with the third highest score, the third highest IQ; and so on through the entire class. When this one-to-one relationship exists between two sets of scores, the index of correlation is 1.00 (perfect positive correlation).

It is possible to discover by observation of these scores that there is a tendency for the pupils who have the higher scores also to have the higher IQ's; or the pupils who have the lower scores to have the lower IQ's. Since a one-to-one relationship does not prevail completely between these two sets of scores, the correlation is less than 1.00 but it is positive. There are two commonly used techniques for computing the coefficient of correlation. One of these, the Product-Moment method, has a high reliability, although it is relatively difficult to compute. Its symbol is r. The other technique, the Rank-Difference method, has a lower reliability, but its computation is relatively simple. Its symbol is p. For the data in Table 29, $p = .75$ and $r = .82$. (See Table 29a for computation of p)

Utilization of the coefficient of correlation. A classroom teacher rarely needs to compute a coefficient of correlation. It is desirable to understand its connotation, however. Reference to correlations is made in explanations of the results of research studies. A constructor of a standardized test usually reports concerning the coefficient of correlation of his test with other similar measuring instruments. The higher the coefficient of correlation between his test and another reliable and valid test of the same function, the more reliable and valid his test will be.

For example, the person in charge of testing in a high school wished to substitute a more recently constructed test of intelligence for others that formerly had been administered. There was some objection among the faculty to the change. According to the manual of this test, it correlated well with other tests of intelligence. To check further the reliability and validity of the test under question, it and three other approved tests were administered to the same group of students. Intercorrelations of the four tests then were computed. It was found that this test had a high coefficient of correlation with each of the others (ranging from .91 to .94).

The computation of the coefficient of correlation usually is the responsibility of a statistically trained person, but an understanding of the coefficient of correlation is needed by all school people.

Scatter diagrams. The direction of the relationship between data can be determined conveniently by plotting each of the pairs of scores on a two-way table. The scores made by the learners and their intelligence quotients are plotted on a scatter diagram in Figure 31.

For this purpose, grouped data are used since less space is required and the effectiveness of the plotting is as great.

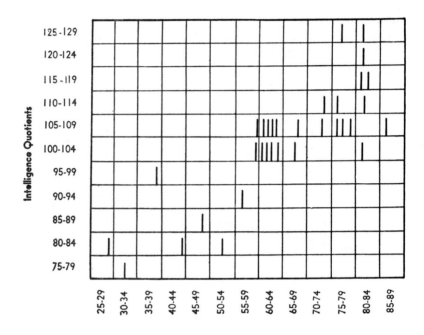

Scores on Reading Test

FIGURE 31. Scatter Diagram of Thirty-Three Paired Scores on an Intelligence Test and a Reading Comprehension Test

If the scores for each pupil are plotted by making the entry in the box that represents the point at which the score from the vertical axis (IQ) meets the score from the horizontal axis (Reading), a scatter diagram is formed that will show at a glance the closeness of the relationship. If the marks tend to follow a line from the lower left-hand (low score) to the upper right-hand (high score), there is evidence of a relatively high coefficient of correlation, or close relationship. However, if the scores are scattered throughout the diagram, there is evidence of little relationship among the scores. The coefficient of correlation can then be expected to be low. If the plotted scores of the two tests seem to fall into a diagonal pattern that extends from the upper left to the lower right, a negative relationship would be indicated.

Rank-difference method illustrated. We shall use the data in Table 29 to find the correlation between the test scores and the IQ's. First we rank the reading comprehension scores and place them in the table. Since they are already arranged in a descending order they are easy to rank. Next, on a separate sheet of paper, we arrange the IQ scores in a descending order and rank them. This rank position is then placed in its proper place in Table 29a.

TABLE 29a.   Computation of Correlation between the Scores Made by 30 Students on Reading Test and Intelligence Test

Student's Initials	Reading Score	IQ Score	Rank Reading	Rank IQ	Rank Difference	D²
NK	59	116	1	5.5	4.5	20.25
DS	53	127	2	1	1	1
WF	49	119	3	4	1	1
RH	46	120	4	3	1	1
KP	45	125	5	2	3	9
AZ	44	116	6.5	5.5	1	1
PS	44	112	6.5	8.5	2	4
RF	36	110	8	10	2	4
DV	34	104	9	21	12	144
MD	32	105	10	18.5	8.5	72.25
ES	31	101	11	27	16	256
RF	29	112	13	8.5	4.5	20.25
CA	29	106	13	16	3	9
SG	29	107	13	13	0	0
ET	27	107	16	13	3	9
VC	27	104	16	21	5	25
GD	27	104	16	21	5	25
CJ	25	106	19	16	3	9
JA	25	114	19	7	12	144
SC	25	108	19	11	8	64
ED	23	102	21.5	24.5	3	9
LL	23	102	21.5	24.5	3	9
JD	21	106	23	16	7	49
RR	20	103	25	23	2	4
FH	20	105	25	18.5	6.5	42.25
HZ	20	101	25	27	2	4
MC	19	107	27	13	14	196
SD	17	101	28	27	1	1
VP	15	85	29	30	1	1
RS	11	94	30	29	1	1
					Total	1135

With the Rank-Difference method, the formula for finding the correlation is:

$$p = 1 - \frac{6 \, \Sigma \, D^2}{N(N^2 - 1)} \qquad p = 1 - \frac{6(1135)}{30(900 - 1)}$$

$$p = 1 - .25$$

$$p = .75$$

QUESTIONS AND TOPICS FOR DISCUSSION

1. Explain what is meant by a standardized test.
2. Why should a teacher be interested in the extent of reliability of a standardized test?
3. By reference to a particular test, explain what is meant by its validity.
4. After your class has taken a test, ask your instructor to give the class scores so that all the class members can determine the median, the mode, and the mean of the marks on this test.
5. The following scores were earned on a test in child psychology: 92, 69, 82, 90, 84, 68, 80, 54, 90, 72, 95, 86, 90, 83, 93, 79, 54, 75, 65, 57, 83, 64, 74, 80, 76, 80, 72, 80, 91, 81, 88, 62, 77, 82, 73, 72.
   a. Compute the median and the mean, using ungrouped data.
   b. Make a frequency table of the scores by using a step-interval of 4.

SELECTED REFERENCES

Baron, D., and Bernard, H. W., *Evaluation Techniques for Classroom Teachers,* McGraw-Hill, New York, 1958.

Blommers, P., and Lindquist, E. F., *Elementary Statistical Methods in Psychology and Education,* Houghton Mifflin, Boston, 1960.

Garrett, H. E., *Statistics in Psychology and Education,* 5th ed., McKay, New York, 1961.

Garrett, H. E., *Testing for Teachers,* American Book, New York, 1959.

Koenker, R., *Simplified Statistics,* McKnight and McKnight, Bloomington, Ind., 1961.

Manuel, H. T., *Elementary Statistics for Teachers,* American Book, New York, 1962.

Peatman, J. G., *Introduction to Applied Statistics,* Harper and Row, New York, 1963.

Tate, M. W., *Statistics in Education,* Macmillan, New York, 1955.

Walker, H., and Lev, J., *Elementary Statistical Methods,* Holt, New York, 1957.

17 Appraisal and Reporting of Pupil Progress

The one school duty in which the teacher is least sure of her ability to perform is in the area of assigning pupils' marks. Marks are not absolute measures of achievement but represent the philosophy that underlies their determination. The parent or the school administrator who reads the marks on a pupil's report form may not interpret them according to the values or standards of the teacher who entered them.

Teachers have never been absolutely sure of the purpose of marks. With the introduction into the marking system of an attempt to synchronize a mark with the ability of the child, even more confusion has been experienced in this respect by both the teacher and the parents. Nevertheless, out of attempts to make marks more realistic and humane are emerging the kinds of report that represent qualitative as well as quantitative values.

Functions of Classroom Tests and Examinations

Although standardized tests are of great value, they cannot be used adequately for the testing and appraising that need to be done in connection with day-to-day teaching. Tests made by the classroom teacher, called teacher-made tests, generally are used to measure achievement progress for grading purposes. The teacher-made test is adapted better than standardized tests for small units of learning and can be pointed by the teacher to include any area of learning. It then meets one basic principle of testing, i.e., to measure the extent of the learning. Teachers, therefore, need to have a high degree of proficiency in the construction of adequate teacher-made tests.

Teacher-made tests differ from standardized achievement tests in several ways, although they have some elements in common.

A Teacher-Made Test	*A Standardized Test*
1. Is constructed for use in a specific teaching-learning situation.	1. Is constructed for use in any teaching-learning situation in which the content of the test is covered.

A Teacher-Made Test	A Standardized Test
2. Tends to have questions directly related to details of learning situation.	2. Is usually general in its application to subject matter.
3. May or may not be valid or reliable.	3. If well constructed, has a high degree of validity and reliability.
4. May contain either short-form or essay-type questions.	4. Is usually limited to short-form questions.
5. Does not have norms or standards of achievement to which the performance of testees can be compared.	5. Affords norms of performance, based upon many cases, with which individual results can be compared.
6. Is usually a group test.	6. May be either an individual or a group test.
7. May be used for diagnostic, survey, or pretesting purposes.	7. May be diagnostic, prognostic, or survey.[1]

The giving of tests and examinations no longer is limited in purpose to the measuring of achievement at the end of learning units and to the ascertaining of whether the pupil has mastered sufficient learning content to pass the course. Modern educational theory and practice emphasize the importance of the use of tests as a vital part of the teaching-learning process. Preliminary tests are helpful to instruction in learning areas, such as arithmetic and spelling. By means of these tests (teacher-made or standardized), the teacher can discover the learning status of each member of his class. For example, if the class, as a unit, is found to be weak in subtraction and strong in addition, the teacher can apply remedial teaching techniques that will benefit the entire class. If only a few are found to be weak in addition, however, he is confronted with the problem of giving remedial help to those few pupils.

The type of test that is used will influence the study methods of the learner. The learner on the upper-grade or high-school level wants to know ahead of time whether the test is to be an essay or an objective type. Tests give learners an opportunity for expression. To this extent, testing programs serve to motivate learning. The essay type is better suited to fulfill this purpose than is the objective type test.

[1] See L. D. Crow, H. E. Ritchie, and A. Crow, *Education in the Secondary School*, American Book Company, New York, 1961, pp. 388–389.

Diagnosis of learning difficulties is one of the important functions of tests, either standardized or teacher-made. The more effectively errors can be located, the better the teacher will be able to help the learner overcome his difficulty. Learning hurdles may differ among learners. The teacher should correct test papers himself so that he may become intimately acquainted with the type of mistakes made by each pupil. When the teacher discovers that many pupils in his class have made the same kind of mistakes, he may come to appreciate the fact that his teaching can be the cause of the difficulty.

Another function of classroom tests is that they furnish a basis for marks and progress reports. These marks are as valid and as reliable as the tests on which they are based. Hence correct test construction becomes extremely important. The form of a test, the number of included items, and the length of the test are fundamental to its value as a basis for school marks.

Learners are interested in the progress they are making. When tests are administered and the papers scored, the results should be given to the learners as soon as possible after the test has been taken. Many objective type questions can be marked by the pupils immediately after the test is completed by having them exchange papers. The class discussion that follows makes it possible to correct errors at once. This procedure may have a greater motivating effect than returning the corrected papers at a later date.

Although the final examination is a teacher check on effectiveness of teaching, its use as a means of learner motivation is still an undecided issue. Some school people claim that the time taken for a final examination might better be used otherwise; others believe that the final examination fits into the concept of whole learning because it covers the entire term's or year's work. Hence the learner who prepares for it is confronted with the whole course. As he reviews, in preparation to take this examination, he makes use of the whole method of learning in a way that stimulates further integration of learning. Through this final effort, the serious student integrates his learning in a way that ordinarily does not take place earlier.

This comprehensive approach to larger units of learning materials results directly from the learner's effort at understanding and remembering as much of the material of the term as is possible. It enables him to see relationships that may not have been appreciated earlier when he engaged in piecemeal study of smaller units of work. There are significant differences among individual learners in the extent of integration that takes place through the reviewing of learning materials. The bright learner discovers new relationships; the slow learner is likely to employ rote memory.

Bases of Evaluating Pupil Progress

A mark is issued to the learner to help him evaluate the adequacy of his learning activities. The mark may record progress as a percentage on the basis of a hundred or as a letter that represents a step interval of several per cents. A teacher may attempt to show each pupil his degree of achievement in comparison with the level of other members of the class; he may compare individual performance with the norm of a standardized test. The comparison procedure, for example, may indicate that the pupil is in the highest one-tenth of his class, or that he is at the point below which the marks of 75 per cent of other pupils fell (seventy-fifth percentile). Each pupil wants to know how he rates in relation to other members of his class.

Importance of standards. It is important to know the standards used by the teacher in his assigning of marks. A teacher may have a tendency to give higher marks to children who are co-operative and who create no disturbance in class than he gives to those pupils who are troublemakers. A pupil who was an ideal school citizen because she was industrious, was prompt in submitting home work, and displayed a good attitude earned excellent marks both in elementary school and in high school. Her brother, who was not so co-operative, received lower marks in the elementary and in the secondary school which they both attended. Nevertheless, although he was one year younger and one grade behind his sister, he demonstrated by his performance on many standardized tests that his ability level is higher than his sister's.

To allow a pupil's attitude or behavior to be reflected in a mark that is supposed to represent success in learning performance is a temptation to some teachers. A mark in a subject should have a reliable meaning. It should represent a learner's achievement in that subject—his status in terms of knowledge, ability, skill, or accomplishment in it. An A in arithmetic should represent a definite quality of attainment in arithmetic. The mark may be flexible in terms of the ability of other members of the class in that it is not based strictly on a 100 per cent standard of perfection. The lowest score or mark in any particular learning area should go to the pupils whose learning performance indicates that they are least proficient. The marks between the best and poorest should be distributed ac-

Lakewood, Ohio
The Public Schools
Kindergarten-First Grade

PERSONAL AND SOCIAL HABITS

Report Period

SOCIAL HABITS

	1	2	3	4
1. Co-operates well with others				
2. Is courteous in speech and manner				
3. Is obedient				
4. Practices self-control				
5. Is dependable				
6. Respects property of others				
7. Shows good sportsmanship				
8. Is considerate of others				
9. Respects authority				
10.				

WORK HABITS

11. Begins and completes work promptly				
12. Depends upon himself				
13. Follows directions carefully				
14. Is critical of own work				
15. Gives satisfactory attention				
16. Achieves according to his ability				
17. Has materials ready				
18. Works in neat and orderly manner				
19. Makes valuable contributions				
20.				

HEALTH HABITS

21. Is clean				
22. Apparently gets sufficient sleep				
23. Is neat in personal appearance				
24. Keeps good posture				
25. Wears appropriate clothing				
26. Is active and alert				
27. Observes safety rules				
28.				

EXPLANATION OF PERSONAL AND SOCIAL HABITS

1. An "A" opposite a habit indicates outstanding success for which the child should be commended by the parents.

2. A check mark means that improvement is needed, and that a conference with the teacher might help the child.

3. Blank spaces show that adjustment is satisfactory. Therefore a large majority of the spaces will have no marks.

cording to the degree of excellence between the two extremes of achievement.

Fine class spirit and attitude can be recognized in other ways but should not be included in achievement rating. Items may be included on the report cards to give attention to such factors as: social behavior, health habits and work habits, and attitude shown toward the learning situation. Marks that are assigned must be understood by all who read them—pupils, parents, and administrators. Some of the modern attempts to introduce factors of encouragement into pupil evaluation are illustrated in progress reports for Kindergarten-First Grade, Lakewood, Ohio. See page 451.

The form represents the items on the check list and the explanations of personal and social habits. There are four report periods. Space is provided for the comments of teachers and parents at each reporting period.

Variability in teachers' marks. If all teachers utilized the same standards concerning the value to be assigned to the answer to every question on a test, there probably would be greater agreement among teachers' marks. However, if, in an arithmetic problem, for example, one teacher believes that any error in the solution should earn a zero for the answer, and another teacher believes that one error should earn a penalty of only 10 per cent, it is not difficult to understand that most of the marks given by the latter will be higher than any of the former. Marks, therefore, become a matter of a teacher's philosophy. Greater agreement among teachers on these basic factors is essential to uniformity of marks.

Several studies have been made to demonstrate the variability of marks among teachers. A final examination paper in first-year English, on the high-school level, was rated by 142 teachers of English. The scores assigned to one paper ranged between 64 and 98. In another investigation, a final examination in mathematics was rated by 118 teachers of mathematics. This paper received ratings that ranged from 28 to 92. In a third study it was found that the model answer sheet was mixed among some history papers that were being rated by teachers of history. This model was given a failing grade by one of the raters. These studies lead to the conclusion that there are wide variations among teachers in the assigning of marks. The results of these studies emphasize the necessity of greater objectivity and accuracy in pupil evaluation.

Students soon learn that one teacher is a higher (easier) marker than another. If the mark he receives is more important to a student than is knowledge of the subject, he enrolls in the class of the teacher who gives the higher marks. Marking standards vary also among departments and among schools. Girls often receive higher marks in high school than do boys because of their more co-opera-tive attitude and greater willingness to study. Yet, the median score on a psychological examination often is slightly lower for girls than for boys. This has been true at Brooklyn College for more than twenty years. The high-school marks for entering girls are higher, on the average, than those for boys, yet the girls score lower on the entrance test which is administered to all freshmen.

Distribution of marks. No matter how highly selected or how homo-geneous a group of bright learners may be, there usually is evi-enced a range in the scores that are made by the members of the group. Even though the learners represent a highly selected group, the marks tend to be distributed according to a percentage basis. Hence the pupils who receive the lower marks are compared unfa-vorably with some of the members of a slower class in the same school who receive higher marks in the same subjects, although their learning ability is less than that of the honors-class students. This is the chief reason why some learners do not like to be placed in the honors class.

For example, in a certain high school, the requirements for admis-sion to "honors" classes included the possession of an IQ of 110 or better and the attainment, during the previous school terms, of final marks that were 85 or better (on a 110 per cent basis). These honors classes were organized in terms of IQ's and past learning achieve-ment only. The teachers of the classes insisted upon high standards of achievement. Hence learning pressures were great and learner competition ran high. In this learning situation, the students who had been admitted on a basis of the minimum 110 IQ's and 85 aver-ages experienced considerable difficulty in keeping up with some of their classmates whose IQ's and averages were much higher. Consequently, in comparison with the others, their class marks sometimes fell to the 70's. Thereupon (also because of teacher pressure) they became very much discouraged. Many of these students were expecting to be candidates for admission to colleges that required a high scholastic average for admission. Emotional-ized tensions resulted from a combination of the fear that their marks would fall below college-entrance requirement standards, and a feeling of humiliation caused by the fact that mentally slower pupils in regular classes were receiving higher marks than did these "honor" students.

The dean of the school often was implored by these young people to transfer them to regular classes. As a mental-hygiene procedure, this permission was granted in those cases of students whose emotional status was such that they could not adjust to the pressures of which they were the victims. In the case of some "honors" teachers, however, the removal of such students meant that a few more able students in their classes fell into the 70 per cent group because of the teachers' attitudes toward mark distribution. They seemed to believe that to have every member of the class achieve successfully was an indication of insufficient learning challenge. Hence one or more pupils had to be given a seventy. Moreover, other phases of personality, in addition to high IQ and success in learning achievement in a heterogeneously organized class, should be considered in the placement of young people into "honors" classes.

There are several percentage schemes that give a distribution of marks. The percentage distribution tends to be fair to the learner, since it can be used regardless of the difficulty of the material. In the utilization of this technique, teaching effectiveness also is taken into consideration.

Teachers should decide upon the kind of distribution that they want to use as a basis of marks. They also must decide whether the lowest percentage point should be regarded as a failure or as poor but satisfactory achievement. The following distribution plans based upon letter ratings are among those widely used for assigning marks.

TABLE 30.   Various Plans for the Distribution of Marks

MARK	PERCENTAGE DISTRIBUTION OF MARKS					
	1	2	3	4	5	6
A	10	7	5	5	15	10
B	20	24	25	20	25	25
C	40	38	40	50	45	55
D	20	24	25	20	10	10
F	10	7	5	5	5	0

Distribution plan number 6 is one in which no failures are found; distribution plan number 2 is considered by some school people to represent a normal distribution of five letter divisions. A relatively normal distribution probably will result among large learning groups heterogeneously organized. These conditions are not characteristic of a small, homogeneous group, all of the members of which are mentally alert and are equally interested in the subject studied. The fact that there are no failures does not necessarily indicate that the teacher is a "high" marker. In Plan 6 there is no provision for failures, but a mark of "C" is assigned to more than half the pupils.

It is a recognized fact that college instructors vary in their marking standards as much as and probably more than high-school teachers. For example, the students of a particular college represent a highly selected and homogeneous group. Yet, there is variation of final letter marks assigned the members of five classes respectively, by five instructors of the same subject during the same semester. The prerequisites for admission to this course include the successful completion of two years of college study, in addition to at least one basic course in the area of the subject-matter field of the elected course. Any differences in learning readiness among the 168 students taking the course would be similar for all classes. Hence the final marks should be relatively high and show the same distribution. In Table 31 are presented the final letter marks in subject ———, semester ———, of five classes, each of which was taught by a different instructor.

TABLE 31.   Final Marks of Five College Instructors
(Same Subject, Same Semester)

MARK	CLASS 1	CLASS 2	CLASS 3	CLASS 4	CLASS 5	NUMBER OF STUDENTS
A	10	6	9	2	5	32
B	15	16	15	16	7	69
C	11	14	9	14	12	60
D	0	1	0	0	4	5
F	0	0	0	0	2	2
Total	36	37	33	32	30	168

A study of this table shows that there was some agreement among the individual instructors, especially in the A, B, and C marks. In general, the majority of the students earned a mark of C or higher. This could be expected in an elected course for which students are ready. The instructor of Class 4 apparently expects more from an "A" student than do the instructors of Class 1 and Class 3. The "hardest" marker, of course, is the instructor of Class 5. Although his class is the smallest, with greatest opportunity for guidance of individual students, he is the only instructor to assign failing marks (two) and to "give" four of the five "D's." The instructors of Classes 1 and 3 would seem to be the "easiest" markers. The implications of the comparisons presented in Table 31 are representative of the habitual marking patterns of these five instructors.

Value of Cumulative Records

It is customary for schools to start and to keep up-to-date a *cumulative record* for every member of the learner population. Records should include important items concerning a pupil from the time he enters the lower school until he is graduated from high school. Pupil needs cannot be diagnosed unless or until the right kind of information is recorded in organized form for utilization by teachers and other school personnel.

The term *cumulative record* refers to the combining into one form of the various types of records that, in the past, were kept separately. It is "a record of information concerned with the appraisal of the individual pupil—usually on a card, sheet, folder, cards in an envelope, or some combination of such—and kept in one place." Some of the school records that usually are included in the cumulative record may be kept in separate duplicate form for use by particular members of the school staff.

Items included in a cumulative record. The number and kinds of items to be included in a cumulative record depend upon the functions to be served by it and by the attitude toward these functions of the school people who are responsible for its construction and utilization. Some of these cumulative records are extremely elaborate. They include data that deal with most, if not all, of the conditions, situations, and activities associated with learning progress about which data are available. Other records are relatively simple. They contain only pertinent data that are more or less objective; other more personal items are kept in separate files.

The items usually included in a cumulative record are classified here in broad categories:

A. *Identifying data*
    Name
    Date of birth, based upon
      official evidence

Place of birth
Sex
Home address
Photograph

B. *Personal data*

Names of parents or guardians

Occupation of parents or guardians

Birthplace of parents

Number and sex of all siblings

C. *Scholarship*

School marks by years and subjects

Special identification of failures

Rank in class, with number in class (especially graduating class)

D. *Ratings on standardized tests, etc.*

General intelligence scores

Achievement test scores

Other test scores

Personality ratings

E. *School attendance*

Days present and absent each year

Record of lateness

Record of schools attended, with dates

F. *Health*

Serious physical or health deviations

Record of vaccinations, etc.

G. *Educational and vocational experiences*

Part-time employment

Vocational plans

Educational plans

Special aptitudes, music, art, etc.

H. *General school relations*

Cocurricular activities

Awards earned

Special projects

Counseling experiences: name of counselor, notes of counselor

Anecdotal reports, etc.

Using the cumulative record card. To keep up-to-date all the various items is a time-consuming job, involving the participation of many faculty members. Some items of personal information have no place on a general cumulative record that is easily accessible to all members of the faculty, and, perhaps, to students. Some of the items, especially those dealing with part-time work, apply especially to record-keeping on the secondary- and higher-school levels. It also is customary in most schools to keep the complete health record separately, including in the cumulative record only those physical and health conditions that are of interest to teachers and counselors who plan programs of study or who are responsible for adjusting school conditions to the needs of a handicapped young person. The inclusion in the record of temporary illnesses, for example, has doubtful value.

It must be kept in mind that the cumulative record card is an official document that remains in the school's archives for many years. It is possible that many years after an individual has left the school, a member of the school staff may need to refer to the record to provide information to possible employers or to others. Situations or conditions that were important while the individual was a pupil of the school no longer may have significance, but may be reported by a school clerk or administrative officer who never had met the person. It is the authors' philosophy that nothing except objective, factual data should be entered on a cumulative record card. All information of a personal nature, including anecdotal records, personality evaluations, home conditions, parental relations, and similar materials, should be kept in the files of the guidance or administrative staff, and be destroyed within a reasonable lapse of time after the discharge of the pupil.

Regardless of the kinds of information included in a cumulative record, *all items must be accurate.* Difficulties often are experienced by teachers and young people because errors in reports have been allowed to creep into the record. Elementary-school records usually are transferred to the next higher school, and pertinent information copied on the record cards of the latter school. Copying errors are frequent, unless each item is checked. It also may happen that parents give incorrect information to the school. Such data as correct spelling of the name and accurate date of birth, for example, should be checked by reference to official birth certificates or other legal documents. Moreover, there are instances of incorrectly-copied marks, ratings, and other information. The recording of the results of standardized testing materials should include the name of the test and the *date of its administration.* The reason for this is obvious.

Accurate and up-to-date cumulative records have great value as background materials that can assist teachers, parents, school counselors, and outside agencies to provide for every pupil whatever he needs to help him adjust to learning and other life situations. Teachers and counselors refer constantly to these records. They are useful in parent-school conferences. Whether young people themselves should have access to their records is a matter of disagreement among school people.

Reporting Learner Progress

Teachers might not mind rating learner progress if it were not for the fact that report cards have to be made out. Most current marking and reporting methods are the causes of widespread dissatisfaction among teachers. Many innovations have been introduced by school people to alleviate some of the annoying aspects of reporting learner progress and to introduce more realism into the reports. Teachers are expected to be fair to their pupils, yet they are charged by the administration to employ definite reporting procedures. They may not be certain that they have complied with given instructions or that they have been fair or accurate in reporting the progress of each pupil.

Reports to parents. Reporting to parents is one of the most difficult teacher-parent responsibilities. Much thought and effort have gone into attempts to improve progress reports that are sent to parents. It can be said with confidence that no report is of value to parents unless its purpose and the information it contains can be understood by them. As a means to get away from percentage- or letter-rated report cards, there is much experimental utilization of reports that give descriptive statements relative to the progress of a child. To the teacher these newer reports may be quite meaningful; unless they are understood equally well by parents, they have little value.

Some types of report cards that are sent to parents have done more than anything else to bring about misunderstanding between parents and teachers, parents and their children, and teachers and their pupils. Parents find it difficult to feel friendly toward or enthusiastic about a teacher who, if the child has done poorly in school, sends a formal report to the effect that their child lacks intelligence, interest, or industry, or a combination of these. The report card often is the basic cause of the breaking off of good relationships with the school. It sets up a triangle of parent, child, and teacher; in the presence of the child the parents become critics of the school and of the teacher. When a child receives an unsatisfactory report of school progress, parents may scold, withdraw privileges, or otherwise punish the child. This parental attitude may lead to no other result than the child's building negative attitudes toward the school and the teacher. Such attitudes are almost certain to lessen rather than increase learning achievement.

To secure more accurate measures of pupil progress, it has been customary to indicate on the report card a mark for behavior. This practice has some value in that the overt behavior of the learner is not reflected in the reported evaluation of his progress in subject-achievement. Formal letter rating of effort, achievement, and conduct, such as, A, B, C, etc., has no diagnostic or prognostic value, however.

New-Type Report Forms

We cannot stress too strongly the importance of devising report-to-parent techniques that are psychologically sound. The authors are engaged in a study of experimental procedures that are in progress in many schools throughout the country. They have found that considerable thought is being given by school leaders to ways of improving the method of reporting to parents and that in many school systems the ultramodern report forms are being modified to meet parental objections. These school personnel express their belief, however, that new reporting forms are needed to help parents gain a better understanding of the school's purposes and practices and to achieve more co-operative relationships. To the present, experimentation in this field appears to be greater on the elementary- and junior high-school levels. Some attempted changes in reporting are evidenced on the senior high-school level but, for the most part, traditional reporting forms still are used.

Various new forms have been obtained by the authors from many schools. One of these newer report forms already has been included in this chapter.

One of the recent attempts to construct meaningful reports to parents of elementary-school children is being made at Montclair, N. J. Separate forms have been constructed for Grades 2 and 3; and for Grades 4, 5, and 6. There is included also a "Growth Plan," that accompanies the report of progress for Grades 4, 5, and 6.

Letters as Reports to Parents

Letters or modified letters are being used to report to parents. If the teacher cannot meet parents personally, he can write specific statements for the parents to read. The utilization of the letter procedure need not wait for a formal report period; a letter report can be sent to parents whenever the teacher has something definite to report. It also can be used at specific report periods. These so-called letters take many forms, from a blank sheet of paper on which the teacher makes a statement, to a special form which contains blank spaces to be filled in by the teacher, according to definite areas of interest and available space on the form.

Many school systems are introducing the letter-type report for the kindergarten and first through the sixth grades. On these report forms, provision is made for reporting on: Personal and Social Habits (Lakewood, Ohio); Social Growth, Growth in Skills and Understanding (New Rochelle, N. Y.); Work Habits, Social Habits,

THE PUBLIC SCHOOLS
MONTCLAIR, NEW JERSEY

Report of Progress

Name
_____

School
_____

Grade _____ Year _____

Dear Parents:

Teachers and administrators have the same interest that you do—the development of your child's talents and capabilities. We want to work with you toward that goal.

This "Report of Progress" is the teacher's evaluation of your child's growth as revealed by his responses in the school situation. It is hoped that this report will help you to understand your child's abilities and needs, and to encourage his continued achievement.

This report will come to you three times during the school year. In addition, your child's teacher will schedule a mid-year conference.

You are cordially invited to visit your school and to talk with your child's teacher and principal.

C. E. Hinchey
Superintendent of Schools

Form A   For Grades 2, 3

461

The items below represent personal habits and social attitudes which the school tries to develop. The appraisal at the right records your child's performance in school activities.	FIRST			SECOND			THIRD		
	Usually	Sometimes	Seldom	Usually	Sometimes	Seldom	Usually	Sometimes	Seldom
HEALTHFUL LIVING (Mental and Physical) Keeps reasonably neat and clean									
Maintains good posture									
Shows evidence of sufficient rest									
Is cheerful and pleasant									
RELATIONSHIP WITH OTHERS Practices courtesy									
Respects rights and opinions of others									
Claims only his share of attention									
Is careful of property and materials									
Works well with others									
Accepts guidance from persons of experience									
Shows good sportsmanship									
Practices self-control									
Is a good leader									
Is a good follower									
Makes constructive contributions									
WORK HABITS Begins work promptly									
Follows directions									
Completes work on time									
Checks work									
Is neat and orderly in his work									
Works independently									
Uses free time wisely									
Assumes responsibility									
Shows initiative									
Refrains from talking unnecessarily									

	1st Report	2nd Report	3rd Report
Times Tardy			
Days Absent			

For Grades 2 to 6

The following statements define academic objectives. At the right is given the school's estimate of your child's progress relative to his ability and his past achievement.	FIRST				SECOND				THIRD			
	Outstanding progress	Progress compares favorably with ability	Improving, but can do better	Progress much below ability	Outstanding progress	Progress compares favorably with ability	Improving, but can do better	Progress much below ability	Outstanding progress	Progress compares favorably with ability	Improving, but can do better	Progress much below ability
SKILLS, KNOWLEDGE, UNDERSTANDING												
LANGUAGE Expresses ideas well in speech												
Uses correct English												
Speaks distinctly												
Writes thoughts in complete sentences												
READING Reads well to others												
Understands what he reads												
Is able to work out new words												
Reads library books												
SPELLING Learns words in spelling lessons												
Spells well in written work												
HANDWRITING												
Forms letters correctly												
Writes plainly and neatly												
ARITHMETIC Shows growing knowledge of fundamentals												
Uses what he knows in solving problems												
Is accurate in computation												
PHYSICAL EDUCATION Cooperates in organized group activities												
Is growing in skills												
ART ACTIVITIES Has ideas												
Uses various media in art												
MUSIC Takes part in singing												
Enjoys rhythmic activities												
Shows growth in music activities												
SOCIAL STUDIES AND SCIENCE Takes part in class discussions												
Is able to use simple reference materials												
Is learning important facts												
Shows interest in nature and science												
Is alert to news events												
Offers contributions												

For Grades 2 to 6

First Report

Teacher's supplementary comments:

Parent's reply to the teacher's comments, and information which may help to enlarge the school's understanding of the pupil.

MY GROWTH PLAN

While I .... expect to improve in many things, I am checking here those on which I plan to work hardest now. I hope my teachers will make comments or suggestions which they think will help me in any of my work.

Class Goals	✓	My Next Steps	✓	My Next Steps
My Health Habits				
Keep myself neat and clean				
Sit and stand well				
My Relationship with Others				
Work well with others				
Play well with others				
Accept guidance from persons of experience				
Show consideration for others				
My Work Habits				
Listen carefully and follow directions				
Work well alone				
Complete and check my work				
My Skills, Knowledge and Understanding				
Language				
Speak so others understand me				
Write so others understand me				
Read with understanding				
Spell correctly				
Write neatly				
Arithmetic				
Compute accurately				
Reason in arithmetic problems				
Physical Skills				
Improve my skills in games				
Understanding the world				
Use many different kinds of art materials				
Take part in music				
Read many different kinds of books				
Take part in the study of science				
Try to understand the people of all lands				

[Much of the value of this GROWTH PLAN depends on *conferences*.]

and Health Habits (Kent, Ohio); Personal Habits, Social Growth, and Work Habits (Massapequa, N. Y.); Work-Study Habits, Social Attitudes, and Physical Education (Great Neck, N. Y.); Work Habits and Group Relations (Syracuse, N. Y.); Social Habits, Work Habits, and Health Habits (Dallas, Texas). Blank spaces on the report letter permit the teacher and the parent to point their comments to the particular needs of the child.

Another type of modified letter is in the form of a folder which consists of five identical sections, one to be used at each of five marking periods. This form, used in Dallas, Texas, gives uniformity to the teacher's report, yet it allows him to apply his remarks to the status of the child's work.

If a teacher has kept anecdotal records and other necessary data about his pupils, he will be in a position to write an interesting letter to the parents. A shortcoming of the letter technique is that one teacher is able to write an interesting letter, but another teacher, who perhaps is just as capable, does not seem to have the facility to express in writing what he might like to say. The latter may be able to do much better in a personal conference. Furthermore, an overburdened teacher may find letter writing to be an added chore for his already busy day. Hence he is tempted to prepare copies of several form letters, which he sends to the many parents.

Parent-Teacher Conferences

In most school systems, parent-teacher interviews are used to supplement the written reports that are made regularly to parents. Through the conference approach, the teacher can discover any problems that the child experiences in the home; he also can clarify for the parents the child's school achievement status.

The interview can be fruitful to the teacher as a means of studying parents. If he has available time, he may visit the home for the interview. One of the most successful teachers known to the authors makes it a policy to visit the home of each of his pupils by appointment. By doing this, the teacher reduces the potential difficulties of his classwork considerably. His pupils get to know him in a different way from the way in which pupils in other classes know their teachers. These visits bring about a firsthand understanding of problems faced by the learner, the teacher, and the parent. A home-visit by a young female teacher in a crowded school community may not be advisable, however.

Whether an interview is conducted in the home or in the school, consideration should be given to the topics of conversation that would be appropriate. Parents can be rich sources of information if they are given a chance to talk. Teachers should try to discover something about the emotional reactions of parents, the extent to which parents can be expected to co-operate in a behavior problem, the degree to which the parents understand the child and his problems, the aspirations which the parents have for the child, their relationships with the child, the disciplinary measures that are used in the home, and the attitudes of the members of the family toward the school and its teachers.

Parents who experience opportunities to talk freely with teachers about current happenings, sometimes offering objective criticisms of school procedures, can come to have the kind of respect for the teacher that will induce parents to talk confidentially with him. Contrariwise, if parents receive harsh criticism or sarcasm from teachers, they may become so aroused emotionally that they will be unwilling or unable to co-operate with the teacher in the solution of a school problem situation in which their child is involved. A teacher can learn much in a parent-teacher interview by practicing the art of being a good listener.

In some school systems an attempt is being made to dispense with the formal cards for the kindergarten and first grade. In Winnetka, Ill., the conference is used for all reporting for the kindergarten through the second grade, and as a supplement to reporting in the higher grades. The parent-teacher interviews are more effective than are formal written reports. In a conference, the teacher can be specific in his interpretation of ratings that appear on the report card. In the interview, both the teacher and the parents come to understand the value of accurate data concerning the child's strengths and weaknesses. The conference gives the parent an opportunity to improve his understanding of the school's program.

It is necessary for every principal and teacher to gain the co-operation of parents, but even the best home-school relations will not always change children into co-operative human beings who never get into mischief or never fail to do their homework. Parents often are blamed if their children get into trouble in school. If children fail to complete their homework, forget their books, turn in untidy papers, or talk back to teachers, one of the first things some teachers think of doing is to place the blame on the parents. Parents, on the other hand, say that they send their children to school; it is the responsibility of school people to provide the kind of activities in the classroom that will be stimulating to active pupils.

Very young children appreciate the attention given by the family to their school interests. However, as the pupil emerges from childhood through preadolescence and into adolescent years, he becomes less interested in having his parents give too close supervision to his school activities. Yet, whatever is done in home-school relations is carried on for the benefit of the child. This can be accomplished through a better understanding between the teacher and the parents of what constitutes good education.

Group meetings between parents and teachers long have been the practice in home-school relations. The recent trend to organize small group meetings is a step toward greater individualization and more personal relations between parents and teachers. Such meetings encourage parents and teachers to talk over mutual problems in a face-to-face situation. Many of these small meeting opportunities are provided at the time of the monthly Parent-Teacher Association meeting. Here, over a cup of coffee or other light refreshments, the teacher and the parents become better acquainted and evaluate whatever problems need exploration.

Example of a teacher-parent interview. We have elaborated on the possibilities of improved school-parent relationships that are inherent in teacher-parent interviews. Before we consider the many problems and situations that can be discussed profitably in an interview relationship, we present what might be regarded to be a typical interview between a teacher and a parent.

> Teacher—Good morning, Mrs. M. I'm glad you were able to visit us. I've been wanting to meet you.
> Mother—I'm sorry I couldn't come sooner, but I'm very busy.
> T—Yes, I know how busy mothers are these days with so many things to do and to take care of. I wanted to talk with you about Steven.
> M—Is he in any trouble?
> T—Oh no, he isn't in any trouble. It's just that I believe he isn't progressing in his school work as rapidly as he could.
> M—There are times when I might be able to help him with his school work, but he tells me that he hasn't any homework.
> T—Yes, that's true. We don't assign formal homework to children in the second grade.
> M—I don't understand why his work isn't as good as the other children's. He's not a dull child.
> T—I agree with you; Steven certainly isn't a dull child. There must be some other reason to account for his slow progress.

M—Sometimes when I'm home, he seems to sit quietly as if he were in a dream world.

T—Aren't you at home when Steven arrives home from school?

M—No. I work in one of the neighborhood stores, and I'm on duty at that time. That's why I found it so difficult to come to see you.

T—I didn't know that. Do you get Steven ready for school in the morning? I sometimes wonder if he has had a good breakfast, and some mornings his personal appearance needs improvement.

M—Maybe it is my fault that he doesn't get his breakfast and that he doesn't get dressed properly. You see I work afternoons at the store, and I sleep until about nine in the morning.

T—Oh. Does your husband take care of Steven in the morning?

M—No. My husband leaves the house very early in the morning.

T—Do you have other children?

M—Yes, a girl two years older than Steven.

T—Does she take care of him?

M—She tries to, but she bosses him and they quarrel quite a bit. After all she's very young. Steven is such an unhappy child. Sometimes I wish that something could be done for him. I feel so helpless about it all.

T—Maybe the two of us can help him. Remember I mentioned that Steven wasn't progressing very well in school. Maybe his daily breakfast and his appearance might have something to do with it.

M—I really don't think those things are so important. I believe that if he can learn to read and write, he'll get along somehow.

T—But examinations have shown that children *do* learn better and are happier and, of course, healthier when they're well fed and properly dressed.

M—Well, maybe I could find time to help him with his reading and writing, but he doesn't bring his books home from school.

T—We usually don't allow the children to take their books home. We believe that when a child is happy, well-fed, and dressed properly, he will learn at school. Your son is a very likable and bright youngster. In fact, at times when he appears to be a little more at ease, he contributes to the class discussions. He shows promise of developing into an excellent pupil.

M—Maybe I should talk this over with my husband. Do you have any suggestions for helping Steven?

T—I think it's a good idea to talk this over with your husband. I know you both want to do the best for your children. Before you leave, however, I want to give you some word and number games that you can play with Steven. I also think that Steven might enjoy trips to the library, where he can find books he might like.

M—Thank you; you've been very helpful.

T—Thank you for coming in; I've enjoyed talking with you. Good-bye, and come again.

In this interview the teacher discussed several significant facts about home conditions. The mother promised to co-operate with the school. In follow-up interviews, more specific matters can be discussed. In addition, both the teacher and the mother gained an understanding of the problems of the other in relation to Steven.

Topics for interviews. The interviews that are held between teachers and parents may include discussion concerning a variety of topics; the most important are those that pertain to the specific problems which arise in connection with the child or children of the parents. Langdon and Stout selected a list of discussion-situations that may be initiated either by the teacher or by the parents themselves.

Situations initiated by the teacher:

1. Child is absent a great deal and teacher believes that schoolwork is suffering.
2. Child is finding his schoolwork so easy that teacher believes there must be more challenge.
3. Child shows some special talent which teacher believes should be given attention.
4. Teacher needs information about the child who has moved from another community.
5. Teacher believes child needs some help in school subjects.
6. Teacher just wants to get acquainted with the parents.
7. The teacher has asked the parents to discuss the school's new reporting system.
8. Teacher wants the parents to give help in the school.
9. Teacher wants to plan with the parents the necessity of, and changes needed, to go on a half-day session because of overcrowded conditions.
10. The child has been misbehaving; the teacher wants to talk with the parents about it.

Situations initiated by the parents:

1. Parents are dissatisfied with the way reading is taught.
2. Parents believe that the school is too free, that the children do too much as they please.
3. Parents come to demand that something be done because other children pick on their child.
4. Parents are concerned relative to the grades their child is getting.
5. Parents object to the amount of homework the child has to do.
6. Parents object to the fact that no homework is assigned.
7. Parents believe that the teacher should know about a family emergency that may affect the child's schoolwork.
8. Parents seek the teacher's help concerning a problem with the child at home.
9. Parents believe that school parties are lasting too late and wish that the school would do something about it.
10. Parents are planning a trip that will cover several weeks; they wish to make arrangements to take the child out of school.
11. Parents are dissatisfied with the behavior of the children on the school bus.
12. Parents want the child to skip a grade.[1]

Concerning what parents want to know, Hymes offered the following suggestions:

1. First, a parent wants to feel proud of his child's school. He can't get excited if school is just school, an empty name. He will appreciate any facts which give his child's school a special setting. . . .
2. No parent likes being in the dark, or being taken by surprise. School schedules and school costs have to be fitted into family budgets of time and money. Parents appreciate facts which let them plan wisely. . . .
3. A parent feels confidence if he knows something about the people who are taking his place from 9 to 3. The human beings who touch his child's life are mighty important people. . . .
4. Parents want to break through the sound barrier. They don't like to feel shut out of their child's life. School is their child's life. Parents want to know: What are you driving at? What are you trying to do? What is your reasoning?

[1] Adapted from G. Langdon and I. W. Stout, *Teacher-Parent Interviews*, copyright, 1954, by Prentice-Hall, Inc., New York, 1954, pp. 78–106. Reprinted by permission.

Where do you leave off, and where do parents come in? . . .

5. Parents want the best for their children. No mother or father can possibly be comfortable if he thinks someone is "experimenting" with his child, or trying out "new things." Parents want to understand what is going on; once they understand they are very likely to say "Fine!" (or have an even better idea!). . . .

6. Parents want to know your hopes and your headaches. They can help, if they are informed. And *they* have hopes and problems too. . . .

7. Most of all, every parent wants to know: How is my youngster doing? How does he stack up? How is he behaving? What do you think of him? What do you think we ought to do next? [1]

Self-Rating by Parents

Most parents want to be good parents. They are interested in the welfare of their child, and usually are willing to co-operate with their child's teacher. When things do not go well with their child, they may blame themselves for the situation. Yet, they do not know wherein they have failed to meet their parental responsibilities. They are eager to check their deeds and misdeeds according to standards of what can constitute good parental attitudes.

Report cards for parents. Recently, the authors prepared report cards for parents. They were devised for the purpose of alerting parents to desirable behavior and attitudes toward their children. Included are the following areas of interest: *home relationships, social relationships, school attitudes,* and *job careers.* We present *Home Relationships* and *School Attitudes.*

Home Relationships

Directions: Answer each question with one of these words:

Never	Sometimes
Always	Often
Rarely	Usually

Be honest with yourself:

Good Example: Do You—

1. Exhibit bad manners before your son or daughter?
2. Have husband-wife disputes in the presence of your children?

---

[1] J. L. Hymes, Jr., "Parents Want to Know These Things About a School," *National Education Association Journal,* Vol. 43, No. 5, May, 1954, pp. 279–280. Reprinted by permission.

  3. Set them an example of proper dress and good manners?
  4. Keep the house neat and clean?
  5. Gossip about other people?

Manners: Do You—

  6. Allow your boys or girls to be late for meals?
  7. Welcome their friends in the home?
  8. Criticize them in the presence of visitors?

Self-reliance: Do You—

  9. Expect your child to agree with your political views?
  10. Restrict him in his choice of friends?
  11. Give him intelligent sex education?
  12. Expect him to accept your decisions?

Responsibilities: Do You—

  13. Give your boy or girl definite work to do in the home?
  14. Treat him (or her) as an adult?
  15. Help him plan the expenditure of money?
  16. Permit him to decide his activities at home?

Your Attitude: Do You—

  17. Give your child reasons for denying requests?
  18. Feel misunderstood?
  19. Give in to his whims?
  20. Secure the confidence of your child?

School Attitudes

Study: Do You—

  1. Provide Bill and Joan with a quiet nook for home study?
  2. Help them arrange a time schedule for homework?
  3. Interrupt them when they are studying?
  4. Let them neglect homework?
  5. Expect marks beyond their ability?

School: Do You—

  6. Insist that they get to school on time?
  7. Encourage co-operation with teacher and classmates?
  8. Allow them to object to courses they are taking?
  9. Induce them to settle their own school problems?
  10. Encourage them to be critical of their teachers?
  11. Inspire them to think their school is tops?
  12. Help them adjust to the realities of school life?

Home: Do You—

  13. Pamper them at home, so they're spoiled brats at school?

14. Help them overcome their fear of examinations?
15. Worry about how well they will do at examination time?
16. Act as quizmaster during examination reviews, when requested?
17. Expect performance of household duties, as well as homework?

Finances: Do You—

18. Give them an allowance sufficient to cover school activities?
19. Try, within your means, to have them appear as well as their classmates?
20. Expect them to work part time while going to school? [1]

The parents' readiness to learn has been important in the improvement of parent-teacher relations. As the teacher and the parent learn to work together, much can be done to aid the child toward satisfactory behavior and greater achievement. Parents can absorb the deficit side of their child's performance if they first are permitted to know what the good points are. Any warranted commendation of the improvement or achievement of the child is desired and appreciated by them.

Factors of Importance in Promotion

Learning progress should be continuous. Traditionally, progress in formal education has followed a kind of educational ladder that represents artificial divisions of school experiences into grade and school levels. The successful learner is promoted from one step of the ladder to the next at "fixed" promotional periods. The utilization of this procedure is not conducive to best learning achievement. Too often the earning of promotion is the chief incentive that is employed by a teacher to motivate study and class co-operation. Promotion should be thought of as placement for learning purposes, not as punishment for misdeeds or rewards for good behavior.

The 100 per cent promotion plan attempts to eliminate the teacher's use of the threat of failure as a method to gain obedience. According to modern theory, a child is placed in the grade or class where he can make most progress in learning. We are committed to grade placement as the basis of formal school progression. Yet, we are trying to work out plans whereby a child on any ability

[1] L. D. Crow, and Alice Crow, "Report Cards for Parents," *Better Homes and Gardens,* April and May, 1947. Reprinted by permission.

level may participate in the educational experiences of the school at different rates, without breaking his yearly promotion sequence. For example, a child in a fifth-grade class may be at different learning levels in his various subjects—arithmetic, reading, etc.

In the schools of large cities where there are three or more classes to a grade, this can be done by organizing the classes of a grade in terms of the relative achievement levels of the pupils of that grade. Hence the learning of one class of the grade might be much higher than that of another. This form of grade organization is not possible in a small school that has only one class in a grade.

It is good psychology to retain the grade plan even though a child has not mastered learning material as well as the average student of the grade. The child is happy; the parents are satisfied; school personnel can educate the child on the level of his experience and, at the same time, keep his learning continuous even though his progress differs from that of other pupils in his class. Any promotional plan that takes recognition of individual differences tends to lessen the headaches of the teachers, the parents, and the children themselves.

The underlying psychological principle of continuous promotion is that, except in cases of extreme retardation, more desirable social development is achieved by the ten-year-old child who is with his peer-age group in the fifth grade, than if he were with younger children in the second grade. Although the ten-year-old child's subject achievement level may be that of second-graders, in the higher grade he is profiting from participation in other developmental experiences that are as important to him as is the achievement of mastery in subject-matter material.

Visual grading. By adapting the principle of normal distribution to small groups, the pitfalls of the application of the normal curve can be minimized. Visual grading is based on the utilization of the following criteria: (1) a comprehensive measurement program, (2) a symbol of comparison between student achievement and established standards, (3) a realistic approach, and (4) a knowledge of procedures by all concerned: students, faculty, and parents.

Visual grading can be valuable when properly used and interpreted. These valuable outcomes include (1) the use of all types of scores, (2) the provision of a uinform basis of comparison, (3) the consistency of grades from teacher to teacher, (4) the realistic factor of grades, and (5) the fact that visual grading consumes less time than many other methods. One of the Charts (See Figure 32) taken from the booklet *Visual Grading*[1] will serve to illustrate the form and use of this method. The scores of each of three classes are presented separately. There also is given the combined scores of all three classes. The teacher can use the combined scores to aid him to determine the point which should divide the A from the B; the B from the C; and so on. After the dividing points have been determined, the instructor can easily assign the appropriate letter grade to each student according to his score.

QUESTIONS AND TOPICS FOR DISCUSSION

1. State the values and weaknesses in comparing learning progress in two systems through the administration of the same achievement test.
2. What use can a teacher make of the results of different instruments of evaluation in adapting his teaching to individual learners?
3. List at least five values of a teacher-prepared test.
4. Indicate the cautions that should be observed in the construction of a teacher-prepared test.
5. To what extent should teacher success be determined by pupil performance on standardized tests?
6. Explain the reasons for the wide range in marks assigned by teachers to essay questions. If possible, have the members of your class rate an answer to an essay question. A teacher in the elementary or high school might provide you with a question. Discuss your findings.
7. Where should school records be kept?
8. Study the report card presented in the chapter and indicate any changes for improvement.
9. Enumerate the values of the cumulative record card.
10. Visit an elementary school or a high school to become acquainted with the report forms that are used to report to parents. Compare them with one or more of those mentioned in the chapter.
11. What purposes are served by keeping records and reporting marks?
12. What is your opinion of a plan of distributing marks according to one of the distribution methods presented in this chapter?
13. Compare the reporting forms found in this chapter with those received by you when you attended elementary school. With those received by your parents when they went to school, if any of those cards still are available.

[1] K. L. Russell, *Visual Grading*, Educational Filmstrips, Huntsville, Texas, 1959

FIGURE 32. Chart Illustrating a Method of Combining Scores from Several Sections of the Same Course Taught by the Same Teacher

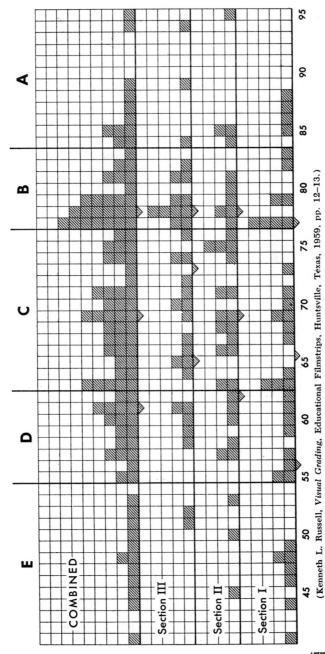

(Kenneth L. Russell, *Visual Grading*, Educational Filmstrips, Huntsville, Texas, 1959, pp. 12–13.)

477

14. Explain why a letter report to the parents is better adapted to reporting progress of the young child than of an older child.
15. Attend a parent-teacher meeting during an "open house" and listen in on some of the conferences held between teachers and parents.
16. Suggest ways for improving marking and reporting.

SELECTED REFERENCES

Cronbach, L. J., and Dreuth, P. J., *Mental Tests and Cultural Adaptation.* Humanities, N.Y., 1972.

Budd, W. C., *Educational Measurement and Evaluation.* Harper and Row, N.Y., 1972.

Griffiths, S. D., and Downes, L. W., *Educational Statistics for Beginners.* Barnes and Noble, N.Y., 1970.

McDonald, M., *Teacher's Messages for Report Cards.* Fearon, Belmont, Calif, 1971.

Popham, W. J., and Sirotnik, K. A., *Educational Statistics: Use and Interpretation,* 2nd ed. Harper and Row, N.Y., 1973.

Russell, K. L., *Visual Grading.* Educational Filmstrips, Huntsville, Texas, 1960.

Smith, F. W., and Adams, S., *Educational Measurement for the Classroom Teacher.* Harper and Row, N.Y., 1972.

Wick, J. W., *Educational Measurement.* Charles Merrill, Columbus, Ohio, 1973.

Wittrock, M., *Evaluation of Instruction: Issues and Problems.* Holt, Rinehart & Winston, N.Y., 1970.

PART VI

The Role of the Teacher
in Education

18 Development of Teaching Effectiveness

Present-day emphasis upon the importance of a teacher's possessing suitable personality qualities, extensive and intensive background knowledge, and understanding of human growth and maturation and of psychological principles of teaching and learning is a relatively recent trend in preparation for teaching. Traditionally, the sole teaching requirement was knowledge of the subject matter to be taught. A young person who had mastered the 3R's was eligible to teach young children. Those men and the few women who had earned a college degree with honors in their major field of study were considered to be highly qualified to teach in the secondary schools and colleges.

Although the training period for elementary-school teaching gradually was extended to include education on the secondary-school level, it was not until the twentieth century that serious attention was given to the fact that teacher preparation means more than the mastery of subject matter. Revolutionary changes in teacher education stemmed from the results of psychological studies of child development and the propounding of the thesis that the teacher teaches the child through subject matter rather than teaching subject matter to the child.

Broadening Concepts of Teacher Preparation

More than ever before in history, parents and other community leaders now recognize the significance in the life of an individual of his childhood and youth experiences. The years spent in schooling are viewed as a period during which the child and adolescent are developing those attitudes, skills, and knowledges that not only benefit them during their growing-up years, but also prepare them for constructive adolescent adjustment. Since the strength of the nation depends upon the kind and quality of youth education, teacher effectiveness is a matter of primary social concern.

Areas of teacher competence. The trend in teacher education is toward an increasing emphasis upon (1) the personal qualities and self-control possessed by the candidate for teaching, (2) his understanding of child nature and development, (3) his cultural sensitivity, (4) his ability to learn and apply psychological principles of teaching, and (5) his mastery of the subject matter and skills of his teaching field. In its broadest connotation, effectual teacher preparation and continued teacher development begin during the early school days and continue so long as a man or woman engages in teaching-learning activities in the school.

As could be expected, the number of post-high-school years devoted to specific preparation for entrance into teaching is steadily increasing. In some states, to become a teacher in the elementary school requires four years of college study; a high-school teacher must have completed a five-year program of study. The length of time devoted to teacher preparation may be increased in all states. We know that the kind and amount of schooling a person experiences become a tremendous influence upon his attitudes and behavior. More important, however, are the personal potentialities that he brings to his school experiences on any level of education. The prospective teacher is no exception. The kind of person he is before he begins his direct teacher preparation is a fundamental factor of his degree of later teaching effectiveness.

Personal qualifications for teaching. Is a good teacher born or made? The truth of the matter probably is that a successful teacher gives evidence of desirable innate qualities and appropriate teacher-education. Before a person begins his professional training, he should believe that he possesses some of the personal qualities that are fundamental to success in teaching.

A high-school senior or a college student who has not yet chosen his vocation might well ask himself if he is the kind of person to become a teacher. The National Association of Manufacturers prepared a self-evaluation questionnaire for the purpose of helping young people discover whether they are personally qualified to become teachers. It is suggested that a good teacher possesses these five basic qualities: "(1) a strong desire to learn; (2) a strong desire to teach; (3) an interest in people, especially young people; (4) the ability to get along with people, especially young people; (5) good character." [1]

If the interested person can answer affirmatively most of the questions in the four areas included in the questionnaire, he may be

[1] *Your Career in Teaching,* copyright, 1953, by National Association of Manufacturers, New York, p. 9. Reprinted by permission.

a fine prospect for the teaching profession. The self-rater is admonished, however, not to be discouraged by some "No" answers.

Desire to Learn

1. Do you enjoy reading books, magazines, newspapers?
2. Do you like to browse in a library?
3. When turning the pages of a newspaper, do you find something interesting on practically every page?
4. When looking up a word in the dictionary, do you often find yourself stopping to see the meaning of other words, too?
5. Do you ask lots of questions of grownups whose intelligence you admire?
6. Do you enjoy solving puzzles, especially those that teach you something, such as crossword puzzles?
7. Do you like to take things apart and put them back together to see what makes them work?
8. Do studying and learning come easy to you when you really get interested in a subject?
9. Do you often go deeper into a subject than is necessary to pass the course?
10. Are your school grades generally better than average especially when you're really interested in the subject and the teacher?

Desire to Teach

11. Do your friends come to you for help when in trouble?
12. Do you give help readily?
13. Do people generally take your advice to heart?
14. Do you give advice sympathetically, without poking fun or making sarcastic remarks?
15. Do children interest you enough to keep answering their endless questions?
16. Are you a leader in Scouting or similar groups?
17. Do you enjoy explaining things to your parents, or younger brothers or sisters, or your friends?
18. When somebody seems "dumb" and just doesn't seem to get what you're talking about, do you remain patient and go on trying to explain?

Getting Along with People

19. Are you free of temper tantrums and irritability?
20. Do you get along with parents, brothers and sisters?
21. Do you have a good sense of humor—even when the joke's on you?
22. Are you a good loser?
23. Do you have a lot of friends?

24. Are you a good team player, even when you're pushed back out of the spotlight?

Good Character

25. Do you feel strongly about such matters as human worth and dignity, freedom from oppression, rights of private property, civic duties?
26. No matter how you express it, do you believe in the brotherhood of man and the Fatherhood of God?
27. Would you refrain from lying or stealing even though you thought you could get away with it?
28. Do you avoid bragging?
29. Do you take good care of your appearance? Health? Physical condition?
30. Do you attend your church or synagogue regularly? [1]

Teaching represents a form of social service. Hence the kind of interpersonal relationships that a teacher is able to engender with his colleagues and especially with his pupils and their parents is a major phase of his degree of success in teaching.

Pre-teaching education. As has been suggested earlier, teacher preparation involves more than the subject matter to be taught. The modern teacher's responsibilities are not limited to the evaluation of the kind of learning that represents book study alone. He is a co-operative participant in the learning and living activities of his pupils, and he extends his influence beyond the classroom into the school community. Hence he needs to know and to appreciate the many aspects of modern world and American culture in general and the specific patterns of the subcultures of the community in which his pupils live.

To enrich their cultural background, teacher-trainees in most college and other teacher-education institutions devote their first two years of study to what is generally referred to as the liberal arts. Upon this basic background of general academic study is built whatever is considered appropriate teacher preparation in the areas of psychological, sociological, and educational theory and practice.

The practical value of the education that prospective teachers receive depends upon the kind and quality of the curricular offerings of our teacher-education institutions. Considerable thought and energy have been devoted to the minimum educational requirements that are essential to the training of those persons whose

[1] *Ibid.*, p. 11. Reprinted by permission.

occupational choice is teaching. Since education is a state function, teacher-preparation requirements in the form of college credits are decided at the state level. In most instances, however, the local teacher-education institution, operating under the supervision of the state authorities, is given freedom of planning within the framework of prescribed courses. In other words, a teacher-education institution does not operate under a rigidly prescribed state curriculum. It evolves its own particular curriculum that must be approved by responsible authorities in the state department of education.

Since teachers are likely to teach as they have been taught or as they are being taught to teach, teacher education exerts a potent influence upon the achievement of teaching effectiveness. Teachers need help in learning how to deal with children; they should possess an adequate wealth of subject matter; they must become acquainted with teaching materials and learn how to use them; they should develop a co-operative attitude toward all who come into contact with them in any way; parents, supervisors, co-workers, and members of the school community. Basically, teaching efficiency develops on the job as teachers work with their pupils. Yet, teacher-trainees benefit from participation in firsthand experiences with young people before they assume actual teaching responsibilities.

The integration of theory and practice. For many years school people have recognized the value of including student-teaching as an integral part of teacher education. There is a growing trend toward providing more and better opportunities for teacher-trainees to observe the learning activities of young and older children, and to participate, with regular classroom teachers, in teaching-learning situations. Through these actual classroom experiences the trainee is enabled to apply in practice what he learns as theory.

Another valuable experience for teacher-trainees is that of working with children and adolescents in community agencies. In 1948 one of the authors had the opportunity to organize a program of community experience that gave teacher-trainees the privilege of going directly into community centers and other social agencies in Brooklyn. In these agencies they received firsthand experience in working with children. This project began as a voluntary student experience. It was considered so valuable, however, that later it was incorporated as a basic part of the teacher-education program.

Brooklyn College students who are preparing to teach now are required to devote from two or three hours weekly for a period of a year to participation in community agency activities.

The significance of and the extent of the plan can be understood better through a reading of the stated aims of the program. A copy of this statement is given to all participating teacher-trainees and to all social agency supervisors.

COMMUNITY EXPERIENCE PROGRAM OF BROOKLYN COLLEGE

Statement of Aims of Education Students

To agency supervisors:

In order to help the supervisors understand what the college wants its education students to get out of their volunteer experience, the following list of values has been drawn up out of the statements of the instructors and the students. An attempt has been made to list the more important values first. The college hopes that a beginning of learning will take place in some of the following areas:

1. Getting to know boys and girls. ("Getting a 'feel' for youngsters.")
2. An increase in the feeling of competence in dealing with a group.
3. Acceptance of and adjustment to the supervising relationship.
4. Self-assessment by the student: discovering the degree of ability he has to take a new role; discovering emotional inadequacies and strengths in himself.
5. Learning something of the group process: interpersonal relations as well as indigenous leadership.
6. Some insight into the motivations of individual children or youth and of differences between individuals.
7. Reassessment of the student's own purposes and fitness for a teaching career.
8. Understanding of the role of the parent.
9. Appreciation of neighborhood influences on members of a group, both institutional influences and those of the informal associations.
10. Sensing the meaning of class in American cities: what it means to be poor.
11. A beginning of facility at handling materials.
12. Sense of the need for controls and of democratic ways of instituting them.
13. An insight into cultural differences in talking about sex and in sex as a factor in group relations.

Present-day teacher-education programs reflect the broadening concept of pre-teaching preparation. As a result cf their many and varied educational experiences, most young men and women begin their teaching careers with a creditable degree of confidence in their ability to guide the learning experiences of their pupils. Teacher neophytes go to their classrooms with some understanding of learner needs, of the differences of abilities, interests, and backgrounds among pupils, and with training in techniques of learner motivation, subject-matter presentation, and achievement evaluation. Moreover, if they have been helped during their training experiences to develop appropriate self-adjustments, their attitudes toward their pupils and their teacher-pupil relationships will be a definite asset to them.

Personal and Professional Growth of the Teacher

At one time, it was believed that a person's education was completed when he received a diploma or was granted a degree. This attitude is changing; hence classes in adult education are becoming increasingly popular. It is even more important for professional persons to acquaint themselves with the changes taking place in their particular fields. Since a teacher is responsible for meeting the personal and cultural needs of all the pupils whom he teaches successively, he must continue to improve his personal attributes as well as to keep informed concerning changes in world affairs. Not only must he become thoroughly oriented to his work as a beginning teacher, but he also needs to be a learner as well as a teacher throughout his teaching life.

Orientation of the beginning teacher. More than one hundred thousand new teachers enter the classrooms of the nation annually. Some of these are beginning their teaching career; others are new to a particular school or school system. It is only recently, however, that formal plans have been considered for the orientation of beginning teachers into the work of the profession, or for the induction of new teachers into a school. In New York City alone, more than two thousand newly appointed teachers are inducted annually into the profession. At the time of this writing, the members of New York City's Board of Education, recognizing the urgency of the problem, have inaugurated plans for implementing an orientation program for newly appointed teachers.

To greet the new teacher, to make him feel at home in his job, and to provide him with help in becoming acquainted with the policies and problems of the school, several new procedures are employed. The plan is to select a school in each district in which newly appointed teachers will be oriented to their teaching responsibilities and helped to strengthen their personal qualities and teaching approaches during their probationary experiences. Each will have general supervision by an assistant superintendent and direct supervision by highly efficient teachers.

The in-service growth of the teacher begins with orientation procedures whereby self-reliance is developed through the gaining of an understanding of local practices and procedures. Orientation of teachers includes: (1) helping the teacher become acquainted with school routine and achieve adjustment to school relationships; (2) acquainting him with community attitudes, cultural backgrounds, and social and business life, and (3) giving him a thorough understanding of the school's aims, methods, and procedures.

The important objectives of orientation are to give the teachers who are new to a school the security of knowing what to do and when, and the feeling that the teacher and his family are a part of the school and community. In addition, orientation procedures should serve to unite the entire staff into one group that is working toward the fulfillment of the educational goals of the school.

Instead of trying to give too much material in too short a space of time, such as half a day, the orientation program is increased in many instances to a week. The more urgently needed orientation is given in one or two days before the regular school session begins, and a program of continued orientation is conducted throughout the first year. The procedures used vary with the seriousness of teaching-learning problems, the size of the school, and the number of new teachers involved.

Various procedures have been found to be helpful in providing for the orientation of the beginning teacher. Basic to all of them, however, are genuine friendly interest and helpfulness on the part of the administration, teachers, and community. A suggested program that might be helpful in the orientation of a new teacher to his duties in a small town having a population of about twenty thousand is presented here. It includes most of the considerations that need to be included in any good program of orienting a new teacher. The responsibilities of both community groups and faculty groups are included.

1. *Community groups may:*
   a. Assist in finding suitable living quarters.
   b. Introduce teachers to members of the community through receptions, picnics, or other special functions.

    c. Provide information about the economic and social life of the community.

    d. Invite teachers to join community organizations.

    e. Invite teachers to attend the church of their choice.

2. *Faculty groups may:*

    a. Introduce teachers to their professional associates.

    b. Appoint "big brothers" to familiarize new teachers with school routine.

3. *Preschool conferences or workshops may:*

    a. Clarify the teacher's responsibilities.

    b. Explain the school's objectives, program, organization, and routine.

    c. Find out the new teacher's special talents with a view of providing an early opportunity for their use.

4. *Community directories may contain:*

    a. Maps of the community and the district.

    b. Local bus schedules and routes.

    c. Lists of religious, medical, shopping, banking, and recreational facilities.

    d. Information on resources such as industries, civic leaders and facilities, historical spots, and visual aids.

5. *Faculty handbooks may contain:*

    a. School bus schedules.

    b. Special school regulations.

    c. Personnel policies of the board.

    d. Staff roster.

    e. Building floor plans.

    f. Class schedules.

    g. Fire and air defense instructions.

    h. Practical suggestions for class management.[1]

Professional growth of the teacher. The primary function of a teacher is to guide the learning of young people. This statement has been repeated several times in preceding discussions. In order to perform his major function adequately, he needs to keep abreast of the times, both culturally and professionally. Most men and women who enter the teaching profession are interested in furthering their professional growth.

    The authors recall a teacher who some forty years ago was teaching a fourth-grade class in an elementary school. She had been teaching that grade for thirty-five years. During that time, she had

---

[1] *The First Three Years of Teaching*, The State Education Department, Albany, New York, May, 1952, pp. 18–19.

taught several generations of the same families. Each succeeding generation had used the same textbooks and followed the same learning techniques. In many ways she was an excellent teacher. When it was decided to introduce a new and more psychologically organized arithmetic textbook for the fourth grade, however, she refused to use it and retired from teaching. She would have nothing to do with these new "fads and frills." Old books and old methods were good enough for her.

Teachers today display a very different attitude. They read educational journals. They become members of professional organizations; many teachers participate actively in one or two of these organizations. They attend national, state, and local educational conventions and conferences, and they, contribute to the programs.

They spend summers, evenings, or Saturdays in continued preparation toward meeting their duties and responsibilities. These efforts are encouraged by boards of education. Some school boards insist upon further study as a condition to be met for salary increments. Moreover, many teachers are motivated by their interest in keeping up with the newer educational ideas to avail themselves of the in-service courses that are offered by teacher-training colleges or schools of education, or by the more experienced members of the school staff.

Through in-service teacher education, not only can a teacher improve his knowledge or skill in the field of his present teaching, but he also can prepare himself for entrance into a school activity other than the one in which he now is employed. Many teachers who still are in their probationary period (usually the first three years) may wish to continue their study so that they may be recommended for tenure. To develop the attitude of study is one of the greatest assets of a teacher.

Teachers in large cities usually are more able to take advantage of in-service opportunities during the regular school year than are those who are teaching in smaller places. At present, this situation is being changed somewhat. Many of the universities, responding to the needs and interests of teachers, have organized extension courses which may be taken by teachers in their own city, sometimes in their own school building. The airplane has made it possible to offer such courses at centers that may be many hundreds of miles from the campus. To make certain that regular campus standards are maintained for these off-campus courses, several universities have established the policy of assigning their regular staff members to one or more of these extension courses as a part of a semester's teaching load. Other qualified, off-campus instructors also are used.

Library facilities of some off-campus courses are inadequate. Hence books need to be transported from long distances in order to provide the students with sufficient research and study material.

Membership in educational organizations. A teacher who has a professional attitude will want to join one or more professional organizations. The size of his salary limits the number of such organizations he is able to join. As a rule, a teacher should be able to afford membership in one national association, one state association, and one local association. In addition, he may find that he is able to be active in an association of his area of teaching. The *Educational Directory* (1953–1954) of the U. S. Office of Education lists approximately five hundred organizations that are national or regional in scope, and slightly more than one hundred that are statewide.

On the national level, the largest organization is the National Education Association, which is an organization of teachers, administrators, and others engaged or actively interested in educational work. Its announced purpose is, "To advance the interests of the teaching profession, promote the welfare of children, and foster the education of all the people." The power and influence of this organization are growing constantly. In 1918, the association numbered among its members approximately ten thousand. Since then its growth has been tremendous; its present membership is approximately seven hundred thousand; its goal is a membership of one million.

Each of these organizations includes various subdivisions or committees that are organized to meet the respective interests of school people. Alert, forward-looking teachers seek membership not only in the organization itself but also in a subdivision or committee. To join one of these organizations is not sufficient, however. Teachers who become known as educational leaders are active participants in the work of the organization. Some teachers join many organizations but are little more than dues-paying members. Other teachers are not affiliated with any organization, except perhaps a local group of which they become a member under administrative compulsion. Most teachers are active in these organizations, however. Many contribute to, as well as read carefully, the educational journals published by the various professional groups.

The Service Activities of the Teacher

The successful teacher-neophyte wants to follow teaching as his life's work. Hence he looks forward to the time when he has earned tenure. One of the most discouraging aspects of teaching is a lack of tenure. The emotional strain which many teachers have experienced has been great because the renewal of their contract was based upon the whim of a supervisor. Many states have enacted tenure laws that protect the teacher against unwarranted criticism or dismissal. As is true of certification, however, tenure rights are accompanied by certain teacher responsibilities. It is as important for a teacher as it is for a superintendent to respect the provisions of his contract. When all standards are maintained, including adequate preparation and good personal and professional relations, teaching rightfully can be considered to be a profession.

Teaching as a service. The keynote to any profession is its avowed purpose to give service to others. Teacher responsibility for pupil welfare has increased to the extent that the public is coming to recognize teaching as a profession. The behavior and attitude of the teacher determine the extent to which he receives the respect of parents and other members of the community, and of his professional colleagues. Long established professions such as law and medicine have codes of ethics to be respected by all their members. The National Education Association also has adopted a code of ethics that serves as a guide for the behavior of teachers. In this code the relations of the teacher to the profession are stated as follows:

Article III—Relations to the Profession

Section 1. Each member of the teaching profession should dignify his calling on all occasions and should uphold the importance of his services to society. On the other hand, he should not indulge in personal exploitation.

Section 2. A teacher should encourage able and sincere individuals to enter the teaching profession and discourage those who plan to use this profession merely as a steppingstone to some other vocation.

Section 3. It is the duty of the teacher to maintain his own efficiency by study, by travel, and by other means which keep him abreast of the trends in education and the world in which he lives.

Section 4. Every teacher should have membership in his local, state, and national professional organizations, and should participate actively and unselfishly in them. Professional growth and personality development are the natural product of such professional activity. Teachers should avoid the promotion of organization rivalry and devisive competition which weaken the cause of education.

Section 5. While not limiting their services by reason of small salary, teachers should insist upon a salary scale commensurate with the social demands laid upon them by society. They should not knowingly underbid a rival or agree to accept a salary lower than that provided by a recognized schedule. They should not apply for positions for the sole purpose of forcing an increase in salary in their present positions; correspondingly, school officials should not wait to give deserved salary increases to efficient employees until offers from other school authorities have forced them to do so.

Section 6. A teacher should not apply for a specific position currently held by another teacher. Unless the rules of a school system otherwise prescribe, he should file his application with the chief executive officer.

Section 7. Since qualification should be the sole determining factor in appointment and promotion, the use of pressure on school officials to secure a position or to obtain other favors is unethical.

Section 8. Testimonials regarding teachers should be truthful and confidential, and should be treated as confidential information by the school authorities receiving them.

Section 9. A contract, once signed, should be faithfully adhered to until it is dissolved by mutual consent. Ample notification should be given both by school officials and teachers in case a change in position is to be made.

Section 10. Democratic procedures should be practiced by members of the teaching profession. Co-operation should be predicated upon the recognition of the worth and the dignity of individual personality. All teachers should observe the professional courtesy of transacting official business with the properly designated authority.

Section 11. School officials should encourage and nurture the professional growth of all teachers by promotion or by other appropriate methods of recognition. School officials who fail to recommend a worthy teacher for a better position outside their school system because they do not desire to lose his services are acting unethically.

Section 12. A teacher should avoid unfavorable criticism of other teachers except that formally presented to a school official for the welfare of the school. It is unethical to fail to report to the duly constituted authority any matters which are detrimental to the welfare of the school.

Section 13. Except when called upon for counsel or other assistance, a teacher should not interfere in any matter between another teacher and a pupil.

Section 14. A teacher should not act as an agent, or accept a commission, royalty, or other compensation, for endorsing books or other school materials in the selection or purchase of which he can exert influence, or concerning which he can exercise the right of decision; nor should he accept a commission or other compensation for helping another teacher to secure a position.

Teacher-staff relationships. Included in the Code of Ethics are statements that emphasize the professional attitudes that should characterize teacher-staff relationships. No human being is perfect; there are certain to be differences of opinion and possible conflicts among the members of a group who work so closely with one another. Teachers want security in their profession, and they appreciate working conditions that include co-workers who are co-operative and superiors who are sympathetic. The personality of the teacher is important, not only in his relationship with his pupils but also in his relationships with his fellow teachers. Every teacher should experience sufficient security-status in his position so that bickerings and jealousies among teachers can be reduced to a minimum.

There is no place in the school for gossip. The light conversation of teachers as they meet during lunch period or in the school corridors should not be directed toward the bad behavior of pupils in the school. Individual pupils need to be discussed, at times; such discussions should take place during conference hours, and on an objective, impersonal basis. It is a professional responsibility of the teacher to do whatever he can to promote pupil welfare. Hence he should apprise appropriate staff members concerning pertinent data that are related to pupil adjustment. These data should never be broadcast among all members of the faculty, however.

It is not undesirable for a teacher to try to further his professional status; it is unprofessional for him to take an unfair advantage of a co-worker. For example, in order to make a good impression on the principal, a teacher presented evidence of her success in helping her children improve their handwriting. Her evidence consisted of the class's handwritten papers at the beginning of the year and those submitted by the children at the end of the year. The teacher failed to report that the children had written the first papers in great haste but had been warned by her to write the last papers carefully and in their best handwriting. Too often, teachers are tempted to bolster their own *egos* at the expense of the reputation of a co-worker. Sometimes, teachers engage in self-aggrandizing practices without malicious intent. The results of their behavior nevertheless are harmful.

The happy teacher is one who has the personality qualities that enable him to establish friendly relationships with all members of the school staff. The principal is the most important member of the school personnel from the standpoint of authority; hence the teacher should maintain a respectful attitude toward him and the authority he represents. There is a place for honest disagreement between the two on professional matters, however. The teacher should attempt, tactfully, to sell his principal on a plan, procedure, or idea that he believes will benefit the school, rather than criticize the principal adversely in the presence of other teachers, if the two are not in agreement concerning school matters.

For a school to be smooth-running, the teachers must function efficiently. If there is a guidance unit in the school, each teacher has some responsibility to it. The teacher who submits reports on time, attends required meetings, co-operates on matters that concern the school, and is punctual in attendance is an asset to a school and is effective in his classroom. If a teacher is sharply critical of school procedures, or of administrators and fellow teachers, it is likely that he is an inefficient and dissatisfied person.

Teacher attitudes in the classroom. Pupil-and-teacher relations are many-sided; pupils are a constant source of stimulation to the teacher. If the teacher shows leadership and if pupils have the ability to learn, the enthusiasm of the former stimulates young learners to appreciate the value to them of activities associated with learning. Teachers influence the dress, the conduct, the ideas, and ideals of developing individuals. The teacher's mode of thinking, speech, gestures, and interests inevitably exert their influence on learners. If a child admires and respects his teachers, he imitates their behavior consciously and deliberately. The responsibility for teachers to become worthy of imitation is great.

As a teacher works with children and adolescents, he lives within a pattern of professional responsibilities. Essentially, it is his responsibility to encourage a free play of mental activity on current controversial issues. Yet, he has the larger responsibility so to influence his learners that they become indoctrinated in the bases and framework of a democratic way of life.

The responsibilities of a teacher in his relations with pupils are set forth in the "Code of Ethics of the National Education Association of the United States" as follows:

Article I—Relations to Pupils and the Home

Section 1. It is the duty of the teacher to be just, courteous, and professional in all his relations with pupils. He should consider their individual differences, needs, interests, temperaments, aptitudes, and environments.

Section 2. He should refrain from tutoring pupils of his classes for pay and from referring such pupils to any member of his immediate family for tutoring.

Section 3. The professional relations of a teacher with his pupils demand the same scrupulous care that is required in the confidential relations of one teacher with another. A teacher, therefore, should not disclose any information obtained confidentially from his pupils, unless it is for the best interest of the child and the public.

Section 4. A teacher should seek to establish friendly and intelligent co-operation between home and school, ever keeping in mind the dignity of his profession and the welfare of the pupils. He should do or say nothing that would undermine the confidence and respect of his pupils for their parents. He should inform the pupils and parents regarding the importance, purposes, accomplishments, and needs of the schools.

A teacher's understanding of the accustomed thinking patterns of his pupils is important. He cannot assume that their experiences and interests parallel his own youthful attitudes. As a result of the rapid changes which are taking place on the local, national, and international scene, present situations are vastly different from what they were formerly. Consequently, some of the experiences of modern children are very different from the childhood and adolescent experiences of their teachers.

Today, teachers are working with learners who are stimulated constantly by what they read in the newspapers, hear on the radio, see on television or at the movies, or pick up on the streets. Some aspects of these media are undesirable. The present tremendous increase in juvenile delinquency may be caused by the attitudes that young people acquire from these asocial stimuli. The confused thinking that is found among adults inevitably is reflected in the attitudes of students.

The teacher himself is likely to possess certain biases or prejudices that have resulted from his experiences with media of communication. Regardless of what a teacher's point of view may be concerning controversial issues, it is his professional responsibility to encourage among his pupils an objective nonpartisan attitude toward such issues. It is unethical for a teacher to attempt to impose his opinion upon the thinking of young people in matters that deal with political, economic or social situations, conditions, or relationships.

Parent-teacher relationships. The National Congress of Parents and Teachers reports a membership of approximately six million. Parent-teacher associations are found in all communities throughout the United States. Although the attendance is voluntary, some teachers who attend such meetings do so under professional compulsion rather than because of their personal interest.

Parent-teacher associations and parent associations are exerting a positive influence on the schools. They are helpful in many ways: during a war period, parents help guard the school building from the entrance of any intruder; during the regular school year they assist the principal and the teacher in many ways and on many projects. If the school needs equipment that the board of education cannot provide out of its budget, the parent-teacher association can launch a project to raise the money. If the principal needs advice on policy, the leaders of the association usually are most co-operative in working together for the good of the entire school. We must not blind ourselves, however, to the possibility of the undue influence that a strong PTA can bring to bear on school policy if there is difference of opinion as to what the official policy of the school should be.

The teacher who wishes to confer with the parents of his pupils usually attends parent-teacher meetings, so that co-operation can be achieved. Some teachers accomplish their purpose of meeting parents through a systematic program of inviting parents to visit them at the school. This is not always possible, however; some working parents are not free to come to school during the day. Unfortunately, an open school night, when all parents are invited to visit the school to talk with the teachers of their children, may bring out only one of the parents; the other must remain at home to "baby sit."

Teacher community relationships. Teaching responsibilities extend beyond the reach of the four walls of the school building. Earlier, we referred to the experiences that are made available to students in pre-teaching education. The prospective teacher has a right to expect that the institution which prepares him to teach will equip him to enter his teaching activities with basic techniques to meet both his school and community responsibilities. Teachers need to understand and to accept the customs of the particular community in which their pupils have been reared.

The teacher in a small community has an excellent opportunity to become well acquainted with the families of his pupils. Therefore, he soon comes to understand family and community traditions and customary ways of doing things. In addition, the teacher is expected to participate in community activities. He also comes to know the occupational opportunities that are available in the community for the graduates of the school.

In large cities the situation is very different. Even though the teacher has lived in the city for many years, he may not be acquainted with the neighborhood conditions of the school in which he is teaching. More than that, the various schools of the city may be organized differently and may employ different teaching procedures. Hence, as a part of his pre-teaching educational experiences, the trainee should gain some knowledge of the school philosophy and the neighborhood customs of those areas of the city in which he may expect to teach.

This need of student-trainees is met partly by a program of community experiences. Through close contacts with the public schools and their parent-teacher associations, the college instructors can learn much about the various communities in which their graduates probably will teach. As a result of class discussions concerning these matters, the teacher-trainees can gain some insight into what they will meet when they start to teach. Their student-teaching experiences also are helpful.

There are many aspects of community life which the teacher can understand only when he is teaching in one of the schools of the community, however. Hence it is important that he participate in community or neighborhood activities. Through such participation he can gain the co-operation of parents and other community members. He can discover what the community has to offer young people in recreational facilities and occupational opportunities. Teacher-community relationships represent an important area of a teacher's professional activities.

Need for Teacher Self-Appraisal

Every professionally-minded teacher wants to succeed in his teaching activities and relationships. Even the best teacher may be tempted to continue routine behavior that, at one time, was satisfactory and satisfying. To avoid routine patterns of teaching attitudes and behavior, the teacher should keep alert to constantly changing educational theory and practice, as well as to cultural changes. Rather than to be overcritical of or overenthusiastic about new ideas, however, the effective teacher is open-minded concerning that which is good in either old or new philosophies or procedures.

A conscientious and service-minded teacher is interested in an evaluation of his teaching success, either through supervisor appraisal of his work or by means of his own self-appraisal. To help a teacher evaluate his professional worthwhileness, the utilization of the following questionnaire is suggested.

Teacher Improvement Questionnaire

Directions: This is a self-rating questionnaire for teachers. Examine your attitudes and present practices by responding honestly to each of the statements. Read each statement carefully. If the statement describes your customary attitude or practice, answer "Yes." Otherwise, answer "No."

1. I try to become acquainted with the interests, attitudes, and out-of-school activities of each of my pupils.
2. I am willing to admit, any time and any place, that I am a teacher.
3. I am willing to listen to the point of view expressed by a colleague.
4. I avoid criticizing a co-worker adversely.
5. I am willing to have other teachers visit my classes.
6. I try to visit another teacher's class in my school at least once a year.
7. I try to visit a class in another school at least once in five years.
8. I keep abreast of the newer methods of reporting to parents.
9. I contribute to professional literature.
10. I co-operate with teacher-education institutions in the education of new teachers.
11. I try to visit the parents of my pupils once each year.
12. I use audio-visual aids available in my subject field.
13. I am willing to try out teaching techniques used successfully by my fellow teachers.
14. I am willing to experiment with new curricula and teaching techniques.
15. I know about and am open-minded toward changes in educational policies and practices.
16. I participate in discussion during faculty meetings in my school.
17. I take at least one yearly in-service course.

18. I keep myself informed concerning the results of psychological and educational research.
19. I am an habitual reader of at least one educational journal.
20. I am a member of the National Education Association.
21. I am a member of one or a few educational organizations.
22. I participate in constructive community activities.
23. I spend some time each week in social and recreational activities.
24. I engage with fellow teachers in constructive professional discussions.
25. I participate in, or attend sports and other athletic activities.
26. I participate in wholesome social activities with persons who are outside the teaching profession.
27. I try to attend, yearly, at least four good plays and four musical productions.
28. I try to keep informed about current books and to read, yearly, at least three nonprofessional books.
29. I read, each year, and evaluate at least three current professional books.
30. I keep myself informed concerning new theories or practices in my special teaching field.
31. I co-operate with appropriate community agencies.
32. I try to be objective and friendly in my relationships with pupils, parents, and co-workers.
33. I recognize and fulfill my citizenship responsibilities, especially in the matter of voting.
34. I attend nonpartisan political meetings, and discover all that I can about candidates for political office, regardless of political affiliation.
35. I read several newspapers, daily, to keep informed concerning important happenings, and differing newspaper points of view.
36. I am selective in my choice of radio, television, and motion-picture programs.
37. I am alert to national, state, and local legislation.
38. I read regularly at least two unprejudiced magazines that deal with political, economic, and social conditions.
39. I am an active member of a religious organization.
40. I am keenly interested in the welfare of teachers in all parts of the country.

A teacher who could respond to each of these forty items with an unequivocally affirmative answer would be a "paragon of perfection." There probably are few teachers who find it possible each year to engage in all the suggested self-improving activities.

Some of the items represent the customary practices of many teachers, however. To *know* what to do can motivate one *to do*. As teacher-trainees read this list of items, they at least can resolve to start the practice of some of them before they begin to teach. Later, as teachers, they can concentrate on other self-improving activities.

QUESTIONS AND TOPICS FOR DISCUSSION

1. Justify the thesis that all teachers should keep themselves informed concerning the present social, political, and economic happenings.
2. Recall two of your teachers, one of whom you were very fond, another whom you may have disliked. Compare them from the point of view of background, flexibility of attitudes, and the like.
3. Discuss the advantages of observing the teaching of other teachers in the same grade or subject level.
4. Prepare a short essay on the topic: "The Best Teaching I Ever Had."
5. Outline a plan by which the facilities in the community in which you live can be utilized better by the school.
6. Discuss ways in which the civic and social organizations in the community can be of service in improving education.
7. Prepare summary statements of five recent articles in professional journals.
8. Arrange a conference with a community leader or with the head of one of the social agencies of a city. Be prepared to tell the class about the purposes, activities, program, and achievements of the organization.
9. Discuss the advisability of requiring all students who are preparing to teach to participate in experiences in community agencies of the kind referred to in the chapter.
10. State as many reasons as you can for requiring in-service education of teachers.
11. Study the aims and purposes of two local teachers' organizations. How do they differ?
12. What arguments can you present for and against joining the National Education Association?
13. What orientation did you experience upon your admission to high school? To the college you attended? To the school in which you are teaching?
14. How can an individual know whether or not he should teach?
15. What values can result from close adherence to a code of ethics for teachers?
16. Compare the requirements for teacher certification of any five states. What differences do you find among them?
17. In what ways can the teaching profession be helped by tenure laws?
18. To what extent should there be screening of candidates for teaching?

SELECTED REFERENCES

Burrup, P. E., *Teacher and the Public School System*, 3rd ed. Harper and Row, N.Y., 1972.

Carter, L. J., and Cheers, A. L., *Teaching-Learning Process*. Exposition Press, Jericho, N.Y., 1973.

Corey, G., *Teachers Can Make A Difference*. Charles Merrill, Columbus, Ohio, 1973.

Crow, L. D., *Introduction to Education*, 3rd ed. Christopher, North Quincy, Mass., 1974.

Day, T. F., *Teacher Retirement in the United States*. Christopher, North Quincy, Mass., 1971.

Deane, N., *Teaching with a Purpose: 1974 Impression*, 5th ed. Houghton Mifflin, Boston, 1974.

Gatti, D., and Gatti, R., *Teacher and the Law*. Prentice Hall, Englewood Cliffs, N.J., 1972.

Gorman, A. H., *Teacher and Learner: The Interactive Process of Education*, 2nd ed. Allyn and Bacon, Boston, 1972.

Hess, B. D., Croft, D. J., *Teachers of Young Children*. Houghton Mifflin, Boston, 1972.

Hilsum, S., *Teacher at Work*. Fernhill, N.Y., 1972.

Howe, R., *Teacher Assistants*. William C. Brown, Dubuque, Iowa, 1972.

Langdon, C., and Stout, I. W., *Teacher-Parent Interviews*. Prentice Hall, Englewood Cliffs, N.J., 1954.

Miller, W. C., and Newbury, D. N., *Teacher Negotiations: A Guide for Bargaining*. Prentice Hall, Englewood Cliffs, N.J., 1970.

Myers, D. A., *Teacher Power: Professionalization and Collective Bargaining*. Lexington, Maine, 1973.

NEA, *Teacher Tenure and Contracts*. NEA, Washington, D.C., 1973.

Ryans, D. C., *Characteristics of Teachers*. American Council on Education, Washington, D.C., 1960.

19   *Adjustment Aspects of Teaching*

The pattern of a teacher's interpersonal and intersocial relationships is many-sided. The effective teacher is able to adapt his personal preferences, interests, and modes of behavior to the stimulus-situations that constitute the social milieu of the school and the school community in which he serves. Unless a teacher understands and practices the principles of good mental hygiene, he may become the victim of various emotion-disturbing experiences. He constantly is beset by the demands of the young and of older individuals that he devote his time and energy to the meeting of their needs, interests, cultural mores, and educational standards. It is extremely important, therefore, that a teacher possess emotional stability and achieve adequate adjustment to the mental-health hazards inherent in teaching.

Personal and Social Adjustment of the Teacher

The person who aspires to become a teacher must be the possesser of definite qualities that will enable him to deal successfully with the problems of human relations. From morning until night, over week ends and during summer vacations, he constantly is concerned with those human relationships that are allied to his professional service.

Personal adjustments. There are personal qualities that serve well the individual who aspires to teach. It is difficult to enumerate these in isolation, since the total personality becomes vital to effectiveness of teaching. To the layman or to the college student, teaching appears to be a sinecure. The layman thinks of the school holidays; the student believes that teaching is an easy activity. He knows that he is right; he has been a student for many years and has observed how simple it is to carry out the responsibilities of a teacher. That is, he *knows* this until his first term of student-teaching. Then he comes face-to-face with the realization that if proper stimulation is given and adequate plans made for pupil motivation, a great deal of energy is required. He discovers that teaching actually is hard work.

The person who does not enter the teaching profession mainly for the purpose of earning a living is the one who has interest in others and in the affairs of the community and who has some enthusiasm for his work. The enthusiastic, purposeful teacher enjoys the opportunity to live a full and rich life as he works with his pupils, co-workers, and superiors, the parents of his pupils, and other community members.

Many personal qualities can be suggested as desirable for an individual who teaches. Among these qualities are included: good health, intelligence, good speech, flexibility, integrity, emotional stability, cheerfulness, courtesy, ability to get along with people, ability to do creative thinking, kindliness, co-operativeness, sense of humor, patience, sincerity, and enthusiasm. The list could be extended to include many other personal qualities, but those mentioned are sufficient to suggest the type of personal characteristics that predispose toward success in teaching.

Although professional qualities are related indirectly to personal characteristics, they also are important as representative of a good teacher. A good teacher is expected to help the pupil develop self-control, direct pupil study, maintain pupil interest, measure achievement, sponsor out-of-class activities, stimulate thinking, use community resources, master improved teaching techniques, use special teaching aids, motivate work effectively, and ask questions that stimulate thinking.

The desirable qualities of a teacher, both personal and professional, were described in the words of Henry Van Dyke when he paid tribute to the unknown teacher.

I sing the praise of the unknown teacher. Great generals win campaigns, but it is the unknown soldier who wins the war. Famous educators plan new systems of pedagogy, but it is the unknown teacher who directs and guides the young. He lives in obscurity and contends with hardship. For him no trumpets blare, no chariots wait, no golden decorations are decreed. He keeps the watch along the borders of darkness and makes the attack on the trenches of ignorance and folly. Patient in his daily duty, he strives to conquer the evil powers which are the enemies of youth. He awakens sleeping spirits. He quickens the indolent, encourages the eager, and steadies the unstable. He communicates his own joy in learning and shares with boys and girls the best treasures of his mind. He lights many candles which, in later years, will shine back to cheer him. This is his reward. Knowledge may be gained from books; but the love of knowledge is transmitted only by personal contact. No one has ever deserved better of the republic than the unknown teacher. No one is more worthy to be enrolled in a democratic aristocracy, "king of himself and servant of mankind." [1]

The good teacher is a worthwhile person. He has an excellent outlook on life. He is successful in meeting situations. A teacher's pleasures, joys, friendships, fears, enemies, prejudices, and his habits of speech and dress are as much a part of his teaching as any subject matter or method employed. His personal qualities aid or hinder him as he teaches both by example and precept.

The good teacher has the kind of integrity that helps him to do what is right rather than what may be expedient. Too many teachers, however, may be willing to take advantage of circumstances to promote their own interests. Teachers, like any other human beings, have their temptations. When they yield, they are cited as horrible examples, and rightly so, since the youth with whom they work are great imitators of behavior. The individual whose character is weak should not seek to teach, or he should be eliminated by the faculties of teacher-training institutions as they screen their candidates for admission.

The teacher is expected to have high ideals. His personal standards are to be worthy of imitation. Included among the qualities that represent high ideals are honesty, courage, charity, chastity, loyalty, and fairness. Personal standards, however, may lie somewhere between one extreme and the other. Few of us, including teachers, are absolutely loyal, charitable, and honest in all possible situations. Thus, there is a range in, and complexity of, moral and social standards.

Social and emotional adjustment. Teachers, like many other professional workers, are constantly in the public eye. They have countless opportunities to build up stimulating social contacts in their professional and civic relationships. Through teacher and other civic organizations, they experience challenging opportunities for leadership. Satisfaction results from working with others and from talking with their former students—those men and women whose lives they have influenced. Although teaching provides many

[1] Henry Van Dyke, "The Unknown Teacher," in *Journal of the National Education Association*, January, 1927, p. 15. Reprinted by permission of NEA.

opportunities for earning these and related rewards, a teacher should not expect his work alone to bring him complete social acceptance or complete personal satisfaction.

There is a tendency for teachers to share their social life almost exclusively with other teachers. Opinions differ concerning the extent to which they should fraternize with other members of their profession. Some believe that, in order to insure acquaintance with many life areas, the persons selected for social purposes should be men and women whose interests lie outside the teaching profession. Teachers tend to gossip about faults in their profession; if they are in the company of people engaged in other vocations, they are less likely to carry this idle talk very far.

Like other occupations, teaching has become more and more specialized. This has a narrowing rather than a broadening effect. Hence a teacher can gain in social stature by separating his school life from his social life. There are advantages, however, in continuing associations with other persons whose interests are similar to one's own. Teachers should make and hold friendships with their professional workers. Great satisfaction can result from close social contacts with other school personnel in spite of the fact that when they get together they tend to "talk shop." If they can elevate their conversation to the level of discussing broad educational issues, considerably more good than harm can be derived from their social life together.

Teachers need social relaxation in a form that takes them from their work. Among recreational activities that relieve nervous tension are activities such as: the cultivation of hobbies, enjoyment of dramatics, music, and traveling, and playing bridge or canasta. It is possible for good social adjustment to result from engaging in numerous out-of-school activities. If the teacher is interested in sports, continued study, research or writing, he expands his chance of meeting, in social situations, members of his profession other than those with whom he associates daily. Conflict and a general attitude of dissatisfaction with life may result if a teacher believes that he is hindered by the demands of his work from taking part in desired avocational activities.

Teachers resent having their social activities limited by the attitudes of the community in which they teach. We have moved a long way, however, from what formerly was expected from teachers in their private lives. At one time, the personal and social life of the teacher was given consideration to the extent that provisions concerning it were written into his contract. For example:

I promise to take a vital interest in all phases of Sunday-school work, donating of my time, service, and money without stint for the uplift and benefit of the community. I promise to abstain from all dancing, immodest dressing, and any other conduct unbecoming a teacher and a lady. I promise not to go out with any young men except in so far as it may be necessary to stimulate Sunday-school work. I promise not to fall in love, to become engaged, or secretly marry. . . . I promise to sleep at least eight hours a night, to eat carefully, and to take every precaution to keep in the best of health and spirits in order that I may be better able to render efficient service to my pupils.[1]

Few requirements of this kind are imposed today. Teachers are expected to meet ethical standards, be good American citizens, and co-operate in community activities. The teacher needs a restful and satisfying counterchallenge to his arduous and energy-consuming work of guiding wholesome and successful learning. If teachers are afforded social and recreational activities, they can continue to be enthusiastic and dynamic stimulators of learners in the classroom.

Importance of Teacher-Pupil Relationships

The major function of the teacher is to guide learners in acquiring knowledge and ways of behaving. The success of this guidance function rests upon many factors, important among which are the teacher's knowledge of the nature and needs of learners, and his understanding of the particular conditions that influence the learning process. For these there can be no substitute. Interest in children and in the activity of teaching also are important, yet it takes more than interest alone to assure success in teacher-pupil relationships.

Teacher attitudes toward pupils. The beginning teacher is faced immediately with the problem of giving direction to learning and to child behavior. New teachers, especially, discover that what has been learned in psychology courses can give only a mental orientation to the problems that arise in daily meetings with children. In spite of extensive research, there still are problem areas about which available data are inadequate. The teacher will bring to his job whatever background of training and experience he has gained so far, in terms of what psychologists believe to be correct training.

[1] Quoted by E. W. Knight in *Education in the United States*, 3rd rev. ed., Ginn & Co., Boston, 1951, pp. 360–361. Reprinted by permission.

This background of knowledge, enriched by whatever observational or other experiences the individual has had in working with children, constitutes the human equipment with which the teacher faces his class. As teachers gain greater understanding of the inner lives of their pupils, they become more sensitive to the conditions and situations with which the boys and girls of today are seriously concerned.

The teacher becomes a parent substitute, especially for the young child in school. The teacher should become the child's friend and earn the confidence of the young person. The child should be able to go to his teacher with his joys and his troubles; he should feel free to tell his teacher of his hopes and his fears; he should seek his teacher's advice, with the knowledge that he can anticipate sympathetic understanding and wise counsel.

Often it is wiser for a child to confide in a teacher than it is for him to take his problems to his parents. In spite of the friendliness of relatives, there usually is an objectivity in teacher-pupil attitudes that encourages wholesome behavior. The adolescent is concerned especially with what the thinking patterns are of the larger society to which he is attempting to adjust. He uses the teacher as an avenue of discovery as he attempts to find out what the teacher's attitudes are toward things in general and toward himself in particular. He looks to the teacher for security.

Improvement of teacher-pupil relationships. Teachers want to be admired and respected by their pupils. In order to achieve pupil-acceptance, the teacher needs to display those characteristics that were listed earlier. In order to exert a desirable influence upon learners, a teacher should give time and attention to improve his own personal assets to the end that they will exert positive rather than negative effects upon young people.

Many of the problems that are experienced by teachers in their relationships with their pupils are rooted in the many factors of influence that have been discussed throughout this book. In summary, the ways in which teacher-pupil relationships can be improved include: smaller classes; improved teaching procedures; more homogeneous grouping of pupils; greater teacher insight into young people's abilities, interests, and attitudes; more effective counseling services; and greater administrative, parent, and community co-operation. These conditions constitute ideal school situations. Budgetary allowances and other practical considerations often make it impossible to realize all of these ideals.

Teacher-Co-worker Relationships

Every organized teaching situation involves teacher-supervisor relationships. A supervisor is any person in authority who evaluates the work of the teacher in any way or gives assistance to him in the improvement of his teaching efficiency. Supervision also includes the evaluation of the effectiveness of learning outcomes and the offering of suggestions to improve learning conditions. The supervisor and teacher, therefore, work very closely together for the purpose of inspiring learners toward their best achievement.

Characteristics of a good supervisor. The act of supervising involves a personalized situation. Hence there is ever present in the situation the potential of clashes of attitudes, ideas, and interests, and even of personalities. Differences among teachers in personal ambitions, basic training and experience, and temperament sometimes have dynamic possibilities; under a weak supervisor these differences may destroy the effectiveness of supervision. A good supervisor will exhibit the traits that make him a welcome visitor to a classroom. He will have achieved a satisfactory degree of self-control, will be open-minded, and have a clear and broad perspective.

Among the personal qualities of a good supervisor can be listed: cheerfulness, courtesy, flexibility and integrity; emotional stability; ability to get along with people, and an understanding of social standards; ability to do creative thinking and to express ideas in good English, and a broad outlook that is coupled with leadership ability. Professional qualities include such understandings as are related to cultural background, evaluation techniques, and teaching procedures and processes. The supervisor also should possess the following qualities: ability to assist teachers with material and techniques, an attitude of liking and respecting young people, enthusiasm for the profession of teaching, tolerance toward the professional views of others, desire for self-improvement, and an attitude of justice and fair-mindedness.

A good supervisor demonstrates through his attitude and behavior that he possesses sympathetic understanding, is alert to the conditions and problems at hand, is willing to try to see the problem from the teacher's viewpoint, is inclined to give the teacher a second chance, and shows that he, too, can learn and improve. He attempts to be without bias and tries to be as eager to learn from those he supervises as he is to assist them in developing their techniques, attitudes, or points of view.

Teacher adjustment to supervisors. It is normal for teachers to want to be in the good graces of those who make judgments about them and who have the authority to assign them to various duties. For the most part, teachers tend to co-operate with their principals and other supervisors. Unfortunately, fear enters into the relationships between the teacher and his supervisor a great deal more than it should. The fault lies with both the supervisor and the supervised. The supervisor is in a position of authority and must take the lead in establishing good rapport between the two; the teacher is on the defensive.

If the supervisor's attitude is one of kindly concern for the welfare of his teachers and their pupils, and if the teachers recognize his suggestions as helpful in the improvement of their teaching techniques, they seek his advice and counsel. When the mental-set of the teacher toward supervisors is one of trust and sincerity, the supervisor has done much to establish a satisfactory relationship between himself and the supervised. Adjustment problems between the two will be reduced if the teacher is helped to maintain his self-respect at all times.

Among the situations that create conflict between teachers and supervisors are: (1) the extent to which the position was gained on merit, (2) the attitude of the supervisor toward many details of teaching and school management, (3) the extent to which the teachers are invited to participate in school policy-making, and (4) any display of favoritism on the part of the supervisor. Teachers resent supervisor appointments based upon political considerations. They are critical of supervisors who are consistent faultfinders. They wish to be able to offer suggestions for the policy of the school. They are easily disturbed at the overemphasis on the part of the supervisor of the excellent qualities of a favored teacher, especially if those qualities are ignored or overlooked in other teachers.

Teacher-teacher adjustments. The attitudes displayed by one teacher toward another reflect mainly the kind of school spirit that has been engendered by the administrative and supervisory officers of the school. In any group of people who are working together, there is likely to be some personality conflict. If all the teachers of the school are expected to assume their respective responsibilities, there need be little or no display, on the part of any teacher, of resentment toward another staff member. The inefficient or dissatisfied teacher, however, is likely to be in conflict with his co-workers as well as with his supervisors and pupils.

Aspects of Teacher Maladjustment

From time to time, articles appear in the newspapers concerning the large number of maladjusted teachers. Although the actual number of problem teachers is small, the fact that there may be even one in a school is enough to advertise that fact. Just as one bad apple in a basket is one too many, so is one maladjusted teacher in a school.

Many teachers possess personality qualities that are serious handicaps in their work. They may be too sensitive to warranted criticism, or they may become sarcastic and unfriendly in their school relations. These attitudes impair their effectiveness as teachers. Fortunately, the percentage of the mentally ill among the teaching profession is far less than that for the population as a whole. Nevertheless, the harm that can be done by an emotionally disturbed teacher is greater than that done by another person who is not responsible for the care and education of others.

Causes of teacher maladjustment. Teacher-training institutions are responsible for the preparation of persons who have teaching potential and who are well adjusted emotionally. Because the strains of teaching are severe, however, a well-adjusted beginning teacher may succumb to these strains, especially if he takes his job too seriously. During his working hours, a teacher is constantly under nervous tension. To be responsible for the behavior of others is a tension-producing situation, especially if the teacher is faced with great pressure from a supervisor. The teacher who worries or becomes anxious about possible failure to meet the standards set by the principal or the ideals he has set for himself may build up tensions within himself that become personally devastating.

Sometimes, a conscientious teacher allows attitudes of discouragement or of frustration to be built up because of his failure to help his learners perform successfully. Nervous strains are experienced particularly by a beginning teacher who is unsure of himself, who has not yet built up a reputation of being a good teacher, and who may be unduly afraid to earn administrative disapproval if mistakes are made. As he gains experience, he is able to take things in his stride and to allow himself time for relaxation.

The conscientious teacher is never totally free from the responsibilities of his job. He constantly seeks new ways to improve his work; he always is aware of the problems and interests of his pupils. To him, teaching is an all-day job; even his vacations are not completely free from his work. In the long run, it is worry, not challenging work, that may undermine the physical, the mental, and the emotional health of the teacher.

Many factors contribute to a teacher's apparent failure. If his first teaching experience has been in a situation that is an unusually difficult one, he may meet many problems that can hinder his personal and professional adjustment. For example, a teacher-trainee became so discouraged during her student-teaching experience that she decided to give up teaching. This girl was above average in her studies, possessed an attractive and winning personality, and was known for her co-operativeness and her generosity of time and energy in working with and for others. For her student-teaching she was assigned to a very difficult school and to one of the worst classes in that school. Although she had ability, she was not prepared to meet this situation. She became disheartened, her health failed, and she lost interest in teaching. She could not be convinced that the failure may have been in the situation, not in herself. A potentially good teacher was lost to the teaching profession.

The quality of leadership in a school is important to teacher morale and mental health status. Within two months, a principal who is nonunderstanding can cause half of his teachers to decide that they cannot work under his leadership. Recently, an excellent teacher, who has been known for her ability to work with various administrators, asked for a transfer to another school because of the policy, personality, and practices of a new principal who had been appointed to the school in which she had been teaching. "As is the principal, so is the school" has many facets. Unpsychological supervision may contribute greatly to the mental and emotional disintegration of a teacher.

With increasing years of service, a teacher may lose his earlier enthusiasm; his teaching becomes mechanical. He may seem to hate his work and his pupils. He may become an unhappy and frustrated martinet who continues his teaching as a matter of habit and as a means of earning a living. If a teacher develops into the type who has little control over his class, either he may be forced to give up the work or he may suffer a nervous breakdown. He may try to continue his teaching. He resents his young tormentors, yet he is incapable of remedying the situation.

The factors that contribute to the personal maladjustment of the teacher have been summarized in a research bulletin of the National Education Association. They suggest the following: "(1) overpressure of required work, (2) underpay, (3) insecurity of tenure, (4) constant sharing of the burdens of others, (5) puritanic restrictions on out-of-school activities, (6) repressive, autocratic administration and supervision, (7) aloofness on the part of the general public, (8) necessary attention to numerous details, and (9) the constant association with immature minds." [1]

Some teacher maladjustments. Fortunately, most teachers adjust to their work, their pupils, their supervisors, or any or all frustrating forces that can be found in the teaching situation. As teachers go about their duties, their attitudes are reflections of their experiential backgrounds. Whenever maladjusted behavior manifests itself in the classroom, the children are the victims and the ones who suffer most. In an attempt to discover significant examples of teacher maladjustment, the authors, over a period of many years, have collected examples of teacher maladjustment as these have been experienced by their college students during their earlier school years. Some of the cases reported by these teacher-trainees are pathetic and almost beyond belief.

We shall limit to a brief descriptive statement the content of some of the reported examples of maladjusted teacher behavior.

1. An elementary-school teacher refused to meet her class because she had been "told" by the spirits that she should not talk. She spent the school day in the school library until she was retired for mental disability.

2. A junior-high school teacher refused to perform a routine duty to which he had been assigned and threw his school keys into the principal's office. Pupils of this teacher reported that sometimes he acted queerly in class; he often stood at the window with his back to the class; he refused to answer pupils' questions; he repeated the same statement several times; he had the habit of giving a home-study assignment and, on the following day, insisting that the assignment was different from what he had told them.

3. A high-school teacher was accustomed to make derogatory remarks concerning the family, home conditions, and personality of a student who did not answer questions in the words or form desired, even though the answers were correct.

4. A third-grade teacher punished even the slightest infrac-

[1] *The Status of the Teachng Profession*, National Education Association, Research Bulletin, 1940, 18, No. 2, p. 71. Reprinted by permission.

tion of a class rule by requiring the miscreant to sit under the teacher's desk for several hours, or to stand with his arms raised for an hour or until he collapsed. She pasted labels over the mouth of a child who whispered, and strapped a child to his seat if he wriggled.

5. A high-school teacher could not tolerate staying in the same room for more than twenty minutes. He would assign "busy work" that required an hour or more to complete, and then leave the room. If all the work had not been completed when he returned at the end of the twenty minutes, he became violent. He threw books at the pupils, broke their pencils, and tore pages from their notebooks.

6. A junior-college instructor continually complained about the coldness of her classroom, even, during warm weather. She was accustomed to wear several sweaters or coats, one over the other. She would send for the custodian to repair the radiator in the room. When he arrived, she would accuse him of making "improper advances" toward her. She also told the women students to avoid men, but she embarrassed the young men in the class by her endearing remarks to them.

7. A high-school teacher either refused to turn in routine reports or delayed completing them for several weeks. She explained her behavior by insisting that "No one can order me around." She also was accustomed to leave her class and the school at any time during the day for "personal business." When she did this, she neglected to inform any administrative officer of her intention. She also contended that her students refused to do any work in her class, "just to spite me."

8. If one of the students in a certain high-school teacher's class were having difficulty with a problem in mathematics, the teacher would sit with the student at the latter's desk for an entire recitation period to make sure that the boy understood it. Meanwhile, the remainder of the class were allowed to do as they pleased. His response to a supervisor's objection to his conduct was: "I was taught to take care of individual needs!"

These descriptions of abnormal teacher behavior represent only a few of the many that could be presented. Some of the teachers described were sincere in their efforts to do what they thought was best for the learners. Two of them had been excellent beginning teachers. All of them were referred to mental hospitals for observation and therapy.

It is unfortunate that any child should be placed in a learning situation in which teacher behavior as described has dominated the classroom for a term or a year. Even allowing for exaggerations,

these reported experiences reveal the fact that a few badly maladjusted persons enter the teaching profession and continue in it.

In many instances the undesirable effects of teacher maladjustment
appear to be cumulative, since most of the causes are concerned
with older teachers. The toll of many years of experience is high
for those who are unable to withstand the occupational hazards
involved. Laymen rarely appreciate the amount of nervous energy
expended during a long teaching career by men and women who,
hour-by-hour, day-by-day, and year-by-year, attempt to mold the
lives of many young people, each of whom exemplifies a different
degree of learning ability and a different set of behavior patterns.

Preservation of Mental Health

Fortunately, teaching experiences generally are satisfying and
healthful, rather than disturbing and maladjustive. The dominant
reason for a person's entering the teaching profession is the fact
that he likes to work with young people. Although he may experience many tension-producing situations, the teacher who learns
how to diversify his activities during his out-of-school hours is
enabled thereby to maintain good mental health.

Effect of fear and worry. In spite of constant exposure in the classroom to disease potentials, the physical health of teachers is relatively good. In fact, good physical health is basic to good mental
health and to successful teaching. Fear and worry are the two factors that undermine a teacher's confidence and that may lead to
mental ill-health. Teachers must learn to exercise control of these
emotions in relation to disciplinary matters, and the principal of the
school should try to lessen or to remove the fears and worries in
order to motivate teachers toward better teaching. Teachers should
be stimulated to be as happy as possible in their work. There should
be little excuse for the utilization by an administrator of fear as an
inducer of teacher co-operation or of respect for authority.

The present provisions of teacher tenure have helped to reduce
the fear of loss of position because of the whims of a supervisor.
Teachers need the feeling of security that goes with the assurance
that they cannot be dropped from their positions if they find themselves in disagreement with their supervisors. This has helped to
bolster their self-esteem and to encourage a feeling of independence.

Developing a wholesome attitude. The teacher must adopt an attitude
of assuming responsibility for his vocational choice, his teaching

behavior, and his success. The forward-looking teacher is the person who does not try to place the blame for his shortcomings on others. The teacher who looks to himself first when things go wrong is the one who is likely to find a way to resolve whatever conflict, frustration, or other problems may be present. When the teacher believes that he is receiving what his efforts earn for him, he is developing the kind of personality that will absorb any difficulties he meets.

To be well adjusted, the teacher needs friends, he needs to have his work recognized and approved; above all, he needs to believe that he is attaining a satisfactory degree of success. Success in one's work is a great morale builder. The person who is stimulated by satisfying experiences as he works at his job is likely to have few adjustment problems. If the teacher keeps abreast of the new ideas in his field, if he reads the professional journals and books that suggest new ideas, and if he displays the attitude that he can improve his teaching, he is likely to develop the personal strength to parry the blows that otherwise would frustrate him.

Although teachers' salaries have not been large, a definite effort must be made not to spend more than is received. Most teachers who go into needless debt find that this tends to harass them at all times. An obligation to relentless debtors is a source of constant worry. Teachers should be careful not to borrow from co-workers or superiors; they should be just as careful not to lend to others. The relatively large number of teachers who are involved in badly-managed financial affairs is very discouraging. If proper attitudes are to be developed in the classroom, the teacher cannot afford to be burdened with worry, no matter what its cause.

The improvement in salaries, in pension provisions, and in recreational facilities has helped teachers to have a better attitude toward their profession. There still are aspects of their working conditions that disturb them greatly. Insufficient clerical help, inadequate equipment in the schools, lack of co-operation of their administrators in the handling of behavior problems, heavy pressure of work required, restrictions on outside activities, and the multiplicity of other details that they are expected to complete are frustrating factors. Any improvement in teaching conditions will improve the mental health of the teacher.

A teacher who suffers a blow to his self-esteem should try deliberately to compensate for it as soon as possible. He might do something that he will enjoy, especially if this previously has bolstered his self-esteem. If a difficult and fearsome experience is ahead of

him, such as teaching a lesson for critical evaluation, he might prepare himself thoroughly for it, including his skeleton plans for the
lesson. After this has been completed, he should turn to something
else that will absorb his thoughts and energy. When he is able to
relax, he demonstrates to himself that he has confidence in what he
is about to do. Of course, he cannot predict all that will happen
during a class session. These uncertainties are part of any lesson,
but the teacher who has fortified himself with thorough preparation is ready and able to meet these situations as they arise. Thus
can teachers avoid many experiences that otherwise might lead to
frustration.

Menninger offered the following suggestions to teachers as hints
on good mental health:

Staying Well Mentally

Although there is no sure-fire method for the prevention of
personality maladjustment, most people can maintain good
mental health. Mental health depends not on being free of
problems but on facing and solving them.

The most important factor in your personal happiness and
effectiveness is your ability to get along well with other people.
This ability really depends on whether you *can love* and *are
loved* more than you hate. And by love we mean family affection and friendship, as well as love of husband or wife. Difficulties and unhappiness almost always are related to the fact
that one does not give and receive enough love to balance
hate.

To be mentally healthy, and to help children attain good
mental health, you must get satisfaction from life. Satisfactions
come from filling your personal needs, from making wishes
come true. You can get satisfaction from creating a beautiful
product, from carrying out a plan, doing a worthwhile job, or
working toward an important goal.

The amount of satisfaction you get from life depends largely
on *your* own ingenuity and self-sufficiency. People who wait
for life to supply their satisfaction usually find boredom instead. You can achieve greater satisfaction if you:

Stand aside and look at how you may be contributing to
your own unhappiness. (You may be too dependent or too
aggressive).

Do something out of the ordinary now and then. Use your
imagination—explore new ideas and activities.

Make a serious effort to find ways of doing your main job
better.

Recreate and refresh yourself. The more fun you have in

your leisure, the better it is for you. Everyone needs time to do what he wants, with full freedom of conscience to be happy in his own way.

Develop the art of friendliness. Most of the joys of life, and sorrows, too, depend on how you get along with other people. Friends can be your greatest source of satisfaction—your strong support in times of crisis.

Finally, take a look at your life goals. If you have a goal that is high enough and worthy enough, your achievement will come with your growth toward emotional maturity.

You are emotionally mature to the extent that you:

Find greater satisfaction in giving than in receiving.

Form satisfying and permanent loyalties in give-and-take relationships.

Use your leisure creatively.

Contribute to the improvement of your home, school, community, nation, and world.

Learn to profit from your mistakes and successes.

Are relatively free from fears, anxieties, and tensions.

No one needs emotional maturity more than parents and teachers. We can hardly expect our children to be more mature adults than we are ourselves. If we hope to have a healthy, happier, more effective—*more mature*—next generation, we must come closer to maturity ourselves.[1]

Self-evaluation. The emotionally stable teacher is not impulsive. He attempts to solve his adjustment problems calmly and intelligently. He is willing to take some of the responsibility for difficulties that may arise in the teaching-learning situation. He examines himself and his behavior to discover wherein he has failed to gain pupil cooperation. Usually, these self-examinations are relatively haphazard. A teacher probably could do a better job of self-evaluation if he were to utilize a list of specific questions concerning his personal and professional equipment. A monthly evaluation on a check list such as the one on pages 519 and 520 may add to teacher satisfaction and effectiveness.

If the teacher is frank in his responses to these questions, he is likely to become aware of his shortcomings and to improve his teaching through correcting as many of them as he can. The enthusiastic and friendly teacher is the teacher who is admired by children. Various studies have been made concerning teacher traits that

[1] W. C. Menninger, "Self-understanding for Teachers," *National Education Association Journal*, Vol. 42, No. 6. September, 1953, p. 333. Reprinted by permission.

PERSONAL AND PROFESSIONAL QUALITIES
OF A TEACHER

	Below Average	Good	Excellent
Personal Qualities			
Attitudes, and interests			
Are you accurate and dependable?			
Are you optimistic and cheerful?			
Are you friendly and co-operative?			
Are you kind and emotionally stable?			
Are you enthusiastic and forceful?			
Are you adaptable and open-minded?			
Are you sincere and loyal?			
Are you resourceful?			
Do you possess a sense of humor?			
Do you exhibit a sense of justice?			
Are you tactful?			
Are you industrious?			
Are you, in general, a sociable person?			
Are you interested in children?			
Are you interested in teaching?			
Personal appearance			
Do you wear clothes that are clean, pressed, and free from unpleasant odors?			
Do you wear clothes that fit you and are attractive?			
Do you make sure that your handkerchief is clean and fresh?			
Do you give proper care to your hair?			
Do you give proper care to your teeth?			
Do you stand and sit according to correct posture?			
Speech qualities			
Is your voice quality adequate?			
Is your rate of speech neither too fast nor too slow?			
Do you pronounce words correctly?			
Do you use proper inflection?			
Is your voice properly modulated?			
Professional qualities			
Do you stimulate pupil interest?			
Do you stimulate pupils to think?			
Do you provide for individual differences?			
Do you measure pupil achievement?			
Do you sponsor out-of-class activities?			

PERSONAL AND PROFESSIONAL QUALITIES
OF A TEACHER
(Continued)

	Below Average	Good	Excellent
Professional qualities (*Continued*)			
Do you assist pupils toward achieving good study methods?			
Do you develop pupil self-control?			
Do you possess an excellent subject-matter background?			
Do you make adequate preparation for each day's work?			
Do you know and use improved teaching techniques?			
Do you keep informed on current social and political affairs?			
Do you utilize community resources?			
Do you show an interest in community affairs?			
Do you give appropriate home-study assignments?			
Do you formulate good questions for class discussion?			
Do you strive for self-improvement?			

are liked by learners. Among the most significant qualities are those in the area of human relations; students like teachers who are friendly, good-natured, interested in learners, attractive in appearance, and who have a good sense of humor.

The public provides schools for the benefit of learners, and teachers are employed for the purpose of guiding the learners. Good human relations should be established between teachers and learners as soon as possible. Except on the college level, learners seldom have an opportunity to choose their teachers; classes are organized and qualified teachers are assigned to teach the learners in them. Personality clashes may arise between teachers and pupils. However, if the teacher's attitude is objective but understanding, most conflicts that arise in the classroom can be resolved easily.

Value of Satisfaction in Teaching

First of all, a teacher should earn enough money to provide for himself and his family the necessities and some luxuries of life. Fortunately, there are many satisfactions in teaching that extend far beyond those of monetary returns. William Lyons Phelps attempted to set forth some of the reasons for young people to want to teach, when he wrote the following:

> I do not know that I could make entirely clear to an outsider the pleasure I have in teaching. I had rather earn my living by teaching than in any other way. To my mind, teaching is not merely a life work, a profession, an occupation, a struggle: it is a passion. I love to teach. I love to teach as a painter loves to paint, as a musician loves to play, as a singer loves to sing, as a strong man rejoices to run a race. Teaching is an art—an art so great and so difficult to·master that a man or a woman can spend a long life at it, without realizing much more than his limitations and mistakes and his distance from the ideal. There never has been in the world's history a period when it was more worthwhile to be a teacher than in the twentieth century; for there was never an age when such vast multitudes were eager for an education or when the necessity of a liberal education was so generally recognized. It would seem as though the whole world were trying to lift itself to a higher plane of thought.[1]

The prestige inherent in professional status and the opportunities afforded for service to others provide the inner satisfactions to an individual that motivate him or her to be willing to engage in teaching, even if its monetary rewards are not so high as those in other occupational areas. The sheer joy that comes from working with children or older learners offers its own rewards. The receiving of words or other signs of appreciation from those who have been one's students comes as a source of satisfaction to the receiver. For example the following note speaks for itself as an illustration of the intrinsic rewards of teaching. A teacher who had completed a graduate program of study in guidance wrote:

> It seems as though there are many things to thank you for as a result of my attendance at ——— College. However, what seems to stand out is your faith in my ability to go on and your encouragement when things seemed overwhelming. When I look back now and wonder how I did it, I know you played a large part in it. The last six months, especially, I was nearer the giving-up point than at any other time. So many other things seemed working against me. I am happy now that I kept going—if for no other reason than that I feel much more secure in my daily work. Certainly here, too, you have given us a pattern of what guidance really is.

[1] Edwin A. Lee (ed.), *Teaching as a Man's Job, Phi Delta Kappan,* Bloomington, Ind., 1938, p. 56. Reprinted by permission.

Probably, many teachers of the past and present have felt more than repaid by the receipt of such expressions of gratitude for the energy they have expended because of their great interest in the younger or older learners with whom they have worked. Sometimes, young people hesitate to express their appreciation of a teacher's efforts in their behalf, lest they appear to be seeking continued help from the teacher. Other boys and girls do not want to call special attention to themselves for fear that schoolmates may interpret any such expressions as attempts to gain teacher favor. However, teachers appreciate receiving sincere expressions of gratitude from their pupils. Such experiences represent intrinsic teaching rewards and help a teacher maintain good mental health.

QUESTIONS AND TOPICS FOR DISCUSSION

1. Name several excellent teachers in your state; nation. Come to class prepared to support your choices.
2. Name several past or present outstanding teachers of your school. What reasons can you give for their success?
3. What do you believe are the greatest rewards in teaching?
4. In what ways do high ideals and sound character aid a teacher?
5. Prepare a list of personality traits of a successful teacher.
6. List the personality traits of the teacher liked best by you.
7. Describe the maladjusted behavior, if any, of a teacher you have had. What effect did his behavior have upon you and the other members of the class?
8. Evaluate the social status of teachers in your community.
9. Give arguments for and against a teacher's promotion to a position of authority in the school in which he has been teaching.
10. Who is the best judge of a teacher's efficiency: himself, his students, or his supervisors? Explain.
11. Why are rest and recreation so important to a teacher?
12. Why are good professional relationships among the school staff important?
13. To what extent should a teacher stand up for his ideas relative to school policy that directly affects him in his class work?
14. What professional faults exist among teachers?
15. To what extent should teachers participate in the meetings of parent-teacher groups?
16. To what extent should teachers seek or accept the confidences of their pupils?
17. Name the traits that you would like to find in a supervisor.
18. What supervisor traits are disliked by teachers?
19. Why do teachers sometimes believe that supervision is less difficult than teaching?
20. Evaluate yourself on the teacher-rating scale in the chapter.

SELECTED REFERENCES

Bernard, H. W., *Mental Health in the Classroom*. McGraw-Hill, N.Y., 1970.

Brubaker, D., *Teacher as Decision Maker*. William C. Brown, Dubuque, Iowa, 1970.

Crow, L. D., *Psychology of Adjustment*. Knopf, N.Y., 1967.

Drayer, A., *Teacher in a Democratic Society*. Charles Merrill, Columbus, Ohio, 1970.

Greene, M., *Teacher as Stranger: Educational Psychology for the Modern Age*. Wadsworth, Belmont, Calif., 1972.

Jennings, H. H., *Sociometry in Group Relations*, rev. ed. American Council on Education, Washington, D.C., 1960.

Jourard, S. M., *Personal Adjustment*, 2nd ed. Macmillan, N.Y., 1963.

Keezer, W. B., *Mental Health and Human Behavior*, 3rd ed. William C. Brown, Dubuque, Iowa, 1971.

Rosenshine, B., *Teaching Behaviors and Student Achievement*. Fernhill, N.Y., 1971.

Simpson, R. H., *Teacher Self-Evaluation*. Macmillan, N.Y., 1966.

Spadek, B., *Beaching in the Early Years*. Prentice Hall, Englewood Cliffs, N.J., 1972.

Washkin, Y., and Parrish, L., *Teacher-Pupil Planning for Better Classroom Learning*. Pitman, N.Y., 1967.

Wechsler, H., et al, *Social Psychology and Mental Health*. Holt, Rinehart & Winston, N.Y., 1970.

Wenar, C., *Personality Development from Infancy to Adulthood*. Holt, Rinehart & Winston, N.Y., 1971.

Wiggins, J. S., et al, *Psychology of Personality*. Addison-Wesley, Boston, 1971.

20 Teacher Counseling and Learner Adjustment

Throughout our discussions of the learning process and learner adaptation to learning requirements, situations, and conditions, we refer to the teacher's responsibility *to guide* the learner toward the achievement of successful learning outcomes. To the uninitiated, "learning" usually is interpreted to refer to the memorization of factual material and, less often, to the acquiring of necessary skills. To the psychologist and educator, to learn implies the development of or improvement of all the reactions that constitute an individual's behavior patterns in every area of life activities. Hence guidance and counseling are significant aspects of teacher responsibilities.

Adjustment Problems of the Learner

We know that a growing young person, without adult assistance, cannot attain satisfactory adjustments to the demands that are made upon him by the factors and forces inherent in his physical environment and his cultural milieu. Each learner represents a unique personality: a total of potentialities, needs, wants, interests, and background experiences. Every child or adolescent, therefore, must be aided to learn whatever he can learn, in whatever way is best for him to learn, for the purpose of becoming a personally and socially adjusted member of his group or groups.

The general purport of our treatment of human development in relation to the learning process has been to stress the reasons for and the ways in which individual learners can be stimulated toward satisfactory and satisfying adjustment to life requirements. In this chapter is presented a pinpointing overview of the teacher's responsibility to meet individual learner needs, the various methods or techniques that can be utilized to implement the task, and the school personnel and outside agencies that share with the teacher the responsibility of assisting learners to resolve problems of adjustment. These problems center primarily (1) around one or more phases of a person's life pattern, and (2) in one or more major areas of experience. Problems of adjustment that are rooted in personal

524

characteristics and problems associated with environmental situations and conditions do not represent a dichotomy, however. A young person's abilities, attitudes, and overt behavior reflect the interrelationship that exists between personal characteristics and experiential situations and conditions.

Problems associated with personal characteristics. A young person's progress may be retarded by poor adjustment or lack of adjustment to learning situations that is caused by the presence of a problem which is associated particularly with one or more of the following personal characteristics or conditions: physical condition or health status, intelligence level, degree of emotional control, habitual attitudes, social and vocational interests and ambitions, ethical standards and appreciation of religious values, and accustomed modes of overt behavior. Rarely does any one of these personal characteristics, of itself, function as a problem stimulator.

Habitual behavior, insofar as it is not acceptable to the other members of the individual's class or school group, can reflect the presence of a problem that needs to receive attention from the teacher or from other school personnel. In Chapter 8 are considered some of the more common behavior "problems." If we attempt to discover the underlying causes of these problems, however, we find that overt behavior patterns are the resultants of problem conditions within the individual. These are related to one or more of the characteristics that are listed here.

What has been said about behavior refers also to problems that are rooted in habitually displayed antisocial or self-referred attitudes. The interrelations and interactions of a learner's personal characteristics are potent factors of learner adjustment and maladjustment.

Problems associated with areas of experience. When or if a child or adolescent gives evidence of suffering from one or another personal adjustment problem, he needs help in its resolution. If the problem is the resultant of a serious physical handicap, or of extremely retarded mental status, he needs to learn how to meet life requirements insofar as his physical or mental limitations permit him to do so. If the problem is functional rather than organic, emotional reconditioning is as important as, if not more so than, the improvement of motor skill, conceptual understanding, or creative expression. Those teaching techniques and learning approaches associated with the solving of personal problems differ from those applied in more "academic" teaching-learning situations in that they should be more personalized than they are in other areas of learning, and that there may be greater necessity to relate the problem to factors that are inherent in home, school, work, and/or social experiences and relationships.

Home conditions. Many of the adjustment problems of young people seem to reflect unhygienic home conditions. Parental attitudes and home and family situations that may lead to a young person's experiencing problems that need resolution include: family jealousies and dissensions; overindulgent, indifferent, or too strict parents; frequent moving of the family from one section of the city or country to another; too many or too few home duties; differences in ethical standards or religious affiliations among family members; low moral status; lack of home co-operation with the school or the community; homes broken by divorce or the death of a parent; homes that represent a culture that is foreign to that of the school community, and extremely low socio-economic status.

The first six years of a child's life are very important. Hence the six-year-old child who is a product of a home in which there are maladjustive factors is likely to reflect these unfavorable home conditions in undesirable attitudes and behavior patterns. Yet, teachers sometimes are amazed at the extent to which a child's undesirable habit patterns can be reconditioned through the efforts of understanding teachers. At the same time, home influences may be so strong that there is little that teachers and counselors can do for the child unless he can be removed from unhealthful home surroundings. In most states, the parents have the legal right to decide where their child shall live. Hence school people are helpless in such situations unless, by court action, the child is placed in an institution or foster home because of extreme parental neglect of or cruelty to the child, or gross immoral behavior on the part of one or both parents.

School experiences. A learner may experience difficulties in adjusting satisfactorily to his learning experiences for one or more of several reasons. Some of these interfering factors can be and are overcome with the help of teachers who are alert to disturbing influences. With the aid of the administrative officers and counselors of the school, a teacher may be able to encourage whatever changes are needed to help the learner make a better adjustment to his learning activities. Other learner problems may represent a complex of conditions that cannot be improved by the school without the assistance of parents or other community agencies.

There are certain common situations or conditions that have been found by teachers to retard or to interfere with a young person's satisfactory adjustment to learning requirements. Among these are: lack of interest in school work or in specific school subjects; school curricula that are not graded appropriately to the learner's level of intelligence; too much or too little teacher assistance; poor study habits; too long or too difficult home-study assignments; too much or too little competition among learners in terms of ability to compete; fear of failure; learner-teacher antagonisms; inadequate home-study conditions; too much or too little participation in the school's sports program or other cocurricular activities, or out-of-school social activities; uncertainty about, or parent-child conflict concerning, vocational choice and preparation, and too great or too little parental interest in the child's school activities or learning progress. Some of these problems are experienced especially by secondary-school learners; some of them result from learner attitudes that have their roots in home-stimulated recognition of what should constitute desirable life values.

One of the most important functions of teachers and school counselors is to recondition the attitudes of some young people toward an appreciation of the value to themselves of achieving success in whatever educational opportunities are made available for them. Occupational requirements, social pressures, and educational encouragement are responsible for the fact that the upper limit of compulsory school attendance now ranges between the ages of sixteen and eighteen. There is a trend toward a school-leaving age of eighteen, except in emergency home conditions or in the case of a learner's giving evidence of inability to profit from further formal school learning. In every secondary school, however, can be found boys and girls whose one ambition is to leave school for a job, even though they are not yet prepared to perform adequately in any kind of job. Youth attitudes of this kind place upon school people the responsibility either to try to change a young person's attitude toward the value of education, or to offer a vocationally pointed curriculum that will prepare him for a job in which he has some chance of success.

Problems of occupational adjustment. Relatively simple or extremely serious vocational problems are encountered by most adolescents. Assistance in a solution becomes the responsibility of high-school personnel. The first step, of course, is for the young person to decide upon an occupational field in which he is interested. Hence counselors and teachers need to acquaint him with available work opportunities. They then try to guide his interest into one or another field, in terms of his degree of intelligence and special aptitude, opportunities for obtaining training toward meeting specific job requirements, and available openings for entrance into the field of the young person's choice.

Vocational counseling is not easy. Problems that may arise both for the counselor and the counselee deal with one or more of the following: indecision of the young person concerning which field to enter (he may be interested in many occupations, or in none); too low or too high vocational ambitions in relation to possessed ability; parental interference; strong personal interests; insufficient, ineffective, or prejudiced teacher counseling; inadequate opportunities for appropriate training, or too high cost of training; oversupply of workers in a chosen field; difficulties of job application or individual inability to meet job requirements, especially in the areas of adaptability to supervision of work activities or worker-worker relationships. School people may succeed in helping a young man or woman select, prepare for, and obtain a job. The counseling task is not completed unless school counselors follow up their former students' degree of success on the job and help them solve their occupational problems until the young workers give evidence of mature and satisfying adjustment in their work activities.

Problems related to social and civic adjustment. There are still some vocal groups of taxpayers who raise strenuous objections to the "wasting" of public monies on what they call educational fads and frills. The school activities about which these citizens usually complain are the opportunities now being provided by most schools for learner participation in out-of-class social gatherings, such as school-sponsored dances and parties, intramural sports, and civic projects that take them out of the school into the community. Present educational philosophy is concerned with teaching the *whole child.* Learning activities, therefore, cannot be limited to classroom mastery of subject matter and skill improvement.

Every individual needs to know his community and be prepared to perform his citizenship duties adequately. From childhood through all of his adult years, he will be concerned about his relationships with his fellows. Hence he needs to experience school situations in which he learns to participate with his peers and elders in social projects that are similar to those in which he now engages outside of school, and which he will continue to experience during all of his life span. School people are giving an increasing amount of attention to these areas of learning. Yet, attitude or behavior differences among young people may lead to problem-arousing conditions that include: intolerant or asocial attitudes; unwholesome relations between the sexes, or lack of association with the opposite sex; excessive or insufficient participation in the school's out-of-class activities; unwise choice of commercially organized recreational activities, or overparticipation in them; insufficiency of community-sponsored recreational activities, and apathy toward school citizenship responsibilities or undesirable attitudes or behavior in relation to them.

Adult attitude toward problems of adjustment. We repeat for emphasis that any adjustment problem experienced by an individual of any age is not caused by only one factor of influence that lies either within the total personality pattern or in his areas of experience. Many people fail to recognize the interrelationships that exist among all the inner and external elements that are provocative of satisfactory or unsatisfactory life adjustments.

During a discussion of juvenile delinquency, for example, questions concerning the causes of young people's asocial attitudes and behavior are certain to arise. Each discussant is likely to become emphatic in his explanation of youthful escapades in terms of *one* factor which may be: divorce of parents, lax discipline in school, excessive attendance at motion pictures, too much free time, too few community-organized recreational activities, low economic status, too high economic status, poor biological heritage, corrupt government, adult example of self-indulgence or crime, or any other *one* cause that, to the individual giving it as a reason for all delinquency, seems to be the obvious or superficial factor of a particular situation that has come to his attention.

Some teachers who are studying to become school counselors give evidence of a similar lack of insight concerning the complex nature of the factors that are basic to problematic situations, as these are experienced by children, adolescents, or adults. As a means of alerting their students to these complexities of interacting elements, the authors are accustomed to ask their students, in a course on principles and practices of guidance, to prepare anecdotal reports of problems of adjustment, each of which appears to be rooted in *one* specific maladjustive factor. The students soon discover, as they prepare their reports and then discuss them in class, that not one cause but many possible causes may seem to operate toward the arousal of a problem of adjustment. They also become aware of the fact that a specific situation or condition that is considered generally to be a significant factor of maladjusted behavior may be a motivator of undesirable behavior for one individual but may serve as a challenge to another to overcome the difficulty and thereby strengthen his character.

Another phase of the project referred to in the preceding paragraph deals with what can be done by the teacher or counselor to remove or to ameliorate unfavorable experiential conditions or to help in the reconditioning of attitudes or behavior. As a result of discussions concerning specific and general therapeutic techniques, these graduate students, many of whom are experienced teachers, invariably come to the conclusion that there is no easy remedy for the improvement or cure of a problematic adjustment situation. They agree that desirable changes can be effected only by means of parent-school-community co-operation, careful administration of valid and appropriate evaluating techniques, and expert counseling.

Psychological and Educational Aspects of Counseling

Whenever or wherever individuals live together as a group, there can be found among them one or a few of the members who are especially able and willing to help other members solve their problems. Since the beginning of formally organized education, there have been teachers to whom young people have brought their problems for the help that, through actual or vicarious experience, they had discovered would be given them. There are teachers and other adult leaders who, without special training, appear to be sensitive to difficult situations and conditions and to display an exceptional power to understand problematic situations and keen insight concerning ways in which problems may be resolved.

There are limits to the help that can be given by any one person in the meeting of all of the many kinds of adjustment problems that may occur, however. Informally given, friendly advice or counseling can have great value in some instances. When they need it, young people should receive the kind of help that can be offered only by trained teacher-counselors who are working in the framework of a functionally organized program of guidance and counseling services.

The counseling attitude. Throughout the discussion to this point, the word *help* has been used to connote that which the teacher or counselor does in relation to a young person and his problem. Other suggestions follow. However, the adult does *not* direct; he does *not* tell the child or young person what he would do if he were in the other person's situation. The teacher-counselor does *not* scold or express sentimental sympathy; he does *not* display shock, disgust, or any other strong emotional reaction.

What does he do? Through what he says and refrains from saying, or through what he does and does not do is evidenced a recognition of the fact that the problem is the young person's problem and that only he can solve it, except for the removal or amelioration of situations or conditions that are outside his power to control. If unfavorable environmental elements can be changed, it is the responsibility of the home, the school, and the community to do something constructive about the situation. If nothing can be done to remove or mitigate undesirable external factors, the problem of adjusting to these conditions remains the responsibility of the young person himself. The counselor can do no more than to motivate the young person to "grin and bear it."

The guidance point of view. Educationally, we are committed to the point of view that the learner and his needs constitute the core of a school's teaching and administrative activities. The meeting of many of a young person's needs centers around what can be and is done for him by way of the teaching-learning process that takes place in the classroom. Classroom activity represents only one area of school responsibility, albeit a very important phase of the child's or adolescent's learning experiences. Everyone associated with the school shares with every other member of the school personnel the function of helping each pupil to achieve self-dependence, self-control, and self-realization, within the framework of the home, the school, and the community.

The guidance point of view refers to the kind of attitude displayed and the kind and amount of assistance provided by every member of the school staff, in conjunction with other community leaders. The help given should be best fitted to meet any one or more of the problems of individual learner adjustment that were listed earlier in the chapter. The implications of the guidance point of view can be summarized briefly thus:

> According to the guidance point of view . . . the school helps to bring to bear on the individual those influences that stimulate and assist him, primarily by his own efforts, to develop to the maximum degree consistent with his capacities. In other words, the institution offers activities and employs procedures through which the individual is encouraged to make the most of himself.

In line with the guidance viewpoint, the school recognizes that the effectiveness of the entire group depends upon the effectiveness of each individual who is a member of that group. If the individual is not achieving as well as he might, he to that extent handicaps the development of the group as a whole.[1]

We now can ask ourselves what is meant by *guidance* as a function of the school. Stated simply, guidance can be interpreted to include whatever is done for an individual to *help* him in the solution of whatever difficulties or problems he may encounter in any area of his life activities, and relationships, and (insofar as it is possible) to *prevent* the arousal of any such difficulties or problems. In another discussion of the functions of guidance and school counseling, the authors have said:

> Education interpreted either as *process* or *product* is an *individual* matter. The child, adolescent, or adult himself must make the changes within himself which he recognizes to be desirable. The function of the teacher can be no more than to make available to the learner opportunities of value to him in his self-education. He needs to be stimulated to want to learn, to be helped to discover what things he should learn, and to be encouraged to progress satisfactorily in his learning. The educational process takes place within the individual, and educational products are evidenced in his behavior.
>
> What then is the relation of guidance to education? Guidance constitutes those factors *outside* the individual that are made available to him in his own search for self-development. In its broadest connotation, guidance can be regarded as a form of education. In its more specific interpretation, it includes all those techniques of counseling and all those bodies of information that can help the individual to help himself.[2]

It is evident that guidance services (1) require that guidance and counseling be organized in such form that duplication of effort and activity is eliminated or reduced to a minimum, (2) begin early in the child's educational experiences, and (3) represent some areas of assistance that are common to all educational levels, but include other services that are peculiar to specific age and school levels, in terms of specific activities and approaches.

[1] J. A. Humphreys, and A. Traxler, *Guidance Services*, Science Research Associates, Chicago, 1954, p. 7. Reprinted by permission.
[2] L. D. Crow, and A. Crow, *An Introduction to Guidance*, 2nd ed., American Book Company, New York, 1961, pp. 16–17.

Importance of organizational plan. Informal counseling has value. The help that is given by an interested and understanding teacher or other adult may stimulate a young person to make wholesome changes in his attitudes or modes of behavior. This is especially true if a difficulty is related to a specific situation not rooted in fundamental personality deficiencies or damaging environmental conditions. However, no *one* teacher has the ability or the authority to provide the kind of school climate that is conducive to the prevention of pupil-problem arousal. In fact, not even a guidance-minded administrator can establish a completely wholesome or hygienic school atmosphere, unless he is able to obtain the intelligent and cheerful co-operation of *every member of the school personnel*, including the teachers, administrators, special counselors, clerks, and custodial staff.

Robert H. Mathewson, the Program Director of the Graduate Guidance and School Counseling program of the four Colleges of the City of New York, wrote:

> Authorities are in agreement today as to underlying principles and as to what constitute desirable practices in guidance and counseling. Roughly, this common core of professional belief may be designated as the pupil personnel point of view, with guidance services in a prominent, if not central, position of responsibility in the pupil personnel organization of the school and system. Guidance provides individual service to all children and deals with a core of commonly recurring needs and problems in the process areas of: Self-understanding, direction and development; personal-social adjustment, educational and vocational orientation. The chief guidance processes are: appraisal, interpretation and recording of individual characteristics and needs; analysis and evaluation of needs, problems and other aspects of individual persons and situations; counseling and other forms of personal intercommunication for educative ends; special forms of group work; collection and use of information; co-ordination of organized procedures and processes so that the whole guidance process may relate optimally to individual developmental, adjustive and orientational needs.[1]

On all school levels, guidance services, broadly interpreted, are concerned with teacher attitudes, subject matter mastery and cur-

[1] R. H. Mathewson (ed.), *The Program of Study and Course Outlines*, Graduate Training Program in Guidance and School Counseling, Division of Teacher Education, Board of Higher Education, New York, 1953. Reprinted by permission.

ricular adjustments that are adapted to individual abilities, interests and needs, and in-and-out-of-class activities suited to the learner's level of emotional and social development. Included also are: provision of and maintenance of a school plant, and of health care that will insure for every young person a healthful school environment; orientation of young people to their next step in the educational ladder; vocational selection and preparation; the resolution of personal problems of adjustment, frustrations, and conflicts experienced by any pupil, and the reconditioning of asocial and personally harmful behavior characteristics. The fulfillment of all these objectives requires the services of many guidance workers, each of whom not only has received training that is appropriate to his special guidance responsibilities, but also has achieved a recognition of the relationship of his particular area of service to other guidance activities.

Guidance and counseling are not synonymous terms. Among guidance services can be included all the various areas of activities that have to do with learner welfare. Counseling, as a phase of guidance, deals with the personal relationships of the counselor with young people, individually or in groups, through the utilization of evaluating techniques (observation, testing, and case studies) and interviewing. Although the general objectives of guidance and many of the tools employed by counselors are similar for all school levels, certain guidance emphases and approaches differ from level to level.

Guidance of the young child. During the early years of the child, the guidance services provided for him center first in the home. When we refer to parental rearing of young children, it might be more accurate to describe parents' activities as those of *guiding* the child. Later, nursery-school and kindergarten teachers share with the parent the responsibility of introducing the child to the process of adapting himself to the requirements of an enlarging social world. Here the needed guidance activities include those of the teacher, the school nurse, and pediatrician and, of course, the parents. On this level, except in the case of the small child who already has become the victim of maladjustive influences, the main objective of guidance is prevention of difficulties. The youngsters are motivated to achieve self-awareness and self-confidence in their reactions to stimulating objects and situations and in their relations with their peers and older people.

Guidance on the elementary-school level. Until recently, the concept of guidance excluded services on the elementary-school level. The teacher was expected to be responsible for whatever learning, conditioning, or reconditioning was needed by the individual pupils in his class. Since in the past the functions of education on this level were limited primarily to the mastery of rudimentary knowledges and skills, other phases of development, such as the emotional and the social, were considered to be the responsibilities of parents. Whatever attitude and behavior patterns the child developed as a result of his school experiences were considered merely to be concomitants of the real business of learning. The display by a child of undesirable attitudes and/or teacher-and-class-disturbing conduct resulted in pupil punishment.

Our increasing concern with child development and adjustment has broadened our concept of the objectives of elementary education and consequently our recognition of the need to provide guidance and counseling services for elementary-school children. The classroom teacher, however, remains the center of the teaching and counseling of the supposedly normal child. Unless the teacher's class is large, he is in a position to know the strengths and weaknesses of each of his pupils. He can utilize the techniques that are suggested in Chapter 14 for the gaining of greater insight concerning likenesses and differences in development among and within his pupils.

There still are elementary schools in which the teacher is responsible for the development of the whole child and all the difficulties of adjustment that may appertain thereto. In most modern elementary schools, however, the principal and his administrative or supervisory assistants assume some responsibility for individual child welfare. They co-operate with the teachers in the reconditioning of child behavior and often take major responsibility for the provision of more healthful environmental conditions. Practically every school has the services, at least on a part-time basis, of a doctor and a nurse. Relatively few elementary schools are fortunate enough to have the full or part-time services of a psychologist or of a trained counselor to administer needed individual tests and to co-operate with teachers who are attempting to help disturbed children.

Some guidance-minded principals of elementary schools so organize teaching schedules that personally-qualified and guidance-trained teachers are released from some of their regular classroom duties to serve as teacher counselors. Their guidance responsibilities include (1) to help other teachers administer testing instruments, either periodically or when special testing is needed; (2) to interview children and parents, and, (3) in co-operation with a visiting psychologist or counselor, to plan and conduct programs of teacher and parent education. These programs are aimed at the development among teachers and parents of guidance-minded attitudes in their relationships with children. In addition, most elementary schools keep cumulative records of pupil progress that include not only subject-matter "marks" earned by the pupil but also his status in other developmental or adjustment areas.[1]

One important guidance function deals with the orientation of first-grade children to school experiences. Children who have attended nursery schools and/or kindergartens find the transfer to the elementary-school level to be relatively easy. In some school systems, the first grade becomes a kind of kindergarten extension in which learning activities represent the continuation of those experienced in the kindergarten, except that they gradually are increased in difficulty to meet increasing maturational ability to perform.

Serious adjustment difficulties may be experienced by the child who comes directly from the sheltered environment of the home into a strange and possibly overwhelming new world. It usually is difficult for a six-year-old to tear himself away for a whole day from his accustomed home activities which, by this age, may be following a definite and satisfying pattern. Moreover, during these first six years, so close a bond may have developed between the child and his mother that neither can tolerate a separation from the other for a whole school day. Hence there is need for a planned program of orientation for the parent as well as for the child.

Guidance on the secondary-school level. Guidance as a phase of or adjunct to education had its beginnings in what is referred to, generally, as vocational guidance of high-school graduates and dropouts. There still are people who use interchangeably the terms *guidance* and *vocational guidance*. It is only recently that guidance has come to be interpreted broadly to include organized assistance toward adjustment in all life areas.

As can be expected, guidance and counseling services on the secondary-school level are an enlargement of services and follow a more definitely planned organizational pattern than usually needed

[1] For a detailed consideration of cumulative records, see Chapter 17.

on the lower-school levels. The preventive and therapeutic aspects of guidance or personnel services must be geared to the changing and increasing adaptations to new and different experiences that are characteristic of adolescence. Guidance workers are hoping that more effective help given by parents and elementary-school teachers may lead to greater readiness on the part of young people to adjust to the problems inherent in adolescent "growing up." Even if these hopes are realized, adolescents need counselor assistance to help them adapt to certain situations and conditions peculiar to the adolescent period.

There is a growing trend in many school systems away from the traditionally organized pattern of the educational ladder in which the first twelve years of schooling are divided into eight years of elementary schooling and four years of high school. Various school systems are experimenting with differing patterns of organization, some of which include the college years. The form of organization that now is receiving general acceptance, however, is the six-three-three plan, by which is meant that the child spends six years in the elementary school, three years in a junior high school, and the last three years of his precollege or prework education in a senior high school.

The fundamental purpose for inserting the junior high-school level between the lower and upper schools was guidance-pointed. Recognition of the fact that many young people dropped out of high school at the end of their freshman year caused educators to attempt to provide a means of easing the difficult problems of adjustment that were experienced by young people when they transferred from an elementary school in their home community, in which they were well known, to a high school. The new school might be far removed geographically from their home. They were required to adapt themselves to new subjects of study, many new teachers, a large student body, and an unaccustomed daily class schedule. The establishment of junior high schools seemed to be a way of eliminating some of these difficulties. The in-between schools were organized to meet the following significant purposes:

1. That an educational environment suitable for the preadolescent and early adolescent years might be provided.
2. That economy of time in education might be made possible.
3. That a gradual transition from the elementary school to the high school might be achieved.
4. That pupils might be kept in school rather than allowed to drop out at the end of the eighth year.

5. That social needs might be met in terms of individual differences in abilities and interests.
6. That opportunities for vocational and educational guidance might be provided.
7. That facilities for educational and vocational exploration might be set up.[1]

Provision is made in some junior high schools for mentally superior young people to complete the three-year program in two-and-a-half or two years. In large cities, the number of available junior high schools is sufficient to avoid children's traveling long distances to school. The setting up of facilities for educational and vocational exploration would seem to have excellent guidance implications. Actually, however, all that usually can be accomplished is that the counselor suggests the kind of senior high school which would be best for the junior high-school graduate. Unfortunately, parents and young people still regard a vocational school as a dumping ground for "dumbbells." Hence any suggestion by the counselor that a particular child might benefit from study in a vocational high school more than he could from pursuing a program in an academic high school often is disregarded by the parents and the child. There are parents, however, who are counseled unwisely by teachers to enter their child in a vocational school and then discover that their child belonged in an academic school.

The interests and special abilities of preadolescents and young adolescents usually are relatively uncertain; vocational counseling during the junior high-school years must be general, in terms of possible potentialities. Except in rare cases, it takes considerable thought and time for a young person to decide definitely what his occupational field should be. Some people reach an advanced age without making an adequate decision. In spite of some inadequacies, however, the establishment of junior high schools has been a step toward the realization of guidance-pointed educational objectives.

In many respects, the organization and conduct of guidance services on the junior and senior high-school levels are similar. There are a few significant differences that can be presented briefly. Older adolescents tend to become increasingly self-dependent, although they do not always use their newly experienced independence wisely. Hence they need tactful adult counseling. Widening social experiences, both within and outside the school,

[1] L. D. Crow, and A. Crow, *An Introduction to Guidance*, 2nd ed., American Book Company, New York, 1961, p. 230.

may interfere with the giving of proper attention to their school studies. The extent to which adolescents of either sex become unduly interested in members of the opposite sex may give rise to emotional disturbances, frustrations, or conflicts that interfere with accustomed habits of behavior. As the adolescent approaches young adulthood he becomes increasingly concerned with vocational choice and preparation. These various characteristics of adolescent development and adjustment often lead to the need, on the part of the teen-ager, for the kind and amount of counseling assistance that is not required of counselors on the lower-school levels.

One could enlarge upon the specific emotion-arousing situations and conditions that are faced by adolescents. Throughout this book, the mental hygiene and guidance points of view are stressed. Hence, at this point, we summarize the many functions that constitute guidance services on the secondary-school level. They include:

1. Visits to "feeding schools" to acquaint upper-grade children with the high school's curricular and cocurricular offerings.
2. Preadmission conferences with new entrants, for advisement purposes.
3. Orientation of new students.
4. Administration of appropriate testing programs.
5. Preparation and utilization of adequate and reliable cumulative records for all students.
6. Suggestions concerning additions to or changes in curriculum offerings to meet the learning needs of particular students.
7. Provision for and sponsoring cocurricular activities, and encouragement of pupil participation in them.
8. Planning and sponsoring of group conferences with students, teachers, or parents.
9. Provision for individual conferences with students.
10. Provision of pertinent and up-to-date materials for student and counselor use: college and other bulletins, books and pamphlets dealing with occupational information, etc.
11. Care of student health.
12. Educational and vocational counseling of all students.
13. Placement service for graduates, dropouts, and former students.
14. Follow-up of former students.
15. Co-ordination of all guidance and counseling services of teachers, administrative officers, and special counselors.
16. Co-operation with parents and community agencies; such

as child guidance clinics, welfare and recreational agencies, religious leaders, industrial plants and business houses, etc.

17. Sponsorship of alumni groups.
18. In-service training of teachers toward the development of the guidance point of view, and of skill in counseling.
19. Research by the guidance personnel concerning the evaluation of their existing program, and possible improvement of it.

These guidance functions should be organized appropriately but not rigidly. Each guidance program should develop out of the major needs of the school. For example, a small school system in which both levels—elementary and secondary—are housed in the same building would not need to make extensive plans for pre-registration and orientation counseling. Preregistration and orientation need to be planned carefully for young people, in a large city, who come from many different lower schools and who are not acquainted with the purposes, curricular offerings, and method employed in the new and strange secondary school. In a smaller town, recreational and social activities of young and old may be centered in the school building; hence the students participate in these activities as a matter of course. In large cities, there are so many commercially organized recreational opportunities that adolescents may find the social activities of the schools to be dull and uninteresting, even though the latter would have greater value in helping them develop wholesome social interrelationships.

The past ten years have witnessed a tremendous rise among school people of interest in the offering of guidance services to young people. Many administrative officers on all school levels have started to establish guidance programs in their schools. Unfortunately, too many of these programs have been patterned almost exactly upon a particular program that appeared to function successfully in another school or school system. The blind following of what may meet the guidance requirements in one situation may fail miserably in another.

Pertinent suggestions are offered for the establishment of a program of guidance and counseling services in any particular school. These suggestions are based upon the psychological factors that operate in any group interrelationships.

1. Faculty members, parents, and the young people themselves should come to understand the implications of guidance and school counseling. The Regents' Citizens Council

of New York State, having completed an intensive one-year study of the improvement of guidance services in the high school, had this to say concerning the role of guidance:

"The Regents' Citizens Council therefore advocates the large expansion of guidance but our committee would like to make clear at the outset just what it means by 'guidance.' *By this word, we mean a service to pupils and their parents of an informational and counseling nature*—a service which will result in placing more 'round pegs in round holes,' and which will conserve human resources. We do not mean that specialists should attempt to determine for boys and girls the answers to the educational, vocational, and personal problems of boys and girls. In the first place, one person is rarely competent to make such decisions for another. In the second place, no one can either predict accurately the numbers of persons who will be needed in the future in various occupations or appraise precisely the potential abilities of adolescents. In the third place, even if 'guidance' were much more of an exact science than it is, the American way is the way of free choice for the individual; it is not the way where careers and lives are dictated by others. Our goal is to open horizons, not to 'channel' people, to point out opportunities, rather than to make decisions for young people." [1]

2. The school staff, parents, and students should determine, co-operatively, what are the particular guidance needs of the young people, so that each member of the student population can be helped to become a round peg in a round hole. Again quoting from the Council's report:

"Guidance can reduce and prevent the number of course failures by pupils and can thereby reduce the amount of 're-peating' of subjects and courses; it can help pupils develop individual goals and objectives; *it can help the schools to locate the needs of individual communities for training opportunities."* [2]

3. A committee, consisting of the principal, teachers, and possibly including the superintendent and selected parents, plans the program, arranges for available space in the building for guidance rooms, and decides upon the number and kinds of outside personnel needed to implement the program, as well as the kind and amount of available material and equipment.

4. Various committees then can be organized. These might include, if possible, all the members of the faculty who, in

[1] "Improving Guidance Service in High Schools," Regents Citizens Advisory Council on the Readjustment of High School Education, Albany, 1954, p. 6.
[2] *Ibid.*, p. 5.

terms of their particular interest, choose the respective committee on which they will serve. The functions of each of these committees will be to study guidance needs in its particular area of study, and to advise the principal, the special counselors, and fellow teachers concerning their findings.

5. The program is organized, and appropriate teachers and other counselors are assigned their counseling duties.

6. The program should be organized simply and should be sufficiently flexible to permit needed organizational or functional changes to be made from time to time.

A program of guidance services that emerges from group cooperative thinking is likely to become an effective phase of the teaching-learning activities of the school. Guidance programs that are superimposed from above rarely meet all of the school's guidance needs. Extremely important is the fact that the purposes of a superimposed program will not be understood by teachers or by young people. Its services may be disregarded or resented by those who should benefit from them. Although the guidance program represents a formal organization of services, the activities of the program should be shared by all concerned, including the students. Some young people in a school can do an excellent job as counseling aides.

Personnel of School Guidance Services

A recognition of the guidance and counseling needs of the young people who constitute the learner population of a particular school or school system is important. Equally valuable is a flexible organization of appropriate guidance and counseling services. A complete understanding by the guidance personnel of the counseling needs of the school and an excellent organizational plan will fail to achieve desired objectives, however, if any of the various members of the counseling personnel are inadequately trained to meet their specific responsibilities, or if they lack suitable personality qualities. In a counselor's relationships with young people, their parents, other members of the school staff, and community leaders, he must display, in his overt behavior, skill in the application of needed techniques; attitudes of intelligent understanding of conditions and situations; warmth and flexibility in his dealings with young people, and co-operation with his fellow workers, both in and out of the program itself.

Personnel included in a guidance program. We referred earlier to the fact that the superintendent of a school system, the principal of a school and his administrative assistants, and staff committees constitute a group of persons who are vitally concerned with the organization and implementation of school guidance services. The functions of the members of this group are general. Specific guidance services usually are carried on by the members of a group who, respectively, are assigned to assume particular responsibilities. These guidance workers or counselors constitute the *guidance staff*. A fully-staffed guidance program includes the services of the following individuals: (1) A director of guidance activities, chairman of guidance, or dean, (2) Home-room prefects or recitation teachers, (3) Teacher counselors, (4) Director of cocurricular activities and his assistants, (5) Specialists (full-time or part-time)— doctor, dentist, nurse, psychologist, psychiatrist, social worker, and vocational and placement counselor, (6) Attendance Officer, (7) Parents, (8) Religious leaders, and (9) The personnel of health, welfare, and guidance agencies.

To this list can be added community leaders in business and industry and in recreational activities. The relations of these community leaders to the school guidance program differ in function and attitude from those that exist among the staff members. The attitude of community leaders who are outside the program itself should be that of co-operation with the school staff. Industrialists and businessmen invite school groups to visit their plants or offices so that the young people can become acquainted at firsthand with the work activities; they may employ graduates and dropouts on a full-time basis or accept students of co-operative high schools on a part-time-experience basis; they may keep the school informed concerning the successful achievement of former students, and they may offer suggestions to the school concerning improved methods to be used in the teaching of the skill subjects, or of needed attitude changes to be encouraged among young people. Leaders of recreational projects, such as community recreational programs, can be of great assistance to the school personnel as attempts are made to adjust sports or other recreational programs to the leisure-time needs of young people of different age and interest levels. They also can help the school meet the adjustment problems of some pupils.

There are many leaders of religious organizations who work closely with school counselors. The authors have had experience with pastors who make it part of their ministerial responsibility to know the schools which their young people attend, talk to their young parishioners about their school interests, and meet with school counselors to discuss ways to resolve individual or group problems that involve undesirable attitudes or behavior. In some school communities, one or more religious leaders are members of the school board. Community co-operation always is helpful; the extent to which this is or can be made available to the school's guidance staff rests primarily upon the displayed attitudes of the staff itself toward them.

We have stressed the fact that each counselor should operate within his special field of service. This kind of interstaff relationship may not be adhered to, or it may be followed too strictly.

In a high school that is known to the authors, the guidance services are well organized to meet every possible learner need that might arise. With few exceptions, faculty members are commendably guidance-minded, and guidance and counseling responsibilities involve much teacher participation. Each participant is proud of his share in carrying out the school's objective to help every young person develop to the utmost whatever he possesses of ability to become a well-informed, constructive young man or woman.

Unfortunately, many of the teacher-counselors seem to believe that they personally are responsible for all the guidance activities of the school. Each of these teacher-counselors, without conferring with other members of the staff, attempts to meet all of a boy's or girl's problems, regardless of the fact that some of the difficulties do not lie within his area of responsibility. Hence too many young people become confused as a result of too many and too varied counseling approaches to the remedying of their difficulties.

In another school, all the counselors had been very carefully warned to keep out of another counselor's territory. Hence, in a counseling situation, a counselor would refrain from answering a simple question or offering a minor suggestion; he would insist that, if the counselee wanted certain information, he should make an appointment with the appropriate counselor. This procedure is timewasting. Moreover, a young person might want the question answered or the suggestions made *at that particular moment,* but might forget it later or be unwilling to take the trouble to seek out the other counselor.

Counselors should agree on a middle course. Each counselor or other member of the guidance staff has his own "niche," but guidance services must be fluid. Without overstepping his rightful limits of responsibility, every guidance-minded staff member will do all that he can to help a young person when the latter *needs the help.* Periodic staff conferences are valuable as means to co-ordinate guidance services.

It is not the purpose of this discussion to consider at length the specific duties of the respective members of a school guidance and counseling staff. This information can be obtained from any one or more of the books included in the *Selected References* at the end of the chapter. We are concerned primarily in focusing attention upon the various media of guidance and counseling that are available in modern schools for all young and older learners who need help to achieve good physical, mental, emotional, or social adjustment.

The Guidance Role of the Teacher

No matter how simple or elaborately organized a school guidance program may be, the teacher remains the key person. The influence of his personal attributes, his attitudes and activities, and his relationship with his pupils permeates every phase of the school's guidance and counseling services. His degree of interest in learners and of insight into their problems will determine the extent of his helpfulness as a teacher-counselor or as a classroom teacher.

The functions of the teacher-counselor. As we said earlier, in many elementary and secondary schools certain teachers are released from some of their regular teaching obligations to serve as teacher-counselors. On the elementary level, a few teachers are assigned to various grade-combinations, e.g., grades one through three, and grades four through six. Their particular function is to assist the teachers to employ a mental-hygiene approach in their dealings with children. Special problems of adjustment are referred to the teacher counselor, who then does whatever he can to remedy the situation. Failing in his efforts, he refers the child to the proper person or agency. The teacher-counselor also co-operates with parents to bring about a child's improved health, learning or attitude status.

On the secondary level, a teacher-counselor usually is assigned to a special grade level or learning area. He attempts to guide the learners in his group: to plan their subject schedule, to decide upon their future plans, to join school cocurricular activities, and to care for their physical and mental health. Adolescents often bring to the teacher-counselor many of their personal problems, such as parent-child relations, dating, grooming, spending of money, and interest in part-time employment.

Some schools cannot afford a trained vocational and placement counselor whose responsibility it would be to alert young people to occupational opportunities and job requirements and to place them in suitable part-time or full-time jobs. If there is no full-time or part-time vocational counselor in the school, the teacher-counselor of a group of students may have to assume this responsibility. In some schools one teacher-counselor is assigned to provide vocational counseling for all interested students, regardless of their grade level or curriculum area.

The teacher-counselor's guidance functions are extremely important. In most secondary schools, budgetary allowance for guidance services is extremely meager. Consequently, teaching schedules are so tight that any time that is taken from the regular teaching schedule of a teacher-counselor results in an increase in size of recitation classes. We already have referred to the value, to both the learners and the teacher, of small classes. This psychological principle is recognized by all teachers. Hence there is general resentment among teachers if the administration assigns so many hours of released time to teacher-counselors that thereby the regular teaching load is increased substantially. Consequently, teacher-counselors usually have insufficient time to counsel students, meet with parents, and complete satisfactorily every task that is required for the proper exercise of their duties. The interested and conscientious teacher-counselor too often feels impelled to devote an undue amount of time to his counseling activities, before and after school and during his lunch period.

Counseling functions of the classroom teacher. The classroom teacher is the most important factor in the school life of the child. In the teacher's daily associations with a young person, he is afforded an opportunity to discover the learner's attitude and behavior strengths and weaknesses. It is to the teacher that the young person first brings his problems or difficulties. It is the teacher who either can help in the solution of the difficulty or refer it to the teacher-counselor. It is the teacher who can supply the members of the guidance staff with firsthand information concerning a counselee. The classroom teacher also can implement recommendations that result from pupils' contacts with counselors. Many group-therapy activities can be provided by the classroom teacher. Guidance-minded classroom teachers represent the *alpha* and *omega* of guidance and school counseling. Teacher responsibility for young people's school and life adjustment begins with teacher-guided learning in the early school grades and continues until the learner has reached a mature level of self-dependence and self-control.

Counselor training. Most teacher-education programs reflect a mental-hygiene approach. Beginning teachers usually recognize their responsibility to promote child or adolescent welfare. Many teachers do not know what to do, however, when they are faced with a problem situation in which a child or an adolescent needs adult help.

The New York State Regents' Citizens Council recommends that "students in the teacher education institutions should be given some training in the principles and practices of guidance."[1] Many of us, who have been in close contact with nonguidance-minded teachers and who have observed ineffective school guidance procedures, heartily agree with the opinion expressed by the Council.

In an increasing number of states, the completion of an adequate training program, including some supervised counseling experience, is required of any teacher who desires to participate in counseling activities. Interest in and understanding of the developing child are needed by anyone who attempts to teach or to counsel him. These personal qualities are not sufficient, however. To be an effective counselor, the teacher needs to be self-controlled and emotionally stable. In addition, he must possess appropriate knowledge and skill competencies in the field of guidance and counseling as well as successful teaching experience.

Special Guidance Projects

In an increasing number of schools, especially in large city school systems, provision is being made to meet the particular guidance needs of young people. At present, there are a number of worthwhile guidance projects in the process of experimentation. A few of these projects are described here briefly.

Early identification. In the past, all entrants into the elementary school were assumed to be relatively similar in their ability to meet their basic learning needs. It now is realized that young children differ widely in their learning potentialities. Hence attempts are made in the early grades (usually first, second, and third) to discover how and to what extent the youngsters can be expected to profit from instruction. Through testing and observation of

[1] Ibid., p. 11.

learning progress, teachers and teacher-counselors try to discover individual differences among the children and adapt learning programs accordingly. Special attention is given to the provision of enrichment and other stimulating approaches for those children identified as possessing high learning potential.

Disadvantaged children. In most urban school systems wide economic and social differences exist among the members of the school population. Some parents can provide many enriching experiences for their children by way of social activities, acquaintance with neighborhood educational facilities, and travel beyond the home environment. The children of economically and socially deprived homes are denied such advantages, however. In order to meet this lack, higher horizons programs are being initiated. Teachers and teacher-counselors co-operate in helping these children become better acquainted with the world about them. Visits are made to various places of interest in the community. Through appropriate reading, the utilization of carefully selected motion pictures and television programs, and other educationally enriching aids, these pupils are introduced to interesting phenomena that take them outside their home environment.

Guidance of underachievers. It is well known that school performance below full capacity to learn is characteristic of too many mentally superior young people. Many schools are attempting to discover and help solve the problem of underachievement. School counselors, in co-operation with classroom teachers, study the personal history, the classroom behavior, the observable interest pattern of these students. They give special attention to any problems of adjustment. Through individual and group conferences, consultation with parents, and appropriate changes in subject programs, and the like, counselors attempt to motivate underachievers to work up to their potential.

Credit for advanced standing. Some colleges are co-operating with neighboring senior high schools in an advanced educational program for mentally superior senior students. The college admits these students to certain regular college courses before their graduation from the lower school, allowing college credit for courses completed successfully. College and high school counselors work together closely in this project.

Meeting the drop-out problem. Some adolescents drop out of high school before graduation because of lack of success in school work and/or desire to be engaged in remunerative work. According to one program of meeting this problem, drop-outs under eighteen years of age are readmitted to certain high schools where they are given a study program adjusted to their abilities and interest. Another program affords a young person the opportunity to continue an appropriate schedule of studies during a shortened school day, the rest of which is spent at a job which has been selected by his counselor in accordance with the student's interest and job potentiality.

QUESTIONS AND TOPICS FOR DISCUSSION

1. The concept of guidance can be so broad as to include all education. Explain.
2. What are some of the reasons for the introduction of formal guidance into the school system?
3. What is meant by education of the whole person? Explain.
4. Why did organized guidance have its beginning on the high-school level?
5. What values can accrue from having a well-trained guidance staff in the elementary school?
6. Present arguments for and against counselors' continuing to engage in part-time classroom teaching.
7. Enumerate school activities for which the guidance office can assume responsibility.
8. Show specific ways in which a loosely organized guidance program might lead to duplication of effort.
9. Differentiate between group guidance and individual guidance.
10. Discuss the teacher's role in the guidance program.
11. Explain the role of the principal in the guidance program.
12. Name three kinds of problems which should be referred by school counselors to other community agencies.
13. Discuss and evaluate: Disciplinary problems should not be handled directly by the dean or chairman of guidance.
14. Show that the case study and the interview can become integral phases of counseling responsibilities.
15. Outline a guidance program for home room periods.
16. State the values and limitations of organized guidance.
17. Compare the guidance problems and programs of a small school with those of a large school on the following levels: elementary, junior high school, senior high school. What major differences appear?

SELECTED REFERENCES

Barr, J. A., *The Elementary Teacher and Guidance*. Holt, Rinehart & Winston, N.Y., 1958.

Bennett, M. E., *Guidance and Counseling in Groups*. McGraw-Hill, N.Y., 1963.

Brown, W. F., *Student to Student Counseling*. University of Texas Press, Austin, Texas, 1972.

Crow, L. D., Crow, A., *Organization and Conduct of Guidance Services*. David McKay, N.Y., 1966.

Dinkmeyer, D. C., *Guidance and Counseling in the Elementary School*. Holt, Rinehart & Winston, N.Y., 1968.

Downing, L. N., *Guidance and Counseling Services*. Charles Merrill, Columbus, Ohio, 1970.

Fedder, R., *Guidance in the Homeroom*. Teachers College Press, N.Y., 1967.

Goodman, S. I., *Guidance Counselor: Elementary, Junior High School & Senior High School*. Arco, N.Y., 1972.

Gowan, J. C., *Guidance of Exceptional Children*, 2nd ed. David McKay, N.Y., 1972.

Herr, E., and Cramer, S. H., *Guidance of the College Bound*. Appleton-Century-Crofts, N.Y., 1968.

Hill, G. C., and Luckey, E. B., *Guidance for Children in the Elementary School*. Appleton-Century-Crofts, N.Y., 1969.

Lee, J. M., and Pallone, N. J., *Guidance and Counseling in Schools*. McGraw-Hill, N.Y., 1966.

Maier, N. R., *The Appraisal Interview*. Wiley, N.Y., 1958.

Nordberg, R. B., *Guidance: A Systematic Approach*. Random House, N.Y., 1970.

Perrone, P. A., et al, *Guidance and the Emerging Adolescent*. Intext, Scranton, Pa., 1970.

Peters, H. J., and Shertzer, B., *Guidance: Program Development and Management*, 2nd ed. Charles Merrill, Columbus, Ohio, 1969.

Shelton, B. O., *Teaching and Guiding the Slow Learner*. Prentice Hall, Englewood Cliffs, N.J., 1971.

Appendix

Recommended Films

2—The Fundamentals of Human Development

Principles of Development (McGraw-Hill, 16 minutes). Outlines the fundamentals of growth and change from early infancy, revealing that development follows a pattern that is continuous, orderly, and predictable.

Heredity and Pre-Natal Development (McGraw-Hill, 21 minutes). Describes the fertilization of the ovum by the sperm cell at conception and traces the development of the fetus until delivery.

Human Reproduction (McGraw-Hill, 20 minutes). Presents facts concerning the human reproductive system and the process of normal human birth.

Human Growth (Brown Trust, 19 minutes). Traces human growth and development of the organism from mating through pregnancy and birth.

3—Physical, Mental, and Emotional Development

Growth: A Study of Johnny and Jimmy (Int Flm Fd, 43 minutes). Presents the developmental pattern of twins, with emphasis upon a comparison of their behavior to the age of eight years. Traces the interrelation between maturation and practice, especially in the motor functions.

Growth of Adaptive Behavior (Ebf, 15 minutes). Presents Dr. Arnold Gesell's study of the finer motor co-ordinations during a child's first five years.

Life with Baby (McGraw-Hill, 18 minutes). Presents Dr. Arnold Gesell's study of children's mental and physical growth; aids adults and older children to gain a better understanding of a young child's growth pattern.

Why Won't Tommy Eat? (Can Nfb, 16 minutes). Suggests that the basis of feeding habits is laid in early infancy. Weaning, introduction of solid foods, self-feeding, and other methods of feeding are shown.

4—Personal and Social Development during Childhood (Ages and Stages Series)

He Acts His Age (McGraw-Hill, 14 minutes). Examines the play habits of children from one to fifteen years of age and presents some characteristics of each age group.

Terrible Twos and the Trusting Threes (McGraw-Hill, 20 minutes). Presents a close examination of the growing years between two and four.

Angry Boy (Int Flm Bur, 32 minutes). A ten-year-old boy strikes out blindly at life to relieve the turmoil of his emotions that result from hostility toward his parents.

Children's Emotions (McGraw-Hill, 22 minutes). The major emotions of childhood—fear, anger, jealousy, curiosity, and joy—are described, and methods of dealing with them are explained.

Early Social Behavior (Ebf, 11 minutes). Presents Dr. Arnold Gesell's study of the behavior of children in various social situations, especially in the home.

Emergence of Personality (Ebf, 30 minutes). Indicates ways in which differences in personality, including the impact of heredity and environment, can be explained.

Experimental Studies in Social Climates of Groups (Int Flm Bur, 30 minutes). Presents a comparison of the effects upon boys' behavior of various forms of group organization.

Fears of Children (Int Flm Bur, 32 minutes). Dramatizes some of the emotional problems of Paul, a normal five-year-old boy. Paul's fears of the dark, of being alone, and of new situations are shown as they affect his everyday life.

Meeting Emotional Needs of Childhood (Nyu, 33 minutes). Concerns the development in the child of sensitivity to and responsibility for adult community living.

Preface to a Life (Uwf-Castle, 29 minutes). Portrays the influence parents have on a child's developing personality, from birth to adulthood.

5—Personal and Social Development during Adolescence

Are You Ready for Marriage? (Coronet, 16 minutes). Describes a very young couple, whose marriage is objected to by the girl's parents. The couple have about decided to elope when they agree first to discuss their problem with the counselor at the church.

Children of the City (Bis, 30 minutes). Portrays the problem of juvenile delinquency and how it is handled in a Scottish city.

Children on Trial (Bis, 62 minutes). Tells the story of two boys and a girl, repeat offenders, who are sent to approved schools for the rehabilitation of juvenile delinquents.

Choosing for Happiness (McGraw-Hill, 14 minutes). Tells about Eve and her cousin, Mary, who are concerned with the choice of a mate but in their evaluation of boys find a flaw in all of them.

Developing Self-reliance (Coronet, 10 minutes). Shows how self-reliance is essential to all successful endeavor.

Farewell to Childhood (Int Flm Bur, 20 minutes). Describes a normal teen-ager, full of the emotions typical of adolescence, who longs for independence and the privileges of adulthood.

Friendship Begins at Home (Coronet, 14 minutes). Shows adolescents the ways in which they can develop desirable attitudes and behavior in their relations with other members of the family.

Shy Guy (Coronet, 12 minutes). Demonstrates the value of friendliness as a means of improving a shy adolescent's social adjustment.

6—Dynamics of Human Behavior and Learning

Children Growing Up with Others (Uwf-Castle, 30 minutes). Shows the development of self-reliance in children in their group relations.

Motivating the Class (McGraw-Hill, 19 minutes). A student-teacher learns that motivation is essential to good teaching.

This Is Robert (Nyu, 80 minutes). Traces the development of Robert, an aggressive, "difficult" child, from his arrival in nursery school at two up through his first year in a public school at seven.

Unconscious Motivation (Assoc Flm Artists, 38 minutes). Demonstrates how unconscious motives can influence and direct our everyday thoughts, feelings, and actions.

7—Personal and Social Bases of Adjustment

Experimental Studies in Social Climates of Groups (Iowa St U, 30 minutes). Presents a comparison of the effects upon boys' behavior of various forms of group organization.

The Feeling of Hostility (McGraw-Hill, 27 minutes). Gives a detailed analysis from early childhood of the causes of a young woman's inner maladjustment and her final readjustment through her occupational activities.

The Feeling of Rejection (McGraw-Hill, 23 minutes). Tells the story of a twenty-three-year-old neurotic who is helped by psychiatric treatment.

Overcoming Worry (Coronet, 10 minutes). Story about a teen-age boy who is worried about his father who has become very nervous and irritable.

Overdependency (McGraw-Hill, 32 minutes). Shows how the ordinary life problems of a young married man stem from a childhood of too much dependence on his mother and sister.

Social Development (McGraw-Hill, 16 minutes). Presents an analysis of social behavior at different age levels and the reasons underlying the changes in behavior patterns as the child develops.

8—Adjustment through the Development of Self-Discipline

Children Growing Up with Others (Uwf-Castle, 30 minutes). Shows the development of self-reliance in children in their group relations.

Life with Junior (McGraw-Hill, 18 minutes). Depicts the happenings of an average day in the life of a school-age child.

Maintaining Classroom Discipline (McGraw-Hill, 14 minutes). Treats various methods of handling classroom situations and emphasizes the development of desirable behavior controls.

Problem Children (Penn State U, 20 minutes). Shows the effects of home and school relationships upon the personality of two children.

9—Learning: Principles, Theories, and Transfer Values

How To Think (Coronet, 14 minutes). Presents situations in which a boy has a chance to make use of his ability to concentrate in the solution of practical problems.

How We Learn (Coronet, 10 minutes). Portrays the main principles which are basic to effective learning.

Learning from Class Discussion (Coronet, 10 minutes). Stresses the value of properly phrased questions in effective learning.

11—Acquiring Skill Competence

Exercise and Health (Coronet, 11 minutes). Shows how participation in exercise and athletics aided in overcoming a particular difficulty.

Football (DHB, 25 minutes). It has slow motion, animated diagrams, posed plays, and some action shots. Directed and planned by D. H. Bible.

Football Fundamentals (Coronet, 11 minutes). Shows various techniques used in playing football.

Matt Mann's Swimming for Boys (Coronet, 19 minutes). Shows top swimming techniques.

Matt Mann's Swimming for Girls (Coronet, 11 minutes). Shows four basic strokes for beginners.

Learning to Swim (United States Department of Agriculture, 20 minutes). Basic techniques for learning to swim.

13—Individual Differences in Learning

Discovering Individual Differences (McGraw-Hill, 25 minutes). Shows how the teacher gets to know and understand each child and shows how the teacher adapts her teaching program to meet individual needs.

Individual Differences (McGraw-Hill, 23 minutes). Shows how Roy, a shy, slow learner, adjusts to the school situation with the guiding hand of the teacher.

Making Learning More Meaningful (McGraw-Hill, 12 minutes). Shows how a teacher helped her pupils develop skills in arithmetic as they were learning to understand something about economic activities.

Motivating the Class (McGraw-Hill, 19 minutes). Problems faced by a young student-teacher and procedures followed to meet them are presented in the setting of a geometry class.

Teacher and Pupils Planning and Working Together (McGraw-Hill, 19 minutes). Shows how a teacher enlisted the co-operation of the pupils in developing working plans for the day.

14—The Study of the Learner in the Classroom

Guidance Problems for School and Home (Tchrs Col, 18 minutes). Attempts to give parents and teachers an understanding of some of the causes of a child's poor home and social adjustment.

Learning to Understand Children: Part I, A Diagnostic Approach (McGraw-Hill, 21 minutes). Presents in detail the diagnostic techniques used by the teacher to discover the causes of the social maladjustment of one of her pupils, Ada Adams. *Part II, A Remedial Program* (23 minutes). Describes the remedial techniques employed by the teacher for Ada Adams' rehabilitation.

Understanding Children's Play (Nyu, 10 minutes). Designed to understand and help children through observation of their use of toys and play materials.

15—Functions and Techniques of Evaluation

Aptitudes and Occupations (Coronet, 16 minutes). Shows the extent to which possession of ability in a given field can be determined.

Children Are Creative (Int Flm Bur, 33 minutes). Shows motivation, creative work, and evaluation of finished product in an elementary art class.

Testing the IQ (Int Flm Bur, 18 minutes). Shows the administration of the revised Stanford-Binet test and the calculation of the IQ.

16—Interpretation of Learner Progress

Using Analytical Tools (McGraw-Hill, 14 minutes). Shows how analytical instruments can be used to evaluate adolescent behavior.

18—Development of Teaching Effectiveness

Teaching (Mahnke, 11 minutes). Shows the contributions of teachers to the nation.

Tips for Teachers (Jam Handy, 20 minutes). Personality, preparation, and presentation are dramatized.

Broader Concepts of Method (McGraw-Hill, 16 minutes). Part I, Developing Pupil Interest; Part II, Teacher and Pupil Planning Work Together.

Principles of the Art and Science of Teaching (Iowa State U, 55 minutes). Shows the development of an assignment: including the setting up of objectives, selecting content and activities, and adapting procedures.

Preparation of Teachers (Uwf-Castle, 20 minutes). Stresses the need for desirable personality traits in teachers.

What Greater Gift? (Nea, 28 minutes). Presents the teacher as a professional person and shows something of the nature of teaching.

19—Adjustment Aspects of Teaching

The Teacher as Observer and Guide (Tchrs Col, 20 minutes). Indicates ways in which the teacher can help pupils solve their problems, improve their learning, and develop desirable character traits.

A Better Tomorrow (Uwf-Castle, 20 minutes). Shows desirable teaching and learning opportunities in New York City.

Maintaining Classroom Discipline (McGraw-Hill, 14 minutes). Treats various methods of handling classroom situations and emphasizes the development of desirable behavior controls. Also shows how pupil behavior reflects teacher attitudes.

20—Teacher Counseling and Learner Adjustment

A Job for Bob. (B&F Comm, 30 minutes). Tells the story of an ambitious young man who was helped by guidance to find and to adjust to a job commensurate with his abilities.

Choosing Your Occupation (Coronet, 16 minutes). Presents desirable vocational guidance techniques.

Counseling—Its Tools and Techniques (Mahnke, 22 minutes). Presents the techniques used by the efficient guidance counselor.

Counselor's Day (McGraw-Hill, 11 minutes). Presents the activities of a counselor.

Diagnosis and Planning Adjustments in Counseling (McGraw-Hill, 18 minutes). Shows the need of understanding the problem or difficulty before recommending or utilizing therapy.

Finding Your Life Work (Mahnke, 22 minutes). Presents the necessary thinking and planning of a boy in relation to his vocational choices, as these are compared to the experiences of an expert fisherman.

Guidance Problems for School and Home (Tchrs Col, 18 minutes). Attempts to give parents and teachers an understanding of some of the causes of a child's poor home and social adjustment.

Problem of Pupil Adjustment, Part I—The Dropout: A Case Study (McGraw-Hill, 20 minutes). Part II—*The Stay-In: A School Study* (McGraw-Hill, 19 minutes). Shows how a school can hold its students.

Psychological Implications during the Clinical Visit (Nyu, 20 minutes). Gives the effect upon children's emotional attitudes of a visit to the New York Infirmary for Women and Children.

Recreational and Occupational Therapy (Uwf-Castle, 13 minutes). Describes the work done by hospitals and community agencies in occupational therapy, and projects in social recreation.

Marriage Series (McGraw-Hill,) *Choosing for Happiness* (14 minutes), *It Takes All Kinds* (20 minutes), *This Charming Couple* (19 minutes), *Who's Boss?* (16 minutes), *Marriage Today* (22 minutes).

Suppliers of Films and Recordings

Assoc Flm Artists	Associated Film Artists, 30 N. Raymond Ave., Pasadena 1, Calif.
B&F Comm	Broadcasting and Film Commission, National Council of Churches, 220 Fifth Ave., New York 1, New York
Bis	British Information Services, 30 Rockefeller Plaza, N. Y. 20, N. Y.
Brown Trust	E. C. Brown Trust, 220 S. W. Alder St., Portland 4, Oregon
Can Nfb	National Film Board of Canada, 630 Fifth Ave., N. Y. C., N. Y.
Coronet	Coronet Instructional Films, 65 E. South Water St., Chicago 1, Ill.
Ebf	Encyclopaedia Britannica Films, 1150 Wilmette Ave., Wilmette, Ill.
Flms Inc	Films Incorporated, subsidiary of Ebf.
Jam Handy	Jam Handy Corp., 2821 E. Grand Blvd., Detroit 11, Mich.
Int Flm Bur	International Film Bureau, Suite 308–316, 57 E. Jackson Blvd., Chicago 4, Illinois
Int Flm Fd	International Film Foundation, 345 E. 46 St., N. Y. 17, N. Y.
Iowa St U	State University of Iowa, Bureau of Visual Instruction, Iowa City, Iowa
Mahnke	Carl F. Mahnke Productions, 215 E. 3 St., Des Moines 9, Iowa
McGraw-Hill	McGraw-Hill Book Co., Text Film Department, 330 W. 42 St., N. Y. 36, N. Y.
Nea	National Education Association, Press and Radio Section, 1201 Sixteenth St., N.W., Washington 6, D. C.
Nyu	New York University, Film Library, 26 Washington Place, N. Y. C., N. Y.
Penn State U	Pennsylvania State College, State College, Penna.
Tchrs Col	Teachers College, Bureau of Publications, Columbia University, 525 W. 120 St., N. Y. 27, N. Y.
Usda	United States Department of Agriculture, Washington, D. C.
Uwf-Castle	United World Films, 1445 Park Ave., N. Y. 29, N. Y.

Author Index

561

478

414

Subject Index